817.008   Roy Blount's book of
           Southern humor.

$27.50

DATE			

Also by Roy Blount, Jr.

About Three Bricks Shy—And the Load Filled Up

Crackers

First Hubby

What Men Don't Tell Women

Not Exactly What I Had in Mind

It Grows on You

Camels Are Easy, Comedy's Hard

Now, Where Were We?

One Fell Soup

Soupsongs/Webster's Ark

Roy Blount's Book of Southern Humor

Roy Blount's Book of Southern Humor

Edited by

Roy Blount, Jr.

W · W · Norton & Company · New York · London

First Edition

The text of this book is composed in Perpetua, with the display in Nadall and Felix Titling.
Composition and manufacturing by the Haddon Craftsmen, Inc.

Library of Congress Cataloging-in-Publication Data
Roy Blount's book of Southern humor / [edited] by Roy Blount, Jr.
    p.   cm.
    1. Southern States—Humor. I. Blount, Roy.
PN6231.S64R69   1994
817.008′0975—dc20   94-18611

ISBN 0-393-03695-2

W. W. Norton & Company, Inc., 500 Fifth Avenue, New York, N.Y. 10110
W. W. Norton & Company Ltd., 10 Coptic Street, London WC1A 1PU

1 2 3 4 5 6 7 8 9 0

To Jesse Roy Dellea.
About time the family had another Southerner.

Contents ✤

ACKNOWLEDGMENTS 15
INTRODUCTION 19

SECTION ONE: MY PEOPLE, MY PEOPLE (HOW'S YOUR MAMA 'N' THEM?)

"Nobody Loves Me but My Mother" B. B. KING 41
"Mama's Memoirs" BAILEY WHITE 41
"I Blame It All on Mamma" JOSEPH MITCHELL 43
Making the Honky-tonks with Mama LOUIS ARMSTRONG 50
"I Get Born" ZORA NEALE HURSTON 55
from *Raney* CLYDE EDGERTON 59
from *No Time for Sergeants* MAC HYMAN 66
According to Bubba DAN JENKINS 72
"Papa Was a Democrat" TED POSTON 77
"A Late Encounter with the Enemy" FLANNERY O'CONNOR 84
from *The Redneck Bride* JOHN FERGUS RYAN 92
Dying Properly LISA ALTHER 101
from *Confessions of a Failed Southern
    Lady* FLORENCE KING 104
"The Fortunate Spill" MARILYN NELSON WANIEK 113
"Levitation with Baby" MARILYN NELSON WANIEK 115
Fighting for Folks NIKKI GIOVANNI 116

*Selection titles in quotation marks are the original titles; those without quotation marks have been devised by the editor for this volume.

from *A Confederacy of Dunces*   JOHN KENNEDY TOOLE 126

from *Baby Doll*   TENNESSEE WILLIAMS 133

Mary Grace's Reception   NANCY LEMANN 139

"The Beard"   FRED CHAPPELL 147

Modern Baptist Bible Study   JAMES WILCOX 157

"Typical"   PADGETT POWELL 164

"More Carters"   ROY BLOUNT, JR. 172

SECTION TWO: HERE BE DRAGONS, OR HOW COME THESE BUTTERBEANS HAVE AN ALLIGATOR TASTE?

"A Coon Huntin' Story"   JERRY CLOWER 183

"The Fish and the Edsel"   JERRY CLOWER 186

"Newgene and the Lion"   JERRY CLOWER 187

"Rat Killin' "   JERRY CLOWER 188

"Rats in the Corn Crib"   JERRY CLOWER 189

"Alligators"   MARJORIE KINNAN RAWLINGS 190

"A Chicken Story"   RAY WASHINGTON 197

"He Is My Horse"   ANONYMOUS 200

"False Alarm"   DAVE BARRY 200

Animal Deals   RAY LUM AS TOLD TO WILLIAM FERRIS 203

"Simon Slick's Mule"   ANONYMOUS 207

"Brother Rabbit Conquers Brother Lion"   JOEL CHANDLER HARRIS 208

" 'Heyo, House!' "   JOEL CHANDLER HARRIS 211

"Aunt Tempy's Story"   JOEL CHANDLER HARRIS 213

"Why the 'Possum's Tail Is Bony"   A BILOXI INDIAN AS TOLD TO JAMES OWEN DORSEY 217

"Toot and Teat"   BAILEY WHITE 220

"Turkeys"   BAILEY WHITE 222

"The King of the Birds"   FLANNERY O'CONNOR 224

"Song to Oysters"   ROY BLOUNT, JR. 232

from *Keeper of the Moon*   TIM MCLAURIN 233

"Parson John Bullen's Lizards"   GEORGE WASHINGTON HARRIS 235

"A Day with the Vet"   GREGORY JAYNES 241

"Kudzu East and West and South"   FRANK GANNON 242

"A Sensible Varmint"   DAVY CROCKETT 245

Section Three: Lying, and Other Arts of Communication

"Georgia Theatrics"   A. B. Longstreet   251

Fort Worth Golf (from Dead Solid Perfect)   Dan Jenkins   253

"Country Golf"   Garrison Keillor   257

A Dickey Story   George Garrett   264

"The Ordeal of Lonnie Register"   William Price Fox   266

"Coley Moke"   William Price Fox   270

from Mules and Men   Zora Neale Hurston   277

from Shuckin' and Jivin'   Various Black Virginians as told to Daryl Cumber Dance   286

Dozens   Richard Wright   292

"New Dirty Dozen"   Memphis Minnie   294

"A Night at the Ugly Man's"   Johnson J. Hooper   295

from You All Spoken Here   Roy Wilder, Jr.   299

"Wrong Number"   Roberto G. Fernandez   304

"X-ing a Paragrab"   Edgar Allan Poe   305

"The Ransom of Red Chief"   O. Henry   311

"Poetic Gems"   John Shelton Reed   320

"In Memorial"   J. Gordon Coogler   325

from Car   Harry Crews   325

"Between the Lines"   Lee Smith   331

"I Don't Eat Dirt Personally"   Roy Blount, Jr.   341

Gertrude   Randall Jarrell   344

Head to Head with the Champ   Hunter S. Thompson   346

Willie Didn't Want a Lot of Confusion Backstage   Larry L. King   352

A Position on Whisky   Noah S. Sweat   358

Letters from Hollywood   Nunnally Johnson   359

"Petrified Man"   Eudora Welty   364

"Keela, the Outcast Indian Maiden"   Eudora Welty   375

"Nineteen Fifty-five"   Alice Walker   382

"The King of Jazz"   Donald Barthelme   394

A Jerry Lee Session   Nick Tosches   398

Womp Bomp a-Loo Momp   Richard Penniman and Bumps Blackwell   400

Alabama Dimensions   TOM WOLFE 405
"Diddie Wa Diddie"   BLIND BLAKE 407

SECTION FOUR: BLACK AND WHITE, AND OTHER
POLITICAL STRIPES

"Look at That Gal . . ."   JULIAN BOND 413
Bookie Odds Favored the Union   ISHMAEL REED 414
Relating to Skillet and Fode   WILLIAM ALEXANDER PERCY 420
"Slim in Atlanta"   STERLING A. BROWN 427
"Slim Hears 'The Call' "   STERLING A. BROWN 429
"Sporting Beasley"   STERLING A. BROWN 435
"The Vertical Negro Plan"   HARRY GOLDEN 436
The Rise of Lester Maddox   MARSHALL FRADY 438
"Mrs. James"   ALICE CHILDRESS 447
"The Pocketbook Game"   ALICE CHILDRESS 448
"Tuskegee Airfield"   MARILYN NELSON WANIEK 449
"Women's Locker Room"   MARILYN NELSON WANIEK 451
"Dave's Neckliss"   CHARLES W. CHESNUTT 452
"Bill Arp Addresses Artemus Ward"   CHARLES HENRY SMITH 463
"Earl Long's Finest Moment"   A. J. LIEBLING 466
Rogue Truth   BILLY BOWLES AND REMER
                                                   TYSON 471

"Johnson"   RUSSELL BAKER 479
"Tough as Bob War and Other Stuff"   MOLLY IVINS 487
"Hair Dupe"   MOLLY IVINS 491
"Cracker-Barrel Reveries on the Tune 'Pax
   Americana' "   JONATHAN WILLIAMS 492
"Uncle Iv Surveys His Domain from His
   Rocker of a Sunday Afternoon as Aunt
   Dory Starts to Chop the Kindling"   JONATHAN WILLIAMS 494
"The Spoon Story"   DAVE GARDNER 494
"Chicken Every Sunday"   DAVE GARDNER 496
"The Rolls-Royce Story"   DAVE GARDNER 496
"Observations on American Indians"   DAVE GARDNER 497

SECTION FIVE: HOME ON THE ROAD

"Georgia on a Fast Train"	BILLY JOE SHAVER	503
On an Empty Stomach	LOUIS ARMSTRONG	504
from *Norwood*	CHARLES PORTIS	505
"Uncle Willy"	WILLIAM FAULKNER	513
"A Guest's Impression of New England"	WILLIAM FAULKNER	528
"The Hoosier and the Salt Pile"	WILLIAM TAPPAN THOMPSON	530
from *Vibration Cooking*	VERTAMAE SMART-GROSVENOR	533
The Neshoba County Fair	JILL CONNER BROWNE	541
from *Eating in Two or Three Languages*	IRVIN S. COBB	544
Raftmen's Passage	MARK TWAIN	546
"The Private History of a Campaign That Failed"	MARK TWAIN	556
"Taming the Bicycle"	MARK TWAIN	570
"If I Had a Boat"	LYLE LOVETT	576
"Confused Motorist"	JUSTIN WILSON	577
"Sizing Him Up"	JUSTIN WILSON	578
"Georgia Dust"	JOHN OLIVER KILLENS	579
"Old Dry Frye"	RICHARD CHASE	580
"Lamar Fountain Is Free"	GREGORY JAYNES	583
"One Last Cheer for Punk Kinkaid"	JAMES SEAY	587
Hustling Here and There	JELLY ROLL MORTON AS TOLD TO ALAN LOMAX	590
Meeting Hemingway	KATHERINE ANNE PORTER	597
"First Carolina Said-Song"	A. R. AMMONS	599
"Second Carolina Said-Song"	A. R. AMMONS	600

SECTION SIX: MIND AND HEART AND SOUL

"Precious Memories"	JOHN SHELTON REED	607
"The Ballad of Charles Whitman"	KINKY FRIEDMAN	609
"Knowing He Was Not My Kind yet I Followed"	BARRY HANNAH	611
"T for Texas (Blue Yodel No. 1)"	JIMMIE RODGERS	615

"Jackson"   BILLY EDD WHEELER AND JERRY
              LIEBER   617

"Empty Bed Blues"   BESSIE SMITH   618
"My Old Man and the Grass Widow"   ERSKINE CALDWELL   620
"Dang Me"   ROGER MILLER   624
"Saint Roxie"   FERROL SAMS   626
"A Little Full"   FERROL SAMS   628
"Grass Turned Out Green"   MARILYN NELSON WANIEK   629
"Love"   ZORA NEALE HURSTON   630
"Jambalaya (on the Bayou)"   HANK WILLIAMS   632
"Sister's Comin' Home/Down at the
    Corner Beer Joint"   WILLIE NELSON   633
from Hairdo   SARAH GILBERT   634
"The Hills of Zion"   H. L. MENCKEN   640
"Last Laugh"   ROBERT PENN WARREN   645
from Praying for Sheetrock   MELISSA FAY GREENE   647
"Spanish Pipedream"   JOHN PRINE   649
"Judgment in the Sky"   JERRY CLOWER   651

Copyright Acknowledgments   655

Index   665

ACKNOWLEDGMENTS

People whose suggestions or whose writing about Southern humor have been helpful to me in compiling this book include Lisa Howorth of the Center for the Study of Southern Culture, Eric Sundquist of the University of California at Los Angeles, Vereen Bell of Vanderbilt University, Jerry Elijah Brown of Auburn, James M. Cox of Dartmouth, M. Thomas Inge of Michigan State, John Ruskey of the Delta Blues Museum in Clarksdale, Mississippi, Gerald Howard of Norton, and such private-citizen readers as Ruth Porter, Polly King, Bruce Tucker, Ruff Fant, Dave Marsh, Pauline Kael, and Ann Lewis.

I found it useful as well as unacademically entertaining to take part in a symposium on Southern humor at Milsaps College, whose participants included John Shelton Reed of the University of North Carolina at Chapel Hill, James Cobb of the University of Tennessee, William Ferris of the Center for the Study of Southern Culture, Trudier Harris of Emory University, Anne Goodwin Jones of the University of Florida ("The Incredible Shrinking You-Know-What: Southern Women's Humor"), William Koon of Clemson, and Johanna Shields of the University of Alabama–Huntsville.

For biographical and other background information I have consulted a number of reference works, including *Southern Writers: A Biographical Dictionary,* edited by Robert Bain, Joseph M. Flora, and Louis D. Rubin, Jr.; *Blues Who's Who: A Biographical Dictionary of Blues Singers,* by Sheldon Harris; *The Encyclopedia of Southern Culture,* edited by Charles Reagan Wilson and William Ferris; *Woman with Guitar: Memphis Minnie's Blues,* by Paul and Beth Garon; Justin Kaplan's *Mr. Clemens and Mark Twain;* and Bill C. Malone's *Country Music U.S.A.* Other sources are mentioned in my introduction and notes.

But I daresay I neglected to consult all sorts of important sources whose omission from this roster is a reflection on me, not them. What I mainly did was dig around for two years in my bookshelves and record collection at home; in the stacks of the New York Society Library and (one pleasant afternoon) of the Joint University Libraries at my alma mater, Vanderbilt; and in bookstores around the South. Nice work if you can get it.

If only I could have gotten permission to include selections from Cormac McCarthy (he doesn't allow himself to be excerpted) and Richard Pryor (Mudbone wasn't available). Well, as Adam said when he and Eve left Paradise for the rest of the world, you can't have everything.

Roy Blount's
Book of
Southern Humor

INTRODUCTION

Here's what I figured:
• The Confederacy plus Kentucky.
• Funny on paper without pictures.
• And *various*. I wanted the world to know Southern humor in many different forms.

I also aspired to historical sweep. So I began at the beginning, with Virginia planter and colonial politician William Byrd (1674–1744). Byrd never set himself up as a humorist—the first thing he published was a serious scientific paper entitled ''An Account of a Negro Boy That Is Dappled in Several Places on His Body with White Spots.'' But he is the earliest Southerner still surviving in American lit. He is also the earliest American-born writer still regarded as witty.

Byrd wrote stuff that is still lively—about confronting bears, pulling his own tooth in the wilderness (not even any doors around), discussing the afterlife with a redskin, and feeling up a tavern wench. His poem ''Upon a Fart'' is not bad at all, and I would be pleased to present it as the first breath of Southern humor except that it was written when Byrd was residing in England dabbling in Queen Anne–period satire. His funniest stuff, today, is to be found in his matter-of-fact (matter-of-fact to *him,* apparently) secret diaries. Here is how I would boil those diaries all down into one day's entry:

> I lay abed late and rogered my wife to effect a reconciliation. I ate boiled milk for breakfast. Several of my negroes died. In the evening I attended the Governor's ball and danced with Mrs. Russell and Colonel Sm-th's son, who cut a

queer figure. The Governor wore the worst trousers of anyone present. I had good thoughts, good humor, but indifferent health, Thank God Almighty. I dreamed of a coffin being thrown through the door and a beaver emerging.

I say boiled down—in the original, for instance, the beaver and the coffin appear on different days. Byrd expressed moral reservations about slavery. On the other hand, I gather from the diaries that he and his wife argued by whipping each other's favorite attendants. I don't want to anthologize anybody who acted like that.

Now that I am an anthologist, I have more sympathy for other anthologists, even those (may they come up out of their dirt like waterlogged earthworms and shrivel into crisps under the suddenly reemergent sun) who have left me out of their anthologies of *anything*. (Have I not written tellingly enough about, say, basketball, or love?)

But Lord knows no anthologist has ever had it as hard as I have. Southern humor is an irregular thing to collect. Most of the funniest Southern writers have not been tight genre-minded sprinters in the Benchley-White-Thurber-Perelman *New Yorker* tradition; they have been longer-winded than that, and they have mixed humor in with everything from bloody murder (Flannery O'Connor) to anthropology (Zora Neale Hurston). Many comic Southern novels (mystery writer Carl Hiassen's, for example) are uproarious in the context of their plots but resist excerpting. A number of interesting contemporary Southern writers (Lewis Nordan, for example) take humor off into a kind of epiphanistic lyricism that recommends them, I would say, to some other choir than this one. The blues is full of humor but most of it depends on vocal inflections never meant to register on a page. Mounting an expedition into Southern humor—there is a lot of uncharted territory out there—and emerging with a tidy treasury of amusement would be like disappearing into the Amazon jungle and coming back toting a representative petting zoo.

Kiss my foot, however, if I haven't gathered a world of wonderful stuff here. What I would like to do now is to quote some of my favorite passages, such as this one from Clyde Edgerton's novel *Raney:*

> "Young people nowadays will go to almost any length," said Aunt Naomi. "I don't know what it's all coming to. Who ever heard of so much burning, beating, and stabbing, and my Lord, I can't imagine what Papa would done to me had I come home with a blue lightning bolt tattooed on my kneecap. Why he would—"
>
> "It's on the inside of her knee," says Mama.
>
> "Why he would have skint me alive."
>
> Up walked Charles all of a sudden and said we'd better come to the house, that Norris had a fish hook hung in his *nose . . . with the worm still on the hook.* We followed him to the cottage. I couldn't imagine.

But you will come to these passages right along. (You will also find out more about the hook, the worm, and Norris's nose.) The thing that is incumbent upon me, now, I guess, is to say a few words *about* Southern humor. All right, then. That passage from *Raney* exhibits several features which you might call typical:

• Characters bringing themselves abundantly to life through their fascination with other characters' deplorability.

• Careful attention to exactly how people talk ("would done" is nice).

• Close interaction with fish, bait, and other forms of animal life.

• People saying "I can't imagine," meanwhile imagining like a house afire.

• Young boys named something like Norris. Or could be a young girl. Norman Mailer's wife is Southern, named Norris. If it's a boy it's funnier. If it's a girl, it's destiny: she's just about going to have to go off away from home and do something her parents couldn't imagine.

The trouble is, *typical* (see Padgett Powell's story by that title) is not a term you use to describe something you approve of, in the South.

"Uncle Porter Junior has gone and lost Daddy's boat *and* motor, *and* drowned himself, trying to drown the new kittens."

"Well if that ain't just typical."

Southerners are too *sportive* with words—frolicsome and competitive—to use them as neutral analytical terms. I hate it when I am out on what is known as an author tour, and some hard-nosed interviewer tries to outflank my shameless book-mongering by asking questions designed to get to the bottom of humor: what *is* funny, after all; why *do* we laugh; and how did I, personally, get to be supposedly hilarious?

Sometimes I try hard to be responsive to these questions; sometimes I try hard to make it clear why I believe that my being responsive to these questions would be a bad idea; in either case the interviewer eventually looks at me as though he or she wishes I would quit.

So I do. If I am in luck, the next question is "Do Southerners laugh at different things than Northerners do?"

"Yes," I say. "Northerners."

But that is just a joke. At the bottom of Southern humor lies this fundamental truth: that nothing is less humorous, or less Southern, than making a genuine, good-faith effort to define and explain humor, particularly Southern humor.

Why particularly Southern humor? There you go, you're trying to draw me into something that we will both regret. If I had the sense that God gave a goose (and God knows God didn't give a goose much sense), I would introduce this anthology by declaring, with simple dignity, "I'm Southern, I'm a humorist, in my book this is Southern humor."

If I had that kind of sense, however, I would not be here before you today.

I would be a humor *consultant*—that's where the money is, getting paid by the hour for advice on improving corporate risibility. When you're a consultant you speak with authority, because you and your clients are wearing the same suit. (Maybe your tie is different, has little understated monkeys instead of spots.) "Give your company a funny name," I would be saying, only at greater length in order to stretch out the billable time.

"Well, we're not sure we want to do *that*. Owenco, Inc., is a pretty established name in virtual fundware, and old man Owen is still very much—"

"Oink Oink? Your name is Oink Oink and you come to *me*? Never mind. Give your employees funnier names, then."

"Well, we tried that, but a lot of them didn't like it. And we don't believe in running too roughshod over our people's feelings just for the sake of building their morale through humor. Do you?"

"Believe in it?" I would riposte. "Hell, I've . . . ."

That's what the old boy said, you know, when somebody asked him if he believed in infant baptism:

"Believe in it? Hell, I've seen it done!"

For the sake of argument, let's call that statement the quintessential Southern Zen koan. I first heard it some years ago in Yazoo City, Mississippi. What I was doing in Yazoo City is a pretty good story, involving the then President of the United States and an unaccommodating commode, and if I were a less self-effacing person I would have included the written version of that story in this book, but like I say I am *not* less self-effacing, and anyway I had to make some room for Mark Twain. Actually I believe I will quote, from that story, an ancillary story I was told by a Yazoo City native I knew in college, Spencer Gilbert:

"The first time I flew over town in an airplane, coming back from college, I looked down on the top of a water tank, and a sign on it said YAZOO CITY. That was the first time it ever occurred to me that those letters together look funny."

The point of Spencer's story, I believe, for our purposes here, is that you have to get back a certain distance from things to see them as comical. And if you live in a part of the country where folks are traditionally liable to hit or shoot you if you get brash with them, and vice versa, then it's a good idea to maintain a certain distance from everybody all the time (which is not to say that you aren't eternally devoted to these people, or sick and tired of them, or both). Let's hold on to that thought—although actually the story is easier to hold on to than the thought. Let's hold on to *that* thought.

If you were to ask me why there have been so many humorists in the South, I might cite this Appalachian folk story recorded by Loyal Jones:

A man came home after working late one night and found his wife in bed and his best friend hiding in the closet.

"Why, John, what are you doing in there?" he asked.

"Well, Bert," his friend answered. "Everybody has to be somewhere."

To that story I would append three stipulations:

First: I was born in Indianapolis. I say this because I don't want somebody popping up waving a certified copy of my birth certificate in an effort to cast this entire collection in doubt. I was born in Indianapolis because the Libby canned goods company transferred my Florida Panhandle father and my Mississippi mother to the Midwest for two years just to complicate my future résumé. My forebears on both sides are Southern as far back as there are unburned courthouses, and I grew up in Georgia from the age of eighteen months. I have been to the Delta, the French Quarter, the Okefenokee, civil rights demonstrations, Klan rallies, juke joints, a rattlesnake roundup, backstage at the old Opry, Willie Nelson's hotel room, Son Thomas's porch, Chet Atkins's golf tournament, Mean Joe Greene's rec room, Bear Bryant's office, George Jones's car, and everywhere else in the South except your mama's wedding, 'cause there weren't no men there, 'cause we all knew better than to get caught like that. Now I live in New York and Massachusetts, but that is because when I'm in the South I wander around wondering where I can get the *New York Times,* and when I'm in the North I wander around wondering where I can get some okra, and I would rather think about some okra than the *New York Times.*

Second: Of the 114 writers in this collection, fewer than 20 of them would be described as humorists. Being humorous in the South is like being motorized in Los Angeles or argumentative in New York—humorous is not generally a whole calling in and of itself, it's just something that you're in trouble if you aren't.

Third: I do not think of Southern as some kind of outlandish separate category of human life. Hey, I had a Southern *mother.* I had a Southern first-grade teacher. I went through measles and puberty in the South. Maybe it's because I'm Southern that I get a certain thrill out of these lines from a postbellum poem called "I'm a Good Old Rebel":

> I hates the Yankee nation
> And everything they do,
> I hates the Declaration
> Of Independence too.

On the other hand, maybe I get that thrill because I learned to appreciate early in life—in the South—both the Pledge of Allegiance and the American tradition of nothing sacred. (Believe in free speech? Hell, I've heard it *denounced*.) Granted, Southern tradition is full of *dumb* sacred things. But Southerners love America—except for its government—all the more because many of our great-great-granddaddies damn near licked it. Incidentally, a Southerner *wrote* the Declaration of Independence. (These truths be self-evident? Hell, I've held 'em myself!) So don't talk to me, about whatever it was we were talking about.

If you want to, you can say that Southern humor deals with "typical" concerns of the region: dirt, chickens, defeat, family, religion, prejudice, collard greens, politics, and diddie wa diddie. But are not these concerns, boiled down, pretty much like everybody else's? Of course, Southerners boil them down (speaking figuratively, except with regard to collard greens and diddie wa diddie) with hamhock in the pot; although not so much anymore, because believe it or not we too have heard about low-density lipids. But we still know that eating right is more than a matter of molecular chemistry. As the eponymous hero of Charles Portis's novel *Norwood* says to some boys he comes upon on a sidewalk of New York, as they are toasting marshmallows over a smoldering mattress: "They ain't going to taste like anything cooked over hair."

Demographically, we still fry a lot. Is frying a defining characteristic of the South? A boiled New England dinner eases its way into your system the same way a New England sentence does: without calling much attention to itself. Whereas a dinner of fried panfish (fins and all) and hushpuppies and fried yellow squash says *hot damn, here I am. I got the grit and I got the grease, come on.* . . . And while eating fried things Southerners will often talk about them, even talk *with* them—and I don't mean just that some of us will talk with food in our mouths, excuse me. I mean we will *have conversations with our food.*

That's right. We will pick up a crispy-fried bluegill and say, "My, you're nice. I believe I remember hooking you in particular. Hope you enjoyed that cricket as much as I'm about to enjoy you." And then somebody else will put on the voice of the (just-caught) fish and say, "You can take me home and clean me and eat me, B'rer Fox, but whatever you do, donnnn't throw me back up under them lily pads." Maybe we will usually do that to nonplus Yankees who may be at the table; but here is what we *will* do: we will chew on our choice of *words,* engage in dialogue with our words, roll them around in our mouth, enjoy them for the peculiar artifacts or organisms that they are. And toss a bunch of them scooters protogrammatically together in one sentence like frogs, rabbits, turkeys, cats, snakes, Chihuahuas, katydids, wasps, and several other kinds of bugs and dogs in a confined area just to see what they will do. Believe in split infinitives? Hell, I have known infinitives to actually just, truth of the matter, near about evermore before God in broad daylight purely . . . Let's just say I have known infinitives to. To the point where the infinitive was scattered to the winds like an opened-up sack of feed, *and the person speaking didn't even necessarily know what an infinitive was.*

I know I overdid that last paragraph. On purpose, to make a point: Southern humor is usually better when it is trying to do justice to the nature of things than when it is trying to be comical. We see this in Hank Williams: "Did you ever see a robin weep?" is funnier, though it fits right in with the genuine pain of "I'm So Lonesome I Could Cry" than anything in "Kaw-li-ga," the ditty about the romantically frustrated wooden Indian.

Before I got off into extending infinitives into infinity and all, the point I was making was that words in the South have lives of their own. Here's another of Loyal Jones's Appalachian stories:

> A girl from the country went into town and got a job with a lawyer's family who were pretty high-faluting. The girl cooked, cleaned the house, and did the wash and that sort of thing. The daughter in the family got engaged to a young man up the street.
> One day the lady of the house called to the hired girl, "Have you seen my daughter's fiancé?"
> "No, she ain't put it in the wash yet."

Let's get back to that infant baptism story. What is essentially Southern-humorous about it? One thing is, it's a deep-structural pun, which vivifies and confounds an abstraction by getting physical with it. (Compare the country song title "If I Said You Had a Beautiful Body, Would You Hold It Against Me?") Another thing is, it involves religion. I am not a Southern Methodist anymore, though I was strenuously brought up to be; but I still find myself, as you may have noted above, invoking the Lord. That is because you can't invoke nothing.

Compare the infant baptism story to that well-known *Eastern*-religious koan "What is the sound of one hand clapping?" Southerners don't have to sit mulling that one over. Given the meaning of the word "clapping," there isn't any such thing as one hand doing it. And never has been, except that time when John was sitting out in the yard meditating and his wife said, "John, when are you going to come in here and work on our relationship?" and John said, "What is the sound of one hand clapping?" and she said *Wap* upside his head with the flat of her palm.

Possibly one hand *trying* to clap in thin air is a low, barely detectable whushy sound, maybe something that only a cat could hear. Have you ever noticed how a cat's ears will do—moving around, cocking at various angles, those little hairs sticking out all different ways—when people in the same room can't hear a thing? Personally I think the cat is just trying to get attention, but who knows. I don't think a person could hear one hand clapping against a high whistling wind, even. It's not something I've ever heard. Once I talked to a man who claimed that his wife was driving him crazy because she couldn't tell the difference between the phone ringing on television and the phone ringing there in their house in real life. An unusual dysfunction, but maybe it was part of the Lord's plan. Maybe one afternoon the phone rang on a rerun of *All in the Family* and she picked up her phone—thinking it was ringing—just before it *would have actually* rung if she hadn't picked it up, but since she did pick it up, her line was busy when somebody was trying to call her to tell her something filthy that she had lived too Christian a life to have to hear. We don't know. We just don't know.

If you're not clapping against anything you're not clapping for anything either, because you're not clapping, you're just waving; of course, if somebody sees you doing it she might think you're waving at her. Might be worth a try. It's the same with invocation—and if it's the Lord you're invoking instead of, say, Heidegger, then you are empowered to move along a lot quicker from story to story. I've seen it done.

Here's *another* Loyal Jones story:

> A woman moved from Kentucky to Dayton, Ohio. One day a fire started in her house, and she called the fire department.
> "Hello, I've got a fire out here in my house."
> "Okay, where is it?"
> "It's in the kitchen."
> "I mean, how do we get to it?"
> "Well, you come in off the back porch or through the living room, either one."
> "No, I mean, how do we get from here where we are to you out where you are?"
> "Ain't you got one of them big red trucks?"

If you are willing to live with the fact that everything is phenomenal—and you are able to bear in mind, meanwhile, that nobody with any sense ever expected the phenomenological to be logical (because how the hell can it be, when words, the very things the phenomenologist is trying to comprehend phenomena *with,* are phenomena themselves, and wait a minute, isn't the phenomenologist one too, *him*self?)—then there you have Southern humor in a nutshell, except surely you have more sense than to want anything as strong as Southern humor to be packed down that tight. And how about the phenomenologist's mama? She was a sight in this world. I can just hear her now—"Son, don't you come into this house talking about *ab ovo,* that ain't the way you were raised and you know it."

We can't hold ourselves out at arm's length, brethren—and when you consider that I don't have any more rigorous idea of what I am talking about than a man I knew in Georgia did when he realized, while going eighty miles an hour downhill, that the fire ants had got all up inside his motorcycle leathers, you will see why I say: far be it from me to sit here calmly summing Southern humor up.

Others might sum it up, unthinkingly, as crackerishness. But that fiancé won't wash. One thing we need to get straight about Southern humor— Southern culture generally—is that it is Africo-Celtic, or Celtico-African.

According to the scholarly work *Cracker Culture: Celtic Ways in the Old South,* by Grady McWhiney (which I believe in absolutely because it makes me feel less pale), the South was originally settled not predominantly by Anglo-Saxons (as was the North) but by wild, oral, whiskey-loving, unfastidious, tribal, horse-racing, government-hating, Wasp-scorned Irish and Welsh and pre-Presbyterian Scots.

Who then brought in Africans. The ferment that produced Southern culture has *not* been a matter of Wasp civilization guiltily but angrily at odds with (while depending upon) enforced black labor. It has been a profoundly confused struggle to determine who is less like New England—Sut Lovingood or Mudbone, Jerry Lee Lewis or Little Richard. Crackers never did admit that they were oppressors. They could always put that off on Washington. (The fact that Washington, outside the embassies, is in most respects a Southern town, organized around government instead of, say, sawmills, is something that I suppose Northerners might call an irony.) What it came down to was that blacks, after all the exploitation and co-optation they had submitted to, proved in the crunch to be *more Southern.* Years after the news showed white mobs chanting in defiance of desegregation, the following jump-rope rhyme was recorded among black children in east Texas:

> Two, four, six, eight,
> We ain't gonna integrate.
> Eight, six, four, two,
> Bet you sons-of-bitches do.

When Rob Slater's class of high school students in Winston-Salem, North Carolina, rebelled against a Northern-devised intelligence test by making up their own "In Your Face Test of No Certain Skills" and sent it up to the testers, who scored C's and D's on it, I counted it as not just a racial but also a regional victory. One question was "Who is buried in Grant's Tomb?" The correct answer was "Your mama."

The civil rights movement, I grant you, was an all-American constitutional triumph (as far as it went) that could not have been achieved without the help of Northern media and activists. But in the local courthouses and on the TV news, where it counted, it was a struggle to prove who were the truest fundamentalists, black ones or white ones—resulting in an explosive Africo-Celtic fusion (King versus Connor) like the Uncle Remus stories (slave instructing Harris), like *Gone with the Wind* (Hattie McDaniel and Butterfly McQueen supporting the O'Haras), like country music (the Delta Blues seeping into mountain ballad), like Elvis (soul giving body to white gospel keening), like Mark Twain (Jim on the raft with Finn).

(Incidentally, if you wonder whether Southern humor is important enough to devote a whole book to, you might bear in mind that Ernest Hemingway said all of modern American literature grew out of *Huckleberry Finn*.)

What have black Southerners and white Southerners always had in common, aside from the soil and the sweet potatoes and the heat and the possums and just about everything else but rhythm and money and rights? They have had orality. They have had a sense that English—as American infants of whatever ethnicity (and baptized or not) realize when they smile in their first recognition of words—is a comically physical thing for earthy people who bypassed the Enlightenment to wrap their mouths around.

"Nigger, your breed ain't metaphysical," wrote Robert Penn Warren in a 1945 poem—to which Sterling A. Brown riposted, "Cracker, your breed ain't exegetical." Don't white folks ever get the last word? I guess the rule of thumb is, if the first word is "nigger," no. (Warren and Brown were both fine and enlightened writers, but Brown was funnier.)

Let me interject here a story from my experience. I don't mean it to prove anything absolutely positive about Southern race relations, Lord knows: I was attacking Southern race relations in print, in the South (for all the good it did anybody but me), before I was a legal adult. Southern racism is full of double binds ("We ain't heard *our* Negroes say nothing about freedom") that have been as damnably confining as the infant baptism koan is (sort of) liberating.

But here's what happened. Twenty years ago, I was lying flat on my back in the woods in the middle of the night in Arkansas with a po-white man whose conversation I had been enjoying for a couple of hours. While we waited for his dogs to start going *ba-oooo* in the distance to signify that they were on the trail of a raccoon, we talked about various things. Suddenly, out of the blue (or actually the darkness), he said, "I hate niggers."

My heart sank. "You *do?*" I said.

"Well," he said, sounding surprised that I was surprised, and then he started talking about black people he had known all his life, had swum with as a boy and walked the woods with as a man. Nothing he said was progressive or even sufficiently respectful, but none of it sounded hateful, more like fascinated. And finally he said, "This colored feller Tooley, I'll bring him a possum, 'cause I don't eat 'em. And he'll carry on, 'Lawd, Mr. Bobby, that thing got teeth on him, that thing is ugg-leeeee, Lawd, I always has been mos' bewary of a possum, *hoooo.'* And then be John Brown if I don't come back the next day and Tooley has already cooked that thing and eat it all down to the bones and sucked whatever po' marrer there may *be in* possum bones out of them.'' What seemed to stick in this man's craw about black people was that they could get more out of a wild animal than he could, on an even smaller budget.

I wish I could pull leprechauns and Yoruba tricksters, Brother Dave Gardner and Little Richard, George Wallace and Stokely Carmichael together into one unified theory of Crackro-African or Africo-Cracker mischief and indirection, but I'm not exegetical enough.

I will say this: I read *The Signifying Monkey,* Henry Louis Gates, Jr.'s, book about African-American vernacular irony—which Gates with linguistic nicety calls ''Signifyin(g)''—and its traditional uses in fostering tough intimacy among blacks and protecting slaves' pride against white violence. And I kept thinking that this was a lot like Southern white irony and its traditional uses in fostering tough intimacy among whites and protecting them against each other and the overbearing North. (To the extent that Southern white irony is a defense against blacks, on the other hand, it is Br'er Bear trying to position himself against Br'er Rabbit.) ''Cracking'' is a Scots and Irish term for pointed boastful joshing and also an African-American synonym for ''Signifyin(g).'' One thing I hope this anthology bears out is the kinship, grossly abused but persistent, between humor of the crackers and humor of the brothers. Without gainsaying that ''lynch'' comes from a Virginia Irishman's name.

Maybe in some parts of the world, or even of this country, words are taken as givens or as things that grow naturally in the dictionary. But to Southerners (as to Africans and Irishmen I have sat at tables with), language is the sound of the tongue and the mind clapping, with an understandable tendency to lose the beat, especially in print. We wrestle with our words the way we do with our children, so as to get syncopated with them.

Here's a story Zora Neale Hurston heard in Florida. A man sent his daughter off to school for seven years, and when she came back he sat her down and began to dictate a letter:

> '' 'Dear Brother, our chile is done come home from school and all finished up and we is very proud of her.' ''
> Then he ast de girl ''Is you got dat?''
> She tole 'im ''yeah.''
> ''Now tell him. . . . 'Our mule is dead but Ah got another mule and when Ah say (clucking sound of tongue and teeth) he moved from de word.'
> ''Is you got dat?'' he ast de girl.
> ''Naw suh,'' she tole 'im.
> He waited a while and he ast her again, '' 'You got dat down yet?''

"Naw, suh, Ah ain't got it yet."

"How come you ain't got it?"

"Cause Ah can't spell (clucking sound)."

"You mean to tell me you been off to school seben years and can't spell (clucking sound)? Why Ah could spell that myself and Ah ain't been to school a day in mah life. Well jes' say (clucking sound), he'll know what you mean and go on wid de letter."

Writing isn't all language, tooby sho. People who pronounce upon Southern culture cite "sense of place" and "sense of character." Well, Southern humorists have been more likely to ramble than to settle into small-town society, but they have rambled through a physical world, of not just routes but roads, not just areas but woods and neighborhoods, and they have gotten themselves thoroughly embroiled along the way with the horses or the vehicles that they rode through on. When they have put down roots, it has been in settlements where people have known each other for quite likely a lot longer than they ever wanted to, so that they have had ample time, material, and audience for fashioning themselves and each other into characters.

But that doesn't mean that the cream of Southern humor nestles warmly in the South. Traditionally, the Southern writer has had this great advantage: he or she might be not only the only writer in town but also the only free-range reader. Hard-core book larnin' is your town's name written on top of the water tower, up there for strangers to see. So a writer in the South is less likely to be tripping over other writers, less likely to be reduced to writing about what's already paginated. The air is full of unwritten stories ripe for translation to the page. And before the neighbors discover that they have been immortalized, they or the writer may well be safely dead.

Hardly anybody in this book has been sustained in his or her vocation by Southern audiences and media. Of course, artists naturally aspire to national exposure and compensation, but most of these writers, white and black, have had to get a foothold outside the South before they could speak the rough truths that were self-evident to them as Southerners. "Southern Comfort," muses Blanche Du Bois on seeing that brand name on a bottle. "How can that be, I wonder?"

You won't hear a humorous Southern writer proclaiming, like James Joyce in exile from Ireland, that he or she means to "forge in the smithy of my soul the uncreated conscience of my race." Here's what Joseph Mitchell, tobacco-country legend of *The New Yorker,* recently told National Public Radio:

One of the greatest things. . . . One time the state of North Carolina gave me a gold medal. My youngest daughter jokes with me a good deal, and she read in the paper that I had been awarded a gold medal, by the state of North Carolina?

> And she got on the phone, said, "Daddy, I see that you're still foolin' 'em."
> Well I can't tell you how that made me. . . . The idea that I'm half a swindler
> delights me more than the literary stuff—though I'm very glad to see these
> things, God knows, and all that. But at the same time, the feeling that I'm
> foolin' the population pleases me too. You see when you write these stories,
> you're not writin' 'em for, God forgive me, posterity, you're writin' 'em for a
> weekly magazine hopin' some people will laugh at it, see? If I had sat down and
> said, "I'm going to try and write some literature," do you know what a mess
> that would've been? Can you imagine? But it's accidental, the fact that some-
> body will *re-read* these things? That makes me feel, I tell you—that people will
> go into a store and . . . The damn book costs a lot of money!

That was Mitchell telling the plain truth, but also Signifyin(g). When it comes down to anthology time, the test of humor is whether it will keep.

What makes most Southern humor rot? Not meanness—Sut Lovingood is rough as a cob, Mark Twain damned the human race, Faulkner said a good book was worth any number of old ladies, didn't anybody mess with Memphis Minnie, and Katherine Anne Porter once praised Eudora Welty for "her blistering humor and her just cruelty" in "Petrified Man." Nothing is less enduringly savory than narrow-mindedness that tries to pass for geniality. Whereas a tang of meanness may be a preservative—vinegar for pickling real fellow feeling and love of the world. Mean as in biting, mean as in common, mean as in signify.

Nothing's funny unless it smacks of delight. But what surely leads to spoil-age in Southern or any other humor is condescension—or, as Porter put it (describing what Welty eschewed), "that slack tolerance or sentimental ten-derness . . . that amounts to criminal collusion between author and charac-ter." The Southern humorists who put me off are those who rest their crabby/maudlin appeal upon the assumption that certain of their characters (for instance, themselves) are just about the most precious *thangs*. . . .

Too much Africo-Celtic blood has been shed for Southern humor to be good *and* cozy. The precious thang in any kind of writing is slippery exacti-tude, such as we see in that infant baptism story. Here's a master-slave ex-change that Mel Watkins cites in his book on African-American humor:

> "You scoundrel, you ate my turkey."
> "Yes, suh, Massa, you got less turkey but you sho nuff got mo' Nigger."

The word "Nigger," there, digests too many shifting layers to ever settle. When writing keeps, it's not because it finds a niche but because it keeps on moving. Zora Neale Hurston observed that "the colored preacher, in his cooler passages, strives for grammatical correctness, but goes natural when he

warms up. . . . The congregation wants to hear the preacher breathing."
Believe in it? Heard it done. Now from the white side of the aisle hear
Knoxville, Tennessee, newspaper columnist Jimmie Dykes:

> Once, somewhere in Georgia, somebody was watching the rednecks dance. It
> seemed like they were all bouncing around differently. He asked a good ol' boy
> nearby what was the trouble. "Hell," he said, "they ain't dancin' to the music.
> They're dancin' to the words."

If there's anything to which abstract correctness does not apply, it's humor.
Almost everything is funny to somebody, and nothing makes everybody laugh.
The New Yorker, in the days when it was the standard-bearer of American
humor, never appreciated Flannery O'Connor, for God's sake. I once heard
O'Connor say she had no patience for Dickens. I daresay there are funny
writers whom I don't get. For a white boy I do get the blues (Lord, Lord)—
here's a verse from "You Got to Love Her with a Feeling," by Tampa Red:

> You know the cop took her in, she didn't
> Need no bail—
> She shook it for the judge, he put
> The cop in jail.

Judging boils down to feeling. From some of the notes that precede the first
appearance of each author in the following pages, you may gather that a high
percentage of the writers included are people I have had a drink with (not even
mentioning sherry with Flannery O'Connor, tea with Bailey White, buttermilk with Jerry Clower, bourbon with Jim Wilcox), but that was not a
criterion, I just get around. I have in fact left out or underrepresented certain
friends and personally favorite writers, just to prove my Olympian detachment—that's my story and I'm sticking to it.

One piece that is not in this book still nags at me: "The Shape of a Year,"
an odd brief essay by an obscure Louisianan named M. C. Blackman. Bill
Whitworth of Arkansas, editor of *The Atlantic Monthly,* recommended this
piece to me as something that had somehow always stuck with him. I found it
in a 1948 issue of *The New Yorker,* and read it, and it stuck with me. It describes
Blackman's way of visualizing, mentally, a calendar year. It for certain would
have added to this collection's variety.

However, it did not pertain to any of the Confederate states or Kentucky (it
was set in a New York cocktail party and in Blackman's cerebrum), it wasn't
funny, exactly, and it needed the little drawing, by Blackman, that went with
it. Whitworth didn't know much about Blackman, except that newspaper
colleagues called him Inky. I looked up several brief small-town Louisiana

reminiscences by Blackman, published in *The New Yorker* and elsewhere. They were more nostalgic than humorous. Still I kept thinking that this man figured into Southern humor some way.

M. C. Blackman sounds like a rap artist's cognomen, but of course this was way back before rap. On the acknowledgments page of *You All Spoken Here,* by Roy Wilder, Jr., I noticed the name Marion Cyrenus Blackman. Yes, Wilder wrote me, that was Inky. Wilder had known him, in New York newspaper circles, as a source of some Southern-speech lore, also as a loner and a drinker of spritzers (hardly a Southern taste). Wilder said Charles Portis might have some information about Inky. I wrote to Portis, who responded that he knew Blackman "slightly at the *Herald Tribune,* where he was a veteran of the old rewrite bank. So slightly that I thought his name was Blackie Inkman for about a year." Portis said Blackman had worked at the *Arkansas Gazette* in the 1930s, and he returned from New York to Little Rock "to retire (not knowing a soul, I believe) and took city buses all over town, just for the ride. I happened to see him one day on a bus stop bench. Doubled back in my car and made a couple of passes to make sure it was Blackie or Inky. Picked him up and took him somewhere but he said not to pick him up again."

There, I knew the man was a key to something. The one thing all the pieces collected here have in common is that, after having read them over several times, I would like right now to pick up any one of them again.

P.S. As far as historical sweep goes, the most influential Southern institutions today, I guess, are Wal-Mart, CNN, the forthcoming Atlanta Olympics, mostly soulless country music, and a feel-your-pain policy-wonk President. Country music can still be good, though. Jimmy Dale Gilmore sings, "I would've killed myself, but it made no sense/Committin' suicide in self-defense." And Bill Clinton is slick, he's up to things, and he comes from a humorous mama. When somebody asked her how it felt when one of her husbands shot at her, she said, "About like when *anybody* shoots at you." There have been all kinds of connections between the South and humor, over the years, that people aren't widely aware of. Oliver Hardy was a Georgian born and raised. He left Milledgeville to seek his fortune in the movies shortly before Flannery O'Connor was born there. Charlotte Moorman, who made a name for herself in New York by playing the cello topless back when that was considered outrageous, was from the South. Did you know that Margaret Dumont, who was so funny in Marx Brothers movies because she was *so* humorless, was born in Atlanta? George Herriman, creator of Krazy Kat, was born in New Orleans. Jim Henson, creator of the Muppets, grew up in the Delta. And here's something my friend Slick Lawson down in Nashville told me, that a man told him, just the other day, about another man who was bald: "I've seen more hair on a bar of soap down at the Holiday Inn." Holiday Inns started in the South too—and now, finally, there's something funny about them. In any self-respecting library, by the way, you can find William Byrd's fart poem, on page 245 of *Another Secret Diary of William Byrd of Westover,* edited by Maude H. Woodfin. According to that poem, Maids at Court in the days of Queen Anne and Sir Isaac Newton did something with farts, for amusement (I don't know, but sounds like Byrd may have seen it done), that you may have assumed nobody but awful old Southern boys ever did. Lit them. The Maids' were blue too.

Oh, but that's too low a note to end on. If you want to read something *inspiring* about Southern humor, read Ralph Ellison's essay "An Extravagance of Laughter" (too long and complex to be reprinted here), in his book *Going to the Territory.* After a Southern boyhood and three years of studying music at Tuskegee Institute, in 1936 Ellison moved to New York, where he loved the freedom but found himself astounded by bad manners on the subway and by the fact that he missed some things about the South. One evening his hero and new-found Harlem friend Langston Hughes invited him to take in a play. Until he arrived at the theater, Ellison didn't know that the play—his first exposure to Broadway—was *Tobacco Road,* Jack Kirkland's long-running adaptation of the Erskine Caldwell novel. "Had I been more alert," he says in the essay, "it might have occurred to me that somehow a group of white Alabama farm folk had learned of my presence in New York, thrown together a theatrical troupe, and flown north to haunt me. But being dazzled by the lights," and so on, Ellison settled back to watch white trash dramatized on the Great White Way. When he saw Ellie May and Lov "uttering sounds of animal passion" and "floundering and skittering back-to-back across the stage," he fell into a laughing fit that embarrassed Hughes and disrupted the proceedings. When other patrons in the balcony saw that this person reduced to helpless laughter was black, they began to "howl and cheer," but theatergoers down below, who couldn't see him, reacted huffily. As for the actors, they "were now shading their eyes and peering open-mouthed toward the balcony." Ellison felt "as though I had been stripped naked, kicked out of a low-flying plane onto an Alabama road, and ordered to laugh for my life." Though part of him was mortified, the rest of him doubled over and straightened back up and doubled over again and wheezed and choked in laughter—all the more convulsively because he was recalling an apropos in-joke that Tuskegee students would elaborate among themselves.

The story was that since African-Americans in small Southern towns "were regarded as having absolutely *nothing* in their daily experience which could possibly inspire *rational* laughter," and since a given black person did, however, sometimes find something hilarious even while crossing the town square, he would at such a moment leap headfirst into a "laughing barrel," where he was "apt to double up with a second gale of laughter—and that triggered, apparently, by his own mental image of himself laughing at himself upside down.'' To their dismay, respectable white citizens would find themselves joining in this laughter—which would cause the embarreled laugher to laugh all the harder, which would cause the whites to suspect that ''in some mysterious fashion the Negro involved was not only laughing at *himself* laughing, but was also laughing at *them* laughing at his laughing against their own most determined wills. And if such was the truth, it suggested that somehow a Negro (and this meant *any* Negro) could become with a single hoot-and-cackle both the source and master of an outrageous and untenable situation.''

Finally, reduced to tears, Ellison calmed down. He sat there in the balcony awash in ''embarrassment, self-anger, ethnic scorn, and at last a feeling of comic relief. And all because Erskine Caldwell compelled me to laugh at his symbolic, and therefore nonthreatening, Southern whites, and thus he shocked me into recognizing certain absurd aspects of our common humanity.''

All together now, if you will, let's roll out the barrel.

SECTION ONE

MY PEOPLE, MY PEOPLE
(HOW'S YOUR
MAMA 'N' THEM?)

The Benefits of the Married State

It supplies the world with population
Without which we would be awful;
It does all this, besides it makes copulation
A virtue, when under circumstances lawful.

—Col. *W.C. Falkner*
   (William Faulkner's great-grandfather)

B. B. KING

The great guitarist and singer Riley B. King (the "B. B." was an early shortening of "Blues Boy") grew up on a Mississippi Delta plantation. He had an aunt named Jemima who introduced him to the blues. What do his friends call him? Well, I once heard Ray Charles call him "B." This little ditty, which he improvised at a 1970 recording session, starts us off on a suitably conflicted, fundamental note.

"Nobody Loves Me but My Mother"

Nobody loves me but my mother
And she could be jivin' too.
Nobody loves me but my mother
And she could be jivin' too.

Now you see why I act funny Baby
When you do the things you do.

BAILEY WHITE

Bailey White is a first-grade teacher who lives with her mother, Rose, in Thomasville, Georgia. In her soft-voiced National Public Radio commentaries about south Georgia life, she sounds rather venerable, but when her best-selling collection of those pieces, Mama Makes Up Her Mind, propelled her into celebrity in 1993, she was revealed to be forty-one and younger-looking than that, even. In print, the folks she writes about and also her prose have considerable snap. She is said to generate more letters than any other NPR commentator. "Some of them are from nuts," she told the New York Times. *"I got one that was just words on a page. She said, 'Dear Harley Davidson White,' and then she told me about her laundry and how she had not gotten correct change. I got a very sad letter once from a woman after I'd written about an old aunt who went crazy. This woman wrote and said she knew exactly how that aunt felt, she could feel it happening to her, that she was a forty-one-year-old spinster. . . . I wrote her back and said that I, too, was a forty-one-year-old spinster, and I didn't find it all that bad and to cheer up."*

"Mama's Memoirs"

For years we've been trying to get Mama to write her memoirs. She actually started once. She was writing them on old envelopes with a blue ballpoint pen. But she would make her grocery list on the other side of the envelope, and she kept leaving her memoirs at the checkout counter of Piggly Wiggly.

We bought Mama an electric typewriter, but the persistent hum made her nervous. "I can't stop and think with that humming," she said, glaring at the machine. "I feel like it's saying, 'Type, you old fool!' " Then my sister tried to train Mama to use a word processor. But she kept mashing the wrong buttons, and she ended up with three pages of dollar marks in her early childhood and a nine everywhere there should have been a space. And her account of the birth of her younger sister, Eleanor, turned out with every letter that should have been capital, small, and every letter that should have been small, capital—which, she said, gave a false sense of importance to the event.

"What I really need," she said, "is that old Underwood upright typewriter that used to sit under the sink." But my niece, Lucy, had taken that typewriter to college in Atlanta and had abandoned it when she got her first computer. So Mama had a good excuse not to write her memoirs.

Then, one summer, while cleaning out the attic of an old aunt in Saltville, Virginia, I found another Underwood upright typewriter. My aunt said I could have it, if I could just get it down from the attic and home on the train. The typewriter is the shape and size of a sperm whale. My aunt's husband, a newspaper journalist, had wrestled it up into the attic and then did. I rigged up a series of winches and pulleys and got it down.

Then I practiced different ways of carrying that typewriter. I'm strong for my size, so the sheer weight of it wasn't the problem. But if you tilt it the wrong way, the bell will ding and the carriage will swoop down and whack you on the knee. And I had to be fast and agile, because the train barely pauses at my station in Georgia. If you're not at the door with your bags and ready to leap off when the train begins to brake, you end up the next morning in Fort Lauderdale.

With the help of several gallant, old-fashioned uncles and a fluttering chorus of their wives making little shrieks and swapping yarns about hernias, I got the typewriter onto the train in Richmond. Then I was on my own. I staggered down the aisle to my assigned seat and plopped down beside a very alert looking young woman. "For my mother's memoirs," I gasped. The alert look changed to a kind of guarded disgust, and she clamped the headset of her portable tape player over her ears and began viciously reading a short story in her *New Yorker* magazine. I could barely hear the squeak of Beethoven's Fifth Symphony.

After a while I began to feel the flow of blood to my feet shut off, and I realized that I was going to have to get the typewriter off my lap and onto the overhead rack. I did it in two heaves, one to chest height, then up and onto the rack. At one point everything went black inside my head except for one bright light behind which I thought I could see my dead uncle, the journalist, dressed in white robes and beckoning earnestly to me across a deep valley. When I opened my eyes, my seatmate was gone. Only her *New Yorker* magazine was left, the pages still rustling. Later I heard her down the aisle, arguing with the attendant about assigned seats.

It was late at night when we got to Georgia. A nice man from Ludowici had moved over to sit by me. "Your mama can type?" he asked.

"My mama can do anything," I said.

"Yeah," he said, "my mama is like that, too. But the one thing she can't do is type." He helped me get the typewriter off the train as it paused for its one instant.

We keep the typewriter on the kitchen table. Mama acts like she doesn't know it's there. But sometimes, late at night, I see a light on in the kitchen, and I hear a sound like somebody is out there cracking oysters open with a rock. And then I know Mama is writing her memoirs.

JOSEPH MITCHELL

Anyone who thinks of Southern humor as parochial should bear in mind that the man most often called the quintessential New Yorker writer is a deep-dyed North Carolinian. Too poor at math to master the rapid calculations involved in his family's cotton and tobacco business, Joe Mitchell came to the big city at twenty-one, the day after the 1929 stock market crash, and made a vocation of his great ear for talk. Most of his profiles of raffish characters (collected in 1992 in the best-selling Up in the Old Hotel) *have been set in New York, but he also wrote several semifictional recollections of life back home, including "I Blame It All on Momma." "Life is a mess," Mitchell said at the age of eighty-four, "but you wouldn't want to miss it."*

"I Blame It All on Mamma"

Mrs. Copenhagen Calhoun, who lives on a riverbank watermelon farm in Black Ankle County, about a mile from the town of Stonewall, is the only termagant I have ever admired. She has no fondness for authority and is opposed to all public officials, elected or appointed. Once a distinguished senator came to Stonewall and spoke in the high-school auditorium; just after he finished telling how he made it a practice to walk in the footsteps of Thomas Jefferson, she stood up and said, "Senator, you sure are getting too big for your britches." A mayor of Stonewall once tried to get her fired from her job as cook in the station restaurant of the Charleston, Pee Dee & Northern Railroad. A woman who got drunk in public, he said, was a disgrace to the town. She kept her mouth shut until he came up for reelection; then she went up and down Main Street making speeches which helped defeat him. "Why, the stuck-up old hypocrite!" she said in one of her speeches. "He goes to the country club on Saturday night and gets as drunk as a goose on ice, and Sunday morning he stands up in the Methodist choir and sings so loud the whole church echoes for a week." She believes that public officials are inclined to overlook the fact that Americans are free, and when she is brought into court for disturbing the peace she invariably begins her address to the judge by stating, "This is a free country, by God, and I got my rights." She has a long tongue, and Judge Elisha Mullet once said she could argue the legs off an iron pot. She has many bad qualities, in fact, and her husband often complains that she has made his life a hell on earth, but when I go back to Stonewall for a visit and find that she is still insisting on her rights, I always feel better about the vigor of democracy.

I was in the tenth grade when I became one of her admirers. At that time, in 1924, she was unmarried and had just come up from Charleston to cook in the station restaurant. It was the only restaurant in Stonewall; railroad men ate there, and so did people from the sawmill, the cotton gin, and the chewing-tobacco factory. After school I used to hang around the station. I would sit on a bench beside the track and watch the Negro freight hands load boxcars with bales of cotton. Some afternoons she would come out of the kitchen and sit on the bench beside me. She was a handsome, big-hipped woman with coal-black hair and a nice grin, and the station agent must have liked her, because he let her behave pretty much as she pleased. She cooked in her bare feet and did not bother to put shoes on when she came out for a breath of fresh air. "I had an aunt," she told me, "who got the dropsy from wearing shoes in a hot kitchen." Once I asked her how she came to be named Copenhagen. "Mamma named all her babies after big towns," she said. "It was one of her fancy habits. Her first was a boy and she named him New Orleans. Then my sister came along and she named her Chattanooga. Mamma was real fond of snuff, and every payday Pa would buy her a big brown bladder of Copenhagen snuff. That's where she got my name."

One Friday night, after Miss Copey had been working at the restaurant a couple of months, the station agent wrote her a pass and she went down to Charleston to see her family. When she returned Monday on the 3:30, she was so drunk the conductor had to grab her elbows and help her down the train steps. She paid no attention to him but sang "Work, for the Night Is Coming." She bustled into the kitchen, kicked off her shoes, and began throwing things. She would pick up a pot and beat time with it while she sang a verse of the hymn, and then she would throw it. "Work till the last beam fad-eth, fad-eth to shine no more," she would sing, and then a stewpot would go sailing across the room. I stood at a window and stared. She was the first drunken woman I had ever seen and the spectacle did not disappoint me; I thought she was wonderful. Finally the chief of police, who was called Old Blunderbuss by the kids in town, came and put her under arrest. Next day she was back at work. In the afternoon she came out to sit in the sun for a few minutes, and I asked her how it felt to get drunk. She gave me a slap that almost knocked me off the bench. "Why, you little shirttail boy," she said, "What do you mean asking me such a question?" I rubbed my jaw and said, "I'm sorry, Miss Copey. I didn't mean any harm."

She leaned forward and held her head in her hands like a mourner and sat that way a few minutes. Then she straightened up and said, "I'm sorry I slapped you, son, but that was a hell of a question to ask a lady. Drinking is a sad, sad thing, and I hate to talk about it. I was a liquor-head sot before I got past the third grade, and I blame it all on Mamma. I had the colic real often when I was a little girl, and to ease the pain Mamma would take Pa's jug and measure out half a cup of liquor and sweeten it with molasses and dose me with it, and I got an everlasting taste for the awful stuff. If I knew then what I know now, I would've got up from my sickbed and knocked that liquor outa my mamma's hand." She sighed and stood up. "Still and all," she said, and a broad smile came on her face, "I got to admit that it sure cured my colic."

Miss Copey had not worked at the restaurant long before she got acquainted with Mr. Thunderbolt Calhoun. He has a watermelon farm on the bank of

Shad Roe River in a section of the county called Egypt. He is so sleepy and slow he has been known as Thunderbolt ever since he was a boy; his true name is Rutherford Calhoun. He is shiftless and most of his farm work is done by a Negro hired boy named Mister. (When this boy was born his mother said, "White people claim they won't mister a Negro. Well, by God, son, they'll mister you!") Mr. Thunderbolt's fifteen-acre farm is fertile and it grows the finest Cuban Queen, Black Gipsy, and Irish Gray watermelons I have ever seen. The farm is just a sideline, however; his principal interest in life is a copper still hidden on the bank of a bay in the river swamp. In this still he produces a vehement kind of whiskey known as tanglefoot. "I depend on watermelons to pay the taxes and feed me and my mule," he says. "The whiskey is pure profit." Experts say that his tanglefoot is as good as good Kentucky bourbon, and he claims that laziness makes it so. "You have to be patient to make good whiskey," he says, yawning, "and I'm an uncommonly patient man."

After Miss Copey began buying her whiskey from him, she went on sprees more often; his whiskey did not give her hangovers or what she called "the dismals." At least once a month, usually on a Saturday afternoon, she would leave her kitchen and walk barefooted down Main Street, singing a hymn at the top of her voice, and she seldom got below Main and Jefferson before she was under arrest. Most of the town drunks meekly paid the usual fine of seven dollars and costs or went to jail, but Miss Copey always took advantage of the question "What have you got to say for yourself?" First she would claim that the right to get drunk is guaranteed by the Constitution, and then she would accuse the judge of being a hypocrite.

"I got a right to let loose a hymn when I feel like it," she would say. "That don't harm nobody. Suppose I do make a little noise? Do they put 'em in jail for blowing the whistle at the sawmill? And anyhow, I don't drink in secret. There's nothing so low-down sorry as a man that drinks in secret. You're a secret sot, Judge Mullet, and don't try to deny it."

"I like a drop now and then, to be sure," the Judge would reply, "but that don't give me the right to run up and down the highways and byways in my bare feet."

"Now you're trying to tell me there's one law for a judge and another for a railroad cook," Miss Copey would say triumphantly. "That's a hell of a way for a judge to talk."

Miss Copey had been cooking in the station restaurant about two years when a stovepipe crumpled up and fell down on her head, stunning her. It made her so angry she quit her job and threatened to sue the railroad for a thousand dollars. She settled out of court, however, when a claim agent offered her a check for seventy-five. "I haven't got the patience to fight a railroad," she said. She cashed the check, insisting on having the sum in one-dollar bills, and hurried out to Mr. Thunderbolt's to buy a Mason jar of tanglefoot. When he saw her roll of bills he said he felt they ought to celebrate. He drew some whiskey out of a charred-oak keg that had been buried in the swamp for five years, and they sat in rocking chairs on the front porch and began to drink to each other. After an hour or so, Mr. Thunderbolt told her he was a lonesome man and that he had grown mighty damned tired of Mister's cooking. He wound up by asking her to be his wife. Miss Copey broke down and sobbed. Then she said, "I'll make you a good wife, Thunderbolt. We better hurry to town before the courthouse closes. If we wait until you're sober, I'm afraid you'll change your mind." Mister drove them to Stonewall in Mr. Thunderbolt's old Ford truck. They stopped at Miss Copey's rooming house and picked up her trunk; then they went over to the courthouse and were married. Judge Mullet was surprised by the marriage but said he guessed Mr. Thunderbolt's star customer wanted to get closer to the source of supply. For a week the bride and groom went fishing in Shad Roe River in the morning, got drunk in the afternoon, and rode about the country in the Ford truck at night. Then, Saturday morning, Miss Copey woke up, looked out a window, and saw that the figs were ripe on the door-yard bushes; she shook her husband awake and said, "The honeymoon's over, Thunderbolt. I got to get busy and can them figs before they drop on the ground."

For a couple of months, Miss Copey was a model wife. That autumn I hunted squirrels practically every afternoon in the swamp that runs alongside Mr. Thunderbolt's farm, and I used to stop by and see her. She showed me scores of jars of watermelon-rind pickles and fig preserves she had canned and arranged on the cellar shelves. She had spaded a pit in the back yard for barbecues, and in the corncrib she had a big barrel of scuppernong grapes in ferment. She had bought four Rhode Island Red hens and four settings of eggs, and she had a yardful of biddies. She proudly told me that every night when Mr. Thunderbolt came home from the swamp, worn out after a day of squatting beside his still, he found a plate of fried chicken and a sweet-potato pie on the kitchen table waiting for him.

After a while, however, she began to get bored. "It's too damned still around here," she told me one evening. "I need some human company. Sometimes a whole day goes past and I don't get a single word out of Thunderbolt. He lived by himself so long he almost lost the use of his tongue." There is a Baptist church a half mile up the river, and one lonesome Sunday she attended a service there. She picked an unfortunate time, because there was a fight in progress in the congregation. In fact, at that period, which was the autumn of 1926, there was dissension in many rural Baptist churches in the South over the ceremony of immersion. One group believed a convert should be immersed three times face forward in the still water of a pond and the other favored a single immersion in the running water of a river. The opposing

groups were called the Trine Forwardites and the Running Riverites. Miss
Copey became a churchgoer merely because she wanted to sing some hymns,
but she soon got mixed up in this theological wrangle. The second Sunday she
attended services she was sitting in a back pew when a man got up and
advocated changing the name of the church from Egypt Baptist to Still Water
Trine Forward Baptist. He said any sensible person knew that a calm pond was
more spiritual than the troubled waters of a river. This did not seem right to
Miss Copey; she arose and interrupted him. "Jordan wa'n't no pond," she
said. "It was a running river. On that rock I stand." "That's right, sister!"
exclaimed a man up front. "You hit the nail on the head." He went back and
asked Miss Copey to come forward and sit with the Running River faction.
"Why, I'll gladly do so," Miss Copey said. "What's this all about, anyhow?"

Presently the argument between the factions grew bitter, and Miss Copey
arose again and suggested singing "On Jordan's Stormy Banks," a revival
hymn. The leader of her faction said, "Let's march out of this church as we
sing that hymn." Thereupon seven men and women marched up the aisle.
Miss Copey got up and followed them. In the yard outside, they held a
meeting and decided to organize a new church and call it the Running River
One Immersion Baptist. "You can meet at my house until you locate a more
suitable place," Miss Copey suggested. "Let's go there now and sit on the
porch and do some singing. I feel like letting loose a few hymns." The
Running Riverites were pleased by this suggestion. With Miss Copey leading,
they marched down the road singing "There Is a Green Hill Far Away."
When Mr. Thunderbolt saw them heading up the lane, he was sitting on the
porch, playing his harmonica. He leaped off the porch and fled to the swamp.
Miss Copey arranged chairs on the porch and announced that her favorite
hymns were "There Is a Fountain Filled with Blood" and "The Old Time
Religion Is Good Enough for Me." All afternoon they sang these hymns over
and over. At sundown Miss Copey said, "If you're a mind to, we'll meet here
again next Sunday. We'll show those Trine Forwardite heathens!" Then the
meeting ended. Late that night Mr. Thunderbolt came in, raging drunk.
"Listen, you old hoot owl!" he shouted. "If you bring them hymn-singers to
this house again, I'll leave you and never come back!" "Don't threaten me,
you drunk old sinner," Miss Copey said. "You start threatening me, I'll pull a
slat out of the bed and fracture your skull."

Next Sunday afternoon the hymn-singers held another meeting on Miss
Copey's porch, and that night Mr. Thunderbolt did not come home at all.
Monday night he was still missing. Early Tuesday morning, Miss Copey went
down to Mister's cabin and found that he was missing too. She looked in the
barn and found that the Ford truck was gone. On my way home from the
swamp that afternoon I stopped by to see her, and she was sitting on the front
steps, moaning. There was a carving knife in her lap. "I'll cut his black heart

out," she said. "I'll put my trademark on him. The wife-deserter!" I sat down and tried to comfort her. Presently two of the hymn-singers came up the lane. "How are you this fine fall day, sister?" one called out. Miss Copey ran out to meet them. "You come another step closer, you old hymn-singers," she said, "and I'll throw you in the river! You've turned a man against his wife! You've broke up a happy home!" After a while we went in the house and she made some coffee. We were sitting on the back porch drinking it when Mister drove up in the Ford truck. "Hey there, Miss Copey!" he yelled. "They got Mr. Thunderbolt in jail down in Charleston." "Why, bless his heart," said Miss Copey. She ran in the house and got her hat and her purse. "Get back in that truck," she said to Mister, "and take me to him." The three of us climbed in the seat.

In Charleston, the jailer let us go in and see Mr. Thunderbolt. He was lying in his cell playing his harmonica. He was in fine spirits. He told us the hymn-singing had made him so angry he had ordered Mister to drive him to Charleston. There was a moving-picture theatre near the place they parked the truck, and Monday night he decided to go in and see a show; he had never seen a moving picture. Mary Pickford was in it, he said, and he became so absorbed in her troubles that he crouched way forward in his seat and got a cramp in his left leg. At first he tried not to notice it, but when he could bear it no longer he decided to try the old-fashioned remedy of kicking the cramp out. He got out in the aisle, held on to an end seat, and began kicking backward, like a mule that is being shod. All the time he kept his eyes on the picture. "I didn't want to miss a thing," he said. People began to yell for him to sit down, he said, and an usher hurried up and told him to stop kicking. "Please go away and don't bother me," he told the usher. The usher got the manager and together they grabbed him. "I couldn't properly defend myself," Mr. Thunderbolt told us. "I couldn't fight them two busybodies and keep up with what was happening to Miss Mary Pickford and kick the cramp out of my foot all at the same time. It was more than any one human could do." The usher and the manager hustled him to the lobby, and when he realized he wouldn't be able to see the rest of the picture, he put all his attention on self-defense and knocked the two men flat. Then a policeman came and arrested him for disorderly conduct.

"Why, it's a damned outrage, honey," Miss Copey said. "I'm going right down and bail you out."

"Just a minute," Mr. Thunderbolt said. "You're not going to bail me out until I get your solemn promise to leave them hymn-singers alone. It's real quiet in this jail."

"Oh, hell, Thunderbolt!" said Miss Copey. "I threw them hymn-singers in the river before I left home."

LOUIS ARMSTRONG

Not only was Louis Armstrong one of the greatest figures in American music, he could also write. The typescript of Satchmo, My Life in New Orleans, *from which is taken the following account of getting to know his mother better, resides in the archives of the Institute of Jazz Studies at Rutgers. According to Dan Morgenstern's introduction to the book, no one else could have typed it: "His approach to language, spelling, and syntax—even his touch on the typewriter—is inimitable." He often closed personal letters with "Red beans and ricely yours."*

Making the Honky-tonks with Mama

I have been fortunate in working with musicians who did not drink too much when they were working. That can certainly cause a lot of trouble. I had my first experience when I started working in big time early in life. I had no idea how bad a guy can feel after a night of lushing. I was seventeen years old when my comrades carried me home to Mayann dead drunk. She was not bored with me at all, even though I was sick. After she had wrapped cold towels with ice in them around my head she put me to bed. Then she gave me a good physic and told the kids to go home.

"The physic will clean him out real good. After he has put one of my meals under his belt in the morning he'll be brand new."

Sure enough, that was just what happened.

My mother was always a quick thinker when she had to help people who were seriously sick. She came from a little town in Louisiana called Butte. Her parents had all been slaves, and she had been poor all her life. She had had to learn everything the hard way. My father was a common laborer who never had anything all his life. Mayann's parents could not afford doctors, and when any of the kids was sick they would gather herbs down by the railroad tracks. After these had been boiled down, the children drank them or rubbed their bodies with them. Believe me, the cure worked like magic. The sick kid was well in a jiffy and ready to start life over again.

I was so embarrassed to have Mayann see me drunk that I apologized again and again.

"Son," she told me, "you have to live your own life. Also you have to go out into this world all by your lone self. You need all the experiences you can get. Such as what's good and what's bad. I cannot tell you these things, you've got to see them for yourself. There's nobody in this world a better judge for what's good for your life than you. I would not dare scold you for taking a few nips. Your mother drinks all the liquor she wants. And I get pretty tight sometimes. Only I know how to carry my liquor to keep from getting sick."

Then she went on to explain to me what I should do if I got the urge again. She would not make me promise never to drink; I was too young to make such a resolution.

"Son," she added, "you don't know yourself yet. You don't know what you are going to want. I'll tell you what. Suppose you and I make all the honky-tonks one night? Then I can show you how to really enjoy good liquor."

"That would be fine, mama," I said. "That would be just grand, going out with my dear mother and having lots of fun together."

I felt like a real man, escorting a lady out to the swellest places in our neighborhood, the honky-tonks. All that week at work I looked forward to my night off. Then I could take Mayann out and she would show me how to hold my liquor. . . .

On the night my mother and I went out cabareting we went first to Savocas' honky-tonk at Saratoga and Poydras Streets. This was the headquarters and also the pay office for the men working on the banana boats down at the levee. Lots of times I had stood in line there after working on those boats. And many times I went right in to the gambling table and lost my whole pay. But I didn't care—I wanted to be around the older fellows, the good old hustlers, pimps and musicians. I liked their language somehow.

Savocas' was known as one of the toughest joints in the world, but I had been raised in the neighborhood and its reputation did not bother me at all. Everybody knew my mother and me. Mayann used to do washing and ironing for the hustling gals and the hustlers, and they paid well. . . .

When the girls were hustling they would wear real short dresses and the very best of silk stockings to show off their fine, big legs. They all liked me because I was little and cute and I could play the kind of blues they liked. Whenever the gals had done good business they would come into the honky-tonk in the wee hours of the morning and walk right up to the bandstand. As soon as I saw them out of the corner of my eye I would tell Boogus, my piano man, and Garbee, my drummer man, to get set for a good tip. Then Boogus would go into some good old blues and the gals would scream with delight.

As soon as we got off the bandstand for a short intermission the first gal I passed would say to me: "Come here, you cute little son of a bitch, and sit on my knee."

Hmmmm! You can imagine the effect that had on a youngster like me. I got awfully excited and hot under the collar. "I am too young," I said to myself, "to even come near satisfying a hard woman like her. She always has the best of everything. Why does she pick on me? She has the best pimps." (I always felt inferior to the pimps.)

I was always afraid of the hustling gals because of my experience with the chick who pulled her bylow knife on me and stabbed me in the shoulder. Still the whores continued to chase me. Of course I must admit I just couldn't resist letting some of the finer ones catch up with me once in a while.

However, let's get back to the night Mayann and I went out sporting 'em up. After we left Savocas' we went to Spanol's tonk around the corner. As soon as we entered everybody gave us a big hello.

"Where you been keeping yourself?" they all asked Mayann. "You are a sight for sore eyes."

Then they all shouted: "Mother and son are making the rounds tonight. We all ought to have good luck."

"Give me a twenty dollar card," one of the big-shot gamblers hollered to the game keeper. "I feel very, very lucky tonight."

Mother and I did not have a chance to spend much money that night. Everybody kept pouring whiskey down into our stomachs. It was the first time they had ever seen us together.

All the time Mayann kept explaining to me how to hold my liquor. I took it all in and said "Yes, mom's" to everything she told me. I was anxious to learn everything I could. At my boss' joint Henry Matranga asked us to have a drink on the house.

"You have a fine boy," he told Mayann. "He is well liked by everybody who comes to my place. We all predict he will be a very fine musician some day. His heart is in it."

Mayann poked out her chest with pride.

"Thank God for that," she said. "I was never able to give my son a decent education like he deserved. I could see he had talent within him from a wee youngster. But I could not do very much about it, except just pray to the Lord to guide him and help him. And the Lord has answered my prayers greatly. Am I proud of my boy? God in heaven knows I am. And many thanks to you, Mr. Matranga, for letting him work at your place, knowing he did not have the experience he needed. But you tolerated him just the same and the Lord will bless you for it. I shall remember you every night when I say my prayers. With all you people pulling for Louis, the way you all are doing, he just can't miss."

Just then Slippers, the bouncer, came into the bar and yelled: "Hello,

Mayann. What in the world are you doing out on the stroll tonight?''

When she told him we were making the rounds he thought it was the cutest thing he had seen in a long time. Then he insisted that we have a drink with him.

By this time my mother and I were getting pretty tight, and we had not visited even half of the joints. But we were determined to make them all; that was our agreement and we intended to stick to it. Besides we were both having a fine time meeting the people who loved us and spoke our language. We knew we were among our people. That was all that mattered. We did not care about the outside world.

Slippers, who should have been in the back room keeping an eye on the bad men, stayed on at the bar with us. He just had to tell Mayann how good I was on that quail.

''Mayann, that boy of yours should really go up North and play with the good horn blowers.''

''Thanks, Slippers,'' Mayann said, downing another drink and stuttering slightly. ''Thanks, Slippers. You know . . . I'm proud of that boy. He's all I got. He and his sister, Mama Lucy. Of course his no good father has never done anything decent for those children. Only their stepfathers. Good thing they had good stepfathers, or else I don't know what those two children would have done.''

Mayann downed another drink, and just as she did somebody in the back room shouted:

''Slippers! Slippers. Come real quick. There's a bad man from out of town who won't pay off his debts.''

Slippers made one leap to the rear. In less than no time he was running the guy to the door by the seat of his pants. He gave him a punch on the chops, saying: ''Get the hell out of here, you black son of a bitch, and don't come back again, ever.''

That was that. Nobody dared to mess around with Slippers. He was a good man with a pistol and he knew how to handle his dukes. He could fight fair and he could fight dirty, whichever his victim preferred. But he was as nice a fellow as God ever made. I loved him just as though he had been my father. Whenever I was around fellows like Slippers or Black Benny I felt secure. Just to be in their company was like heaven to me.

After the guy had been thrown out we finished our drinks. At least we tried to finish them for they were lined up like soldiers. We said good night to Matranga and the crowd and were on our merry way to Joe Segretta's at Liberty and Perdido, the street that became so famous that Duke Ellington wrote a tune about it.

Segretta served extract of Jamaica ginger for fifteen cents a bottle. Everybody was buying this jive and adding it to half a glass of water, so Mayann and

I joined in. That drink gave you just what you would expect; it knocked you flat on your tail. I could see that Mayann's eyes were getting glassy but she still asked me: "Son, are you all right?"

"Sure, mother. I'm having lots of fun."

"Whenever you get ready to go home just let me know and we will cut out."

For some reason or other I was fresh as a daisy. From the way I was holding up you would have sworn I was immune to the lush. Mother and I had two of those bottles of Jamaica ginger each, and by that time it was getting real late. I could see that mother was getting soused, but I did not want to go home without stopping at Henry Ponce's place across the street. He, as you know, was the good-looking Frenchman of the old Storyville days, and Joe Segretta's competitor. Joe would have rather been bitten by a tiger than see Henry Ponce walk the streets.

Henry Ponce thought a good deal of me and I admired him too. I used to love to see those real beautiful women of all colors who came to the Third Ward especially to see him. Of course they did not like the neighborhood he was in, after he had been run out of Storyville, but they loved him. These women used to tip us plenty to play the tunes they liked. There is no doubt about it, Ponce was a mighty man. When you are talking about real operators who really played it cool, think of Henry Ponce.

The minute mother and I stepped into his joint he spied me and ran out from behind the bar to greet me. He did not know Mayann, so I introduced her.

"I am so very glad to meet you," Ponce said right away. "You are the mother of a real good boy. He has nice manners, he works with all his heart and he has never given me an ounce of trouble. I am certainly glad to meet you. Your boy is ambitious and he is anxious to get somewhere. I watched him closely when he was working for me from eight in the evening to four in the morning. I knew that he used to work all day long at the coal yard. I could not understand how he could keep it up. He is serious about his career, I want you to understand that."

The bartender brought us a round of drinks and we downed these too. Then the three pieces which had replaced our band started jumping a tune and Mayann and I danced. I noticed she was yawning, but I did not say a word.

After the dance was over we went back to our table to finish our drink. When we got up to go, Mayann started over to say good night to Henry Ponce. She was weaving a little and after she had taken a half dozen steps she fell flat on her face. Not realizing I had had as many as she, I went over to pick her up. As I leaned over I fell right on top of her. Everybody in the place broke out laughing. My mother had a good sense of humor, drunk or sober, and she joined in with the laughter. Everybody was in stitches, including me.

Stepfather Gabe was standing across the street at Joe Segretta's corner. When he had gone home he had found we were out and he was looking for us when somebody told him to go over to Ponce's place. When he saw what had happened he joined in the laughter and picked us up. He straightened Mayann's hat and hair as best he could, and led us to the door with a big smile on his face for everybody. He stopped to shake hands with Ponce and tell him what a swell gentleman he was. He thanked him for giving me a chance to play when an older musician would have given better service. Ponce told Gabe that an older musician did not have what this youngster had—sincerity and a kind of creative power which the world would eventually recognize. Gabe did not understand all those big words, but he thanked Ponce and went out supporting both mother and me with his strong arms.

When we started going down the street toward home, which was not over a block away, it was about daybreak and there were only a few stragglers on the street. We were weaving badly as we walked and we pulled Mr. Gabe from one side of the sidewalk to the other as we lurched. Any of the passers-by who saw us must have thought Gabe was as drunk as Mayann and me. However, he was very good natured about the whole business.

"Son," Mayann said, "I am convinced that you know how to hold your liquor. Judging by what happened last night you can take care of yourself. I feel that I have found out just what I wanted to know. You can look out for yourself if anything happens to me."

I felt very proud of myself.

ZORA NEALE HURSTON

Hurston was born in 1901 in the all-black town of Titusville, Florida. She went on to become an important figure in the Harlem Renaissance, to investigate voodoo in Haiti, and to write a splendid novel set in a town such as Titusville, Their Eyes Were Watching God. *The following is taken from her 1942 memoir* Dust Tracks on a Road. *"Every phase of Negro life is highly dramatised," she wrote once. "No matter how joyful or how sad the case there is sufficient poise for drama. Everything is acted out." This says a good deal about the energy of Southern humor black and white.*

"I Get Born"

This is all hear-say. Maybe some of the details of my birth as told me might be a little inaccurate, but it is pretty well established that I really did get born.

The saying goes like this. My mother's time had come and my father was not there. Being a carpenter, successful enough to have other helpers on some jobs, he was away often on building business, as well as preaching. It seems that my father was away from home for months this time. I have never been told why. But I did hear that he threatened to cut his throat when he got the news. It seems that one daughter was all that he figured he could stand. My sister, Sarah, was his favorite child, but that one girl was enough. Plenty more sons, but no more girl babies to wear out shoes and bring in nothing. I don't think he ever got over the trick he felt that I played on him by getting born a girl, and while he was off from home at that. A little of my sugar used to sweeten his coffee right now. That is a Negro way of saying his patience was short with me. Let me change a few words with him—and I am of the word-changing kind—and he was ready to change ends. Still and all, I looked more like him than any child in the house. Of course, by the time I got born, it was too late to make any suggestions, so the old man had to put up with me. He was nice about it in a way. He didn't tie me in a sack and drop me in the lake, as he probably felt like doing.

People were digging sweet potatoes, and then it was hog-killing time. Not at our house, but it was going on in general over the country like, being January and a bit cool. Most people were either butchering for themselves, or off helping other folks do their butchering, which was almost just as good. It is a gay time. A big pot of hasslits cooking with plenty of seasoning, lean slabs of fresh-killed pork frying for the helpers to refresh themselves after the work is done. Over and above being neighborly and giving aid, there is the food, the drinks and the fun of getting together.

So there was no grown folks close around when Mama's water broke. She sent one of the smaller children to fetch Aunt Judy, the mid-wife, but she was gone to Woodbridge, a mile and a half away, to eat at a hog-killing. The child was told to go over there and tell Aunt Judy to come. But nature, being indifferent to human arrangements, was impatient. My mother had to make it alone. She was too weak after I rushed out to do anything for herself, so she just was lying there, sick in the body, and worried in mind, wondering what would become of her, as well as me. She was so weak, she couldn't even reach down to where I was. She had one consolation. She knew I wasn't dead, because I was crying strong.

Help came from where she never would have thought to look for it. A white man of many acres and things, who knew the family well, had butchered the day before. Knowing that Papa was not at home, and that consequently there would be no fresh meat in our house, he decided to drive the five miles and bring a half of a shoat, sweet potatoes, and other garden stuff along. He was there a few minutes after I was born. Seeing the front door standing open, he came on in, and hollered, "Hello, there! Call your dogs!" That is the regular way to call in the country because nearly everybody who has anything to watch has biting dogs.

Nobody answered, but he claimed later that he heard me spreading my lungs all over Orange County, so he shoved the door open and bolted on into the house.

He followed the noise and then he saw how things were, and, being the kind of a man he was, he took out his Barlow Knife and cut the navel cord, then he did the best he could about other things. When the mid-wife, locally known as a granny, arrived about an hour later, there was a fire in the stove and plenty of hot water on. I had been sponged off in some sort of a way, and Mama was holding me in her arms.

As soon as the old woman got there, the white man unloaded what he had brought, and drove off cussing about some blankety-blank people never being where you could put your hands on them when they were needed.

He got no thanks from Aunt Judy. She grumbled for years about it. She complained that the cord had not been cut just right, and the belly-band had not been put on tight enough. She was mighty scared I was going to have a weak back, and that I would have trouble holding my water until I reached puberty. I did.

The next day or so a Mrs. Neale, a friend of Mama's, came in and reminded her that she had promised to let her name the baby in case it was a girl. She had picked up a name somewhere which she thought was very pretty. Perhaps she had read it somewhere, or somebody back in those woods was smoking Turkish cigarettes. So I became Zora Neale Hurston.

There is nothing to make you like other human beings so much as doing things for them. Therefore, the man who grannied me was back next day to see how I was coming along. Maybe it was pride in his own handiwork, and his resourcefulness in a pinch, that made him want to see it through. He remarked that I was a God-damned fine baby, fat and plenty of lung-power. As time went on, he came infrequently, but somehow kept a pinch of interest in my welfare. It seemed that I was spying noble, growing like a gourd vine, and yelling bass like a gator. He was the kind of a man that had no use for puny things, so I was all to the good with him. He thought my mother was justified in keeping me.

But nine months rolled around, and I just would not get on with the walking business. I was strong, crawling well, but showed no inclination to use my feet. I might remark in passing, that I still don't like to walk. Then I was over a year old, but still I would not walk. They made allowances for my weight, but yet, that was no real reason for my not trying.

They tell me that an old sow-hog taught me how to walk. That is, she didn't instruct me in detail, but she convinced me that I really ought to try.

It was like this. My mother was going to have collard greens for dinner, so she took the dishpan and went down to the spring to wash the greens. She left me sitting on the floor, and gave me a hunk of cornbread to keep me quiet. Everything was going along all right, until the sow with her litter of pigs in convoy came abreast of the door. She must have smelled the cornbread I was messing with and scattering crumbs about the floor. So, she came right on in, and began to nuzzle around.

My mother heard my screams and came running. Her heart must have stood still when she saw the sow in there, because hogs have been known to eat human flesh.

But I was not taking this thing sitting down. I had been placed by a chair, and when my mother got inside the door, I had pulled myself up by that chair and was getting around it right smart.

As for the sow, poor misunderstood lady, she had no interest in me except my bread. I lost that in scrambling to my feet and she was eating it. She had much less intention of eating Mama's baby, than Mama had of eating hers.

With no more suggestions from the sow or anybody else, it seems that I just took to walking and kept the thing a-going. The strangest thing about it was that once I found the use of my feet, they took to wandering. I always wanted to go. I would wander off in the woods all alone, following some inside urge to go places. This alarmed my mother a great deal. She used to say that she believed a woman who was an enemy of hers had sprinkled ''travel dust'' around the doorstep the day I was born. That was the only explanation she could find. I don't know why it never occurred to her to connect my tendency with my father, who didn't have a thing on his mind but this town and the next one. That should have given her a sort of hint. Some children are just bound to take after their fathers in spite of women's prayers.

CLYDE EDGERTON

One of the many fresh and endearing aspects of Clyde Edgerton's first novel, Raney, *is that it portrays a literal-thinking Free Will Baptist—Raney Bell, of Bethel, North Carolina—with uncondescending affection. After the book appeared in 1985, the fundamentalist college where Edgerton was teaching fired him over it. Presumably because Raney does loosen up some. She marries an Episcopalian. I gave this book a blurb: "If I were single, I'd marry it." I doubt I could deal with all the in-laws involved as well as the book does, though.*

from *Raney*

We get married in two days: Charles and me.

Charles's parents are staying at the Ramada—wouldn't stay with any of us—and today me, Mama, Aunt Naomi, and Aunt Flossie ate lunch with Charles's mother, Mrs. Shepherd. And found out that she's, of all things, a vegetarian.

We ate at the K and W. Mrs. Shepherd wanted to eat at some place we could sit down and order—like a restaurant—but Aunt Naomi strongly suggested the K and W. She said the K and W would be more reasonable and the line wouldn't be long on a Thursday. So we ate at the K and W.

I got meatloaf, Mama got meatloaf (they have unusually good meatloaf—not bready at all), Aunt Naomi got turkey, Aunt Flossie got roast beef, and Mrs. Shepherd, Mrs. Shepherd didn't get any meat at all. She got the vegetable plate.

When we got seated Mama says, "I order the vegetable plate every once in a while myself."

"Oh, did you get the vegetable plate?" says Aunt Naomi to Mrs. Shepherd.

"Sure did," says Mrs. Shepherd. "I've stopped eating meat."

We all looked at her.

"I got involved in a group in Atlanta which was putting together programs on simple living and after a few programs I became convinced that being a vegetarian—me, that is—made sense."

Somehow I thought people were *born* as vegetarians. I never thought about somebody just *changing over*.

"What kind of group was that?" asks Mama.

"Several Episcopal women. I'm originally Methodist, but—"

"Naomi!" says this woman walking by holding her tray. "Good gracious, is this all your family?" Her husband went ahead and sat down about three tables over—picked a chair with arms.

"It sure is," says Aunt Naomi. "Let me introduce you. Opal Register, this is my sister-in-law, Doris Bell." (That's Mama.) "You know Doris, don't you?"

"Oh, yes. I think we met in here one time. Right over there."

"And this is her daughter, Raney, who's getting married Saturday."

"Mercy me," says Mrs. Register. She had on big glasses with a chain, little brown curls on the top of her head, and too much lipstick. "You're at the start of a wonderful journey, honey," she says. "It was thirty-seven years for me and Carl the twenty-first of last month. I hope your journey is as happy and fulfilling as ours."

"And this is Mrs. Millie Shepherd, the groom's—groom-to-be's—mother. She's up from Atlanta, Georgia."

"Atlanta!" says Mrs. Register.

"And this is Flossie Purvis, Doris's sister. And ya'll, this is Opal and Carl Register," said Aunt Naomi, pointing toward Mr. Register who had started eating over at his table. He smiled, with food in his mouth. You couldn't see any though.

"Atlanta!" said Mrs. Register again. "You don't know C. C. Lawrence, do you?"

"No, I don't think I do," said Mrs. Shepherd.

"C. C. works at one of the big banks in Atlanta. He got a law degree and a business degree—one right after the other. His mama and daddy didn't think he'd ever finish—and them working at Liggett and Myers. He went—"

"Opal," Mr. Register calls out. "Sit down and eat."

"Well, nice to have met you," said Mrs. Register. "Good luck on that wonderful journey, honey," she says to me.

When Mrs. Register was out of hearing distance, Mama says, "Mr. Register just had a prostrate operation and I don't think he's recovered."

"Prostate," says Aunt Flossie.

"Is it?" says Mama. "Prostate? Oh. You know, I've always liked him better than her. She always makes so much out of every little thing."

The conversation went from the Registers to prostrate operations back around to eating meat.

"You know," says Aunt Naomi, "once in a while I've gone without meat, but I got so weak I thought I'd pass out."

"Well, that happens a bit at first," Mrs. Shepherd says. "But after a few days that usually goes away. It's a matter of what you get used to, I think. The body adjusts."

"I'd be afraid I couldn't get enough proteins," says Mama.

"Oh, no," says Mrs. Shepherd. "There are many protein substitutes for meat. Beans—soybeans, for example—are excellent."

"My next door neighbor, Lillie Cox, brought me some hamburger with soybean in it," said Aunt Naomi, "when I had the flu last winter, and it tasted like cardboard. She's always trying out the latest thing."

"I couldn't do without my meat," says Mama. She was fishing through her tossed salad for cucumber—and putting it on her plate. "I'd be absolutely lost without sausage for breakfast. Cole's sausage. The mild, not the hot. Do they have Cole's in Atlanta?"

"I don't think so. I really don't know."

"Do you get the patties or the links?" Aunt Naomi asks Mama.

"The patties—Thurman don't like the links; they roll off his plate."

We all laughed. Even Mrs. Shepherd, so Mama stretched it out. "Every time we go to Kiwanis for the pancake supper he'll lose one or two links. Because of the way he eats his pancakes—pushes them all around in the syrup. Last time one rolled up under the edge of Sam Lockamy's plate, and for a minute there we couldn't find it. Then Sam swore it was his."

"I guess you have less cholesterol if you don't eat meat," says Aunt Naomi.

"There are health advantages," said Mrs. Shepherd. "And also our women's group has been concentrating on how eating less meat can help curtail hunger in the third world."

"On another *planet?*" says Aunt Naomi.

"Oh, no. Developing nations," says Mrs. Shepherd. She finished chewing and swallowed. "Developing nations."

"What I don't understand," says Aunt Naomi, "is that if they don't eat their own cows, like in India, then why should we send them ours? They wouldn't eat ours, would they? Or maybe they *would* eat American meat."

"We wouldn't send meat to India, of course; we'd send grain and other staple goods. The fewer cows we eat the less grain we'll need to feed cows, so there will be a greater grain surplus."

Aunt Naomi blew her nose on this Kleenex she had been fumbling with. She had a cold. She can get more nose blows on one Kleenex than anybody I ever saw. She always ends up with this tiny corner which she slowly spreads out, then blows her nose into.

We'd finished eating so I said, "Aunt Naomi, you get more nose blows out of one Kleenex than anybody I've ever seen in my life."

"I probably won't be able to sing Sunday," she said. She sings in the church choir. "This cold just drags on and on and on."

"Ain't it nice the way Raney and Charles play music together," says Mama to Mrs. Shepherd. I was relieved to get off the meat subject.

"Yes, it is," says Mrs. Shepherd.

"I think it's wonderful," says Aunt Naomi.

"They sound real good together," says Aunt Flossie.

Music is what brought me and Charles together. He plays banjo and collects old songs from the mountains. When I sang for the faculty at the college Christmas dinner he was there—he's the assistant librarian—and he came up afterward and complimented my singing. He was real nice about it. And has been ever since. Charles is the kind of person who is real natural around people—and is smart as he can be.

Then I met him again when I went to the library to check out a record. They have a good collection, thanks to Charles. One thing led to another and the first thing you know we're playing music together. We've had three or four performances. Kiwanis and such. Charles calls them gigs.

"Charles sent me a tape," says Mrs. Shepherd. "You two sound really good together. You have a beautiful voice, Raney."

I thanked her.

Charles is learning to sing too. We harmonize on two or three songs. He's improving gradually. He plays good banjo. He don't *look* like a banjo picker, but he sounds good.

"I don't know what I'm going to do without Raney singing around the house, and helping out with Norris and Mary Faye," says Mama, looking at me.

"Mama, I'm twenty-four years old," I said.

There's a big gap between me and my little brother, Norris, and sister, Mary Faye. Norris is eight and Mary Faye is eleven. Mary Faye picks on Norris all the time, but sometimes he deserves it.

"How many children do you have, Mrs. Shepherd?" says Aunt Flossie.

"One," says Aunt Naomi.

"Please call me Millie," says Mrs. Shepherd. "All of you," she says, and smiles. "You too, Raney, if you're comfortable with that. I have only one," she says. "Charles is the only one."

. . . .

Monday morning, Mama and me cooked eggs, bacon, grits, and biscuits. After breakfast, Daddy, Uncle Nate, and Charles took Mary Faye and Norris fishing at the pier. Me, Mama, Aunt Naomi, and Aunt Flossie cleaned up the dishes, put on our bathing suits, got towels and suntan lotion, and walked to the beach. We were all planning to meet back at the cabin for lunch.

About the time we got settled on a nice even spot, along came this Marine with a woman who had a blue lightning bolt tattooed on the inside of her knee.

They sat down on this white towel—too little for both of them—beside some college students. The waves were crashing, so I know they couldn't hear us talk.

"I declare I don't think I've ever seen a woman with a tattoo," says Mama.

"Where?" says Aunt Naomi.

"On the inside of her knee."

"No, *where? Where* is she?"

"Oh. Right over there."

"He looks like a soldier."

"He's a Marine from Camp Lejune," I said. "I can tell by the way his hair's cut."

"I don't see no tattoo on her," says Aunt Naomi.

"Wait a minute and you will," says Mama.

"There it is," says Aunt Flossie.

"Well, I'll be dog," says Aunt Naomi. "Don't that beat all? A blue lightning bolt. Do you reckon she drew that on there with a ball point pen?"

"Not unless she can draw mighty good," says Mama. "Course a lightning bolt ain't all that hard to draw. I remember from school."

"Now can you imagine," says Aunt Naomi, "Some woman walking into a tattoo parlor with a bunch of men standing around, hiking up her dress and saying I want a blue lightning bolt tattooed right here on the inside of my knee? Can you imagine that?"

"Well, I sure can't," says Mama. "But she looks like she's been in plenty places like that. I mean she looks like she's spent a good deal of her life indoors in some back room."

"Well, she could be a you-know-what," says Aunt Naomi.

The woman was pale and skinny with black hair stringy wet from swimming. She lit a cigarette and when she pulled it out of her mouth she laughed smoke at something the Marine said I could see some of her teeth were rotten.

"Young people nowadays will go to almost any length," said Aunt Naomi. "I don't know what it's all coming to. Who ever heard of so much burning, beating, and stabbing, and my Lord, I can't imagine what Papa would done to me had I come home with a blue lightning bolt tattooed on my kneecap. Why he would—"

"It's on the inside of her knee," says Mama.

"Why he would have skint me alive."

Up walked Charles all of a sudden and said we'd better come to the house, that Norris had a fish hook hung in his *nose*. He said that on Mary Faye's first cast, Norris was walking behind her and the hook caught him, as clean as day, in his left nostril—*with the worm still on the hook*. We followed him to the cottage. I couldn't imagine.

We walk in and there sits Norris in a straightback chair, crying, with Uncle

Nate down on his knees trying to see in Norris's nose and Norris trying to hold his head still but not being able to on account of crying.

Norris rolls his eyes to look at us when we walk in. Standing there beside him is Mary Faye, holding a rod and Zebco reel with a line leading to Norris's nose where the hook is stuck in his nostril with a live worm half in and half out. It won't bleeding though. Daddy is standing behind Uncle Nate, watching.

"I say we ought to take him to the hospital," says Charles.

"Wait a minute," says Uncle Nate, "if the barb ain't in we can pull it right out."

"If the barb ain't in, it would've fell out, wouldn't it?—with that great big worm on there," says Aunt Flossie. "He must weigh half a pound."

"You don't need that much worm to catch a fish," says Aunt Naomi.

"I think we ought to take him to the hospital," says Charles.

"I agree," I said. In many ways Charles is very clear-headed.

"Well, if I can just—" said Uncle Nate, reaching up toward Norris's nose. Norris lets out this short yell and puts his hand in front of his face.

Uncle Nate stands up and looks around at everybody.

"Take him to the hospital," says Charles.

"I don't think so," says Uncle Nate.

Tears are dropping off the worm. A drop of blood appears.

"It's bleeding," says Charles. "What's wrong with taking him to the hospital?"

"That's the worm bleeding," says Uncle Nate.

"How do you know that?" asks Charles.

"Cause it's a blood worm. They're supposed to bleed. That's what it's called: a blood worm. That's what it says where you buy them on the pier: blood worms, $2.00 a dozen."

"Gosh, they've gone up," says Aunt Naomi.

"Well, suppose it *is* the worm," says Charles. "What can you lose by taking him to the hospital?"

"The worm or Norris?" says Mary Faye.

"Norris," says Charles.

"If Norris goes, the worm goes," says Aunt Naomi.

"To start with," says Uncle Nate to Charles, "you're going to lose about fifty dollars. Second, you're going to lose a chance to do something for yourself instead of some overpaid doctor doing it."

Charles walked out the door. Again.

Then Daddy took over. "Now, wait a minute," he said. "Everybody sit down. No. No, not you, Mary Faye. You stand right there and hold the pole, honey." He pulled a chair in front of Norris's chair and sat down. "You all go on about your business. I want to talk to Norris a few minutes. Let me have the rod and reel, Mary Faye. Now, Mr. Norris. I'll bet that nose hurts, don't it?''

Norris nodded his head.

''Why don't you stand up real easy.''

Norris stood up, stretching his neck out and holding his head still like a dog smelling a dead snake, his hands hanging down by his sides with his fingers spread like he was afraid of touching something gooey—or like he *had* touched something gooey.

''Okay,'' said Daddy, ''I'll tell you what let's do—do you want to get that old worm out of there?''

Norris nodded his head up and down, easy.

''Now the first thing I want you to do is give me your hand.''

Norris reached out his hand and Daddy took it in his hand and massaged it around and around. ''Now you just relax. We'll get that old worm right out of there in no time flat. You think about that little sting as a mosquito bite.''

Norris nodded his head up and down. A tear dropped.

''Now you take holt of the line right here—that's right. Right there. That's good. Now you just move your hand up along the line until it gets up to that little hook. Okay. Now. You relax and I'm going to wrap my hand around your hand and help you out a little bit.''

Norris nodded up and down, slow. His eyes were getting bigger.

''Hold your head real still and we'll—''

Daddy nudged up and then down, and that hook came right out—as pretty as you please.

.   .   .   .

When we finished singing, Uncle Nate told about the Christmas Uncle Pugg went to Raleigh to sell wreaths and holly and mistletoe and got lost and was too proud to ask anybody the way home. He slept that night in a church and the next morning the preacher saw him come out and asked him if he was the man who'd come to fix the steps. Uncle Pugg said he was. He had his tools in a box in the wagon. He fixed the steps and the preacher asked him to fix the roof and so he did that. Then the preacher asked him if he brought the window to put in. Uncle Pugg said he didn't but that a man over in Bethel had the window and could the preacher tell him how to get there. The preacher told him, and Uncle Pugg came on home.

MAC HYMAN

No Time for Sergeants was a big hit when it came out in 1954. So was the Broadway play and the TV special and the 1958 movie, which made a star of Andy Griffith in the role of Will Stockdale, the least defensive Southerner ever involved in our national defense. (A supporting part in the film was played by Don Knotts, who went on to be Andy's deputy in Mayberry, on TV.) Mac Hyman, a native of Cordele, Georgia, died young without becoming an important Southern writer, but he created something fine in Will's sweet-natured way of infuriating persons from other parts of the country with his invulnerable assumption that a backwoods Georgian is as good as, no better than, anybody else. At one point after his induction, an Army psychiatrist says to him, "I don't think I would ever want to live in your rotten state. How about that?" Will replies: "Well, I guess you know where you want to live. Besides that, things is getting right crowded around home anyhow. Some folks moved in not long ago about two miles down the road from us and land ain't as cheap as it once was. So it really don't make no difference to me whether you live there or not, not that we wouldn't be mighty glad to have you." In this excerpt, Will is recruited.

from *No Time for Sergeants*

The thing was, we had gone fishing that day and Pa had wore himself out with it the way he usually did when he went fishing. I mean he went at it pretty hard and called the fish all sorts of names—he lost one pretty nice one and hopped up in the boat and banged the pole down in the water which was about enough to scare a big-sized alligator away, much less a fish, and he spent most of the afternoon after that cussing and ranting at everything that happened. And all he caught was one catfish which warnt much bigger than the worm he was using, and he got finned by that, so by the time I brought the boat back in, he was setting in the front with the back of his neck red and his jaws moving in and out, the way he gets when he is upset, not speaking to me at all.

So after we walked the four miles back to the house, he didnt care to eat right then, so he set down on the porch and pulled his hat down over his eyes and leaned his head back against the post to doze a bit which I've seen him do for as long as four hours on the straight sometimes. So I seen he was settled for a while and I got out my harp and begun playing a few pieces. And in a little bit, he was snoring and his foot was patting up and down in time to the tune I was playing, so I played a fast one and watched it bounce a bit, and then a slow one to calm him down again—anyhow, I was kind of enjoying it as it was quiet by that time; it was about sundown and the dogs was laying around the yard only opening their eyes every once in a while to make sure one of them didnt get fed before the other one, and the chickens was clucking easy and comfortable about the yard, and the fields across the way were kind of pink-colored the way they get sometimes when the sun is going down, so I was kind of enjoying the quiet and all, and taking it real easy that way, when all of a sudden I seen my dog Blue raise up his head and perk his ears and set there a minute, and then stare at me with this real puzzled *look* on his face.

Well, I wouldnt have thought nothing of it if it had of been any other dog, but Blue warnt the kind of dog that ever looked puzzled about anything much. I mean he was one of the smartest dogs I ever seen in my life and pretty stuck-up about it too—like when he points a bird for you, he makes out it warnt *nothing* for him to do and acts kind of casual about it and all and watches you with this real disgusted look on his face—I mean I dont guess he had ever come right out and showed he was puzzled about anything much before in his life before then.

So I really couldnt figger it for a minute. I stopped playing and listened and didnt hear nothing at first, and it was a few seconds before I made it out myself. What it was, was this far off moaning sound somewhere, and then it come to me what was bothering Blue because it sounded like a *car* to me. So I knowed why he was puzzled then because I dont guess he has seen no moren two cars in his whole life and they was more like wagons than they was cars, and I guess you might as well say that one of them *was* a wagon because this one that my uncle had didnt have no motor in it and he usually just hitched a mule to the front to pull it along, and a lot of folks would probably think it was just a wagon, and especially a *dog* would. So Blue must have thought it was a motorboat or something and couldnt figger what it was doing coming from that direction as the river was way down behind the house and there warnt nothing in front but a road, and not much of a road at that, only some weeds with ruts on either side, and he had sense enough to know that no boat would be coming down *that* way; so he was right puzzled about it all right.

Anyhow, the sound kept getting louder and the other dogs started whining and looking around at me, and the chickens begun trotting this way and that like they do when a storm is coming up, and I stood up on the lookout for it. Then it sounded like it was almost roaring, and about that time it heaved into sight around the edge of the woods. And you should have heered the racket set up then. The dogs got to barking and howling and the chickens started squawking, running this way and that, and then the car come busting up in front of the place with dust behind it in long billows, turning and heading right toward the house like it was aimed for it. Blue took off for the woods with most of the hounds running ducktailed behind him, barking and looking back over their shoulders; the chickens went around in circles trying to dodge it, which was probably as good a way as any with the car wobbling the way it was; they darted here and there, only most of them never made any headway at all and got knocked aside and went fluttering off, all but one that went straight up in the air and came down on the hood and set there right calm for a second, thinking she had got out of the way of it, but then turning and seeing the *house* heading for her, and setting up about twice as much of a ruckus about that.

So it was pretty much of a surprise to me too because for a minute there it looked like the car warnt going to stop at all. I mean it come heading right for us and didnt begin to stop until it was about thirty feet from the porch; and then it jolted with dust blowing up past it, and stopped, and jumped forward again and finally come to a halt, and then the door slammed and this little, fat, round-faced fellow come walking through the cloud of dust talking just as hard as he could. I mean that's just the way he done too. All you could hear was the door slam and see him coming through the dust with his mouth going. You couldnt hear what he was *saying,* though—all you could hear was sounds and see his mouth moving because there was so much racket all around, and it really was surprising. I mean it looked like he was raving somehow—he was either doing that or preaching and it didnt seem natural to me that a fellow would come riding up in a car that way and jump out and start preaching even though I did know one fellow who used to jump at you from behind the bushes and start preaching—but it didnt seem that way somehow; and with all the racket going on, you couldnt tell what he was doing.

Anyhow, Pa usually warnt in so good a humor when he woke up easy and casual—I mean it usually took him a half hour or so to manage it and he warnt in much of a humor *then;* and waking up with dogs barking and chickens howling and a man stomping up and talking that way was pretty much of a shock to him any way you look at it. I seen his eyes blinking and his jaws moving before he was halfway up; then he stood there a second, shaking his head trying to get his bearings, and looking down at the fellow like he hadnt ever seen anything like him in his life before. And all this time the man kept on talking—I caught the words ". . . want to see Will Stockdale; now is that you or aint it because I've been riding for . . ." but that was all I could make out—but he kept on with it, and then he raised one finger up and started wiggling it at me, saying something else, but about that time Pa lit into him with about the only thing he could think of at the time, I guess, being half-asleep the way he was; he yelled out, "Dont you pint your finger in my boy's face!"

So that kind of stopped the fellow for a second; he turned and looked at Pa and Pa's face turned a little redder, and then he bellowed it out again, "Dont you pint your finger in my boy's face!" which should have quieted him down for a while, only it didnt, because the next thing I knowed, there he was telling Pa he just ought to keep out of the whole thing, that he was there to see me and not him, and that it warnt Pa's business.

"Not my business?" Pa said. "Just what in the hell do you mean by that, sir?"

"Look," the fellow said. "I came out here to see this boy and I . . ."

"Just what do you mean, not my business," Pa said to him; and for a minute he was leaned so far over him, it looked like he might just fall right on top of him.

But then the fellow come back with something else, and Pa kept coming back at him. The fellow was trying to tell what he wanted to see me about and I got right curious, only he never got to finish because all Pa could talk about was him going around pointing his finger in my face, and it warnt much of an argument with both of them talking about different things that way and all.

But finally Pa out-yelled him and got him onto his argument, but then the fellow said that it was his finger and my face and it was his business where he pointed it, and Pa come back with, "Not on my property, it aint," and then the fellow got off the point again and said if he had property like ourn, he sho wouldnt go around bragging about it, and then Pa come back by saying, "I dont care about that but one thing I aint going to stand for as long as I am a man is having somebody going around pinting their fingers in people's faces on my property," which was a pretty long thing to say in one bellow and left him so wore out he was kind of gasping before he finished.

But then the other fellow managed to get in a few more words, and he said, "Look, I dont care nothing about all that and I didnt come out here to talk to you nohow. I'm from the draft board and I'm out here to see this boy and that's our business and . . ."

"By God, on my property . . ." Pa said.

"That aint got nothing to do with it," the man said. "If this boy knows what's good for him, he'll get in that car right now and head back to town with me and we wont have any more trouble about it. You folks out here think just because you live ten thousand miles from town, you dont have to do things like anybody else, but I'm here to tell you different. I've been over roads that aint even been discovered yet and down trails that nothing but a horse and wagon has been down, and t his is the third time I've tried to find this place, and I mean it's the last time too!"

And he kept on like that for a pretty good while and kept Pa from busting in again, but then he said, "I've wrote you four letters and havent had an answer to none of them and you neednt say you cant read neither because you could have got somebody to read them to you, so that aint no excuse!" which was about the most *foolish* thing he could have said, it seemed like to me, because Pa warnt going to take that from nobody.

And he didnt neither. He drawed himself up real quick with his eyes all lit up and looked down on the fellow and just bellowed out at him, "By God, sir, do you mean to stand here and say to my face that my son cant *read!*"

"Now look," the fellow said.

"Do you mean to come busting up here and not say Howdy or nothing and say my son cant *read* and expect him to go hopping in that car like you said? Do you think my son who has gone to school and has read more times than you could shake a stick at couldnt answer a puny little ole letter if he wanted to? By God, man, let me tell you . . ."

"All right," the fellow said. "Then there aint any excuse at all for him not answering them letters . . ."

"Letter?" Pa said. "By God, sir, I dont think I can stand to listen to any more of this . . ."

"Well, that's all right with me. Now . . ."

"Nosir!" Pa said. "What you think dont mean nothing to me, but I'm going to make you eat them words just the same. Will, you go in the house and get that book and lets see about this thing here and now and not have no more foolishness about it."

And he stood there with his arms folded and his mouth clamped together, so there warnt nothing much I could do but go get it; and when I got back, he hadnt budged, so I set down on the steps and opened it up. Then Pa said, "Go ahead, Will," without even looking at me, and so I read him a couple of pages out of it. It was about this little boy named Tony who wanted a pony and how he went to work for a man so he could buy it, but he never made enough money, so the man finally just *give* it to him because he worked so hard. But I never got to the end of it because Pa raised up his hand all of a sudden, and I stopped, and he lowered his hand and said, "All right, that's enough of that one. Now go in and get the Bible and let's hear a few of them words in there."

"Now look, I dont care anything about that," the fellow said. "I . . ."

"Go on, Will," Pa said. "I want to get this here thing straightened out once and for all, by God."

So I went in and got the Bible and when I come back out, Pa still had his arms folded, so I set back down on the steps and give him a dose of that one too. I read him a few lines about that fellow that warnt a nigger but was called Abraham, and I done pretty good with it, I think, only I didnt get to finish it neither because the fellow busted in again, saying, "I've had enough of all this.

I'm asking you for the last time now. Are you going to get in that car and go back into Callville with me or are we going to have to come out here and get you?''

And that set Pa off again so that he done some pretty fierce cussing right up in the man's face and asked him what he *meant* by that and all; and when the fellow said, ''I mean just what I say. They'll come out here and take him if he dont come with me and they can do it too!'' it looked like Pa was going to tear into him all of a sudden. He rared back with his chest poking out and his face turning red and lifted his fist up and bellowed out, *''Off my property!''* so loud that the fellow's face turned right *white*. He started going backward, looking at Pa with his eyes wide, while Pa kept making these noises in his throat; and then he turned and headed for the car and slammed the door and started driving out just about as fast as he had been coming in before.

Pa was right wild by that time, too; he run around until he found himself a rock and he heaved it at the car just as it was turning off onto the road, but he missed it and hit my dog Blue instead, as Blue was just coming out of the woods about that time, so that Blue looked right at him and gave this yelp and headed back for the woods again; and by the time Pa could find another rock, the car was gone and there warnt nothing left but dust floating across the ditch.

Anyhow, after things settled down a bit, Pa was right wore out from it all. He set down on the steps to rest, looking weak and trembly all over; he kept shaking and turning white in the face and when I tried to talk with him, he didnt have nothing to say. He would just rub his hands over his face and shake his head and lean back against the post again.

But after a little bit, he begun to feel better and talk some, even though he didnt sound much like the same man as before. He shook his head and looked at the ground and spoke real soft and sad, and said how it warnt right for folks to act that way. He said it was sinful to get mad with folks too, and he felt right bad about it. He said, ''Will, why dont you read a little more out of that Bible again?'' and I said, ''Yessir, why dont you just rest a while,'' and reached over and got it and read to him for a spell. He set there listening, nodding his head up and down, and I read a part with a lot of big words in it, and I done pretty good with it, I think. I throwed in a lot of Thees and Thous and Verilys and things like that, and when I hit some of the big names, I just called them Sam or Joe or whatever come into my head, but he didnt know the difference; he nodded his head up and down, looking like he felt better already. I read, ''And he saideth verily thee unto thou,'' and he cleared his throat and said, ''That's the truth, too, Will. That's the truth.''

DAN JENKINS

As a person who grew up being called "Bubba" around home from the time I got a sister, I took offense when Bill Clinton and Al Gore were referred to slightingly as the "Double Bubba" ticket, but when Sen. Daniel Moynihan referred to certain of President Clinton's public statements as "boob bait for the Bubbas," he may have had a point. Now that white Southerners don't do much plowing in the neck-burning hot sun, "Bubba" seems to have replaced "redneck" as a blithely employed ethnic slur. It's hard to deny that a certain prevalent mind-set is roughly evoked by the term, however. Dan Jenkins, native of Forth Worth, is an eminently funny sportswriter who has written several raucously comic novels including most notably the first duly ribald sports book, Semi-Tough. *In the 1993 book* Bubba Talks, *from which I quote here, Jenkins rounded up the Bubba school of thought. Having hung out in bars with Jenkins a good deal over the years, I may have said some things like these myself. I want y'all to know I didn't mean them. Nor, I'm willing to grant, did any of our fine Irish-American legislators who may have lapsed, in their own wise, from multiculturalism occasionally.*

According to Bubba

RELATIVES

It is very hard to keep all of your relatives straight when you only see them at funerals or sometime around Christmas.

Bubba still gets R.T. and Vermelle mixed up with V.G. and Wrenella. They're on his daddy's side, but R.T. and V.G. are both bald-headed and Vermelle and Wrenella never breathe, they just talk.

Bubba thinks Alma Lea and Milton are the ones who moved to Thorp Springs, but that could be Vineta and Cecil. Alma Lea collects figurines and Vineta frames her jigsaw puzzles, or it could be the other way around.

It could well be Milton who complains the most about diabetes, although Cecil has it, too.

Wilma and Mary Margaret are definitely sisters. One is married to Floyd and one is married to Doyle. Floyd and Doyle both like to stare at carpets.

Aunt Mozelle used to be able to keep it all straight, but she got mad about an antique lamp in somebody's will and hasn't spoken to anybody in the family for fifteen years.

FATHERS

The thing Bubba remembers best about his daddy is how his daddy never talked to anybody in the family as much as he talked to the TV set.

This gave him something in common with most other daddies, actually.

Bubba's daddy would come home from work every night and sit in the same chair and eat his dinner off the same tray. It was from this vantage point that he could tell Ironside who the kidnapper was, or tell Kojak to watch out for that crazy sumbitch hiding in the closet with a knife.

Mostly, however, Bubba's daddy talked to news commentators and all of the vagrants and foreigners who turned up on the news every evening.

There was definitely a news broadcast on TV if Bubba overheard his daddy saying any of the following things:

1. "That's a crock."
2. "There's a liberal for you."
3. "I don't believe you can sell any of that crap in *this* house tonight."
4. "That's right. All of you lay down in the street now."
5. "Well, I've got a suggestion for *you,* hoss. If you don't like it here, why don't you get your ass on over there to Mozambique?"

Bubba's daddy almost never saw anything good on the TV news.

Patsy Claire swears to this day that it was those I-raqis and I-ranians who caused his heart attack and killed him.

MOTHERS

Generally, Bubba says, they fall into two categories.

Dark room, headache.

Sunny porch, no headache.

Bubba's Mama

They don't make women like Bubba's mama anymore. If Bubba had to pin it down, he'd say they stopped about when the microwave oven came along.

There was never a household problem Bubba's mama couldn't handle with a smile. She cooked and cleaned and picked up and held down a part-time job all her life. She never got sick. As a matter of fact the only time she ever even had to lie down on the bed for a minute or two was when Florence died—she loved that Lab.

Bubba's mama was a great lady in all ways, and she left Bubba with a wonderful legacy, which was the recipe she invented for chicken fried bacon.

> Dip pieces of bacon in milk.
> Dredge in flour.
> Sprinkle salt and pepper.
> Place in cold skillet on hot stove.
> Turn once.
> Remove when brown.
> Serve with Bisquick biscuits.

Bubba can still hear his mama's voice talking about her invention.

"The bacon don't shrink, and all the fat is preserved inside the crispy brown crunchy coating."

She was about half saint is all she was.

Newspapers

After all these years, Bubba says, you would think somebody might know how to put out a decent newspaper.

Start with your average front page.

The top half is about a group of maniac foreigners who are throwing bombs at each other to see who can wind up with the most pairs of Gucci loafers and cable channels.

The bottom half tells you two things. It sheds new light on a tollbooth controversy that will obviously have a dire effect on mankind, and it brings you up-to-date on the city councilman who accidentally parked in a handicap zone and has hell to pay.

Nothing of interest on all those inside pages of the first section, unless you care about the storm that blew all the Taco Bells off Mombasa.

Nobody has ever read an editorial, it goes without saying, and the columns on that page across from the editorials don't matter to anybody who's not living in Israel.

Over in the business section, it's business as usual. The Dow and the prime and the deficit are deeply concerned that two and five-eighths may not equal one and three-fourths, although it's a good sign that four and one-third is more than three and two-fifths. Locally, your lessees and lessors are still at it.

Go to the lifestyle section and there's the old wood-carver again, sitting in front of her haunted house.

Bubba's not sure he would even subscribe to a daily paper if it weren't for the sports pages and TV log.

CHINA

Small wonder your Chinamen are inscrutable, Bubba says. They talk in pictures.

If you could understand it, you would know that Fu Wong is saying to his wife, Ching Ling, "Honey, let's get dressed up tonight in our oblong boxes with slanty slashes and go eat some of those triangles with curliques we like over at the leaning rectangle with the dipping roof. We better drive your Doodle. My Hieroglyphic is low on gas."

HARDWARE STORES

"I don't know what you call it, but have you got one of those things that's about this long and has a deal that curves around and looks kind of like—well, it looks a little like *that,* I think—except it's supposed to be bigger, with a knob or something on top, and a wooden handle, and there's a thing you ought to be able to pull *up* with, you know, in case you're trying to . . . I'll tell you what. Just forget it. I'm gonna have to go back home and see what the fuck she's talking about."

SEXUAL HARASSMENT

Bubba is all for doing whatever it takes to put an end to sexual harassment. It is a disgusting thing, he says, and he knows what he's talking about because he has been a victim of it himself on more than one occasion.

He vividly remembers that night when Maxine Shaw rubbed up against him at The Blue Note and said:

"I want to fuck you, Bubba. If you fuck me, I won't tell your wife. If you don't fuck me, I'll tell your wife you did."

Bubba vows to fight on the side of feminists to destroy this dreaded epidemic.

Girlfriends

It's been Bubba's experience that your best girlfriends, those that last the longest, are the ones who are happily married to somebody else.

This is the girlfriend who lets you know up front that she's strictly in it for the adventure, like you are.

A girlfriend is not a mistress, incidentally. Your good mistresses are expensive to maintain, and Bubba would rather spend his money on a new set of Hogan irons.

Girlfriends are not always as good-looking as wives, but they're certainly more good-natured, which, by and large, is why they become girlfriends in the first place.

It's always a sad day, however, when the girlfriend suddenly turns out to be not so happily married and not so good-natured.

All you can do in this unfortunate moment, Bubba says, is heave a sigh, shake your head, and quietly say to yourself, "Oh, Christ—here we go."

Dogs

To Bubba's way of thinking, there aren't many things more entertaining than rolling around on the carpet with a slick-haired dog.

Dogs have many splendid virtues, he says.

1. They are entirely sympathetic about your problems at the office.
2. They enjoy hearing about your golf game, hole by hole, shot by shot.
3. They like the same TV programs you do.
4. Food will square most any differences you have with them.
5. They hardly ever object to anything on moral grounds.

TED POSTON

Poston grew up in Hopkinsville, Kentucky. From the 1930s through the '60s, he worked for the New York Post—*the first black person to have a lasting career as a reporter on a major metropolitan daily paper. In 1940 he was appointed to Franklin D. Roosevelt's "Negro Cabinet." Over the years he also set down ten semifictional childhood reminiscences, some of which appeared in Langston Hughes's* Book of Negro Humor. *They were never collected into a book, however, until 1991, seventeen years after his death, when the University of Georgia Press brought out* The Dark Side of Hopkinsville. *Hard to see why it took so long.*

"Papa Was a Democrat"

Papa was the only Negro Democrat in our Hopkinsville, Ky., or in the whole state of Kentucky for that matter. And this made it very difficult for me in my first years at the Booker T. Washington Colored Grammar School.

For while Rat Joiner, Tack-Haired Baker and the rest of my friends had only to put up with "playing the dozens" (that is, having your opponents say nasty things about your mother), my enemies always ended all arguments with me by yelling:

"Your Pappy's a Democrat."

At first, I didn't know exactly what a Democrat was, but I gathered it was regarded as something dirty in our colored community. So I was always forced to carry the argument one step further by busting my opponent in the nose.

But there was no fence built around my nose either, so I didn't always win the argument by this strategem.

I didn't take the matter up immediately with Papa, though, even after my first half dozen bloody noses. I guess I was sort of afraid he might answer "Yes" if I put the question to him directly. And then where would I be?

But the real reason was that Papa was a busy man—being Professor Ephraim Poston, Dean of Men at the Kentucky State Industrial College for Negroes at Frankfort, Ky.—and he only got home every other week-end.

And on those rare occasions when he arrived, he didn't have too much time for me, the last of his 11 children. And very little time for the other 10 either.

For, as the first Negro college graduate in Hopkinsville, Ky.—he'd finished Walden College down in Nashville long before the turn of the century—he believed in fulfilling his community responsibilities.

And one of these responsibilities was to settle all the arguments and bets on any constituted dispute of facts which had arisen during his absence in Frankfort.

In fact, the only way we children knew for sure sometimes that Papa was due in town on Saturdays was when our front porch started filling up early in the morning with disputants on both sides.

All the sporting men would stand on the left-hand side of the steps, putting their bets into neutral hands and waiting for Papa to render his immutable decisions.

The seekers after truth and the more respectable disputants would range themselves comfortably in the swing and benches on the porch itself and ignore the riff-raff down the steps.

Papa would finally arrive, put his carpet bag in the living room, and then stroll out to meet his callers.

The routine never varied. First there were the usual amenities. Who had been feeling poorly? How were things with the Elks?

(I remember Papa asked the latter question once of Mr. Ezekial Quarles, our long-time Imperial Potentate. And when Mr. Quarles replied, "Well, 'Fesser Poston, the Elks ain't doing so well right now. . . ." Papa consoled him as quick as a flash with: "Gee, I'm sorry to hear it, Zeke. I didn't know you lost the last election. Who is Imperial Potentate now?")

But after the amenities were over, the elders would get in their questions.

The opening gambit was always reserved for Mr. Freddie Williams, who had been First Deacon of the Virginia Street Baptist Church ever since we bought the structure from the white folks.

"Well, Professor Poston," he would start, "Just how do you spell this 'Nebbie-ker-neezer'?"

And Papa would say, "N-e-b-u-c-h-a-d-n-e-z-z-a-r."

"Now ain't that something?" Mr. Williams would ask, sneaking a look at the piece of paper he had in his hand. And if he had it written down right, he'd smirk at Mr. Ronald Childress, the first elder of the Dirt's Ave. African Methodist Episcopal Church.

(Being men of religion, the deacons and elders never made a *bet*. But they challenged each other by saying "I'll *bound* you a million that such-and-such ain't so.")

Then Mr. J. B. Petty, our local insurance man who fancied himself as Hopkinsville's best Negro historian, would show off his erudition by asking:

"Now, Professor Poston, what was the name of that proud African tribe who boasted that they all remained jet black even in slavery, and that no white folks' blood had ever coursed through their veins?"

And Papa would hesitate thoughtfully before answering. And then he would say:

"Well, J.B., I don't think it was any *particular* African tribe that made the boast. It was just a number of individual slaves from various tribes who boasted that their blood lines were pure.

"As a matter of fact, they often called themselves 'Salt Water Negroes,' meaning that their racial strain was as undiluted then as it was the day their forebears were brought in shackles over the ocean."

And while everybody stood aghast at Papa's knowledge, he would break the spell by saying:

"But, J.B., I don't think you have to worry about that. You took good pains to see that none of your children would be salt water Negroes."

And both front porch and lawn would break out in raucous laughter. For although his intimates sometimes joked Mr. J. B. Petty that he was so dark at birth that his mother didn't find him for five months, everybody knew that he was inordinately proud of his marriage to Miss Aurelia Scott. For few white folks and no Negroes at all were lighter than Miss Aurelia in Hopkinsville, Ky.

But soon the historians and theologians would be disposed of, and the sporting men would get down to business.

Smoky Smith, who wore his black Stetson hat without a dent anywhere in the crown, and a starched blue denim jumper over his black serge tailor-made pants, was always the first in this category. Nobody ever dared challenge his precedence.

"Now, Mr. Eph," Smoky would say, "What were the odds on the Jack Johnson–Jeff Willard fight?" and then facetiously, "Who won?"

And although Papa was not a betting man himself, he'd say:

"The odds, as I recall them, were 8 to 5 on Willard. And I seem to remember that Johnson won."

The laughter had hardly subsided after Smoky collected his bet when somebody like Set-the-Meat Jones would ask:

"And how many years did George Dixon fight before he hung up his gloves?"

And Papa would come back with: "Just about 21 years, Edward." (Papa never used the more descriptive nicknames.) "I think he fought his first fight in 1886 and hung up his gloves for good in 1906—the same year little Ted here was born."

And then the questions would go on to Joe Gans, Sam Langford, the original Joe Walcott and other of our pugilists of note. I can never remember a question about a white fighter in all these sessions, or about a bout where a Negro got licked.

Neither can I ever remember anybody checking back on Papa. If Professor said it was so, it was so. Papa did have a prodigious memory and if anybody ever caught him wrong, they didn't have nerve enough to tell him so.

So it was understandable that I waited six weeks—and eight bloody noses—before I screwed up my courage enough to raise the question which had been racking my brain (not to mention rocking my head in daily combat) at the Booker T. Washington Colored Grammar School.

And I probably wouldn't have had nerve enough to ask it even then if I hadn't been forced to take on a double-header the day before in the Booker T. playground.

It had started out as a simple fight between me and Copper-Mouth Papa Peterson. Only he wasn't called Copper-Mouth then, but just plain Oscar. It was only in later years when he became a sporting man that he got the nickname Copper-Mouth Papa.

Allison Williams gave it to him that day Oscar came back from Louisville where, as a sporting man, he had had extensive dental work done. But he was nicknamed for life when Allison cried:

"Look at that doggone Oscar. He's got a mouth full of gold teeth. And ain't no two of them the same color. They got to be *copper.*"

I don't remember exactly what the original argument was between me and Oscar that day at Booker T. Washington Colored Grammar School. But when he could think of nothing else to say, he yelled at me in scorn:

"And anyway, your Pappy's a Democrat!"

And I let him have it right where the gold teeth were later to appear.

It wasn't my first set-to with Oscar. And I had no doubt that I could take him again. And I would have too if Leonardius Wright hadn't chosen that minute to put his two cents worth in.

Leonardius was my rival for the affections of pretty little Sarah Williams, and he'd had it in for me ever since he learned I was writing her love letters too in our Third Grade Class. So when me and Oscar locked horns in the playground, Leonardius started cheering Oscar on.

"Let him have it, Oscar," he was yelling from the sidelines, "Give him a *white* eye."

Now Leonardius knew that was wrong, and that he had deliberately broken an unwritten convention. Nobody as high yaller as Leonardius was supposed to raise the complexion question with nobody as dark as me—although Mama always insisted I was a pretty chocolate brown.

Anyway, I turned to glare at Leonardius out of my right eye and Oscar landed a haymaker in my left before I could turn back again.

So I forfeited the fight to Oscar on a matter of higher principle, and caught up with Leonardius just before he scampered through the back door of the Booker T. Washington Colored Grammar School.

And then I proceeded to give him two *black* eyes as a lesson for the future.

Therefore, early the next morning when the signifiers started gathering on our front porch to await Papa's fortnightly arrival, I hurried down to the L. & N. railroad station so I could stroll back home with him and have a few minutes alone.

And as we walked away from the station—where Papa had spent a few minutes settling a couple of bets between Mr. Sam Owens, the baggage clerk, and Mr. Edward Wynn, our colored porter—I took the bull by the horns.

"Papa," I said without preamble, as we approached Ninth and Campbell Streets, "Are you a Democrat?"

He considered the question with his usual deliberation and then said:

"Why no, son. I'm neither a Democrat nor a Republican. I just vote for men and measures. Party labels mean nothing to me."

I mulled this over for another block—in both hope and despair—and ventured another query:

"But, Papa, didn't you ever vote for the Republicans some time?"

"Come to think of it," he rejoined, "I don't think I ever did. They never nominated a Republican around here that I thought was worth voting for."

I mulled over that until we got to Second and Vine Streets, only three blocks from home. And then I ventured:

"Miss Hazel Green, our Third Grade teacher, says our colored citizens shouldn't vote for the Democrats. She said it ain't fair to Mr. Abraham Lincoln."

Papa chuckled to himself as we walked over the little bridge at Gulley Street. But finally he said:

"Son, I never voted against Mr. Lincoln. He hasn't been on the ballot for years and years as far as I know. Matter of fact, I was a little tyke just about your age when John Wilkes Booth shot Mr. Lincoln dead."

"Dead?" I echoed automatically. And then I shut up. I knew that my history book in the Booker T. Washington Colored Grammar School said something about Mr. Lincoln being shot, but you would never have guessed that he was dead—from the way our leading politicians and teachers talked about him.

But we were home by that time and I was carrying Papa's carpet bag into the living room as Mr. Freddie Williams was preparing to ask the day's first question.

I never raised the question again with Papa, but I found out later that it was not by any means a dead issue in his mind.

On his next trip home, for instance, he brought me a new history book he'd ordered from way up North—as far up there as Cleveland or some such place. And it taught me a lot of things I'd never learned in Booker T. Washington Colored Grammar School.

I started to wonder, for one thing, if Mr. Robert E. Lee was *really* a better general than old Ulysses Simpson Grant (for whom one of my brothers was named).

I also began to have my doubts about Mr. Stonewall Jackson and to question for the first time whether that blood-thirsty old rascal, General Sherman, actually ate pure and innocent little white babies for breakfast every morning as he made his march through Georgia.

But Papa wasn't content just doing this to *me*. He carried the whole matter further. He started pushing his twice-monthly front porch seminars far beyond the usual questions and answers, and began talking to our visitors about "men and measures" and local politics.

Oddly enough, it was the sporting men down on the front lawn who first started listening. They didn't care who was Mayor or City Clerk or Circuit Judge.

But they were a little fed up with Mr. Sidney Lanier Jenkins, our Republican sheriff in Christian County. It seemed that in recent weeks, Mr. Jenkins— or his collectors—had doubled the ante the sporting men had to pay for running an innocent little poker or pitty-pat game, or for selling a little "mountain dew" corn liquor, or even for just keeping out of jail.

But nobody seemed to pay Papa no real mind until the returns were counted in that next April's elections. And, come and behold, the whole Republican ticket was elected—with the sole exception of Mr. Jenkins. And when they counted up the votes out on Dirt's Avenue and Lovier's Hill where most of the sporting people lived, they found out that 113 colored citizens had voted Democratic for the first time, while Sheriff Jenkins had lost the county-wide race by only 103 votes.

Papa was pretty put up by the whole thing. But Mama didn't seem too happy. For while Papa was back up in Frankfort the next week, she heard the rumors that were going around the town.

It seemed that Cock-Eye Watson and Ozie Jones, the two colored citizens who used to collect his graft for Sheriff Jenkins, felt that Papa had done them a personal disservice in getting their boss defeated. And they boasted they weren't going to take it lying down.

In fact, every time they got high in Pete Postell's saloon—where drinks for them were no longer on the house—they boasted that they were going to shoot that Eph Poston dead the next time they saw him.

Papa didn't pay them no mind in spite of Mama's apprehensions. But the reports got so widespread that Judge Hezekiah Witherspoon, our local Republican leader, heard about them. And he sent word to Mama to have Papa come straight to his office the next time he came home.

Papa did and Judge Witherspoon came right to the point.

"Eph," he said, Papa told us later, "You are a Democrat—God knows why—and you've never done us no good. But you are also one of our leading colored citizens. And we are not going to have our good colored citizens bothered by no riff-raff."

Then he reached in his roll-top desk and handed Papa two big horse pistols.

"You take these guns and go right out there and shoot those two Nigras dead. And I'll see that nobody does a thing about it."

Papa had never owned a pistol in his life, but he was too polite to offend Judge Witherspoon. So he picked up the guns with mixed emotions. For one thing, he knew that Judge Witherspoon hadn't been too unhappy about the defeat of Sheriff Jenkins. For Mr. Jim Williams, our courthouse janitor, had told him the Judge had long been dissatisfied with the way Sheriff Jenkins was splitting his "take."

For another, Papa knew he wasn't going to shoot anybody.

But I didn't learn the sequel until late the next afternoon when I was digging fishing worms under the back porch and Mama and Papa were sitting up there in the shade talking things over.

"I've never felt so silly in my life," Papa was telling Mama. "There I was walking down Sixth Street with two big horse pistols in my pockets. And I knew I'd never bring them home.

"So as I was passing Pete Postell's Saloon, I got an idea. I'd give the pistols to Pete and he could dispose of them as he saw fit.

"But when I walked in the bar with those two big pistols in my hands, the first two people I saw were Cock-Eye Watson and Ozie Jones.

"We all saw each other at the same time. But they took one look at those big horse pistols and almost broke each other's necks in scrambling out the back door family entrance. They actually tore one side off the swinging doors."

Mama chuckled quietly, but by the next day the story was all over town. One wag swore on his oath that:

"Ozie and Cock-Eye didn't stop running until they got to the L. & N. Station. And then they took the first thing out of there smoking. It turned out to be a Pullman conductor with a pipe in his mouth. But they rode him as far as Evansville, Indiana, before they found out their mistake."

I always doubted that Papa's detractors left town that fast. But nobody ever saw them around anymore after that night.

And anyway, the incident solved my own personal problem.

For nobody else for the rest of our school term dared insult the son of Two-Gun Eph Poston—even if his father *was* a Democrat.

FLANNERY O'CONNOR

Granted that it culminates in the cold-blooded murder, one by one, of an entire family, I'd say that the most deeply humorous Southern short story is O'Connor's "A Good Man Is Hard to Find," which is also one of the most widely anthologized American stories. For this book I've selected a lesser-known story, in which only one person dies and perhaps there are more funny lines. The year before she died, I visited her at her home in Milledgeville, Georgia. She said a hired man on the farm had said something to her about a "scrootch owl." "Don't you mean a screech owl?" she asked him. No, he said, a scrootch owl: one of those owls that lands on a limb close to another bird and then scrootches over and scrootches over until he can grab him in his talons. That's my Flannery O'Connor story. She was a wonderful writer, whose redemptive delight in depravity, a fusion of Southern dirt-commonness and dark no-nonsense religious enthusiasm, attains such a pitch as to bring awful back down to its roots in awe. Southern humor ain't just kidding. And what an ear she had! Sometimes I'll just be sitting around thinking idly about final things and a line from one of her stories will pop into my head—"The monks of old slept in their coffins," "Jesus thown everything off balance," "Shut up Bobby Lee, it's no real pleasure in life"—and I'll feel chastened, but better.

"A Late Encounter with the Enemy"

General Sash ws a hundred and four years old. He lived with his granddaughter, Sally Poker Sash, who was sixty-two years old and who prayed every night on her knees that he would live until her graduation from college. The General didn't give two slaps for her graduation but he never doubted he would live for it. Living had got to be such a habit with him that he couldn't conceive of any other condition. A graduation exercise was not exactly his idea of a good time, even if, as she said, he would be expected to sit on the stage in his uniform. She said there would be a long procession of teachers and students in their robes but that there wouldn't be anything to equal *him* in his uniform. He

knew this well enough without her telling him, and as for the damm procession, it could march to hell and back and not cause him a quiver. He liked
parades with floats full of Miss Americas and Miss Daytona Beaches and Miss
Queen Cotton Products. He didn't have any use for processions and a procession full of schoolteachers was about as deadly as the River Styx to his way of
thinking. However, he was willing to sit on the stage in his uniform so that
they could see him.

Sally Poker was not as sure as he was that he would live until her graduation. There had not been any perceptible change in him for the last five years,
but she had the sense that she might be cheated out of her triumph because she
so often was. She had been going to summer school every year for the past
twenty because when she started teaching, there were no such things as
degrees. In those times, she said, everything was normal but nothing had been
normal since she was sixteen, and for the past twenty summers, when she
should have been resting, she had had to take a trunk in the burning heat to the
state teachers' college; and though when she returned in the fall, she always
taught in the exact way she had been taught not to teach, this was a mild
revenge that didn't satisfy her sense of justice. She wanted the General at her
graduation because she wanted to show what she stood for, or, as she said,
"what all was behind her," and was not behind them. This *them* was not
anybody in particular. It was just all the upstarts who had turned the world on
its head and unsettled the ways of decent living.

She meant to stand on that platform in August with the General sitting in his
wheel chair on the stage behind her and she meant to hold her head very high
as if she were saying, "See him! See him! My kin, all you upstarts! Glorious
upright old man standing for the old traditions! Dignity! Honor! Courage! See
him!" One night in her sleep she screamed, "See him! See him!" and turned
her head and found him sitting in his wheel chair behind her with a terrible
expression on his face and with all his clothes off except the general's hat and
she had waked up and had not dared to go back to sleep again that night.

For his part, the General would not have consented even to attend her
graduation if she had not promised to see to it that he sit on the stage. He liked
to sit on any stage. He considered that he was still a very handsome man.
When he had been able to stand up, he had measured five feet four inches of
pure game cock. He had white hair that reached to his shoulders behind and he
would not wear teeth because he thought his profile was more striking without
them. When he put on his full-dress general's uniform, he knew well enough
that there was nothing to match him anywhere.

This was not the same uniform he had worn in the War between the States.
He had not actually been a general in that war. He had probably been a foot
soldier; he didn't remember what he had been; in fact, he didn't remember
that war at all. It was like his feet, which hung down now shriveled at the very

end of him, without feeling, covered with a blue-gray afghan that Sally Poker had crocheted when she was a little girl. He didn't remember the Spanish-American War in which he had lost a son; he didn't even remember the son. He didn't have any use for history because he never expected to meet it again. To his mind, history was connected with processions and life with parades and he liked parades. People were always asking him if he remembered this or that—a dreary black procession of questions about the past. There was only one event in the past that had any significance for him and that he cared to talk about: that was twelve years ago when he had received the general's uniform and had been in the premiere.

"I was in that preemy they had in Atlanta," he would tell visitors sitting on his front porch. "Surrounded by beautiful guls. It wasn't a thing local about it. It was nothing local about it. Listen here. It was a nashnul event and they had me in it—up onto the stage. There was no bob-tails at it. Every person at it had paid ten dollars to get in and had to wear his tuxseeder. I was in this uniform. A beautiful gul presented me with it that afternoon in a hotel room."

"It was in a suite in the hotel and I was in it too, Papa," Sally Poker would say, winking at the visitors. "You weren't alone with any young lady in a hotel room."

"Was, I'd a known what to do," the old General would say with a sharp look and the visitors would scream with laughter. "This was a Hollywood, California, gul," he'd continue. "She was from Hollywood, California, and didn't have any part in the pitcher. Out there they have so many beautiful guls that they don't need that they call them a extra and they don't use them for nothing but presenting people with things and having their pitchers taken. They took my pitcher with her. No, it was two of them. One on either side and me in the middle with my arms around each of them's waist and their waist ain't any bigger than a half a dollar."

Sally Poker would interrupt again. "It was Mr. Govisky that gave you the uniform, Papa, and he gave me the most exquisite corsage. Really, I wish you could have seen it. It was made with gladiola petals taken off and painted gold and put back together to look like a rose. It was exquisite. I wish you could have seen it, it was . . ."

"It was as big as her head," the General would snarl. "I was tellin it. They gimme this uniform and they gimme this soward and they say, 'Now General, we don't want you to start a war on us. All we want you to do is march right up on that stage when you're innerduced tonight and answer a few questions. Think you can do that?' 'Think I can do it!' I say. 'Listen here. I was doing things before you were born,' and they hollered."

"He was the hit of the show," Sally Poker would say, but she didn't much like to remember the premiere on account of what had happened to her feet at it. She had bought a new dress for the occasion—a long black crepe dinner dress with a rhinestone buckle and a bolero—and a pair of silver slippers to wear with it, because she was supposed to go up on the stage with him to keep him from falling. Everything was arranged for them. A real limousine came at ten minutes to eight and took them to the theater. It drew up under the marquee at exactly the right time, after the big stars and the director and the author and the governor and the mayor and some less important stars. The police kept traffic from jamming and there were ropes to keep the people off who couldn't go. All the people who couldn't go watched them step out of the limousine into the lights. Then they walked down the red and gold foyer and an usherette in a Confederate cap and little short skirt conducted them to their special seats. The audience was already there and a group of UDC members began to clap when they saw the General in his uniform and that started everybody to clap. A few more celebrities came after them and then the doors closed and the lights went down.

A young man with blond wavy hair who said he represented the motion-picture industry came out and began to introduce everybody and each one who was introduced walked up on the stage and said how really happy he was to be here for this great event. The General and his granddaughter were introduced sixteenth on the program. He was introduced as General Tennessee Flintrock Sash of the Confederacy, though Sally Poker had told Mr. Govisky that his name was George Poker Sash and that he had only been a major. She helped him up from his seat but her heart was beating so fast she didn't know whether she'd make it herself.

The old man walked up the aisle slowly with his fierce white head high and his hat held over his heart. The orchestra began to play the Confederate Battle Hymn very softly and the UDC members rose as a group and did not sit down again until the General was on the stage. When he reached the center of the stage with Sally Poker just behind him guiding his elbow, the orchestra burst out in a loud rendition of the Battle Hymn and the old man, with real stage presence, gave a vigorous trembling salute and stood at attention until the last blast had died away. Two of the usherettes in Confederate caps and short skirts held a Confederate and a Union flag crossed behind them.

The General stood in the exact center of the spotlight and it caught a weird moon-shaped slice of Sally Poker—the corsage, the rhinestone buckle and one hand clenched around a white glove and handkerchief. The young man with the blond wavy hair inserted himself into the circle of light and said he was *really* happy to have here tonight for this great event, one, he said, who had fought and bled in the battles they would soon see daringly re-acted on the screen, and "Tell me, General," he asked, "how old are you?"

"Niiiiiinnttty-two!" the General screamed.

The young man looked as if this were just about the most impressive thing that had been said all evening. "Ladies and gentlemen," he said, "let's give the General the biggest hand we've got!'' and there was applause immediately and the young man indicated to Sally Poker with a motion of his thumb that she could take the old man back to his seat now so that the next person could be introduced; but the General had not finished. He stood immovable in the exact center of the spotlight, his neck thrust forward, his mouth slightly open, and his voracious gray eyes drinking in the glare and the applause. He elbowed his granddaughter roughly away. ''How I keep so young,'' he screeched, ''I kiss all the pretty guls!''

This was met with a great din of spontaneous applause and it was at just that instant that Sally Poker looked down at her feet and discovered that in the excitement of getting ready she had forgotten to change her shoes: two brown Girl Scout oxfords protruded from the bottom of her dress. She gave the General a yank and almost ran with him off the stage. He was very angry that he had not got to say how glad he was to be here for this event and on the way back to his seat, he kept saying as loud as he could, ''I'm glad to be here at this preemy with all these beautiful guls!'' but there was another celebrity going up the other aisle and nobody paid any attention to him. He slept through the picture, muttering fiercely every now and then in his sleep.

Since then, his life had not been very interesting. His feet were completely dead now, his knees worked like old hinges, his kidneys functioned when they would, but his heart persisted doggedly to beat. The past and the future were the same thing to him, one forgotten and the other not remembered; he had no more notion of dying than a cat. Every year on Confederate Memorial Day, he was bundled up and lent to the Capitol City Museum where he was displayed from one to four in a musty room full of old photographs, old uniforms, old artillery, and historic documents. All these were carefully preserved in glass cases so that children would not put their hands on them. He wore his general's uniform from the premiere and sat, with a fixed scowl, inside a small roped area. There was nothing about him to indicate that he was alive except an occasional movement in his milky gray eyes, but once when a bold child touched his sword, his arm shot forward and slapped the hand off in an instant. In the spring when the old homes were opened for pilgrimages, he was invited to wear his uniform and sit in some conspicuous spot and lend atmosphere to the scene. Some of these times he only snarled at the visitors but sometimes he told about the premiere and the beautiful girls.

If he had died before Sally Poker's graduation, she thought she would have died herself. At the beginning of the summer term, even before she knew if she would pass, she told the Dean that her grandfather, General Tennessee Flintrock Sash of the Confederacy, would attend her graduation and that he was a hundred and four years old and that his mind was still clear as a bell. Distinguished visitors were always welcome and could sit on the stage and be introduced. She made arrangements with her nephew, John Wesley Poker

Sash, a Boy Scout, to come wheel the General's chair. She thought how sweet it would be to see the old man in his courageous gray and the young boy in his clean khaki—the old and the new, she thought appropriately—they would be behind her on the stage when she received her degree.

Everything went almost exactly as she had planned. In the summer while she was away at school, the General stayed with other relatives and they brought him and John Wesley, the Boy Scout, down to the graduation. A reporter came to the hotel where they stayed and took the General's picture with Sally Poker on one side of him and John Wesley on the other. The General, who had had his picture taken with beautiful girls, didn't think much of this. He had forgotten precisely what kind of event this was he was going to attend but he remembered that he was to wear his uniform and carry the sword.

On the morning of the graduation, Sally Poker had to line up in the academic procession with the B.S.'s in Elementary Education and she couldn't see to getting him on the stage herself—but John Wesley, a fat blond boy of ten with an executive expression, guaranteed to take care of everything. She came in her academic gown to the hotel and dressed the old man in his uniform. He was as frail as a dried spider. "Aren't you just thrilled, Papa?" she asked. "I'm just thrilled to death!"

"Put the soward acrost my lap, damn you," the old man said, "where it'll shine."

She put it there and then stood back looking at him. "You look just grand," she said.

"God damm it," the old man said in a slow monotonous certain tone as if he were saying it to the beating of his heart. "God damm every goddam thing to hell."

"Now, now," she said and left happily to join the procession.

The graduates were lined up behind the Science building and she found her place just as the line started to move. She had not slept much the night before and when she had, she had dreamed of the exercises, murmuring, "See him, see him?" in her sleep but waking up every time just before she turned her head to look at him behind her. The graduates had to walk three blocks in the hot sun in their black wool robes and as she plodded stolidly along she thought that if anyone considered this academic procession something impressive to behold, they need only wait until they saw that old General in his courageous gray and that clean young Boy Scout stoutly wheeling his chair across the stage with the sunlight catching the sword. She imagined that John Wesley had the old man ready now behind the stage.

The black procession wound its way up the two blocks and started on the main walk leading to the auditorium. The visitors stood on the grass, picking out their graduates. Men were pushing back their hats and wiping their foreheads and women were lifting their dresses slightly from the shoulders to keep them from sticking to their backs. The graduates in their heavy robes looked as if the last beads of ignorance were being sweated out of them. The sun blazed off the fenders of automobiles and beat from the columns of the buildings and pulled the eye from one spot of glare to another. It pulled Sally Poker's toward the big red Coca-Cola machine that had been set up by the side of the auditorium. Here she saw the General parked, scowling and hatless in his chair in the blazing sun while John Wesley, his blouse loose behind, his hip and cheek pressed to the red machine, was drinking a Coca-Cola. She broke from the line and galloped to them and snatched the bottle away. She shook the boy and thrust in his blouse and put the hat on the old man's head. "Now get him in there!" she said, pointing one rigid finger to the side door of the building.

For his part the General felt as if there were a little hole beginning to widen in the top of his head. The boy wheeled him rapidly down a walk and up a ramp and into a building and bumped him over the stage entrance and into position where he had been told and the General glared in front of him at heads that all seemed to flow together and eyes that moved from one face to another. Several figures in black robes came and picked up his hand and shook it. A black procession was flowing up each aisle and forming to stately music in a pool in front of him. The music seemed to be entering his head through the little hole and he thought for a second that the procession would try to enter it too.

He didn't know what procession this was but there was something familiar about it. It must be familiar to him since it had come to meet him, but he didn't like a black procession. Any procession that came to meet him, he thought irritably, ought to have floats with beautiful guls on them like the floats before the preemy. It must be something connected with history like they were always having. He had no use for any of it. What happened then wasn't anything to a man living now and he was living now.

When all the procession had flowed into the black pool, a black figure began orating in front of it. The figure was telling something about history and the General made up his mind he wouldn't listen, but the words kept seeping in through the little hole in his head. He heard his own name mentioned and his chair was shuttled forward roughly and the Boy Scout took a big bow. They called his name and the fat brat bowed. Goddam you, the old man tried to say, get out of my way, I can stand up!—but he was jerked back again before he could get up and take the bow. He supposed the noise they made was for him. If he was over, he didn't intend to listen to any more of it. If it hadn't been for the little hole in the top of his head, none of the words would have got to him. He thought of putting his finger up there into the hole to block them but the hole was a little wider than his finger and it felt as if it were getting deeper.

Another black robe had taken the place of the first one and was talking now and he heard his name mentioned again but they were not talking about him, they were still talking about history. "If we forget our past," the speaker was saying, "we won't remember our future and it will be as well for we won't have one." The General heard some of these words gradually. He had forgotten history and he didn't intend to remember it again. He had forgotten the name and face of his wife and the names and faces of his children or even if he had a wife and children, and he had forgotten the names of places and the places themselves and what had happened at them.

He was considerably irked by the hole in his head. He had not expected to have a hole in his head at this event. It was the slow black music that had put it there and though most of the music had stopped outside, there was still a little of it in the hole, going deeper and moving around in his thoughts, letting the words he heard into the dark places of his brain. He heard the words, Chickamauga, Shiloh, Johnston, Lee, and he knew he was inspiring all these words that meant nothing to him. He wondered if he had been a general at Chickamauga or at Lee. Then he tried to see himself and the horse mounted in the middle of a float full of beautiful girls, being driven slowly through downtown Atlanta. Instead, the old words began to stir in his head as if they were trying to wrench themselves out of place and come to life.

The speaker was through with that war and had gone on to the next one and now he was approaching another and all his words, like the black procession, were vaguely familiar and irritating. There was a long finger of music in the General's head, probing various spots that were words, letting in a little light on the words and helping them to live. The words began to come toward him and he said, Dammit! I ain't going to have it! and he started edging backwards to get out of the way. Then he saw the figure in the black robe sit down and there was a noise and the black pool in front of him began to rumble and to flow toward him from either side to the black slow music, and he said, Stop dammit! I can't do but one thing at a time! He couldn't protect himself from the words and attend to the procession too and the words were coming at him fast. He felt that he was running backwards and the words were coming at him like musket fire, just escaping him but getting nearer and nearer. He turned around and began to run as fast as he could but he found himself running toward the words. He was running into a regular volley of them and meeting them with quick curses. As the music swelled toward him, the entire past opened up on him out of nowhere and he felt his body riddled in a hundred places with sharp stabs of pain and he fell down, returning a curse for every hit. He saw his wife's narrow face looking at him critically through her round gold-rimmed glasses; he saw one of his squinting bald-headed sons; and his mother ran toward him with an anxious look; then a succession of places—Chickamauga, Shiloh, Marthasville—rushed at him as if the past were the only future now and he had to endure it. Then suddenly he saw that the black procession was almost on him. He recognized it, for it had been dogging all his days. He made such a desperate effort to see over it and find out what comes after the past that his hand clenched the sword until the blade touched bone.

The graduates were crossing the stage in a long file to receive their scrolls and shake the president's hand. As Sally Poker, who was near the end, crossed, she glanced at the General and saw him sitting fixed and fierce, his eyes wide open, and she turned her head forward again and held it a perceptible degree higher and received her scroll. Once it was all over and she was out of the auditorium in the sun again, she located her kin and they waited together on a bench in the shade for John Wesley to wheel the old man out. That crafty scout had bumped him out the back way and rolled him at high speed down a flagstone path and was waiting now, with the corpse, in the long line at the Coca-Cola machine.

JOHN FERGUS RYAN

Someone once described Ryan's writing as "like something carved into a bus-station bench." It ain't fancy to be sure, but the unabashed low-downness of its merriment—a great antidote to wispily sentimental quasi-folk nostalgia for down-home values—is so infectious that I can read it over and over. Ryan, from Arkansas, is a retired probation officer in Memphis. The Redneck Bride *is his high-water mark to date.*

from *The Redneck Bride*

Mrs. Tate let Yancey into the house and led him down the hall to the back and showed him a large, cool room with a lot of good furniture in it.

"Ten dollars a week," she said.

"I'll take it," said Yancey.

"Before you can move in, I'll need to ask you some questions. I never saw you before. You're not a local boy. You may have come here planning to get my breath while I'm asleep . . ."

"Aw ma'am, you don't need to worry about anything like that. I'm just a reporter for the *Tomcat*. Mr. Turmath told me you rented rooms . . .''

"Don't move," whispered Mrs. Tate, freezing. "Hold real still. Hold real still and he won't jump you."

"Jump me?" asked Yancey.

"The dog. He's right behind you. He don't know you. That's all. He's just uncertain."

Mrs. Tate moved away from her chair slowly, toward the open door behind Yancey. There in the doorway, a very large German shepherd dog was crouched, ready to spring. She moved slowly toward the dog and slowly reached out her arm to the door and shut it slowly as the dog began to growl, deep within his bowels. She continued to slowly shut the door until it was a foot away from the jamb; then she shut it very fast and clicked the lock. The dog let out a fierce, frustrated growl of rage, ran down the hall, pushed open the front door, ran out to Yancey's car, grabbed the front bumper in his teeth and shook it vigorously. Yancey and Mrs. Tate watched him through the window in the living room.

"I bought him for a bad dog," she said.

"How bad is he? He looks dangerous to me!"

"A woman living alone needs protection. I read about all that killing and raping and knocking in the head in Memphis. I read every word. It's just a matter of time until it spreads down here to Bloat. When it gets here, that dog will take care of it."

"He looks dangerous to me!"

"He was in the army. He's an old army dog."

"I say he's too dangerous. How am I going to get in my car?"

"I'll call him off and lock him in the hall."

"I don't know about renting a room here, with that dog. I'm afraid he might jump me if I were to come in late some night."

"I don't allow nobody here to keep late hours. Are you a Christian?"

"I guess so."

"You guess so! When the Lord comes, he'll want to know definite!"

"Is there anyone else in Bloat who rents rooms?"

"Just me. Most people are glad to rent here, in a Christian home where they'll be safe."

Mrs. Tate had attachments on every door and window in the house that played music-box tunes every time one of them was opened. She also had some kind of electrical device that switched the floor lamps on and off, all over the house, all night long, to make burglars outside think there were people up and moving around inside. At intervals during the night, a tape recording of the voices of loud, rough men was played through a loudspeaker under the eaves on the second floor of the house.

"I believe there's a burglar in the yard, Spike!"

"Let me at him," replied a gravelly voice. "I'll get hold of him and make him sorry he tried to rob this house!"

"Better take this axe with you!"

Then there would follow the sound of police whistles and gunshots, all taped and played through the loudspeaker.

"I guess I'll take the room," said Yancey. He was getting tired and Tubby Turmath had ordered him to return at once to the *Tomcat* office and help get out the next day's edition.

"You say you're a Christian?"

"Yes, ma'am."

"Church of Christ?"

"Uh . . . Methodist."

"Methodist? I won't allow cigar smoking in my house!"

"No, ma'am."

"All right. You can move in."

Yancey paid Mrs. Tate ten dollars, a week's rent, and she went outside and locked the dog in a shed until Yancey could get his luggage in the house.

After changing his clothes, Yancey reported back to the *Tomcat* office and relieved Davy Sue's brother Frank, who went home for supper. Yancey was alone in the office, writing up a notice of a De Molay pie supper, when the telephone rang.

"*Tomcat* office," he answered.

A colored man's voice on the other end of the line said, "Rafe, Jr. was arrested this afternoon for rape."

"Rafe, who?" asked Yancey.

"Rafe Junior Munger. He was arrested this afternoon for rape. Wrecked a car and puked on a Stingray. He's in jail right now. This is a friend."

The voice hung up. It had been the owner of the beer joint with no name calling, the one whose place had been rammed by Rafe, Jr. in the Pimp. Big Rafe had refused to stand good for the repairs. Big Rafe had told the owner he could sue him if he did not like it.

Yancey telephoned the jail and Marshal Hazel Catfield answered.

"This is Duane Yancey down at the *Tomcat*. I hear you got Rafe Junior Munger in there."

The marshal assumed the story was out and told all.

"How do you spell your name, marshal? I want to make sure I get it right in the *Tomcat*."

Hazel Catfield had never had his name in the *Tomcat* and was thrilled by the prospect. "You going to put my name in the paper?"

"Yes sir!"

"That'll be mighty nice!"

"Do I have all the facts, now, before I hang up?"

"Well, sir, like I said, we've got evidence enough to send Rafe, Jr. to Parchman for life. It was one of the most awful crimes in the history of this county. I've been marshal for twenty years and I've seen some bad men in my day, but never nothing like Rafe, Jr.!

"We found three hundred thousand dollars' worth of hard drugs under the back seat of his car," said the marshal, beginning to get carried away. "We figger the Mafia's in on it and that Rafe, Jr. was fixing to take that girl across a state line as part of an interstate call-girl ring."

The marshal was really wound up and talked on for another ten minutes, throwing in charges of arson, damage to real property, suspected buggery, and hints of connections with several unsolved murders.

"Thanks, marshal," said Yancey.

"My pleasure. Be sure now you spell my name right. It's CATFIELD. Lot of times, people think it's HATFIELD. It's CATFIELD. C-A-T. CATFIELD."

"Yes sir'. I got it!" said Yancey.

Yancey wrote two thousand words on the Rafe, Jr. story, full of the colorful details given him by the marshal, and set it up for the front page under the headline:

RAFE MUNGER, JR. HELD ON RAPE, DOPE,
DRUNK CHARGES. MURDER LINK SUSPECTED.
FACES LIFE AT PARCHMAN.
SPORTY PIMP TOTALLED.

Tubby Turmath returned from the Country Club about eight-thirty P.M. Friday night and started looking through the stories on his desk. When he saw the story about Rafe, Jr., he yelled to Yancey.

"Hey, Weak-Eyes! Get your butt in here!"

"Yes sir, Mr. Turmath?"

"Where'd you get all this stuff about Rafe, Jr.?"

"Checked it out after I got a tip on the phone."

"Boy—Weak-Eyes—We can't run nothing like this, even if it's true. We'd get our ass sued off if we was to run this . . ."

At that moment, Big Rafe walked in the *Tomcat* office, tired and played out after his busy and unpleasant day. He had one final mission to accomplish before he could go home and to bed. He had to be sure there would be nothing in the *Tomcat* about Rafe, Jr.'s troubles.

Tubby Turmath and his wife, Mona Mutt Turmath, were partners with Big Rafe, along with Dr. Dennis Dennis, the dentist, and his wife, Baxter Dennis, in the company that was trying to get the Roller Board Roadside Inn franchise.

"Tubby, can I see you alone?" asked Big Rafe.

"Weak-Eyes, get your butt on out of here, so's we can talk bidness."

Big Rafe shut the door to Tubby's office behind Yancey as he left.

"Tubby, I need a favor," he said. "It's a favor for me, but it's in your own interest, as well. Rafe, Jr. did a damn-fool thing this afternoon. Out foon with that Sula Measles. Wrecked her car. Drunk. You know Rafe, Jr."

"You want it kept out of the *Tomcat?*" asked Tubby.

"Not just for me, Tubby. For you and Mona, as well."

"I gottcha!"

"You and Mona have just as big an interest in this as I have. If it was to get out that my boy was no-count, if it was to get back to Roller Board's home office that he's had the past he's had, it would mean the end of any franchise down at the Cloverleaf."

"Sure would at that!" said Tubby. "Sure as Hell would!"

"So, if you could keep it out of the *Tomcat,* you see, we'd both stand to gain."

"I gottcha! Sure, we'll keep it out. That's what owning a paper is for!"

.   .   .   .

Alta Munger, wife of Big Rafe and mother of the felon Rafe, Jr., sat in the den of the Munger home, a split-level ranch style with double carport, on Alta Drive, two blocks off Main Street. When Big Rafe had laid out the subdivision, he had named the street after her. He named the street behind it Rafe, Jr. Drive.

It was ten-thirty Friday evening, and Alta Munger was working the cross-word puzzle that appeared daily in the Memphis *Commercial Appeal.* For a puzzle in a Memphis newspaper, it was very difficult, with words like "Italian River," two letters Down, and "Russian Coin," five letters Across. Alta Munger was not bright, but she finished it, in about an hour, every evening. She forced it. Sometimes she would put two letters in one square. It did not matter to her if it made sense, as long as every block had a letter in it.

Big Rafe drove up outside, entered the house by the side door in the carport, and stepped into the kitchen. He opened the refrigerator and took out a cold can of Diet Seven-Up, popped the top, and went into the den.

Big Rafe sat down. There was nothing said between them for a moment or two. Finally, "Rafe, Jr. is in trouble again."

"I know. I heard. What is it this time, exactly?"

"Drunk driving. We can count on that. Wrecking a car. Totalled out a sporty little Pimp. With factory air. Sula Measles, she's claiming he raped her. He tried to run Senator Oscar S. Baymule off the road. Rape, assault, drunk driving, attempted murder. He's going to be sent away this time. There's nothing I can do to save him. Money's going to mean nothing. Oscar S. Baymule is going to see him put away.''

Alta continued to force the crossword puzzle.

"Parchman?" she asked.

"I'm afraid so."

More silence, then Alta spoke. "I'd almost rather he be in the pen than to be married to that Davy Sue Merkle, that snake chunker's daughter! I had my heart set on him marrying the Queen of Delta Gamma Gam!"

"I wish you'd see Davy Sue's good side!"

"That's just another bidness deal, you fixing up that marriage! Who'd ever believe you'd marry off your son to a bony, ninety-pound tomboy just because she can add up a column of figures!"

"Not only just add! Subtract! Divide! Multiply! That girl is a walking IBM calculator! She's a genius! And smart, too! I want her to be in charge of the books when I get the Roller Board Inn going. You've gotta have a bookkeeper! That's the first lesson you learn in bidness. Books's gotta be kept! Why, I'll have a dozen Roller Board Inns before it's over, maybe two dozen! There'll be books and more books to keep and Davy Sue will keep them and I'll trust her because she'll be family! She'll be my daughter-in-law!"

Alta threw down her crossword puzzle. "You and your deals! Your big plans have ruined my life! Rafe, I'm borne to death! I'm miserable! I wish it was like it was, back in the beginning! I want to go back to the days when all you had was eight or ten nigger rent houses!"

"A man's gotta keep on moving, Alta. I've told you that, time and again. Onward and onward. Richer and richer."

"Well, at least, there'll be no wedding as long as Rafe, Jr. is in jail."

Big Rafe shook his head. "You're wrong there. The wedding'll take place, as scheduled. By proxy. It's all been taken care of. There'll be a proxy for Rafe, Jr. I've already had it put in the paper. Rafe, Jr. got called up by the National Guard and a fraternity brother from Ole Miss is going to stand in for him."

"You did what?" asked Alta, in shock. "A proxy?"

"I had to. The Roller Board deal will fall through if it gets out up in Memphis about Rafe, Jr. You know how Roller Board won't give a franchise to anyone without good morals all the way down the line."

"All the same," said Alta, "I'm not going to the wedding! I am not going to set foot in that Merkle house and make like I'm happy about it!"

Big Rafe smote his forehead. "You've got to go! The Executive Vice-President will want to meet you! You know that! You've got to go!"

"I will NOT go!" said Alta, and she left the room.

Big Rafe sat there in the den, drinking Diet Seven-Up and trying to think of an angle.

He thought of one! The Executive Vice-President did not know what Alta Munger looked like. He would hire a woman to pose as his wife! Big Rafe smiled, for the first time that day.

"Rafe Munger!" he said aloud to himself. "When it comes to working angles, they ain't a suh mitch in northwest Mississippi to hold a candle to you!"

.   .   .   .

An old pickup truck, battered and dented, with no state license plates, only a metal tag bought at Stuckey's that read, "GOD IS THE ANSWER," moved slowly down Main Street, from the water tower toward the road out to the Barrow Pits. Ricey Fitts was at the wheel, holding it with his left hand. In his right hand was a duck caller, the kind for sale in a Sears sporting goods department. Whenever he saw a Negro woman on the street, he slowed down as he went past her, put the duck caller to his lips and quacked obscenely.

Ricey Fitts was the only man from Bloat, Mississippi, ever to hold a state office in the Veterans of Foreign Wars.

He drove up and down Main Street three times, then pulled up and angle-parked in front of the Spit Cafe. It was about eight o'clock in the morning and the Spit was filling up with regulars. Ricey Fitts sat at a table with three old friends: one, a man who drove the "bottle" gas truck; one, a salesman for Dixie Midget Corn Meal; and the third, a foreman at the axe-handle factory before he retired.

Ricey ordered coffee and started looking around.

A stranger sat at the table next to him, a heavy, fleshy man about thirty, with curly blonde hair. At first glance, he looked fat, but on second glance, just big. It was Jackie Bad Ass, a professional wrestler out of Memphis, who had been in Jackson, Mississippi, the night before, wrestling for the Southern Heavyweight Championship.

Jackie Bad Ass had a big tattoo, Jesus choking an eagle, on his upper right arm and he was wearing leather sandals with lots of brass rings and studs on them. He was finishing breakfast, four eggs, fried over light, and was sopping up the yellow with buttered toast.

Ricey Fitts noticed the stranger's sandals.

"That's something I ain't never seen before," he said to his friends. "Sandals on a man."

The three friends turned to look at Jackie Bad Ass's sandals.

"Sandals on a man. That means just one thing," said Ricey Fitts. "There sits a fruit!"

"Our Lord and Savior wore sandals!" said the corn meal salesman. "I seen pitchurs in the Bobble!"

"Sandals on a man," repeated Ricey Fitts. "There sits a fruit!"

Jackie Bad Ass heard him say it. He set a piece of toast dripping with egg yolk back on his plate, wiped his lips with a paper napkin, and turned around and faced Ricey Fitts.

"Did I hear you say that I might be wearing a fruit's shoe?" he asked.

Ricey Fitts got flustered. "No sir! All I said was, that's one thing I never have seen before, sandals on a man!"

"How'd you like to have one of them up between the cheeks of your ass?" asked the wrestler.

Ricey Fitts turned away from Jackie Bad Ass and said, under his breath, to his friends, "He may be a fruit but he talks just like you and I do!"

.   .   .   .

"Sandals on a man don't mean a fruit!" said Mom. "It's when a man carries uh numbrella that he's a fruit!"

Big Rafe had walked over to the Mink Motel to pick up Rixie Leaptrot and Bunny and take them to the Spit Cafe for breakfast. He stopped at the desk.

"What room's Mr. Leaptrot in?" he asked.

"I moan' a kill you!" said the clerk.

Big Rafe adjusted his glasses and took another look at the clerk.

"Oh, is that you, Coy?" he asked. "Still not feeling any better?"

Coy's father, Coy Mink, Sr., appeared and said, "Your friend's in number 12. Sorry, Mr. Munger, about Coy. He's taking treatments."

"I understand," said Big Rafe.

Coy Mink, Sr. leaned across the desk and whispered in Big Rafe's ear, "Sometimes I worry, with him having keys to the rooms and all."

Big Rafe found his new friends awake. Rixie Leaptrot was in the bathroom, shaving his ear lobes.

The three of them walked out past the desk. Rixie Leaptrot cut his eyes in the direction of Coy Mink, Jr., who sat behind the desk, honing a Bowie knife on an Arkansas stone.

"That boy's not all there!" he said. "Dangerous, I say!"

"He's taking treatments," said Big Rafe.

Over breakfast—hot cakes, waffles with blueberry syrup and dairy butter, King Cotton Baby Link sausages, orange juice and coffee—Big Rafe laid out plans for the coming week.

"I put it out that Rafe, Jr. got called up overnight by the National Guard. I told them Bunny here was a frat brother at Ole Miss and a two-time winner of Mr. Popularity and that he was going to stand up for Rafe, Jr. at the wedding."

Bunny had a second helping of everything.

"That boy," asked Big Rafe, in a whisper. "Can't he talk?"

"Bunny's a mute, that's what he is," said Rixie Leaptrot. "He can hear like a bell but he can't say a word."

"Ain't that awful!" said Big Rafe. "Awful! A good-looking fella like him. MORE COFFEE, BUNNY?"

"I'll have a cup, Big Rafe," said a woman who walked up to the table and sat down, uninvited. It was Wolfena Poppenbarger, Society Editor of the *Titus County Tomcat*. She was about fifty, had prominent teeth and wore green eye shadow and lots of gold bracelets with bangles and charms on them. Miss Poppenbarger smoked a cigarette in a short holder and wore sequined eyeglasses that made her look like The Cat Woman.

If she had stepped out on the streets of Bloat in her bangles and green eye shadow in the old days, twenty years ago, she would have been brought up before the Justice of the Peace, old man Fritz Pitts, and fined ten dollars for appearing in the trappings of a harlot. Judge Pitts once fined a famous colored band leader ten dollars for driving through Bloat, Mississippi while barefooted and it made Walter Winchell. For the last two years of his life, Judge Pitts had cancer of the mouth and had to be fed with an air hose.

"What's happened to Rafe, Jr.?" asked Wolfena Poppenbarger, after she sat down. "Is he in some kind of trouble? I hear he's in trouble again. It's nothing to do with that sporty little Pimp that's been pulled into Blackie's Body Shop, is it? I hear it's totalled out and that Rafe, Jr. was seen driving it yesterday afternoon."

"Rafe, Jr. is not in any trouble, Wolfena," said Big Rafe, smiling paternally. "He's been called up by the National Guard. Secret Mission. Don't know when he'll be back."

"What about the wedding? I read in the *Tomcat* this morning that it was going ahead, with a proxy to stand up for Rafe, Jr. How can that be?"

"This here's the proxy," said Big Rafe, pointing to Bunny. "Mr. . . . er . . ."

"Whitesides," said Rixie Leaptrot. He stood up and extended his hand to Wolfena Poppenbarger. "I'm Rixie Leaptrot and this here is Bunny Whitesides. My folks was circus people."

"Bunny was a frat brother of Rafe, Jr.'s at Ole Miss," said Big Rafe, "and a two-time winner of Mr. Popularity."

Wolfena Poppenbarger extended her hand to Bunny.

"Bunny's got a bad throat this morning and can't talk," said Big Rafe.

"You say Rafe, Jr. is not in any trouble?" she asked.

"Not a bit," said Big Rafe. "Just off serving his country."

"Maybe so," she said. "Maybe so. All I know is, the Methodist Church Young People were not allowed to roller skate on the jail floor last night, and it the night they were supposed to crown the Queen!"

"You got me!" said Big Rafe, throwing up his hands.

LISA ALTHER

If you want to read about a really erotic football game (the denouement, which involves a cucumber, is also interesting), I recommend the excerpt from Kinflicks *chosen by Mordecai Richler for his anthology* The Best of Modern Humor. *This excerpt is more specifically Southern.*

Dying Properly

My family always has been into death. My father, the Major, used to insist on having an ice pick next to his placemat at meals so that he could perform an emergency tracheotomy when one of us strangled on a piece of meat. Even now, by running my index fingers along my collarbones to the indentation where the bones join, I can locate the optimal site for a tracheal puncture with the same deftness as a junky a vein.

The Major wasn't always a virtuoso at disaster prediction, however. When I was very young, he was all brisk efficiency, and made no room whatsoever for the unscheduled or the unexpected. "Ridiculous!" he would bark at Mother as she sat composing drafts of her epitaph. "Do you want to turn the children into a bunch of psychotics like the rest of your crazy family?" Perhaps, like my southern mother, you have to be the heiress to a conquered civilization to take your own vulnerability seriously prior to actually experiencing it. At least if you were born, as was the Major, in 1918 B.B. (Before the Bomb).

Whatever the reason, the Major's Cassandra complex developed later in life. He was a carpetbagger by profession, brought to Hullsport, Tennessee, from Boston to run the chemical plant that is the town's only industry. During the Korean War the plant, with its acres of red brick buildings and forests of billowing smoke stacks, was converted from production of synthetic fabrics to munitions; there were contracts from the federal government and top-secret contracts with the laboratories at Oak Ridge. On summer evenings, the Major used to take us kids out for cones of soft ice cream dipped in chocolate glaze, and then to the firing range where the new shell models were tested. Licking our dripping cones, we would watch proudly as the Major, tall and thin and elegant, listing forward on the balls of his feet, signaled the blasts with upraised arms, like an orchestra conductor cuing cymbal crashes.

Shortly after the conversion of the plant to munitions, the Major experienced his own personal conversion, and in a fashion that even an experienced aficionado of calamity like Mother could never have foreseen: He caught his platinum wedding band on a loose screw on a loaded truck bed at the factory and was dragged along until his ring finger popped out of its socket like a fried chicken wing being dismembered. Then his legs were run over by the rear wheels. There he lay, a fallen industrial cowboy, his boot caught in a stirrup, trampled by his own horse. . . .

When the Major emerged from his casts, a metamorphosis had occurred: He was no longer bold and brash. In fact, the first project he undertook was to renovate the basement family room into a bomb shelter as a surprise for Mother's birthday. *Her* reaction to the atmospheric nuclear tests going on all over the world then was to join a group in Hullsport called Mothers' Organization for Peace. MOP consisted of a dozen housewives, mostly wives of chemical plant executives who'd been exiled to Hullsport for a dreary year as grooming for high managerial posts in Boston. MOP meetings consisted of a handful of women with abrasive Yankee accents who sipped tea and twisted handkerchief corners and insisted bravely that Russian mothers *must* feel the same about strontium 90 in *their* babies' bones.

The Major, sneering at MOP, kept going with his bomb shelter. We kids were delighted. I took my girl friends down there to play house; and we confronted such ethical issues as whether or not to let old Mr. Thornberg next door share our shelter when the bomb dropped, or whether to slam the door in his miserly face, as he did to us on Halloween nights. Later we girls took Clem Cloyd and the acned boys from Magnolia Manor development down there to play Five Minutes in Heaven. While the others counted outside, the designated couple went into the chemical toilet enclosure to execute the painful grinding of braces that left us all with raw and bruised mouths . . . but in love. And in high school I brought dates down for serious sessions of heavy petting. In fact, I broke the heart of Joe Bob Sparks, star tailback of the Hullsport Pirates and body beautiful of Hullsport Regional High School, by forfeiting my maidenhead to Clem Cloyd one night on the altarlike wooden sleeping platform, double-locked behind the foot-thick steel door, while Mother and the Major slept on blissfully unaware upstairs.

Soon, no situation was too safe for the Major to be unable to locate its potential for tragedy. Death to him was not the inevitable companion of one's later years, the kindly warden who freed each soul from its earthly prison. Death to him was a sneak and a cheat who was ever vigilant to ambush the unwary, of whom the Major was determined not to be one. In contrast to Mother, who regarded Death as some kind of demon lover. The challenge, as she saw it, was to be ready for the assignation, so that you weren't distracted during consummation by unresolved earthly matters. The trick was in being both willing to die and able to at the same time. Dying properly was like achieving simultaneous orgasm.

Mother had many photographs, matted in eggshell white and framed in narrow black wood, on the fireplace mantle in her bedroom. As I was growing up, she would sit me on her lap and take down these yellowed cracked photos and tell me about the people in them, people who had already experienced, prepared for it or not, this ultimate fuck with Death. Her grandmother, Dixie Lee Hull, in a blouse with a high lace neck, who had cut her finger on a recipe card for spoon bread and had died of septicemia at age twenty-nine. Great-uncle Lester, a druggist in Sow Gap, who became addicted to cough syrup and one night threw himself under the southbound train to Chattanooga. Cousin Louella, who dove into a nest of water moccasins in an abandoned stone quarry at a family reunion in 1932. Another cousin who stuck his head out of a car window to read a historical marker about the Battle of Lookout Mountain and was sideswiped by a Mason-Dixon transport truck. It was always so unsatisfying to rage at her in a tantrum, as children do, "I *hate* you! I hope you *die!*" She'd reply calmly, "Don't worry, I will. And so will you."

At spots in our decor where lesser women would have settled for Audubon prints or college diplomas, Mother hung handsomely framed and matted rubbings of the tombstones of our forebears, done in dark chalk on fine rice paper. The Major always planned family vacations around business conferences so that expenses would be tax deductible and so that he wouldn't have to spend long stretches trapped with his family. Mother used to coordinate his meetings with trips for the rest of us to unvisited gravesites of remote relations. I spent most of my first seventeen summers weeding and edging and planting around obscure ancestral crypts. Mother considered these pilgraimages to burying plots around the nation as didactic exercises for us children, far superior to the overworked landmarks, like the Statue of Liberty, on the American Freedom Trail.

Apparently a trait like fascination with eschatology is hereditary. At any rate, it seems to run in *our* family. Mother's ancestors, however humble their circumstances (and most of them were in very humble circumstances, being dirt farmers and coal miners), invested a great deal of thought and money in their memorials to themselves. In any given cemetery, the most elaborately carved urns and weeping willows and hands pointing confidently to heaven invariably belong to my ancestors. Also the most catchy epitaphs: "Stop and look as you pass by. / As you are now, so once was I. / As I am now, so you will be. / Prepare to die and follow me." Mother considered that one, by a great-great-aunt named Hattie, the pinnacle of our family's achievement. Mother had dozens of trial epitaphs for herself, saved up in a small black loose-leaf notebook. The prime contender when I left home for college in Boston was, "The way that is weary, dark and cold / May lead to shelter within the fold. / Grieve not for me when I am gone. / The body's dark night: the soul's dawn."

When Mother wasn't working on her epitaph, she was rewriting her funeral ceremony. "Let's see——" she'd say to me as I sat on the floor beside her mahogany Chippendale desk dressing my doll in black crepe for a wake, "Do you think 'A Mighty Fortress Is Our God' should go before or after 'Deus Noster Refugium'?" I'd look up from my doll's funeral. "You won't forget, will you, dear?" she'd inquire sternly. "The agenda for my memorial service will be in my upper right-hand desk drawer."

Or she'd repolish her obituary and worry over whether or not the Knoxville *Sentinel* would accept it for publication. I have since come to understand her agony. When my classmates were taking frantic notes on penile lengths in first term Physiology 110 at Worthley College, I was diligently preparing the wording of my engagement announcement in the margin of my notebook: "Major and Mrs. Wesley Marshall Babcock IV of Hullsport, Tennessee, and Hickory, Virginia, take pleasure in announcing the engagement of their daughter Virginia Hull Babcock to Clemuel Cloyd. . . ." Years later, when the time finally came to dust off this draft and replace the name of Clemuel Cloyd with Ira Bliss, I discovered that the Boston *Globe* wouldn't print it, in spite of the fact that I'd read their damned paper dutifully every Sunday for the two years I'd been in college there. What could bring more posthumous humiliation than to have your obituary rejected by a paper like the Knoxville *Sentinel?*

FLORENCE KING

Florence King's cranky conservative essays have many fans, but I prefer her rather heartier recollections of family life. She says her ancestors arrived in tidewater Virginia in 1662. The Atlanta Journal-Constitution *said her* Confessions *left "more Old South traditions in shreds than Gen. William T. Sherman." If only Sherman had done his work in such a pleasure-giving way. Maybe it was a Northern thing, Sherman's grimness. What if Nathan Bedford Forrest, say, had cut a swath northeasterly from Gettysburg to the sea? Don't get me wrong: I'm glad he didn't. But I'll bet the devastation would have had more panache.*

from *Confessions of a Failed Southern Lady*

There are ladies everywhere, but they enjoy generic recognition only in the South. There is a New England old maid but not a New England lady. There is a Midwestern farm wife but not a Midwestern lady. There is most assuredly a California girl, but if anyone spoke of a California lady, even Phil Donahue and Alan Alda would laugh.

If you wish to understand the American woman, study the Southern woman. The sweetening process that feminists call "socialization" is simply a less intense version of what goes on in every Southern family. We call it "rearing." If the rearing is successful, it results in that perfection of femininity known as a lady.

I was reared. On the day in 1948 that I got my first period, my grandmother gave me a clipping. I suppose it came from the Daughters' magazine since she never read anything else. It said:

> When God made the Southern woman, He summoned His angel messengers and He commanded them to go through all the star-strewn vicissitudes of space and gather all there was of beauty, of brightness and sweetness, of enchantment and glamour, and when they returned and laid the golden harvest at His feet, He began in their wondering presence the work of fashioning the Southern girl. He wrought with the golden gleam of the stars, with the changing colors of the rainbow's hues and the pallid silver of the moon. He wrought with the crimson that swoons in the rose's ruby heart, and the snow that gleams on the Lily's petal. Then, glancing down deep into His own bosom, He took of the love that gleamed there like pearls beneath the sun-kissed waves of a summer sea, and thrilling that love into the form He had fashioned, all heaven veiled its face, for lo, He had wrought the Southern girl.

That my mother referred to this paean as "a crock of shit" goes far to explain why Granny worked so hard at my rearing. She was a frustrated ladysmith and I was her last chance. Mama had defeated her but she kept the anvil hot for me and began hammering and firing with a strength born of desperation from the day I entered the world until the day she left it.

This is the story of my years on her anvil. Whether she succeeded in making a lady out of me is for you to decide, but I will say one thing in my own favor before we begin.

No matter which sex I went to bed with, I never smoked on the street.

My ladylike adventures have taken me from Seattle to Paris, but last year I was carried back to Tidewater Virginia, which my ancestors helped to unsettle.

A romantic version of my address can be found on the first page of Thackeray's *Henry Esmond,* which kicks off with a description of the Esmond family's royal grant "in Westmoreland County between the Rappahannock and Potomac rivers." It was the only book I ever read that Granny did not tell me to get my nose out of. Though she hated "bluestockings"—her name for female intellectuals, who could never be ladies—she actually read a few pages of it herself, muttering, "Esmond . . . Esmond . . . do I know any Esmonds?"

Being an Englishman, my father was singularly unimpressed by Granny's ancestors, so I knew he was getting ready to enjoy himself. I met his dancing eyes and read the message in them: *Don't tell her it's a novel.* We let her go on until she was saying, "It was Samuel Esmond who married my great-great-grandfather's half-sister." Preening herself, she added, "Our royal grant was next to theirs."

. . . .

Near the end of the sixth grade we were given an IQ test without being told what it was. The teacher, a huggybear, became so unhinged by the mere thought of a sabot being tossed into her leveling machine that she spent most of the morning praising the forthcoming test in an Aeschylean speech that sounded like Clytemnestra compulsively telling everyone who would listen that she had never, no never, committed adultery.

"I have some good news! You're going to take the most wonderful test tomorrow. It's going to be *fun!* I'll bet you think that's too good to be true, don't you? Well, it *is* true—how about that? Now, it's a *leetle* bit different from what you're used to. You have to use a special pencil, and you'll be timed. But it has lots of pictures of things like, oh, slices of pie and circles and squares and such. And best of all—oh, I know you'll be happy to hear this—you won't get a grade on it!"

"Then why are we taking it?" I asked.

I got the look all Cassandras get. "To help you get used to grownup tests," the huggybear replied, forcing a laugh. "You're growing up and going to junior high."

After the test, Peg and I compared notes. Considering our long-standing mutual aid pact wherein I copied her math and she copied my spelling, our reactions were not surprising.

"I finished the pies way ahead of time," she said, "but I only got halfway through the part with the story and the list of words."

"I was the other way around. The story and words were easy but the pies got on my nerves."

"You were supposed to figure out which pieces made a whole circle and which were the extra ones that didn't fit."

"I know. That's why they got on my nerves."

"I bet they're trying to find out what we're good at."

"But they already know."

A voice behind us spoke.

"They're trying to find out who's smart and who's dumb so they'll know what track to put us in when we get to junior high."

It was Ann Hopkins, the only girl in the sixth grade able to wear a skirt without suspenders to hold it up. She was what Granny called "over-developed."

"What's a track?" I asked.

"There's 7A1, 7A2, 7A3, and 7A4. Four is smartest, three is next-to-smartest, two is average, and one is dumb. I want to be in 7A2 so I can be popular. Average kids are always the most popular." Her eyes widened. "It's even more important for girls to be average. Boys don't like smart girls but you have to be smart enough to ask the right questions when a boy is explaining something to you, so that's why I want to be average. You get the most dates."

On a hot rainy September morning, Peg, Helen, and I walked to Powell Junior High just above 14th and Park Road. My New Look transparent plastic raincoat, the last word in postwar fashion, was so long that water dripped off the hem directly into the top of my socks. We squished into the building and followed the signs to the auditorium and took seats. At nine the principal entered, followed by four women teachers. He mounted the podium and unfolded some papers.

"I will call the names of those of you assigned to 7A4. When you hear your name, rise and stand by the wall until the group is complete."

Our three names were not among the ones he called. When the intellectual plutocrats had left with their new homeroom teacher, the principal began on the 7A3s. We were in it, and so was Ann Hopkins. As we made our way to the wall, Peg and I exchanged a resigned glance.

"Words," she said.

"Pies," I replied.

Ann groaned at the thought of being next-to-smartest instead of average.

A pretty blond teacher named Miss Ogilvy beckoned us to follow her. As I squished moistly behind her I admired the way her New Look skirt swirled glamourously in undulating waves near her ankles. It also stayed up on her hips, while mine was pinned to my undershirt. To complete the contrast, she looked as fresh as a daisy and I was beginning to smell. It was the plastic raincoat. Some amazing new synthetic chemical, as yet unperfected, was wafting from it like vapor from a cesspool. I sniffed at my forearm and nearly gagged. Whatever it was, it had clung tenaciously to me.

In homeroom, Miss Ogilvy arranged us alphabetically, made a seating chart, assigned lockers, gave us our class schedules, and asked for someone to act as class chaplain for the daily Bible reading. I scrunched down and concealed my face in my stinking arms, terrified that she would pick me because I looked— yes, *looked*—like a class chaplain. Ann Hopkins volunteered for the job and I breathed again.

When the first period bell rang we remained seated because our first class was English and Miss Ogilvy was also our English teacher. After issuing us our books, she passed out composition paper and told us to write a theme on one of the topics she listed on the blackboard. They were: "What I Did This Summer," "What I Want to Be When I Grow Up," and "My Family."

I had no idea what I wanted to be when I grew up. Ann Hopkins did. I glanced over and saw her scrawling "Wife and mother" in her purple ink and circling the dot over the *i* in her customary way. She and I had already clashed over her ambitions. For all I had heard about ancestors, I had no wish to be one. The idea of having children so they could have children so *they* could have children frightened me. It seemed so pointless, like that blissful measure of time in Heaven that so comforted the devout: "If a bird transferred every grain of sand on every beach, grain by grain, and dropped them in the ocean, that is the beginning of eternity."

I derived comfort from what I called "overness," possibly because Herb's Socratic dialogues always ended in such neat, inescapable conclusions. Thinking of him, I decided to write on "My Family."

> My grandmother lives with us. She is my mother's mother, but new people moving into our building always guess it wrong. They think my father is her son instead of her son-in-law because he's so polite to her. When I didn't catch a mother-in-law joke on the radio, Aunt Charlotte said it was because I never saw the kind of stuff that usually goes on between a man and his mother-in-law. Granny's friends like my father, too. They are all Daughters. When they come to see her, he always tells them little things about history that they like. Tessie Satterfield, who brought me into this world, calls my father a prince among men. Jensy, the colored woman who works for us, says they broke the mold when they made my father. The librarians at Mount Pleasant all like him, too. All women like my father but he doesn't have any men friends. I guess that's because he's so nice.

I felt I could have done better if only I had not smelled. My arms had absorbed most of the chemical and reeked at the slightest movement; trying to contain it had affected my penmanship as well as my thoughts. When the bell rang I rushed into the girls room and washed myself wherever the raincoat had touched me, but the smell remained, at least in my imagination.

I could not afford a lapse like this. I was used to being a pariah for flattering reasons, but now I was a real pariah and it made me feel vulnerable. Dimly I sensed that a female with a personality like mine has to make sure that she looks and smells good at all times, or as Henry Adams put it: "Those who study Greek must take pains with their dress." So far I had kept the watery moles in a state of resentful awe, but if I stank, their mood would change to scorn and I would be powerless. Nobody cared how a loner boy smelled, but a girl who is a misanthrope must be nice to be near.

The raincoat fiasco traumatized me so much that I did something completely out of character: I took Granny's long-ignored advice on ladylike graciousness and tried to be friendly.

The object of my sudden warmth was a late enrollee named Harriet Mudd, who stalked into homeroom the next morning and thrust her card at Miss Ogilvy. She had muscular shoulders, thick glasses, and tiny black eyes with an odd bright shine. Her complexion was taupe and her demeanor grim.

"I'm afraid all the lockers have been assigned, Harriet," said Miss Ogilvy, "but I'm sure one of the girls would be happy to share hers with you." She turned to us. "Do I have a volunteer?"

Every female hand in the room shot up. All the Virginless American dynamos were eager to practice goodness without clout. It felt strange not being the only one with my hand down, but this sort of thing happens to the best of us. Ann Hopkins was waving her arm frantically and I nearly tore mine out of its socket as I hacked desperately at the air near Miss Ogilvy's face.

"All right, Florence, thank you. Please take Harriet out in the hall and show her your combination."

I rose triumphantly and gave Harriet a bright smile. Her face remained immobile. I told myself she was just shy. As I worked the combination lock, she seemed to be listening for a click like safecrackers in the movies; her eyes, minuscule to begin with, turned into mere pinpoints. She reached into her sacklike purse for a small black notebook, wrote down the combination, then replaced the notebook with a swift, secretive gesture. She uttered not a word the whole time but I looked on her silence as a challenge to my newly acquired charm. I would soon have those taupe toes curling.

She spoke her first sentence to me at three-fifteen that afternoon when I tried to put a book on the locker shelf.

"You touch this locker again and I'll kill you."

I looked around; she couldn't possibly be talking to me—this sort of thing never happened to gracious ladies who made everybody happy. But there was no one else in the hall; I was alone with my new friend. She grabbed my books off the shelf and threw them at me.

"My Pop was a war hero," she growled. "He drove a tank for Patton. He killed lots of people and he showed me and my brother how to do it. You smear axle grease on an icepick and stick it straight in their heart. When you pull it back out, the grease seals the hole so it don't show and the doctor thinks you died of something natural."

She dipped into her haversack and pulled out an evil-looking pointed instrument and a can stamped WESTERN AUTO STORES.

"That's for you if you don't stay away from this locker."

She slammed the door shut and jerked her head toward the stairs, taking no chances that I would sneak back and open it after she was gone. I decided not to argue with her. A girl who called her father Pop was capable of anything. I descended the stairs, my spine crawling at the sound of her ponderous tread behind me.

Peg and Helen were waiting for me outside.

"Why are you taking all those books home?"

"Er, I have a lot of homework."

"Already? It's only the second day of school."

I almost told them about the death threat but I hated to publicize my defeats, especially one I had volunteered for. How would it look if I admitted to a falling out with my new lockermate after only five hours? Even the chronically unpopular took longer than that to get a feud going, and this was more than a feud. Needing time to think, I brushed off their questions and changed the subject to one guaranteed to absorb us all the way home: pubic hair.

I spent the evening with the story on the tip of my tongue. Each time I almost told it, I considered the consequences and stopped. I could not tell Granny. An uncomprehending veteran of my social wars, she would only say, "What did you *do* to the poor child to upset her so?" I could not tell Herb. He was for good news, like report cards. There was something almost sacrilegious about the idea of going to Herb for help in this sort of crisis; it would have been a travesty, like using a fine linen napkin to wash a car. Herb was a luxury, like Ashley, and the situation clearly called for a necessity.

That meant Mama, but I did not see how she could rescue me this time. Harriet was not a teacher or a tombstone but a girl my age, and Mama could not move in on a kid, even a monster kid. Besides, in a funny way I was afraid that if she met Harriet they would take a liking to each other. After all, they were both loaded for bear; I had a fleeting fantasy of the two of them going out on a rampage together and having a grand old time. The knowledge that they were sisters under the skin was painful, like having a brother whom Mama loved better than me. While Harriet was not a boy, she was much closer to being one than I was, so she loomed in my mind as the son Mama had wanted.

That night I lay in bed reviewing my options. The most direct solution, guaranteed to please Mama, was to beat Harriet up. There were two holes in this approach that no amount of axle grease could close. First, although I was taller, Harriet was much stronger; it would be no exaggeration to describe her figure as burly. Second, how could I, with my long history of peer problems, walk into junior high on the third day of school and start slamming the new girl around for no apparent reason? When the dust settled I would, of course, reveal my reason, but how would it sound? "She threatened to stick an icepick in my heart." Who would believe it? Harriet would only deny it. A search of her haversack would bear me out, but that solution was flawed, too. Violent people invariably have an animal shrewdness that I knew I lacked. Somewhere between the fray and the principal's office Harriet, like Lizzie Borden, would find some way to get rid of her incriminating weapon, leaving me holding the icepickless and greaseless bag.

A quieter solution was to tell Miss Ogilvy in private, but that would bring me up against the same credibility problem. Teachers are old hands at childish hyperbole. "She threatened to stick an *icepick* in your *heart?*" "Yes, ma'am." If I had known Miss Ogilvy better she might—I say *might*—have believed me, but after only three days? No. Not in 1947. Schools were peaceful places in those days.

My third option was to call Harriet's bluff, but having looked into those glittering peppercorns that passed for eyes, I didn't dare risk it. She *might* stab me. I was afraid of her but more afraid of what she represented. Like all members of the shabby genteel class, I hated low-class people. Being a shabby genteel Southerner only intensified this prejudice; we are bottomless wells of aristocratic disdain and empty thimbles of aristocratic power. All we can do is badmouth poor white trash.

For the remaining days of that week I carried my books everywhere. Nobody paid any attention; I was always carrying books. As long as the weather stayed warm I could count on not being noticed, but what would happen if I started carrying a coat around I did not know.

By happy chance I never found out. My problem was solved suddenly and permanently on Saturday morning when Granny opened the newspaper and uttered a cry of despair.

"Oh, the poor little soul! Did you know a girl named Harriet Mudd? It says she went to your school."

Her past tenses were music to my ears. I jumped up and read over her shoulder.

BRONZE STAR WINNER AND FAMILY
KILLED IN COLLISION WITH TRAIN;
SUICIDE RULED

Cumberland, Md.—A speeding B&O freight train took the lives of Albert J. Mudd, his wife, and their two children Friday night when the decorated 3rd Army veteran drove onto the tracks here. Witnesses said Mudd, who had been under psychiatric care at Walter Reed Hospital, shouted "Here I come, Georgie!" and crashed through a lowered signal bar in an apparently deliberate attempt to end his life.

The story went on to list the names and schools of Harriet and her brother. It was true. Somebody Up There liked me.

"Did you know her?" Granny asked sorrowfully.

"Just a little," I said, struggling to keep a grievous expression on my face.

"Mudd . . ." she said pensively. "That's an old Maryland name. Was she descended from that doctor who was involved in the Lincoln assassination?"

"She could have been."

In homeroom on Monday morning, Ann Hopkins, who had already lectured me on the need to show boys how deep the waters of womanly emotion ran, burst into tears and simulated a fainting spell. That the boys looked distinctly uncomfortable escaped her notice. Miss Ogilvy, no believer in letting students verbalize their finer feelings, insisted on an immediate end to the display and called for a constructive response.

"Flowers!" Ann sobbed. "We have to send flowers!"

"That would be appropriate," said Miss Ogilvy. She looked around in that way teachers have when they are getting ready to appoint a volunteer. My hand was down but now there was a clear logic to her choice.

"Florence, since you were Harriet's lockermate, would you take up a collection and stop by the florist's this afternoon?"

I went up and down the aisles gathering nickels and dimes, my smile muscles aching from suppression. When I had all the money together, we voted on what kind of flowers to send. It should have been over then, but Ann Hopkins still had some more womanly feeling to let out.

"Miss Ogilvy, I think Florence should lead us in prayer."

Miss Ogilvy handed me the Bible and I read the Twenty-third Psalm, all the while thinking that the death of the Mudd family was the greatest event in the history of genetics since Mendel crossed his peas. I was in a state of delirious joy the whole day, but I had to hide it. All the girls went round with dolorous faces and spent lunch hour talking in hushed tones about what a wonderful person Harriet had been. None of them chose to remember that they had known her for only four days, and that during this time she had not even said hello to them. They competed with each other to deliver the most moving testimonial to her basic sweetness; what she was *really* like, "deep down" and "inside" and "in her heart." Each girl *knew* how warm and friendly Harriet had been, and I, who did know, had to keep quiet.

By lunch hour the next day, the Legend of Harriet Mudd had sprung up like a Nashville hit. It was the human comedy, female version; being unable to find the essential goodness in Harriet was an admission that there was no goodness in oneself, so all the girls in our homeroom related tender little stories about her: some thoughtful favor she had done them, something sweet she had said to them, a cute joke she had told. And I, to whom she had spoken as Cato to Carthage, had to keep quiet.

Do you think that's all I had to endure? Read on with me, the best is yet to be. When I got home that afternoon, Granny was wearing her good black hat.

"Change into your church dress, we're going to pay a call at the funeral parlor. I've invited Mrs. Bell to go with us."

The caskets were closed, of course, so Mrs. Bell did not have a very good time. It was a shame, because she would have been the ideal person to help me realize my fantasy of folding Harriet's taupe fingers around an icepick. Picturing the scene in my mind, I doubled over and Granny patted my shaking shoulders, so I had to pretend I was crying.

The other mourners were extremely fat women with mean mouths and red-faced men with little pieces of toilet paper stuck on razor nicks. Granny gave them a dubious glance.

"These people look right trashy to me but we must pay our respects."

"We're all equal in death," said Mrs. Bell.

Granny was so pleased by my show of womanly grief that she added an extra dollar to her share of my allowance that week. Of far greater value was the lesson I learned from the whole ungodly mess: I never again tried to make myself liked.

MARILYN NELSON WANIEK

Waniek teaches English at the University of Connecticut, but the Louisiana State University Press has published her books of poems (including Mama's Promises *and*

The Homeplace), and her roots are in the South. Her father was one of the black World War II aviators known as the Tuskegee Airmen (her poem about him appears later in this book). You wouldn't call her a humorist, but some of her poems have a lift very like that of hilarity.

"The Fortunate Spill"

Note: Traditionally, black-eyed peas are served on New
Year's Eve: each black-eyed pea one eats brings luck.

> *Well!* Johnnie thinks. *He has his nerve!*
> *Crashing this party! What stuck-up conceit!*
> *Passing his induction papers around;*
> *another Negro whose feet never touch the ground.*

> His name is Melvin Nelson. In his eyes
> the black of dreams sparkles with laughing stars.

> Johnnie agrees to play. And it defies
> all explanation: she forgets five bars!
> *This cocky, handsome boy?* she asks her heart.
> *For good luck all year,* Melvin says, *you've got to fart.*

> They eat elbow to elbow, in a crowd
> of 1942's gifted black youth.
> His tipsy bass-clef voice is much too loud.
> Hers trebles nervously: to tell the truth,
> she's impressed.

> *I'll be a man up in the sky,*
> he confides. She blurts out, *Hello, Jesus!* And they die
> with laughter.

> But the joke catches him off-guard:
> he spills the black-eyed peas into her lap.
> *Oh Lord,* he mumbles, but she laughs so hard
> both recognize the luck of their mishap.

> And I watch from this distant balcony
> as they fall for each other, and for me.

"Levitation with Baby"

The Muse bumped
against my window this morning.
No one was at home but me
and the baby. The Muse said
there was room on her back for two.
Okay, I said, *but first I've got to*

Pack his favorite toys.
Small ones are the best:
that way he can sit and play quietly
as the earth slides out from under our feet.
Let's see, somewhere there's
a wind-up dog with a drum
that sometimes keeps him busy
ten minutes or more.
And we'd better take some books.

Disposable diapers,
pre-moistened towelettes,
plastic bags,
and I'll pack a lunch.
Peanut butter and crackers
are nutritious,
and the crumbs brush right off.

While I was packing his lunch
the baby got hungry,
so I put him in his high chair,
unpacked the crackers,
and gave him some.
He threw the third one down,
so I took him out,
wiped the high chair,
wiped the floor under and around the chair,
wiped the window next to it,
and wiped his fingers and face.
Then I took off his pants,
shook them out,
and wiped the soles of his shoes.

I filled two plastic bottles,
changed his diaper,
and got him dressed.
I washed my hands.
I sat down at my desk.
Okay, I said. *Now
I'm ready for takeoff.*

As he cried for a bottle
I saw my next-door neighbor,
shirtless, in the pants he wears
to work in his garden,
scribbling furiously on the back of a paper bag
as he ascended over the roof of his house
on the Muse's huge, sun-spangled wings.

NIKKI GIOVANNI

Nikki Giovanni was born in Knoxville, Tennessee. The following is taken from
Gemini, *her "Extended Autobiographical Statement on My First Twenty-five Years of
Being a Black Poet." She doesn't take any prisoners.*

Fighting for Folks

My father was a real hip down-home big-time dude from Cincinnati who,
through a screw-a-YWCA-lady or kiss-a-nun program, was picked up from
the wilds of the West End (pronounced deprived area), where he was wreak-
ing havoc on the girls, and sent to college, mostly I imagine because they
recognized him as being so talented. Or if not necessarily talented, then able
to communicate well with people. He was sent to Knoxville College in Tennessee. Nestled lovingly in the bosom of the Great Smoky Mountains in the
land of Davy Crockett and other heroes of Western civilization is Knoxville,
Tennessee. Knoxville, in those times, was noted for *Thunder Road* starring
Robert Mitchum and/or Polly Bergen of Helen Morgan fame; but when my

father boarded the train to carry him back to his spiritual roots (it was just like my great-grandfather to be the only damned slave in northeastern Tennessee) all he saw were crackers—friendly crackers, mean crackers, liberal crackers, conservative crackers, dumb crackers, smart crackers and just all kinds of crackers, some of whom, much to his surprise, were Black crackers. He hit the campus, "the Nigger the world awaited," shiny head (because Afros were not in vogue), snappy dresser with the one suit he had and a big friendly smile to show them all that just because he was in the South he wasn't going to do like a lot of people and cry all the time and embarrass the school. In walks the fox.

Swishing her behind, most likely carrying a tennis racket and flinging her hair (which at that time hung down to what was swishing) was the woman of the world, the prize of all times—Mommy. Mommy has an illustrious background. Her family, the Mighty Watsons, had moved to Knoxville because my grandmother was going to be lynched. Well, the family never actually said she was going to get lynched. They always stressed the fact that traveling late at night under a blanket in a buggy is fun, and even more fun if a decoy sitting in a buggy is sent off in another direction with Uncle Joe and Uncle Frank carrying guns. They told us the guns were to salute good-bye to Louvenia, my grandmother, and John Brown ("Book") Watson, my grandfather.

If I haven't digressed too much already I want to say something about Grandpapa. He was an extremely handsome man. Grandmother got the hots for him and like any shooting star just fell and hit *splash*. Now, we in the family have always considered it unfortunate that Grandfather was married to another woman at that time. And Grandmother, to make matters even more urgent, would not give him none. Grandfather considered that more unfortunate than his marriage. And since he was the intellectual of the family, hence "Book," he assessed the situation and reached the logical conclusion that he should marry my Grandmother.

The Watsons were quite pleased with Louvenia Terrell because she was so cute and intelligent, but what they didn't know and later learned to their chagrin was that she was terribly intolerant when it came to white people. The Watson clan was the epitome of "Let's get along with the whites"; Grandmother was the height of "We ain't taking no shit, John Brown, off nobody." So the trouble began.

First some white woman wanted to buy some flowers from Grandmother's yard, and as Grandmother told it they were not for sale. She didn't make her living growing flowers for white people. The woman's family came back later to settle it. "John, yo' wife insulted ma wife and we gotta settle this thang." Grandpapa was perfectly willing to make accommodations but when the only satisfactory action was Grandmother's taking twenty-five buggy-whip lashes, he had to draw the line. "Mr. Jenkins, we've known each other a long time. Our families have done business together. But this is too much." "John, we've gotta settle this thang.'' And about that time Uncle Joe, who always liked to hunt, came out of Grandpapa's house with his gun and powder and asked if he could be of any help. The Jenkinses left. The Watsons stayed up all night with a gun peeking from every window. The guns in those days were not repeaters so the youngsters in the family had been given complete instructions on how to clean and load in the shortest time possible. I'm told by my granduncles there was a general air of disappointment when nobody showed. After almost a week of keeping watch things reverted to normal. Grandpapa says the white dude told him later they didn't need the flowers anyway.

Then one Sunday afternoon Grandmother and Grandpapa were out strolling when a Jewish merchant asked them to come look at his material. He owned one of those old stores with bolts and bolts of material because most clothes were made, not store-bought. Well, they looked and looked. Grandmother had him pull bolts from way up high to way down low. Then she got bored and told Grandpapa she was ready to go.

MERCHANT: You mean you're not going to buy anything?

GRANDMOTHER [innocently]: No.

MERCHANT: You mean you had me pull all this material out and you're not going to buy anything?

GRANDMOTHER [a little tired]: My husband and I were walking down the street minding our own business when you asked us to come in. We did not ask you.

GRANDFATHER [wary of the escalation in the exchange]: Let's go, Louvenia.

GRANDMOTHER [as she generally did when she was in an argument]: Hell, it's his own fault. [To the merchant] Nah, we don't want none of your material.

GRANDFATHER [pinching and kicking at her]: Let's go, Louvenia.

MERCHANT [in the background screaming obscenities]: I'll have you horse-whipped for talking to me this way.

GRANDMOTHER [really wolfing now]: You and which cavalry troop? My husband will kill you if you come near me!

GRANDFATHER [almost in tears]: Let's go, Louvenia.

They hurried to spread the alarm of impending danger. A woman in the next county had recently been lynched and her womb split open, so there was no doubt in Grandfather's mind that the whites might follow through this time. A family meeting was called and all agreed that Grandmother and Grandfather (most especially Grandmother) had to leave Albany, Georgia. The sooner the better. When night came they climbed into a buggy, pulled a blanket over themselves and slept until they reached the Tennessee border. Having no faith in southern Tennessee they began again by public transportation to head North. The intention was to go to Washington, D. C., or Philadelphia, but when they found themselves still in Tennessee they agreed to settle at the first reasonable-sized town they came to—Knoxville. Grandfather settled Grandmother in a good church home and went back to Albany, where he taught school, to finish the term out. Grandfather was like that.

Now, Mommy was an intellectual, aristocratic woman, which in her time was not at all fashionable. She read, liked paintings, played tennis and liked to party a great deal. Had she been rich she would have followed the sun—going places, learning things and being just generally unable to hold a job and be useful. But Mommy made just one bad mistake in the scheme of things—she sashayed across the Knoxville College campus, hair swinging down to her behind, most probably carrying a tennis racket, and ran into a shiny-head Negro with a pretty suit on. He, being warm and friendly and definitely looking for a city girl to roost with, introduced himself. I have always thought that if his name hadn't been exotic she would never have given him a second thought; but Grandfather, whom my mother was so much like, had a weakness for Romance languages and here comes this smiling dude with Giovanni for a name. Mommy decided to take him home. . . .

For a four-year-old I was a terror. Mostly this was because my big sister, Gary, would wolf all the time, then come running in from school, throw her books down and scream at my mother, "JUST LET ME GO GET THEM—JUST LET ME AT THEM!" And Mommy, digging the whole scene, would say, "Gary, have a glass of milk and some graham crackers and let's talk about your day." And Gary would say, "But Peggy's waiting outside. I gotta go fight." And I, sitting on the top porch waiting for Gary to come home, would already have adequately handled the situation. Since it was a thrice-weekly occurrence at least, I kept a large supply of large rocks on the top porch. And as Gary crossed the front porch I had started pelting Peggy and her gang with my pieces. So by the time Gary put her books down and called out how she had to fight, I had them on the run. For a four-year-old I was beautiful. Peggy and her gang would always run out of my reach and call up, "YOU TELL GARY WE'LL GET HER! YOU AIN'T ALWAYS HOME!" Then they'd leave.

By the time Gary had changed clothes and had her first glass of milk it was all over. Mommy innocently asked where I had been, telling me, "Gary's home." And I said, "Yeah, Peggy chased her again. But I took care of it." "Kim, you've got to quit fighting so much. You'll be five soon and in school yourself. And you've got to control yourself."

"I'm glad Kim got that ole Miss Yella," Gary piped up from her plate. "She's always picking on somebody." "Somebody's always wolfing," Mommy said. "And who are you to call anybody yellow?" "Well, at least my hair don't hang all the way down to the ground." "Doesn't. Doesn't hang. And Kim, you'll have to quit storing those rocks on the porch. Gary can fight her own battles." "Yes, Mommy."

The summer passed rather happily with Peggy and sometimes Skippy chasing Gary from piano lessons. I always thought Gary was tops. She is very smooth, with the older sister style that says I-can-do-anything, you know? And I thought she could. "Kim," she said, taking me aside in the back yard, "you know why I don't fight? It's not that I'm scared or something—but I'm a musician. What if my hands were maimed? What if I were injured or something? Then Dr. Matthews couldn't give me lessons anymore. Then Mrs. Clarke couldn't give me rehearsals anymore. Why, their families would starve. Walter and Charles couldn't wear clothes. The studio would close down. And the world would be deprived of a great talent playing 'Claire de Lune.' You understand, don't you?" And I did. I swear I did. All I wanted from this world was to protect and nourish this great talent, who was not my cousin or best friend or next-door neighbor but my very own sister.

We lived in Wyoming, Ohio, which is a suburb of Cincinnati, which some say is a suburb of Lexington, Kentucky. But we liked it. The sidewalks run broad and clear; the grass and mud intertwine just enough to let you be a muddy little lady; and there were those magnificent little violets that some called weeds and that I would pick for Mommy to put in her window vase.

Most of the summer was spent running and swinging and making believe. I did learn the hard way not to make-believe and swing at the same time. I was going way up high. People were standing at the bottom marveling at me. "She doesn't spell or read as well as Gary," they said, "but clearly she's an Olympic contender at swinging." They were amazed. Then I fell out of the swing. I wasn't so hurt as I was hurt. Swinging was my strong point. It's really a cruel life when your strong point falls through. But I had a backup. Gary had taught me how to read and write a little and I could count to ten in French, Okinawan and Pig Latin. I knew no matter what, I was going to knock kindergarten out. When fall finally came I was overprepared. I had even practiced nap time.

I woke up that morning bright and early to a solid cold cereal breakfast. You see, I had early recognized the importance of getting away from the hot-cereal-Father-John's-Tonic syndrome. The older you are the less they—i.e., parents—care what you eat until you get married or something. Then they—i.e., lovers—start the whole parent syndrome all over again. So I had told Mommy in no uncertain terms—*cold cereal, no toast, no Father John's and plenty of coffee.* She at least let me have the corn flakes.

She also insisted on taking me to school. Surely that was an insidious move on her part. I had planned to walk with Gary and let everybody know that just because I was going to school I wasn't going to be no lady or nothing like that. What I had done to Peggy last year I could do again.

You see, the winter before, Mommy had let me go meet Gary from school. That had been right after Christmas. Gary had taken the sled to school because we had finally gotten snow in January. I was going to meet her and ride home. Mommy had bundled me in my brown snowsuit and airplane hat pulled over my ears and mittens (though I had been insisting on gloves for some time) and a big scarf. Mommy took her job of mommying quite seriously and never wanted me to catch cold or something. I practically rolled down the stair and, gaining momentum, bounced along Burns Street, making the turn at Pendry past Mrs. Spears's house, just barely turning Oak and managing by the grace of God to stop in front of Oak Avenue school. Gary alighted from the side door with the sled and Peggy on her heels. We put her books on the beautiful beige sled with the magnificent red streak and started home, Peggy and the three goony girls a respectful distance behind.

"What will we do if they bother us?" Gary asked. "I'll beat her up." "Well, it's different when we're home but we've got the sled to look out for." "Don't worry, Gary, I'll beat her up." "Well, she better not hurt you or I'll deal with her myself." "Oh, no, Gary. Don't you get in it. I can beat Peggy all by myself." Even then I couldn't bear the thought of someone's laying uncaring, irreverent hands on her. "I can handle it." We turned the corner.

Pendry is one of those little suburb streets that they always show when they want to convince you Negroes want to live next door. The sidewalks are embraced by cut grass in the summer and a clean blanket of snow in the winter. All the houses have front yards and white steps leading to them. Mostly they are brick houses, except the Spearses had a white frame one. As we turned onto Pendry the gang moved up on us since no one from the school could see. "Look at the stuck-up boobsie twins," they started. "Mama had to send the baby to look out for the coward."

"Don't say anything," I advised. "You always say something to make them mad. Maybe they'll just leave us alone." We made it past the house where we never saw the people and started by Dr. Richardson's. "They walk alike, talk alike and roll on their bellies like a reptile," they chanted. There had been a circus that year and everybody had gotten into the barker thing. "Just look at them, folks. One can't do without the other." And they burst out laughing. "Hey, old stuck-up. What you gonna do when your sister's tired of fighting for you?" "I'll beat you up myself. That's what." Damn, damn, damn. Now we would have to fight. "You and what army, 'ho'?" *'Ho'* was always a favorite. "Me and yo' mama's *army,*" Gary answered with precision and dignity. "You talking 'bout my mama?" "I would but the whole town is so I can't add nothing." They sidled up alongside us at the Spears's. "You take it back, Gary." Deadly quiet. "Yo' mama's so ugly she went to the zoo and the gorilla paid to see her." "You take that back!" "Yo' mama's such a 'ho' she went to visit a farm and they dug a whole field before they knew it was her."

Peggy swung and I stepped in. Peggy had long brown hair that she could easily have sat on if she wasn't always careful to fling it out of the way. She said it was her Indian ancestry. She swung her whole body to hit Gary as her goony girls formed a circle to watch. And as she swung I grabbed her hair, and began to wrap it around my hand, then my arm. I had a good, solid grip. Gary stepped back to watch the action. Mrs. Spears went to call Mommy. The next clear thing I remember is Mommy saying from a long, long way away, ''Let her go, Kim,'' and Peggy being under me and me wondering why it was so cold. I, at four, had defeated Peggy Johnson. And she was bad. As Mommy fussed me home that was all I could think about. I had won. Now that that was established the rest would be simple.

So Mommy walked me to school telling me how nice the kids were and how I would enjoy it and I was thinking whether Peggy would remember last year and how I could make sure she knew the same would hold true. She must not, no one must touch my sister. ''You must realize Gary is in the fifth grade and can fight for herself. You'll have enough to do just taking care of yourself. Your sister isn't a dummy. She skipped, didn't she? And she's not a weakling. She beats you up when you have arguments and I don't want any repetition of what happened last year. OK?'' ''Yes, Mommy.'' ''I'm counting on you, Kim. It's very important you give the children a chance. You can't always run around with Gary and her friends. Make some of your own. If you give them a chance they'll just love you as much as your father and I do. OK?'' ''Yes, Mommy.''

''Mrs. Hicks is a wonderful woman.'' ''I remember Aunt Willa, Mommy. I like her and Elizabeth Ann.'' Sometimes I played with Elizabeth Ann even though she was younger than I. Aunt Willa was super. She played Pekeno at our house and sometimes they let me deal since I was always up and meddling. Aunt Willa would always pay you when you gave her a good hand. Some of Mommy's friends would just say, ''Good dealing,'' and some would say, ''Kim, why aren't you in bed?'' But Aunt Willa was all right. She was always straight. You could really go to kindergarten with a lady like that. ''And remember everybody in class doesn't know her like you do. So what are we going to call her?'' ''Mrs. Hicks,'' I pronounced very distinctly, ''just like you said I should.'' ''That's my big girl.'' Mommy squeezed my hand and looked relieved. Adults are certainly strange. They always do things they don't want people to remember but they never remember not to let you see them doing it. I mean, if they cared in the first place, it would have gone down differently. But what the hell—I would call Aunt Willa Mrs. Hicks and be good because I dug the whole game. Even then. From a low vantage point.

I was bouncing up the stairs prepared to knock them dead when Mommy opened the door and I looked at all those little faces. I broke down. I didn't know these people. They didn't look like they were seeing a woman with a mission. My God!! They might not even care. I started crying. Mommy, in the usual vanity that mothers possess, thought I didn't want to leave her but that wasn't it at all. I was entering a world where few knew and even fewer would ever understand my mission. Life is a motherfucker. Mommy—four eleven, ninety pounds after Christmas dinner—walked out of that kindergarten room a little taller, a bit prouder . . . her baby girl really cared. The kids, in their usual indifferent way, stated, "Kim is a crybaby." I wanted to shout at them all—*"You dumbbumbs"*—but I restrained myself by burying my head in Aunt Willa's lap and softly pleading, "What shall I do?" Aunt Willa hit upon the saving idea: Go get Gary.

In She strode—like Cleopatra on her barge down the Nile, like Nefertiti on her way to sit for the statue, like Harriet Tubman before her train or Mary Bethune with Elenora; my big sister came to handle the situation. You could feel the room respond to her presence. It could have been San Francisco at the earthquake, Chicago as Mrs. O'Leary walked to her cow, Rome as Nero struck up his fiddle, Harlem when Malcolm mounted the podium; Gary came to handle the situation. Looking neither right nor left she glided from the door, her eyes searching for the little figure buried in Aunt Willa's skirt. "Kim"—her voice containing all the power of Cicero at the seashore, Elijah at the annual meeting—"Kim, don't cry." And it was over. Tears falling literally pulled themselves back into my eyes. In a gulp, with a wipe of the hand, it was over. "I'll walk you home for lunch. Come on, now, and play with the other kids. There's Donny, Robert's brother, and Pearl. They want to play with you." The pain, the absolute pain of wanting to be eight years old and in the fifth grade and sophisticated and in control. I could have burst! "I'm sorry." "Don't worry about it. Mommy just wouldn't want you to cry." She turned her full gaze on me. "I've got to go back to class now." She paused. Of course I understood. Oh, yes. I understood. "See you at lunch," she whispered. And as majestically as she had come—red turtleneck sweater, white short socks and yes, sneakers (I still had to wear high-top shoes)—she vanished through the door. And I had been chosen to nourish this great woman, to protect her and perhaps, should I prove worthy, guide her.

For some reason, probably a blood thing, I was always good with my hands . . . and feet . . . and teeth . . . and I had a very good eye. If this wasn't the age of Black Power I would possibly attribute that to my Indian blood, but now I'm sure it goes straight to my Watusi grandfather and Amazon great-grandaunt. Skippy, an old enemy who I later learned planned to marry Gary, was pulling her hair and marking her knees up with his ballpoint. Gary would tell me of these things laughingly and I would exclaim, *"It's so wrong of him to abuse you,"* not to mention, in such a white way, "I will take care of it." She assured me, "It's all right, Kim. He's just teasing." But mine was not a world of frivolity. He was disturbing the genius. He was, in fact, not just disrespectful, because that at least means you understand the position; was not in reality just insolent, because that just means you are jealous—he was common! I had no choice. I called him out.

I would imagine no boy likes to be called out by a kindergartner, especially on the playground . . . especially to a marble duel. Plus he recognized what I didn't—he was in a trick. If he defeated me, he was supposed to. If he lost—my God! A nine-year-old boy losing? To me? My God! In deadly calm I drew the circle.

Now, our family was never what anyone could call well off. Mommy didn't work, but that was because the money would have been spent in babysitting fees. Gus, our father, held down a couple of jobs, which meant we rarely saw him. Grandmother had never actually worked either, but we're from a small town and Grandpapa was a schoolteacher—of Latin actually—which says a lot about our pretensions. But despite hard times, depressions, lack of real estate, we had passed, from generation to generation since we had first been brought to these shores, a particular semiprecious jewel that was once oblong in shape. It was originally brown with a green tint. In order to conceal it successfully through several hundred years of slavery we had worn it in odd places. It had been rounded off through the sweat and kisses of generations of Giovanni-Watson ancestors. We consulted it for every important and quite a few unimportant events and decisions.

When I decided to challenge Skippy I snuck the jewel from my mother's hiding place. As I drew the circle and stood back I was all confidence. There was no chance for the poor fellow. "You go first," I generously offered with the assurance of Willy McCovey at third base nodding to the pitcher to play ball. A sure winner. "No, you go first." Quietly, with a Huey Newton kind of rage. "You can go on." Smiling, prancing like Assault at the Derby. "You go on, Kim. You should get at least one chance." "One chance!" I knelt and spotted. There was no stopping me. I shot marbles from between my legs and over my back. I put a terrible double spin on my shot that knocked his cat's-eye out and came back for his steelie. I was baaaaad. I shot from under my arm and once while yawning. Good God! There was no way to defeat me! I rose from the earth brushing off the little specks that clung to my dress, tip chest two miles out. "And if you mess with my sister again I'll deal with you on a physical level." I was ready for anything. He squared off. "You keep it up, Kim, and somebody's gonna really get you." I half stepped back. "You, Mighty Mouse? You?" Sure, all the kids knew I could handle myself but teachers never know anything. I had him in a double bind. All the grown-ups ever saw was big brown eyes, three pigtails and high-top white shoes. He would really catch it if they saw him fighting—me especially. My stock in trade was that I looked so innocent. So he backed down. I understand his problem now, but then—a chicken at the top of the pecking heap—I ruled the roost. And as I sauntered happily up Oak Avenue, turned on Pendry, passed the Spears's house and headed for Burns Avenue I was feeling *très* good. Plus Mommy gave me my very favorite cold lunch—liverwurst with mayonnaise dripping from the raisin bread. Too much! I was prepared to take a long nap. I was prepared to work the number problems Gus had left for me. I was ready for everything . . . but Gary's reaction at 3:30.

"HOW COULD YOU DO THAT TO HIM?" "Who?" "HOW COULD YOU? MOMMY, KIM'SPICKINGONMYFRIENDS!" "Who, Gary?" My God! Her absolute displeasure. No "Hi." No "How'd it go today?" No approving smile. "Who, Gary?" "MOMMY, SHE MADE SKIPPY LOOK LIKE A FOOL!" "Skippy?" "YOU SHOULD HAVE SEEN HER!" "But he was picking on you." "I AM MORTIFIED!" "Mortified?"

My world was coming to an end. And all because of Skippy. I would handle this right away.

I ran out of the house like a pig runs when a Muslim comes, near rage. Absolute rage. "SKIPPYYY!" All the way down to his house. With just a brief stop for some sort of weapon. I don't actually remember picking up that piece of cement but it was there—along with my trusty broomstick that Flappy had made for me. I flew down to the corner, though of course being careful to stay on my side of the street. "SKIPPYYY! COME OUT! I WANT TO FIGHT YOU!" And there he was. Buck teeth, pants hanging off, sneakers and all. "COME ON OUT." He was ready. I could see he had been building his supply of rocks. He threw. But missed. I ducked and started running back and forth. "COME ON OVER." "YOU KNOW I CAN'T CROSS THE STREET." My father and Skippy's father had made an agreement that I couldn't cross the street since I fought and beat Skippy a lot. But he was in a rage. "TRY TO MAKE ME LOOK LIKE A FOOL, OLE SILLY GIRL. I'LL GET YOU." "COME ON OVER." I was a streak of energy. I was the fire after the A bomb fell. All heat and light. "COME ON OVER." And he did. I wanted to devour him. To kill him slowly. To punish him beyond words able to describe the emotion. He looked both ways and was on my territory. Like the Black panther I leaped. And he feinted and landed a solid blow. I never felt it. I clawed at his face and pulled his shirt loose. *"Youtoremyshirtl'llkillyou!"* And he bit me. We fell onto the lawn and people were all around. We squared off and I heard Mommy say, "I hope he gets her." It crushed my will. I had been prepared to draw blood. Gary was mad and Mommy was rooting for the opposition. He swung and landed flat on my nose. Blood spurted, as blood is wont to do. I didn't cry or even really feel hurt. I just looked at him, then picked up my broomstick and set off for home. People started consoling Mommy but she was just saying, "I'm glad. Maybe Kim'll learn she can't fight Gary's battles." And I was crushed. I walked from Mrs. Williams' house to mine without family, friends or loved ones. No one understood what I had tried to do. No one. I thought of *Beautiful Joe* and *Mistress Margaret*, *Heidi* and the *King of the Golden River*. And conceived of myself in that league. I think I smiled as I opened the door.

JOHN KENNEDY TOOLE

When A Confederacy of Duces *was published in 1980, I thought it was wonderful in its comic desperation—farcicality for dear life—and that it richly deserved its Pulitzer Prize. Other people felt the book's acclaim derived from the story behind it: in despair after the manuscript was rejected, Toole committed suicide at the age of thirty-two, and it wasn't until seven years later that his mother pressed the messy bundle of pages upon Walker Percy, who was astounded to find in it, as he later wrote, "a gargantuan tumultuous human tragicomedy." After watching a videotaped interview of Toole's mother noodling at the piano and rather coquettishly denouncing New York Jews, I was if anything even more impressed with what the author had done with what he was up against in life. The irony of this woman's role in bringing such a caricature of herself into the world added what seemed to me at the time organic resonance. On rereading the book recently, however, I was astounded to find that much of the afflatus had gone out of it, that it no longer seemed to transcend its source in sexual confusion and mother-hatred. (Toole's first novel, a negligible work later published as* The Neon Bible, *ends in matricide.) All that being said, however, the book does distinctively render a variety of Newawlins accents, it does have high moments, Ignatius Reilly remains stuck in my mind, and no treasury of Southern humor would be complete without a piece of him.*

from *A Confederacy of Dunces*

A green hunting cap squeezed the top of the fleshy balloon of a head. The green earflaps, full of large ears and uncut hair and the fine bristles that grew in the ears themselves, stuck out on either side like turn signals indicating two directions at once. Full, pursed lips protruded beneath the bushy black moustache and, at their corners, sank into little folds filled with disapproval and potato chip crumbs. In the shadow under the green visor of the cap Ignatius J. Reilly's supercilious blue and yellow eyes looked down upon the other people waiting under the clock at the D. H. Holmes department store, studying the crowd of people for signs of bad taste in dress. Several of the outfits, Ignatius noticed, were new enough and expensive enough to be properly considered offenses against taste and decency. Possession of anything new or expensive only reflected a person's lack of theology and geometry; it could even cast doubts upon one's soul.

Ignatius himself was dressed comfortably and sensibly. The hunting cap prevented head colds. The voluminous tweed trousers were durable and permitted unusually free locomotion. Their pleats and nooks contained pockets of warm, stale air that soothed Ignatius. The plaid flannel shirt made a jacket unnecessary while the muffler guarded exposed Reilly skin between earflap and collar. The outfit was acceptable by any theological and geometrical standards, however abstruse, and suggested a rich inner life.

Shifting from one hip to the other in his lumbering, elephantine fashion, Ignatius sent waves of flesh rippling beneath the tweed and flannel, waves that broke upon buttons and seams. Thus rearranged, he contemplated the long while that he had been waiting for his mother. Principally he considered the discomfort he was beginning to feel. It seemed as if his whole being was ready to burst from his swollen suede desert boots, and, as if to verify this, Ignatius turned his singular eyes toward his feet. The feet did indeed look swollen. He was prepared to offer the sight of those bulging boots to his mother as evidence of her thoughtlessness. Looking up, he saw the sun beginning to descend over the Mississippi at the foot of Canal Street. The Holmes clock said almost five. Already he was polishing a few carefully worded accusations designed to reduce his mother to repentance or, at least, confusion. He often had to keep her in her place.

She had driven him downtown in the old Plymouth, and while she was at the doctor's seeing about her arthritis, Ignatius had bought some sheet music at Werlein's for his trumpet and a new string for his lute. Then he had wandered into the Penny Arcade on Royal Street to see whether any new games had been installed. He had been disappointed to find the miniature mechanical baseball game gone. Perhaps it was only being repaired. The last time that he had played it the batter would not work and, after some argument, the management had returned his nickel, even though the Penny Arcade people had been base enough to suggest that Ignatius had himself broken the baseball machine by kicking it.

Concentrating upon the fate of the miniature baseball machine, Ignatius detached his being from the physical reality of Canal Street and the people around him and therefore did not notice the two eyes that were hungrily watching him from behind one of D. H. Holmes' pillars, two sad eyes shining with hope and desire.

Was it possible to repair the machine in New Orleans? Probably so. However, it might have to be sent to some place like Milwaukee or Chicago or some other city whose name Ignatius associated with efficient repair shops and permanently smoking factories. Ignatius hoped that the baseball game was being carefully handled in shipment, that none of its little players was being chipped or maimed by brutal railroad employees determined to ruin the railroad forever with damage claims from shippers, railroad employees who would subsequently go on strike and destroy the Illinois Central.

As Ignatius was considering the delight which the little baseball game afforded humanity, the two sad and covetous eyes moved toward him through the crowd like torpedoes zeroing in on a great woolly tanker. The policeman plucked at Ignatius' bag of sheet music.

"You got any identification, mister?" the policeman asked in a voice that hoped that Ignatius was officially unidentified.

"What?" Ignatius looked down upon the badge on the blue cap. "Who are you?"

"Let me see your driver's license."

"I don't drive. Will you kindly go away? I am waiting for my mother."

"What's this hanging out your bag?"

"What do you think it is, stupid? It's a string for my lute."

"What's that?" The policeman drew back a little. "Are you local?"

"Is it the part of the police department to harass me when this city is a flagrant vice capital of the civilized world?" Ignatius bellowed over the crowd in front of the store. "This city is famous for its gamblers, prostitutes, exhibitionists, anti-Christs, alcoholics, sodomites, drug addicts, fetishists, onanists, pornographers, frauds, jades, litterbugs, and lesbians, all of whom are only too well protected by graft. If you have a moment, I shall endeavor to discuss the crime problem with you, but don't make the mistake of bothering *me*."

The policeman grabbed Ignatius by the arm and was struck on his cap with the sheet music. The dangling lute string whipped him on the ear.

"Hey," the policeman said.

"Take that!" Ignatius cried, noticing that a circle of interested shoppers was beginning to form.

Inside D. H. Holmes, Mrs. Reilly was in the bakery department pressing her maternal breast against a glass case of macaroons. With one of her fingers, chafed from many years of scrubbing her son's mammoth, yellowed drawers, she tapped on the glass case to attract the saleslady.

"Oh, Miss Inez," Mrs. Reilly called in that accent that occurs south of New Jersey only in New Orleans, that Hoboken near the Gulf of Mexico. "Over here, babe."

"Hey, how you making?" Miss Inez asked. "How you feeling, darling?"

"Not so hot," Mrs. Reilly answered truthfully.

"Ain't that a shame." Miss Inez leaned over the glass case and forgot about her cakes. "I don't feel so hot myself. It's my feet."

"Lord, I wisht I was that lucky. I got arthritis in my elbow."

"Aw, no!" Miss Inez said with genuine sympathy. "My poor old poppa's got that. We make him go set himself in a hot tub fulla berling water.''

"My boy's floating around in our tub all day long. I can't hardly get in my own bathroom no more.''

"I thought he was married, precious.''

"Ignatius? Eh, la la,'' Mrs. Reilly said sadly. "Sweetheart, you wanna gimme two dozen of them fancy mix?''

"But I thought you told me he was married,'' Miss Inez said while she was putting the cakes in a box.

"He ain't even got him a prospect. The little girl friend he had flew the coop.''

"Well, he's got time.''

"I guess so,'' Mrs. Reilly said disinterestedly. "Look, you wanna gimme half a dozen wine cakes, too? Ignatius gets nasty if we run outta cake.''

"Your boy likes his cake, huh?''

"Oh, Lord, my elbow's killing me,'' Mrs. Reilly answered.

In the center of the crowd that had formed before the department store the hunting cap, the greed radius of the circle of people, was bobbing about violently.

"I shall contact the mayor,'' Ignatius was shouting.

"Let the boy alone,'' a voice said from the crowd.

"Go get the strippers on Bourbon Street,'' an old man added. "He's a good boy. He's waiting for his momma.''

"Thank you,'' Ignatius said haughtily. "I hope that all of you will bear witness to this outrage.''

"You come with me,'' the policeman said to Ignatius with waning self-confidence. The crowd was turning into something of a mob, and there was no traffic patrolman in sight. "We're going to the precinct.''

"A good boy can't even wait for his momma by D. H. Holmes.'' It was the old man again. "I'm telling you, the city was never like this. It's the communiss.''

"Are you calling me a communiss?'' the policeman asked the old man while he tried to avoid the lashing of the lute string. "I'll take you in, too. You better watch out who you calling a communiss.''

"You can't arress me,'' the old man cried. "I'm a member of the Golden Age Club sponsored by the New Orleans Recreation Department.''

"Let that old man alone, you dirty cop,'' a woman screamed. "He's prolly somebody's grampaw.''

"I am,'' the old man said. "I got six granchirren all studying with the sisters. Smart, too.''

Over the heads of the people Ignatius saw his mother walking slowly out of the lobby of the department store carrying the bakery products as if they were boxes of cement.

"Mother!" he called. "Not a moment too soon. I've been seized."

Pushing through the people, Mrs. Reilly said, "Ignatius! What's going on here? What you done now? Hey, take your hands off my boy."

"I'm not touching him, lady," the policeman said. "Is this here your son?"

Mrs. Reilly snatched the whizzing lute string from Ignatius.

"Of course I'm her child," Ignatius said. "Can't you see her affection for me?"

"She loves her boy," the old man said.

"What you trying to do my poor child?" Mrs. Reilly asked the policeman. Ignatius patted his mother's hennaed hair with one of his huge paws. "You got plenty business picking on poor chirren with all the kind of people they got running in this town. Waiting for his momma and they try to arrest him."

"This is clearly a case for the Civil Liberties Union," Ignatius observed, squeezing his mother's drooping shoulder with the paw. "We must contact Myrna Minkoff, my lost love. She knows about those things."

"It's the communiss," the old man interrupted.

"How old is he?" the policeman asked Mrs. Reilly.

"I am thirty," Ignatius said condescendingly.

"You got a job?"

"Ignatius hasta help me at home," Mrs. Reilly said. Her initial courage was failing a little, and she began to twist the lute string with the cord on the cake boxes. "I got terrible arthuritis."

"I dust a bit," Ignatius told the policeman. "In addition, I am at the moment writing a lengthy indictment against our century. When my brain begins to reel from my literary labors, I make an occasional cheese dip."

"Ignatius makes delicious cheese dips," Mrs. Reilly said.

"That's very nice of him," the old man said. "Most boys are out running around all the time."

"Why don't you shut up?" the policeman said to the old man.

"Ignatius," Mrs. Reilly asked in a trembling voice, "what you done, boy?"

"Actually, Mother, I believe that it was he who started everything." Ignatius pointed to the old man with his bag of sheet music. "I was simply standing about, waiting for you, praying that the news from the doctor would be encouraging."

"Get that old man outta here," Mrs. Reilly said to the policeman. He's making trouble. It's a shame they got people like him walking the streets."

"The police are all communiss," the old man said.

"Didn't I say for you to shut up?" the policeman said angrily.

"I fall on my knees every night to thank my God we got protection," Mrs. Reilly told the crowd. "We'd all be dead without the police. We'd all be laying in our beds with our throats cut open from ear to ear."

"That's the truth, girl," some woman answered from the crowd.

"Say a rosary for the police force." Mrs. Reilly was now addressing her remarks to the crowd. Ignatius caressed her shoulder wildly, whispering encouragement. "Would you say a rosary for a communiss?"

"No!" several voices answered fervently. Someone pushed the old man.

"It's true, lady," the old man cried. "He tried to arrest your boy. Just like in Russia. They're all communiss."

"Come on," the policeman said to the old man. He grabbed him roughly by the back of the coat.

"Oh, my God!" Ignatius said, watching the wan little policeman try to control the old man. "Now my nerves are totally frayed."

"Help!" the old man appealed to the crowd. "It's a takeover. It's a violation of the Constitution!"

"He's crazy, Ignatius," Mrs. Reilly said. "We better get outta here, baby." She turned to the crowd. "Run, folks. He might kill us all. Personally, I think maybe *he's* the communiss."

"You don't have to overdo it, Mother," Ignatius said as they pushed through the dispersing crowd and started walking rapidly down Canal Street. He looked back and saw the old man and the bantam policeman grappling beneath the department store clock. "Will you please slow down a bit? I think I'm having a heart murmur."

"Oh, shut up. How you think I feel? I shouldn't haveta be running like this at my age."

"The heart is important at any age, I'm afraid."

"They's nothing wrong with your heart."

"There will be if we don't go a little slower." The tweed trousers billowed around Ignatius' gargantuan rump as he rolled forward. "Do you have my lute string?"

Mrs. Reilly pulled him around the corner onto Bourbon Street, and they started walking down into the French Quarter.

"How come that policeman was after you, boy?"

"I shall never know. But he will probably be coming after us in a few moments, as soon as he has subdued that aged fascist."

"You think so?" Mrs. Reilly asked nervously.

"I would imagine so. He seemed determined to arrest me. He must have some sort of quota or something. I seriously doubt that he will permit me to elude him so easily."

"Wouldn't that be awful! You'd be all over the papers, Ignatius. The disgrace! You musta done something while you was waiting for me, Ignatius. I know you, boy."

"If anyone was ever minding his business, it was I," Ignatius breathed. "Please. We must stop. I think I'm going to have a hemorrhage."

"Okay." Mrs. Reilly looked at her son's reddening face and realized that he would very happily collapse at her feet just to prove his point. He had done it before. The last time that she had forced him to accompany her to mass on Sunday he had collapsed twice on the way to the church and had collapsed once again during the sermon about sloth, reeling out of the pew and creating an embarrassing disturbance. "Let's go in here and sit down."

She pushed him through the door of the Night of Joy bar with one of the cake boxes. In the darkness that smelled of bourbon and cigarette butts they climbed onto two stools. While Mrs. Reilly arranged her cake boxes on the bar, Ignatius spread his expansive nostrils and said, "My God, Mother, it smells awful. My stomach is beginning to churn."

"You wanna go back on the street? You want that policeman to take you in?"

Ignatius did not answer; he was sniffing loudly and making faces. A bartender, who had been observing the two, asked quizzically from the shadows, "Yes?"

"I shall have a coffee," Ignatius said grandly. "Chicory coffee with boiled milk."

"Only instant," the bartender said.

"I can't possibly drink that," Ignatius told his mother. "It's an abomination."

"Well, get a beer, Ignatius. It won't kill you."

"I may bloat."

"I'll take a Dixie 45," Mrs. Reilly said to the bartender.

"And the gentleman?" the bartender asked in a rich, assumed voice. "What is his pleasure?"

"Give him a Dixie, too."

"I may not drink it," Ignatius said as the bartender went off to open the beers.

"We can't sit in here for free, Ignatius."

"I don't see why not. We're the only customers. They should be glad to have us."

"They got strippers in here at night, huh?" Mrs. Reilly nudged her son.

"I would imagine so," Ignatius said coldly. He looked quite pained. "We might have stopped somewhere else. I suspect that the police will raid this place momentarily anyway." He snorted loudly and cleared his throat. "Thank God my moustache filters out some of the stench. My olfactories are already beginning to send out distress signals."

After what seemed a long time during which there was much tinkling of glass and closing of coolers somewhere in the shadows, the bartender appeared again and set the beers before them, pretending to knock Ignatius' beer into his lap. The Reillys were getting the Night of Joy's worst service, the treatment given unwanted customers.

"You don't by any chance have a cold Dr. Nut, do you?" Ignatius asked.
"No."

"My son loves Dr. Nut," Mrs. Reilly explained. "I gotta buy it by the case. Sometimes he sits himself down and drinks two, three Dr. Nuts at one time."

"I am sure that this man is not particularly interested," Ignatius said.

"Like to take that cap off?" the bartender asked.

"No, I wouldn't!" Ignatius thundered. "There's a chill in here."

"Suit yourself," the bartender said and drifted off into the shadows at the other end of the bar.

"Really!"

"Calm down," his mother said.

Ignatius raised the earflap on the side next to his mother.

"Well, I will lift this so that you won't have to strain your voice. What did the doctor tell you about your elbow or whatever it is?"

"It's gotta be massaged."

"I hope you don't want me to do that. You know how I feel about touching other people."

TENNESSEE WILLIAMS

Few filmscripts read well, but Baby Doll *was written by the most important playwright produced by the South. When the movie came out in 1956,* Time *magazine called it "just possibly the dirtiest American-made motion picture that has ever been legally exhibited." "It's not quite all that," Pauline Kael has written, "but it is a delight." The most disturbing event of Tennessee Williams's childhood, apparently, was his family's move from Columbus, Mississippi, where he was born and where they lived in gentility with his beloved grandparents, to St. Louis, where his father—scion of an old Tennessee family—worked in a shoe factory. Think twice, then, Southern parents, before you move your children out of the South. I'm not saying you shouldn't do it—Lord knows the American theater could use another real genius.*

from *Baby Doll*

1] INTERIOR. DAY.

A voluptuous girl, under twenty, is asleep on a bed, with the covers thrown off. This is Baby Doll Meighan, Archie Lee's virgin wife. A sound is disturbing her sleep, a steady sound, furtive as a mouse scratching, she stirs, it stops, she settles again, it starts again. Then she wakes, without moving, her back to that part of the wall from which the sound comes.

2] INTERIOR. DAY. CLOSE SHOT. BABY DOLL.

She is a little frightened of what sounds like a mouse in the woodwork and still doesn't sound like a mouse in the woodwork. Then a crafty look.

3] INTERIOR. DAY. FULL SHOT.

She gets up, as the sound is continuing, and moves stealthily out of her room.

4] HALL. DAY. FULL SHOT.

She comes out of her room and just as stealthily opens the door to an adjoining room and peeks in.

5] CLOSE SHOT. BABY DOLL.

Astonished and angry at what she sees.

6] WHAT SHE SEES. ARCHIE LEE MEIGHAN.

He is crouched over a section of broken plaster in the wall, enlarging a space between exposed boards with a penknife. Unshaven, blackjowled, in sweaty pajamas. On the bed table behind him is a half-empty bottle of liquor, an old alarm clock, ticking away, a magazine called Spicy Fiction *and a tube of ointment. After a moment he removes the knife and bends to peer through the enlarged crack.*

7] CLOSE SHOT. BABY DOLL.

BABY DOLL: Archie Lee. You're a mess.

8] ARCHIE LEE.

He recovers.

9] BABY DOLL.

BABY DOLL: Y'know what they call such people? Peepin' Toms!

10] FULL SHOT. ARCHIE LEE'S BEDROOM.

ARCHIE: Come in here, I want to talk to you.

BABY DOLL: I know what you're going to say, but you can save your breath.

ARCHIE [*INTERRUPTING*]: We made an agreement . . .

BABY DOLL: You promised my daddy that you would leave me alone till I was ready for marriage. . . .

ARCHIE: Well?

BABY DOLL: Well, I'm not ready for it yet. . . .

ARCHIE: And I'm going crazy. . . .

BABY DOLL: Well, you can just wait. . . .

ARCHIE: We made an agreement that when you was twenty years old we could be man and wife in more than just in name only.

BABY DOLL: Well, I won't be twenty till November the seventh. . . .

ARCHIE: Which is the day after tomorrow!

BABY DOLL: How about your side of that agreement—that you'd take good care of me? GOOD CARE OF ME! Do you remember that?! Now the Ideal Pay As You Go Plan Furniture Company is threatening to remove the furniture from this house. And every time I bring that up you walk away. . . .

ARCHIE: Just going to the window to get a breath of air. . . .

BABY DOLL: Now I'm telling you that if the Ideal Pay As You Go Plan Furniture Company takes those five complete sets of furniture out of this house then the understanding between us will be canceled. Completely!

11] ARCHIE LEE. AT WINDOW.

He is listening. We hear the distant sound of the Syndicate Cotton Gin. Like a gigantic distant throbbing heartbeat. Archie Lee puts the window down. He crosses to the mirror, dolefully considers his appearance.

BABY DOLL: Yeah, just look at yourself! You're not exactly a young girl's dream come true, Archie Lee Meighan.

[*The phone rings downstairs. This sound is instantly followed by an outcry even higher and shriller.*]

BABY DOLL: Aunt Rose Comfort screams ev'ry time the phone rings.
ARCHIE: What does she do a damn fool thing like that for?

[*The phone rings again. Aunt Rose Comfort screams downstairs. The scream is followed by high breathless laughter. These sounds are downstairs. Archie Lee exits.*]

BABY DOLL: She says a phone ringing scares her.

12] HALL.

[*Archie lumbers over to a staircase, much too grand for the present style of the house, and shouts down to the old woman below.*]

ARCHIE: Aunt Rose Comfort, why don't you answer that phone?

13] DOWNSTAIRS HALL.

[*Aunt Rose comes out of the kitchen and walks towards the hall telephone, withered hand to her breast.*]

AUNT ROSE: I cain't catch m'breath, Archie Lee. Phone give me such a fright.
ARCHIE [*FROM ABOVE*]: Answer it.

[*She has recovered some now and gingerly lifts the receiver.*]
AUNT ROSE: Hello? This is Miss Rose Comfort McCorkle speaking. No, the lady
    of the house is Mrs. Archie Lee Meighan, who is the daughter of my
    brother that passed away . . .

[*Archie Lee is hurrying down the stairs.*]
ARCHIE: They don't wanta know that! Who in hell is it talking and what do they
    want?
AUNT ROSE: I'm hard of hearing. Could you speak louder, please? The what?
    The Ideal Pay As—

[*With amazing, if elephantine, speed, Archie snatches the phone from the old woman.*]
ARCHIE: Gi'me that damn phone. An' close the door.

[*The old woman utters her breathless cackle and backs against the door. Archie speaks in a hoarse whisper.*]
ARCHIE: Now what is this? Aw. Uh-huh. Today!? Aw. You gotta g'me more

time. Yeah, well you see I had a terrible setback in business lately. The Syndicate Plantation built their own cotton gin and're ginnin' out their own cotton, now, so I lost their trade and it's gonna take me a while to recover from that. . . .

[*Suddenly.*]

Then TAKE IT OUT! TAKE IT OUT! Come and get th' damn stuff. And you'll never get my business again! Never!

[*They have hung up on him. He stands there—a man in tough trouble. Then abruptly starts massaging his exhausted head of hair.*]

AUNT ROSE [*TIMIDLY*]: Archie Lee, honey, you all aren't going to lose your furniture, are you?

ARCHIE [*HOARSE WHISPER*]: Will you shut up and git on back in the kitchen and don't speak a word that you heard on the phone, if you heard a word, to my wife! And don't holler no more in this house, and don't cackle no more in it either, or by God I'll pack you up and haul you off to th' county home at Sunset.

AUNT ROSE: What did you say, Archie Lee, did you say something to me?

ARCHIE: Yeah, I said shoot.

[*He starts upstairs. Aunt Rose cackles uneasily and enters the kitchen. Suddenly, we hear another scream from her. We pan with her, and reveal Old Fussy, the hen, on top of the kitchen table pecking the corn bread.*]

14] UPSTAIRS HALL.

Archie is heading back to his bedroom. Baby Doll appears in a flimsy wrapper at the turn of the stairs crossing to the bathroom.

BABY DOLL: What made her holler this time?

ARCHIE: How in hell would I know what made that ole woman holler this time or last time or the next time she hollers.

BABY DOLL: Last time she hollered it was because you throwed something at her.

[*She enters bathroom. Archie Lee stands in doorway.*]

ARCHIE: What did I ever throw at Aunt Rose Comfort?

BABY DOLL [*FROM INSIDE BATHROOM*]: Glass a water. Fo' singin' church hymns in the kitchen. . . .

[*We hear the shower go on.*]

ARCHIE: This much water! Barely sprinkled her with it! To catch her attention.

She don't hear nothing, you gotta do somethin' to git the ole woman's attention.

[*On an abrupt impulse he suddenly enters the bathroom. Sounds of a struggle. The shower.*]
BABY DOLL: Keep y'r hands off me! Will yuh? Keep your hands off . . . Off.

[*Archie Lee comes out of the bathroom good and wet. The shower is turned off. Baby Doll's head comes out past the door.*]
BABY DOLL: I'm going to move to the Kotton King Hotel, the very next time you try to break the agreement! The very next time!

[*She disappears. . . .*]

15] *CLOSE SHOT. ARCHIE LEE WET. DISSOLVE.*

16] *ARCHIE LEE.*

He is seated in his 1937 Chevy Sedan. The car is caked with pale brown mud and much dented. Pasted on the windshield is a photo of Baby Doll smiling with bewilderment at the birdie-in-the-camera. Archie Lee is honking his horn with unconcealed and unmodified impatience.

ARCHIE [*SHOUTING*]: Baby Doll! Come on down here, if you're going into town with me. I got to be at the doctor's in ten minutes. [*No answer.*] Baby Doll!!!

[*From inside the house. Baby Doll's voice.*]
BABY DOLL: If you are so impatient, just go ahead without me. Just go ahead. I know plenty of ways of getting downtown without you.
ARCHIE: You come on.

[*Silence. The sound of the Syndicate Gin. Archie does a sort of imitation. His face is violent.*]
ARCHIE: Baby Doll!!!

[*Baby Doll comes out on the sagging porch of the mansion. She walks across the loose boards of the porch through stripes of alternate light and shadow from the big porch pillars. She is humming a little cakewalk tune, and she moves in sympathy to it. She has on a skirt and blouse, white, and skintight, and pearl chokers the size of golf balls seen from a medium distance. She draws up beside the car and goes no farther.*]
ARCHIE: You going in town like that?
BABY DOLL: Like what?

ARCHIE: In that there outfit. For a woman of your modest nature that squawks like a hen if her *husband* dast to put his hand on her, you sure do seem to be advertising your—

BABY DOLL [*DROWNING HIM OUT*]: My figure has filt out a little since I bought my trousseau AND paid for it with m'daddy's insurance money. I got two choices, wear clo'se skintight or go naked, now which do you want me t'—

ARCHIE: *Aw, now, hell! Will you git into th' car?*

[*Their angry voices are echoed by the wandering poultry.*]

BABY DOLL: I will git into the rear seat of that skatterbolt when you git out of the front seat and walk around here to open the door for me like a gentleman.

ARCHIE: Well, you gonna wait a long time if that's what you're waiting for!

BABY DOLL: I vow my father would turn over in his grave. . . .

ARCHIE: I never once did see your father get out and open a car door for your mother or any other woman. . . . Now get on in. . . .

[*See wheels about and her wedgies clack-clack down the drive. At foot of drive she assumes a hitchhiker's stance. A hot-rod skids to a sudden and noisy stop. Archie Lee bounds from his car like a jack rabbit, snatching a fistful of gravel as he plummets down drive. Hurls gravel at grinning teen-age kids in hot-rod, shouting incoherently as they shoot off, plunging Baby Doll and her protector in a dust-cloud. Through the dust . . .*]

ARCHIE: Got your license number you pack a—

DISSOLVE.

NANCY LEMANN

In her novel Lives of the Saints, *Lemann's New Orleans is different from that of either John Kennedy Toole or Tennessee Williams. Hers is a dottiness highly refined, as pellucidly pungent as a good raw oyster's juice.*

Mary Grace's Reception

Mr. Walter Stewart came up and put his arms around me. I couldn't reach his cheek to kiss, but tried awkwardly, and succeeded in pressing my glasses lens into his cheek.

But he took my hand and said, "You are very dear to me, young lady."

Large, beefy, and handsome, with watery blue eyes, he invited me back into the house—or rather, ordered me in. Then he took me into his duck-hunting room and showed me his rifles. I politely admired his rifles, and he launched into a soliloquy about hunting and the thrill of the chase. Then he went off to stand on the front lawn of his mansion, where he called out to passersby—"My daughter is a delicate magnolia blossom!" or "I love my baby doll!"—in his gravel-voiced baritone. "She's my favorite, you know!" he advised the public. "She was always my favorite."

.   .   .   .

"The thing I remember most vividly from my youth," Mrs. Stewart the elder was saying to me, "is that little red hat which I wore in the summer of . . . 1912. It went with a blue suit. I remember it vividly," she said, her eyes rapturous. We were talking about what hats we wore when we were fifteen. What shoe sizes her friends wore in 1910, minute details of clothing, recalled to her the Mystery of Life and filled her with the greatest zest. She was in her eighties and had a perfect memory for her attire through the years, but could not remember things in a normal conversation.

"What do you do, Louise?" she said to me.

"I'm working in a law firm now."

"Oh, how nice."

"Well, it isn't exactly the nicest thing you could ever think of, but it's—"

"Now, what was it again, dear—what was it that you do?"

"Oh. Well—that is, I work in a law firm."

"Now let me just get this straight. You work in a law firm . . . downtown?"

"Yes, uh, it is downtown, yes."

"Well, why don't the young people want to just stay home and read?"

"Oh, I wouldn't mind doing that at all."

"You wouldn't? Well, I think that's very nice. Do you work, though?"

"Do I work?"

Claude walked up and started overwhelming Mrs. Stewart with his politeness. He was always polite. It was one of his greatest traits. It is hard to be truly polite. It is an elegant trait.

I felt like I was going into a stupor. I could hear Mr. Stewart quoting from a famous book he owned that he always quoted from, which was a history of the battles of the Civil War written entirely in verse. It filled me with dread.

"Let me tell you something about women," I could hear Mr. Stewart saying. "You have to treat women gently because they're weak. Young girls should be sheltered. They shouldn't be allowed to have affairs. One affair, and they're ruined. I pity women. After one affair, they're ruined. Who would want them?''

Oh, God, I thought. He was a law professor and had a tendency to lecture on all occasions. He often aired his private views for the benefit of large groups. He took a particular relish in quotation. I could hear him quoting from the Bible:

'' 'Woman, thou shouldst ever go in sackcloth and mourning, the eyes filled with tears. Thou hast brought about the ruin of mankind.' ''

He was looking remorsefully into the eyes of some poor unsuspecting woman standing next to him, to gain a histrionic effect. As though off in a reverie, he turned dazed eyes on his youngest son.

"Peter, I'll tell you what Jeb Stuart used to say." Mr. Stewart looked raptly off into space. '' 'All I ask of fate is that I may be killed leading a cavalry charge.' ''

.   .   .   .

Mrs. Stewart, next to me, was talking about who married who in 1910. Claude returned and sat down, chewing a bottle cap. Pensively, he took out the pack of cigarettes and started to divide the foil part from the paper part, leaving a pile of strips on the table.

"Could you please tone it down a little?" I said.

"Yes, enough silliness," he said. "Now I must suffer." He clutched his throat and pretended to be having a strangulation fit.

"If that weren't so amusing, one might laugh," I said darkly—but confused. . . .

"I find it so terribly amusing," he said, "that I'm terribly amused. I find this terribly amusing."

"I find this rather immature," I said. "If this weren't so unbearably immature, maybe I would—"

"I feel very mature right now. I feel extremely mature."

He put his hand on my knee. I just stared at it in a stupor.

"The way your slip was showing," he said, "it reminded me of the South."

Mrs. Stewart the elder was just sitting there with a rhapsodical expression in her eyes. Probably recalling the famous pink kid evening bag she used to carry in 1915. Suddenly, there was a booming voice above the crowd:

"LET US HAVE FAITH THAT RIGHT MAKES MIGHT, AND IN THAT FAITH, LET US, TO THE END, DARE TO DO OUR DUTY AS WE UNDERSTAND IT!"

It was Mr. Stewart.

His wife went across the room, I saw, over to his party.

"Walter, please," she said.

"Let the dead bury the dead!" Mr. Stewart boomed. "Poets, war—war, poetry—"

"Walter, please, come over here, dear," said his wife, who led him away from the group. She had an instinct for his breakdowns, such as the one that was swiftly impending. She took his arm. He stumbled. Everyone in the vicinity looked at the floor with embarrassed expressions.

Mrs. Stewart the elder was still staring off into space. She had that same glazed expression that her son had. Then she rose and was just standing there.

.   .   .   .

"Keep an eye on Tom," said Claude to me, getting up. Everyone was always telling you to keep an eye on Tom. As I've never seen a person who could get in so much trouble as Tom, I was a little concerned that it was now my job to keep an eye on him. Furthermore, he was the bride's old flame, or one of them. He was acting Extremely Peculiar. The last time I had seen Tom, he was lying down on the floor in a tormented crumple with a lamp shade over his head. He was wearing sunglasses and a suit made out of leather.

Then I found him sitting in his Lonely Splendor in one of the anterooms. He trained a pair of smoldering eyes on me.

"Will you read the first chapter of my novel?" he said.

"Oh, really? That's great."

"It's dedicated to Mary Grace."

"Now, come on, Tom," I said, "get hold of yourself."

He stared at me smolderingly.

"Where *is* Mary Grace?" I said.

"She's probably in the bamboo grove having sex."

"The bamboo grove?"

"Well, you know, that's the type of person she is. She's the type of person who would just go out to the bamboo grove during the middle of a party or during her own wedding and have sex."

"She is? What? But—but—why the bamboo grove, though?"

"It's racy out there, Louise. It's sexy. Out in the bamboo grove."

"God," I said, stunned, wishing I were that type of person.

Mary Grace Stewart, the bride, sailed past the parents of a boy whose life she ruined, who hated her for ruining their son's life, and she just sailed past, brave, undaunted, not caring. However, let me make it clear—not heartlessly uncaring, but on the contrary, specifically brave.

She was finally resolving her troubles, and the havoc she had wrought, by matrimony.

"They don't make them like Mary Grace anymore," said Claude's father fondly, passing by. He shook his head in amusement at the sight of Mary Grace, who left many souvenirs of herself in ruined lives between New Orleans and Boston, including, one might say, Claude. The whole wedding party was populated by the bride's old flames, not to say potential new ones. She had the spark of divine fire, which you find in a face not quite pretty enough.

Mary Grace Stewart was the type of girl you see being dragged screaming from a convertible sports car outside of the bar at the Lafayette Hotel at three in the morning by her father and brothers, and then, the next day, in the bank or shoe store looking as though she had been shedding a lot of tears. She wore conservative clothes with navy blue pumps, neat unwrinkled skirts, and alligator belts. I always used to see her standing in line at the bank looking like she was about to burst into tears, or going to buy shoes uptown with a vacant stare.

She always looked voluptuous and as though she were about to become hysterical. I could picture her bursting into tears at home while putting together some conservative outfit, her stockings hanging across a drawer and the room in disarray, an overgrown banana tree extending in through an open window, in this tropic setting, and the maid singing soul songs downstairs.

. . . .

Mr. Collier, Claude's father, a mild and elegant man, was standing in a conversation at the bar. He was talking to a woman of about fifty, quite beautiful, but with a wildly crestfallen expression as though embossed onto her face, the lines of it were so deep. It was Mrs. Sully Legendre. She was married to a famous playboy.

Mrs. Sully Legendre had a jazzy way of talking, and would preface her remarks with *Kiddo, Baby,* or *Fella*. It seemed inappropriate, her saying to the dignified Mr. Collier, "Baby, just lemme tell you this . . ." and then she would make some jazzy, cynical remark. She would look at him inquiringly with her crestfallen face, but Mr. Collier was not forthcoming on the subject. He would never say anything bad about anyone.

Mrs. Legendre continued in a crestfallen vein, delivering some cynical maxims pertaining to marriage. Mr. Collier nodded stiffly, coughed, pretended to be thinking it over. He puffed on his cigar. He looked at her gently.

"Never marry a man with a weak chin, Fella," she concluded grimly.

"Quite right," said Mr. Collier mildly.

Mr. Collier was a man who always wore seersucker suits that he had had for about fifty years and which were always wrinkled and faded to a kind of yellow color. He and Claude looked alike in that their suits were always wrinkled and looked as though they had come from someone else's closet in a prep school in 1920. But that is about as far as the comparison goes, because Mr. Collier and Claude—they were not alike.

Mr. Collier was always trying to interest me in unexpected key changes in arias and oratorios. He was obsessed with Homer, and went around speaking in ancient Greek. He was conducting studies in Rhapsody. His ambition was to become a Rhapsode. What is a Rhapsode? What, indeed. It is a person who memorizes the entirety of Homer in the ancient Greek and goes around reciting it.

At the office, Mr. Collier would write papers for his eccentric club, which met monthly at Antoine's in the Quarter in a private room, where scholarly men in white tie and tails delivered to each other strange treatises. Mr. Collier was writing a paper called "Rhapsody." He would Xerox these papers and send them to me. Before that he wrote a paper called "Ecstasy." Imagine, the most mild-mannered man in the world writing something called "Ecstasy." But then when you read what he wrote, you found out that it was all about obscure metric configurations in ancient Greek. This, to him, was ecstasy.

.   .   .   .

Mr. Collier and Mr. Stewart had been together from kindergarten through law school.

"How *are* you, Louis?" Mr. Stewart asked Mr. Collier in a confidential tone when Mrs. Legendre had left.

"Well, that's fine, just fine," said Mr. Collier vaguely.

"You look well," said Mr. Stewart.

"You can't tell a book by its cover, old man," said Mr. Collier, never one to accept a compliment under any circumstance.

Mr. Stewart directed a rather gloomy gaze on Claude, who was still sitting with Mr. Stewart's mother, apparently filling her with hilarity and inexpressible mirth. They looked like they were having the time of their lives.

Mr. Stewart looked at them darkly.

"I've been hearing some things about Claude," Mr. Stewart said to Mr. Collier. "I hear he's been spending a lot of his time at the racetrack."

"Claude is not using his abilities," said Mr. Collier.

Mr. Collier trained an eye of amused benevolence on his son Claude. Mr. Collier had a soft spot for Wastrel Youth. In fact, it was one of his favorite episodes in life. He always said—trying to get the lingo, in his dignified old age—that the young people should "find themselves."

"I'd like to see that boy at the law school, Louis."

"He's finding himself, Walter," said Mr. Collier, ecstatic. He loved wastrel youths, but he loved his sons to a degree approaching beatitude. The combination—his sons plus wastrel youth—was almost too much for him.

.   .   .   .

The garden was still populated by the crowd, arranged in deck chairs around the green-and-white striped tents, in the steamy night. Some ancient couples sat in well-lit corners of the room beside the garden, which was now dazzlingly lit. Old-time jazz from the orchestra was wafting by, the instruments in languid unison, giving the effect of that buffoonish hedonism which you find only in New Orleans.

Claude was still sitting between Mrs. Stewart the elder and her daughter-in-law, who were discussing, at interminable length, the blue dress which one of them had almost worn.

Mary Grace was conducting a violent flirtation with George Sweeney in a corner of the garden.

As for the bridegroom, he was not in evidence. We found him sitting in an anteroom at an empty table crooning a song to some empty chairs. A stricken expression passed across Claude's face when he saw this. With a beleaguered step, Claude went over to Henry and talked to him for a while, consoling him. Then they both came striding out, and Henry, looking strangely sunny, paced resolutely to the French doors and then on outside to claim the bride.

. . . .

We went over to the bar. "Here come the boy I raised," said Chester, the old butler, in a reverential whisper.

"How are you, heart?" said Claude in that kind voice, and they shook hands.

In his suit and tie, Claude looked slightly unusual, so old-fashioned, a little stark, in his dark suit and overstarched white shirt, with a sodden, gin-like fragrance as though he had taken too long of a shower, a Southern habit originally brought on by fear of heat.

"That boy is an angel on earth," said Chester, watching Claude, practically with tears in his eyes.

Everyone's grip on his emotions was deteriorating.

"Stop, dawlin. Wait," said Chester to me. "That boy is the only chance you'll ever get to see an angel on earth."

Mr. Sully Legendre was weaving toward us. He had silver hair parted in the middle, making melodramatic wings on either side of his face, and a glamorous silver mustache. The society column in the newspaper referred to him as "the hyper-handsome Sully Legendre."

This hopeless burden fell on his wife. That girl got her heart broke.

He gazed at us with his heavy-lidded eyes, and then screamed in a maniacal voice, "BABY!"

Then he clasped me to his bosom.

"CLAUDE, DAWLIN!" he screamed to my companion.

Heads turned. Silence fell upon suddenly hushed conversations. It was as though Mr. Sully Legendre were returned, at last, from the Odyssey.

"BABY!" he screamed again in histrionic amazement and joy. "IT'S LOUISE

BROWN!'' he scramed, and stood riveted in amazement.

The man was plainly falling apart.

Claude made normal remarks and pretended that everything was normal—and Mr. Legendre subsided somewhat, though he still displayed the mock-amazed congeniality of New Orleanians confronted with the spectacle of one another.

.   .   .   .

I heard Mary Grace's voice:

"Jane, can I have some crème de menthe?"

There was a silence.

"No, Mary Grace, you cannot have some crème de menthe," said a sober voice, that of Mrs. Collier.

There were some muffled voices. There was a crash.

"I LOVE YOU, GODDAMNIT! BECAUSE I LOVE YOU, GODDAMNIT!" Henry's voice could be heard to scream from the vicinity.

Mr. Stewart was delivering another lecture on The Woman Question.

"Why, Walter," interrupted his wife, "how can you?"

"Barbara, Barbara, you'll never understand." He glared at her. "Men have ambitions, where women just have longings."

No one tried to argue, as they had all known him for decades. It was just his personality.

Henry Laines was also falling apart. He was made that way. He was made to scream wild declarations of love to women in dressing rooms and gardens, and then throw pots and pans on them. And then he was made to get in rages and have jazz music and crashes coming out of his apartment across the garden and have nothing in his icebox except an old head of broccoli.

Life ran high in Mary Grace, and I admired her for that—it takes generosity to love, no matter what the circumstance, and she had loved many. But she was in a state of Total Chaos, among the madcap palms and honorable oaks, as society shed its bloodshot eyes upon the scene.

Everyone was leaving. The wastrel-youth contingent was making plans to meet later at the Lafayette Hotel for binges.

I was walking down the Garden District street, watching everyone "tank up," as my companion put it, in their cars, in alleys, and walking down the street, everyone with their plastic cups and glasses washing liquor down their throats. People were sitting in parked cars about to take off, but pouring liquor down their throats, first.

Tom, the bride's old flame, was strewn upon the ground, tangled up in the wires of his Walk-Man, passed out underneath his car.

So when the wastrel-youth contingent had departed, the old sat at tables in the house, with some of the men in tuxedos, against the ancient walls, with brandy glasses and cigars, a more than pretty sight, and looked back to view with fond dismay the crises of their own youth.

FRED CHAPPELL

One thing about editing an anthology, you feel like you ought to go ahead and read various people you've been halfheartedly meaning to get around to for years. Fred Chappell I had long known of as a noted underappreciated Southern poet, novelist, critic, professor of English; but let's face it, there are a lot of people who answer that description in the South. As I examine my conscience now, I wonder whether I may also have been put off by the name Fred. I have known nice people named Fred, but, well, you'll notice there's no other writer in this book named Fred. Totally irrational! When I started researching for this book, I picked up The Fred Chappell Reader *and, hey—he's an old boy from Canton, North Carolina, who writes great wild well-made but unacademic stuff. There's a poem called ''My Grandmother Washes Her Feet'' and another one, ''My Father's Hurricane'':*

> *It even blew your aunt's glass eyeball out.*
> *It blew the lid off a jar of pickles we'd*
> *Been trying to unscrew for fifteen years.*

I want to thank this book for getting me to Chappell before I died.
   (After reading him, I met him, and we unscrewed a jar.)

''The Beard''

Uncle Gurton's beard had a long and complex history, but I will try not to bore us with much of that. Enough to say that it was a fabled beard and that when my father and I heard that Uncle Gurton was coming to visit we were thrilled at the prospect of viewing the legendary fleece.

''How long is that beard of his now?'' my father asked my grandmother.

She smiled a secret smile. "Oh, I wouldn't have no idea," she said. "But he's been growing it for forty years or more and ain't once yet trimmed it. That's what I hear tell."

"And he's coming here to our house to visit?" I asked.

"That's what Aunt Sary says in her letter." She held up the scrawled bit of paper, but not close enough for us to read the writing.

"And when is he going to get here?"

"She wouldn't know about that. You'll just have to wait."

"Hot damn," my father said. "If this ain't the biggest thing since Christmas. We're going to make that old man plenty welcome."

"Now, Joe Robert, don't you be deviling Uncle Gurton," she said. "Leave him in peace."

"Oh, I wouldn't harm a hair of his face," he said. "When you say he's coming?"

She smiled again. "You'll just have to wait till he shows up."

Show up is exactly what Uncle Gurton did. We heard no car or truck arrive, and he didn't walk into the house or knock at the door. One Tuesday noon he was just there, standing under the walnut tree in the side yard and staring at our chopblock and pile of kindling as if he'd never seen such objects upon the face of the earth. An apparition, he simply became present.

The three of us raised our heads from our dinner plates at the same time and saw him, and a spooky feeling came over us.

"What in the world is *that?*" my father asked.

"Uncle Gurton," said my grandmother in her serenest voice.

His back was toward us, so that all we could tell was that he was a very tall man, his white head bare, and dressed in faded overalls and a green plaid shirt, as lean and narrow as a fence rail, and warped with age and weather. Then, as if presenting himself formally to our gaze, he turned around.

I was profoundly disappointed. The famous beard that he had been working on for forty years and more, the beard that was the pivot of so many stories, was tucked down inside his overalls bib.

My father and I had made bets whether it would hang down to his belly button or all the way down to his knees, and now we couldn't say.

But even apart from his beard he was an extraordinary-appearing person. His arms were too long for his shirt sleeves and his hands dangled out like big price tags. His overalls legs were too short and his skinny legs went naked into his high-topped brogans. His long hair was white and hung down both sides of his ruddy sharp-featured face. The beard, as purely white as a morning cloud, went down behind his overalls bib, and what happened to it after that, what it truly looked like, only Uncle Gurton and the almighty and omniscient God could say.

"Jess," my grandmother said, "go out and welcome Uncle Gurton to the house."

"Please, ma'am, no," I said. Uncle Gurton was too famous in my mind. It would have been easier to shake hands with Lou Gehrig.

"He does look kind of fearsome," my father said. "I'll go gather him in."

He went out and talked and Uncle Gurton gave him one short nod and then they came into the house. When the old man entered our small alcove dining space he looked even taller and odder than he had outdoors. His head nearly scraped the low ceiling.

My grandmother told him how glad we were to see him and how we hoped he would stay a long time, and asked him to sit and eat with us. Which he did with right goodwill. She brought flatware and a glass of buttermilk and a plate piled full of green beans, cornbread, and fried rabbit. Then she sat down at the end of the table and began to question him.

"How is Aunt Jewel getting along?" she asked.

Uncle Gurton smiled and was silent.

She waited a space of time and asked, "How is Cousin Harold doing?"

He gave her a smile as warm and friendly as the first, and as informative as a spoon.

In a while she lit on the correct form. "Has Hiram Williams got him a good tobacco crop set out?" He smiled and gave a vigorous affirmative shake of his head. After this, she asked questions that could be answered yes or no, and Uncle Gurton would nod a cheerful Yes or wag a downcast No.

And all during this exchange he was feeding voraciously. Great heaping forkfuls went into his hirsute mouth with mechanical accuracy and rapidity. A sight awesome to behold. My father kept filling his plate and Uncle Gurton kept emptying it. My father described it later: "The way he was forking at it, and with all that hair around his mouth, I kept thinking it was a man throwing a wagonload of alfalfa into a hayloft."

He finished by downing a whole glass of buttermilk. We came to find out that buttermilk was his sole beverage, breakfast, dinner, supper. He never touched anything else, not even water.

He edged his chair back from the table.

"Uncle Gurton, won't you have a little something else?" my grandmother asked.

"No thank you," he said. "I've had an elegant sufficiency; any more would be a superfluity."

That was his one saying, the only one we ever heard him utter, and he was as proud of it as another man might be of a prize beagle. He said this sentence at the end of every meal, and we came to realize that he got mighty upset, his whole day was lusterless, if you didn't ask him to have a little more something, and give him occasion to say his sentence.

My father's mouth flew open like a phoebe's after a fly. His eyes lit up with surprise. "Would you mind saying that again, Uncle Gurton?" he asked. "What you just said?"

Uncle Gurton gave him a sweet warm smile and disappeared.

I don't mean that he dissolved into nothingness before our watching eyes like a trick ghost in a horror movie. But he evaded my father's request with one of those silent smiles, and when we had got up and scraped our dishes into the slop bucket and stacked them on the drainboard of the sink and turned around, Uncle Gurton was gone. His chair was angled back from the table, his red and white checked napkin folded neatly and laid in the seat, and he was nowhere to be seen. If it weren't for the soiled plate with the knife and fork primly crossed and the empty streaked glass, we might not have believed that he had been there. No footsteps of departure, no sound of the side door, nothing.

"Our Uncle Gurton has got some interesting ways about him," my father said.

"Poor old soul," my grandmother murmured.

This habit of absenting and distancing himself we learned to know as an integral part of Uncle Gurton's character, as one with the man as his silence. You would sight him on the ridge of the pasture above the farther barn, his stark figure scarecrowlike against the sky and leaning into the wind, and then if you glanced off into the pear tree to see a bluejay, he was no longer on the ridge when you looked again. Snuffed out of the present world like a match flame. Translated into another and inevitable dimension of space. What? Where? When was he? He was an enigma of many variations, and his one answer, silence, satisfied them all as far as he was concerned.

"There's one thing, though, you can be certain of," my father said. "He won't miss a mealtime."

And this was true. As soon as the first steaming dish of corn or squash or squirrel burgoo was set out, Uncle Gurton *arrived* from whatever mystery world otherwise absorbed him.

My father kept testing him. "Uncle Gurton," he said, "this afternoon Jess and me have got a little fence mending to do along the back side of the far oatfield. Restring some barbwire, reset a few posts. How'd you like to go along and keep us company?"

There was the smile, sweet and friendly and utterly inscrutable.

My father rephrased the question. "I mean," he said, "would you be willing to go along with us, maybe lend a hand?"

Uncle Gurton nodded.

My father leaned back in his chair. "That's fine," he said. "We'll go catch us a smoke out on the porch here after lunch and then we'll go on over to the oatfield."

What distracted us? When we finished eating and tidied up a bit, Uncle Gurton was gone again. The folded napkin, the crossed knife and fork; and no Uncle Gurton.

"I'm going to get me a moving picture camera," my father said. "Because I want to find out how he does that. I believe that it's a truly rare gift that he has."

He pondered the matter all the way out to the fence line, the roll of barbwire hoisted on his shoulder and bouncing on the burlap-sack pad with every stride. I walked at his side, toting the awkward posthole diggers and the wire stretcher. "I put the question to him wrong," he said at last. "I didn't ask him was he actually going to go with us, but was he *willing* to go."

"What's the difference?" I said.

"He was willing to go, all right, but he was even more willing not to."

At the top of the high second hill of the pasture we turned to look back. There in the dusty road between the house and the first barn, as steady as a mailbox post, stood Uncle Gurton.

I dropped the posthole diggers with a loud clatter. When we looked again, the road was empty.

"No, a movie camera wouldn't capture it," my father said. "It would take some kind of invention that is beyond the capacity of present-day science."

We were resting from the fence work. We sat in the shade of a big red oak and watched the wind write long cursive sentences in the field of whitening oats.

"One question we don't need to ask," my father said. "Whether he sleeps with his beard inside or outside the covers. Stands to reason that a man who would tuck his beard down in his overalls will sleep with it under the covers."

"How long do you reckon it is?" It was the thousandth time I had asked that question.

"Before he got here, I would've guessed it was a foot and a half," he said. "And then when I saw him first, I'd've said two feet. But now the more I don't see it the longer it gets. I've been imagining it four or five feet easy."

"You really think it's all that long?"

"I've got to where I'll think anything when it comes to that beard."

"If it's that long he has to let it run down his britches leg," I said. "Which one you think, left or right?"

"Kind of a ticklish decision," he said. "Maybe he divides it up, half down one leg, half down the other."

"You reckon it's the same color all over?"

He gave me a level look. "Jess, for anything I know, it's green and purple polka-dotted under them overalls and he's got it braided into hangnooses. But I'll tell you what. I'm bound and determined to see that beard, every inch of it. I'll never sleep easy again till I do."

"How are you going to do that?"

"I'll let you know."

It was three days later, the hour before suppertime, when he revealed his grand and cunning design. He took a thumb-sized blue bottle out of his pocket. "You see this? This is our beard-catcher; this is going to turn the trick."

"What is it?"

"It's a sleeping draught I got from Doc McGreavy."

Doc McGreavy was our veterinarian, an old man who lived with his wife in a dark little house three miles from us, at the very end of the road where the mountainside pines took possession and human habitation left off.

"What are you going to do?"

"Slip it in his buttermilk. When he goes to bed he'll sleep as sound as a bear wintering in. Then we'll have us a look at that beard."

"You think it'll work?"

"Doc says it'll lay a horse down, he's put many a horse to sleep with it. I'll give Uncle Gurton just a little bit. We won't be hurting him any."

"You sure?"

He was impatient. "Sure I'm sure."

And so at supper my father kept close watch on Uncle Gurton's buttermilk. When he had drunk off the first glass, my father picked it up. "Here," he said, "let me get you some more, Uncle Gurton." He tipped me an evil wink and I knew he was going to drop the powders.

Uncle Gurton nodded and flashed the friendliest smile in his smile box, and when the buttermilk came he drained it in two swallows. My father looked so gleeful I was afraid he'd bust out laughing and spoil it all.

Then I was afraid he'd got hold of the wrong powders because nothing seemed to be happening. Uncle Gurton was as bright-eyed silent as ever and was forking into the stewed tomatoes with devastating effect. But in a few minutes I saw that his eyes were growing faraway cloudy and the lids were drooping.

"Have another piece of cornbread," my father suggested.

"No thank you," he said. "I've had an elegant sufficiency—"

But he didn't say on to *the superfluity* and we knew we had him. He rose from the table and stumbled through the kitchen and out the door, headed down the hall for the stairway. He didn't cross his knife and fork on the plate, and the checked napkin lay on the floor where he'd dropped it. My father retrieved it and laid it by his plate.

My grandmother followed his progress with curious eyes. "Uncle Gurton is right strange-acting. I wonder is he feeling poorly."

"Aw, he's okay," my father said. "He's just plumb tuckered from appearing and disappearing out of thin air all day."

We cleaned and stacked our dishes and then retired to the side porch where my father smoked his cigarette after meals.

"We going to see the beard now?" I asked.

"Better give him a little while, make sure he's sound asleep. Let's go out to the shed a minute."

In the woodshed he took a dusty kerosene lantern off a hook and shook it to hear if there was oil in the reservoir. He reached an old motheaten blue sweater off a nail and wiped the cobweb off the lamp. "We'll need this if we're going to be good and sneaky," he said. He brought the lamp and the sweater and we returned to the porch and he smoked two slow cigarettes and we watched the first stars pierce the western sky. The far hills went hazy blue and then purple-black.

"Let's go," he said, and we opened the forbidden door and tiptoed through the dark sun parlor. The souvenir teacups rattled on the glassed-in shelves. It was stale in here and dusty. I was afraid I'd sneeze and trumpet our crime to the world at large.

We entered into the dark stairway hall and stood for a moment to listen. My father struck a kitchen match with his thumbnail and lit the wick and let the shell down. The pale orange light made our shadows giant on the walls, and everything was strange in here in the hallway, all silent, and in the stairwell above in the hovering darkness. I felt a way I'd never felt before, like a thief or a detective. My breath was quick, the pulse tight in my temples.

We climbed the stairs one careful step at a time. Our shadows fell behind us and washed up on the far wall and the shadows of the banister posts spun like ghostly wheel spokes. My father held the lantern by his side in his left hand and I hid in his right-hand shadow, moving when he did.

We paused at the top of the stairs and he raised the lantern. The door to Uncle Gurton's room was at the end of the hall and we edged toward it. Every snap and squeak of the floor made me fearful; I was certain we'd be discovered. What could we say to Uncle Gurton or my grandmother when they found us? I realized, maybe for the first time, that my father wasn't always the safest protection in the world.

At that fateful door we stopped and held our breaths to listen. My father began to ease the door open, turning the knob slowly, slowly, until it ceased and the door swung open upon blackness. We heard the sound of heavy breathing and I felt relieved to know we hadn't poisoned the old man to death. My father had wrapped the wool sweater around the lantern and now he rolled it up from the bottom, showing a little light at a time.

We needn't have been so precisely stealthy. Uncle Gurton's mouth was open and, lying flat on his back, he uttered a gurgling half-snore. We could have dropped a wagonload of tin kettles on the floor and he wouldn't have stirred an ounce.

I was impressed by how Uncle Gurton lived. There were a few shirts on hangers in the open closets and one shirt hung on the back of a chair by the foot of the bed. In front of this chair his battered brogans sat, a sock dangling out of the top of each. And that was all I saw there. He led a simple existence.

My father handed me the lantern and we advanced to the edge of the bed. After giving me one significant and thrilling glance, he began to turn the sheet down from under the old man's chin. We were dismayed to discover that Uncle Gurton slept in his overalls. He wore no shirt; his naked freckled arms lay flat beside him, but the blue denim bib still hid what we had schemed so anxiously to disclose. My father rolled the sheet down to Uncle Gurton's waist, then leaned back from the bedside.

He gave me another look, this one of bewilderment and frustration. Little beads of sweat stood on his forehead. I shrugged. I was ready to leave, figuring Uncle Gurton was just one too many for us. He was a coon we couldn't tree.

But we'd come too far for my father to let it go. He reached and unhooked the gallus on the far side; then loosed the one nearer. Then he inched the bib down.

We were not disappointed; it was everything we had come to see. A creeklet of shining white lay over Uncle Gurton's skinny chest and gleamed in the lantern light like a drawer of silver spoons. It was light and dry and immaculately clean—a wonder because we'd never known Uncle Gurton to bathe. We'd never seen him do much but eat.

I thought the beard was marvelous, and I couldn't regret all our trouble and terror. It was like visiting a famous monument—Natural Bridge, Virginia, say; and I felt a different person now I'd seen it.

But the great question went begging. How long was it? We couldn't tell, and there didn't seem to be any way to find out unless we stripped him naked or tugged the beard to light by handfuls.

We stood gazing dejected until the beard began to move. It was a movement hard to distinguish. At first I thought it was flowing away to the foot of the bed like a brook, and then I thought it was rising like early mist over a pond. My father clutched my shoulder and I knew he saw this motion too.

Then suddenly it was out upon us, billow on billow of gleaming dry wavy silver beard, spilling out over the sheet and spreading over the bed like an overturned bucket of milk. It flowed over the foot of the bed and then down the sides, noiseless, hypnotic. There was no end to it.

I felt it stream over my shoe tops and round my ankles and it was all I could do to stifle a shriek. I dropped the lantern and my father bent and picked it up before it could set fire to the beard, to the house. We retreated, stepping backward quickly, but always facing the bed. We were afraid to turn our backs on that freed beard.

Now over Uncle Gurton's torso it began to rise into the air, mounding up dry and white and airy. It was like seeing a frosty stack of hay rising of its own volition out of the ground. Little streamers of beard detached from the mass and began to wave in the air like the antennae of butterflies. They searched around the tall flat headboard of the bed and went corkscrewing up the curtain drawstrings. In just a moment the beard had curled in and out, around and over, the chair in the middle of the floor like wisteria overtaking a trellis.

At last my father said something, speaking out loud. *My God,* was what he said.

"Let's please leave," I said. The flow of beard was up to my calves now and I was afraid it would start wrapping around my legs the way it had gone over the chair. Then what would happen?

"Go on," my father said. "I'm right behind you." Then he pointed and said *My God* again.

Over the bed the beard had climbed until it was like a fogbank, only more solid, and threatened to topple forward. But it was still sliding underneath in sheets off the bed like a small waterfall, and now out of that misty mass and down over the edge of the bed came a birchbark canoe with two painted Cherokee Indians paddling with smooth alacrity. Above them, out of the mist-bank of beard, flew a hawk pursued by a scattering of blackbirds. We heard a silvery distant singing and saw a provocative flashing and then a mermaid climbed out of the beard and positioned herself in the streaming-over straight chair. She did not seem to see my father and me, but gazed into some private distance and sang her bell-like song; the hair that fell over her shoulders, hiding her breasts, was the same color as Uncle Gurton's beard.

Behind the mermaid's singing all sorts of other sounds emerged, squeaks and squawks, chatterings, chitterings, muffled roars, howls, and thunderings: the background noises in a Tarzan movie. In the corner of the room was a sudden and terrific upheaval and a great mass of beard lifted to the height of the ceiling, then subsided to ominous silence. We glimpsed the movement of a huge indistinct bulk beneath the surface, moving stately-swift toward the far wall.

"What's that?" I whispered.

My father said *My God* once more and then murmured, "I believe to my soul it's a damn big white whale."

"I really think it's time to get out of here."

"I do believe you're absolutely right, Jess," he said. He pointed at three dark sharp triangles cutting through the surface. "Sharks in here too. Well, that settles that. We'd better go, I reckon."

He slipped the lantern bail up over his shoulder and dropped the old wool sweater. It floated for a moment on the surface of the silver hair and suddenly submerged. Something had snatched it under, I didn't want to know what.

We made our way to the door, lifting our feet high, and after a minute of straining together, managed to push the slowly closing door against the wall. The river of beard was already out into the upper hall, spreading both ways along the corridor. We stopped at the top of the stairs and my father unslung the lantern from his shoulder and held it up. The beard was flowing steadily down the steps, and the footing on the stairway looked plenty treacherous.

"What do you think?" I asked.

"I don't know. I don't trust it."

"I know what," I said. "Let's slide down the banister."

"Yeah, that's the ticket," he said. "I'll go first and hold the lantern for you. You can see your way down better."

"I'll go first."

"Stay right here and watch if I get down okay." He clenched the tin wire bail in his teeth. Then he straddled and lifted his feet and slid to the bottom pretty nifty. But he hit the newel post there hard and I knew if he hadn't had a mouthful of lantern bail I'd have heard some hair-singeing curses. He got off and stepped back, holding the lantern with one hand and rubbing his ass with the other. "Come on," he said, "you can make it just fine."

But as I was getting set to mount the banister, my left foot tangled in a wavelet of beard and I pitched forward. I was sure I was drowned or strangled, but my right hand on the banister held me up and I twisted over and got hold with my left hand and pulled myself up. Then I got on and slid down.

"I was worried about you for a second there," he said. "Come on, let's go."

"I was a little worried myself."

The beard was only shoe top deep down here and we went padding through it into the little sitting room, then through the kitchen hallway and out the back door.

In the yard stood a startling black apparition, but when my father held the lantern toward it, it was only my grandmother standing straight and narrow and angry in a wine-colored bathrobe. "What have you boys been doing?" she asked.

We said nothing and turned to look at the house. The upstairs windows were packed solid white with beard, and there were trailers coming out of the downstairs kitchen windows, and from the chimney a long flamelike banner of it reached toward the stars and swayed in the cold breeze.

"We just wanted to see Uncle Gurton's beard," I told her.

She clucked her tongue. "Well, do you think you've seen enough of it?"

My father looked at her and gave a deep and mournful sigh. "Yes ma'am," he said. "I've seen an elegant sufficiency. Any more——" He choked on a giggle like a bone in his throat. "Any more would be a superfluity."

JAMES WILCOX

Until recently I was even more ignorant with regard to James Wilcox (from northern Louisiana) than I was with regard to Fred Chappell. I was under the impression that I had read part of a Wilcox novel and didn't like it. The human mind is a funny thing. Once I actually did start reading a Wilcox novel, I read all six of them, and then looked up his short stories in back issues of The New Yorker. *Probably the best of the novels is* Sort of Rich, *but the funniest are* Modern Baptists, North Gladiola, *and* Miss Undine's Living Room. *You can't do justice to any of them by quoting an excerpt, because they get better as you get to know the characters and as the seemingly flighty narrative develops spooky retrospective coherence. But here, from* Modern Baptists, *goes:*

Modern Baptist Bible Study

That evening after work Donna Lee had dinner at her parents' house, which was roomy and comfortable, but plain-looking, almost severe, when seen from the street. Mrs. Keely had forgotten she had invited her daughter to dinner; this meant that Mr. Keely had to do without seconds on his favorite dish, stuffed peppers. During the meal Donna Lee's father, an officer at the Tula Springs Savings and Loan Association, gazed vacantly out the bay window whenever the conversation lagged.

"How was work?" Mrs. Keely asked for the third time as she passed her daughter the coleslaw. Donna Lee's mother was a little distracted because she was trying to keep the names of the gods and goddesses straight in her mind. She had a test on Monday at St. Jude State College, where she was auditing classes in mythology and abnormal psychology.

"Mother."

"Oh, yes," Mrs. Keely said vaguely. In her early sixties, she was a striking woman, buxom, with a head of long snow-white hair gathered in a chignon.

Donna Lee envied her mother's knack of appearing gracious and composed no matter how she was feeling.

"Dad, have you ever heard of the Calydonian boar?" Mrs. Keely said to her husband, who was humming—unconsciously, as usual—"Three Blind Mice." Hypnotherapy, a birthday gift from Donna Lee, had failed to cure him of this awful habit. Mr. Keely, though, assumed he *was* cured and was always surprised when someone asked him to stop humming.

"Yes?"

"I asked if you had heard of the Calydonian boar." Mrs. Keely dabbed at her cheek with a napkin; she dabbed frequently during meals, even though there was nothing to dab at but a spotless creamy-white cheek. "This boar was a dreadful beast, very large and unpleasant. Many, many good people were upset by it. So one day the men of the town gathered together and said—"

"What town?" Mr. Keely asked. "There's some pretty big boars right outside Ozone."

"Don't interrupt. Anyway, there was a young lady, renowned as a top athlete—"

"Mother," Donna Lee said.

"She threw the javelin as far as—"

"Mother, you put sugar in the coleslaw."

"I forgot you were coming to dinner."

"But it's not just me. Think of Dad. He's overweight, he's got high blood pressure, and you feed him sugar."

"Oh, I'm so tired of sugar. That's all we ever talk about, sugar and chemicals."

"Look what time it is," Mr. Keely said, glancing up at the cuckoo clock over the sideboard. When she was eight years old, Donna Lee had stolen the cuckoo, then lost it, so that now only a silent stick of wood, its perch, heralded the hour. "They'll be here any minute."

"Who's they?" Donna Lee asked.

"Dad's Bible study class," Mrs. Keely said. "He's always volunteering our house."

"We rotate, dear," Mr. Keely said patiently. He scratched absently at a freckle on his broad face.

"Well, I don't understand why you can't rotate yourselves over to the church hall. That's what it's there for."

"Did you get any refreshments like I told you?"

"Last time they crumbed up my living room so bad," Mrs. Keely said to Donna Lee, pretending not to have heard him, "Moab and I never did get it back to normal. I kept on discovering little crumbs behind the cushions. Hey, Dad, where are you going?"

Mr. Keely, halfway out of his chair, sank back into it. "Dr. Henry's."

"Must you feed them?"

"Oh, Mother, I'll go." Donna Lee got up.

Her father handed her a few bills from his wallet. "Be sure and get enough. They like that blue-cheese dip. And get the king-size Fritos. Not the little ones. And plenty of root beer and 7-Up. Here, take another five, just in case."

"Finish this slaw for me," Mrs. Keely said to her husband, and then, as Donna Lee was going out of the dining room, she called out, "Don't be extravagant."

The door to the cuckoo clock opened, and the stick came out.

"Oh, look, Leon," Mrs. Keely said, peering out the bay window. "She's taking your bike, and it doesn't have a light."

Mr. Keely began humming again.

Donna Lee sat in the kitchen with her mother, who had her Edith Hamilton open on the oak table, while the men talked about the Bible in the next room. Donna Lee kept threatening to go in there and tell them what *she* thought of that Bible. "It really gets me, Mother. The ones who are the worst racists are always quoting the Bible."

Mrs. Keely highlighted a passage in her book with a yellow Marks-a-Lot.

"How Dad can associate with those people, I don't know."

Mrs. Keely looked up, her bright-blue eyes full of puzzlement. "I wonder, did Moab say she was going to buy some Top Job?" Moab came twice a week to help Mrs. Keely clean.

Suddenly the men in the living room burst into laughter.

"Probably just told a nigger joke," Donna Lee commented.

"Dear, please," her mother said with a pained expression.

"I saw Mrs. Jenks today. You know, that woman who writes for the paper."

"Oh, yes. I'm always running into her at the beauty parlor."

"Do you realize her poor handyman is starving to death? Right here in Tula Springs we've got someone starving to death. And she won't even sign him up for food stamps."

"Well, dear, you *know* what people buy with food stamps—the most expensive brands. Just the other day, at the A&P, the woman right in front of me had two bottles of Progresso olive oil. Progresso. Why, I wouldn't dream of anything but that unlabeled kind. It's such a blessing, all that no-brand food they have. They're in the white cans, Donna Lee."

"Mother, can you be real for a minute? This man must weigh only seventy, eighty pounds. It's too awful. I told Mrs. Jenks it was like Auschwitz."

"I hope you didn't." The freezer on the other side of the spotless kitchen began to clank; Mrs. Keely gave it a worried look. "That's not a very nice thing to say to someone. Poor Mrs. Jenks has to manage all by herself."

"Ha, that's a joke. She's got maids coming out of her ears, black women who should be going to college, not ironing a silly old woman's underwear."

The kitchen door swung open. Mr. Keely came in and started going through the cupboards over the sink he was allowed to use when he needed to scrub his hands after yard work. The other sink, newly done over in stainless steel, was off limits.

"What are you looking for?" Mrs. Keely asked.

"I thought we had some potato chips," he said vaguely, his back to them. "Cookies, anything."

"Really, Leon, after all the trouble Donna Lee went to," Mrs. Keely said, shaking her head. Donna Lee had decided the Bible class didn't need junk food, and brought back apples, carrots, and cauliflower instead.

"Dad, can I come listen in?" Donna Lee asked.

"You let your father be," Mrs. Keely said.

"Dad?"

With a dejected air Mr. Keely gave up the search. "What, honey? Well, sure."

"But it's a *men's* Bible class," Mrs. Keely objected. "It's time Donna Lee was on her way home. I can't get any studying done with her around."

"Ann, you know Donna Lee is welcome here anytime she wants, for as long as she wants. It's her house." He winked at his daughter. "You know your mother doesn't mean it."

"Foolishness," Mrs. Keely said, returning to her book.

"Dr. McFlug, I believe you know my daughter, Donna Lee." Donna Lee held out her hand to the old doctor, whose stiff, lusterless dyed brown hair, worn stylishly long, fooled people into thinking it was a wig. Tall and spindly, he didn't seem to realize what she intended until she grabbed his hand and gave it a firm, manly squeeze. The other men remained standing until Donna Lee pulled up the bench from the Mason & Hamlin baby grand and sat down. Next to her father on the oversize couch was Mr. Binwanger, Tula Springs's ex-mayor, and beside him, Mr. Dambar, the owner of the creosote plant out on the Old Jefferson Davis Highway. Squeezed into her mother's favorite wing chair was a fat, florid-faced man she had never met before who was introduced to her as Mr. Randy. In the Windsor chair sat his brother-in-law, Mr. Gaglioni, who didn't look very Baptist to Donna Lee.

"This is his first time," Mr. Randy said to her, jerking a thumb at his brother-in-law, who smiled weakly back at her. "He's my new assistant manager over at Sonny Boy. Want to help him mix and mingle. Say hello, Sal."

"Hello," the young man mouthed silently. He sat stiff as a board, his back not touching the chair.

"Gentlemen," Mr. Keely said after clearing his throat, "since we're all agreed you are an exceptionally bright, intelligent group of citizens, I'm sure you'll welcome the addition tonight of a pretty face," He gestured toward his daughter, who gave him a sour look. She had tried, tried very hard, but despite her best efforts, it seemed her father would never recover from the Dale Carnegie course he had taken thirty years ago.

"Dr. McFlug," Mr. Keely said, unfazed by his daughter's look, "I believe we were all enjoying your reading. Where did we leave off?"

The old doctor glared at his Bible and brought it up to within an inch of his face. " 'Moreover there were at my table an hundred and fifty of the Jews and rulers, beside those that came unto us from among the heathen that are about us. Now that which was prepared for me daily was one ox and six choice sheep; also fowls were prepared for me, and once in ten days store of all sorts of wine: yet for all this required not I the bread of the governor, because the bondage was heavy upon this people.' "

Donna Lee leaned forward on the bench, her eyes closed, listening hard. When Dr. McFlug paused to mop his brow with his handkerchief—he put a lot into his reading, each word sounding heavy as a brick—she raised her hand. "Did you say that this man ate a whole ox every day?" she asked.

"And some sheep and chickens," Dr. McFlug said.

"Well, no wonder he doesn't require the bread of the governor, not after all that. My God, who is this man?"

"Nehemiah," Dr. McFlug said, reaching for the apple juice Donna Lee had provided.

"Now, Donna Lee, the ox wasn't just for him," her father said with an anxious smile. "There were two hundred other people at his table."

"An hundred and fifty," Dr. McFlug corrected, then held up the book again. " 'Think upon me, my God, for good, according to all that I have done for this people.' "

"Some good," Donna Lee put in. "He takes the choice sheep and fowl and leaves everyone else the bread."

"I think you're missing the point," Dr. McFlug said calmly. "Nehemiah was engaged in building a wall at that time. He was a good governor."

"Would you think it good," Donna Lee persisted, "if Mr. Binwanger had taken all the meat from your table when he was mayor and left you nothing but bread?"

" 'Bread' probably means something else," Mr. Dambar said. He was a good-looking man who sometimes took Mr. Keely shrimping in Lake Pontchartrain. "At least in this passage 'bread' doesn't mean actual bread."

"Neither do I," Donna Lee said, smiling at Mr. Binwanger, who, having had his mind elsewhere for the past half hour, smiled back at her. Mr. Binwanger would probably be reelected mayor, mainly because of his law-and-order campaign. He promised to give Tula Springs a police force, although where he'd find the money for it, God only knew. Tula Springs couldn't even afford to get the sewer main fixed over on South Street where the live oak roots had busted through a culvert.

"Pardon me, Mr. Dambar," Dr. McFlug said coolly, professionally, "but I believe if Nehemiah said bread, he meant bread. We just can't go substituting words in Scripture, now, can we?"

"Correct," Donna Lee said, scooting the piano bench a little closer. "Either you believe what's written there, just like it says, or you don't. Either it's the word of God, or it isn't."

Dr. McFlug nodded solemnly while Mr. Keely opened his mouth to say something, then shut it. A vague, low hum stirred the air.

Mr. Randy's pudgy fingers strayed to the plate of raw cauliflower next to his chair, violating one of Mrs. Keely's edicts: If you touch it, you must eat it. Fiddling with the cauliflower, he said, "This is Pickens's fault. He was supposed to do Nehemiah this week, read up on it for us. And it's twice he's skipped out having us over to his house. Sal, *here,*" he concluded, handing his brother-in-law a handful of white flowerets.

"Mr. Gaglioni," Donna Lee said, "what do you think about the bread?"

His back still away from the chair, his mouth full of cauliflower, the young man looked with a pained expression at his brother-in-law. Mr. Randy scowled at him. "Don't ask Sal here nothing, Miss Keely," Mr. Randy said, rubbing a huge, bushy eyebrow with his knuckle. "He still hasn't caught on to the language too good."

"Oh, sorry," Donna Lee said, getting up. "Would everyone like more apple juice?"

"How about Dr Pepper?" Mr. Randy asked.

"I'm afraid all we have is apple juice."

"All right, I'll take some of that."

When Donna Lee returned from the kitchen, where she had a quick spat with her mother, who had been eavesdropping on the Bible class, Mr. Binwanger was explaining to Mr. Dambar the best way to skin a catfish: "You got the nail hammered in the tree, head high. Okay, next you hook the cat up there by its gill, right? Then slice just around the gills with your knife, grab off a piece of skin with your pliers, then yank down for all you're worth. Oh, thank you, hon," he said, taking a glass of juice from Donna Lee. "Best if you skin it while the bugger's still kicking."

"Gentlemen," Mr. Keely said, "I believe Dr. McFlug was saying something very intriguing."

Dr. McFlug took a gulp of the apple juice that Donna Lee had just set down in front of him, then another large gulp. "An ox divided into a hundred and fifty portions would probably be equal to about a pound of meat per man. I trust Miss Keely would not find this offensive, one pound per day, probably not much more than thirteen hundred calories.''

''Dr. McFlug,'' Donna Lee replied as he finished the apple juice in a few more gulps, ''since when do oxen weigh only a hundred and fifty pounds?''

''We aren't counting the head and legs and insides. Only the choice meat.''

''Let's say that's another hundred and fifty, the ox still weighs only three hundred pounds. I defy you to show me a three-hundred-pound ox. Plus there's all that sheep and fowl.''

''I think you're missing the point,'' Mr. Keely said.

''Dad, an ox weighs at least a thousand pounds, maybe even a ton.''

Mr. Keely leaned forward and took the bible from Dr. McFlug's lap. ''Here,'' he said, pointing a thick finger at the text. ''It says there were a hundred fifty Jews *'beside those that came unto us from among the heathen.'* So you see, Donna Lee, that could mean there were a thousand all together.''

''More, please,'' Mr. Gaglioni said to Donna Lee, holding out his empty glass.

''Sal,'' Mr. Randy reprimanded.

''Say, while you're up, maybe you could get me some more too,'' Dr. McFlug said. ''I'm parched.''

Donna Lee went back to the kitchen and while her mother wasn't looking poured a healthy dose of vodka into the two glasses, which she then filled with apple juice. When she had gone back to the kitchen earlier, she had decided to give Sal a little booze because she couldn't stand to see someone sitting so straight that his back wouldn't touch the chair. Then she had decided Dr. McFlug could use something to loosen him up too. The rest of the men, like good Baptists, got straight apple juice.

In the living room catfish had strayed into the conversation again. When Mr. Keely steered them back to Nehemiah, Mr. Binwanger sagged back against the sofa cushions with a glazed look in his eyes.

''Boy, where's your manners?'' Mr. Randy said as Mr. Gaglioni drained his glass in a few gulps.

Dr. McFlug looked sharply at Mr. Randy. After polishing off his third glass of apple juice Dr. McFlug began to sound like the Bible even when he wasn't reading. If God willed, he proclaimed to Donna Lee, an ox could weigh three hundred pounds.

''*Prego, signora.*'' Mr. Gaglioni held out his glass to her. She stood up and took his and Dr. McFlug's into the kitchen for refills.

When Donna Lee returned, the ox had shrunk from three hundred to fifty pounds, then one pound—if God willed. No one seemed too concerned with the one-pound ox except Mr. Keely, who had an odd look on his face as he strained to follow Dr. McFlug's inspired commentary.

When she saw that Mr. Gaglioni was slouching comfortably in his chair,

Donna Lee excused herself and went into the kitchen to say good night to her mother.

"Are they using the coasters I put out?" Mrs. Keely asked without looking up from her book.

"Bye, Mother," Donna Lee said from the door.

"They better not leave any rings on my furniture," she said as her daughter closed the door behind her.

PADGETT POWELL

Powell, who lives and teaches in Gainesville, Florida, was nominated for a National Book Award when his first novel, Edisto, *came out in 1984. Those who think they can sum up the average old white boy of the South by calling him a Bubba should read this story.*

"Typical"

Yesterday a few things happened. Every day a few do. My dog beat up another dog. He does this when he can. It's his living, more or less, though I've never let him make money doing it. He could. Beating up other dogs is his thing. He means no harm by it, expects other dogs to beat him up—no anxiety about it. If anything makes him nervous, it's that he won't get a chance to beat up or be beaten up. He's healthy. I don't think I am.

For one thing, after some dog-beating-up, I think I feel better than even the dog. It's an occasion calls for drinking. I have gotten a pain in the liver zone, which it is supposed to be impossible to feel it. My doctor won't say I can't feel anything, outright, but he does say *he* can't feel anything. He figures I'll feel myself into quitting if he doesn't say I'm nuts. Not that I see any reason he'd particularly cry if I drank myself into the laundry bag.

I drank so much once, came home, announced to my wife it was high time I went out, got me a black woman. A friend of mine, well before this, got in the laundry bag and suddenly screamed at his wife to keep away from him because she had *turned* black, but I don't think there's a connection. I just told mine I was heading for some black women pronto, and I knew where the best ones were, they were clearly in Beaumont. The next day she was not speaking, little rough on pots and pans, so I had to begin the drunk-detective game and open the box of bad breath no drunk ever wants to open. That let out the black women of Beaumont, who were not so attractive in the shaky light of day with your wife standing there pink-eyed holding her lips still with little inside bites. I sympathized fully with her, fully.

I'm not nice, not too smart, don't see too much point in pretending to be either. Why I am telling anyone this trash is a good question, and it's stuff it obviously doesn't need me to tell myself. Hell, I know it, it's mine. It would be like the retired justice of the peace that married me and my wife.

We took a witness which it turned out we didn't need him, all a retired JP needs to marry is a twenty-dollar tip, and he'd gotten two thousand of those tips in his twenty years retired, cash. Anyway, he came to the part asks did anyone present object to our holy union please speak up now or forever shut up, looked up at the useless witness, said, "Well, hell, he's the only one here, and *y'all* brought him, so let's get on with it." Which we did.

This was in Sealy, Texas. We crossed the town square, my wife feeling very married, proper and weepy, not knowing yet I was the kind to talk of shagging black whores, and we went into a nice bar with a marble bartop and good stools and geezers at dominoes in the back, and we drank all afternoon on one ten-dollar bill from large frozen goblet-steins of some lousy Texas beer we're supposed to be so proud of and this once it wasn't actually terribly bad beer. There was our bouquet of flowers on the bar and my wife was in a dressy dress and looked younger and more innocent than she really was. The flowers were yellow, as I recall, the marble white with a blue vein, and her dress a light, flowery blue. Light was coming into the bar from high transomlike windows making glary edges and silhouettes—the pool players were on fire, but the table was a black hole. All the stuff in the air was visible, smoke and dust and tiny webs. The brass nails in the old floor looked like stars. And the beer was 50¢. What else? It was pretty.

She's not so innocent as it looked that day because she had a husband for about ten years who basically wouldn't sleep with her. That tends to reduce innocence about marriage. So she was game for a higher stepper like me, but maybe thinks about the cold frying pan she quit when I volunteer to liberate the dark women of the world.

I probably mean no harm, to her or to black women, probably am like my dog, nervous I won't get *the chance*. I might fold up at the first shot. I regret knowing I'll never have a date with Candice Bergen, this is in the same line of thought. Candice Bergen is my pick for the most good to look at and probably kiss and maybe all-you-could-do woman in the world. All fools have their whims. Should an ordinary, daily kind of regular person carry around desire like this? Why do people do this? Of course a lot of money is made on fools with pinups in the backs of their head, but why do we continue to buy? We'd be better off with movie stars what look like the girls from high school that had to have sex to get any attention at all. You put Juicy Lucy Spoonts on the silver screen and everybody'd be happy to go home to his faithful, hopeful wife. I don't know what they do in Russia, on film, but if the street women are any clue, they're on to a way of reducing foolish desire. They look like good soup-makers, and no head problems, but they look like potatoes, I'm sorry. They've done something over there that prevents a common man from wanting the women of Beaumont.

There are many mysteries in this world. I should be a better person, I know I should, but I don't see that finally being up to choice. If it were, I would not stop at being a better person. Who would? The girls what could not get dates in high school, for example, are my kind of people now, but *then* they weren't. I was like everybody else.

I thought I was the first piece of sliced bread to come wrapped in plastic then. Who didn't. To me it is really comical, how people come to realize they are really a piece of shit. More or less. Not everybody's the Candy Man or a dog poisoner. I don't mean that. But a whole lot of folk who once thought otherwise of themself come to see they're just not that hot. That is something to think on, if you ask me, but you don't, and you shouldn't, which it proves my point. I'm a fellow discovers he's nearly worth disappearing without a difference to anyone or anything, no one to be listened to, trying to say that not being worth being listened to is the discovery we make in our life that then immediately, sort of, ends the life and its feedbag of self-serious and importance.

I used to think niggers were the worst. First they were loud as Zulus at bus stations and their own bars, and then they started walking around with radio stations with jive jamming up the entire air. Then I realized you get the same who-the-hell-asked-for-it noise off half, more than half, the white fools everywhere you are. Go to the ice house: noise. Rodeo: Jesus. Had to quit football games. There's a million hot shots in this world wearing shorts and loud socks won't take no for an answer.

And un*like* high school, you can't make them go home, quit coming. You can't make them quit playing life. I'd like to put up a cut-list on the locker-room door to the world itself. Don't suit up today, the following:

And I'm saying I'd be in the cut myself. Check your pads in, sell your shoes if you haven't fucked them up. I did get cut once, and a nigger who was going to play for UT down the road wouldn't buy my shoes because he said they stank—a nigger now. He was goddamned right about the toe jam which a pint of foo-foo water had made worse, but the hair on his ass to say something like that to me. I must say he was nice about it, and I'm kind of proud to tell it was Earl Campbell wouldn't wear a stink shoe off me.

Hell, just take what I'm saying right here in that deal. *I'm* better than a nigger who breaks all the rushing records they had at UT twice and then pro records and on bad teams, when I get *cut* from a bad team that names itself after a tree. Or something, I've forgotten. We might have been the Tyler Rosebuds. That's the lunacy I'm saying. People have to *wake up*. Some do. Some don't. I have: I'm nobody. A many hasn't. Go to the ice house and hold your ears.

This is not that important. It just surprised me when I came to it, is all. You're a boob, a boob for life, I realized one day. Oh, I got Stetsons, a Silverado doolie, ten years at ARMCO, played poker with Mickey Gilley, shit, and my girlfriends I don't keep in a little black book but on candy wrappers flying around loose in the truck. One flies out, so what? More candy, more wrappers at the store. But one day, for no reason, or no reason I know it or can remember anything happening which it meant anything, I stopped at what I was doing and said, John Payne, you are a piece of crud. You are a common, long-term drut. *Look* at it.

It's not like this upset me or anything, why would it? It's part of the truth to what I'm saying. You can't disturb a nobody with evidence he's a nobody. A nobody is not disturbed by anything significant. It's like trying to disturb a bum by yelling *poor fuck* at him. What's new? he says. So when I said, John Payne, you final asshole, I just kept on riding. But the moment stuck. I began watching myself. I watched and proved I was an asshole.

This does not give you a really good feeling, unless you are drunk, which is when you do a good part of the proving.

I've been seeing things out of the corners of my eyes and feeling like I have worms since this piece-of-crud thing. It works like this. I'm in a ice house out Almeda, about to Alvin in fact, and I see this pretty cowboy type must work for Nolan Ryan's ranch or something start to come up to me to ask for a light. That's what I *would* have seen, before. But now it works like this: before he gets to me, before he even starts coming over, see, because I'm legged up in a strange bar thinking I'm a piece of shit and a out-of-work beer at three in the afternoon in a dump in Alvin it proves it, I see out the corner of my eye this guy put his hand in his pants and give a little wink to his buddies as he starts to come over. That's enough, whatever it means, he may think I'm a fag, or he may be one himself, but he thinks you're enough a piece of shit he can touch his dick and wink about you, only he don't know that he is winking about a known piece of shit, and winking about a known piece of shit is a dangerous thing to do.

Using the mirror over the bar about like Annie Oakley shooting backwards,

I spot his head and turn and slap him in the temple hard enough to get the paint to fall off a fender. He goes down. His buddies start to push back their chairs and I step one step up and they stop.

"What's all the dick and grinning about, boys?"

On the floor says, "I cain't *see.*"

"He cain't see," I tell the boys.

I walk out.

Outside it's some kind of dream. There's ten Hell's Angel things running around a pickup in the highway like a Chinese fire drill, whatever that is. In the middle by the truck is a by-God muscle man out of Charles Atlas swinging chains. He's whipping the bikers with their own motorcycle chains. He's got all of the leather hogs bent over and whining where he's stung them. He picks up a bike and drops it headfirst on the rakes. Standing there with a hot Bud, the only guy other than Tarzan not bent over and crying, I get the feeling we're some kind of tag team. I drive off.

That's how it works. Start out a piece of shit, slap some queerbait blind, watch a wrestling match in the middle of Almeda Road, drive home a piece of shit, spill the hot beer I forgot about all over the seat and my leg.

I didn't always feel this way, who could afford to? When I was fifteen, my uncle, who was always kind of my real dad, gave me brand-new Stetson boots and a hundred-dollar bill on a street corner in Galveston and said spend it all and spend it all on whores. It was my birthday. I remember being afraid of the black whores and the ones with big tits, black or white, otherwise I was an ace. In those days a hundred dollars went a long way with ladies in Galveston. I got home very tired, a fifteen-year-old *king* with new boots and a wet dick.

That's what you do with the world before you doubt yourself. You buy it, dress up in it, fuck it. Then, somehow, it starts fucking back. A Galveston whore you'd touch now costs the whole hundred dollars, for example, in other words. I don't know. Today I would rather just *talk* to a girl on the street than fuck one, and I damn sure don't want to talk to one. There's no point. I need some kind of pills or something. There must be ways which it will get you out of feeling like this.

For a while I thought about having a baby. But Brillo Tucker thought this up about fifteen years ago, and two years ago his boy whips his ass. When I heard about that I refigured. I don't need a boy whipping my ass, mine or anybody else's. That would just about bind the tit. And they'll do that, you know, because like I say they come out *kings* for a while. Then the crown slips and pretty soon the king can't get a opera ticket, or something, I don't know anything about kings.

This reminds me of playing poker with Mickey Gilley, stud. First he brings ten times as much money as anyone, sits down in new boots, creaking, and hums all his hit songs so nobody can think. He wins a hand, which it is rare, and makes this touchdown kind of move and comes down slowly and rakes the pot to his little pile. During the touchdown, we all look at this dry-cleaning tag stapled to the armpit of his vest. That's the Pasadena crooner.

I was at ARMCO Steel for ten years, the largest integrated steel mill west of the Mississippi, a word we use having nothing to do with niggers for once. It means we could take ore and make it all the way to steel. Good steel. However, I admit that with everybody standing around eating candy bars in their new Levi's, it cost more than Jap steel. I have never seen a Japanese eating a candy bar or dipping Skoal showing off his clothes. They wear lab coats, like they're all dentists. We weren't dentists.

We were, by 1980, out of a job, is what we were. It goes without saying it, that is life. They were some old timers that just moped about it, and some middle-lifer types that had new jobs in seconds, and then us Young Turks that moped *mad*. We'd filler up and drive around all day bitching about the capitalist system, whatever that is, and counting ice houses. We discovered new things, like Foosball. Foosball was one of the big discoveries. Pool we knew about, shuffleboard we knew about, Star Wars pinball we knew about, but Foosball was a kick.

For a while we bitched as a club. We were on the ice-house frontier, Tent City bums with trucks. Then a truckload of us—not me, but come to think of it, Brillo Tucker was with them, which is perfect—get in it on the Southwest Freeway with a truckload of niggers and they all pull over outside the *Post* building and the niggers whip their *ass*. They're masons or something, plumbers. A photographer at the *Post* sees it all and takes pictures. The next day a thousand ARMCO steel workers out of a job read about themselves whipped by employed niggers on the freeway. This lowered our sail. We got to be less of a club, quick. I don't know what any of my buddies are doing now and I don't care. ARMCO was ARMCO. It was along about in here I told my wife I was off to Beaumont for black chicks, and there could be a connection, but I doubt it.

As far as I can really tell, I'm still scared of them in the plain light of day. At a red light on Jensen Drive one day, a big one in a fur coat says to me, "Come here, sugar, I got something for you," and opens her coat on a pair of purple hot pants and a yellow bra.

I say, "I know you do," and step on it. Why in hell I'd go home and pick on a perfectly innocent wife about it is the kind of evidence it convinces you you're not a prince in life.

Another guy I knew in the ARMCO club had a brother who *was* a dentist, and this guy tells him not to worry about losing his job, to come out with him golfing on Thursdays and *relax*. Our guy starts going—can't remember his name—and he can't hit the ball for shit. It's out of bounds or it's still on the tee. And the dentist who wants him to relax starts ribbing him, until our guy says if you don't shut the fuck up I'm going to put this ball down and aim it at *you.* The dentist laughs. So Warren—that's his name—puts the ball down and aims at the dentist, who's standing there like William Tell giggling, and swings and hits his brother, the laughing dentist who wants him to relax, square in the forehead. End of relaxing golf.

Another guy's brother, a yacht broker, whatever that is, became a flat hero when we got laid off because he found his brother the steel worker in the shower with his shotgun and took it away from him. Which it wasn't hard to do it, because he'd been drinking four days and it wasn't loaded.

Come to look at it, we all sort of disappeared and all these Samaritans with jobs creamed to the top and took the headlines, except for the freeway. The whole world loves a job holder.

One day I drove out to the Highway 90 bridge over the San Jacinto and visited Tent City, which was a bunch of pure bums pretending to be unfortunate. There were honest-to-God river rats down there, never lived anywhere but on a river in a tent, claiming to be victims of the economy. They had elected themselves a mayor, who it turns out the day I got there was up for re-election. But he wasn't going to run again because God had called him to a higher cause, preaching. He announced this with shaking hands and wearing white shoes and a white belt and a maroon leisure suit. Out the back of his tent was a pyramid of beer cans all the way to the river, looked like a mud slide in Colombia. People took me around because they thought I was out there to *hire* someone.

I met the new mayor-to-be, who was a Yankee down here on some scam that busted, had left a lifelong position in dry cleaning, had a wife who swept their little camp to where it was smoother and cleaner than concrete. I told him to call Mickey Gilley. He was a nice guy, they both were, makes you think a little more softly about the joint. How a white woman from Michigan, I think, knew how to sweep dirt like a Indian I'll never know. Maybe it's natural. I don't think it's typical, though.

This one dude, older dude, they called Mr. C, was walking around asking everybody if this stick of wood he was carrying belonged to them. He had this giant blue and orange thing coming off his nose, about *like* an orange, which it is why they called him Mr. C, I guess. A kid who was very pretty, built well—could of made a fortune in Montrose—ran to him with a bigger log and took him by the arm all the way back to his spot, some hanging builder's plastic and a chair, and set a fire for him. It's corny as hell, but I started liking the place. It was like a pilgrim place for pieces of shit, pieces of crud.

Then a couple gets me, tells me their life story if I'll drink instant coffee with them. The guy rescued the girl from some kind of mess in Arkansas that makes Tent City look like Paradise. He's about six-eight with mostly black teeth and sideburns growing into his mouth, and she's about four foot flat with a nice ass and all I can think of is how can they fuck and why would she let him. For some reason I asked him if he played basketball, and the *girl* pipes up, *"I played basketball."*

"Where?"

"In high school."

"Then what did you do?" I meant by this, how is it Yardog here has you and I don't.

"Nothing," she says.

"What do you mean, nothing?"

"I ain't done *nuttin.*" That's the way she said it, too.

It was okay by me, but if she had fucked somebody other than the buzzard, it would have been *something.*

I was just kind of cruising there at this point, about like leg-up in Alvin, ready to buy them all a case of beer and talk about hard luck the way they wanted to, when something happened. This gleaming, purring, fully restored, *immaculate* as Brillo Tucker would say, '57 Chevy two-door pulls in and eases around Tent City and up to us, and out from behind the mirrored windshield, wearing sunglasses to match it, steps this nigger who was a kind of shiny, shoe-polish brown, and *exact* color and finish of the car. The next thing you saw was that his hair was black and oily and so were the black sidewalls of his car. Everything had dressing on it.

The nigger comes up all smiles and takes cards out of a special little pocket in his same brown suit as the car and himself. The card says something about community development.

"I am prepared to offer all of you, if we have enough, a seminar in job-skills acquisition and full-employment methodology." This comes out of the gleaming nigger beside his purring '57 Chevy.

The girl with the nice butt who's done nothing but fuck a turkey vulture says, "Do what?"

Then the nigger starts on a roll about the seminar, about the only thing which in it people can catch is it will take six hours. That is longer than most of these people want to *hold* a job, including me at this point. I want to steal his car.

"Six hours?" the girl repeats. "For *what?*"

"Well, there are a lot of tricks to getting a job."

I say, "Like what?"

"Well, like shaking hands."

"Shaking hands." I remember Earl Campbell not buying my stinky shoes. That was okay. This is too far.

"Do you know how to shake hands?" the gleaming nigger asks. Out of the corner of my eye I see the turkey buzzard looking at his girl with a look that is like they're in high school and in love.

"Let's find out," I say. I grab him and crush him one, he winces.

"You know how to shake hands."

"I thought I did."

Who the fuck taught *him* how? Maybe Lyndon Johnson.

He purrs off to find a hall for the seminar, and the group at Tent City proposes putting a gas cylinder in the river and shooting it with a .22.

I've got my own brother to contend with, but we got over it a long time ago. He was long gone when ARMCO troubles let everybody else's brother loose on them. He, my brother, goes off to college, which I don't, which it pissed me off at the time, but not so much now. Anyway, he goes off and comes back with half-ass long hair talking *Russian.* Saying, *Goveryou po rooskie* in my face. It's about the time Earl Campbell has told me he won't wear my cleats because they stink, so I take all my brother's college crap laying down.

Then he says, "I study Russian with an old woman who escaped the Revolution with nothing. There's only one person in the class, so we meet at her house. Actually, we meet in her back yard, in a hole."

"You what?"

"We sit in a hole she dug and study Russian. All I lack being Dostoevsky's underground man is more time." He laughed.

"All I lack being a gigolo," I said, "is having a twelve-inch dick." And hit him, which is why he doesn't talk to me today, and I don't care. If he found out I was in the shower with my shotgun he'd pass in a box of shells. Underground man. What a piece of shit.

That's about it. Thinking of my brother, now, I don't feel so hot about running at the mouth. I'm not feeling so hot about living, so what? What call is it to drill people in their ear? I'm typical.

ROY BLOUNT, JR.

Back during the Carter administration I wrote a book called Crackers *about how strange it seemed to me, a Georgian, for the leader of the Free World to be from that*

state. Not that it seemed strange to me in the same way that it did to a lot of wise
guys from other states. I spent some time with Billy and Miss Lillian and enjoyed
hearing about all the other Carter relatives, but at length I thought it was time for
new ones, so I made some up.

"More Carters"

Velveeta Carter, 36, Bird Swale, Tennessee. "Wail, there's no dat abat it,
we're jis trash. Not mean hateful trash, jis people that don't amant to a whole
lot. My daddy caint read, my momma don't wash, my brothers just kind of
stand arand and say things lack 'shithook' to each other and peek at me in the
bathroom and spit down between their feet till it forms a pool. And, wail, as
far as me, wail, I had a Mexican baby. I don't know *how,* in this *world,* but I did.

"There he is over there chewing on the fly swatter! Jaime, quit that! Give
that to Momma. That child, I declare, I don't know. That's the filthiest thang
in this *house* he could chew on. Jaime, you ain't being raised to chew on no fly
swat!

"But he's a precious little thang and I love him to death and I don't see
where people got the right to look down on us and all. Daddy always taught
us, one thing is—we may not have much but we're good as anybody. We've
got prad, and we've got roots—course I'm the first generation ever to run
into a crad of Mexicans. But my daddy's people been right here since years and
years and years. Course, too, they didn't have nowhere to go.

"And now ar distant relative there is the President. It jis seems lack a
dream. Didn't you lack it when he told that story down in Mexico abat
Monterzumer's Revenge? Lord, we laughed. We was prad that he knew
enough histry to know abat a Mexican king. Must've learned that in the Navy.
I wouldn't've known *what* to say. I would've sho Lord lacked to go down
there with him though."

O. S. "Giblet" Carter, 39, who helps out around Hub and Dr. Bob Span-
gler's fireworks, stuffed baby alligator gifts, and country ham stand on Route
108 out here half a mile or so the other side of Fermit, Georgia, and is only
about eighteen inches tall.

"Hooo, I tell folks I'm exactly the highth of one of Jimmy's ties, you know,
I mean the part down below the neck when it's tied. Rilly though I'm prolly a
little longer. Unless he wears a tie real long. I don't know. Jimmy come in the
place back in '66 when he was arunning for governor. Hoo, yeah. I jumped up
and said, 'Heeyyyo, Jimmy, you know weuz *related?*' He said why fine and kep

looking around for where my voice was coming fum, thought it was just a *pup*pet or somewhat of that order, I 'magine. Folks'll do that when they ain't been around me long.

"M'little feet are s'small, law-dee. Why I can stand on a carrot. Could use me for Jimmy on the TV a lot, when they're in the close-ups. I'm about his size on the average person's screen, and you know with a small man, there's not the distortion as when you're trying to bring somebody large way down to fit the picture. And you know there's a favorance. You mighta thought I *was* Jimmy at a distance or something, wouldn't you? I can sound like him, too. Can't I do Jimmy—hey, Dr. Bob, can't I . . . ?"

"Git down off 'at table, Giblet, and run 'em mice. Like I tode you, now."

A. Don and E. Don Carter, 39, who are the "Two-Headed Four-Armed Three-Legged Gospel-Singing Man" in a traveling show throughout most parts of the country.

"Aw, we ham't seen a sign of Jimmy since the big family union back in '48. I don't think Jimmy's too innersted in us. I say that 'cause, well, it's sorta cool between us. E. Don voted against him."

"I did not neither, A. Don."

"Well, yes, you sure as the H-word did. I tried to tell you, it can't hurt us in the bookings, having kin in the White House. Thought he might summon us on up to appear. Kindly showcase us. Done us a world of good nationally."

"Well, I just liked Mr. Ford."

"Uh-huh, you liked him. I know. E. Don, he votes the man. But this time it wadn't *professional,* E. Don. We got to think of our*sef* sometime. Hear?

"And I tell you what else. I guarantee you—you think old Gerald R. Ford cares two diddlies whether you like him or not? Well? H'm? E. Don?

"I swanny, E. Don, sometimes getting something through to you is like . . . I don't know what."

Sister Muriel Oriola Carter, 50, Far Caverns, Georgia, who speaks in tongues. "I'm not saying it's Jesus; it's not all necessarily the Lord. It could be my momma way back off up in there deep down inside of my sinus—*and* God cherubim seraphim owls powers roots imps dominions. Jigljigljiglj. WOMPH. *Wee sleekit.* I'm the Church of *Poly*glossolalia. *Woo* nawny nawny nawny, h'*Wew* nawny nawnym'narsenal. *Weeee*-geriblerablet.

"*Nawnk nawnk* Molybd'num. K'cockerophylogeno-rogerobomplet. Arbiofi. Toombes. Geriblet. Hootin' Newton nicens tuckoo wotheth bloom me Belchum Yaw Yaw.

"It goes way back. It comes way out. The *door's* on the tip of your tongue. Alveralvry. Phlempopocantata-p'tetre-p'tetl. Jimmy ain't opened it. Jimmy ain't opened it. *Yet.* Not in his *public* utterance. Geriblerablet. Wooo, m'wooom: *sleekit.*

"I tell you this, Buddy-Roe. Women likes it, at certain times, and so does babies."

Chinquapin Carter, 40, Cope, Alabama, whose profession is visions. "Wull *yeah* it's a good living. It *deserves* to be, don't it? Where you going to get that kind of work done today? What does a lawyer do for people, and he gets a *gooood* dollar. He'll probly make better'n I do.

"I might of studied for a lawyer if I knew what I know now.

"How I usually work it, well, people get word to me, you know, and I pull on this whole chicken skin on over my head and look out thoo his little leg holes and move into their attic for a week, ten days, and have the visions that's backed up in there awaiting the adept. Certain number of fat oxens eating certain number of skinny oxens, or young people getting preternaturally wrinkled, or gret huge certain-colored birds across the Milky Way, whatever.

"Haven't been to the White House yet, no. I'd be tickled to—I think I could clear up some things been *bothering* people.

"So, anyway, I'll have a vision for you, give you an idea. Couldn't have a full one on this short of a notice but let's see, well, there's a bear with a flaming head and feet running thoo a bus station, only the bus station is, it's sort of got a funny *tone* to it, it makes this kinda hum, kinda *woooooonnnn . . .*"

Sartrain Lolley Carter, 43, Whack, North Carolina, who is writing a book entitled *A Southerner's Account.* "I know what you're saying. You're saying, Lord help us, another book on the South. But this is the first one *I've* written. Look at it from that point of view.

"I tell you the truth, a lot of these other books, I haven't even read them. *The Mind of the South.* Boy, I tell you. *The Mind of the South.* People will take and just *write a book* about something, won't they?

"Where are you from? Say you're from Illinois. How would you like to read a book, *The Mind of Illinois?*

"Actually I did skim through Cobb and Ringling Fry's book they put out here lately, *The Looks Southern People Get on Their Faces.* But you know, it don't come off anywhere near as well in print as it does when Cobb and Ringling *tell* it, where they can demonstrate the expressions live. Cobb can do forty or fifty 'Pissed Offs' alone. He gets to doing them one after another till—well, one time Ringling broke in on him and said, 'Quit it, Cobb, and gimme a chance to do some "While Hummings" or some "Wondering About Somethings" '; and you should have seen the one Cobb gave him then. Ringling has just about completely given up on cutting in on Cobb when he gets going.

"I don't read books about the South, but I read *Southern books.* Hoooo, people cutting one another with scythes, stealing one another's wooden legs, setting fires, making tarbabies out of one another. I listen to Southern music, but I don't listen to music about the South. See. Matter of fact, I think the Frys entitled their book *The Looks People Get on Their Faces,* and it was the publisher that stuck in the *Southern.*

"I think mostly what I'll write about is women out in the woods nekkid. I never have run into any out there yet, but I've got an idea what it'd be like."

Reverend Dulcent Carter, 43, West Weaver, Indiana. "I believe if there is any way wherein that I perhaps share a leadership quality with that of my relative in the Highest Office, it is in the area of achieving consensus. I am, I believe I can say, a man who can pull a broad spectrum of people's thinking together on an issue. When, for example, I learned on arrival at this pulpit that my predecessor here at First Church, Dr. M. Elmond Whisnant, was suspected of walking out of Wednesday Night Family Fellowship Supper every week with there packed in between his skin and sport shirt sometimes as many as five dozen of Mrs. Hoopy's, our cook here for many years, so wonderful light but butter-rich rolls, I was able to reach and ease and settle and reconcile I would say at least 85 percent of the hearts of our congregation with this way of looking at it: It was sure a shame if he was doing it, and if he wasn't, well, it was sure a shame that anyone would think that he was."

Freeman Carter, 28, Philadelphia, black fugitive. "Well I ain't telling you the whole thing of it 'cause it's family. Anyway nobody ever told me the *whole* thing of it. What I heard, doctor looked at me when I arrived, you know, said '*Uh*-oh.'

"But evybody was real nice, you know the Carters, we was ahead of most folks in the area. Yeah, when I was little, 'bout two or three days old, they sent me on out to Wyomin', that was cool, I could understand that.

"Didn't fit *in* Wyomin' was all. So I run off and come on here to Philly. Kinda lost touch with most of the famly, you know I didn't have no *addresses* for 'em and I wadn't but five. Fell in with some arm robbery, man. Shot a man three times and hit 'im wif a jack hannle, twice. And a great big old man, too. And that was on the *way* to the liquor store. Got nine years in the joint.

"Didn't fit in there either, too well. So I got me a job in the prison bakery, man, baked myself into a twenty-foot pan of cornbread they was making in there for the Cornbread Fest of a nearby town, see, was the Cornbread Capital of the World for that area. 'Cept I couldn't find no way to get out you know until the *ceremony,* man, mayor getting ready to cut it you know and I come busting out of there, people screaming and crying and cornbread evywhere and I was *gone,* Jackson.

"I felt bad about the cornbread and all, it was a community relations projeck, you know, but *what you want me to do?* See, an nen I couldn't really help Jimmy much in the campaign, see, 'cause, you know, I was *wanted.*

"Ony thing of it is, I'd like to get somese endorsements. I'd endorse a little wine. . . .

"But thing is, lot of people be into things that ain't got *brands,* see what I'm saying?

"But that's cool, that's cool.

"I sing, man.

"I'm the ony person I know whooo's
Fum Wyomin' and got the blues.

"Yeah, heh. Yeah, said '*Uh*-oh.' "

SECTION TWO

HERE BE DRAGONS, OR HOW COME THESE BUTTERBEANS HAVE AN ALLIGATOR TASTE?

The Old Hen Cackled

De ole hen she cackled,
An' stayed down in de bo'n.
She git fat an' sassy,
A eatin' up de co'n.
De ole hen she cackled,
Got long yaller laigs.
She swaller down de oats,
But I don't git no aigs.
De ole hen she cackled,
She cackled in de lot,
De nex' time she cackled,
She cackled in de pot.

—Anonymous

JERRY CLOWER

Yazoo City, Mississippi,'s Jerry Clower, former fertilizer salesman turned country comedian, once lost a chain saw commercial because, he explained modestly, "I overwhelmed the saw." He can make the sound—incidental to one of his stories—of a chain saw cutting through a screen door, and his speeches gain considerably also from the way he flings his 270 pounds into them. But I was sure that his best stories would stand up without him on the page. Just as I had confirmed that belief by painstakingly transcribing several of them from his albums, he came out with a book of them, Stories from Home. *I'm not complaining. I spent a good deal of time with Jerry back in 1973, to do a story about him for* Sports Illustrated. *One thing he told me was: "I've seen William Faulkner sittin' talkin' to the reddest of rednecks. I don't know of no country store in Lafayette County he couldn't sit down on a nail keg in front of and whittle. With that little old brown hat on, look like he'd fought a wasp's nest with it. . . ." In the late '60s and early '70s, Clower risked antagonizing a good part of his audience by coming out aggressively for the desegregated public schools as opposed to lily-white Christian academies. When he continued to shop with a white grocer friend of his who belonged to the NAACP and who therefore was patronized by blacks when they boycotted other white Yazoo City businesses in 1969, Clower was denounced by some of his white neighbors. He told one of them, "Go ahead. Call Walter Cronkite on the telephone. And as I come out of the front door, shoot me. And let Walter focus that camera on the blood and say, 'War veteran, father of four, shot down in a free country trying to buy groceries at the store of his choice.'" He doesn't get into politics in his act, but he does make a point of not imitating black voices. When a man came up to tell him how much he enjoyed the story "about the lynx getting ahold of that nigger up in the tree," Clower replied, "What do you mean? John Eubanks was my cousin." Actually, the model for John up in the tree was black, but he wasn't a whole lot poorer than Jerry was when he was growing up and gathering his richest material.*

"A Coon Huntin' Story"

Where I come from—Route 4, Liberty, Mississippi—is twelve miles west of McComb, Mississippi, sixty-five miles due northeast of Baton Rouge, Louisiana, and 116 miles due north of New Orleans, Louisiana. It was there that I first saw the light of day in Amite County, September 28, 1926. Now, as I grew up in that community the only extracurricular activities that we engaged in was to go coon huntin' or to revival meeting if we had our crop laid by. And that's all we did except work.

This particular time that I want to tell you about is one evening when we were going coon huntin'. We had a pack of hounds. When we went to the mill to get our corn ground up, we'd get some ground up for dog bread, and we'd get some ground for just regular cornmeal for human consumption. This particular day we weren't too busy. All we'd done was just cut down a few fence rows, shucked and shelled some corn, went to mill, drew up some water because that was wash day, helped get the sow back what rooted out from under the netwire fence, sharpened two sticks of stove wood real sharp and pegged them down over the bottom wire of the fence where the hogs couldn't root out no more, and had a rat killing. If I'm lying, I'm dying!

Well, this particular day after we got through with the rat killin', I walked out on the front porch and I hollered, "Hooooo, oooooo," and them dogs come out from under the house barking. They knew we was going coon huntin'. I hollered again and my neighbor, way across the sage patch, hollered back. That meant "I'll meet you halfway."

We met in the middle of that sage patch and he had his dogs, Ole Brummy, Queen, and Spot. I had Tory, Little Red, and Ole Trailer. We went down into the swamp and we started hunting. Oh, we was having such a fine time. Caught four great biguns. Then I heard a racket and it scared me, and I whipped my carbide light, what I had wired to my cap, around there, and I was looking in the vicinity of where I heard the racket coming from. The beam of light hit a man right in the face, and it likened to have scared me slap to death because we was hunting on this man's place.

I said, "Mr. Barron, is that you?"

He said, "Yes, Jerry. What are y'all doing?"

"We hunting."

"How many y'all caught?"

"Four great biguns."

He said, "Well, boys, I'm glad to see you. Y'all want to spend the rest of the evening hunting with me and John?"

Well, I looked and lo and behold there was John Eubanks, a man who lived on Mr. Barron's place. John Eubanks was a great American; he was a professional tree climber. He didn't believe (I'm telling you the truth) in shooting no coon out of no tree. It was against his upbringing. He taught us from birth, the day we were born, till the age we would keep listening to him, "Give everything a sporting chance. Whatever you do, give it a sporting chance." He'd been a great conservationist today, if he were here.

John said, "Take a crosscut saw coon hunting with you. When you tree a coon, hold the dog and cut the tree down, or either climb the tree and make the coon jump in amongst the dogs. Give him a sporting chance." A lot of times we'd climb a tree and make a coon jump in amongst twenty dogs, but at least he had the option of whipping all them dogs and walking off if he wanted to. This was strictly left up to the coon.

So I said, "Mr. Barron, we'd be glad to go huntin' with you."

You know, he was a rich man. He had sold a lot of cotton during the First World War for a dollar a pound. He had some world-renowned dogs, and we hollered three or four times and they started hunting. We listened, and Ole Brummy—Ole Brummy didn't bark at nothing but a coon—had a deep voice, and when he cut down on him, it was a coon. Don't worry about no possum or no bobcats, Brummy was running a coon. Ole Trailer, and Ole Highball, and them famous dogs of Mr. Barron's kept right in there with them. And Ole John Eubanks would holler, "Hooooo! Speak to him!"

And my brother, Sonny, hollered, "Hoooo, look for him!"

Oh, it was beautiful! Now y'all get this picture. About that time they treed. We rushed down into the swamp, and there the dogs were, treed up the biggest sweet gum tree in all of the Amite River swamps. It was huge—you couldn't reach around this tree. There wasn't a limb on it for awhile. It was way up there. Huge tree.

I looked around at John, and I said, "John, I don't believe you can climb that tree."

And it hurt John's feelings. He pooched his lips out, got fighting mad. He said, "There ain't a tree in all these swamps that I can't climb."

He got his brogan shoes off and he eased up to that sweet gum tree. He hung his toenails in that bark, and he got his fingernails in there, and he kept easing up the tree, working his way to that bottom limb, and he finally got to it, and he started on up into this big tree.

"Knock him out, John-n-n!"

It won't be long! And John worked his way on up to the top of the tree. Whoo-oo! What a bigun! He reached around in his overalls and got that sharp stick and he drawed back and he punched the coon. But it wasn't a coon—it was a lynx! We called 'em "souped-up wildcats" in Amite County. That thing had great big tusks coming out of his mouth, and great big claws on the end of his feet; and people, that thing attacked John up in the top of that tree.

"Whaw! Ooooo!" You could hear John squalling.

"What's the matter with John?"

"I don't have no idea what in the world's happening to John!"

"Knock him out, John-n-n!"

"What in the world's happening to John?"

"Knock him out, John-n-n!"

"WOW! OOOO! This thing's killing me!"

The whole top of the tree was shaking. The dogs got to biting the bark of the tree and fighting one another underneath the tree, and I kicked 'em and said, "You dogs get away!"

"What's the matter with John?"

"Knock him out, John-n-n!"

"Yow-owooo! This thing's killing me!"

John knew that Mr. Barron toted a pistol in his belt to shoot snakes with. He kept hollering, "Ohhhh, shoot this thing! Have mercy, this thing's killing me! *Shoot this thing!*"

Mr. Barron said, "John, I can't shoot up in there. I might hit you."

John said, "Well, just shoot up in here amongst us. One of us has got to have some relief."

"The Fish and the Edsel"

Newgene Ledbetter was a full-blood, registered, pedigreed liar. I went to a funeral the other day. Somebody said, "Jerry, old Newgene, he's turned over a new leaf. He don't lie every time he opens his mouth."

Newgene was there setting up at the funeral home, about two o'clock in the afternoon. Folks was up at the casket squalling, so I knew I could risk sitting down in there and he wouldn't come over there and tell me no lie.

Well, it wasn't long before he eased over there by me, said, "Jerry, I put this old Edsel car in the lake. I knew it would be a good cover for them old mossy backed bass fish to get in there. I left that Edsel in that lake about six months. I got my rod and reel, I went down there, and I parked my boat right up over that Edsel. I throwed that old plug out there, and about a fourteen-pound big-mouthed bass grabbed it. It run up in the back seat of that Edsel, and I was spooling him in. I'm turning that spool, and I'm tightening up that line, and I'm about ready to pull him out of the back seat of that Edsel, and Jerry, he rolled the window up on me!"

"Newgene and the Lion"

Some folks will take advantage of dogs. They'll be done messed up and done something, and they'll blame it on a dog. Newgene Ledbetter was like that.

Newgene was the meanest Ledbetter of them all. He used to even play dog—get down on his all fours and get up under the front porch. Somebody walked up in the front yard, he'd come out from under there, barking. One day he bit Aunt Daisy DeLaughter on the leg. Uncle Versie beat him. And lie—Newgene would climb a tree to tell you a lie when he could stand on the ground and tell the truth.

I was over there eating supper with them one night. I had been swapping work with the Ledbetters. Am I talking over your head? Swapping work, see, I growed up pore and we didn't have no money. A lot of times we had to get neighbors to come in and help us do work. It's hard to pull a crosscut saw by yourself. And I had been getting Newgene to come and help me saw stove wood. Now I was over there paying back a day's work by helping them dig a dug well.

Aunt Pet Ledbetter said, "Jerry, you want to stay and eat supper with us?" Did I ever! 'Cause she made them big old cathead biscuits, squshed them up with her hands, cooked them golden brown. You bite into one of them, it'd make a puppy pull a freight train.

There I'm sitting, with old Newgene, the lying Ledbetter, and all of the other Ledbetters—Arnell, Burnell, Raynell, W. L., Lanell, Odell, Udell, Marcel, Claude, Newgene and Clovis. We was eating supper, and Newgene jumped and hollered, *"Hahhh!* There's a lion in the yard! There's a lion in the yard. He's gonna eat us up!"

Uncle Versie looked out there and there was a dog in the front yard, a big old collie dog. It was hot summertime and somebody had sheared all the hair off that dog, and had left a ring of hair around his neck and a patch of hair right on the end of his tail. Uncle Versie wheeled around and slapped Newgene down, flat on his back, and stood straddle of him.

He said, "Boy, I done told you about lying. I done begged you to quit. You're a pretty good boy, but you just lie so much I can't depend on you. Newgene, I'm gonna turn it over to the Lord. I don't know nothing else to do but let God take it over. You get up out of that floor, go out yonder in the side room, and you get down on your knees and you beg God to forgive you of the sin of lying. Go now and do it."

Newgene come back in about fifteen minutes. Uncle Versie said, "Newgene, you feel better?"

"Yessir."

"You feel like you can overcome the temptation of lying?"

"Yessir."

"You feel better inasmuch as you told the Lord to help you?"

"Yessir."

Newgene said, "In fact, Papa, while I was out there talking to the Lord, the Lord talked directly back to me."

Uncle Versie said, "Newgene, son, don't lie about God!"

Newgene said, "I ain't lying, no sir. The Lord talked just as plain to me while I was out there as I can hear your voice talking to me right now."

Uncle Versie said, "You mind sharing with us what the Lord told you?"

Newgene said, "No, I don't mind telling you. The Lord told me the first time he saw that dog, he thought it was a lion, too."

"*Rat Killin*'"

It was Monday morning and my mama told me to get on the school bus and tell all of my friends on there that we's gonna have a rat killin' Saturday. I got on the school bus, and I said, "We're gonna have a rat killin' Saturday."

Them folks come from all over the county with their dogs and sticks to help us kill them rats. We had worked our way to the far corner, and there was just a whole bunch of them rats flushed out of that corn crib at the same time. There was so many of them they broke through the ranks and run and got under a big concrete slab. We couldn't get them out from under there. We dug, drawed up water, and poured it down them holes trying to drown 'em.

Directly Uncle Versie Ledbetter, who was the head rat killer in our community, said, "Boys, I tell you what we got to do. If we can get that A-model car over there cranked, and back it up to that concrete slab, we can put that inner tube around the exhaust pipe and run the other end of that inner tube down under that concrete slab. If we get that old car cranked and go to racing that motor, I am told it manufactures something up in that engine that when you gush it down through that exhaust pipe, it will make the rats come out from under there." We got it cranked and revved that motor up. Now, folks, y'all ain't never had no fun unless y'all have stood with a stick waiting for them carbon monoxided, sick rats to come out of the front of that slab. Now that is some fun.

One day while we were having a rat killin', me and my brother, Sonny, was up in the corn crib, a-moving the corn and killin' them rats as we got to 'em. Directly my brother, Sonny, caught a bigun in the throat. It was the hugest rat I have ever seen in all my life. His tail hung way down. It was such a fine rat that my brother, Sonny, wanted to show it to Mama. He jumped out of the corn crib and commenced to running toward the house, hollering, "Mama, Mama, looka here what a rat!"

Now my brother, Sonny, didn't know that Reverend Brock, the Baptist preacher, was in the house visiting with Mama. But Sonny run on in the back door and run in the living room. Mama was sitting over in one corner and the preacher in the other. Now Sonny ain't seen the preacher yet. He rushed on into the living room and said, "Mama, looka here. What a rat! I done whipped him over the head with a ear of corn. I done jobbed him with a hayfork. I done stripped all the hide off of his tail. I done whopped him up and down on the floor of that corn crib. I done stomped him three or four times."

Then Sonny saw the preacher. And he hugged that rat up in his fist, and he commenced to stroking it and crying, "Oh, and then the Lord called the pore thing home!"

"Rats in the Corn Crib"

I was out there at Hollywood doing one of them talk shows, sitting on the couch, and had my feet propped up on the coffee table, watching my turn when I was supposed to go out on television. In walked a lady, and just as she walked in, she grabbed her Adam's apple and screamed "Ahhh, ahhh, ahhh!" Likened to have scared me to death.

I said, "Lady, what's the matter?"

She said, "Oh, look at your boots! Your boots are lizard boots, and some little creature had to be put to death. Some little creature had to be killed to give you your pair of lizard boots."

I said, "No, ma'am, a Greyhound bus run over this lizard. After the Greyhound bus run over this lizard, I run out there in the middle of the highway and fought the buzzards off of it. Then I made me a pair of boots."

She said, "Well, I've heard some of your records and you were talking about brutally killing a little rat."

I said, "Lady, you ain't serious—I mean, you ain't agin killing them rats."

She said, "You don't have to be so brutal."

I said, "Lady, I want to tell you something. This is a true story. Now you listen to me. I know you're a high society, city woman, but it's very obvious you're educated beyond your intelligence. Lady, let me explain something to you. Me and my brother, Sonny, used to work out in the fields. A rain would come and while we couldn't work in the field, Papa would send us to the corn crib and tell us to shuck and shell corn, getting ready to go to mill Saturday to get some cornmeal ground for corn bread. It was bad enough with that old weevil dust getting up in my nose. (Achoo! We'd be sneezing.) But when we'd reach to get an ear of corn and our fingers would touch some wet shucks, we'd look and there'd be a stinking rat's nest messing up that corn crib.

Me and my brother, Sonny, would scoop up that stinking rat's nest, and we'd get them little old slick baby rats out of that nest. We had a big bird dog named Andy, and he was standing on the ground out there, flatfooted. We'd throw them little old slick baby rats out the door, and old Andy would run and catch them whole in his mouth and swallow 'em.''

That lady said, ''Hahhh!'' and broke and run from the dressing room and left me alone.

MARJORIE KINNAN RAWLINGS

Rawlings, who grew up in Washington, D.C., found her subjects as a writer when she moved to the tiny town of Cross Creek in north-central Florida. The Yearling *is her best-known novel about her cracker neighbors, but* When the Whippoorwill, *her 1940 collection of short stories, is a gold mine of folk-telling. The following is an abridgment of one of those stories.*

"*Alligators*"

Bless Katy, I don't know nothing about alligators. You belong to talk to some of them real old-timey Florida 'gator hunters that has messed up with 'em deliberate. I don't never mess up with no alligator. If so chance me and one meets, it's just because he comes up with me—I don't never try to come up with him. There ain't never been but once when me and a alligator met more than accidental.

.   .   .   .

I don't much mind handling a small un. Partickler if it's to torment somebody is worse scairt of 'em than me. Like Br'er Cresey. He hates a varmint or a snake or a 'gator the most of any man I know. I don't never get my hands on a little alligator but I goes to studying: Where can I put him so's Br'er Cresey will get the most good of him? Cresey'll holler like a woman if you catch him just right. A while ago, me and Raymond caught him just right in the post office.

Br'er Cresey was standing back of the delivery window, sorting mail from the 2:10 train. We eases in at the back door and lays a three-foot 'gator just back of his heels and eases out again. Directly the 'gator goes to blowing. A 'gator's the blowingest thing I know of. 'Tain't rightly a blowing, nor yet a sighing, nor even a groaning—you know the way it sounds. It's a damn peculiar sound—partickler in a post office. Cresey looks around and sees nothing. Directly the 'gator heaves another. Cresey looks down between his legs and there's the alligator bopping his lips and blowing.

Now, Cresey come out from behind that delivery window like a man with ants in his breeches. He squealed and whinnied like a Maud mule, and when he sees me and Raymond, he goes to cussing. It's a pure treat to hear Br'er Cresey cussing. He calms down when we takes the 'gator off. He don't know we'd only moved it to the back of the express wagon. The rest ain't so funny. He was so mad, and scairt, too, when he steps on the 'gator in the express wagon, he just picks it up by the tail and pitches it. I happens to be the first thing in the way, and when Br'er Cresey pitches the alligator, bless Katy if it don't land on me and get all wropped around my neck. And I don't enjoy that much more'n Cresey.

.   .   .   .

You understand, it don't do to be too timid with a alligator. It just don't do. You got to know their ways, like them old 'gator hunters do, and you got to be bold according. If a 'gator faces you in close quarters, you got to watch your chance to shut his mouth for him, and when the chance comes, you got to take it or the 'gator'll take his. Like the night me and Raymond was gigging frogs in Black Sink Prairie. Raymond shined his light in a 'gator's eyes and shot him. He was about nine feet long and we dragged him in the boat. I was paddling the boat and Raymond was giggling in the bow. Now, it turned out Raymond had shot the alligator too far down the nose—not backwards to where his brains was. The 'gator wasn't dead—he was only addled.

I hollered to Raymond, "Shine your light back here!"

He shined his light back for me, and here was the 'gator with his mouth wide open. Right there is where a feller'd be in trouble if he was too timid. Raymond held the light steady. The minute the 'gator closed his mouth, I caught him by the lips and held them shut while Raymond finished him with a knife. You can hold a 'gator's lips together with one hand if you catch him with his mouth shut. But once he's got his jaws open, you can't get the purchase to close them again.

Alligators is mighty strong. They're that strong to where they can fool you.

Like John Milliken at Salt Springs last week. We was gigging mullet. I seen a right small 'gator rise and sink. I whammed the gig into him. When I grabbed the gig handle he commenced a-rolling.

I says, "Here, John, hold him."

John takes the gig handle and says, "What is it?"

The 'gator was rolling to beat the devil. I like to fell in the spring, laughing. I says, "Hold him, John—hold him."

The gig was purely playing a tune. It blistered John's hands and like to beat his brains out. How come it wabbling so, the 'gator had done grabbed the gig handle in his mouth. So, with him rolling, it made right hard holding. If a 'gator once shuts down on you, that's his trick—he goes to rolling. If he grabs your arm in the water, say, he goes to rolling. It's like to twist your arm right out of the shoulder.

Now, a 'gator will bite. Don't never let nobody tell you a alligator won't bite. I've knowed several fellers to get bit to hurt 'em. Nub-footed Turner—a twenty-foot 'gator bit his foot off. But generally speaking, a 'gator'll go his way if you'll go yours. But he don't like to be fooled up with. He most particklerly don't like nobody monkeying around his cave.

.   .   .   .

I don't know but what I'd rather be behind an alligator than in front of one, come to think of it. I've seen one outrun a horse through the palmettos and across a flat-woods. Like Uncle Breck. He'd of give a pretty to of been behind the alligator the time it run him. That was over in Gulf Hammock, not far from the Gulf of Mexico. Me and Uncle Breck was to a pond, shooting ducks. The ducks'd circle overhead and we'd shoot 'em so's they'd fall in the woods behind us, and us not have to wade in the pond amongst the alligators. I'll swear, I never seen so many alligators. I reckon there was three hundred heads in sight, all sticking up out of the water. 'Gators just ain't plentiful in Florida now, the way they was then in Gulf Hammock.

I was watching for ducks—shooting and watching. Directly I hears Uncle Breck say, "Oo-o-ee-e!" Then he says, kind of faintified, "Shoot him, Fred— shoot him!" I looks around. Now, what he'd done to him first—if he shot him or what—I don't know, but it was Uncle Breck and the alligator across the woods.

Chasing him? The alligator was really chasing Uncle Breck.

I reckon there's been men has travelled faster than Uncle Breck. I don't reckon there's ever been a man has tried to travel faster. I mean, he was selling out. The 'gator was this high off the ground. . . . They made a turn around a bay tree. They was coming mighty near straight to me.

Uncle Breck calls in a weak voice, "Shoot him, Fred—shoot him!"

The devil of it was, I couldn't shoot the alligator for shooting Uncle Breck.

Directly they hits a log two-three feet high. Uncle Breck jumps it—he hurdled fast and pretty—and the alligator has to take a minute to waddle over it. It didn't stop him—a 'gator'll go right over a five-foot fence—but he couldn't take it as fast as Uncle Breck. The 'gator slowing down for the log give me the first chance, what with laughing and not craving to shoot Uncle Breck, to get a shot at him. And then, bless Katy, Uncle Breck was fixing to tear me down for not shooting sooner!

. . . .

One night me and Nub-footed Turner was at the fish house on Lochloosy. Oh, my, it was a fine night, just as still and pretty. It wasn't too cold, it wasn't too hot. It was just a fine, calm night in the spring of the year. The lake was as still as a glass candle.

Nub says, "I'd just naturally love to go fishing tonight."

I says, "I ain't never really pulled the net since I've owned it, but I'll pull one end of it."

We goes out in the launch and throws the seine, and we takes about two hundred pounds of bream on the first haul. Now, Nub-footed Turner liked to fish on the moon.

He says, "I'd love to make a moon haul. I'd love to pull this seine just at moonrise."

Didn't neither one of us happen to know the time of moonrise.

I says, "We just as good to go on shore and eat."

We goes on back to shore and lights us a oak fire and cooks fish and coffee. Nub-footed Turner, he lays down and goes to sleep. I sets a while watching the east for the moon to rise. I commenced getting cold. Our clothes was wet and I couldn't never sleep right in wet clothes. So I totes up logs and limbs and builds up a big fire. I dried first one side and then t'other. Directly I lays down by the fire and goes to sleep. Now and again I'd raise up and look out east. By then I didn't want to go fishing.

I says, "I hope the moon don't never rise."

I lays down and goes to sleep again. Directly I wakes up, and here the east was done turned red, the moon a half hour high, and day a-breaking.

"Wake up, Nub," I says. "Here 'tis daylight and the moon done rose."

He says, "We'll pull a haul regardless."

We sets out in the launch close to shore in shallow water.

I says, "You jump off; I'll hold the land stake."

We lays the seine.

Now, how come the alligator in the pocket, it was thisaway. When one of them fishermen made a haul he'd do it easy and a alligator'd swim out of the net and sell out through them cypress timbers. Them as knowed this partickler 'gator told me he'd of swum out if he'd had the chance. But I didn't know no better and we worked too fast for him. He didn't get off at the right place.

I ties up the haul, and when the time comes, here I am, pulling away. We had the fish, all right, but directly the net commenced a-banging.

I says, "Nub, I'm tearing all the webbing loose from the lead line. The net's hung up on a log."

He says, "Next time it hangs, leave me see it."

"All right. It's hung."

He looks.

" 'Tain't nothing."

I says, "Listen, Nub, there's a alligator in this net."

He says, "Yeah, but he's a little one. He won't hurt you."

I says, "Are you sure he's a little one?"

I was inside the circle and I had to pull it my way. I had to hold fast on the lead line to keep from losing the fish. The circle got right small.

Directly Nub says, "Wait, Fred."

I says, "Nub, you ain't lied to me?"

Now, we'd done had a couple of snorts, but not enough to where I wanted to catch no alligator.

I says, "Nub, I'm as close to what's in that net as I aim to be. Now, if that 'gator catches you, don't never say a alligator caught you and I goed off and left you. I'm just telling you ahead of time—I'm gone now. I hate to leave you, but I'm gone."

He says, "Come back here with your pistol."

I says, "I'll come a foot closer."

I untied the launch from a cypress tree. I pulls up on the lead line. I shot the .38 where I figured the 'gator belonged to be.

Nub says, "You got him."

All right. I pulls up the seine. I knowed I'd killed him. You ever fished a seine? Well, you have to fish the pocket out. We fished out the pocket.

I says, "Where'd that alligator go?"

About that time something comes up between us.

I says, "Nub, the first man moves is the first man caught!"

That alligator's head was three feet long. He was bopping his lips, and when they was wide open you could of put a yardstick between 'em. His mouth come together. Nub catches his lips.

He says, "Gimme your pistol."

"Here 'tis."

Nub shot him in one eye, one ear and the neck. The 'gator lays quiet. We goes on fishing the net. Then we piled the net on board the boat. We like to turned it over, loading the alligator. We finally got him in, facing to the rear. He had his front legs laying on a seat. Nub, he climbs in the bow of the boat by the 'gator's tail. I got back in the stern on the pile of webbing, me and the 'gator face to face. I reloaded my pistol and picked up one of the twelve-foot oars and Nub takened the other.

Here we go, a-paddling. That alligator commences raising up on his toes on that seat.

I says, "Nub, I'm going to shoot him."

He says, "Fred, don't shoot him! You'll kill me. He'll settle down right where he is."

Sure enough, he did. He settled down. Then he begun winking that good eye at me. He raised up again that high to where I had to look up at him. He settles down and goes to winking. I ain't never objected to nothing much more'n that alligator setting there winking that red eye at me. I shot him in the good eye and in t'other ear, and that quieted him down for a little while. Directly he rared up and give a flounce. He hit that pile of webbing just about the time I left it. Now, if he'd hit where I'd done been, there'd of been no funeral—just a water burial.

We makes it on in to shore. We had about three hundred pounds of fish. Nub takes a fish scoop and goes to shoveling fish.

I says, "Nub, never mind the fish. Let's get this alligator out of this boat."

When I said that, the daggone alligator rared up and knocked that fish scoop out of Nub's hands to where it ain't never been found.

Nub says, "Hand me another scoop."

About then the alligator takened a notion it was time to leave the boat. I want to tell you, the only way we kept him from going out was Nub lost his patience and takened a ax and chopped him through the backbone. He was thirteen feet and nine inches—and he was really hard to kill.

Now, that's just the way it's always been with me and alligators. I don't never mess up with 'em on purpose. No, no; the one time I fooled with one deliberate don't count. No use scarcely telling about it. 'Twasn't nothing in the world but the banana brandy. If 'twasn't for that, hell nor high water couldn't of got me to ride no alligator. And even then, now mind you, even then I didn't, so to speak, figure on doing it. It was old man Crocky aimed to do it. Old man Crocky had done set the Fourth of July to catch the alligator that had been bothering people swimming at Lochloosy Station.

He was a big old 'gator, and by bothering, I mean that when people was swimming he'd come in close enough that they'd come out. Fourth of July used to be a big time at Lochloosy. I've seen five hundred niggers come down for the frolicking and fighting. The first train that come in would unload right peaceable. Then, as t'other trains come in, there was fights all ready, waiting for 'em. I was deputy sheriff at Lochloosy, but 'twasn't no use for one deputy to go in to 'em. It would of takened fifteen or twenty.

This partickler Fourth of July the word had done gone out that old man Crocky was fixing to ride the alligator out of Lake Lochloosy. What with the niggers swarming, and the white folks congregating, there was a crowd on shore like a Baptist baptizing. And you know, old man Crocky never did show up?

Now, I figured, long as there wasn't nothing one deputy could do to stop a crowd from quarrelling, I had the same right as them to enjoy myself on the Fourth of July. And the way I was enjoying myself was drinking banana brandy. You ain't never been high on banana brandy? There ain't nothing more I can say about banana brandy than this: It put me to where I got the idea it was my duty, as deputy sheriff, to take the place of old man Crocky and ride the alligator.

The word went out I was fixing to substitute for old man Crocky. Folks goes to clustering along the shore. I pushes in amongst 'em and I hollers, "Get out of the way! I'm fixing to ride the alligator!"

I remember somebody yelling, "You fixing to ride the alligator or is he fixing to ride you?"

And I can just remember me saying, "You go eat your rations and drink your 'shine, and leave me 'tend to the alligator."

I walks out into the water and goes to swimming. I have the stick in my fist old man Crocky had aimed to use and had left at the fish house. It was big around as my fist, and whittled to a point at both ends. I swims out a ways more. Directly here comes the alligator, starting in to meet me. He's got his jaws open. I swims up to him and feeds him the stick. I jobbed it straight up and down in his mouth to where he couldn't close it. The alligator commences rolling and I stayed with him, rolling too. Him with his mouth held open, it didn't pleasure him, rolling, no more than me. When he quits, I slings one leg over the back of his neck, and here we go, me riding the alligator.

I give him plenty of room. I knowed he wouldn't sink with me, for a 'gator's got sense, and he knowed he'd drown hisself with his mouth open. I put my hands over his eyes so he couldn't see where he was going. I guided him thisaway and that just as good as if I'd been riding a halter-broke mule. The way I turned him, I'd job my thumb in one of his eyes. He'd swing t'other way to try and break his eye loose.

I can just remember, dimlike, the crowd a-cheering and the niggers screaming. I rode the daggone alligator out of Lake Lochloosy and plumb up on shore.

You can see how come it to happen. 'Twasn't nothing in the world but the banana brandy. I didn't have no intention of riding no alligator. I ain't the man you belong to talk to at all. You go talk to some of them fellers that has hunted alligators. I just naturally don't know nothing about 'em.

RAY WASHINGTON

Here's a writer I'll bet you've never read. Ray Washington is a fourth-generation Floridian whose newspaper columns were collected in the book Cracker Florida *in 1983. His latter-day Florida Crackers are shorter-winded than Marjorie Kinnan Rawlings's, but they can tell a story right along.*

"A Chicken Story"

It seemed like Homer Gordon's whole life had led up to one final question of chickens and manhood, and in a subdivided orange grove west of Zephyrhills he rose to the challenge. Homer Gordon felt he had become a doormat for anybody with dirty feet—his first two wives, other women, strangers. But somewhere down deep inside something snapped when Joe Fureigh started his funny business. Homer Gordon was not going to take it any more.

"Now my first old lady," Homer Gordon said, "she did me like you wouldn't do a dog. After being married 19 years and having me three kids, she took to running around. She'd say she was going to a church meeting, and I were damn fool enough to believe it. It's a hard thing to understand, a woman slipping off to see another fellow like that. I packed up and left everything behind."

When Joe Fureigh first bought the trailer in the lot on the next acre in the orange grove Homer Gordon thought he had found a friend. Old Chief growled every time Joe Fureigh came over, but Homer Gordon just told the dog to be still.

"Now my second old lady," Homer Gordon said, "when I met up with her she was separated and I paid for her G——— divorce. We had a son named Max, and she stayed home except for when she took a factory job in Tampa, but she quit that because it weren't air conditioned enough for her. Somewhere she started slipping around on me. She started drinking hard too. I'd have to go down to the G——— jailhouse to bail her out, and I did it too. But the third time they called me down there, I said to hell with it, let her boyfriend pay her way out."

Joe Fureigh admired Homer Gordon's leghorn cross laying hens, so Homer Gordon took him down where he could get his own chickens for 50 cents apiece. Homer Gordon let Joe Fureigh use his rabbit hutch, and when Joe Fureigh's wife wrecked her Mustang, Homer Gordon got some fenders and said he would fix the car at a bargain rate.

"Now there was this one old girl I was going out with some," Homer Gordon said. "She'd come over here and drink beer with me some, and one day she was sitting over there on the couch and she said, 'Homer, I'd like to go up to Dade City and get my daughter and bring her over here to meet you, but I don't have no gas for the car and I don't have no money with me.' All I had was $10, so I said, 'You take this and get you $3 in gas and bring the girl back and bring me the change.' Like the damn fool I always was I sat there watching TV for a couple of hours waiting. I ain't seen that woman since I gave her the $10."

Homer Gordon thought he and Joe Fureigh were pretty good buddies until Joe Fureigh's wife moved out and charged her husband with battery and then filed for divorce. Joe Fureigh refused to pay Homer Gordon the money he owed him for the work on his estranged wife's fenders. Things began to go downhill.

"Now, I'm used to having buddies turn on me," Homer Gordon said. "When I was working construction in Tampa I let these old boys stay over at my house for free. They didn't have no money and they seemed like pretty good old boys so I took them into my house and I fed them and I let them feel like they was right at home till they could get enough money together to get a place of they own. One day I came home and my valuables was all stolen, garbage had done been poured across my floors, and them old boys was long gone. I found my stuff in a pawn shop and had to buy it back."

Homer Gordon was a downtrodden man when Joe Fureigh began his funny business. At first he took it like he had taken it before. When he tried to mow his lawn, he said, Joe Fureigh called him dirty names. He said Joe Fureigh took to threatening him with a shotgun. He said Joe Fureigh took to calling the police on him and making up lies about his dog and his rooster being nuisances.

"He was all around mean and nasty," Homer Gordon said. "But I was used to being treated that way."

When old Chief came yelping home with a hide full of birdshot, Homer Gordon just picked out the pellets and said, "I guess we was meant for abuse, Chief. When you signed on with me you was asking for it."

Things went on like that until one day Homer Gordon said, "enough is enough." It was Homer Gordon's chickens that caused him to say, "enough is enough."

At one time he had owned 14 of the prettiest laying hens between Zephyr-hills and Wesley Chapel. But suddenly they began to disappear, and before he knew what was happening, only six hens were left. That is when enough became enough for Homer Gordon.

He parked his rusted old Chevrolet back down the grove and then sneaked back home and tied old Chief near to the chickens. He turned out the lights in his trailer and went back to the bedroom and waited. Along about three in the morning old Chief commenced to barking and Homer Gordon was out the door with his 18-inch flashlight.

"I saw what looked like old Joe Fureigh, out there with one of my best laying hens," Homer Gordon said. "He cussed me and ran back toward the weeds swinging the chicken around his head and laughing and cussing me out. I knew it was Joe Fureigh by his hunchback walk. You can spot him among a hundred people."

Homer Gordon called the police and showed them the dead chicken for evidence. He had the proof, he told them, and nobody was going to push Homer Gordon around anymore. It was the kind of case a prosecutor would rather not be bothered with, they told Homer Gordon, but he was not even listening. He was a changed man, and he was not going to back down ever again.

Homer Gordon did not back down, either, and pretty soon Joe Fureigh found himself on trial for cruelty to animals and damaging another's property. Across the state of Florida came cries of outrage that taxpayers would have to foot the estimated $3,000 bill for the jury trial of a man accused of wringing a chicken's neck. But Homer Gordon was through with being pushed around, and he would not be swayed.

"See, it's not just the price of a chicken," he told the court.

Joe Fureigh, through his lawyer, told the jury that Homer Gordon was lying about the chicken theft, and even if he was not lying there was nothing cruel about wringing a chicken's neck. The jury sat in judgment for 40 minutes, and returned to announce that Joe Fureigh was guilty as charged. The judge ordered Joe Fureigh to pay Homer Gordon $1 as restitution for the dead chicken.

Homer Gordon spent the dollar and sat under an orange tree with old Chief and talked about how his life had changed.

"Old Joe Fureigh, he couldn't take the shame, and he moved away to Arkansas where he belongs," Homer Gordon said. "Now I don't let no one push Homer George Gordon around. I'm 62 years old and I deserve a little respect. Now people comes up to me and says, 'Homer, you really stood up against that chicken thief. You're a man.'

"Word gets around. People don't mess with you. Radio Shack over in Tampa started sending me a flyer everytime they have a sale."

ANONYMOUS

"He Is My Horse"

One day as I wus a-ridin' by,
Said dey: "Ole man, yo' hoss will die."

"If he dies, he is my loss;
An' if he lives, he is my hoss."

Nex' day w'en I com a-ridin' by,
Dey said: "Ole man, yo' hoss may die."

"If he dies, I'll tan 'is skin;
An' if he lives, I'll ride 'im ag'in."

Den ag'in w'en I come a-ridin' by,
Said dey: "Ole man, yo' hoss might die."

"If he dies, I'll eat his co'n;
An' if he lives, I'll ride 'im on."

DAVE BARRY

*Barry grew up in Pleasantville, New York, but he moved in early adulthood to Miami,
which is south of the South but deserves representation. And the boy is funny. Won a
Pulitzer Prize for being funny in his syndicated column, not just guess-this'll-do funny*

or predictably-cranky funny, but surprisingly funny week in and week out. I believe he has a vocation. He and I are in an authors' rock-and-roll band together, the Rock Bottom Remainders, and I can tell you that Southern audiences liked him on patter and lead guitar when we played Atlanta and Nashville. And not because Southern audiences—at least, the kind of Southern audiences we attracted—would find anybody's booger references funny. In a letter to me Barry has written:

"I think I qualify as at least partly Southern. As you point out, I have dogs, and dogs tend to Southernize a person. I do not mean this in any condescending sense. I mean it in the sense of, you can't be putting on elitist northern airs if your house has dog snot smeared on the windows from the dogs trying to get at the UPS man. (Not that I work mucus into everything.) Also, I have eaten catfish. (I did not care for it, but I ate it.) And more than once I have eaten meals involving 'fixin's.' I have never eaten catfish with 'fixin's,' but I would, if this would qualify me to be in The Norton Book of Southern Humor.* P.S. Is there going to be a Sutton Book of Northern Humor?"

Barry not only has dogs, he does dogs well in writing. Robert Benchley, no Southerner, is his hero, but Barry is more visceral, less detachedly literary, than Benchley; in that sense, more in the Southern tradition. (Otherwise I'd try to finagle Benchley, also one of my heroes, into this book.) Also, Barry has been exposed to rock and roll, which as we all know would be as the sound of clattering cymbals, were it not infused with Southern idiom and rhythms. And he hung around with black people a lot when he was growing up. And of course nobody ever seriously didn't like catfish.

"False Alarm"

The man was standing right outside our master bathroom. He couldn't see Beth and me, standing in the hallway, but we could see him clearly. His face was covered with a stocking mask, which distorted his features hideously. He was dressed all in black, and he had a black plastic bag stuck in his back pocket.

He was using a screwdriver to open our sliding glass door.

You always wonder what you're going to do in a situation like this. Run? Fight? Wet your pants?

I'm not experienced with physical violence. The last fight I had was in eighth grade, when I took on John Sniffen after school because he let the air out of my bike tires. Actually, I didn't *know* that he did this, but he was the kind of kid who *would* have, and all the other suspects were a lot larger than I was.

*The title of this book, until the publisher reconsidered.

The man outside our house was also larger than I am. He jerked the screwdriver sideways and opened the door. Just like that, he was inside our house, maybe six feet from where Beth and I were standing.

Then he saw us. For a moment, nobody spoke.

"CUT!" yelled the director.

"Way to go, Ozzie!" I said to the stocking-masked man. "Looking good! Looking criminal!"

"I'm wondering if his bag is too dark to show up," said Beth.

Everybody wants to be a director.

Anyway, as you have guessed, Ozzie wasn't a real burglar. He was part of a production crew that was using our house to shoot a promotional video for the company that installed our burglar alarm. Here in South Florida it's standard procedure to have burglar alarms in your house, your car, your workplace, and, if you've had expensive dental work, your mouth.

I like having an alarm in our house, because it gives me the security that comes from knowing that trained security personnel will respond instantly whenever I trigger a false alarm. I do this every day at 6 A.M., when I get up to let out our large main dog, Earnest, and our small emergency backup dog, Zippy. I'm always in a big hurry, because Zippy, being about the size of a hairy lima bean (although less intelligent), has a very fast digestive cycle, and I need to get him right outside.

So I fall out of bed, barely conscious, and stagger to the back door, where both dogs are waiting, and I open the door and *BWEEPBWEEPBWEEP* I realize that I have failed to disarm the alarm system.

Now I have a problem. Because within seconds, the voice of a trained security person is going to come out of the alarm control panel, asking me to identify myself, and unless I give her the Secret Password, she's going to cheerfully notify the police. So I stagger quickly over to the panel. But this leaves Earnest and Zippy alone out on the patio. Theoretically, they can get from the patio to our back yard all by themselves. They used to be prevented from doing this by a screen enclosure around the patio, but thanks to Hurricane Andrew, most of this enclosure is now orbiting the Earth. The hurricane did NOT blow away the screen door, however. It's still standing there, and the dogs firmly believe that it's the only way out. So—I swear I'm not making this up—instead of going two feet to the left or right, where there's nothing to prevent them from simply wandering out into the yard, they trot directly to the door, stop, then turn around to look at me with a look that says, "Well?"

"GO OUTSIDE!" I yell at them as I lunge toward the alarm control panel. "THERE'S NO SCREEN ANYMORE, YOU MORONS!"

"I beg your pardon?" says the Cheerful Alarm Lady, because this is not the Secret Password.

"Bark," says Earnest, who is trotting back toward the house, in case I am telling her that it's time to eat.

"Grunt," says Zippy, as his internal digestive timer reaches zero and he detonates on the patio.

We do this almost every morning. We're very dependable. In fact, if some morning I DIDN'T trigger a false alarm, I think the Cheerful Alarm Lady would notify the police.

"You'd better check the Barry residence," she'd say. "Apparently something has happened to Mr. Barry. Or else he's strangling one of his dogs."

So the alarm people have been very nice to us, which is why we let them use our house for the video. It had a great Action Ending, wherein Ozzie runs out our front door, and an armed security man drives up, screeches to a halt, leaps out, puts his hand on his gun and yells "FREEZE!" This is Ozzie's cue to freeze and look concerned inside his stocking. They shot this scene several times, so there was a lot of commotion in our yard. Fortunately in South Florida we're used to seeing people sprint around with guns and stocking masks, so the activity in our yard did not alarm the neighbors. ("Look, Walter, the Barrys planted a new shrub." "Where?" "Over there, next to the burglar.") Anyway, the point is that our house is well-protected. The alarm system is there in case we ever need it, which I doubt we will, because—thanks to Zippy—only a fool would try to cross our patio on foot.

RAY LUM AS TOLD TO WILLIAM FERRIS

William Ferris, of Vicksburg, Mississippi, is director of the Center for the Study of Southern Culture at the University of Mississippi, and a dedicated folklorist. (His Blues from the Delta *is a standard reference.) Ray Lum was a Mississippi mule trader whose reminiscences Ferris recorded between 1971 and Lum's death in 1977. In her introduction to the resultant book,* You Live and Learn. Then You Die and Forget It All, *Eudora Welty called Lum "a man born and bred to the practice of the country monologue." A video of him holding forth is available from the center, but he comes across fine here in Ferris's rendering.*

Animal Deals

One of the toughest people I met in the Delta was Wildcat Stevens. I rode into Leland with a string of horses, and when I went to put my horses up there, Cat come in. He didn't know I was there. He come in, and I was glad to see him. When he started to walk in, I hollered at him, "Hey, Cat."

Called him Cat. Cat was a man that didn't carry a gun. That little old marshal in Leland had a stable, and I was using it for my horses. But this part of his stable where you come in, this part was locked. So Cat come up one day, knocked the lock off, and put his horse in a stall.

Here comes these two officers, both of them with pistols. They come up, and they didn't know Wildcat Stevens. He had just moved to Leland a week or two before. He just went over, slammed them guns out of their hands, just that quick, and throwed them over in the ditch. He had done already brought his horse out, and he just ignored the officers. He says, "Ray, I'll see you tomorrow. I'll be back in about eight or nine o'clock."

There was the officers' pistols over there in the grass. Those were officers in the town, you know. He said, "I'll see you tomorrow."

"You bet. I'll be looking for you, Cat."

And the next day he was right back. He didn't pay no attention to those officers.

Cat came to our livestock barn in Vicksburg one day, and he had a little boy with him about three years old. Mrs. Lum was there that day. Mrs. Lum and I was staying at the barn. We had our living quarters at the barn until we built our home. Anyhow, Cat comes in, and his little boy, coming about three years old, followed him. Here comes a cat running right under the barn. And, goddamn, right under the barn his son went. You never saw a dog go under there no faster. And when he came out, he came out with the cat right in his hands. Mrs. Lum said, "That's a chip off the old block."

So that was that. Little fellow was three years old, and never saw that cat before in his life. When he come out, he had ahold of him, don't you see. That was Wildcat Stevens. He never used a gun, but oh good God, he was powerful when he'd take your hand.

.   .   .   .

I was trading at Mayersville, and I was riding one mule and leading eight or ten mules and horses. I pulled into Mayersville 'cause I had to stop at the store there to get some sardines and crackers. This old man named Meat Myers was running the store, and up comes an organ-grinder. He had this organ grinding and making music, and his little old monkey was dancing around. Old Man

Myers had a great big bulldog that was sitting down looking at the little monkey with his head between his paws. The organ-grinder kept a-grinding.

Old Man Meat didn't give the organ-grinder anything. He didn't give him any nickels or dimes. He didn't like that monkey. The little monkey kept a-dancing and all. When the monkey got over pretty close to the bulldog, Mr. Myers says, "You better not let your monkey get close to that dog. That dog will kill him."

"This monkey can whoop that dog."

"What?"

"Yes. This monkey can whoop that dog."

Oh, the fat was in the fire. "Would you bet on it?"

The organ-grinder run his hand in his pocket, pulled out a fifty-dollar bill and handed me the fifty dollars. Well, Mr. Myers like to tore his pocket off getting his fifty out. When he handed it over, I said, "Your money's turned to water, Mr. Myers." Talking to the man that had the bulldog, "Your money's turned to water."

I knew better. I'd had a monkey. They got ready, and the organ-grinder said, "Get your dog ready."

Mr. Myers said, "He's ready."

He had the big old bulldog back there, and the little old monkey was jumping around. "Cheechee. Cheechee."

The organ-grinder asked Mr. Myers, he says, "You wouldn't mind him having that little pencil, would you, something to kind of protect himself?"

"No, you can give him a cord of wood if you want to."

The organ-grinder give the monkey the little pencil. "All right, he's ready."

"Turn him loose."

Old bulldog surged at the monkey, and the monkey just hopped right up on his back and started jooging him in the ass with that pencil. Kept shoving that pencil in his back end. Well, the bulldog knocked two slats off the fence, run right in under the house, and the little monkey jumped up on the porch. Here the monkey come back. "Cheechee. Cheechee."

The old organ-grinder had done that before and was smart. He says, "Ah, maybe the bulldog didn't have a good chance. You want to give him another try?"

Old Man Meat says, "Give him the money, Ray."

He wasn't going to argue about it. He done seen enough. That settled that deal.

I had a little old monkey once. He would go up a tree, shit in his hand and throw it at you. I'd have a devil of a time trying to get him down. I swapped the son-of-a-gun for a bulldog and swapped the bulldog for a horse. You just have one monkey in life. You don't ever want the second one.

.   .   .   .

. . . Frank says, "Ray, I want to help you a bit. There's a professor here that's been talking about getting a good Hereford bull."

"All right, Frank."

"I'll tell you what I'd like to do. I'd like to bring him here in the morning and let you sell him a bull."

"What ought I to ask for the bull, Frank? Two thousand?"

"Oh hell no. Ask him three thousand."

Three thousand for a hundred-and-fifty-dollar bull. Well, it wasn't a hundred and fifty. I had made Mr. Hughes take two hundred. A two-hundred-dollar bull. It's awful when you have to rob people to make them happy. Down comes the professor. He picked out the bull and just loved him. I said, "I'll let you have him for three thousand, but I'll have to borrow him from you. I'll have to run him through the auction because it won't do to sell stock before the auction."

He said it was all right with him. The next day at the auction I knocked the bull off for four thousand. The professor loved it, you know. He was getting a four-thousand-dollar bull for three. He really did love that bull then. Mr. Hughes said, "Ray, if there's enough professors in the country, you'll get along all right."

.   .   .   .

I met a man in Texas once that had an ostrich. You know an ostrich kicks like a mule. I was out in the man's lot, and I had no business getting close to the son-of-a-bitch. I was in front of him, and damned if he didn't kick me. I said, "That's a helluva note. That's the first time I was ever kicked by an ostrich."

He said, "That's the first time ever I saw him do that."

I was hurt pretty bad. I had to limp around there for quite a while to get it straightened out. He said that was the first he ever saw him kick anybody. I said, "I don't know how come the son-of-a-bitch don't like me."

He picked me out. I just walked in front of him and paid no attention to him, you know. Didn't pay no more attention to him than if he was a turkey or a chicken, and the man said that was very unusual.

.   .   .   .

On that same trip I run into the man who wrote a book about the story of his life. I can't call his name, but he's the man that came to Dallas when he was a right young fellow. He came to Dallas, and this con gang got hold of him and talked him into going and getting them five thousand dollars. He went back to Coleman, Texas, and got the five thousand and comes back and give it to those sons-of-bitches. Then he went back to where they told him they was going to be, and when he looked around there, they was gone. He woke up right then. He was awake from then on.

Well, to cut a long story short, he followed them to England. He killed four of them, and the one that was on the boat, he jumped off the boat, and he killed him too. He got all five of them. Then he wrote a book. He wrote the story of his life and called it *Does a Yokel Wake Up?* And don't you think it didn't sell. I met him and his brother at Coleman, Texas. I bought fifty mules from that man. He was ninety-something years old then, and he was a damn sight more active than I am now. I wish I had that book now. I had the book once, and it was a true story, just as true as the Bible.

ANONYMOUS

"Simon Slick's Mule"

There was a little kicking man,
His name was Simon Slick.
He had a mule with cherry eyes,
Oh! How that mule could kick!

When you'd go up to him,
Mule'd shut one eye and smile,
Then telegram his foot to you
And send you half a mile.

JOEL CHANDLER HARRIS

Harris, of Eatonton, Georgia, was the illegitimate son of an Irish laborer who deserted the boy's mother around the time of his birth in 1848. All his life Harris was an extremely shy, small, red-headed stammerer. When he was thirteen he became a typesetter for a newspaper published on a nearby plantation, where he heard animal tales from slaves. After the war he worked for a series of newspapers, eventually the Atlanta Constitution, *where he began to publish his Uncle Remus stories, about Brer Rabbit and the other creatures. Harris's framing portrayal of the loving relation between storytelling Remus and his white-boy audience seems embarrassingly patronizing today, but his conversion of the oral-tradition stories into a prose of heavy but rich dialect has never been matched, despite a number of attempted latter-day improvements. I became literate myself by looking at Harris's pages while my mother read aloud to me of the Tar Baby and other black-and-white entanglements. That helped make me a Southern writer—by which I mean one who writes, and when necessary spells, from the mouth and for the ear at least as much as from the dictionary and for the eye, and also one deeply influenced by the ways of animals and by race relations.*

"Brother Rabbit Conquers Brother Lion"

"Uncle Remus," remarked the little boy, one day, "papa says that the animals haven't got sure enough sense."

"Did Marse John tell you dat?" asked the old man, letting his shoe-hammer drop from his hands, as though astonishment had rendered him helpless. "Did Marse John set up flat-footed in a cheer and tell you dat de creeturs ain't got sho nuff sense? Ain't he wink his eye when he tell you dat? Ain't you see his chin drap?"

The little boy had seen none of these manifestations, and he said so.

"Well," exclaimed Uncle Remus, with a groan, "I dunner how come Marse John fer ter take on dat away. He used to be a mighty joker when he wuz fus' married; but look like he too ole fer dat kinder doin's now. When you go back up dar, you tell Marse John, dat time he been wid de creeturs long ez I is, he won't set up dar wid a straight face en say dat dey ain't got sho nuff sense. Des ax 'im how dat ole blue sow up dar in de woods pastur' know when ter shake de plum tree. Ax 'im who tol' 'er how ter bump 'er head 'g'inst de floor er de crib en shatter de corn out. En den, when he git thoo tellin' you 'bout dat, ax 'im how dat brindle cow larn't how ter open all de plantation gates wid 'er horn.

"I be blest," continued Uncle Remus, laughing a little, "ef dat cow ain't a sight. Ef Marse John'll des let 'er come in de house, she'll go up sta'rs en onlock his trunk wid 'er horn, en chaw up dat ar claw-hammer coat what he got married in. She mos' sholy will. Co'se de creeturs can't talk none, so folks kin tell what dey say; but ef you gwine ter blame anybody fer dat, blame de folks, don't blame de creeturs.

"Take um up one side en down de yuther, en all 'roun' ez fur ez dey go, en dey got much sense ez folks. Dey ain't got law sense, en dey ain't got buyin' en sellin' sense, but what dey want wid it? What dey gwine do wid it ef dey had it? Tell me dat! De ole cow, she want ter git in de sallid patch, en she know how ter open de gate. De ole sow want ripe plums, en she shake de tree; she want corn, en she bump 'er head 'g'inst de planks en shatter it out. What mo' do dey want? Dey done got der eddycation.

"De littler de creeturs is, de mo' sense dey got, kaze dey bleedzd ter have it. You hear folks say dat Brer Rabbit is full er tricks. It's des de name dey give it. What folks calls tricks is creetur sense. Ef ole Brer Lion had much sense ez Brer Rabbit, what de name er goodness would de balance er de creeturs do? Dey wouldn't be none un um lef' by dis time."

"The Lion couldn't catch Brother Rabbit, could he, Uncle Remus?" said the little boy.

"Now you talkin', honey," exclaimed the old man, enthusiastically. "'Long side er Brer Rabbit ole Brer Lion ain't knee high ter a duck. He mighty strong; he mighty servigrous; but when it come ter head-work he ain't nowhar.

"Dey wuz one time when Brer Lion wuz sorter playin' overseer wid de yuther creeturs. It seem like he got de idee dat all un um got ter pay 'im toll, kaze he de strongest en de mos' servigrous. He claim one out'n eve'y fambly: one sheep fum de sheeps, one goat fum de goats, en one fum all de kinds. Bimeby, atter so long a time, he sont word ter Brer Rabbit dat his turn done come, en Brer Rabbit he sont back word, 'All a-settin'.' Co'se dis make ole Miss Rabbit en all de chilluns feel mighty bad. De chilluns, dey sot 'roun' a-whimperin' en a-snufflin', en ole Miss Rabbit, she went 'bout cryin' en wipin' 'er eyes on 'er apern. But Brer Rabbit, he got up en smoke his seegyar, en tell um for ter quit der 'havishness en l'arn how ter don't.

"He 'low, 'Ole 'oman, ef I ain't back by supper-time, des set my vittles down dar on de h'a'th, so it'll keep sorter warm.'

"Ole Miss Rabbit say, dat stidder wantin' vittles, he'll be vittles hisse'f, en den she snuffle wuss en wuss. But Brer Rabbit he des hoot at 'er, en den he tuck down his walkin' cane en put out fer ter see Brer Lion. De little Rabs, dey holler out, 'Good-by, daddy!' en Brer Rabbit, he holler back, 'So long!' Ole Miss Rabbit, she look atter 'im, she did, en den she flung 'er apern over 'er head, en des boo-hoo.

"But Brer Rabbit, he march down de road ez gay ez ef he gwine ter a frolic. He march on, he did, en des 'fo' he git ter de place whar ole Brer Lion stay at, he hid his walkin' cane in de fence cornder, en rumpled up his ha'r en draw'd hisse'f up twel he look like he ain't bigger'n a poun' er soap atter a hard day's washin'. Den he went whar dey wuz a big, deep spring, a little piece off fum de road, en look at hisse'f in de water. He sort er roach back his years, en make hisse'f look 'umble-come-tumble, en den he draw'd his mouf 'roun' en wunk one eye, en shuck his fist at his shadder in de water.

"He got back in de big road, he did, en crope 'long like he ailin', limpin' fus' on one foot en den on tudder, en bimbeby he come ter de place whar ole Brer Lion stay at. Brer Rabbit sorter drag hisse'f 'long, en make a bow. Brer Lion look at 'im sideways, en ax 'im whar he gwine. Brer Rabbit say he come de mo' willin' kaze it's his turn ter come, en he been feelin' mighty po'ly dis long time. He talk mighty weak en trimbly.

"Brer Lion look at 'im right close, en 'low, 'You won't make a mou'ful. Time I eat you, I'll des be gettin' hongry good.'

"Brer Rabbit say, 'Yasser, I know I ain't fat, en I speck I got lots er fleas on me, but I'm mighty willin'. I got a bad cough, en I'm tired er fallin' off. I'm des about ez fat ez de mule de man had, which he hatter tie a knot in his tail fer ter keep 'im fum slippin' thoo de collar.'

"Brer Lion look at 'im, en study. Brer Rabbit 'uz so skeer'd he talk weaker en weaker.

"He say, 'Whiles I comin' 'long des now, I seed a creetur dat 'uz mos' big en fat ez what you is, en I 'low ter myse'f dat I wish ter goodness I 'uz fat ez he is; so Brer Lion kin make out his dinner.'

"Brer Lion 'low, 'Who is he?'

"Brer Rabbit say, 'I ain't ax 'im 'is name. He 'fuse ter 'spon' ter my howdy, en he look so servigrous dat I put out fum dar.'

"Brer Lion say, 'Come, show me whar he is.'

"Brer Rabbit say, 'I'd do it in a minnit, Brer Lion, but I skeer'd he'll hurt you.'

"Brer Lion sorter bristle up at dis. He 'low, 'Hurt who? Come on, en go wid me whar he is, en I'll show you who'll git hurted, en dat in short order!'

"Brer Rabbit shuck his head. He say, 'You better take me, Brer Lion. I ain't much, but I'm sump'n', en dat ar creetur what I seed will sholy hurt you. He got claws en he got tushes, kaze I done seed um. Don't go whar he is, Brer Lion, ef you got any friendly feelin' fer yo' fambly. Dat creetur will sholy cripple you!'

"Dis make Brer Lion mighty mad. He 'low, 'Git right in de road dar en show me whar he is!'

"Brer Rabbit say, 'Well, ef I bleedzd ter go, Brer Lion, I'll go. I done tol' you, en dat's all I kin do.'

"Dey went on, dey did, en Brer Rabbit tuck Brer Lion ter de spring. When dey got dar, Brer Rabbit look 'roun' en say, 'He 'uz right 'roun' here somers, en he ain't so mighty fur off now, kaze I feel it in my bones.'

"Den he crope up, Brer Rabbit did, en look in de spring. Time he do dis, he fetched a squall en jump back: 'Ouch, Brer Lion! he in dar! Less run! He'll git us, sho!'

"Brer Lion walk up ter de spring en look in. Sho nuff, dar wuz a big creetur lookin' back at 'im. Brer Lion holler at 'im. De creetur in de spring ain't say nothin'. Brer Lion shuck his head; de creetur shuck his. Brer Lion showed his tushes; de creetur grin at 'im. Dey kep' on dis away, twel bimeby Brer Lion git so mad dat he jump in de spring head foremos'. When he in dar he can't git out no mo', en so dar he is, strangled wid de water en drownded fer de want er bofe sense en breff.

"Brer Rabbit, he caper 'roun' dar some little time, en den he put out fer home, en when he git dar, he tuck his chilluns on his knee en tol' um a mighty tale 'bout how he make way wid ole Brer Lion; en all de creeturs hear 'bout it, en dey go 'roun' en say dat Brer Rabbit sholy is got deze 'ere things up here.''

Uncle Remus tapped his forehead significantly, and the little boy laughed.

'' 'Heyo, House!' ''

"I don't think Brother Lion had much sense," remarked the little boy after awhile.

"Yit he had some," responded Uncle Remus. "He bleedzd ter had some, but he ain't got much ez Brer Rabbit. Dem what got strenk ain't got so mighty much sense. You take niggers—dey er lots stronger dan what white folks is. I ain't so strong myse'f," remarked the old man, with a sly touch of vanity that was lost on the little boy, "but de common run er niggers is lots stronger dan white folks. Yit I done tuck notice in my time dat what white folks calls sense don't turn out ter be sense eve'y day en Sunday too. I ain't never see de patter-roller what kin keep up wid me. He may go hoss-back, he may go foot-back, it don't make no diffunce ter me. Dey never is cotch me yit, en when dey does I'll let you know.

"Dat de way wid Brer Rabbit," Uncle Remus went on, after a pause. "De few times what he been outdone he mighty willin' fer ter let um talk 'bout it, ef it'll do um any good. Dem what outdo 'im got de right ter brag, en he ain't make no deniance un it.

"Atter he done make way wid ole Brer Lion, all de yuther creeturs say he sholy is a mighty man, en dey treat 'im good. Dis make 'im feel so proud dat he bleedzd ter show it, en so he strut 'roun' like a boy when he git his fus' pa'r er boots.

" 'Bout dat time, Brer Wolf tuck a notion dat ef Brer Rabbit kin outdo ole Brer Lion, he can't outdo him. So he pick his chance one day whiles ole Miss Rabbit en de little Rabs is out pickin' sallid fer dinner. He went in de house, he did, en wait fer Brer Rabbit ter come home. Brer Rabbit had his hours, en dis wuz one un um, en 'twa'n't long 'fo' here he come. He got a mighty quick eye, mon, en he tuck notice dat ev'ything mighty still. When he got little nigher, he tuck notice dat de front do' wuz on de crack, en dis make 'im feel funny, kaze he know dat when his ole 'oman en de chillun out, dey allers pulls de door shet en ketch de latch. So he went up a little nigher, en he step thin ez a batter-cake. He peep here, en he peep dar, yit he ain't see nothin'. He lissen in de chimbley cornder, en he lissen und' de winder, yit he ain't hear nothin'.

"Den he sorter wipe his mustash en study. He 'low ter hisse'f, 'De pot rack know what gwine on up de chimbley, de rafters know who's in de loft, de bed-cord know who und' de bed. I ain't no pot-rack, I ain't no rafter, en I ain't no bed-cord, but, please gracious! I'm gwine ter fin' who's in dat house, en I ain't gwine in dar nudder. Dey mo' ways ter fin' out who fell in de mill-pond widout fallin' in yo'se'f.'

"Some folks," Uncle Remus went on, "would 'a' rushed in dar, en ef dey had, dey wouldn't 'a' rushed out no mo', kaze dey wouldn't 'a' been nothin' 't all lef' un um but a little scrap er hide en a han'ful er ha'r.

"Brer Rabbit got better sense dan dat. All he ax anybody is ter des gi' 'im han'-roomance, en dem what kin ketch 'im is mo' dan welly-come ter take 'im. Dat zackly de kinder man what Brer Rabbit is. He went off a little ways fum de house en clum a 'simmon stump en got up dar en 'gun ter holler.

"He 'low, 'Heyo, house!'

"De house ain't make no answer, en Brer Wolf, in dar behime de do', open his eyes wide. He ain't know what ter make er dat kinder doin's.

"Brer Rabbit holler, 'Heyo, house! Whyn't you heyo?'

"House ain't make no answer, en Brer Wolf in dar behime de do' sorter move roun' like he gittin' restless in de min'.

"Brer Rabbit out dar on de 'simmon stump holler mo' louder dan befo', 'Heyo, house! Heyo!'

"House stan' still, en Brer Wolf in dar behime de do' 'gun ter feel col' chills streakin' up and down his back. In all his born days he ain't never hear no gwines on like dat. He peep thoo de crack er de do', but he can't see nothin'.

"Brer Rabbit holler louder, 'Heyo, house! Ain't you gwine ter heyo? Is you done los' what little manners you had?'

"Brer Wolf move 'bout wuss'n befo'. He feel des like some un done hit 'im on de funny-bone.

"Brer Rabbit holler hard ez he kin, but still he ain't git no answer, en den he 'low, 'Sholy sump'n' nudder is de matter wid dat house, kaze all de times befo' dis, it been holler'n back at me, Heyo, yo'se'f!'

"Den Brer Rabbit wait little bit, en bimeby he holler one mo' time, 'Heyo, house!'

"Ole Brer Wolf try ter talk like he speck a house 'ud talk, en he holler back, 'Heyo, yo'se'f!'

"Brer Rabbit wunk at hisse'f. He low, 'Heyo, house! whyn't you talk hoarse like you got a bad col'?'

"Den Brer Wolf holler back, hoarse ez he kin, 'Heyo, yo'se'f!'

"Dis make Brer Rabbit laugh twel a little mo' en he'd a drapt off'n dat ar 'simmon stump en hurt hisse'f.

"He 'low, 'Eh-eh, Brer Wolf! dat ain't nigh gwine ter do. You'll hatter stan' out in de rain a mighty long time 'fo' you kin talk hoarse ez dat house!'

"I let you know," continued Uncle Remus, laying his hand gently on the little boy's shoulder, "I let you know, Brer Wolf come a-slinkin' out, en made a break fer home. Atter dat, Brer Rabbit live a long time widout any er de yuther creeturs a-pesterin un 'im!"

"Aunt Tempy's Story"

The little boy observed that Aunt Tempy was very much interested in Daddy Jack's story. She made no remarks while the old African was telling it, but she was busily engaged in measuring imaginary quilt patterns on her apron with her thumb and forefinger—a sure sign that her interest had been aroused. When Daddy Jack had concluded—when, with a swift, sweeping gesture of his wrinkled hand, he cut the cord and allowed Brother Wolf to perish ig- nominiously—Aunt Tempy drew a long breath, and said:

"Dat ar tale come 'cross me des like a dream. Hit put me in min' er one w'at I year w'en I wuz little bit er gal. Look like I kin see myse'f right now, settin' flat down on de h'a'th lis'nin' at ole Unk' Monk. You know'd ole Unk'

Monk, Brer Remus. You bleedzd ter know'd 'im. Up dar in Ferginny. I 'clar' ter goodness, it makes me feel right foolish. Brer Remus, I des know you know'd Unk' Monk.''

For the first time in many a day the little boy saw Uncle Remus in a serious mood. He leaned forward in his chair, shook his head sadly, as he gazed into the fire.

''Ah, Lord, Sis Tempy!'' he exclaimed sorrowfully, ''don't less we all go foolin' 'roun' 'mungs dem ole times. De bes' kinder bread gits sours. W'at's yistiddy wid us wuz 'fo' de worl' begun wid dish yer chile. Dat's de way I looks at it.''

''Dat's de Lord's trufe, Brer Remus,'' exclaimed Aunt Tempy with unc- tion, ''un I mighty glad you call me ter myse'f. Little mo' un I'd er sot right yer un a gone 'way back to Ferginny, un all on 'count er dat ar tale w'at I year long time ago.''

''What tale was that, Aunt Tempy?'' asked the little boy.

''Eh-eh, honey!'' replied Aunt Tempy, with a display of genuine bashful- ness; ''eh-eh, honey! I 'fraid you all'll set up dar un laugh me outer de house. I ain't dast ter tell no tale 'longside er Brer Remus un Daddy Jack yer I 'fraid I git it all mix up.''

The child manifested such genuine disappointment that Aunt Tempy re- lented a little.

''Ef you all laugh, now,'' she said, with a threatening air, ''I'm des gwine ter pick up en git right out er dish yer place. Dey ain't ter be no laughin', kaze de tale w'at I year in Ferginny ain't no laughin' tale.''

With this understanding Aunt Tempy adjusted her headhandkerchief, looked around rather sheepishly, as Uncle Remus declared afterwards in confi- dence to the little boy, and began:

''Well, den, in de times w'en Brer Rabbit un Brer Fox live in de same settlement wid one n'er, de season's tuck'n come wrong. De wedder got hot un den a long dry drouth sot in, un it seem like dat de nat'al leaf on de tree wuz gwine ter tu'n ter powder.''

Aunt Tempy emphasized her statements by little backward and forward movements of her head, and the little boy would have laughed, but a warning glance from Uncle Remus prevented him.

''De leaf on de trees look like dey gwine ter tu'n ter powder, un de groun' look like it done bin cookt. All de truck w'at de creetur's plant wuz all parched up, un dey wa'n't no crops made nowhars. Dey dunner w'at ter do. Dey run dis a-way, dey run dat a-way; yit w'en dey quit runnin' dey dunner whar dey bread comin' frun. Dis de way it look ter Brer Fox, un so one day when he got mighty hankerin' atter sumpin' sorter joosy, he meet Brer Rabbit in de lane, un he ax um, sezee:

'' 'Brer Rabbit, whar'bouts our bread comin' frun?'

"Brer Rabbit, he bow, he did, un answer, sezee:

" 'Look like it mought be comin' frun nowhar,' sezee."

"You see dat, honey!" exclaimed Uncle Remus, condescending to give the story the benefit of his patronage; "You see dat! Brer Rabbit wuz allus a-waitin' a chance fer ter crack he jokes."

"Yas, Lord!" Aunt Tempy continued, with considerable more animation; "he joke, un joke, but bimeby, he ain't feel like no mo' jokin', un den he up'n say, sezee, dat him un Brer Fox better start out'n take der fammerlies wid um ter town un swap off for some fresh-groun' meal; un Brer Fox say, sezee, dat dat look mighty fa'r un squar', un den dey tuck'n make dey 'greements.

"Brer Fox wuz ter s'ply de waggin un team, un he promise dat he gwine ter ketch he fammerly un tie um hard un fast wid a red twine string. Brer Rabbit he say, sezee, dat he gwine ter ketch he fammerly un tie um all, un meet Brer Fox at de fork er de road.

"Sho nuff, soon in de mawnin', w'en Brer Fox draw up wid he waggin, he holler 'Wo!' un Brer Rabbit he tuck'n holler back, 'Wo yo'se'f!' un den Brer Fox know dey 'uz all dar. Brer Fox, he tuck'n sot up on de seat, un all er he fammerly, dey wuz a-layin' under de seat. Brer Rabbit, he tuck'n put all he fammerly in de behime een' er de waggin, un he say, sezee, dat he 'speck he better set back dar twel dey git sorter usen ter dey surrounderlings, un den Brer Fox crack he whip, un off dey wen' toze town. Brer Fox, he holler ev'y once in a while, sezee:

" 'No noddin' back dar, Brer Rabbit!'

"Brer Rabbit he holler back, sezee:

" 'Brer Fox, you miss de ruts en de rocks, un I'll miss de noddin'.'

"But all dat time, bless yo' soul! Brer Rabbit wuz settin' dar ontyin' he ole 'oman un he childun, w'ich dey wuz sev'm uv um. W'en he git him all ontie, Brer Rabbit, he tuck'n h'ist hisse'f on de seat 'long er Brer Fox, un dey sot dar un talk un laugh 'bout de all-sorts er times dey gwine ter have w'en dey git de co'n meal. Brer Fox sez, sezee, he gwine ter bake hoecake; Brer Rabbit sez, sezee, he gwine ter make ashcake.

"Des 'bout dis time one er Brer Rabbit's childun raise hisse'f up easy un hop out de waggin. Miss Fox, she sing out:

> " 'One frun sev'm
> Don't leave 'lev'm.'

"Brer Fox hunch he ole 'oman wid he foot fer ter make 'er keep still. Bimeby 'n'er little Rabbit pop up un hop out. Miss Fox say, se' she:

> " 'One frun six
> Leaves me less kicks.'

"Brer Fox go on talkin' ter Brer Rabbit, un Brer Rabbit go on talkin' ter Brer Fox, un 'twa'n't so mighty long 'fo' all Brer Rabbit fammerly done pop up un dive out de waggin', un eve'y time one 'ud go Miss Fox she 'ud fit it like she did de yuthers."

"What did she say, Aunt Tempy?" asked the little boy, who was interested in the rhymes.

"Des lemme see:

" 'One frun five
Leaves four alive;
" 'One frun four
Leaves th'ee un no mo';
" 'One frun th'ee
Leaves two ter go free;
" 'One frun one,
Un all done gone.' ' "

"What did Brother Rabbit do then?" inquired the little boy.

"Better ax w'at Brer Fox do," replied Aunt Tempy, pleased with the effect of her rhymes. "Brer Fox look 'roun' atter while, un w'en he see dat all Brer Rabbit fammerly done gone, he lean back un holler 'Wo!' un den he say sezee:

" 'In de name er goodness, Brer Rabbit! whar all yo' folks?'

"Brer Rabbit look 'roun', un den he make like he cryin'. He des fa'rly boo-hoo'd, un he say, sezee:

" 'Dar now, Brer Fox! I des know'd dat ef I put my po' little childun's in dar wid yo' folks dey'd git e't up. I des know'd it!'

"Ole Miss Fox, she des vow she ain't totch Brer Rabbit fammerly. But Brer Fox, he bin wantin' a piece un um all de way, un he begrudge um so dat he mighty mad wid he ole 'oman un de childuns, un he say, sezee:

" 'You kin des make de most er dat, kaze I'm a-gwine ter bid you good riddance dis ve'y day;' un sho nuff, Brer Fox tuck'n tuck he whole fammerly ter town un trade um off fer co'n.

"Brer Rabbit wuz wid 'em, des ez big ez life un twice ez nat'al. Dey start back, dey did, un w'en dey git four er five mile out er town, hit come 'cross Brer Fox min' dat he done come away un lef' a plug er terbacker in de sto', en he say he bleedzd ter go back atter it.

"Brer Rabbit, he say, sezee, dat he'll stay en take keer er de waggin, w'ile Brer Fox kin run back un git terbacker. Soon ez Brer Fox git out er sight, Brer Rabbit laid de hosses under line un lash un drove de waggin home, un put de hosses in he own stable, un de co'n in de smoke-house, un de waggin in de barn, un den he put some co'n in he pocket, un cut de hosses' tails off, un went back up de road twel he come ter a quog-mire, un in dat he stick de tails un wait fer Brer Fox.

"Atter w'ile yer he come, un den Brer Rabbit gun ter holler un pull at de tails. He say, sezee:

" 'Run yer, Brer Fox! run yer! You er des in time ef you ain't too late. Run yer, Brer Fox! run yer!'

"Brer Fox, he run'd en juk Brer Rabbit away, un say, sezee:

" 'Git out de way, Brer Rabbit! You too little! Git out de way, un let a man ketch holt.'

"Brer Fox tuck holt," continued Aunt Tempy, endeavoring to keep from laughing, "un he fetch'd one big pull, un I let you know dat 'uz de onliest pull he make, kaze de tails come out un he tu'n a back summerset. He jump up, he did, en 'gun ter grabble in de quog-mire des ez hard ez he kin.

"Brer Rabbit, he stan' by, un drop some co'n in onbeknowns' ter Brer Fox, un dis make 'im grabble wuss un wuss, un he grabble so hard un he grabble so long dat 'twa'n't long 'fo' he fall down dead, un so dat 'uz de las' er ole Brer Fox in dat day un time."

As Aunt Tempy paused, Uncle Remus adjusted his spectacles and looked at her admiringly. Then he laughed heartily.

"I declar', Sis Tempy," he said, after a while, "you gives tongue same ez a lawyer. You'll hatter jine in wid us some mo'."

Aunt Tempy closed her eyes and dropped her head on one side.

"Don't git me started, Brer Remus," she said, after a long pause; "kaze ef you does you'll hatter set up yer long pas' yo' bed-time."

"I b'lieve you, Sis Tempy, dat I does!" exclaimed the old man, with the air of one who has made a pleasing discovery.

A BILOXI INDIAN AS TOLD
TO JAMES OWEN DORSEY

I wanted a Southern Native American story, but none of the Cherokee or Choctaw or Seminole folktales I found struck me as humorous until I looked through a 1938 anthology entitled Humor of the Old Deep South. *I steered clear of the chapters entitled "The Ladies—God Bless 'Em" and "Darkies," but in the chapter of Indian lore I was struck by the following story. The phrase "The Ancient of Opossums," not*

*to mention that mythical figure's song, was of a strangeness that would have enriched
the tradition of Southern humor—and maybe its influence will crop up yet. At any
rate, what kind of collection of Southern humor would it be that had no possum in it?
I have as a matter of fact written about possums myself—was a judge in a possum
show once, in Clanton, Alabama—and let me tell you if you don't know already, a
possum is an animal no less resistant to translation into ordinary English than this
story palpably was in the original Biloxi.*

"Why the 'Possum's Tail Is Bony"

The Ancient of Opossums killed a Wolf, and, after stringing the Wolf's teeth
as a necklace for himself, he walked along singing a song:

> Hama yuxku! Hama yuxku!
> Isu-na hinwa ye!
> Anixanixye.

While he was singing, the Ancient of Wolves came in sight close to him.
"What are you singing?" said he to the Ancient of Opossums.

"Nothing," replied the latter. "I was saying, 'What very pretty flowers are
here!' "

After this conversation, the Ancient of Wolves disappeared, and he and his
people went some distance ahead and hid from the Ancient of Opossums.

Meanwhile the latter walked along singing:

> Xaye pixti! Xaye pixti!
> Hinwa ye! Hinwa ye!
> Anixanixye!

He sang for some time until he thought that he had gone very far from the
Ancient of Wolves. Then he sang again about the Wolf teeth as he was
walking. Just then the Wolf people were coming out of the undergrowth, and
appearing before him. When they appeared near him, they said, "This one
must be he who has killed some of us." So they tied the Ancient of Opossums
and laid him down; whereupon they searched him and found the necklace of
wolf teeth. Then they wished to kill him, but the Ancient of Opossums said,
"If you hit me with any sort of stick I shall not die, but if some persons go to a
dead tree which has the bark peeled off and dig it up by the roots and bring a
stick from that and hit me but once with it I shall die at once and shall not
revive."

Then the Wolf people went to dig up the tree. They left as a guard over the Ancient of Opossums a one-eyed person, who sat there watching him.

Then the Ancient of Opossums in order to play a trick on his guard, said, "Untie me and bring a stick from the dead tree and kill me by hitting me, and be very brave over me as I recline; do so to me and I shall lie dead."

When he had said this, sure enough the one-eyed person untied him, and was thinking of breaking off the fatal stick when the Ancient of Opossums entered a hole in the ground, and thus escaped.

On the return of the Wolf people just at this time they dug into the ground. While they were digging, their foe came in sight at another place. He had painted himself red before he approached them. "Why are you all acting thus?" said he.

At length they replied, "We are doing so because the Ancient of Opossums killed some of us and entered a hole here."

"I will enter," said the Ancient of Opossums, "and after catching him I will bring him out and you all must kill him." Then he entered the hole.

In a little while he emerged bearing a hoe on his shoulder and with his body painted yellow all over. "What are you all doing?" said he, as if he were a stranger.

"We are doing so because the Ancient of Opossums killed some of us and entered this hole," replied the Wolf people.

"I will go in and catch him, and when I bring him out you all must kill him," said the Ancient of Opossums. Again did he enter the hole.

When he thought, "I have gone a long distance," he began to call out, "I am he. I am the one who did it."

But while he thought that he had gone far into the hole, he was in error; for his bushy tail stuck out of the hole in full sight of the Wolf people, who seized it immediately and slipped off the skin.

Therefore the tails of opossums since that day have been nothing but bone.

BAILEY WHITE

"Toot and Teat"

I have an old cousin who has crazy spells. He gets a pinched look around his eyes, and then he'll do something like put his underwear up on top of his head and go downtown. One of his sisters will call my mother on the phone. "Lila?" she'll say, "It's about Luten." Then my mother has to go get Luten and take him to the mental wing of the hospital. They say things to him and do things to him there that we don't know how to say and do, and after five days he goes back home, cured.

Luten has a little wire-haired dog named Helen of Troy who is just as crazy as he is. She keeps thinking she's pregnant. She develops big bosoms of milk and she waddles around the house making sweet little nests in the corners out of Luten's best clothes. But nothing ever comes of it. After a while she loses her hopeful gaze, her bosoms begin to shrink, and next thing we know Luten gets that pinched look around his eyes, Mama puts him in 3 East, and we keep Helen of Troy at our house for five days.

It was during one of those times that our neighbor killed a wild hog and brought its head to my mother. She makes scrapple every winter, an old family tradition, and the recipe calls for a hog head. Usually we get the head from the butcher, all cleaned and cut into chunks that will fit neatly into the pressure cooker. Even my mother, who is a match for almost anything, was daunted by the sight of that giant bristly black dead hog head staring up at her out of the kitchen sink with its little dead hog eyes and its dead hog snout. Dozens of black ticks, sensing that something was amiss with their host, had abandoned ship and were running up my mother's arms. And in a corner of the kitchen, scrambling around in a cardboard box and squealing pitifully at the tops of their lungs, were the two baby pigs our neighbor had dumped on us along with their mother's head. It was the same old story. He had been sure it was a boar hog when he shot, but then . . .

I tried to make the baby pigs feel at home. I tore up rags to make them a soft bed and put a hot water bottle in the box. I mixed milk and honey and tried to feed them with a baby bottle. But they screamed and screamed and screamed as if our cozy kitchen was Hell for Hogs, and all my tender ministrations were sheer torture.

Finally we just had to take a break. I put down the baby bottle and put the screaming, writhing little pig back in its box. Mama gave up her wrestling match with the hog head and washed her hands. We went out of the kitchen, closed the door, and sat down on the porch. Mama began to make a list. "One," she said, "Luten is up at 3 East. Two, Helen of Troy is having a false pregnancy. Three, that fool Darrel has given us a hog head and two baby pigs."

"How is this helping?" I asked.

"Be quiet. It's helping," Mama said. "I'm getting organized."

We sat. Mama was thinking. We could barely hear the screeching of the baby pigs, and in a flower bed somewhere in the yard, Helen of Troy was scratching out a nest. Finally Mama sat up straight. "I've got it," she said. "Go get that dog."

I found Helen of Troy lying in a hollow of straw in the lily bed. She looked at me with that sweet pregnant gaze and wagged her tail. It almost made tears come to my eyes. Why couldn't she ever learn? I gathered her and her bosoms out of the nest and took her in the house. Mama was peering into the pig box with a meat cleaver in one hand and a sharpening stone in the other. The pigs are right, I thought, looking around the kitchen. Here are murder, mayhem, the implements of torture, and disappointed dreams. This is hell.

Then Mama took Helen of Troy out of my arms and put her in the box with the baby pigs. She nuzzled them, wagged her tail, smiled up at us, and lay down. Instantly the squealing stopped. From the box we could hear the contented sounds of suckling, and now and then a deep satisfied sigh.

In the peace and quiet Mama could concentrate on the hog head, and by 2:00 A.M. the freezer was stacked with neat square loaves of scrapple wrapped in aluminum foil, the kitchen was spotlessly clean, the cleaver was put away in its cardboard sheath, and out under the fig tree was a simple pile of white, picked bones.

Three days later they let Luten out of 3 East and he came to get Helen of Troy. We didn't give him all the details. Just his happy, happy dog, her baby pigs, their cardboard box, and a loaf of scrapple. He named the pigs Toot and Teat.

It's been five years now. Luten has not been back to 3 East, and gravidity has lost its allure for Helen of Troy. Toot and Teat are now as big and black as their natural mother was. Luten has trained them to walk sedately by his side. He scratches their backs with two sticks. When he wants them to stop, he stops scratching. And now, when Luten goes downtown, he walks proudly with Toot on one side and Teat on the other. Helen of Troy, on a gold cord, leads the way.

"Turkeys"

Something about my mother attracts ornithologists. It all started years ago when a couple of them discovered she had a rare species of woodpecker coming to her bird feeder. They came in the house and sat around the window, exclaiming and taking pictures with big fancy cameras. But long after the red cockaded woodpeckers had gone to roost in their sticky little holes in the red hearts of our big old pine trees and the chuck-will's-widows had started to sing their night chorus, the ornithologists were still there. After that, there always seemed to be three or four of them wandering around our place, discussing the body fat of hummingbirds, telling cruel jokes about people who couldn't tell a pileated woodpecker from an ivory bill, and staying for supper.

In those days, during the 1950s, the big concern of ornithologists in our area was the wild turkey. They were rare, and the pure-strain wild turkeys had begun to interbreed with farmers' domestic stock. The species was being degraded. It was extinction by dilution, and to the ornithologists it was just as tragic as the more dramatic demise of the passenger pigeon or the Carolina parakeet.

One ornithologist had devised a formula to compute the ratio of domestic to pure-strain wild turkey in an individual bird by comparing the angle of flight at takeoff and the rate of acceleration. And in these sad days, the turkeys were flying low and slow.

It was during this time, the spring when I was six years old, that I caught the measles. I had a high fever, and my mother was worried about me. She kept the house quiet and dark and crept around silently, trying different methods of cooling me down. Even the ornithologists stayed away; but not out of fear of the measles, or respect for a household with sickness. The fact was, they had discovered a wild turkey nest. According to the formula, the hen was pure-strain wild—not a taint of the sluggish domestic bird in her blood, and the ornithologists were camping in the woods protecting her nest from predators, and taking pictures.

One night our phone rang. It was one of the ornithologists. "Does your little girl still have measles?" he asked.

"Yes," said my mother. "She's very sick. Her temperature is 102."

"I'll be right over there," said the ornithologist.

In five minutes a whole carload of them arrived. They marched solemnly into the house, carrying a cardboard box. "102 did you say? Where is she?" they asked my mother.

They crept into my room and set the box down on the bed. I was barely conscious, and when I opened my eyes their worried faces hovering over me seemed to float out of the darkness like giant, glowing eggs. They snatched the covers off me and felt me all over. They consulted in whispers.

"Feels just right, I'd say."

"102, can't miss if we tuck them up close and she lies still."

I closed my eyes then, and after a while the ornithologists drifted away, their pale faces bobbing up and down on the black wave of fever.

The next morning I was better. For the first time in days I could think. The memory of the ornithologists with their whispered voices and their bony, cool hands was like a dream from another life. But when I pulled down the covers, there staring up at me with googly eyes and wide mouths were sixteen fuzzy baby turkeys and the cracked chips and caps of sixteen brown speckled eggs.

I was a sensible child. I gently stretched myself out. The egg shells crackled and the turkey babies fluttered and cheeped and snuggled against me. I laid my aching head back on the pillow, and closed my eyes. "The ornithologists," I whispered. "The ornithologists have been here."

It seems the turkey hen had been so disturbed by the elaborate protective measures that had been undertaken in her behalf that she had abandoned her nest on the night the eggs were due to hatch. It was a cold night. The ornithologists, not having an incubator to hand, used their heads and came up with the next-best thing.

The baby turkeys and I gained our strength together. When I was finally able to get out of bed and feebly creep around the house, the turkeys peeped and cheeped around my ankles, scrambling to keep up with me, and tripping over their own big spraddle-toed feet. When I went outside for the first time, the turkeys tumbled after me down the steps and scratched around in the yard while I sat in the sun.

Finally, in late summer, the day came when they were ready to fly for the first time as adult birds. The ornithologists gathered. I ran down the hill, and the turkeys ran too. Then, one by one, they took off. They flew high and fast. The ornithologists made V's with their thumbs and forefingers, measuring angles. They consulted their stop watches and paced off distances. They scribbled in their tiny notebooks. Finally they looked at each other. They sighed. They smiled. They jumped up and down and hugged each other. "100 percent pure wild turkey!" they said.

Nearly forty years have passed since then. In many ways the world is a worse place now. But there is a vaccine for measles. And the woods where I live are full of pure wild turkeys. I like to think they are all descendants of those sixteen birds I saved from the vigilance of the ornithologists.

FLANNERY O'CONNOR

When I visited O'Connor in 1963 she gave me two feathers from her peacocks. Then I went off to graduate school, left them in my closet at home, and my mother—who Lord knows did a lot for me as well—must have thrown them out. I sure wish I had them today. I'd display them with more pride, even, than their original bearers did.

"The King of the Birds"

When I was five, I had an experience that marked me for life. Pathé News sent a photographer from New York to Savannah to take a picture of a chicken of mine. This chicken, a buff Cochin Bantam, had the distinction of being able to walk either forward or backward. Her fame had spread through the press, and by the time she reached the attention of Pathé News, I suppose there was nowhere left for her to go—forward or backward. Shortly after that she died, as now seems fitting.

If I put this information in the beginning of an article on peacocks, it is because I am always being asked why I raise them, and I have no short or reasonable answer.

From that day with the Pathé man I began to collect chickens. What had been only a mild interest became a passion, a quest. I had to have more and more chickens. I favored those with one green eye and one orange or with overlong necks and crooked combs. I wanted one with three legs or three wings but nothing in that line turned up. I pondered over the picture in Robert Ripley's book, *Believe It or Not,* of a rooster that had survived for thirty days without his head; but I did not have a scientific temperament. I could sew in a fashion and I began to make clothes for chickens. A gray bantam named Colonel Eggbert wore a white piqué coat with a lace collar and two buttons in the back. Apparently Pathé News never heard of any of these other chickens of mine; it never sent another photographer.

My quest, whatever it was actually for, ended with peacocks. Instinct, not knowledge, led me to them. I had never seen or heard one. Although I had a pen of pheasants and a pen of quail, a flock of turkeys, seventeen geese, a tribe of mallard ducks, three Japanese silky bantams, two Polish Crested ones, and several chickens of a cross between these last and the Rhode Island Red, I felt a lack. I knew that the peacock had been the bird of Hera, the wife of Zeus, but since that time it had probably come down in the world—the Florida *Market Bulletin* advertised three-year-old peafowl at sixty-five dollars a pair. I had been quietly reading these ads for some years when one day, seized, I circled an ad in the *Bulletin* and passed it to my mother. The ad was for a peacock and hen with four seven-week-old peabiddies. "I'm going to order me those," I said.

My mother read the ad. "Don't those things eat flowers?" she asked.

"They'll eat Startena like the rest of them," I said.

The peafowl arrived by Railway Express from Eustis, Florida, on a mild day in October. When my mother and I arrived at the station, the crate was on the platform and from one end of it protruded a long, royal-blue neck and crested head. A white line above and below each eye gave the investigating head an expression of alert composure. I wondered if this bird, accustomed to parade about in a Florida orange grove, would readily adjust himself to a Georgia dairy farm. I jumped out of the car and bounded forward. The head withdrew.

At home we uncrated the party in a pen with a top on it. The man who sold me the birds had written that I should keep them penned up for a week or ten days and then let them out at dusk at the spot where I wanted them to roost; thereafter, they would return every night to the same roosting place. He had also warned me that the cock would not have his full complement of tail feathers when he arrived; the peacock sheds his tail in late summer and does not regain it fully until after Christmas.

As soon as the birds were out of the crate, I sat down on it and began to look at them. I have been looking at them ever since, from one station or another, and always with the same awe as on that first occasion; though I have always, I feel, been able to keep a balanced view and an impartial attitude. The peacock I had bought had nothing whatsoever in the way of a tail, but he carried himself as if he not only had a train behind him but a retinue to attend it. On that first occasion, my problem was so greatly what to look at first that my gaze moved constantly from the cock to the hen to the four young pea-chickens, while they, except that they gave me as wide a berth as possible, did nothing to indicate they knew I was in the pen.

Over the years their attitude toward me has not grown more generous. If I appear with food, they condescend, when no other way can be found, to eat it from my hand; if I appear without food, I am just another object. If I refer to them as "my" peafowl, the pronoun is legal, nothing more. I am the menial, at the beck and squawk of any feathered worthy who wants service. When I first uncrated these birds, in my frenzy I said, "I want so many of them that every time I go out the door, I'll run into one." Now every time I go out the door, four or five run into me—and give me only the faintest recognition. Nine years have passed since my first peafowl arrived. I have forty beaks to feed. Necessity is the mother of several other things besides invention.

For a chicken that grows up to have such exceptional good looks, the peacock starts life with an inauspicious appearance. The peabiddy is the color of those large objectionable moths that flutter about light bulbs on summer nights. Its only distinguished features are its eyes, a luminous gray, and a brown crest which begins to sprout from the back of its head when it is ten days old. This looks at first like a bug's antennae and later like the head feathers of an Indian. In six weeks green flecks appear in its neck, and in a few more weeks a cock can be distinguished from a hen by the speckles on his back. The hen's back gradually fades to an even gray and her appearance becomes shortly what it will always be. I have never thought the peahen unattractive, even though she lacks a long tail and any significant decoration. I have even once or twice thought her more attractive than the cock, more subtle and refined; but these moments of boldness pass.

The cock's plumage requires two years to attain its pattern, and for the rest of his life this chicken will act as though he designed it himself. For his first two years he might have been put together out of a rag bag by an unimaginative hand. During his first year he has a buff breast, a speckled back, a green neck like his mother's, and a short gray tail. During his second year he has a black breast, his sire's blue neck, a back which is slowly turning the green and gold it will remain; but still no long tail. In his third year he reaches his majority and acquires his tail. For the rest of his life—and a peachicken may live to be thirty-five—he will have nothing better to do than manicure it, furl and unfurl it, dance forward *and backward* with it spread, scream when it is stepped upon, and arch it carefully when he steps through a puddle.

Not every part of the peacock is striking to look at, even when he is full-grown. His upper wing feathers are a striated black and white and might have been borrowed from a Barred Rock fryer; his end wing feathers are the color of clay; his legs are long, thin, and iron-colored; his feet are big; and he appears to be wearing the short pants now so much in favor with playboys in the summer. These extend downward, buff-colored and sleek, from what might be a blue-black waistcoat. One would not be disturbed to find a watch chain hanging from this, but none does. Analyzing the appearance of the peacock as he stands with his tail folded, I find the parts incommensurate with the whole. The fact is that with his tail folded, nothing but his bearing saves this bird from being a laughingstock. With his tail spread, he inspires a range of emotions, but I have yet to hear laughter.

The usual reaction is silence, at least for a time. The cock opens his tail by shaking himself violently until it is gradually lifted in an arch around him.

Then, before anyone has had a chance to see it, he swings around so that his back faces the spectator. This has been taken by some to be insult and by others to be whimsey. I suggest it means only that the peacock is equally well satisfied with either view of himself. Since I have been keeping peafowl, I have been visited at least once a year by first-grade schoolchildren, who learn by living. I am used to hearing this group chorus as the peacock swings around, "Oh, look at his underwear!" This "underwear" is a stiff gray tail, raised to support the larger one, and beneath it a puff of black feathers that would be suitable for some really regal woman—a Cleopatra or a Clytemnestra—to use to powder her nose.

When the peacock has presented his back, the spectator will usually begin to walk around him to get a front view; but the peacock will continue to turn so that no front view is possible. The thing to do then is to stand still and wait until it pleases him to turn. When it suits him, the peacock will face you. Then you will see in a green-bronze arch around him a galaxy of gazing, haloed suns. This is the moment when most people are silent.

"Amen! Amen!" an old Negro woman once cried when this happened, and I have heard many similar remarks at this moment that show the inadequacy of human speech. Some people whistle; a few, for once, are silent. A truck driver who was driving up with a load of hay and found a peacock turning before him in the middle of the road shouted, "Get a load of that bastard!" and braked his truck to a shattering halt. I have never known a strutting peacock to budge a fraction of an inch for truck or tractor or automobile. It is up to the vehicle to get out of the way. No peafowl of mine has ever been run over, though one year one of them lost a foot in the mowing machine.

Many people, I have found, are congenitally unable to appreciate the sight of a peacock. Once or twice I have been asked what the peacock is "good for"—a question which gets no answer from me because it deserves none. The telephone company sent a lineman out one day to repair our telephone. After the job was finished, the man, a large fellow with a suspicious expression half hidden by a yellow helmet, continued to idle about, trying to coax a cock that had been watching him to strut. He wished to add this experience to a large number of others he had apparently had. "Come on now, bud," he said, "get the show on the road, upsy-daisy, come on now, snap it up, snap it up."

The peacock, of course, paid no attention to this.

"What ails him?" the man asked.

"Nothing ails him," I said. "He'll put it up terreckly. All you have to do is wait."

The man trailed about after the cock for another fifteen minutes or so; then, in disgust, he got back in his truck and started off. The bird shook himself and his tail rose around him.

"He's doing it!" I screamed. "Hey, wait! He's doing it!"

The man swerved the truck back around again just as the cock turned and faced him with the spread tail. The display was perfect. The bird turned slightly to the right and the little planets above him hung in bronze, then he turned slightly to the left and they were hung in green. I went up to the truck to see how the man was affected by the sight.

He was staring at the peacock with rigid concentration, as if he were trying to read fine print at a distance. In a second the cock lowered his tail and stalked off.

"Well, what did you think of that?" I asked.

"Never saw such long ugly legs," the man said. "I bet that rascal could outrun a bus."

Some people are genuinely affected by the sight of a peacock, even with his tail lowered, but do not care to admit it; others appear to be incensed by it. Perhaps they have the suspicion that the bird has formed some unfavorable opinion of them. The peacock himself is a careful and dignified investigator. Visitors to our place, instead of being barked at by dogs rushing from under the porch, are squalled at by peacocks whose blue necks and crested heads pop up from behind tufts of grass, peer out of bushes, and crane downward from the roof of the house, where the bird has flown, perhaps for the view. One of mine stepped from under the shrubbery one day and came forward to inspect a carful of people who had driven up to buy a calf. An old man and five or six white-haired, barefooted children were piling out the back of the automobile as the bird approached. Catching sight of him they stopped in their tracks and stared, plainly hacked to find this superior figure blocking their path. There was silence as the bird regarded them, his head drawn back at its most majestic angle, his folded train glittering behind him in the sunlight.

"Whut is thet thang?" one of the small boys asked finally in a sullen voice.

The old man had got out of the car and was gazing at the peacock with an astounded look of recognition. "I ain't seen one of them since my grandaddy's day," he said, respectfully removing his hat. "Folks used to have 'em, but they don't no more."

"Whut is it?" the child asked again in the same tone he had used before.

"Churren," the old man said, "that's the king of the birds!"

The children received this information in silence. After a minute they climbed back into the car and continued from there to stare at the peacock, their expressions annoyed, as if they disliked catching the old man in the truth.

The peacock does most of his serious strutting in the spring and summer when he has a full tail to do it with. Usually he begins shortly after breakfast, struts for several hours, desists in the heat of the day, and begins again in the late afternoon. Each cock has a favorite station where he performs every day in the hope of attracting some passing hen; but if I have found anyone indifferent to the peacock's display, besides the telephone lineman, it is the peahen. She seldom casts an eye at it. The cock, his tail raised in a shimmering arch around him, will turn this way and that, and with his clay-colored wing feathers touching the ground, will dance forward and backward, his neck curved, his beak parted, his eyes glittering. Meanwhile the hen goes about her business, diligently searching the ground as if any bug in the grass were of more importance than the unfurled map of the universe which floats nearby.

Some people have the notion that only the peacock spreads his tail and that he does it only when the hen is present. This is not so. A peafowl only a few hours hatched will raise what tail he has—it will be about the size of a thumbnail—and will strut and turn and back and bow exactly as if he were three years old and had some reason to be doing it. The hens will raise their tails when they see an object on the ground which alarms them, or sometimes when they have nothing better to do and the air is brisk. Brisk air goes at once to the peafowl's head and inclines him to be sportive. A group of birds will dance together, or four or five will chase one another around a bush or tree. Sometimes one will chase himself, end his frenzy with a spirited leap into the air, and then stalk off as if he had never been involved in the spectacle.

Frequently the cock combines the lifting of his tail with the raising of his voice. He appears to receive through his feet some shock from the center of the earth, which travels upward through him and is released: *Eee-ooo-ii! Eee-ooo-ii!* To the melancholy this sound is melancholy and to the hysterical it is hysterical. To me it has always sounded like a cheer for an invisible parade.

The hen is not given to these outbursts. She makes a noise like a mule's bray—*heehaw, heehaw, aa-aawww*—and makes it only when necessary. In the fall and winter, peafowl are usually silent unless some racket disturbs them; but in the spring and summer, at short intervals during the day and night, the cock, lowering his neck and throwing back his head, will give out with seven or eight screams in succession as if this message were the one on earth which needed most urgently to be heard.

At night these calls take on a minor key and the air for miles around is charged with them. It has been a long time since I let my first peafowl out at dusk to roost in the cedar trees behind the house. Now fifteen or twenty still roost there; but the original old cock from Eustis, Florida, stations himself on top of the barn, the bird who lost his foot in the mowing machine sits on a flat shed near the horse stall, there are others in the trees by the pond, several in the oaks at the side of the house, and one that cannot be dissuaded from roosting on the water tower. From all these stations calls and answers echo through the night. The peacock perhaps has violent dreams. Often he wakes and screams "Help! Help!" and then from the pond and the barn and the trees around the house a chorus of adjuration begins:

Lee-yon lee-yon,
Mee-yon mee-yon!
Eee-e-yoy eee-e-yoy!
Eee-e-yoy eee-e-yoy!

The restless sleeper may wonder if he wakes or dreams.

It is hard to tell the truth about this bird. The habits of any peachicken left to himself would hardly be noticeable, but multiplied by forty, they become a situation. I was correct that my peachickens would all eat Startena; they also eat everything else. Particularly they eat flowers. My mother's fears were all borne out. Peacocks not only eat flowers, they eat them systematically, beginning at the head of a row and going down it. If they are not hungry, they will pick the flower anyway, if it is attractive, and let it drop. For general eating they prefer chrysanthemums and roses. When they are not eating flowers, they enjoy sitting on top of them, and where the peacock sits he will eventually fashion a dusting hole. Any chicken's dusting hole is out of place in a flower bed, but the peafowl's hole, being the size of a small crater, is more so. When he dusts he all but obliterates the sight of himself with sand. Usually when someone arrives at full gallop with the leveled broom, he can see nothing through the cloud of dirt and flying flowers but a few green feathers and a beady, pleasure-taking eye.

From the beginning, relations between these birds and my mother were strained. She was forced, at first, to get up early in the morning and go out with her clippers to reach the Lady Bankshire and the Herbert Hoover roses before some peafowl had breakfasted upon them; now she has halfway solved her problem by erecting hundreds of feet of twenty-four-inch-high wire to fence the flower beds. She contends that peachickens do not have enough sense to jump over a low fence. "If it were a high wire," she says, "they would jump onto it and over, but they don't have sense enough to jump over a low wire."

It is useless to argue with her on this matter. "It's not a challenge," I say to her; but she has made up her mind.

In addition to eating flowers, peafowl also eat fruit, a habit which has created a lack of cordiality toward them on the part of my uncle, who had the fig trees planted about the place because he has an appetite for figs himself. "Get that scoundrel out of that fig bush!" he will roar, rising from his chair at the sound of a limb breaking, and someone will have to be dispatched with a broom to the fig trees.

Peafowl also enjoy flying into barn lofts and eating peanuts off peanut hay; this has not endeared them to our dairyman. And as they have a taste for fresh garden vegetables, they have often run afoul of the dairyman's wife.

The peacock likes to sit on gates or fence posts and allow his tail to hang down. A peacock on a fence post is a superb sight. Six or seven peacocks on a gate are beyond description; but it is not very good for the gate. Our fence posts tend to lean in one direction or another and all our gates open diagonally.

In short, I am the only person on the place who is willing to underwrite, with something more than tolerance, the presence of peafowl. In return, I am blessed with their rapid multiplication. The population figure I give out is forty, but for some time now I have not felt it wise to take a census. I had been told before I bought my birds that peafowl are difficult to raise. It is not so, alas. In May the peahen finds a nest in some fence corner and lays five or six large buff-colored eggs. Once a day, thereafter, she gives an abrupt *hee-haa-awww!* and shoots like a rocket from her nest. Then for half an hour, her neck ruffled and stretched forward, she parades around the premises, announcing what she is about. I listen with mixed emotions.

In twenty-eight days the hen comes off with five or six mothlike, murmuring peachicks. The cock ignores these unless one gets under his feet (then he pecks it over the head until it gets elsewhere), but the hen is a watchful mother and every year a good many of the young survive. Those that withstand illnesses and predators (the hawk, the fox, and the opossum) over the winter seem impossible to destroy, except by violence.

A man selling fence posts tarried at our place one day and told me that he had once had eighty peafowl on his farm. He cast a nervous eye at two of mine standing nearby. "In the spring, we couldn't hear ourselves think," he said. "As soon as you lifted your voice, they lifted their'n, if not before. All our fence posts wobbled. In the summer they ate all the tomatoes off the vines. Scuppernongs went the same way. My wife said she raised her flowers for herself and she was not going to have them eat up by a chicken no matter how long his tail was. And in the fall they shed them feathers all over the place anyway and it was a job to clean up. My old grandmother was living with us then and she was eighty-five. She said, 'Either they go, or I go.' "

"Who went?" I asked.

"We still got twenty of them in the freezer," he said.

"And how," I asked, looking significantly at the two standing nearby, "did they taste?"

"No better than any other chicken," he said, "but I'd a heap rather eat them than hear them."

I have tried imagining that the single peacock I see before me is the only one I have, but then one comes to join him; another flies off the roof, four or five crash out of the crêpe-myrtle hedge; from the pond one screams and from the barn I hear the dairyman denouncing another that has got into the cowfeed. My kin are given to such phrases as "Let's face it."

I do not like to let my thoughts linger in morbid channels, but there are times when such facts as the price of wire fencing and the price of Startena and the yearly gain in peafowl all run uncontrolled through my head. Lately I have had a recurrent dream: I am five years old and a peacock. A photographer has been sent from New York and a long table is laid in celebration. The meal is to be an exceptional one: myself. I scream, "Help! Help!" and awaken. Then from the pond and the barn and the trees around the house, I hear that chorus of jubilation begin:

> Lee-yon lee-yon,
> Mee-yon mee-yon!
> Eee-e-yoy eee-e-yoy!
> Eee-e-yoy eee-e-yoy!

I intend to stand firm and let the peacocks multiply, for I am sure that, in the end, the last word will be theirs.

ROY BLOUNT, JR.

"Song to Oysters"

> I like to eat an uncooked oyster.
> Nothing's slicker, nothing's moister.
> Nothing's easier on your gorge
> Or, when the time comes, to dischorge.
> But not to let it too long rest
> Within your mouth is always best.
> For if your mind dwells on an oyster . . .
> Nothing's slicker. Nothing's moister.
>
> I *prefer* my oyster fried.
> Then I'm sure my oyster's died.

TIM MCLAURIN

McLaurin, who lives in Chapel Hill, North Carolina, is the only novelist and memoirist I know who has gone around displaying a reptile show, at schools and so on. He keeps his own snakes in his garage, and sometimes around the house. I've seen them.

from *Keeper of the Moon*

When the forest in my home country had been reduced to one last acre, my Uncle Bill will be in the middle of those trees, dressed in his hunting camouflage and stalking whatever game has retreated there. He is the very mold of a Southern sportsman.

Bill is a big man, a little round in his belly from the thousands of Coca-Colas he has drunk over the years, his jaw forever packed with chewing tobacco. His arms are thick from moving around crates of soft drinks, his voice loud; with his black hair and sideburns he looks a little like Elvis might today if he'd kept on driving a truck. He is only ten years older than me, so I remember well as a child his weekend visits, a roughneck young teen who detested school and longed to live a life like Daniel Boone. He was quick to act on impulse, and has always been accident-prone.

An alligator bit him once. This was in the sixties when pet stores still sold unusual animals like horned toads, spider monkeys, and baby South American alligators. Bill came for the weekend, lugging a sack stuffed with a few clothes and a cardboard box that contained an eighteen-inch young gator.

The alligator, like most of his breed, was quick to bite. Bill liked to show off by teasing the alligator with a pencil and watching it snap. I had just begun my own interest in reptiles and was fascinated by the creature, its large, slow-blinking eyes, fat belly, and rough hide.

On our kitchen table, Bill fed the alligator small pieces of fish. He had caught a few small perch in the creek behind our house and cut them into small fillets. He'd drop a fillet in front of the gator and watch it bend its neck and gobble down the meat. Watching was better than seeing a Saturday-morning Godzilla movie.

One of the pieces of fish fell on top of the alligator's head. The alligator shook a couple of times trying to dislodge the meal, but the damp meat stuck fast to his skin. Bill, acting very brave in front of his audience of nephews and niece, slowly extended his hand with the intention of flicking the food off the gator's snout.

Apparently alligators have a wide circle of vision. Bill's finger was an inch away from the morsel of food when the beast lunged upwards and snapped, clamping firmly on a knuckle. Bill shouted and flung up his arm, gator in tow. When his arm reached the zenith high over Bill's head, the gator's teeth ripped out of Bill's flesh, and the momentum slung the reptile completely across the room. The alligator slammed into the wall high above the stove, bounced off, and fell smack-dab into a large pot where butter beans were boiling. He was instantly killed. We stood there in front of the pot and watched the alligator float up and down in the rolling water while Bill cussed, his finger gushing blood. Finally Karen went and got my mother, who fished the gator out of the beans with a spoon. We were not of the finances to throw out a large pot of butter beans and ate them with fascination that night at being flavored with alligator stock. Bill buried the scalded alligator in the pasture after praying it went to hell for biting his finger.

Bill's ability to maim himself has continued all his life. He carries several scars on his hands from knife cuts. Once, soon after he was married and Michael was born, a shotgun he was holding discharged and blew a hole through the couch where a minute before his wife and child had sat. Recently, he was firing a .22 caliber rifle when the bullet ricocheted and somehow fantastically came to lodge between his front teeth. Still, despite his tendency toward mishap, he is a fine hunter, keen of eye and born with the patience to sit motionless in a tree stand for hours in freezing weather waiting out a deer. He has also taught himself the art of taking his kills and mounting them so well that they seem to live again. If I was lost in the Alaska wilderness, he is a man I'd like to have as my partner.

GEORGE WASHINGTON HARRIS

Harris grew up in Knoxville, Tennessee, received in all eighteen months of schooling, did some metalworking, was appointed captain of a Mississippi steamboat at the age of twenty-one in 1835 (the year Mark Twain was born), failed as a farmer, got into newspapering and secessionist politics, wandered about the collapsing South with his wife and children during the war, and is reputed to have uttered the word "poisoned" on his deathbed in 1869. On the side he wrote satirical sketches, the best of which involved Sut Lovingood, a self-described "nat'ral born durn'd fool." At Sut's funeral, Parson Bullen said: "We air met, my brethering, to bury this ornery cuss. He had hosses, an' he run 'em; he had chickens, an' he fit 'em; he had kiards, an' he played 'em. Let us try an' ricollect his virtues—ef he had any—an' forgit his vices—ef we can. For of sich air the kingdom of heaven!" Not a bad sendoff, considered the parson's personal experience with the man (see below). The collected Sut stories influenced Twain and Faulkner and were called by Edmund Wilson "by far the most repellent book of any real literary merit in American literature." I don't think they're so repellent. Harris is the hairiest, the most headlong, and the most abidingly funny of the Old Southwest humorists. His dialect is so dense, though, that even I, who enjoy dialect past all reason, have trouble wading through it. So I have taken the liberty of thinning it out a bit here.

"Parson John Bullen's Lizards"

$8 DOLLARS REWARD

Attenshun Belevers and Constables! Ketch 'Im! Ketch 'Im!

This cash will be paid in corn, or other projuce, to be collected at or about nex camp-meetin, or *tharafter,* by any one what ketches him, a certun one SUT LOVINGOOD, dead or alive, or ailin, and safely give said devil over to the pertectin care of Parson John Bullen, or left well tied, for the reason of said devil personly discomfortin the wimen very powerful, and scarin folks generly a heap, and bustin up a promisin big warm meetin, and makin the wicked laugh, and worse, and worse—insultin the parson awful.

JOHN BULLEN, THE PARSON

I found written copies of the above proclamation stuck up on every blacksmith shop, saloon and store door in the Frog Mountain Range. Then I found Sut himself in a good crowd in front of Capehart's Saloon, and as he seemed to be about in good tune, I read it to him.

"Yas, George, that there dockyment is in dead earnest sartin. Them hardshells over there want me the worst kinda way, powerful bad. *But,* I spect eight dollers won't fetch me, neither would eight hunderd, because there's none of 'em fast enough to ketch me, nor their hosses neither by the livin' jingo! Say, George. Much talk 'bout this fuss up where you been?"

For the sake of a joke, I said yes, a great deal.

"Jis' as I spected, durn 'em—they all git drunk and scare their fool selfs nigh onto death, and then lay it onto me, a poor innersent youth, and as sound a believer as they is. Light down, ole feller, and let that roan of yourn blow a little, and I'll 'splain this cussed misfortunate affair: it has ruinated my caracter as a pious pusson in the s'ciety roun' here, and is a-spreadin' faster'n measles. When ever you hear any of em a-spreadin' it, give it the damn lie square, will you? I ain't done nuffin to one of 'em. It's true, I did sorter frustrate a few lizards a little, but they ain't church members, as far as I knows.

"You see, last year I went to the big meetin' at Rattlesnake Springs, and were a-sittin' in a nice shady place convarsin wif a frien' of mine, in the huckleberry thicket, jis' doin' nuffin to nobody and makin no fuss, when, the fust thing I remembers, I woke up from a trance what I had been knocked into by a four-year-old hickory stick, held in the paw of ole Parson Bullen, durn his alligator hide; and he were standin' astraddle of me, a-foamin' at the mouf, a-chompin' his teeth—gesterin' with the hickory club—and a-preachin' to me so you coulda hearn him a mile, about sartin sins gen'rally and my wickedness pussonly; and mentionin' the name of my frien loud enough to be hearn to the meetin'-house. My poor innersent frien were done gone and I were glad of it, for I thought he meant to kill me right where I lay, and I didn't want her to see me die."

"Who was she, the friend, Sut?"

Sut opened his eyes wide.

"Who the devil and durnation tole *you* that it were a she?"

"Why, you did, Sut—"

"I *didn't,* durn if I did. Ole Bullin done it, and I'll have to kill him yet, the cussed, infernal ole tale-bearer!"

"Well, well, Sut, who was she?"

"None of y-u-r-e b-i-s-n-i-s-s, durn your little anxious face! I *sees you* a-lickin' your lips. I *will* tell you one thing, George; that night, a neighbor gal got a all-fired, overhanded stroppin' from her Mam, wif a stirrup-leather. An' ole Passun Bullin, he'd et supper there, and what's wuss'n all, that poor innersent skeered gal had done her level best a-cookin it for him. She begged him, a-trimblin and a-cryin not to tell on her. He et her cookin, he promised her he'd keep quiet—and then went straight and tole her Mam. Warn't that real low down? Wolf-mean? The durned infernal hippercritical, pot-bellied, scaley-hided, whisky-wastin, stinkin ole groun-hog. But I paid him plum up for it.

"Here's the way I did it. At the nex big meetin at Rattlesnake—las' week it were—I were on hand as solemn as a ole hat. I had my face drawed out into the shape and perportion of a ironin-board, pint down. I come on the con- victed sinner so puffeckly that a ole observin she-pillar of the church said to a ole he-pillar, as I walked up to my bench:

" 'Law sakes alive, if there ain't that *orful* sinner, Sut Lovingood, pierced plum through. Who's next?'

"You see, by golly, George, I *had* to promise the old tub of soap-grease to come and have myself converted, jis to keep him from killin me. An as I knowed hit wouldn't interfere with the relation I bore to the drinkin places roun' there, I didn't care a durn. I jis wanted to git *nigh* ole Bullen, once unsuspected, and this were the bes' way to do it. I took a seat on the side steps of the pulpit, and kivvered as much of my stretched face as I could with my han's, to prove I were in earnest. It took powerful well, for I hearn a sorter thankful kind of buzzin all over the congregation. Ole Bullen hisself looked down at me, over his ole copper specs, and it said jis' as plain as a look could say: 'You am there, are you—durn you, it's well for you that you come.' I thought sorter diffrent from that. I thought it woulda been well for *him,* if I hadn'ta come, but I didn't say it jis then. There were a monstrous crowd in that grove, for the weather were fine, and believers were plenty roun' about Rattlesnake Springs. Ole Bullen motioned, and they sung that hymn, you know:

> *"There will be mournin, mournin here, and mournin there.*
> *On that dreadful day to come.*

"Thinks I, ole hoss, can it be possible enybody has tole you what's agwine to happen; and then I thought that nobody knowed it but me, and I were comforted. He nex took hisself a tex pow'fly mixed wif brimstone, and trimmed wif blue flames, and then he opened. He commenced onto the sinners; he threatened em orful, tried to skeer 'em wif all the worst varmints he could think of, and arter a while he got onto the idear of Hell-sarpents, and he dwelt on it some. He tole 'em how the ole Hell-sarpents would sarve em if they didn't repent; how cold they'd crawl over their nakid bodies, and how like onto pitch they'd stick to 'em as they crawled; how they'd wrap their tails roun' their necks chokin' close, poke their tongues up their noses and hiss into their ears. This were the way the sarpents were to sarve menfolks. Then he turned onto the wimmen: tole 'em how the sarpents'd coil into their bosoms, and how they would crawl down under their frock-strings, no matter how tight they tied 'em, and how some of the oldest and worst ones would crawl up their laigs, and travel *onder* their garters, no matter how tight they tied *them,* and when the two armies of Hell-sarpents met, *then*—

"That las' remark *fetched* 'em. Of all the screamin, and hollerin, and loud cryin, I ever hearn begun all at once, all over the hole groun jis as he hollered out that word *'then.'*

"He kep on a-bellerin, but I got so busy jis' then that I didn't listen to him much, for I saw that my time for action had come.

Now you see, George, I'd cotched seven or eight big pot-bellied lizards, and had 'em in a little narrer bag, what I had made a-purpose. Their tails all at the bottom, and so crowded for room that they couldn't turn roun'. So when he were a-ravin onto his tiptoes, and a-poundin the pulpit wif his fist— unbenownst to anybody, I untied my bag of reptiles, put the mouth of it under the bottom of his britches-laig, and set to pinchin their tails.

Quick as gunpowder they all tuck up his bare laig, makin a noise like squirrels a-climbin a shellbark hickory. He stopped preachin right in the middle of the word 'damnation,' and looked for a moment like he were a-listenin for somethin—sorter like a ole sow does, when she hears you a-whistlin for the dogs.

"The terrific shape of his features stopped the congergation's shoutin and screamin; instantly you coulda hearn a cricket chirp. I give a long groan, and held my head atwixt my knees. He give himself some orful open-handed slaps wif fust one hand and then tother, about the place where you cut the bes' steak outen a beef.

"Then he'd give a vigrous rough rub where a hoss's tail sprouts; then he'd stomp one foot, then tother, then bofe at once. Then he run his hand atween his wais'band and his shirt and reached way down and roun wif it; then he spread his big laigs, and give his back a good rattlin rub agin the pulpit, like a hog scratches hisself agin a stump, leanin into it pow'ful, and twitchin, and squirmin all over, as if he'd slept in a dog bed or on a pissant hill.

"About this time one of my lizards, scared and hurt by all this poundin' and feelin' and scratchin', popped out his head from the parson's shirt-collar next to his ole brown neck, and were a-surveyin the crowd, when ole Bullen struck at him—jis too late, for he'd dodged back again. The hell-deservin ole rascal's speech now come to him, and says he, 'Pray for me brethren and sistern, for I is a-rasslin wif the great inimy right now!' And his voice were the mos' pitiful, tremblin thing I ever hearn. Some of the wimmen give a panther yell, and a young doctor wif ramrod laigs leaned toward me monstrous knowin-like, and says he, 'Clear case of Delicious Tremenjus.'

"I nodded my head and says I, 'Yas, speshly the tremenjus part, and Ise afeared it ain't at its worst.'

"Ole Bullen's eyes were a-stickin out like two buckeyes flung agin a mud wall, and he were a-cuttin up more shines than a cockroach in a hot skillet. Off went the clawhammer coat, and he flung it ahind him like he were a-goin into a fight; he had no jacket to take off, so he unbuttoned his galluses and vigrously flung the ends back over his head. He shed his shirt overhanded and then flung it straight up in the air, like he jis wanted it to keep on up forever; but it lodged onto a oak tree, and I seed one of my lizards wif his tail up a-racin about all over that ole dirty shirt, scared too bad to jump.

"Then he give a sorter shake, and a stompin kind of twist, and he come outer his britches. He took 'em by the bottom of the laigs, and swung 'em roun' his head a time or two, and then brought 'em down chest-flap up over the front of the pulpit. You coulda hearn the smash a quarter of a mile! Nigh onto fifteen shortened biscuits, a boiled chicken wif its laigs crossed, a big double-bladed knife, a hunk of terbacker, a cob-pipe, some copper ore, lots of broken glass, a cork, a sprinkle of whisky, a oil-can, and three lizards flew permiscuously all over that meetin-groun', outen the upper end of them big flax britches. One of the smartest of my lizards lit head-fust into the bosom of a fat woman as big as a skinned hoss and nigh onto as ugly who sot thirty yards off a-fannin herself wif a turkey tail. Smart to the last, by golly, my lizard immejitly commenced runnin' down the center of her breas'bone, and kep on, I speck. She was jis boun' to faint; and she did it fust-rate—flung the turkey-tail up in the air, grabbed the lap of her gown, give it a big hoistin' and fallin' shake, rolled down the hill, tangled her laigs and garters in the top of a huckleberry bush wif her head in the branch, and jis lay still.

"She were interestin, she were, until a serious-lookin, pale-faced woman hung a nankeen ridin skirt over her and the huckleberry bush. That were all that were done towards bringin' her to, that I seed.

"Now ole Bullen had nuffin left on him but a pair of heavy, low-quartered shoes, short woollen socks, and eel-skin garters. His scare had drove him plum crazy, for he felt roun' in the air, above his head, like he were huntin' somethin' in the dark, and he bellered out, 'Brethren, brethren, take care of yourselves, the Hell-sarpents *has got me!*'

"When this come out, you coulda hearn the screams to Halifax. He jis spit in his han's, and loped over the front of the pulpit *kerdiff!* He lit on top of and right among the most pious part of the congregation. Ole Missus Chaneyberry was caught wif her back to the pulpit, sorter stoopin' forward. He lit astraddle of her long neck, a-shuttin' her up wif a snap, her head atwix her knees, like

shuttin' up a jackknife. And he set into gittin' away his level durnednest; he
went in a heavy lumberin' gallop, like a ole fat wagon hoss scared by a
locomotive. When he jumped a bench he shook the earth. The bonnets and
fans cleared the way and jerked most of the children wif 'em, and the rest he
scrunched. He opened a perfeckly clear track to the woods, through every
livin' thing. He weighed nigh onto three hundred, had a black stripe down his
back like onto a ole bridle rein, and his belly were about the size and color of a
beef paunch, and it a-swingin' from side to side; he leaned back from it, like a
little feller a-totin' a big drum, and it made a sound I could hear where I was.
There were cramp-knots on his laigs as big as walnuts, and mottled splotches
on his shins; and takin' him all over, he minded me of a durned crazy ole
elephant, possessed of the devil, rared up on its hind end and jis' *gittin'* from
some immejit danger or tribulation. He did the loudest, and scariest, and
fussiest runnin' I ever seed, to be no faster than it were.

"Well, he disappeared in the thicket jis' bustin'—and all the noises you
ever hearn were made there on that campgroun': some wimmen screamin'
(they were the scary ones); some laughin' (they were the wicked ones); some
cryin' (they were the fool ones); some tryin' to git away wif their faces red
(they were the modest ones); some lookin' after ole Bullen (they were the
curious ones); some hanging close to their sweethearts (they were the sweet
ones); some doin' nothin' (they were the waitin' ones and the most dangerous).

"I took a big scare myself after a few rocks and fruit spattered onto the
pulpit nigh unto my head; and as the Lovingoods knows nuffin but to run when
they gits scared, I jis' put out for the swamp. As I started, a black bottle of
whiskey smashed agin a tree in front of me after missin' the top of my head
about a inch. Some durned fool done this, who had more zeal than sense; for I
say that any man who would waste a quart of even cheap spirits for the chance
of knocking a poor ornery devil like me down wif the bottle is a bigger fool
than—"

"Did they catch you, Sut?"

"Ketch thunder! *No sir!* Jis' look at these here laigs! Scare me, hoss, jis'
scare me, and then watch me while I stay in sight, and you'll never ax that fool
question agin. Why durn it, man, that's what the eight dollars is for.

"Ole Barebelly Bullen, as they calls 'im now, never preached ontil yesterday, and he didn't have the first durned woman to hear 'im—*they have seed too
much of 'im.* Parsons generly have a pow'ful strong holt on wimmen; but, hoss,
I tell you there ain't many of 'em kin run stark nakid over and through a crowd
of three hundred wimmen and not injure their characters *some.* Anyhow, it's a
kind of show they'd rather see one at a time, and pick the parson at that. His
text yesterday were, 'Nakid I come into the world, and nakid I'm agwine
outen it, if I'm spared ontil then.' He said nakidness warn't much of a sin,

pertickerly of dark nights. That he were a weak, frail worm of the dust, and a heap more such truck. Then he touched onto me; said I were a living proof of the hell-desarvin' nature of man, and that there warn't grace enough in the whole association to soften my outside rind; that I were a lost cause forty years afore I were born, and the best thing they could do for the chuch were to turn out and hunt for me ontil I were shot. And he never touched on Hell-sarpents once in the whole sermon.

"Now I wants you to tell ole Barebelly this for me, if he'll let me and Sally alone, I'll let him alone—awhile; and if he don't, then if I don't lizard him agin I wish I may be dod durned! *Scare him if you kin.*

"Let's go take a drink.

"Say, George, didn't that there Hell-sarpent sermon of his'n have somethin' of a Hall-sarpent application? It looks sorter so to me."

GREGORY JAYNES

My friend Jaynes has been to far corners of the world for Time, Life, *and the* New York Times. *He was on the scene for the* Times *in 1979 when the Ayatollah Khomeini returned to the holy city of Qom. A multitude of roadside Shiites, stretching as far as the eye could see, pounded their feet in the dust as the Ayatollah's procession passed, and here was the last line of Jaynes's account: "And the earth moved." Jaynes has also brought to light a good many facets of Southern culture—for instance, it was he who reported, again in the* Times, *Shelby Foote's stated reason for not appearing on TV interview shows (this was before the Civil War series): "I don't have any of those long socks." Jaynes comes from Memphis and lives in Savannah. His usage of the word "tump" is cited in the latest edition of the* American Heritage Dictionary. *In the '70s he lived for a year back up in the north Georgia mountains and wrote a book about it,* Sketches from a Dirt Road, *from which this selection, and the longer one you will come to directly, is taken.*

"A Day with the Vet"

Jacqueline Smith, our veterinarian, got a call last Saturday from an elderly man whose Chihuahua had been chewed up by a German shepherd. When she went to work on the Chihuahua, which was about to expire, owing to a large cavity in its chest, she found the old man was preparing to shoot the shepherd. The shepherd belonged to his nephew. In return, the nephew was going to shoot the old man's cattle. A minister was called.

The Chihuahua died and Mrs. Smith left the feud in favor of a sick horse, twenty miles to the north. The horse had had a bad case of worms and he was down in his stall. He had no feeling in his hindquarters. A blood clot had caused this situation. It was messy for a while, with the horse's owner, a woman, crying, and Dr. Smith hugging her.

It came down to either investing as much as two hundred dollars for surgery on the old quarter horse, or destroying it. Ultimately, it was decided to destroy it. Dr. Smith, retiring early that night, hoped for no more telephone calls. "It hasn't been my day," she said. The telephone rang, and a woman said, "Would you listen to my parakeet breathe on the phone? He doesn't sound right." Dr. Smith listened but couldn't hear a thing.

FRANK GANNON

Frank Gannon is that rare thing among humorists in the South, a minimalist. His brief essays have appeared in Southern magazines and also The New Yorker. *This one was included in his 1987 collection* Yo, Poe. *As to whether kudzu can be dealt with minimalistically, surely it goes on and on and on enough for itself and Gannon both.*

"Kudzu East and West and South"

This is how it starts.

DOWN HERE WE HAVE THIS PLANT. A VINE, ACTUALLY. IT HAS A KIND OF EXOTIC, FOREIGN-SOUNDING NAME TO IT.

This is, of course, by now enough to make you sick. You've picked up the paper and started reading another goddamn story about kudzu.

Such a whimsical subject, kudzu.

There have been, at this point, a great number of articles and columns about kudzu. In Southern newspapers, for instance, an informal survey placed the number of kudzu articles at "no lower than 32,000 and no higher than a googolplex."

These are all humorous columns, and we love seeing them in the paper. But they all say the same thing: kudzu grows very fast and it is hard to get rid of. That's the deal with kudzu. What else can you say?

But what is the attitude in the ancestral home of kudzu? Does the Eastern world approach the subject of this vine in the same manner?

The answer turns out to be no.

I live in Tallulah Falls, Georgia. We have kudzu here, but my attitude toward it is far different from the Japanese attitude. Let me show you what I mean. Here's a Japanese guy writing about kudzu.

> The rice plant bows
> But not the kudzu
> Get out and burn it, Yukio

Has any poem ever offered a clearer expression of the contrast between East and West?

Consider this haiku. It was written in the seventeenth century, but it speaks like today's headlines.

> Rain sings softly
> That's no excuse
> Get out there, Yukio

Yet one does not have to renounce all earthly goods and move to India and kneel motionless on the soft grass for three years in order to appreciate kudzu. Whatever else it is, and it's probably plenty, the vine is not something that can be easily dealt with, especially by a contemplative type.

> Wonder and ecstasy
> Birds make music
> Get busy, Yukio

Kudzu is many things to many people: a dance, a gladdening of the heart, a summons, a subpoena.

There have been many haikus written on kudzu. They can be appreciated individually, but perhaps their fullest sense can be absorbed when they are read en masse.

Consider this brilliant series, written long ago but on the same afternoon.

I

> What this is
> I do not know
> There is a hell of a lot of it

II

A green vine
With dense leaves
Young man, stop resting

III

A frog looks
The leaves breathe
Get your blowtorch

IV

Shaven-headed Buddhist monks
Appreciate the good work
You are doing with that blowtorch

V

The moon is a kudzu vine
Frozen
In blue ice

VI

The memory of the mirror
Is covered in kudzu vines
It's time to get busy again

A man is like a kudzu vine. He starts out as narrow, self-centered, isolated. His world is a small one. He is an angry little guy. Soon, though, he grows and grows. He covers everything. He becomes boundless. His reach seems infinite. He has his little grubby fingers in everything.

We react. We take the man and have him indicted. We chop the vine down and throw it in the fire. Then we send the man to prison, so that he also "knows his place."

This is the way of kudzu.

DAVY CROCKETT

The legendary Crockett was indeed an east Tennessee bear hunter and Congressman. At thirteen he ran away from home like Huck Finn to escape a drunken father, off into the frontier, and at forty-nine he died like Jim Bowie at the Alamo. What he didn't do was write most of the tall tales attributed to him. But he stands tall in the tradition of Southern humor to some extent as a storyteller and to a great extent as an attributee.

"A Sensible Varmint"

Almost everybody that knows the forest understands perfectly well that Davy Crockett never loses powder and ball, having been brought up to believe it a sin to throw away ammunition, and that is the benefit of a virtuous eddication. I was out in the forest one a'ternoon, and had just got to a place called the Great Gap, when I seed a raccoon setting all alone upon a tree. I clapped the breech of Brown Betsy to my shoulder, and war just going to put a piece of lead between his shoulders, when he lifted one paw, and says he, "Is your name Davy Crockett."

Says I, "You are right for once, my name is Davy Crockett."

"Then," says he, "you needn't take no further trouble, for I may as well come down without another word." And the creatur walked right down from the tree, for he considered himself shot.

I stoops down and pats him on the head, and says I, "I hope I may be shot myself before I hurt a hair of your head, for I never had such a compliment in my life."

"Seeing as how you say that," says he, "I'll just walk off for the present, not doubting your word a bit, d'ye see, but lest you should kinda happen to change your mind."

SECTION THREE

LYING, AND OTHER ARTS OF COMMUNICATION

The Woman's Club in a small town was very culture-conscious, and one day the president proposed that they invite a ballet troupe to come to town and do a program. They voted to explore the idea, and the secretary wrote off to a talent agency for information. They discovered that they had only enough money to have one dancer come and demonstrate. So they asked for the ballerina to come on a certain night. The talent agency, however, got things mixed up and sent a stripper.

The town all turned out for the program. They were quite shocked, of course, at the young woman's performance, but no one had ever seen a ballet. Not wishing to show their ignorance, everybody pretended to enjoy the performance, and they left hastily afterwards so that they would not have to discuss it with one another.

The next day the president of the club and her husband were strolling down the street when they met another member of the club. She asked the president, "How did you like the performance last night?"

She hemmed and hawed and said something about its being interesting and perhaps artistic. The woman then turned to the husband and asked him what he thought.

"I'll tell you this much," he responded. "It was no place to take a nervous man!"

—LOYAL JONES

A. B. LONGSTREET

Augustus Baldwin Longstreet was born in 1790, in Augusta, Georgia. He was a physically ugly, huffy, pious, sneering man, at one time or another a judge, a college president, and a less than silver-tongued Methodist minister. (One of his slaves is remembered for saying, "Mars 'Gustus can't preach, he just gets up and laws it.") And yet his Georgia Scenes, *which appeared anonymously in Mark Twain's birth year, 1835, and which was praised by Edgar Allan Poe in the* Southern Literary Messenger *for its "delineation of Southern bravado," was the first book to get raw Southern backwoods character and speech down in print. Longstreet, who had been away to Yale, never approved of such character and speech—was ostensibly trying, in fact, to put it down—but he couldn't help being fascinated by it. If he hadn't been, he might conceivably be remembered today as Confederate General James Longstreet's uncle.*

"Georgia Theatrics"

If my memory fail me not, the 10th of June, 1809 found me, at about 11 o'clock in the forenoon, ascending a long and gentle slope in what was called "The Dark Corner" of Lincoln. I believe it took its name from the moral darkness which reigned over that portion of the county at the time of which I am speaking. If in this point of view it was but a shade darker than the rest of the county, it was inconceivably dark. If any man can name a trick or sin which had not been committed at the time of which I am speaking, in the very focus of all the county's illumination (Lincolnton), he must himself be the most inventive of the tricky, and the very Judas of sinners. Since that time, however (all humour aside), Lincoln has become a living proof "that light shineth in darkness." Could I venture to mingle the solemn with the ludicrous, even for the purposes of honourable contrast, I could adduce from this county instances of the most numerous and wonderful transitions, from vice and folly to virtue and holiness, which have ever, perhaps, been witnessed since the days of the apostolic ministry. So much, lest it should be thought by some that what I am about to relate is characteristic of the county in which it occurred.

Whatever may be said of the *moral* condition of the Dark Corner at the time just mentioned, its *natural* condition was anything but dark. It smiled in all the charms of spring; and spring borrowed a new charm from its undulating grounds, its luxuriant woodlands, its sportive streams, its vocal birds, and its blushing flowers.

Rapt with the enchantment of the season and the scenery around me, I was slowly rising the slope, when I was startled by loud, profane, and boisterous voices, which seemed to proceed from a thick covert of undergrowth about two hundred yards in the advance of me, and about one hundred to the right of my road.

"You kin, kin you?"

"Yes, I kin, and am able to do it! Boo-oo-oo! Oh, wake snakes, and walk your chalks! Brimstone and ————fire! Don't hold me, Nick Stoval! The fight's made up, and let's go at it. ———— my soul if I don't jump down his throat, and gallop every chitterling out of him before you can say 'quit!' "

"Now, Nick, don't hold him! Jist let the wild-cat come, and I'll tame him. Ned'll see me a fair fight; won't you, Ned?"

"Oh, yes; I'll see you a fair fight, blast my old shoes if I don't."

"That's sufficient, as Tom Haynes said when he saw the elephant. Now let him come."

Thus they went on, with countless oaths interspersed, which I dare not even hint at, and with much that I could not distinctly hear.

In Mercy's name! thought I, what band of ruffians has selected this holy season and this heavenly retreat for such Pandæmonian riots! I quickened my gait, and had come nearly opposite to the thick grove whence the noise proceeded, when my eye caught indistinctly, and at intervals, through the foliage of the dwarf-oaks and hickories which intervened, glimpses of a man or men, who seemed to be in a violent struggle; and I could occasionally catch those deep-drawn, emphatic oaths which men in conflict utter when they deal blows. I dismounted, and hurried to the spot with all speed. I had overcome about half the space which separated it from me, when I saw the combatants come to the ground, and, after a short struggle, I saw the uppermost one (for I could not see the other) make a heavy plunge with both his thumbs, and at the same instant I heard a cry in the accent of keenest torture, "Enough! My eye's out!"

I was so completely horrorstruck, that I stood transfixed for a moment to the spot where the cry met me. The accomplices in the hellish deed which had been perpetrated had all fled at my approach; at least I supposed so, for they were not to be seen.

"Now, blast your corn-shucking soul," said the victor (a youth about eighteen years old) as he rose from the ground, "come cutt'n your shines 'bout me agin, next time I come to the Courthouse, will you! Get your owl-eye in agin if you can!"

At this moment he saw me for the first time. He looked excessively embarrassed, and was moving off, when I called to him, in a tone imboldened by the sacredness of my office and the iniquity of his crime, "Come back, you brute! and assist me in relieving your fellow-mortal, whom you have ruined for ever!"

My rudeness subdued his embarrassment in an instant; and, with a taunting curl of the nose, he replied, "You needn't kick before you're spurr'd. There a'nt nobody there, nor ha'nt been nother. I was jist seein' how I could 'a' *fout.*" So saying, he bounded to his plough, which stood in the corner of the fence about fifty yards beyond the battle ground.

And, would you believe it, gentle reader! his report was true. All that I had heard and seen was nothing more nor less than a Lincoln rehearsal; in which the youth who had just left me had played all the parts of all the characters in a Courthouse fight.

I went to the ground from which he had risen, and there were the prints of his two thumbs, plunged up to the balls in the mellow earth, about the distance of a man's eyes apart; and the ground around was broken up as if two stags had been engaged upon it.

DAN JENKINS

Fort Worth Golf (from Dead Solid Perfect)

By the time I was fifteen years old I was going on twenty-one. I was teeing it up with the bandits like Spec and Tiny and Hope-I-Do and Willard. And a lot of others.

There was a guy at Goat Hills we called Cecil the Parachute because he lunged at the ball and he sometimes flew off the edge of elevated tees. There was Foot the Free, which was short for Big Foot the Freeloader. There was

Quadruple Unreal, who seldom said anything other than "Quadruple unreal" when anybody hit a shot. There was Moron Tom, who spoke all of his words backwards. For example, if Moron Tom said something which sounded like "Cod-e-rac Fockledim," that was basically the pronunciation of Dr. Cary Middlecoff spelled backwards. There was Pablo the Poet, who spoke exclusively in rhymes, as in "You're in my line, porcupine." Or "Think I can't, Cary Grant?"

Among the other headliners were Mister Insurance, who never agreed to take a bad partner; Rain Shed, who got drowned as often as Willard Peacock; and there were Magoo, Matty, John the Band-Aid, Zorro, Jerry the Fog, Simpo, Asbestos Ernie, Pet Shop, Whip Saw, Sausage Man, Baby Slick, Spud, Hit the Silk, Diesel Oil, and Hub Caps.

There were often games with as many as twenty guys in them—three sevensomes, roughly—and everybody would be hitting at once, betting everybody else, automatic one-down presses, every combination of teams, bingle-bangle, whip-saw, do-or-don'ts, baseball, and get-evens on nine and eighteen.

It wasn't any different from most public courses. They all had their vultures, and still do.

As the weeks and months—even years—went by, the games grew crazier and more expensive. We would play from the first tee to the third green, a marathon. We'd play the course backwards. We'd play eighteen holes with only one club. We'd play out of the streets and the front yards. Tee off from the clubhouse roof. Left-handed. One-handed. Blindfolded. One-legged. We'd play in rain, snow, tornados, electrical storms—last one dead wins—or hitting all shots from moving bicycles, carts, and running.

One day a few of us made a big effort to combat the sameness of Goat Hills. We played a marathon over several city streets and through a number of neighborhoods—maybe thirty blocks in all—to the closet of my apartment and into a brown leather loafer.

I was married to Joy at the time and we had a decent enough place to live if you didn't mind some empty beer cans and articles of clothing laying around. And an ice box with a science-fiction movie going on inside of it—starring that master of suspense and chills, the Killer Bologna.

Later, when we totaled up the casualties, we found that Cecil the Parachute had been bitten by a Chow dog after he had climbed over a Cyclone fence to fetch his Spalding Dot out of somebody's fishpond. Hope-I-Do Collins had been forced to withdraw briskly into an alley and then through the back door of the Snap Brim Lounge. He had nailed a 2-iron down Berry Street and broken the windshield on a yellow Plymouth. Magoo, too, had withdrawn after finding his poor old Maxfli in the mouth of an eight-year-old, from which he couldn't manage to dislodge it.

Spec and I were playing along together with the only clubs you needed for a game like this. An old blade putter for hitting off asphalt and getting good roll, and an 8-iron for trouble shots.

As it happened, we found Willard Peacock at a bus stop, thinking he knew how to beat the game.

Willard stood on a corner by the bus stop with a pitching wedge in his hand and a ball on the ground. He was facing the street, taking practice swings.

Stopping to watch Willard for a moment we found out what he was up to.

He would wait for a city bus to pull up, stop, and open the doors. Willard thought he could chip the ball inside the bus, hop in behind it, and make up a lot of distance—several blocks—in only one stroke.

His problem was that he couldn't chip good enough to get one inside the bus, especially with people always getting off.

Spec and I sat down on the grass in front of Devaney's Cleaners and watched Willard's futile efforts through a couple of buses.

Spec finally said, "Willard, you couldn't hit the door of one of them buses if you were the driver tryin' to climb out and go home."

Willard was taking practice swings, and he said:

"If I can get one to stop long enough I can."

Spec said, "Well, I don't know nothin' about the Fort Worth Transit System, of course, but I believe I might be tempted to bet me some money on it."

Willard turned around and said, "On what?"

Spec said, "Well, let me think. What you got in your hand there? An old pitchin' wedge, ain't it?"

Willard nodded.

Spec said, "Tell you what I'm gonna do. . . . I'm gonna bet you that you can't even hit the *bus*. I don't care nothin' about the door."

"The bus?" Willard said. "Anybody could hit the bus."

Spec said, "I'm just gonna give you one try now. You gotta hit the next bus with that pitchin' wedge on one try."

"How much?" Willard said.

"Shit, I'll tell you what," Spec said. "I'm gonna give you $40 to $20. 'Cause I know you're gonna choke up and go sideways."

Willard squinted at Spec.

"Next bus? One try?" Willard said.

"Just hit the bus on one try with that old pitchin' wedge you're usin'," Spec said.

"You got it," Willard said, and he started taking dead solid aim with his practice swings.

Now here came the bus, groaning to a halt, only five yards from Willard. The doors, front and rear, squeaked open, as Willard waggled his club and aimed toward the middle.

Two women stepped down with armloads of groceries, then a man in a baseball uniform, then a Mexican laborer, and then an elderly lady with a package.

As the doors closed, Willard hit the shot.

A puff of dirt came up as he scooped it. But he had swung hard enough that the ball went high into the air, came down on top of the bus, bounced, and then disappeared into the street as the bus pulled away.

"That counts!" Willard shouted. "It hit the roof! Roof's part of the bus! Roof's part of the bus!"

Spec sat there on the grass in front of Devaney's Cleaners, and stuck a weed in his mouth.

"Yeah, it counts," Spec said, "if you're talkin' about hittin' the bus with a golf ball. But what I bet my money on was that you couldn't hit it with that pitchin' wedge."

Spec looked at me and said:

"I didn't see no pitchin' wedge hit no bus, did you, Kenny?"

I was compelled to agree.

Willard Peacock whimpered at first, and then he began to growl.

"Mother jeemy fuckin' cock," Willard said, becoming a light red in the face. "Prick bammer shit gobble kingy fucker turd ass bobby gump."

Willard wadded up a $20 bill and threw it on the ground.

Still blabbering, he took another golf ball out of his pocket, put it down on the ground quickly, and took a violent swing at it, knocking it over the cleaners.

"Got fuckin' ever junk spickin' fart flower bed!" Willard called after the ball.

Then he started chasing it around the corner. But suddenly he stopped. He stood there with his head drooping momentarily.

Then he took a deep breath and said to me:

"Kenny . . . Where in the hell *is* your apartment, anyhow?"

Four of us in the marathon wound up at my apartment about the same time. Spec, Big Foot, Tiny, and me. By the time all of us had managed to hit pitch shots up onto the landing of an outside staircase, and had gotten the shots to bite—and hold—on a welcome mat, and then played our way through the kitchen and into the bedroom, I think I was leading Spec by about three strokes.

"Where is it?" Spec said. "That shoe. Which way?"

Tiny said, "Can't we turn on some more lights?"

And Foot said to himself, "What the shit am I doin' here? I lay 2,037."

I looked in the closet and reported that the brown leather loafer was just to the left of the door, laying down on its side, by a brassiere and a used Kotex.

Foot, Tiny, and I each hit bad shots that either careened off the wall in the closet and came back into the bedroom, or missed the door altogether and went under the bed.

Spec then punched a soft little chip shot which glanced off a cardboard box in the closet, hooked to the left, and went out of sight. We heard it hit the wall, and then roll. And then stop.

When we looked in the closet the ball was inside the brown leather loafer. It was probably the best golf shot I've ever seen.

"Why, lookie here," Spec said. "I done made me some kind of hole-in-one. I believe that's the luckiest thing I ever saw."

All I could think about was that Spec hadn't been around Goat Hills the day before, and the door to the apartment was never locked, and I didn't recall that my loafer had been sitting on its side, at a perfect angle for a bank shot.

I said to Spec, "I don't suppose you've ever practiced that trick before, have you?"

Spec said, "Now ain't that somethin'? Man, I guess there's no trust left anywhere in the world. How am I gonna know we're ever gonna play a silly game like this some day?"

Because he had suggested it, I remembered later.

GARRISON KEILLOR

My friend Garrison Keillor, born 1942, is not Southern. Indeed I feel he has had an unfair advantage as a humorist, in that he was the first one from Minnesota. Before him no one had been funny, nationally at least, about lutefisk, Norwegian bachelor farmers, Lutherans, or for that matter, to the best of my knowledge, snow. If a Southerner comes up with an imaginary Southern locality, it stands in competition with Tobacco Road, Dogpatch, the Okefenokee of Pogo, and Yoknapatawpha. Whereas Garrison's Lake Wobegon is Minnesota, or all the Minnesota anyone need know, for readers and listeners around the world. However, that territory has not been enough for him. In his extraordinary homemade award-winning Saturday-evening public-radio show "A Prairie Home Companion," he has created his own Grand Old Opry. Southern guests have included Willie Nelson, Ernest Tubb, Emmylou Harris, and the Everly Brothers. Once on that program—in a commercial for a Georgia-on-My-Mind Talking Feedcap written by the host and somewhat adapted and partly performed by me—Garrison did the voice of the cap with such verisimilitude that friends of mine who were listening thought it was me talking to myself (only more authentically as the

*cap). So I would be hard pressed to deny that there is a place in this book for Keillor
on golf with country music people. Especially when one of those people is as funny a
Tennesseean as Chet Atkins.*

"Country Golf"

I don't have many friends who have done one thing so well that they're famous
for it and could sit on their laurels if they wanted to, although I do know a
woman who can touch her nose with her tongue, which she is famous for
among all the people who've seen her do it. She doesn't do it often, because
she doesn't need to, having proved herself. I also know a man who wrote a
forty-one-word palindrome, which is about as far as you can go in the field of
writing that reads the same forwards and backwards. And I know Chet Atkins,
who is enplaqued in the Country Music Hall of Fame, in Nashville, and has a
warm, secure spot in the history of the guitar. My own accomplishments fall
into the immense dim area of the briefly remarkable, such as the play I made
on a hot grounder off the bat of my Uncle Don, for which I felt famous one day
in 1957. I backhanded the ball cleanly at third base and threw the aging
speedster out at first, which drew quite a bit of comment at the time, but that
was long ago and plays have been made since that put mine in the shade. It was
a hot July afternoon at Lake Minnetonka, and the Grace & Truth Bible camp
had spent the morning in Deuteronomy, where I have no competence at all,
and then I went out and made that great play. I was not quite fifteen and
generally unaccomplished, so it meant a lot to me. The ball took a low bounce
off the soft turf, and I had to pivot, get my glove down fast, then set my right
foot to throw. The throw got him by a stride. If you had seen this, you would
remember it.

I first met Chet Atkins in 1982, backstage at "A Prairie Home Companion."
He was standing just back of the back curtain, humming to himself, and
reached down and picked up his guitar, like a man slipping into a shirt, and put
his right foot up on a chair and fooled around with a string of tunes that came
to him, including the one he'd been humming. Then we made conversation
about various things, and he asked me if I played golf. I said, "A little." Golf
isn't one of my good subjects. I don't have good memories of it.

He mentioned golf again the next time I saw him, and the time after that,
and he told me to come down to Nashville whenever I felt like playing some
golf with him, and finally, on a Sunday morning toward the middle of May
1984, I flew down for a visit, though golf was the last thing on my mind. In my
hands, golf is a grim, catastrophic game that makes me into someone I don't

want my friends to know—a person who, in fact, I already was when I got on the plane. There had been a sour smell in the air around me for weeks, from a hard winter of sitting in a small room and throwing wads of typing paper at a basket and missing, and I went South to get rid of it. Whenever I feel bad, Southern voices make me feel better, whether it's Dolly Parton or Grandpa Jones or a waitress in a café. When she says "Hi! Haw yew?" I am immediately just fine.

I met Chet about midafternoon at his office on Music Row, down the street from the studio where he made most of his albums and where he produced albums for Willie and Waylon, Eddy Arnold, Porter Wagoner, and dozens of other laureates, and we headed south in his black Blazer to the golf course at Henry Horton State Park, forty-two miles from Nashville, where he was going to play in the annual Acuff-Rose Invitational on Monday and Tuesday. He said he had flown in that morning from doing two shows in Denver with a jazz guitarist named Johnny Smith. "You remember him. He had that big record of 'Moonlight in Vermont' back in the fifties." Acuff-Rose is one of the big music-publishing firms in Nashville, the first in the country devoted to country music, founded in 1942 by Roy Acuff, of "Wabash Cannonball" fame, and the late Fred Rose, Hank Williams' mentor. Chet said that the tournament was just for fun. He had played in it for twelve years. "People in the music industry play, and friends of theirs. They see somebody on the street, they invite him. Everybody's played in it, from the chief of police on down. *You* could play." I said no thanks. He was in a foursome, he said, with Billy Edd Wheeler, the songwriter, and a banker from Columbia named Smalley and his old friend Archie Campbell, the comedian. "Archie was the one who got me first playing golf, back in 1958 or 9. I saw how much fun he had, and I liked to be around him, so I started. I was too old to get good at it, though. You have to start young." Chet was thirty-four or thirty-five at the time, and he's sixty now.

He pointed out Waylon Jennings' house, and Eddy Arnold's, and Tom T. Hall's studio as we drove along, and a church where a woman singer got married whose wedding he played for when he had an upset stomach and who was now divorced. He put a tape in the tape deck. "This is one Billy Edd wrote," he said. A song called "Ode to the Little Brown Shack Out Back." He said, "You remember that record Archie made? 'Trouble in the Amen Corner?' 'Old brother Ira, singing in the choir'? It was a real tearjerker, but it sold a lot, so RCA wanted to put out an album on him—of songs, you know—and we had Boudleaux and Felice Bryant go to work to write him some. They were sitting around writing all these sad songs about the old dog who died and that sort of thing, and finally Felice got sick of it. She said, 'Let's write something *happy*,' so they wrote 'Wish that I was on ol' Rocky Top, down in the Tennessee hills' and that was 'Rocky Top.' The Osborne Brothers recorded it, but Archie takes credit for it. He said to me once, 'They'd never have written it without me, Cock. Without me, there'd be no "Rocky Top." ' "

This pleasant monologue in Chet's soft, East Tennessee tenor took us out in the country down Interstate 65 and to the motel at Horton Park, and included so such more—about musicians and golf, and an old radio faith healer who put his fingers in deaf people's ears and yelled at them to hear, and a squirrel Chet kept for a pet when he was a boy ("He made a nest in our old upright piano and wouldn't come out, so I sat down and played the Lost Chord and he shot straight up in the air and we never saw him again")—that when I finally climbed into bed that evening I had long forgotten what it was that I was feeling bad about when I got on the plane.

When I walked over to the clubhouse after breakfast, it was obvious that Tennessee had had a hard winter, too. Frost had killed most of the Bermuda grass on the greens, where the flags stood in circles of light-brown dust like the spot in the schoolyard where we played Fox and Geese, and the fairways looked worn and ratty for so early in the season. The woods were lush and dense, though, and the foliage of the golfers around the first tee was positively inspiring, their pants in particular. Pinks and yellows and oranges, a pair of peach and one of lilac, and an assortment of plaids such as I've seldom seen outside of the circus, including one that looked like a test for color blindness. They were such a brilliant, cheerful sight I felt sheepish about my quiet good taste in tans. It seemed stingy.

Chet arrived a few minutes later in a blue shirt and bright-green pants, and while he went in the clubhouse to sign up, I sidled up toward the crowd for a closer look. Men in clothes the colors of extravagant good humor strolled around behind the tee, pressing the flesh, putting their arms around each other's shoulders and patting each other on the belly and saying, "You're looking *good.*" Being a writer, I took out my checkbook and made some notes on who was there—songwriters such as Whitey Shafer ("That's the Way Love Goes") and Pee Wee King and Redd Stewart ("Tennessee Waltz," both of them) and Wayne Carson ("Always on My Mind," "She's Actin' Single, I'm Drinkin' Doubles"), and singers Mickey Newbury and Del Reeves, and Buck Trent, the banjo player, and pianist Floyd Cramer—and kept occupied, writing "Sunny, air smells fresh and green" and "1st hole 345 yards" and "F. Cramer sliced into sand trap," until Chet appeared at my elbow, and men came over to pat him, including a tall, lanky man named Howard, who said, "I appreciate you, Chet. I want you to know that. I love you." When Chet introduced me to him, he patted me, too, and said I looked good, which was good news to me. Mickey Newbury told Chet he looked good, and they got to laughing about a man they knew named Walter who promoted a public barbecue by flying over in a plane and dropping a pig in a parachute ("Didn't hurt the pig. Pig got up and walked away"), and about a golf hustler named Titanic Thompson. "He'd make bets with you about anything," Chet said. "He'd bet you he could pitch cards under a door and into a hat. He'd bet you he could toss his door key into the lock. He'd bet fifty thousand dollars on the exact circumference of a rock a hundred feet away. Once he bet he could hit a golf ball a mile, and he did it. On Lake Michigan, after it froze over."

Meanwhile, foursomes of all colors and shapes of golfers straggled one by one up to the business end of the tee, posed for an official tournament photograph, took hefty practice swings, looked down the fairway, and teed off, to the great amusement of the bunch behind them. "God! He hit it!" someone yelled after Pee Wee King chopped a sharp ground ball up the middle. "You look nervous, Wesley," a frizzy-haired man called to Wesley Rose, the son of Fred Rose and president of Acuff-Rose, decked out in green. "You look like it's royalties time." And to a fat man: "You don't *need* anybody to play with—you *are* a foursome." A drive hooked into the woods. "For his next shot, a McCulloch chain saw!" An especially fluorescent pair of orange trousers appeared and bent down to tee up the ball. "His handicap is his pants!" said a man whose own pants resembled wallpaper in a cheap restaurant. "Where'd you get those? From the Highway Department?"

Chet introduced me to Archie Campbell, whom I recognized right away from watching "Hee Haw," and Billy Edd Wheeler, whom I remembered for a song the first few lines of which I've sung hundreds of times to myself ("We got married in a fever, hotter than a pepper sprout. We been talkin' 'bout Jackson ever since the fire went out. I'm goin' to Jackson . . ."), and who looked a little flushed in the hot sun. He sported a lilac ensemble and a yellow visor on his thick sandy hair, which at the moment he was adjusting. Archie, an elegant, silver-haired gent in navy blue with a distinguished black mustache, was smoking a foot-long cigar. "Nicaraguan," he said. I was admiring both of them, the man and the cigar, when Chet said that the fourth partner hadn't shown up yet. "You play," he said. "You can play out of my bag."

"You look like a golfer," said Archie. "Either that or your dog just died."

It occurred to me to say that golf makes me feel bad, but it also occurred to me that I was feeling good enough to afford some misery and that if I begged off I'd feel bad about it later, so when Chet put a driver in my hand and two balls—a white one and a green one—and a white Acuff-Rose tournament hat, I put on the hat, and posed with my partners. "Smile. Look like you're winners," said the photographer. I teed up the white ball, and tried to think of grace and ease. I imagined the ball, its tiny engines revving up, *wanting* to fly, imagined a long, perfect shot, and—as a hush fell on the gallery of pants, who didn't know me well enough to give me a hard time—swung *hard* and sent a high pop fly about where the first-base bleachers would have been. It hung up in the air long enough for me to see more of it than I wanted to, took a fifty-foot-high bounce off the parking lot, and landed in tall grass between the lot and the highway. A bad moment, like a major soup spill, but someone said "That'll teach 'em not to bring their Cadillacs!" and though it wasn't a great line, some of the pants laughed, and I teed up the green ball and drove it a respectable distance into the rough and walked down the fairway to play some golf.

Second chances are fundamental to their game, I found out, including my redemptive second drive and also forgiveness of a bad lie. "Everybody gets to walk his dog in hillbilly golf," Billy Edd told me. "Walking the dog" means moving the ball out of the trees or off of hard dirt and teeing it up on a tuft of grass. He kicked his out of a little hollow.

Archie looked at his ball and said, "I believe I'll walk this one."

"That dog needs walking," said Billy Edd.

My green relief ball stayed in the game the rest of the way. I shot a 7 on the first hole, a triple bogey, and went on to shank a few and top some others, which leaked off at weird angles and made my partners look away and say, *"That's* all right. We all do that," and spent time in the woods shooting trees *(klok!),* and once or twice I thought longingly of my typewriter, which when I type "golf" prints "golf," and not "pgwft" or "xxxxx," but I also made par on one hole, sank a twelve-foot putt, and hit a drive that I still remember. When Chet hit a great drive on the long third, he said, "That felt better than sex and almost as good as eating watermelon." Mine on the dogleg fifth didn't feel as good as *that,* but I did feel something smooth and synchronized that started in my head and in my hips and came together at the ball, and I looked up to see it fifty yards out and rising, sailing, a tiny green star lighting up the bright-blue sky.

"That's a beauty. That's a good layup, hoss. You're going to love that," said Billy Edd. "You know, I could learn to admire you if I just worked at it a little." He set his ball down, squinted, hitched up his lilac pants, wiggled his seat, and uncorked a high one that drifted slowly to the right. "Whoa! Hold up! Draw!" he yelled, dancing to the left to pull it back in bounds. "Work! Stay! Stay! Thou art so fair! Stay!" And it worked, drew back, stayed, and fell fair, and rolled in the short grass in the shadows of the tree line. "I didn't hit that as well as I thought I was going to," he said. "But then I didn't think I was going to."

Then Archie. He tossed his ball in the air, caught it on the back of his hand, let it roll slowly down his arm, flipped it up, caught it, and set it on the tee. "Watch this lick here, boys—the old pro is about to perform," he said. He puffed on the cigar, spat, gave us a big footlight smile, and adjusted the bill of his blue cap to the right to compensate for a slight hook on his previous drive. He addressed the ball with a sweet slow swing, but the cap adjustment was perhaps too much or else the weight of the Nicaraguan cigar was off center, because his drive headed woodsward.

"Over the hill to Grandpa's!" said Billy Edd.

Archie yelled "Don't you *dare!*" and the white dot hesitated, drew back, hung up short of a stand of pine, and fell into the dogleg's knee.

"Look at that! I believe he made it. It's a show, isn't it!" Chet said.

"If you'da hit that perfect, it would've been even better," said Billy Edd.

"All right, I'm going to get serious again now," said Chet. He stood over the ball, bent, took a long, slow backswing, and socked it a little beyond Archie's. "That's the greatest shot I ever saw in my life!" he announced, and added, "But the wind was behind me. And, of course, I'm young."

Chet had told me that he feels a little guilty when he plays well, knowing he's probably playing too much golf and not enough guitar. "The way I'm playing today, though, I guess I must be a pretty good guitar player," he said. "Hiking down the fairway in the sunshine, he looked loose and tan and happy. Archie cruised by in his white cart, trailing a ribbon of fragrant cigar smoke, and when we all got to Archie's ball Chet and Billy Edd had put their heads together and were singing a song:

> Son-a-bitch, I'm tired of living this way,
> Gawdamighty damn.

"Let me take the baritone, Chouster," said Archie, and the three of them sang it. It sounded so good they sang it again. And once more. Archie pulled out a 4-iron. He walked his dog a few feet. "Don't you ever play by our rules with somebody else," he told me, grinning. "You might get shot." That reminded Billy Edd of a story about a hillbilly golfer who walked onto a green and picked up all the dimes. "I remember the first time I ever went on tour, I was with another musician and I picked up the tip he left on the table," Chet said. "I'd never seen anybody leave a tip before. I don't know that I'd ever been in a restaurant before."

Archie said, "You've heard that one about Roy Acuff when he was touring with the Smoky Mountain Boys—the one where they were supposed to stop and have supper at the lady's house?"

I had never stood around in the middle of the fairway listening to jokes before. I kept glancing back at the tee, expecting to see angry golfers waving clubs at us, but nobody appeared. We were all by ourselves, four men standing in the hot sun and laughing. Eventually, Archie shot his second shot, and then Billy Edd. My arms were turning red and my neck, too. I rubbed on some lotion that made me smell like a ripe peach. I stood over my ball, hitched up to swing, and smelled Archie's cigar. I laughed on the backswing, my knees caved in a fraction, and I lifted a chunk of sod like a flying toupee and lofted a high fly ball that landed just short of the pin. It wasn't the play that Uncle Don's grounder was, but if you had seen it you would have clapped. I felt awfully lucky. Even a blind dog gets a little meat from the smokehouse now and then, as someone said later, I forget who.

GEORGE GARRETT

A native of Orlando, Garrett has taught at Rice, Hollins, and the University of Virginia, edited various literary magazines, and written twenty or thirty novels (including the highly praised Death of a Fox), *plays, and volumes of poetry, short stories, and criticism. To look at him, though, you'd think he was a scamp.*

A Dickey Story

I reckon I know dozens, maybe hundreds, of literary anecdotes about James Dickey. That's because I collect them. So do many others, all of us fans of his poetry and his inimitable self-image-making, and sometimes we all get together and spend a happy hour or two just swapping Dickey stories, the new ones and some of the old ones. Someday we are going to have a conference somewhere and just tell Dickey stories. Part of it will be Dickey imitations. Among the writers of whom any one is a potential finalist in a James Dickey impersonation contest are: Richard and Robert Bausch, Henry Taylor, Franklin Ashley, James Seay, Joseph Maiolo, and, of course, Ben Greer. Maybe we can persuade Dickey himself to judge and pick the winner. Greer, a fine novelist who teaches at South Carolina and was, once upon a time, my student and Dickey's too, is the source for the final scene of this one. . . .

Greer was visiting me in Maine. One day, sitting on the front porch, watching the tide in the York River flow in and ebb out (which is the principal activity of any given day), we were tossing back a few and reading magazines and stuff. And one or the other of us found a story in the latest *Time* magazine. Which began, as I recollect, like this: " 'He cursed and reviled me and stated that it was his intention to whip my ass,' testified South Carolina Highway Patrolman L. J. Tippet. . . .'' Etc.

Story was that poet James Dickey, wakened from a snoring sleep amid the wreckage of his totaled Land Rover, which he had run into a large tree, came out swinging and cussing. There wasn't a whole lot to the story except that a very prominent poet had gotten somewhat inebriated, and sometime between four A.M. and a little after five A.M., when the cops happened by, he had plowed into a tree on a quiet residential street. Nobody noticed. Dickey wasn't hurt (for once he'd remembered to buckle up his safety belt). He just hung there, all snarled up in the belt, and fell asleep until the cops came along.

Pretty soon both Ben and I had a lot more material to consider. Friends who knew we cared sent us clippings from the South Carolina papers and even the *Washington Post* (which stated that, according to blood and breathalyzer tests, Dickey was the drunkest human being ever picked up in the state of South Carolina; who knows?). From friends and all the coverage, we learned that Dickey had been arrested and booked, finally, sometime close to six-thirty A.M. (time is very important in this tale). He called home and got his wife. His wife called their lawyer. Lawyer said he could take care of things—Dickey wouldn't even lose his license, but he would have to take a special Drivers' Ed. course. But Lawyer wanted to impress the seriousness of all this on Dickey, so he said he would wait until *after* breakfast to bail out Big Jim. Breakfast, a particularly repellent meal at the jail, was served at seven A.M. Dickey was out and on the way home by seven-thirty A.M.

Now, to appreciate the rest of this, you have to know that one of the things we, his fans, most admire about Big Jim is that he is never daunted. Not ever. Not yet. So anyway, after a while, couple of weeks, Ben Greer returns to South Carolina and pretty soon makes a courtesy call on his old teacher and buddy Jim Dickey. Jim is real glad to see him, breaks out a bottle of bourbon. And they have a few while catching up on this and that. Dickey doesn't tell the story of the night he hit the tree. But he does tell a bunch of stories that begin: "Ben, when I was in prison . . ." And he gets quite excited talking about the need for prison reform and how he and Charles Colson and maybe Clifford Irving are going to form a committee dedicated to prison reform. While all this is going on, Ben notices an expensive notebook on the coffee table. Notebook is labeled: The Prison Poems of James Dickey.

Then all of a sudden Dickey goes into a long story about how he was once a Trusty in prison, with the run of the place, and how one day he went into the empty room where the electric chair is kept. Sat in it. Strapped one arm in place. Sat there and imagined what it would be like to be electrocuted. Very moving scene.

Only trouble was that it comes directly out of Ben Greer's first novel— *Slammer*. Ben is a real nice, polite Southern boy, but this was going too far, taking his own story almost word for word. "Damn it, Jim!" Ben burst out. "There isn't any electric chair in the Columbia city drunk tank!" Dickey blinked briefly, sipped his bourbon, but kept a poker face. Never daunted.

"Ben," he said quietly, "it's a *very small* electric chair. A lot of people don't even know it's there."

Ever since then, we, the fans, have pictured Big Jim sitting on a little bitty electric chair, about the size of a potty chair, a very low-voltage model that would take a week and a half to kill you.

WILLIAM PRICE FOX

When William Price Fox's forty-cent paperback collection of sketches, Southern Fried, *appeared in 1962, it was a fresh blast from the old rowdy out-amongst-'em male Southern humor tradition, which had not been heard from much in print, except self-loathingly in Erskine Caldwell and mythopoeically or incidentally in Faulkner, since . . . hell, I'd say since Mark Twain. Maybe—except for Twain, who abandoned the Confederacy for the West and then the Northeast—the boys got too whipped down by the Yankees and the womenfolk, and too defensive racially, to send any more lizards up Parson Bullen's pants leg for quite a few decades there. But since Fox got the tradition going again, it has flourished at various levels in the work of Dan Jenkins and Larry L. King (and their Texas running mates Bud Shrake and Gary Cartwright, who aren't represented in this book because I couldn't come up with a purely humorous self-contained chunk by either of them), Charles Portis, Harry Crews, Hunter Thompson, Cormac McCarthy, and Barry Hannah. Fox has written novels (*Ruby Red *is my favorite), screenplays, and lots of magazine articles. He teaches at the University of South Carolina in his hometown, Columbia.*

"The Ordeal of Lonnie Register"

When Lonnie Register came into the drugstore and casually announced that he'd just drunk a pint of rubbing alcohol, everybody got pretty excited. Doc Daniels took his pulse, checked his pupils, and crouched down and listened to his heart for a full three minutes.

Doc kept shaking his head and saying he couldn't understand it. He finally stood up and said that Lonnie was all right. Lonnie is a short little fellow no more than five foot five, but he's hard as stone. He has a horseshoe of black hair around the back of his almost flat head and a few strands on top that he combs forward into a fine point. He has fierce bushy eyebrows and small black eyes.

The rubbing alcohol hadn't made him drunk and he strutted up and down the counter eating Lance's peanut-butter-and-cheese crackers.

M. L. Anderson came in and Lonnie sang out, "How 'bout it, M. L.?"

"How 'bout what, Lonnie?"

"Me knocking down a pint of Rub and ain't even sweating."

"That's pretty good, Lonnie. But you better keep out of that sun. . . . What did it cost you?"

"Fifteen, maybe seventeen cents. You can't beat that, can you?"

"I guess not."

Pig Hobson stood at the end of the counter near the potato chips. He waited until Lonnie was through talking. Pig cleared his throat and called Lonnie down to the end. "Lonnie, you feel kinda raspy down in here?"

He pointed to a spot on Lonnie's cowboy scarf three inches below his large Adam's apple.

Lonnie said, "Yeah, Pig. Right there. How'd you know?"

Pig lit his pipe, paused a minute. "Next time you drink Rub you add in a stick of cinnamon and a pinch of chicory."

Lonnie looked puzzled for a minute. He raised his fist and slammed it on the counter. "Goddammit!"

The potato-chip rack fell over. Pig picked it up.

Lonnie shouted, "Dammit, Pig. Why come you do that?"

"Do what?"

"You know what. Always low-rating my stories. That's what."

Pig looked serious. The lids were half closed on his big eyes. "I was merely trying to be helpful."

Pig and Lonnie were door-to-door salesmen for the same company. They sold kerosene lamps, chenille bed spreads, hairbrush and mirror sets, and religious statues and plaques that glowed in the dark. They called on the colored trade and the mill hands that lived in the Strawberry Hill district and down along the canal banks. In order to demonstrate their lamps and phosphorescent articles, they had to make their calls at night.

Lonnie worked six times harder than Pig or, for that matter, anyone else, but he always sold less. Some nights he'd make as many as twenty calls down the dark streets without a sale. Pig would make two calls and he would make two sales.

Anyhow, it was kind of funny and kind of sad about Lonnie Register. The pressure of selling and of selling against Pig would get him, and every six or seven weeks he'd cut loose and start drinking. It would be that spitting-in-the-dirt, below-the-belt, loud, wild-type drunk. The police would have to hit him in the head or strap him down to get him to the jail. He'd get fined fifty dollars and have to work ten days on the gang. He didn't have to wear stripes or hook on to the chain, but there would be a man in a black hat on shotgun and a couple of sleepy-looking bloodhounds out there panting in the heat.

The road gang was doing a lot of work along Mulberry Avenue right in front of the drugstore and about four houses from Lonnie's house. Well, one morning we look out and there's Lonnie on rake with his head down low and his cap down low. He had one eye on his front porch and one eye on the drugstore. His wife had the front door closed. The kids were shut up in the back.

Pig got his name because of his eyes being so small. He didn't have much distant vision. He didn't see poor old Lonnie out there and no one was about to mention it to him. Well, it looked like Lonnie was going to escape detection when all of a sudden his big Labrador rushed through one of the hedges and ran up to Lonnie and jumped all over him. Lonnie tried to shoo the dog away but you know how Labradors are. Well, when Pig saw that he squinted his eyes up and started smiling. He stepped to the front of the store and cupped his hands.

"Hey, Lonnie. Lonnie Register. I thought you were up in Walterboro on business."

Lonnie figured he had to beat Pig down because of the road-gang embarrassment. It was on a Saturday around six. Everybody was in the drugstore. Lonnie told how he had drunk a full quart of Old Crow. How two cops beat him on the head and beat him against the curb and how he had laughed at them. They had to get two more cops to drag him in. How he set fire to the mattress in jail, pulled up the toilet and flooded the floor and shouted so loud they had to put him in a straitjacket and tape his mouth.

Lonnie Register finished his story and stepped back. He looked at Pig. We all looked at Pig.

Pig smiled. You know, that no-teeth, soft, rubbery smile when they're holding four of a kind?

"That's pretty drunk, Lonnie. That's pretty drunk."

We all got in close.

"Yessir, that's what I call a pretty good drunk."

Lonnie's face began to fall. He could read the "but I remember" in Pig's smile. Pig lit his pipe, rolled his eyes around to make sure everyone was present.

"But I remember once . . . it was down in Mobile, Alabama. Any of you boys been there? Yeah, down in Mobile. I'd been drinking that absinthe. You all know that absinthe isn't allowed in the country. But you can get it down in Mobile and a couple of places in New Orleans. I mean you can get it if you

know the right people. Anyhow, you know how drunk I got on that absinthe?"

"How drunk, Pig?"

"I got seat-stabbing drunk. That's how drunk."

"What's that?"

"Well, I came out of this absinthe house. Been there a couple of days or so.
I came out and I couldn't tell if it was sun or moon."

Lonnie eased out of the crowd and went over to the beer case. He didn't
want to hear the rest.

"I got me a cab and sat back. Next thing you know I've got my pocketknife
out and I'm down there stabbing the leather seats. That absinthe was driving
me crazy. You all know I'm a quiet sort. But man, I got loose on that stuff.
Whup—whup, up to the hilt. I stabbed a while then slashed a while. When I
finished up on the seat I started working on the door paneling and the roof.
The cab driver saw me but he was too scared to do anything."

"So that's seat-stabbing drunk?"

"Yessir, that's what it is. Every now and then you'll hear about it. But not
very often."

Lonnie came back. He was lipping the bottle of beer and had a funny look in
his eye. He counted on his fingers to eight.

He shouted, "Damn you, Pig. Damn you anyway."

We grabbed him. Lonnie's voice was strained, hysterical. "Don't worry, I
ain't going to swing at that lying bastard. Listen, you, Pig. You listen."

We cleared a path. They were facing one another. Lonnie was hysterical
and jumping. Pig was calm and packing his pipe.

"Maybe you've been drunker than me. Maybe you've done more and
better of everything than me."

His face was white, his upper lip was wet. He set his beer on the counter.
He was shaking. "But I've got you now, Pig. I've got you."

He counted quickly on his fingers to eight. "Okay, Pig, if you win this one
. . . I won't give you any more trouble."

Pig lit his pipe and closed his eyes. "All right, Lonnie. What you got?"

Lonnie smiled, "I slept in worse places than you."

He was too nervous to pause for an effect.

"One . . . on a pool table with my feet in the end pockets.

"Two . . . in a goat pen.

"Three . . . under a car with the grease dripping on me.

"Four . . . in a chicken coop."

He screamed these last four together: "In bed with four gypsies and a dog.
In a bowling alley gutter. . . . In . . . in . . . in . . . in a refrigerator car at
thirty-two degrees Fahrenheit from Mobile to Atlanta. On a slant tin roof with
my feet in the drain gutter!"

We almost applauded. Lonnie was sweating and his teeth were chattering. He drank his beer and ordered two more.

We asked him questions. How he got out of the refrigerated car. How he got on the roof. He answered them all and kept looking at Pig. We ran out of questions. Lonnie began repeating himself. He ran through the list again. . . .

And then Pig coughed. "I don't suppose any of you fellows every stayed at the Rope?"

"The Rope? What's that?"

"A hotel."

"Where?"

"In Charleston."

You could hear the beer-cooler motor going.

"The Rope is a very famous hotel in Charleston. I'm surprised Lonnie here hasn't stayed there. . . . Well, I mean it's like a hotel in that they charge you. The rates vary. It's thirty-five cents in the early evening, but as it gets later the rates gets lower. Around about midnight you can get a place for a dime."

"A dime?"

"A dime."

"A dime for a room?"

"Well, it's not exactly a room. It's more like a place. The room is long. Oh, say, about seventy feet long, maybe even eighty feet. The best places are in the middle. Cost thirty-five cents to a quarter there. The dime places are all towards the end. It isn't so bad in the middle. It's kind of level there."

"What's kind of level, Pig? You lost me."

"The Rope. This big six-inch hawser line. You know the kind they tie the big ships up with. That's what you sleep on. It runs the length of the room."

"How do you sleep on it?"

"Simple. You just lean over it. Nothing to it. Of course it's easier when you're pretty drunk or pretty tired. It's best when you're both. But you pay the man and you go in. First come, first serve. The dime places are pretty close to the wall and the rope is on an angle. It gets pretty bad out there.

"I was lucky. I got in early and got near the middle. I didn't care much for the clientele but I must say I did get me a pretty good night's sleep. . . ."

We looked around for Lonnie. Doc said he had gone out the back way.

"Coley Moke"

In order to get back to Coley Moke's place outside Monck's Corner, South Carolina, you have to run down a Peevy or a Taylor or another Moke and make him take you back. Charley, Jim and I got us a Taylor and went back one day.

There were too many dogs in the yard to count but there were four runty gray pigs who'd been talked into believing they were hounds. When we petted the dogs we had to scratch the pigs. It was hot and the dogs were panting so Coley led us into his front room. There was a bed and a wood stove in the room and nothing else. No tables, no chairs, no lights; it was the only room in the house.

"Make yourself to home."

And then, "You bring any funny books?"

Charley pulled a roll out of his back pocket. Coley thumbed through them and said, "Fine."

He emptied a Mason jar of corn whisky into a water bucket, placed a tin dipper in the bucket and set it down on the floor.

Three of the older dogs got up on the bed with Coley. One of the little razorbacks tried to make it but couldn't.

We sat down against the wall near the bucket and when we started drinking, Coley started talking.

"See this dog here . . . his name's Brownie."

He was a long thin brown dog; his eyes were closed.

"Well, when I tell him the law is coming he picks up that steel bucket and runs out into the swamp, and I mean he doesn't come back until I call him. Couple of the others would do that for me but they got so they were spilling too much.

"Brownie here knows I got me only one small still going now and he don't waste a drop. One old timer—Trig—he's gone now—would take it out there by the creek. He was a mess. He'd drink a while and then swim a while and then sleep until he was sober and then start in all over again. . . ."

Charley nudged Jim and Jim nudged me. We drank some more.

Coley laughed and rasseled the head of the red bone hound on his left. "This here's Bob, and they don't come any smarter than him. One day he convinced these Federal men he would lead them back to the house. And they followed him. He led them poor bastards between the quicksand and the 'gators and showed them every cottonmouth moccasin in the swamp. He got them so scared they were just begging him to lead them back on the road— any road. They promised him steaks and that they'd never raid me again. Well, sir, Bob kept them going until it was dark and after he walked them over a couple long 'gators that looked like logs he finally put them up on the road. It was the right road but it was about twelve miles from their car. Old Bob sure had himself some fun that night. He told Brownie here all about it and Brownie told me."

Charley took a big drink; Jim and I took a big drink. There was more.

About how Spot and Whip would team up on a moccasin or a rattlesnake and while one faked the snake out of his coil the other would grab him by the tail and pop his head off like a buggy whip.

Jim said, "Man, that is some dog to do that."

Coley began to drink a little more and when he started talking about his wife his voice changed. "Yeah, I suspect I miss that old gal. Wonder what she looks like now. She was something, all right. Up at dawn, cook a first-class meal and then go out and outplow any man and mule in the county and every Sunday, rain or shine we had white linen on the table and apple pie . . . ain't nothing I like better than apple pie.

"Sometimes we didn't speak for a week. It was nice then, real nice. As long as I kept quiet and minded the still and my dogs everything was fine. But we started talking and then the first thing you know we were arguing and then she began to throw the dogs up in my face. Let's see . . . it was right in the middle of the Compression. Right here in this room. She had to go and try and turn me against my dogs. . . . Well, the Compression hit us bad—real bad. I had no money, no copper for the still, and no way of getting any up. I was doing a lot of fishing and hunting then. . . . Yeah, right here . . . oh, it was different then. There were four cane chairs and a dresser and a mirror from Sears Roebuck against that wall, and there was a couple insurance calendars from the Metropolitan Life Insurance Company hanging over there."

He took a big drink. The light was fading but we could still see his face. A bull alligator deep in the swamp rumbled once and decided it was too early.

"Yeah, I was lying here with old Sport. He was Brownie here's father. He was young then and high-spirited and, you know, sensitive. When Emma Louise got up from her chair and came over he must have seen it in her face. They never had gotten along. He crawled off the bed and went outside. If I live to be two hundred, I'll never forget those words. . . .

"She said, 'Coley Moke, you are the sorriest man on God's green earth. Here it is almost winter, we got no money, we got no food, and you just lay there and stare up at that leaky roof. And what's more, you've gone out and taken our last hog and traded it for another dog.' "

Coley smiled and leaned forward. Then his face set mean and hard. " 'Emma, Emma Louise,' I said, 'if I told you once I told you a hundred times. . . . But since you seem to not hear I'm going to tell you one more time. I traded that hog and I got me a dog for the plain and simple reason that I can't go running no fox with no hog.'

"Come on men, drink her up. When that's gone there's more where it came from. And if we get too drunk to walk we can send my old buddy Brownie here."

He rasseled the dog's head. "How about it, boy, what d'you say?"

We drank until it was time to eat. Coley lighted a fire in the wood stove and warmed up some red-horse bread. He served it on folded newspapers and with the little light from the stove we sat back down where we had been sitting and ate.

Later he chased the two pigs outside and we heard their hooves clopping down the porch and on the steps. The pigs slept under the house with the dogs. Coley said they generally got to bed a little earlier than the dogs.

An owl sounded, a bull alligator answered, and the moon glided out of the tall cypress trees in the swamp and the room began to streak with silver light. We slept. . . .

It was raining in the morning and all the dogs and hogs were in the living room. Spot, Trig and Buckles were on the bed with Coley. The two hogs were under the unlit stove and the rest of the dogs were against the wall. Charley, Jim and I were sitting on the floor.

Coley was talking. "Bob's father—that was Earl Brown—he's been dead a long time now. Let's see, next month it'll be eleven years. It doesn't seem like it was that long ago. Eleven years, man, but don't it drive by?"

Charley took a drink and handed me the dipper. I took one and gave it to Jim.

"Buried him out on that hill knuckle in front. He always liked it up there. Some mornings I'd wake up and look out and there he'd be sitting up there just as pretty as you please. All the other dogs would still be sleeping. But not Earl Brown, he was always the first one up.

"He wasn't like the others. Now I ain't saying the others weren't smart, but it was a different kind of smartness. You know how it is with hounds. They'll do anything you tell them. But there's a lot of them that just don't have any initiative. Now that's right where Earl Brown was different. Earl Brown was always trying to better himself, trying to improve himself, you might say.

"I could tell it when he was a pup. The other dogs would fall all over one another getting at the food and when they'd get to it they'd bolt it down like they hadn't eaten in a month. But not Earl Brown, no sir. He'd wait and let them take their places at the trough. Then he'd walk over, slow-like, and commence eating. He wouldn't rush. He even chewed his food longer."

Coley got down off the bed and took a drink. He studied the bottom of the empty dipper.

"Yeah, they don't make any finer dog than Earl Brown."

He put the dipper in the bucket of whisky on the floor and sat back down on the bed.

"That dog was a loner, too. The others would all sleep in the wood box. Sometimes there'd be as many as seventeen all flopped in there on top of one another. But not Earl Brown. From the day that scutter was weaned he slept by himself outside the box.

"I guess I miss Earl Brown as much or more than any of them. He was a marvelous dog, all right. Marvelous, that's what he was.

"I told you how he'd sit up on the hill early in the mornings. Well, he wasn't out there lapping the dew off the grass for nothing. He was working on something.

"Boys, I want you to know what that dog was working on. I wouldn't tell this to just anyone else. They'd say that fool Coley Moke has gone slap out of his mind, living out there with all them dogs.

"First of all I wouldn't have known a thing if it hadn't been for the chickens. But they started making a lot of noise during the night. I thought a weasel or a snake was getting at them so I started watching from the window. It wasn't no weasel and it wasn't no snake. It was two foxes. Big red ones, long as dogs, and five times smarter. But those foxes didn't go inside the coop. They just stood there. They must have been there five minutes and then I thought I saw another fox. I looked again and you know who it was?

"It was Earl Brown. Well sir, those two red foxes and Earl Brown stood outside that chicken coop for ten minutes. My other dogs were all inside the house and they were going crazy. The poor hens were clucking and screeching for help. I didn't know what to do. Finally I heard Earl Brown growl and then the next thing you know the three of them ran off into the woods.

"I kind of figured Earl Brown was setting those foxes up for me to shoot so I decided to wait until he gave me some kind of sign. Well, next night it happened again. Same time, right around three o'clock they came out of the woods. Well, they had their little meeting right outside the coop and then they ran off again.

"Of course, during all this I had to make sure Earl Brown got out at night and my other dogs stayed in. That took some doing. The others all knew that Earl Brown was getting special treatment and they got mad as hell. And they smelled those foxes on him and they wouldn't have a thing to do with him.

"But Earl Brown didn't care what they thought about him. He even liked it better that way. But he got to looking peaked and red-eyed. Like he wasn't getting any sleep. I put a couple extra eggs in his rations. That boy was on a rough schedule. He'd go to sleep around ten with the others but he'd be up at two and off with his friends.

"Things began looking bad. My dogs were giving me a fit to be let out at night. I wasn't getting any sleep. And those hens. Lord, those poor hens were going right out of their minds. They got so nervous they were laying eggs at midnight. The rooster worried so he began losing weight and limping. He got so he wouldn't even crow. They were one sad-looking sight in the mornings. Wouldn't eat, couldn't sleep. I mean it got so bad them hens were stumbling around and bumping into one another.

"I decided to give Earl Brown two more nights and then end it. I was determined to shoot those damn foxes and get my chickens back on some decent schedule.

"And that was the very night it happened. . . .

"Earl Brown stepped aside and let one of those foxes go into the coop. Those poor chickens were so scared and tired. I guess they were relieved when that fox walked in and picked one out. He took a Rhode Island Red. That hen didn't even squawk. Just hung there in his mouth and across that red fox's back like she was glad it was all over. Those chickens slept the rest of the night. It was the first good night's sleep they'd had in three weeks."

Coley stopped. "You boys ain't drinking."

Charley said, "I just this minute put the dipper down."

Coley drank again and hunched himself back up between the dogs. "Well, I figured that was the end for Earl Brown. I saw where he had thrown in with the foxes and I knew it would be best if I shot him and the foxes. I had it worked out in my mind that those three were going to take a chicken a night until I was stripped clean. So I loaded up my four-ten over and under and got the four-cell flashlight ready and waited. I was praying Earl Brown wouldn't run off that night. But two o'clock came and he sneaked out and lit out through the woods. . . . You know what happened?"

"What?"

"They never showed up."

"Never?"

"Never . . . but still every night Earl Brown would leave the house at two. About a week later, I followed that dog out through the woods. I was downwind and I stood behind a big sweet gum and watched them.

"They were out in this little field and the moon was good and I could see everything. They were playing some kind of game out there in that moonlight. The foxes would run and Earl Brown would chase them in little circles. Then the foxes would chase him back and forth. And then it all ended and Earl Brown started back through the woods home.

"Mind you, I said 'started back.' Because the minute that rascal figured those foxes figured he was going home, he doubled back. I tell you that was one funny sight. Here I'm behind one tree and Earl Brown is behind another tree and we're both watching those foxes.

"They were running around in circles and making little barking sounds like they were laughing. I tell you, I don't know when I've been so fascinated. I shore wish I had had me a camera about then.

"All of a sudden it hits me what was going on. Old Earl Brown was picking up the foxes' secret about running. That rascal had paid them foxes to show him something. He'd paid them with that Rhode Island Red and now he was checking on the foxes to make sure he'd got his money's worth. Well, by God, I thought I knew something about hounds and foxes but I was shore

learning something that night standing out behind that sweet gum tree. And
Earl Brown not twenty yards away tipping his head around his tree . . . man,
that was one funny night.

"Well, that running secret ain't easy and Earl Brown had to go back several
nights. And every night he went, I went. It took him, all told, about three
weeks but I'll be dogged if he didn't finally get it."

Coley got off of the bed and squatted down by us. He took another drink
and we followed. He spoke lower now.

"I don't want them dogs hearing the rest of this. They'll get out and try it
out and wind up breaking their necks. It's too tricky. As smart as Earl Brown
was he had a hard time learning it. He took a few pretty bad falls himself
before he got it."

Coley stopped and let the bait trail. . . .

Charley rose to it. "Learned what, Coley?"

Coley spoke even lower than before. "How to run like a fox, that's what.
Oh, that was one fine dog. He set his mind to it and he learned it. He was
marvelous."

Charley was getting jumpy. "What did he learn, Coley? What did he
learn?"

"Don't rush me, boy. You don't know much about foxes, do you, boy?"

"I guess not."

"Well you know a fox can outrun any living dog if he feels like it, don't
you?"

"Yes."

"Usually they don't feel like it. They're too smart to just do straight
running. Most of the time they work in pairs and they get the dogs so confused
they don't know what's going on. They'll be running one way and then all of a
sudden the other fox will pop up from another direction. Hell, they have
signals. Sometimes they'll run the dogs through briar patches, skunk cabbage,
anything, and lots of times round and round in the same circles. A good fox
will give a pack of dogs a fit. Lot of times a fox will hide and when the dog
pack comes by he'll jump in and run along with them. He'll be barking and
carrying on and having himself a marvelous time and the dogs won't know a
thing.

"Oh, them red foxes are smart. And a good running fox on a straightaway,
I mean, no cover, no nothing, can burn a dog down to the ground. He can run
that hound right into the ground and he'll be as fresh as when he started. He
won't even be breathing hard. You think back. You ever seen a tired fox? No.
They don't get tired. And it's all because they got this secret way of running."

Coley was whispering. He really didn't want the dogs to hear. "It's like
this. When a fox runs he only uses three legs. Next time you see one running,
you watch. You gotta look close, those reds are smart devils. They keep it

secret and they only do it when the're off by themselves or when they get in trouble. Kind of emergency you might say.''

Charley said, ''Whoa now. What do you mean three legs?''

''They rotate, that's what they do. They rotate. They run on three and keep rotating. That way they always got one resting. That's why they give the impression that they're limping all the time and got that little hop in their run.''

''Coley,'' Charley said, ''I just can't believe that one.''

Coley jumped up and walked across the room twice. He raised his hand. ''The Lord will snatch out my tongue and strike me dead right here and now if that ain't the God's truth.''

It continued raining . . . and the Lord didn't make a move. . . .

ZORA NEALE HURSTON

After earning a bachelor's degree in 1928 as one of the first students of her race at Barnard, Hurston got a grant to study African-American folklore in Florida and Louisiana. How come graduate students don't produce anthropology like this anymore?

from *Mules and Men*

''Ah know you want to hear some more stories, don't you? Ah know ah feels lak tellin' some.''

''Unh hunh,'' I agreed.

''Don't you know dat's one word de Devil made up?''

''Nope, Ah had never heard about it. It's a mighty useful word Ah know for lazy folks like me.''

''Yes, everybody says 'unh hunh' and Ah'll tell you why.'' He cleared his throat and continued:

Ole Devil looked around hell one day and seen his place was short of help so he thought he'd run up to Heben and kidnap some angels to keep things runnin' tell he got reinforcements from Miami.

Well, he slipped up on a great crowd of angels on de outskirts of Heben and stuffed a couple of thousand in his mouth, a few hundred under each arm and wrapped his tail 'round another thousand and darted off towards hell.

When he was flyin' low over de earth lookin' for a place to land, a man looked up and seen de Devil and ast 'im, "Ole Devil, Ah see you got a load of angels. Is you goin' back for mo'?"

Devil opened his mouth and tole 'im, "Yeah," and all de li'l angels flew out his mouf and went on back to Heben. While he was tryin' to ketch 'em he lost all de others. So he went back after another load.

He was flyin' low again and de same man seen him and says, "Ole Devil, Ah see you got another load uh angels."

Devil nodded his head and said "unh hunh," and dat's why we say it to-day.

.   .   .   .

"A lot of things ain't whut they useter be," observed Jim Presley. "Now take de 'gator for instance. He been changed 'round powerful since he been made."

"Yeah," cut in Eugene Oliver, "He useter have a nice tongue so he could talk like a nat'chal man, but Brer Dog caused de 'gator to lose his tongue, and dat's how come he hate de dog today."

"Brer 'Gator didn't fall out wid Brer Dog 'bout no tongue," retorted Presley.

Brer Dog done de 'gator a dirty trick 'bout his mouth. You know God made de dog and the 'gator without no mouth. So they seen everybody else had a mouth so they made it up to git theirselves a mouth like de other varmints. So they agreed to cut one 'nothers' mouth, and each one said dat when de other one tole 'em to stop cuttin' they would. So Brer Dog got his mouth first. Brer 'Gator took de razor and cut. Brer Dog tole him, "Stop," which he did. Den Brer Dog took de razor and begin to cut Brer 'Gator a mouth. When his mouth was big as he wanted it, Brer 'Gator says, "Stop, Brer Dog. Dat'll do, I thank you, please." But Brer Dog kept right on cuttin' till he ruint Brer 'Gator's face. Brer 'Gator was a very handsome gent'man befo' Brer Dog done him that a way, and everytime he look in de lookin' glass he cry like a baby over de disfiggerment of his face. And dat's how come de 'gator hate de dog.

"My people, my people," lamented Oliver. "They just will talk whut they don't know."

"Go on Oliver."

De 'gator didn't fall out wid de dog 'bout no mouth cuttin' scrape. You know all de animals was havin' a ball down in de pine woods, and so they all chipped in for refreshments and then they didn't have no music for de dance. So all de animals what could 'greed to furnish music. So de dog said he'd be de trumpet in de band, and de horse and de frog and de mockin' bird and all said they'd be there and help out all they could. But they didn't have no bass drum, till somebody said, "Whut's de matter wid Brer 'Gator, why he don't play de bass drum for us?" Dey called Brer 'Gator but he wasn't at de meetin' so de varmints deppitized Brer Dog to go call on Brer 'Gator and see if he wouldn't furnish de drum music for de dance. Which he did.

"Good evenin', Brer 'Gator."

"My compliments, Brer Dog, how you makin' out? Ah'm always glad when folks visit me. Whut you want?"

"Well Brer 'Gator, de varmints is holdin' a big convention tonight in de piney woods and we want you to furnish us a little bit of yo' drum music."

"It's like this, Brer Dog, tell de other animals dat Ah'm mighty proud they wants me and de compliments run all over me, but my wife is po'ly and my chillun is down sick. But Ah'll lend you my drum if you know anybody kin play it, and know how to take keer of it too!"

"Oh, Ah'll do *dat,* Brer 'Gator. You just put it in my keer. You don't have to worry 'bout dat atall."

So de dog took Brer 'Gator's tongue to de ball dat night and they beat it for a drum. De varmints lakted de bass drum so well till they didn't play nothin' else hardly. So by daybreak it was wore clean out. Brer Dog didn't want to go tell Brer 'Gator they had done wore his tongue out so he hid from Brer 'Gator. Course de 'gator don't like it 'bout his tongue so he's de sworn enemy of de dog.

Big Sweet says, "Dat's de first time Ah ever heard 'bout de dawg wearin' out de 'gator's tongue, but Ah do know he useter be a pretty varmint. He was pure white all over wid red and yeller stripes around his neck. He was pretty like dat 'till he met up wid Brer Rabbit. Kah, kah, kah! Ah have to laugh everytime Ah think how sharp dat ole rabbit rascal is."

"Yeah," said Sam Hopkins. "At night time, at de right time; Ah've always understood it's de habit of de rabbit to dance in de wood."

"When Ah'm shellin' my corn, you keep out yo' nubbins, Sam," Big Sweet snapped as she spat her snuff.

Ah'm tellin' dis lie on de 'gator. Well, de 'gator was a pretty white varmint wid coal black eyes. He useter swim in de water, but he never did bog up in de mud lak he do now. When he come out de water he useter lay up on de clean grass so he wouldn't dirty hisself all up.

So one day he was layin' up on de grass in a marsh sunnin' hisself and sleepin' when Brer Rabbit come bustin' cross de marsh and run right over Brer 'Gator before he stopped. Brer 'Gator woke up and seen who it was trompin' all over him and trackin' up his pretty white hide. So he seen Brer Rabbit, so he ast him, "Brer Rabbit, what you mean by runnin' all cross me and messin' up my clothes lak dis?"

Brer Rabbit was up behind a clump of bushes peerin' out to see what was after him. So he tole de 'gator, says: "Ah ain't got time to see what Ah'm runnin' over nor under. Ah got trouble behind me."

'Gator ast, "Whut is trouble? Ah ain't never heard tell of dat befo'."

Brer Rabbit says, "You ain't never heard tell of trouble?"

Brer 'Gator tole him, "No."

Rabbit says: "All right, you jus' stay right where you at and Ah'll show you whut trouble is."

He peered 'round to see if de coast was clear and loped off, and Brer 'Gator washed Brer Rabbit's foot tracks off his hide and went on back to sleep again.

Brer Rabbit went on off and lit him a li'dard knot and come on back. He set dat marsh afire on every side. All around Brer 'Gator de fire was burnin' in flames of fire. De 'gator woke up and pitched out to run, but every which a way he run de fire met him.

He seen Brer Rabbit sittin' up on de high ground jus' killin' hisself laughin'. So he hollered and ast him:

"Brer Rabbit, whut's all dis goin' on?"

"Dat's trouble, Brer 'Gator, dat's trouble youse in."

De 'gator run from side to side, round and round. Way after while he broke thru and hit de water "ker ploogum!" He got all cooled off but he had done got smoked all up befo' he got to de water, and his eyes is all red from de smoke. And dat's how come a 'gator is black today—cause de rabbit took advantage of him lak dat.

"Oh, well, if we gointer go way back there and tell how everything started," said Ulmer, "Ah might just as well tell how come we got gophers." [Gophers are terrapins, or land turtles. —Ed.]

"Pay 'tention to yo' pole, Cliff," Jim Allen scolded. "You gittin' a bite. You got 'im! A trout too! If dat fool ain't lucky wid fish!"

Old Man Jim strung the trout expertly. "Now, Cliff, you kin do all de talkin' you want, just as long as you ketch me some fish Ah don't keer."

"Well," began Cliff:

God was sittin' down by de sea makin' sea fishes. He made de whale and throwed dat in and it swum off. He made a shark and throwed it in and then he made mullets and shad-fish and cats and trouts and they all swum on off.

De Devil was standin' behind him lookin' over his shoulder.

Way after while, God made a turtle and throwed it in de water and it swum on off. Devil says, "Ah kin make one of those things."

God said, "No, you can't neither."

Devil told him, "Aw, Ah kin so make one of those things. 'Tain't nothin' to make nohow. Who couldn't do dat? Ah jus' can't blow de breath of life into it, but Ah sho kin make a turtle."

God said: "Devil, Ah know you can't make none, but if you think you kin make one go 'head and make it and Ah'll blow de breath of life into it for you."

You see, God was sittin' down by de sea, makin' de fish outa sea-mud. But de Devil went on up de hill so God couldn't watch him workin', and made his outa high land dirt. God waited nearly all day befo' de Devil come back wid his turtle.

As soon as God seen it, He said, "Devil, dat ain't no turtle you done made."

Devil flew hot right off. "Dat ain't no turtle? Who say dat ain't no turtle? Sho it's a turtle."

God shook his head, says, "Dat sho *ain't* no turtle, but Ah'll blow de breath of life into it like Ah promised."

Devil stood Him down dat dat was a turtle.

So God blowed de breath of life into what de devil had done made, and throwed him into de water. He swum out. God throwed him in again. He come on out. Throwed him in de third time and he come out de third time.

God says: "See, Ah told you dat wasn't no turtle."

"Yes, suh, dat *is* a turtle."

"Devil, don't you know dat all turtles loves de water? Don't you see whut you done made won't stay in there?"

Devil said, "Ah don't keer, dat's a turtle, Ah keep a 'tellin' you."

God disputed him down dat it wasn't no turtle. Devil looked it over and scratched his head. Then he says, "Well, anyhow it will go for one." And that's why we have gophers!

Everybody began to gather up things. The bait cans were kicked over so that the worms could find homes. The strings of fish were tied to pole ends. When Joe Wiley went to pull up his string of fish, he found a water moccasin stealin' them and the men made a great ceremony of killin' it. Then they started away from the water. Cliff had a long string of fish.

"Look, Gran'pa" he said, "Ah reckon you satisfied, ain't you?"

"Sho Ah'm satisfied, Ah must *is* got cat blood in me 'cause Ah never gits tired of fish. Ah knows how to eat 'em too, and dat's somethin' everybody don't know."

"Oh, anybody can eat fish," said Joe Willard.

"Yeah," Jim conceded grudgingly, "they kin eat it, but they can't git de real refreshment out de meat like they oughter."

"If you kin git any mo' refreshment off a fish bone than me, you must be got two necks and a gang of bellies," said Larkins.

"You see," went on Jim, "y'all ain't got into de technical apex of de business. When y'all see a great big platter of fried fish y'all jus' grab hold of a fish and bite him any which way, and dat's wrong."

"Dat's good enough for me!" declared Willard emphatically. "Anywhere and any place Ah ketch a fish Ah'm ready to bite him 'ceptin' he's raw."

"Me too."

"See dat?" Jim cried, exasperated. "You young folks is just like a passle of crows in a corn patch. Everybody talkin' at one time. Ain't nary one of you tried to learn how to eat a fish right."

"How you eat 'em, Mr. Allen?" Gene Oliver asked to pacify him.

"Well, after yo' hands is washed and de blessin' is said, you look at de fried fish, but you don't grab it. First thing you chooses a piece of corn-bread for yo' plate whilst youse lookin' de platter over for a nice fat perch or maybe it's trout. Nobody wid any manners or home-raisin' don't take de fork and turn over every fish in de dish in order to pick de best one. You does dat wid yo' eye whilst youse choosin' yo' pone bread. Now, then, take yo' fork and stick straight at de fish you done choosed, and if somebody ast you to take two, you say 'No ma'am, Ah thank you. This un will do for right now.'

"You see if you got too many fishes on yo' plate at once, folkses, you can't lay 'em out proper. So you take one fish at de time. Then you turn him over and take yo' fork and start at de tail, liff de meat all off de bone clear up to de head, 'thout misplacin' a bone. You eats dat wid some bread. Not a whole heap of bread—just enough to keep you from swallerin' de fish befo' you enjoy de consequences. When you thru on dat side of de fish turn him over and do de same on de other side. Don't eat de heads. Shove 'em to one side till you thru wid all de fish from de platter, den when there ain't no mo' fish wid sides to 'em, you reach back and pull dem heads befo' you and start at de back of de fish neck and eat right on thru to his jaw-bones.

"Now then, if it's summer time, go set on de porch and rest yo'self in de cool. If it's winter time, go git in front of de fireplace and warm yo'self—now Ah done tole you right. A whole heap of people talks about fish-eatin' but Ah done tole you real."

"Look," said Black Baby, "on de Indian River we went to bed and heard de mosquitoes singin' like bull alligators. So we got under four blankets. Shucks! dat wasn't nothin'. Dem mosquitoes just screwed off dem short bills, reached back in they hip-pocket and took out they long bills and screwed 'em on and come right on through dem blankets and got us."

"Is dat de biggest mosquito you all ever seen? Shucks! Dey was li'l baby mosquitoes! One day my ole man took some men and went out into de woods to cut some fence posts. And a big rain come up so they went up under a great big ole tree. It was so big it would take six men to meet around it. De other men set down on de roots but my ole man stood up and leaned against de tree. Well, sir, a big old skeeter come up on de other side of dat tree and bored right thru it and got blood out of my ole man's back. Dat made him so mad till he up wid his ax and bradded dat mosquito's bill into dat tree. By dat time de rain stopped and they all went home.

"Next day when they come out, dat mosquito had done cleaned up ten acres dying. And two or three weeks after dat my ole man got enough bones from dat skeeter to fence in dat ten acres."

Everybody liked to hear about the mosquito. They laughed all over themselves.

"Yeah," said Sack Daddy, "you sho is tellin' de truth 'bout dat big old
mosquito 'cause my ole man bought dat same piece of land and raised a crop of
pumpkins on it and lemme tell y'all right now—mosquito dust is de finest
fertilizer in de world. Dat land was so rich and we raised pumpkins so big dat
we et five miles up in one of 'em and five miles down and ten miles acrost one
and we ain't never found out how far it went. But my ole man was buildin' a
scaffold inside so we could cut de pumpkin meat without so much trouble,
when he dropped his hammer. He tole me, he says, 'Son, Ah done dropped
my hammer. Go git it for me.' Well, Ah went down in de pumpkin and begin
to hunt dat hammer. Ah was foolin' 'round in there all day, when I met a man
and he ast me what Ah was lookin' for. Ah tole him my ole man had done
dropped his hammer and sent me to find it for him. De man tole me Ah might
as well give it up for a lost cause, he had been lookin' for a double mule-team
and a wagon that had got lost in there for three weeks and he hadn't found no
trace of 'em yet."

"My ole man wouldn't farm no po' land like dat," said Joe Wiley. "Now,
one year we was kinda late puttin' in our crops. Everybody else had corn a
foot high when papa said, 'Well, chillun, Ah reckon we better plant some
corn.' So Ah was droppin' and my brother was hillin' up behind me. We had
done planted 'bout a dozen rows when Ah looked back and seen de corn
comin' up. Ah didn't want it to grow too fast 'cause it would make all fodder
and no roastin' ears so Ah hollered to my brother to sit down on some of it to
stunt de growth. So he did, and de next day he dropped me back a note—says:
"passed thru Heben yesterday at twelve o'clock sellin' roastin' ears to de
angels."

Ulmer says: "Joe Wiley, youse as big a liar as you is a man! Whoo-wee.
Boy, you molds 'em. But lemme tell y'all a sho nuff tale 'bout Ole Massa."

"Go 'head and tell it, Cliff," shouted Eugene Oliver. "Ah love to hear
tales about Ole Massa and John. John sho was one smart nigger."

So Cliff Ulmer went on.

You know befo' surrender Ole Massa had a nigger name John and John
always prayed every night befo' he went to bed and his prayer was for God to
come git him and take him to Heaven right away. He didn't even want to take
time to die. He wanted de Lawd to come git him just like he was—boot, sock
and all. He'd git down on his knees and say: "O Lawd, it's once more and again
yo' humble servant is knee-bent and body-bowed—my heart beneath my knees
and my knees in some lonesome valley, crying for mercy while mercy kin be
found. O Lawd, Ah'm astin' you in de humblest way I know how to be *so*

pleased as to come in yo' fiery chariot and take me to yo' Heben and its immortal glory. Come Lawd, you know Ah have such a hard time. Old Massa works me *so* hard, and don't gimme no time to rest. So come, Lawd, wid peace in one hand and pardon in de other and take me away from this sin-sorrowing world. Ah'm tired and Ah want to go home.''

So one night Ole Massa passed by John's shack and heard him beggin' de Lawd to come git him in his fiery chariot and take him away; so he made up his mind to find out if John meant dat thing. So he goes on up to de big house and got hisself a bed sheet and come on back. He throwed de sheet over his head and knocked on de door.

John quit prayin' and ast: ''Who dat?''

Ole Massa say: ''It's me, John, de Lawd, done come wid my fiery chariot to take you away from this sin-sick world.''

Right under de bed John had business. He told his wife: ''Tell Him Ah ain't here, Liza.''

At first Liza didn't say nothin' at all, but de Lawd kept right on callin' John: ''Come on, John, and go to Heben wid me where you won't have to plough no mo' furrows and hoe no mo' corn. Come on, John.''

Liza says: ''John ain't here, Lawd, you hafta come back another time.''

Lawd says: ''Well, then Liza, you'll do.''

Liza whispers and says: ''John, come out from underneath dat bed and g'wan wid de Lawd. You been beggin' him to come git you. Now g'wan wid him.''

John back under de bed not saying a mumblin' word. De Lawd out on de door step kept on callin'.

Liza says: ''John, Ah thought you was so anxious to get to Heben. Come out and go on wid God.''

John says: ''Don't you hear him say 'You'll do'? Why don't you go wid him?''

''Ah ain't a goin' nowhere. Youse de one been whoopin' and hollerin' for him to come git you and if you don't come out from under dat bed Ah'm gointer tell God youse here.''

Ole Massa makin' out he's God, says: ''Come on, Liza, you'll do.''

Liza says: ''O, Lawd, John is right here underneath de bed.''

''Come on John, and go to Heben wid me and its immortal glory.''

John crept out from under de bed and went to de door and cracked it and when he seen all dat white standin' on de doorsteps he jumped back. He says: ''O, Lawd, Ah can't go to Heben wid you in yo' fiery chariot in dese ole dirty britches; gimme time to put on my Sunday pants.''

''All right, John, put on yo' Sunday pants.''

John fooled around just as long as he could, changing them pants, but when he went back to de door, de big white glory was still standin' there. So he says agin: ''O, Lawd, de Good Book says in Heben no filth is found and I got on his dirty sweaty shirt. Ah can't go wid you in dis old nasty shirt. Gimme time to put on my Sunday shirt!''

"All right, John, go put on yo' Sunday shirt."

John took and fumbled around a long time changing his shirt, and den he went back to de door, but Ole Massa was still on de door step. John didn't had nothin' else to change so he opened de door a little piece and says:

"O, Lawd, Ah'm ready to go to Heben wid you in yo' fiery chariot, but de radiance of yo' countenance is *so* bright, Ah can't come out by you. Stand back jus' a li'l way please."

Ole Massa stepped back a li'l bit.

John looked out agin and says: "O, Lawd, you know dat po' humble me is less than de dust beneath yo' shoe soles. And de radiance of yo' countenance is so bright. Ah can't come out by you. Please, please, Lawd, in yo' tender mercy, stand back a li'l bit further."

Ole Massa stepped back a li'l bit mo'.

John looked out agin and he says: "O, Lawd, Heben is so high and wese so low; youse so great and Ah'm so weak and yo' strength is too much for us poor sufferin' sinners. So once mo' and agin yo' humber servant is knee-bent and body-bowed askin' you one mo' favor befo' Ah step into yo' fiery chariot to go to Heben wid you and wash in yo' glory—be so pleased in yo' tender mercy as to stand back jus' a li'l bit further."

Ole Massa stepped back a step or two mo' and out dat door John come like a streak of lightning. All across de punkin patch, thru de cotton over de pasture— John wid Ole Massa right behind him. By de time dey hit de cornfield John was way ahead of Ole Massa.

Back in de shack one of de children was cryin' and she ast Liza: "Mama, you reckon God's gointer ketch papa and carry him to Heben wid him?"

"Shet yo' mouf, talkin' foolishness!" Liza clashed at de chile. "You know de Lawd can't outrun yo' pappy—specially when he's barefooted at dat."

Joe Wiley says: "Y'all might as well make up yo' mind to bear wid me, 'cause Ah feel Ah got to tell a lie on Ole Massa for my mamma. Ah done lied on him enough for myself. So Ah'm gointer tell it if I bust my gall tryin'.

Ole John was a slave, you know. And there was Ole Massa and Ole Missy and de two li' children—a girl and a boy.

Well, John was workin' in de field and he seen de children out on de lake in a boat, just a hollerin'. They had done lost they oars and was 'bout to turn over. So then he went and tole Ole Massa and Ole Missy.

Well, Ole Missy, she hollered and said: "It's so sad to lose these 'cause Ah ain't never goin' to have no more children." Ole Massa made her hush and they went down to de water and follered de shore on 'round till they found 'em. John pulled off his shoes and hopped in and swum out and got in de boat wid de children and brought 'em to shore.

Well, Massa and John take 'em to de house. So they was all so glad 'cause de children got saved. So Massa told 'im to make a good crop dat year and fill up de barn, and den when he lay by de crops nex' year, he was going to set him free.

So John raised so much crop dat year he filled de barn and had to put some of it in de house.

So Friday come, and Massa said, "Well, de day done come that I said I'd set you free. I hate to do it, but I don't like to make myself out a lie. I hate to git rid of a good nigger lak you."

So he went in de house and give John one of his old suits of clothes to put on. So John put it on and come in to shake hands and tell 'em goodbye. De children they cry, and Ole Missy she cry. Didn't want to see John go. So John took his bundle and put it on his stick and hung it crost his shoulder.

Well, Ole John started on down de road. Well, Ole Massa said, "John, de children love yuh."

"Yassuh."

"John, I love yuh."

"Yassuh."

"And Missy *like* yuh!"

"Yassuh."

"But 'member, John, youse a nigger."

"Yassuh."

Fur as John could hear 'im down de road he wuz hollerin', "John, Oh John! De children loves you. And I love you. De Missy *like* you."

John would holler back, "Yassuh."

"But 'member youse a nigger, tho!"

Ole Massa kept callin' 'im and his voice was pitiful. But John kept right on steppin' to Canada. He answered Ole Massa every time he called 'im, but he consumed on wid his bag.

VARIOUS BLACK VIRGINIANS AS TOLD TO DARYL CUMBER DANCE

Shuckin' and Jivin': Folklore from Contemporary Black Americans, published in 1978, derived from fieldwork done for a doctoral dissertation at Virginia Commonwealth University by Daryl Cumber Dance (the only woman named Daryl I have heard of aside from Daryl Hannah). She gathered stories and verses from black Virginians in colleges, senior citizens' centers, and a penitentiary. Though she doesn't bring to the party an editorial touch as enlivening as Zora Neale Hurston's, she has an ear and—unlike far, far too many assiduous collectors of folktales—knows how to capture vocal rhythms on a page.

from *Shuckin' and Jivin'*

I Ain't Scared o' You

My mother said back in their days, you know, they used to call each other Aunt [pronounced *ahnt*] and everything. They didn't say *Mrs.* Julia Jennings, or Mrs. So and So. They used to call 'em Aunt Julia. So they say, Aunt Julia was awfully scared of thunder storms, and say every time she see a black cloud comin' she would always try to make her way to somebody's house. She say, but that day every house she went to, everybody was gone. Say, she kep' runnin', kep' runnin', kep' runnin', and say she started to the next house, went over there. The lady named Cindy. She say, "Well, I think I'll go over there to Aunt Cindy's house." Say, when she got almost there, the cloud had al-l-l-most caught her. Say, it looked like the cloud was just driving down on her. Say, she looked back there. She say, "GOD! You know I ain't running from you, but I'm just running trying to git whar somebody at. But I ain't scare o' you, 'cause I know you can reach me anywhere I go, but I ain't runnin' from you. I'm just running tryin' to get where somebody live."

Running

A. This fellow say he went out to the battlefield when he was a younger man. Say he was scarry, you know. So when they got out to the battlefield, say the battle had started up, and said a fellow shot at 'im. He heard the bullet pass 'im, and he turned 'round and caught up and passed the bullet.

B. And another fellow say they shot at him out in battle like that, and say one o' those high-powered bullets, say, he felt it slap right back here, SWIP! like that [striking the back of his neck] and say he carried it for 'bout a mile [dramatizing a man running too fast for the bullet to penetrate], and he stumped his toe and fell. The bullet passed on 'cross and kill a mule standing up on the hill.

When I Say ''Scat''

There was a fellow who had about ten or twelve cats at his house, you know, and he had ten little holes in his door. One day he had a lot of visitors to come to his house, you know—men friends. And so one of 'em said to 'im, say, ''John,'' say, ''why is it that you have so many *holes* in that door? You got ten cats, but all of 'em can go out one hole, can't they?''

He say, ''Yeah, but when I say 'Scat!' I mean scat!''

Boo!

Here's a lady who has invited the Pastor of her church to come and have dinner, and then she finds out that her sister in town has taken ill. She's got a daughter about seventeen years old, so she tells her daughter, she said, ''Now, what I want you to do is to act as if I was here. And you feed the Pastor and tell 'im what happened and everything.''

So when the Pastor came she explained it to him and everything. And of course, she cooked just as good as her mother and everything. She had a nice, lovely meal. And after the Pastor had ate, he sat there by the stove in the big chair, and *kept* looking at that young thing switching around. He laid back in that chair, and he watched her. He said, ''Mary Lou!''

She say, ''Yes, Reverend.''

''Have you ever been scared before?''

She say, ''No, Reverend, I haven't.''

He say, ''You gone on upstairs and take off your clothes. I'm gon' come up there and scare you in a minute.''

The Reverend went up there. WHAM! [Slap of the hand to suggest immediate success.] Man, he helped himself. Rev. come down *laughing*. ''Oh-ho, my soul! Young! Tender!''

About five minutes later, he heard a lil' tap on the bannister, say, ''Reverend!''

''Yes.''

''I'd like for you to come on up here and scare me again.''

Reverend went up there and stayed about a hour. He come back down. [Dramatizing a return that is much less energetic and enthusiastic than the last one.] He's beat now! He don't want no more. He sat down with the paper.

Five minutes later he heard another lil' tap on the bannister: ''Reverend.''

''Yes.'' [Exhaustedly.]

''I want you to come up and scare me again.''

He *crawled* up the steps, CRAWLING! He gets up there. He stays up there a hour and a half or two hours. He comes back down [nearly dead and collapses in the chair]. He got the paper upside down.

About ten minutes later he heard a tap on the bannister: "Reverend!"

He reached up there, [hardly a whisper] "Yes."

She say, "I want you to come up here and scare me again."

He say, "Well, BOO, goddamn it!"

Jump on Mama's Lap

Someone came to the door, and the little boy went to the door. His father asked him who was at the door, and he told him the Methodist Minister. So the father said, "Go hide all the liquor."

Then again, there was a knock on the door, and he asked him who was there. And he told him it was the Episcopalian Minister; so the father told him to go hide the food.

The next one came up was a Baptist, and he [the father] told him, say, "Go jump in Mama's lap."

The Ugliest

The animals of the jungle were having a big feast. Of course, the Lion was the king and he was the head of everything. So when it was all over, the Lion rared back and say, "The ugliest thing in this group gon' wash the damn dishes."

So the Monkey start laughing and looking at the Baboon.

He say, "I don't know what in the hell you pointing at me for. You gon' dry 'em."

Yawl Used to It

A white guy and a Black guy were in court for rape, and the man had sentenced both of 'em to hang. So the morning of the hanging, the white guy [was] crying, "Huhnhuhn, they gon' kill us, huhn, they gon' hang us, you know they gon' hang us."

The Black guy say, "Man, why don't you *shet* that noise up. Man, you raped the woman and beat 'er—we did all these things, and the only thing we're getting is our *just* due."

The white guy turned around and say, "Huhn [still crying], yeah, you kin talk. YAWL used to it!"

THE SANDY BOTTOM SHUFFLE

Once there was a lovers' lane and this couple drove in lovers' lane and the cop was following them, but they didn't know it. And this old nigger, he was laying out there half drunk; so the cop drove up to him and said, "Listen, did you see a couple drive by here in a car?"

He said, "Yes, I saw 'em drive by here."

"Well, what did they do?"

Say, "They went through the bushes and they done the Sandy Bottom Shuffle."

So he said, "What do you mean by the Sandy Bottom Shuffle?" Say, "You come to court next Thursday and tell us what you saw on May the seventh."

So they went to court next Thursday, and they called this Negro up on the stand and said, "Tell this court what you saw on May the seventh."

Said, "I was out there lying on the grass in the park, half high, and this couple drove up, and they went through the bushes and they done the *Sandy Bottom Shuffle!*"

The Judge stamped his foot. He said, "Just what do you mean by the Sandy Bottom Shuffle?" He says, "We've got to make an affidavit of this case."

So the nigger asked him, said, "Well, what is an affidavit, Mr. Judge?"

He said, "That's a technicality in law that you *niggers* don't know nothing about. You come back here again next Thursday. We're going to have this trial over."

So next Thursday they went back, and he called him up on the stand again: "Tell us what you saw on the seventh, *nigger!*"

"On May the seventh I saw a couple that drove through the bushes and they done the Sandy Bottom Shuffle."

So the Judge was really mad then. He stamped his foot: "Just WHAT do you mean by the Sandy Bottom Shuffle?"

The nigger say, "That's a technicality in screwing that you *white folks* don't know nothing about."

Court was dismissed!

WAIT TILL I LEARN

Here's a guy sticking mail [dramatizing someone throwing mail in several slots, under one leg, over his head, and so on, with unbelievable speed], BAM! BAM! BAM! BOOM! BANG! He just sticking—all up under his legs! He just stickin' it!

A guy say, "Great-t-t day! That's what I call a *clerk!* That guy kin stick some mail!"

He say [without any interruption in the speedy slinging of mail—under his arms, over his back, under his legs], "Yeah! You wait till I learn where this stuff *really* go! I'm gon' show ya sumpin."

If You Want to Go to Heaven

This Minister was conducting a revival in this big church. And this particular day, the church was *full*. The people had told the Minister in advance that there were a lot of sinners in the church, so the Minister preached a very stirring sermon. And after the sermon, he opened the doors of the church [asked for converts], and no sinners came up. And he was rather indignant because he knew that sinners were in his congregation. So he asked the sinners again to come up—to stand where they were. And no one would stand. So then he said, "Everyone in the church who wants to go to heaven, come over on my right side. Come over here."

So everybody went over there and stood—including the sinners—but one Deacon sat over there and he didn't move.

And so when the Preacher saw this Deacon sitting over there, he say, "Well, Brother Deacon, didn't you hear what I said?"

He say, "Yes."

He say, "Well, uh, I said, 'Everybody who wants to go to heaven, come on this side.' Why didn't you come over?"

He say, "Well, I tell ya, Reverend, I heard what you said. But I thought you were gitting up a trip to go *now*."

Help!

They say that, you know, when—during all this integration period—the South trying to hold up its end, you know. So they went out, and they said, "This T.V. is putting out too much, you know, about Blacks, saying it's so bad down here in Mississippi." So they went out in the back woods as far as they could to get the *dumbest* Negro they could find. And they told him, say, "Look, we gon' pay you fifty dollars to be on television, and *all* you got to tell 'em is how well we white folks treat you down here. That's all! Then you can go on back home. FIFTY DOLLARS! And it'll just take you a few minutes."

They carried him up there and set 'im in front the camera; they say, "We'll tell you when we ready." And they say, "You go ahead."

And say he was settin' there, you know, and he say, "Are you ready? Are you ready?"

They say, "Hold it a minute!" They had *all* the cameras and they had *all* the stations across the country opened up for it. They says, "Go ahead!"

He say, "HELP! HELP! HELP!"

RICHARD WRIGHT

The roots of the dozens—the ritualistic, generally male, competitive back-and-forth exchange of no-holds-barred insults, usually involving inventive comic escalation and each other's mama—are obscure, but research suggests that they go back to Africa and the earliest African Americans, the vast majority of whom were, to their misfortune, Southerners. In the frontier days of the South, whites were also imaginative toe-to-toe vituperators, as we will see in one of our selections from Mark Twain. But the dozens entail a distinctive form of harshly purgative humor. They tend to seem repellent in print, even as incorporated into literature by an important writer such as Richard Wright. In fact, I would suggest that the sensitive reader not read past the missionary chitlins, in the following excerpt from Wright's novel Lawd Today! *Wright, who died in 1963 at the age of fifty-two, grew up in Mississippi and Arkansas. He began to write* Lawd Today! *(working title,* Cesspool*) a few years after he moved from the South to Chicago at the age of nineteen. Wright's straightforwardly harrowing account of his youth, in* Black Boy, *his 1945 autobiography, should be in every American's library alongside* Huckleberry Finn.*

Dozens

"This nigger setting here wearing this purple rag around his throat talking about he's got a plenty shirts. *Some*body wake 'im up!"

Slim and Bob laughed.

"I can change *five* shirts to your *one,*" boasted Jake.

"The onliest way you can do that is to pull off the one you has on *now* and put it on *five* times," said Al.

Slim and Bob laughed again.

"Listen, nigger," said Jake. "I was wearing shirts when you was going around naked in Miss'sippi!"

Slim and Bob opened their mouths wide and slumped deep into their seats.

"Hunh, hunh," said Al. "That was the time when you was wearing your hair wrapped with white strings, wasn't it?"

"White strings? Aw, Jake . . . Hehehe!" Bob could not finish for the idea tickled him so.

"Yeah," said Jake. "When I was wearing them white strings on my hair old Colonel James was sucking at your ma's tits, wasn't he?"

"Jeeesus," moaned Slim, pressing his handkerchief hard against his mouth to keep from coughing. "I told a piece of iron that once and it turned *redhot.* Now, what would a poor *meat* man do?"

Al glowered and fingered his cigarette nervously.

"Nigger," Al said slowly, so that the full force of his words would not be missed, "when old Colonel James was sucking at my ma's tits I saw your little baby brother across the street watching with slobber in his mouth . . ."

Slim and Bob rolled on the sofa and held their stomachs. Jake stiffened, crossed his legs, and gazed out of the window.

"Yeah," he said slowly, "I remembers when my little baby brother was watching with slobber in his mouth, your old grandma was out in the privy crying 'cause she couldn't find a corncob . . ."

Slim and Bob groaned and stomped their feet.

"Yeah," said Al, retaliating with narrowed eyes. "When my old grandma was crying for that corncob, your old aunt Lucy was round back of the barn with old Colonel James' old man, and she was saying something like this: 'Yyyyou kknow . . . Mmmister Cccolonel . . . I jjjust ddon't llike to ssssell . . . my ssstuff . . . I jjjust lloves to gggive . . . iiit away . . .' "

Slim and Bob embraced each other and howled.

"Yeah," said Jake. "I remembers when old aunt Lucy got through she looked around and saw your old aunt Mary there watching with her finger stuck in her puss. And old aunt Lucy said, 'Mary, go home and wash your bloomers!' "

Slim and Bob beat the floor with their fists.

Al curled his lips and shot back:

"Hunh, hunh, yeah! And when my old Aunt Mary was washing out her bloomers the hot smell of them soapsuds rose up and went out over the lonesome graveyard and your old greatgreatgreat grandma turned over in her grave and said: 'Lawd, I sure thank Thee for the smell of them pork chops You's cooking up in Heaven . . .' "

Slim grabbed Bob and they screamed.

"Yeah," drawled Jake, determined not to be outdone, "When my old greatgreatgreat grandma was smelling them pork chops, you poor old great-greatgreat*great* grandma was a Zulu queen in Africa. She was setting at the table and she said to the waiter: 'Say waiter, be sure and fetch me some of them missionary chitterlings . . .' "

"Mmmmm . . . miss . . . missionary chitterlings?" asked Slim, stretching flat on the floor and panting as one about to die.

"Yeah," said Al. "When my greatgreatgreatgreat grandma who was a Zulu queen got through eating them missionary chitterlings, she wanted to build a sewerditch to take away her crap, so she went out and saw your poor old greatgreatgreatgreat*great* grandma sleeping under a coconut tree with her old mouth wide open. She didn't need to build no sewerditch . . ."

"Jeeesus!" yelled Slim, closing his eyes and holding his stomach. "I'm *dying!*"

Jake screwed up his eyes, bit his lips, and tried hard to think of a return. But, for the life of him, he could not. Al's last image was too much; it left him blank. Then they all laughed so that they felt weak in the joints of their bones.

MEMPHIS MINNIE

Lizzie Douglas was born in 1894 or 1896 or 1897 or 1900 in Algiers, Louisiana, and grew up in Walls, Mississippi, just outside Memphis. She never did like the name Lizzie. As Memphis Minnie she became one of the most influential of all bluespersons. She played in the Memphis streets and at fish fries all over, did songs called "Good Soppin'," "Dirt Dauber Blues," "Runnin' and Dodgin' Blues," and "Squat It," lived for a while with a man named Squirrel, proved (by wielding a knife or a pistol or her guitar or whatever else came to hand) that she would brook no foolishness, sometimes sang and chewed tobacco at the same time, bested Big Bill Broonzy and Muddy Waters at different times in Chicago picking and singing contests (Broonzy, however, stole the prize and drank it), liked to play with her skirt hiked up so you could see her nice underclothes, allegedly shot a man's arm off or else cut it off with a hatchet, and according to Cactus Jack Dupree "never had a husband that couldn't play guitar." According to Bukka White, she "was about the best thing going in the woman line." She recorded steadily between 1929 and 1959 and died poor in 1973.

"New Dirty Dozen"

Come all you folks and start to walk,
I'm fixing to start my dozen talk. . . .

Come all of you womens
Oughta be in the can.
Out on the corner stopping every man,
Hollering "Soap is a nickel
And the towel is free,
I'm pigmeat, pappy, now who wants me?"
You's a old mistreater,
Robber and a cheater,
Slip you in the dozens,
Your papa and your cousins,
Your mama do the lordy lord.

Now the funniest thing I ever seen,
Tom cat jumping on a sewing machine.
Sewing machine run so fast,
Took 99 stitches in his yas, yas, yas. . . .

Now I'm gonna tell you
About old Man Bell.
He can't see, but he sure can smell.
Fish-man passed here the other day—
Hollered "Hey, pretty mama,
I'm going your way."

JOHNSON J. HOOPER

*North Carolinian Johnson Jones Hooper is best known for his character Simon Suggs,
an uncouth but also unhypocritical con man—and captain of the Tallapoosa
volunteer militia—whose credo is "It is good to be shifty in a new country." The*

Suggs stories are somewhat too long-winded and waggish for my taste, however. The Ugly Man is less significant and funnier. Hooper, who like others of the old Southwestern humorists contributed his sketches to various Southern newspapers and the Spirit of the Times, *a New York sporting magazine, was a prominent Alabama Whig in the 1840s and '50s. I don't know what Alabama Whiggery stood for, but I am constrained to note that Hooper was by no means above dreadful caricaturing of blacks, in pieces which are not reprinted in anthologies today.*

"A Night at the Ugly Man's"

Supper over, old Bill drew out his large soap-stone pipe, and filling and lighting it, placed it in his mouth. After a whiff or two, he began:

"It's no use argyfyin' the matter—I *am* the ugliest man, now on top of dirt. Thar's narry nuther like me! I'm a crowd by myself. *I allers was.* The fust I know'd of it, tho', was when I was 'bout ten years old. I went down to the spring branch one mornin', to wash my face, and I looked in the water, I seen the shadder of my face. Great God! how I run back, hollerin' for mammy, every jump! That's the last time I seen my face—I daresn't but shet my eyes when I go 'bout water."

"Don't you use a glass, when you shave?" I inquired.

"Glass! Zounds! What glass could stand it?—'twould bust it, if it was an inch thick. Glass!—pish!"

Lucy told her father he was "too bad," and that "he knew it was no sich a thing"; and the old man told her she was a "sassy wench," and to "hold her tongue."

"Yes," he continued; "it's so; I haven't seen my face in forty years, but I know how it looks. Well, when I growed up, I thort it would be the devil to find a woman that'd be willing to take me, ugly as I was—"

"Oh, you was not so *oncommon* hard-favoured when you was a young man," said old Mrs. Wallis.

"ONCOMMON! I tell you when I was ten years old, a *fly wouldn't light on my face*—and it can't be much wuss now! Shet up, and let me tell the 'squire my ixperance."

"It's no use," put in Lucy, "to be runnin' one's self down, that way, daddy! It ain't right."

"Runnin' down! Thunder and lightnin', Luce! you'll have me as good lookin' directly as John Bozeman, your sweetheart."

As he said this, old Bill looked at me, and succeeded in half covering the ball of his left eye, by way of a wink. Lucy said no more.

The old man continued:

"Well, hard as I thort it 'ud be to get a wife, fust thing I knowed, I had Sally here; and she is, or was, as pretty as any of them."

Old Mrs. Wallis knitted convulsively, and coughed slightly.

"However, she never kissed me afore we was married, and it was a long time arter afore she did. The way of it was this: we had an old one-horned cow, mighty onnery (ordinary) lookin', old as the North Star, and poor as a black snake. One day I went out to the lot"—

"Daddy, I *wouldn't* tell *that,*" exclaimed Lucy, in the most persuasive tones.

"Drot ef I don't, tho—it's the truth, and ef you don't keep still, I'll send for Bozeman to hold you quiet in the corner."

Lucy pouted a little, and was silent.

"Yes, I went out to the lot, and thar, sure as life, was my old 'oman, swung to the cow, and the old thing flyin' round, and cuttin' up all sorts o' shines! Ses I, 'What the h—ll are you up to, old 'oman?' And with that she let go, and told me she was tryin' to prac*tize* kissin' on old 'Cherry,' and she thort *arter that* she could make up her mind to *kiss me!*"

"Old man, you *made* that! I've hearn you tell it afore—but you *made* it," said the old lady.

"Well, well! I told her, 'squire, ses I, 'Come down to it now!—hang the cow—shet your eyes!—hold your breath!'—and upon that she bussed me so's you might a heard it a quarter, *and since,* nobody's had better kissin' than me! Now, that was my first ixperance about bein' ugly, arter I was grown, and 'twan't so bad neither!

"The next time my ugly feeturs came into play, was in Mobile; was you ever thar! Worst place on the green yearth; steamboats, oysters, free niggers, furriners, brick houses—hell! *that's* the place! I went down on a flat-boat from Wetumpky, with old John Todd. We had a fust-rate time of it, 'twell we got most to Mobile, and then the d——d steamboats would run so close to us, that the *sloshin'* would pretty nigh capsize us. They done it for devilment. My! how old John cussed! but it done no good. At last, ses I, 'I'll try 'em; ef thar's enny strength in cussin', I'll make 'em ashamed!' So the next one come along cavortin' and snortin' like it was gwine right into us, and did pass in twenty foot! I riz right up on a cotton bag, and ses I to the crowd—which there was a most almighty one on the guards of the boat—ses I, 'You great infernal, racket-makin', smokin', snortin', hell totin' sons of thunder—'

"Afore I could git any furder in my cussin', the crowd gin the most tremenjus, yearth-shakin' howl that ever was hearn—and one fellar, as they was broad-side with us, hollored out, 'It's the old HE UGLY HIMSELF! Great G—d, WHAT A MOUTH!' With that, thar was somethin' rained and rattled in our boat like hail, only hevier, and directly me and old John picked up *a level peck of buck-horn-handled knives!* I'll be darn'd this minit if we didn't!"

Old Mrs. Wallis looked to Heaven, as if appealing there for forgiveness of some great sin her ugly consort had committed; but she said nothing.

"So I lost nothin' by bein' ugly *that* time! Arter I got into Mobile, however, I was bothered and pestered by the people stoppin' in the street to look at me—all dirty and lightwood-smoked as I was, from bein' on the boat."—

"I think I'd a cleaned up a little," interposed tidy Lucy.

"Old 'oman! *ain't* you got nary cold 'tater to choke that gal with! Well, they'd look at me the hardest you ever seen. But I got ahead o' my story: A few days afore, thar had been a boat busted, and a heap o' people scalded and killed, one way and another. So at last, as I went into a grocery, a squad of people followed me in, and one 'lowed, ses he, 'It's one of the unfortunate sufferers by the bustin' of the Franklin,' and upon that he axed me to drink with him, and as I had my tumbler half way to my mouth, he stopped me of a sudden—

" 'Beg your pardon, stranger—but'—ses he.

" 'But—what?' ses I.

" 'Jist *fix your mouth that way again!*' ses he.

"I done it, just like I was gwine to drink, and I'll be cussed if I didn't think the whole on 'em would go into fits!—they yelled and whooped like a gang of wolves. Finally, one of 'em ses, 'Don't make fun of the unfortunate; he's hardly got over bein' blowed up yet. Less make up a puss for him.' Then they all throwed in, and made up five dollars; as the spokesman handed me the change, he axed me, 'Whar did you find yourself after the 'splosion?'

" 'In a flat-boat,' ses I.

" 'How far from the Franklin?' ses he.

" 'Why,' ses I, 'I never seen *her,* but as nigh as I can guess, it must have been, from what they tell me, nigh on to *three hundred and seventy-five miles!*' You oughter 'a seen that gang scatter. As they left, ses one, 'IT'S HIM. *It's the Ugly Man of all!*'

"Knockin' round the place, I came upon one o' these fellers grinds music out'n a mahogany box. He had a little monkey along—the d——dest peartest, least bit of a critter you ever seed! Well, bein' fond of music and varmints, I gits pretty close to the masheen, and d——d ef 'twarn't hard to tell which got most praise, me or the monkey. Howsever, at last, I got close up, and the darn thing ketcht a sight of me and *squalled!* It jumped off'n the box in a fright, and hang'd itself by its chain. The grinder histed it up ag'in, but it squalled more'n ever, and jerked and twisted and run over the keeper, and jumped off'n his back, and hang'd itself ag'in. *The sight o' me had run it distracted!* At last the grinder hilt it to his bosom, and ses he,

" 'Go ways, oagley man—maungkee fraid much oagley!' Ses I, 'Go to h–ll, you old heathen'—(you see he was some sort of a Dutch chap or another)—'if you compare me to your dirty monkey ag'in, I'll throw it hell'ards, and split your old box over your head!' And ses he right off ag'in,

" 'Maungkee ish petter ash dat oagley mans!'

"Ses I, 'Gentle*men*, you heer this crittur compare me, a free Amerakin, to his d——d heathen dumb brute of Afriky'; and with that, I fetched the monkey sailing that sent him a whirlin' about sixty-five yards, over a brick wall, and the next minit the Dutchman and his box was the worst mixed up pile of *rags and splinters* you ever seen in *one* mud-hole! About that time, too, thar was a pretty *up-country* runnin' on top o' them cussed bricks as you'll commonly see. I lay up two or three days, and at last made my passage up to Wetumpky, *in the cabin!*"

"How was that?" I asked.

"An old lady, that was along, 'lowed that it was dangerous for me to stay on the deack, *as I might scare the masheenery* OUT O' JINT. So they tuck me in the cabin afore we started, and I reckon I was treated nigh on to a hundred times, afore we got to Wetumpky."

"That's not the way you told it the last time," remarked Mrs. Wallis.

"Thunder! 'squire, did you ever hear sich wimmen folks—I've hardly had a chance to edge in a word, tonight. Well, my last ixperance was about a year ago. I got ketcht in a hurricane; it was blowin' like the devil, and the thunder and lightnin' was tremenjus—so I gits under a big red-oak, and thar I sot 'twell the lightnin' struck it! I was leanin' agin the tree when the bolt come down, shiverin' and splinterin' all before it. It hit me right here—and then"—

"Good Heavens! did *lightning* disfigure your face so?"

"Disfigure h–ll! No! The lightnin' struck right here, as I was sayin', and then—IT GLANCED!"

"Good Lord look down!" ejaculated Mrs. Wallis.

ROY WILDER, JR.

You can find yet another terrible jokey guide to Southern locutions next to the cash register anywhere just off the Interstate once you get below Maryland. Roy Wilder, Jr.'s, loving studies of colloquialism are less widely available, and good. He's an old newspaperman who holds forth in Gourd Hollow, North Carolina, the state of his birth. Joseph Mitchell said of You All Spoken Here, *which came out in 1984, "I don't think there is a poet alive except perhaps Seamus Heaney who is . . . as able to deal with syntax and other perils of grammar as death-defyingly as many of the anonymous speakers in this book.''*

from *You All Spoken Here*

Tight: Stingy; he's so tight, when he grins his pecker skins back; she makes pancakes so thin they've got just one side to them; he's so tight, when he blinks his eyes his toes curl.

A close chewer and a tight spitter: Same as above.

Close: Parsimonious; miserly; a near man with a dollar.

Snudge: Miser.

Ready with his hat and slow with his money: Courteous and close-fisted.

Wants the earth an' the moon with two strands of bobwire aroun' it—an' it whitewashed: Greedy.

Slick: Sharp; so slippery he'd hold his own in a pond full of eels; he's slicker than a greased eel.

He lies like a rug: He's a flat-out liar; he lies so bad he hires somebody to call his dogs.

His uncle stole my grandpap's horse: You wouldn't trust him behind a broom-straw; he'd steal as you looked at him.

He can see through hog wire: He isn't the smartest gent to come up the road, but he gets the message.

Smart as a tree full of owls: Has more information than a mail-order catalog.

He's all sorts of a feller. He's an expert. (Experts know more of less.)

Few weevils in his wheat: Said of a decent, exemplary citizen.

He stacked muskets at Appomattox: An honorable badge to those who plowed to the end of the row. Ben Ames Williams wrote, ''To have been paroled at Appomattox was not enough, since many of those were weaponless strag-glers. But to have 'stacked muskets at Appomattox' meant that men had not only endured, but had carried their weapons and kept themselves in fighting trim.''

When W. Kerr Scott campaigned to become Governor of North Carolina he appealed strongest to voters whose roots were in the soil. ''Branchhead boys,'' he called them, farmers and townspeople who knew the bust of day, coffee that's saucered and blowed, folks who made a good stagger at honest toil and plowed to the end of the row. Scott campaigned to get the farmer out of the mud, he said, so farm families could get to church and farm children to school.

Soon after taking office he astonished the state by proposing a $200,000,000 bond issue, big money in 1949, for a secondary road program. He would pave farm-to-market roads in each of the 100 counties. The bonds would be amortised by a gasoline tax. The proposal was revolutionary, the reaction mixed. Debate was heated and families were split and friendships were jeopardized.

In this seething setting a branchhead boy in Montgomery County came one day to the crossroads store where he traded and loafed. Some of his peers sat about the wood stove and spat in the spit box and berated Governor Scott and deplored the bond issue and the tax levy. They were in ferment.

"Well," one of the group said, taunting the newcomer, "what do you think of your man Scott now?"

Shifting his cud and eyeballing his questioner, the branchhead boy replied: "Anything my dog trees, I'll eat."

Mudge: Move slowly; work in a leisurely fashion.

Mosey: Drift off, afoot, without hurry; move along.

Cooter around: Knock about; mosey.

Shammuck, shammick: Walk in a slouchy, unsteady manner.

Coat tails a-poppin': In an angry hurry.

With every foot up an' toenails draggin': Hurrying as fast as a pullet anticipating her first egg.

Skedaddle: Git up an' dust; get your ass over the dashboard and go. Skedaddle was used by troops on both sides in the Civil War to describe precipitous departure of the opposition from a fray. Ms. Chesnut said the word was like General Nathan Bedford Forrest's words of command: "In place of 'Boots and Saddles' played by the trumpet, he says; 'Git ready to git! Git!' " Slaveholders often used the term in advertising for runaways.

Secretary of State Cordell Hull, a native of Tennessee, was an accomplished, dignified, and incisive cusser. A lisp lent a lilt to his lacings.

President Franklin D. Roosevelt liked to mimic Mr. Hull's most frequent expletive, "Jethuth Chwith."

Another of the Secretary's frequent comments was "pith ant."

Jonathan Daniels, once of President Roosevelt's White House staff, told us of two instances of Mr. Hull's expression of indignation:

—In remarking on Undersecretary of State Sumner Welles, Mr. Hull said: "Every department has its thun of a bitch but I've got the all-American."

—When Raymond Moley, at the Economic Conference in London in 1933, seemed to undercut him, Mr. Hull said: "That pith ant Moley. Here he curled

up at mah feet and let me stroke his head like a huntin' dog and then he goes and
bites me in the ath.''

Secretary Hull's talent for cussin' got norated nationally with the Japanese
attack on Pearl Harbor when, later that day, the Japanese emissaries, Ambassa-
dor Nomura and Special Envoy Kurusu, called at the State Department and
submitted a prepared statement.

The Japanese were received coldly and formally, as President Roosevelt had
instructed. But before the day was ended the word got out that Mr. Hull had
chastised the visiting diplomats ''in strong Tennessee mountain language.''

We have often wondered what Mr. Hull said when he gave the envoys a
piece of his mind—when he read their titles clear—on that memorable day.

The Secretary, in his memoirs, made a diplomatic disclaimer. He said he told
the Japanese that in 50 years of public service he had ''never seen a document
that was more crowded with infamous falsehoods and distortions.'' He had
heard that he cussed out the envoys, he wrote. ''But the fact is that I told them
exactly what I said above. No 'cussing out' could have made it stronger.''

There Mr. Hull rested his case. The better story to the contrary stayed alive,
however, and speculation continued, for good stories die hard. Years after the
incident, Jonathan Daniels wrote us that Harry Hopkins, President Roosevelt's
close and trusted confidant, ''is authority for the fact or legend'' that Mr. Hull
did indeed use strong Tennessee speech that day to express his indignation.

Most of Mr. Hull's purple passages of that day may be lost to history. But a
single fragment remains.

In about as diplomatic a cussin' as he could lay on, Mr. Hull, in pure East
Tennessee dialect, addressed the envoys as:

''You hick'ry headed pith anths.''

This likker is just right.
If it had been any worse I couldn't drink it.
If it had been any better you wouldn't have give it to me.

—An old saying

Like Claude Harris' mule: Indifferent. ''Naw suh, he ain' blind,'' Claude
Harris said as his mule plowed into a fence paling. ''He jus' don' give a
damn.''

Like a jackass eatin' briars: Grinnin' like a barrel of possum heads.

Like a bug arg'in with a chicken: Useless.

Horse-high, bull-strong, pig-tight, and goose-proof: The fourteen-karat bamboozle. The term applied originally to fences and now pertains to political
and financial schemes. The fourteen-karat bamboozle comment comes from
Seminole Sam, a character in Walt Kelly's matchless Pogo cartoon strip
(5-8-1956). Seminole Sam was based on Colonel Samuel Taylor Moore,
newspaper man, magazine writer, Early Birdman (balloons), and good
companion.

Yellow dog Democrat: A straight ticket man. He'll vote for a yellow dog if he's a Democrat.

Slaunchways, sidegartlin': Slanchwise; antigodlin; slanting; on a diagonal; awry; askew; off the main track; out of square; out of plumb; cattercornered; cattywampused; hip-sheltered; crook-sided; slanchindicular.

Contrarious: Same as above.

Make: Mode, as in "This here make of livin' is too high-falutin' for me. They've got a outhouse in the house, an' they're a-cookin' outdoors."

Hincty, hinchy: Sporty patrons of sporting houses—white, overbearing, pompous, some wearing pearl-buttoned spats with revolvers to match. "God damn it, my guns are ivory handled," said General George S. Patton, Jr., alumnus of the Virginia Military Institute, class of 1907. "Nobody but a pimp from a cheap New Orleans whorehouse would carry one with pearl grips."

Jook, jook joint, jook house: An out-of-the-way oasis, a roadhouse, a pleasure house, a house of ill fame where men and women carry on—drinkin', dancin', singin', gamblin', makin' out.

> Jooking, said Zora Neale Hurston, is playing piano and guitar as done in such resorts. Low down . . . blues . . . The music at first was from guitars—boxes, they were called. Then pianos, and player pianos, and talking machines. Finally, coin-operated phonographs—jook boxes as we know them today.
>
> "Musically speaking," Ms. Hurston said, "the jook is the most important place in America. For in its smelly, shoddy confines has been born the secular music known as blues, and on blues has been founded jazz. The singing and playing in the true Negro style," she said, is jooking.
>
> Ms. Hurston also said that a good jook singer must be able to "hoist a jook song from her belly and lam it against the front door. . . . She must also have a good belly-wobble, and her hips must, to quote a popular work song, 'Shake like jelly all over and be so broad, Lawd, Lawd, and be so broad.' "
>
> Jook should be spelled and pronounced *jook* to rhyme with *cook*. Ms. Hurston, born and raised in Florida where jooks flourished among palmettos and back streets, spelled and pronounced it that way. So did MacKinlay Kantor, another old Florida hand. "I'm damned if I spell the word j-u-k-e," he said. "It wasn't pronounced that way, and it still galls me to hear it or see it employed."

> Fellow sinners, I have preached to you. I have prayed for you, and often exhorted you to flee from the wrath to come; but not withstanding all this, here you now are as drunk as Billy be damned.
>
> If you are determined to go to hell foremost, I am too good a shepherd to desert my flock in the hour of danger, and therefore will go with you.
>
> Landlord, give us something to drink! Come on up, boys.
>
> —An unidentified parson in a combination grocery and groggery in Louisiana

Jerks: An orgiastic religious exhibition in which participants are seized in
religious fervor and "struck down"—jerking and twisting in emotional
spasms, shouting, sometimes collapsing unconscious and almost always
awakening with sins forgiven and full of exhortations for others to join the
throngs of sinners saved.

MacKinlay Kantor told of a woman overcome by religious ecstasy—spraddled
on the ground and out cold. When fellow worshippers sought to move and
revive her, the preacher intervened: "No," he said. "Leave her lay where Jesus
flang her."

ROBERTO G. FERNANDEZ

*The territory below the Mason-Dixon line today is not all juleps and magnolias, it is
also Miami Cubans. Fernandez, who came to the United States from Cuba in 1961,
teaches Hispanic literature at Florida State University. Here is a taste of his fourth
book of fiction and first in English,* Raining Backwards, *whose opening words are*
"WILL THE LAST AMERICAN TO LEAVE MIAMI PLEASE BRING THE FLAG."

"Wrong Number"

"Oigo, halow?"

"Do you think you can go on taking over what's not yours? You people
aren't happy with biting the hand that has fed you for more than twenty-eight
long years, but now you want to suck our blood also. You bastards, for years
you lived off our welfare and then used the money to buy the factories, then
took over the banks to launder your money. How many people have you
squashed to get ahead in this land of the free and home of the brave? How
many unsung native sons have you replaced? This was a wonderful place to live
under the sun, where neighbor helped neighbor. But now, now there's no
sun. You're canning it and selling it overseas!"

"Pepe, is an American. I no know what he says. He spics too fast."

"Raul, tell him Waitaminut."

"Waitaminut.

"He continue spicking."

"Tell him, yes. He must be selling you somesing. You know how they love to sell you sings by telephone and ask cute little questions like how many times you brush your teeth or how many times you go potty and then they ask you if you are regular. Tell him yes to see what else he says, as long as you don't sign anysin is okay, and when you get tired you tell him no-sank-you. It will be good practice for your English."

"Jes?"

"Is no jes, Marielito, is like ee-s."

"Ee-s?"

"Yes! I'm glad you agree, that way it'll be easier when we ship you bastards out of here. Do you realize my brother lost his job because he doesn't spica the español? In our own country and we're fired for not speaking spic. And my cousin Rob Hodel, a God fearing man, even a member of the police force, he married a Spanish woman and do you know what she did? Well, what do you think she did? I'm sure you know. She cleaned him out. Now I hear she's some sort of Latin socialite."

"Hey, Pep, he keep spickin. He sounds like a juke box. I no underestan much. He spic too fast. I sink is about his girlfriend."

"Like I told you before, when you get tired of hearing him, you tell him: 'Che no here. Wrong number.' And remember to tell him sank-you because people here are very polite."

"Ee-s?"

"Yes! The season is open. We're going to purify this land of dregs. You fucking Cubans!"

"Che no here. Wrong number. Sank-you!"

EDGAR ALLAN POE

One of the few words Flannery O'Connor habitually misspelled in her letters was, ironically enough, "humorous." She informed one correspondent that her childhood reading was limited to The Book of Knowledge *and "Slop with a capital S. The Slop period was followed by the Edgar Allan Poe period which lasted for years and consisted chiefly in a volume called* The Humerous Tales of EAPoe. *These were mighty humerous—one about a young man who in his room removed wooden arms, wooden legs, hair piece, artificial teeth, voice box, etc etc; another about the inmates of a lunatic asylum who take over the establishment and run it to suit themselves. This is an influence I would rather not think about." I daresay Ph.D. dissertations have examined this revelation in far more depth than I can aspire to here, but I can tell you that the Poe stories O'Connor refers to are "The Man Who Was Used Up" and "The System of Doctor Tarr and Mister Fether." She herself, of course, wrote a story in which a man steals a woman's artificial leg, and her work might lead some to conclude that she viewed life here on earth as a madhouse run by the inmates. Incidentally, or not, her hometown, Milledgeville, was for many years the site of Georgia's only state mental hospital, or rather (judging from the exposés of conditions there that came out in newspapers periodically during my Georgia youth) snake pit. After mentioning the* Humerous Tales *in another letter, she added that they were "anything but funny." They do have their own peculiar fascination, however. Certainly Poe—whose Southern credentials are that he grew up mostly in Virginia and edited the* Southern Literary Messenger*—is an engrossing writer if you don't worry too much about what wavelength he has taken you off onto. And he certainly fancied himself a humorist at times. His first published writings, and a number of his later ones, satirized reigning literary fashions. As one critic has put it very mildly, "the passage of time has inevitably blunted the thrust of many of these works." But you can see why Flannery O'Connor, in youth and adulthood, had trouble getting some of them out of her mind. This is true for me of the following piece, which appeared shortly before Poe's death in 1849, and which for reasons I can't begin to explain never fails to crack me up. I hxpe that yxu, txx, can enjxy sxmething abxut Pxe's xdd sense xf humxr.*

"X-ing a Paragrab"

As it is well known that the 'wise men' came 'from the East', and as Mr Touch-and-go Bullet-head came from the East. It follows that Mr Bullet-head was a wise man; and if collateral proof of the matter be needed, here we have it—Mr B——was an editor. Irascibility was his sole foible; for in fact the obstinacy of which men accused him was anything but his foible, since he justly considered it his forte. It was his strong point—his virtue; and it would have required all the logic of a Brownson to convince him that it was 'anything else'.

I have shown that Touch-and-go Bullet-head was a wise man; and the only occasion on which he did not prove infallible was when, abandoning that legitimate home for all wise men, the East, he migrated to the city of Alexander-the-Great-o-nopolis, or some place of a similar title, out West.

I must do him the justice to say, however, that when he made up his mind finally to settle in that town it was under the impression that no newspaper, and consequently no editor, existed in that particular section of the country. In establishing the *Tea-Pot,* he expected to have the field all to himself. I feel confident he never would have dreamed of taking up his residence in Alexander-the-Great-o-nopolis had he been aware that in Alexander-the-Great-o-nopolis there lived a gentleman named John Smith (if I rightly remember), who, for many years, had there quietly grown fat in editing and publishing the *Alexander-the-Great-o-nopolis Gazette.* It was solely, therefore, on account of having been misinformed, that Mr Bullet-head found himself in Alex—suppose we call it Nopolis, 'for short'—but, as he *did* find himself there, he determined to keep up his character for obst—for firmness, and remain. So remain he did; and he did more; he unpacked his press, type, etc., etc., rented an office exactly opposite to that of the *Gazette,* and, on the third morning after his arrival, issued the first number of the *Alexan*—that is to say, of the *Nopolis Tea-Pot:*—as nearly as I can recollect, this was the name of the new paper.

The leading article, I must admit, was brilliant, not to say severe. It was especially bitter about things in general—and as for the editor of the *Gazette,* he was torn all to pieces in particular. Some of Bullet-head's remarks were really so fiery that I have always, since that time, been forced to look upon John Smith, who is still alive, in the light of a salamander. I cannot pretend to give *all* the *Tea-Pot*'s paragraphs *verbatim,* but one of them ran thus:—

> Oh, yes!—Oh, we perceive! Oh, no doubt! The editor over the way is a genius—Oh my! Oh, goodness, gracious!—What *is* this world coming to? *O tempora! O Moses!*

A philippic, at once so caustic and so classical, alighted like a bombshell among the hitherto peaceful citizens of Nopolis. Groups of excited individuals gathered at the corners of the streets. Everyone awaited, with heartfelt anxiety, the reply of the dignified Smith. Next morning it appeared, as follows:

> We quote from the *Tea-Pot* of yesterday the subjoined paragraph:—'*Oh, yes!—Oh,* we perceive! *Oh,* no doubt! *Oh,* my! *Oh,* goodness! *O tempora! O Moses!*' Why, the fellow is all *O!* That accounts for his reasoning in a circle, and explains why there is neither beginning nor end to him, nor to anything that he says. We really do not believe the vagabond can write a word that hasn't an o in it. Wonder if this *O*-ing is a habit of his? By the bye, he came away from Down-East in a great hurry. Wonder if he *O*'s as much there as he does here? *O!* it is pitiful.'

The indignation of Mr Bullet-head at these scandalous insinuations I shall not attempt to describe. On the eel-skinning principle, however, he did not seem to be so much incensed at the attack upon his integrity as one might have

imagined. It was the sneer at his *style* that drove him to desperation. What!—
he, Touch-and-go Bullet-head!—not able to write a word without an o in it!
He would soon let the jackanapes see that he was mistaken. Yes! he would let
him see how *much* he was mistaken, the puppy! He, Touch-and-go Bullet-
head, of Frogpondium, would let Mr John Smith perceive that he, Bullet-
head, could indite, if it so pleased him, a whole paragraph—ay! a whole
article—in which that contemptible vowel should not once—not even *once*—
make its appearance. But no;—that would be yielding a point to the said John
Smith. *He,* Bullet-head, would make *no* alteration in his style, to suit the
caprices of any Mr Smith in Christendom. Perish so vile a thought! The *O*
forever! He would persist in the *O*. He would be as *O*-wy as *O*-why could be.

Burning with the chivalry of this determination, the great Touch-and-go, in
the next *Tea-Pot,* came out merely with this simple but resolute paragraph in
reference to this unhappy affair:—

> The editor of the *Tea-Pot* has the *honor* of advising the editor of the *Gazette*
> that he (the *Tea-Pot*) will take an opportunity in to-morrow morning's paper of
> convincing him (the *Gazette*) that he (the *Tea-Pot*) both can and will be *his own*
> *master,* as regards style:—he (the *Tea-Pot*) intending to show him (the *Gazette*)
> the supreme, and indeed the withering, contempt with which the criticism of
> him (the *Gazette*) inspires the independent bosom of him (the *Tea-Pot*), by
> composing for the especial gratification (?) of him (the *Gazette*) a leading article,
> of some extent, in which the beautiful vowel—the emblem of Eternity, yet so
> offensive to the hyper-exquisite delicacy of him (the *Gazette*)—shall most cer-
> tainly *not be avoided* by his (the *Gazette*'s) most obedient, humble servant, the
> *Tea-Pot.* 'So much for Buckingham.'

In fulfilment of the awful threat thus darkly intimated rather than decidedly
enunciated, the great Bullet-head, turning a deaf ear to all entreaties for
'copy', and simply requesting his foreman to 'go to the d——l', when he (the
foreman) assured him (the *Tea-Pot*) that it was high time to 'go to press';
turning a deaf ear to everything. I say, the great Bullet-head sat up until
daybreak, consuming the midnight oil, and absorbed in the composition of the
really unparalleled paragraph which follows:—

> So ho, John! how now? Told you so, you know. Don't crow, another time,
> before you're out of the woods! Does your mother *know* you're out? Oh, no,
> no!—so go home at once, now, John, to your odious old woods of Concord!
> Go home to your woods, old owl,—go! You won't? Oh, poh, poh, John, don't
> do so! You've *got* to go, you know! So go at once, and don't go slow; for
> nobody owns you here, you know. Oh, John, John, if you *don't* go you're no
> *homo*—no! You're only a fowl, an owl: a cow, a sow; a doll, a poll; a poor, old,
> good-for-nothing-to-nobody, log, dog, hog, or frog, come out of a Concord

bog. Cool, now—cool! *Do* be cool, you fool! None of your crowing, old cock! Don't frown so—don't! Don't hollo, nor howl, nor growl, nor bow-wow-wow! Good Lord, John, how you *do* look! Told you so, you know—but stop rolling your goose of an old poll about so, and go and drown your sorrows in a bowl!

Exhausted, very naturally, by so stupendous an effort, the great Touch-and-go could attend to nothing farther that night. Firmly, composedly, yet with an air of conscious power, he handed his MS. to the devil in waiting, and then, walking leisurely home, retired with ineffable dignity to bed.

Meantime the devil, to whom the copy was intrusted, ran upstairs to his 'case', in an unutterable hurry and forthwith made a commencement at 'set-ting' the MS, 'up'.

In the first place, of course,—as the opening word was 'So',—he made a plunge into the capital-*S* hole and came out in triumph with a capital-*S*. Elated by this success, he immediately threw himself upon the little-*o* box with a blindfold impetuosity—but who shall describe his horror when his fingers came up without the anticipated letter in their clutch? who shall paint his astonishment and rage at perceiving, as he rubbed his knuckles, that he had been only thumping them, to no purpose, against the bottom of an *empty* box. Not a single little-*o* was in the little-*o* hole; and, glancing fearfully at the capital-*O* partition, he found *that,* to his extreme terror, in a precisely similar predicament. Awe-stricken, his first impulse was to rush to the foreman.

'Sir!' said he, gasping for breath, 'I can't never set up nothing without no *o*'s.'

'*What* do you mean by that?' growled the foreman, who was in a very ill-humor at being kept up so late.

'Why, sir, there beant an *o* in the office, neither a big un nor a little un!'

'What—what the d——l has become of all that were in the case?'

'*I* don't know, sir,' said the boy, 'but one of them ere *Gazette* devils is bin prowling bout here all night, and I spect *he's* gone and cabbaged em every one.'

'Dod rot him! I haven't a doubt of it,' replied the foreman, getting purple with rage—'but I tell you what you do, Bob, that's a good boy—you go over the first chance you get and hook every one of their *i*'s and (d——n them!) their izzards.'

'Jist so,' replied Bob, with a wink and a frown—'*I'll* be in to em, *I'll* let em know a thing or two; but in de mean time, that ere paragrab? *Mus* go in to-night, you know—else there'll be the d——l to pay, and—'

'And not a *bit* of pitch hot,' interrupted the foreman, with a deep sigh and an emphasis on the 'bit'. 'Is it a *very* long paragraph, Bob?'

'Shouldn't call it a *wery* long paragrab,' said Bob.

'Ah, well, then! do the best you can with it! we *must* get to press,' said the foreman, who was over head and ears in work; 'just stick in some other letter for *o,* nobody's going to read the fellow's trash, anyhow.'

'*Wery* well,' replied Bob, 'here goes it!' and off he hurried to his case; muttering as he went—'Considdeble vell, them ere expressions, perticcler for a man as doesn't swar. So I's to gouge out all their eyes, eh? and d——n all their gizzards! Vell! this here's the chap as is jist able *for* to do it.' The fact is that, although Bob was but twelve years old and four feet high, he was equal to any amount of fight, in a small way.

The exigency here described is by no means of rare occurrence in printing-offices; and I cannot tell how to account for it, but the fact is indisputable, that when the exigency does occur, it almost always happens that *x* is adopted as a substitute for the letter deficient. The true reason, perhaps, is that *x* is rather the most superabundant letter in the cases, or at least *was* so, in old times, long enough to render the substitution in question an habitual thing with printers. As for Bob, he would have considered it heretical to employ any other character, in a case of this kind, than the *x* to which he had been accustomed.

'I *shell* have to *x* this ere paragrab,' said he to himself, as he read it over in astonishment, 'but it's jest about the awfulest *o*-wy paragrab I ever *did* see': so *x* it he did, unflinchingly, and to press it went *x*-ed.

Next morning the population of Nopolis were taken all aback by reading, in the *Tea-Pot* the following extraordinary leader:—

> Sx hx, Jxhn! hxw nxw! Txld yxu sx, yxu knxw. Dxn't crxw, anxther time, befxre yxu're xut xf the wxrds! Dxes yxur mxther *knxw* yxu're xut? Xh, nx, nx! sx gx hxme at xnce, nxw, Jxhn. tx yxur xdixus xld wxxds xf Cxncxrd! Gx hxme tx yxur wxxds, xld xwl,—gx! Yxu wxn't? Xh, pxh, pxh, Jxhn, dxn't dx sx! Yxu've *gxt* tx gx, yxu knxw! sx gx at xnce, and dxn't gx slxw; fxr nxbxdy xwns yxu here, yxu knxw. Xh, Jxhn, Jxhn, if yxu *dxn't* gx yxu're nx *hxmx*—nx! Yxu're xnly a fxwl, an xwl; a cxw, a sxw; a dxll, a pxll; a pxxr xld gxxd-fxr-nxthing-tx-nxbxdy lxg, dxg, hxg, xr frxg, cxme xut xf a Cxncxrd bxg. Cxxl. nxw—cxxl! Dx be cxxl, yxu fxxl! Nxne xf yxur crxwing, xld cxck! Dxn't frxwn sx—dxn't! Dxn't hxllx, nxr hxwl, nxr grxwl, nxr bxw-wxw-wxw! Gxxd Lxrd, Jxhn, hxw yxu *dx* lxxk! Txld yxu sx, yxu knxw, but stxp rxlling yxur gxxse xf an xld pxll abxut sx, and gx and drxwn yxur sxrrxws in a bxwl!

The uproar occasioned by this mystical and cabalistical article is not to be conceived. The first definite idea entertained by the populace was that some diabolical treason lay concealed in the hieroglyphics; and there was a general rush to Bullet-head's residence, for the purpose of riding him on a rail; but that gentleman was nowhere to be found. He had vanished, no one could tell how; and not even the ghost of him has ever been seen since.

Unable to discover its legitimate object, the popular fury at length subsided; leaving behind it, by way of sediment, quite a medley of opinion about this unhappy affair.

One gentleman thought the whole an X-ellent joke.

Another said that, indeed, Bullet-head had shown much X-uberance of fancy.

A third admitted him X-entric, but no more.

A fourth could only suppose it the Yankee's design to X-press, in a general way, his X-asperation.

'Say, rather, to set an X-ample to posterity,' suggested a fifth.

That Bullet-head had been driven to an extremity was clear to all; and in fact, since *that* editor could not be found, there was some talk about lynching the other one.

The more common conclusion, however, was that the affair was, simply, X-traordinary and in-X-plicable. Even the town mathematician confessed that he could make nothing of so dark a problem. X, everybody knew, was an unknown quantity; but in this case (as he properly observed) there was an unknown quantity of X.

The opinion of Bob, the devil (who kept dark 'about his having X-ed the paragrab'), did not meet with so much attention as I think it deserved, although it was very openly and very fearlessly expressed. He said that, for his part, he had no doubt about the matter at all; that it was a clear case that Mr Bullet-head never *could* be persvaded fur to drink like other folks, but vas *co*ntinually a-svigging o' that ere blessed XXX ale, and, as a naiteral consekvence, it just puffed him up savage, and made him X (cross) in the X-treme.

O. HENRY

William Sidney Porter was born near Greensboro, North Carolina, in 1862, moved to Texas when he was twenty, wrote sketches of frontier life, started a comic weekly in Austin called the Rolling Stone, *was indicted perhaps not entirely justly for embezzlement, fled to Honduras, returned home when he learned his wife was dying, went to prison, began to write there under the pseudonym O. Henry, moved to New York upon his release, won fame and riches as an enormously prolific writer of short stories characteristically with surprise endings, and died deeply in debt in 1910. Perhaps the reason he achieved neither solvency nor a lasting place in the literary canon may inferred from a bit of his verse:*

> *I'd rather distribute a coat of red*
> *On the town with a wad of dough*
> *Just now, than to have my cognomen*
> *Spelled "Michael Angelo."*
> *For a small live man, if he's prompt on hand*
> *When the good things pass around,*
> *While the world's on tap has a better snap*
> *Than a big man under ground.*

Some of the stories he dashed off for the popular press, however, include brief quirkily lyrical flights and shifts that anticipate Ring Lardner and even later and more highly literary humorists. And many of his less offhand tales have held their sentimental or comic appeal over the years—for instance "The Gift of the Magi" and this one, set in Dixie.

"The Ransom of Red Chief"

It looked like a good thing; but wait till I tell you. We were down South, in Alabama—Bill Driscoll and myself—when this kidnapping idea struck us. It was, as Bill afterward expressed it, "during a moment of temporary mental apparition"; but we didn't find that out till later.

There was a town down there, as flat as a flannel-cake, and called Summit, of course. It contained inhabitants of as undeleterious and self-satisfied a class of peasantry as ever clustered around a May-pole.

Bill and me had a joint capital of about six hundred dollars, and we needed just two thousand dollars more to pull off a fraudulent town-lot scheme in Western Illinois with. We talked it over on the front steps of the hotel. Philoprogenitiveness, says we, is strong in semi-rural communities; therefore, and for other reasons, a kidnapping project ought to do better there than in the radius of newspapers that send reporters out in plain clothes to stir up talk about such things. We knew that Summit couldn't get after us with anything stronger than constables, and, maybe, some lackadaisical bloodhounds and a diatribe or two in the *Weekly Farmers' Budget*. So, it looked good.

We selected for our victim the only child of a prominent citizen named Ebenezer Dorset. The father was respectable and tight, a mortgage fancier and a stern, upright collection-plate passer and forecloser. The kid was a boy of ten, with bas-relief freckles, and hair the colour of the cover of the magazine you buy at the news-stand when you want to catch a train. Bill and me figured that Ebenezer would melt down for a ransom of two thousand dollars to a cent. But wait till I tell you.

About two miles from Summit was a little mountain, covered with a dense cedar brake. On the rear elevation of this mountain was a cave. There we stored provisions.

One evening after sundown, we drove in a buggy past old Dorset's house. The kid was in the street, throwing rocks at a kitten on the opposite fence.

"Hey, little boy!" says Bill, "would you like to have a bag of candy and a nice ride?"

The boy catches Bill neatly in the eye with a piece of brick.

"That will cost the old man an extra five hundred dollars," says Bill, climbing over the wheel.

That boy put up a fight like a welter-weight cinnamon bear; but, at last, we got him down in the bottom of the buggy and drove away. We took him up to the cave, and I hitched the horse in the cedar brake. After dark I drove the buggy to the little village, three miles away, where we had hired it, and walked back to the mountain.

Bill was pasting court-plaster over the scratches and bruises on his features. There was a fire burning behind the big rock at the entrance of the cave, and the boy was watching a pot of boiling coffee, with two buzzard tail feathers stuck in his red hair. He points a stick at me when I come up, and says:

"Ha! cursed paleface, do you dare to enter the camp of Red Chief, the terror of the plains?"

"He's all right now," says Bill, rolling up his trousers and examining some bruises on his shins. "We're playing Indian. We're making Buffalo Bill's show look like magic-lantern views of Palestine in the town hall. I'm Old Hank, the Trapper, Red Chief's captive, and I'm to be scalped at daybreak. By Geronimo! that kid can kick hard."

Yes, sir, that boy seemed to be having the time of his life. The fun of camping out in a cave had made him forget that he was a captive himself. He immediately christened me Snake-eye, the Spy, and announced that, when his braves returned from the warpath, I was to be broiled at the stake at the rising of the sun.

Then we had supper; and he filled his mouth full of bacon and bread and gravy, and began to talk. He made a during-dinner speech something like this:

"I like this fine. I never camped out before; but I had a pet 'possum once, and I was nine last birthday. I hate to go to school. Rats ate up sixteen of Jimmy Talbot's aunt's speckled hen's eggs. Are there any real Indians in these woods? I want some more gravy. Does the trees moving make the wind blow? We had five puppies. What makes your nose so red, Hank? My father has lots of money. Are the stars hot? I whipped Ed Walker twice, Saturday. I don't like girls. You dassent catch toads unless with a string. Do oxen make any noise? Why are oranges round? Have you got beds to sleep on in this cave? Amos Murray has got six toes. A parrot can talk, but a monkey or a fish can't. How many does it take to make twelve?''

Every few minutes he would remember that he was a pesky redskin, and pick up his stick rifle and tiptoe to the mouth of the cave to rubber for the scouts of the hated paleface. Now and then he would let out a war-whoop that made Old Hank the Trapper shiver. That boy had Bill terrorized from the start.

"Red Chief," says I to the kid, "would you like to go home?"

"Aw, what for?" says he. "I don't have any fun at home. I hate to go to school. I like to camp out. You won't take me back home again, Snake-eye, will you?"

"Not right away," says I. "We'll stay here in the cave a while."

"All right!" says he. "That'll be fine. I never had such fun in all my life."

We went to bed about eleven o'clock. We spread down some wide blankets and quilts and put Red Chief between us. We weren't afraid he'd run away. He kept us awake for three hours, jumping up and reaching for his rifle and screeching: "Hist! pard," in mine and Bill's ears, as the fancied crackle of a twig or the rustle of a leaf revealed to his young imagination the stealthy approach of the outlaw band. At last, I fell into a troubled sleep, and dreamed that I had been kidnapped and chained to a tree by a ferocious pirate with red hair.

Just at daybreak, I was awakened by a series of awful screams from Bill. They weren't yells, or howls, or shouts, or whoops, or yawps, such as you'd expect from a manly set of vocal organs—they were simply indecent, terrifying, humiliating screams, such as women emit when they see ghosts or caterpillars. It's an awful thing to hear a strong desperate, fat man scream incontinently in a cave at daybreak.

I jumped up to see what the matter was. Red Chief was sitting on Bill's chest, with one hand twined in Bill's hair. In the other he had the sharp case-knife we used for slicing bacon; and he was industriously and realistically trying to take Bill's scalp, according to the sentence that had been pronounced upon him the evening before.

I got the knife away from the kid and made him lie down again. But, from that moment, Bill's spirit was broken. He laid down on his side of the bed, but he never closed an eye again in sleep as long as that boy was with us. I dozed off for a while, but along toward sun-up I remembered that Red Chief had said I was to be burned at the stake at the rising of the sun. I wasn't nervous or afraid; but I sat up and lit my pipe and leaned against a rock.

"What you getting up so soon for, Sam?" asked Bill.

"Me?" says I. "Oh, I got a kind of a pain in my shoulder. I thought sitting up would rest it."

"You're a liar!" says Bill. "You're afraid. You was to be burned at sunrise, and you was afraid he'd do it. And he would, too, if he could find a match. Ain't it awful, Sam? Do you think anybody will pay out money to get a little imp like that back home?"

"Sure," said I. "A rowdy kid like that is just the kind that parents dote on. Now, you and the Chief get up and cook breakfast, while I go up on the top of this mountain and reconnoitre."

I went up on the peak of the little mountain and ran my eye over the contiguous vicinity. Over toward Summit I expected to see the sturdy yeomanry of the village armed with scythes and pitchforks beating the countryside for the dastardly kidnappers. But what I saw was a peaceful landscape dotted with one man ploughing with a dun mule. Nobody was dragging the creek; no couriers dashed hither and yon, bringing tidings of no news to the distracted parents. There was a sylvan attitude of somnolent sleepiness pervading that section of the external outward surface of Alabama that lay exposed to my view. "Perhaps," says I to myself, "it has not yet been discovered that the wolves have borne away the tender lambkin from the fold. Heaven help the wolves!" says I, and I went down the mountain to breakfast.

When I got to the cave I found Bill backed up against the side of it, breathing hard, and the boy threatening to smash him with a rock half as big as a cocoanut.

"He put a red-hot boiled potato down my back," explained Bill, "and then mashed it with his foot; and I boxed his ears. Have you got a gun about you, Sam?"

I took the rock away from the boy and kind of patched up the argument. "I'll fix you," says the kid to Bill. "No man ever yet struck the Red Chief but what he got paid for it. You better beware!"

After breakfast the kid takes a piece of leather with strings wrapped around it out of his pocket and goes outside the cave unwinding it.

"What's he up to now?" says Bill anxiously. "You don't think he'll run away, do you, Sam?"

"No fear of it," says I. "He don't seem to be much of a home body. But we've got to fix up some plan about the ransom. There don't seem to be much excitement around Summit on account of his disappearance; but maybe they haven't realized yet that he's gone. His folks may think he's spending the night with Aunt Jane or one of the neighbours. Anyhow, he'll be missed today. Tonight we must get a message to his father demanding the two thousand dollars for his return."

Just then we heard a kind of war-whoop, such as David might have emitted when he knocked out the champion Goliath. It was a sling that Red Chief had pulled out of his pocket, and he was whirling it around his head.

I dodged, and heard a heavy thud and a kind of a sigh from Bill, like a horse gives out when you take his saddle off. A niggerhead rock the size of an egg had caught Bill just behind his left ear. He loosened himself all over and fell in the fire across the frying pan of hot water for washing the dishes. I dragged him out and poured cold water on his head for half an hour.

By and by, Bill sits up and feels behind his ear and says: "Sam, do you know who my favourite Biblical character is?"

"Take it easy," says I. "You'll come to your senses presently."

"King Herod," says he. "You won't go away and leave me here alone, will you, Sam?"

I went out and caught that boy and shook him until his freckles rattled.

"If you don't behave," says I, "I'll take you straight home. Now, are you going to be good, or not?"

"I was only funning," says he sullenly. "I didn't mean to hurt Old Hank. But what did he hit me for? I'll behave, Snake-eye, if you won't send me home, and if you'll let me play the Black Scout today."

"I don't know the game," says I. "That's for you and Mr. Bill to decide. He's your playmate for the day. I'm going away for a while, on business. Now, you come in and make friends with him and say you are sorry for hurting him, or home you go, at once."

I made him and Bill shake hands, and then I took Bill aside and told him I was going to Poplar Cove, a little village three miles from the cave, and find out what I could about how the kidnapping had been regarded in Summit. Also, I thought it best to send a peremptory letter to old man Dorset that day, demanding the ransom and dictating how it should be paid.

"You know, Sam," says Bill, "I've stood by you without batting an eye in earthquakes, fire, and flood—in poker games, dynamite outrages, police raids, train robberies, and cyclones. I never lost my nerve yet till we kidnapped that two-legged skyrocket of a kid. He's got me going. You won't leave me long with him, will you, Sam?"

"I'll be back some time this afternoon," says I. "You must keep the boy amused and quiet till I return. And now we'll write the letter to old Dorset."

Bill and I got paper and pencil and worked on the letter while Red Chief, with a blanket wrapped around him, strutted up and down, guarding the mouth of the cave. Bill begged me tearfully to make the ransom fifteen hundred dollars instead of two thousand. "I ain't attempting," says he, "to decry the celebrated moral aspect of parental affection, but we're dealing with humans, and it ain't human for anybody to give up two thousand dollars for that forty-pound chunk of freckled wildcat. I'm willing to take a chance at fifteen hundred dollars. You can charge the difference up to me.''

So, to relieve Bill, I acceded, and we collaborated a letter that ran this way:

EBENEZER DORSET, ESQ.:

We have your boy concealed in a place far from Summit. It is useless for you or the most skilled detectives to attempt to find him. Absolutely, the only terms on which you can have him restored to you are these: We demand fifteen hundred dollars in large bills for his return: the money to be left at midnight at the same spot and in the same box as your reply—as hereinafter described. If you agree to these terms, send your answer in writing by a solitary messenger tonight at half-past eight o'clock. After crossing Owl Creek, on the road to Poplar Cove, there are three large trees about a hundred yards apart, close to the fence of the wheat field on the right-hand side. At the bottom of the fence-post, opposite the third tree, will be found a small pasteboard box.

The messenger will place the answer in this box and return immediately to Summit.

If you attempt any treachery or fail to comply with our demand as stated, you will never see your boy again.

If you pay the money as demanded, he will be returned to you safe and well within three hours. These terms are final, and if you do not accede to them no further communication will be attempted.

TWO DESPERATE MEN.

I addressed this letter to Dorset, and put it in my pocket. As I was about to start, the kid comes up to me and says:

"Aw, Snake-eye, you said I could play the Black Scout while you was gone."

"Play it, of course," says I. "Mr. Bill will play with you. What kind of a game is it?"

"I'm the Black Scout," says the Red Chief, "and I have to ride to the stockade to warn the settlers that the Indians are coming. I'm tired of playing Indian myself. I want to be the Black Scout."

"All right," says I. "It sounds harmless to me. I guess Mr. Bill will help you foil the pesky savages."

"What am I to do?" asks Bill, looking at the kid suspiciously.

"You are the hoss," says Black Scout. "Get down on your hands and knees. How can I ride to the stockade without a hoss?"

"You'd better keep him interested," said I, "till we get the scheme going. Loosen up."

Bill gets down on his all fours, and a look comes in his eye like a rabbit's when you catch it in a trap.

"How far is it to the stockade, kid?" he asks, in a husky manner of voice.

"Ninety miles," says the Black Scout. "And you have to hump yourself to get there on time. Whoa, now!"

The Black Scout jumps on Bill's back and digs his heels in his side.

"For Heaven's sake," says Bill, "hurry back, Sam, as soon as you can. I wish we hadn't made the ransom more than a thousand. Say, you quit kicking me or I'll get up and warm you good."

I walked over to Poplar Cove and sat around the post-office and store, talking with the chawbacons that came in to trade. One whiskerando says that he hears Summit is all upset on account of Elder Ebenezer Dorset's boy having been lost or stolen. That was all I wanted to know. I bought some smoking tobacco, referred casually to the price of black-eyed peas, posted my letter surreptitiously and came away. The postmaster said the mail-carrier would come by in an hour to take the mail on to Summit.

When I got back to the cave Bill and the boy were not to be found. I explored the vicinity of the cave, and risked a yodel or two, but there was no response.

So I lighted my pipe and sat down on a mossy bank to await developments.

In about half an hour I heard the bushes rustle, and Bill wobbled out into the little glade in front of the cave. Behind him was the kid, stepping softly like a scout, with a broad grin on his face. Bill stopped, took off his hat and wiped his face with a red handkerchief. The kid stopped about eight feet behind him.

"Sam," says Bill, "I suppose you think I'm a renegade, but I couldn't help it. I'm a grown person with masculine proclivities and habits of self-defense, but there is a time when all systems of egotism and predominance fail. The boy is gone. I have sent him home. All is off. There was martyrs in old times," goes on Bill, "that suffered death rather than give up the particular graft they enjoyed. None of 'em ever was subjugated to such supernatural tortures as I have been. I tried to be faithful to our articles of depredation; but there came a limit."

"What's the trouble, Bill?" I asks him.

"I was rode," says Bill, "the ninety miles to the stockade, not barring an inch. Then, when the settlers was rescued, I was given oats. Sand ain't a palatable substitute. And then for an hour I had to try to explain to him why there was nothin' in holes, how a road can run both ways and what makes the grass green. I tell you, Sam, a human can only stand so much. I takes him by the neck of his clothes and drags him down the mountain. On the way he kicks my legs black-and-blue from the knees down; and I've got to have two or three bites on my thumb and hand cauterized.

"But he's gone"—continues Bill—"gone home. I showed him the road to Summit and kicked him about eight feet nearer there at one kick. I'm sorry we lose the ransom; but it was either that or Bill Driscoll to the madhouse."

Bill is puffing and blowing, but there is a look of ineffable peace and growing content on his rose-pink features.

"Bill," says I, "there isn't any heart disease in your family, is there?"

"No," says Bill, "nothing chronic except malaria and accidents. Why?"

"Then you might turn around," says I, "and have a look behind you."

Bill turns and sees the boy, and loses his complexion and sits down plump on the ground and begins to pluck aimlessly at grass and little sticks. For an hour I was afraid of his mind. And then I told him that my scheme was to put the whole job through immediately and that we would get the ransom and be off with it by midnight if old Dorset fell in with our proposition. So Bill braced up enough to give the kid a weak sort of a smile and a promise to play the Russian in a Japanese war with him as soon as he felt a little better.

I had a scheme for collecting that ransom without danger of being caught by counterplots that ought to commend itself to professional kidnappers. The tree under which the answer was to be left—and the money later on—was close to the road fence with big, bare fields on all sides. If a gang of constables should be watching for any one to come for the note they could see him a long way off crossing the fields or in the road. But no, sirree! At half-past eight I was up in that tree as well hidden as a tree toad, waiting for the messenger to arrive.

Exactly on time, a half-grown boy rides up the road on a bicycle, locates the pasteboard box at the foot of the fence-post, slips a folded piece of paper into it and pedals away again back toward Summit.

I waited an hour and then concluded the thing was square. I slid down the tree, got the note, slipped along the fence till I struck the woods, and was back at the cave in another half an hour. I opened the note, got near the lantern and read it to Bill. It was written with a pen in a crabbed hand, and the sum and substance of it was this:

> Two Desperate Men.
> Gentlemen: I received your letter today by post, in regard to the ransom you ask for the return of my son. I think you are a little high in your demands, and I hereby make you a counter-proposition, which I am inclined to believe you will accept. You bring Johnny home and pay me two hundred and fifty dollars in cash, and I agree to take him off your hands. You had better come at night, for the neighbours believe he is lost, and I couldn't be responsible for what they would do to anybody they saw bringing him back.
>
> Very respectfully,
> Ebenezer Dorset.

"Great pirates of Penzance!" says I; "of all the impudent—"

But I glanced at Bill, and hesitated. He had the most appealing look in his eyes I ever saw on the face of a dumb or a talking brute.

"Sam," says he, "what's two hundred and fifty dollars, after all? We've got the money. One more night of this kid will send me to bed in Bedlam. Besides being a thorough gentleman, I think Mr. Dorset is a spendthrift for making us such a liberal offer. You ain't going to let the chance go, are you?"

"Tell you the truth, Bill," says I, "this little he ewe lamb has somewhat got on my nerves, too. We'll take him home, pay the ransom, and make our get-away."

We took him home that night. We got him to go by telling him that his father had bought a silver-mounted rifle and a pair of moccasins for him, and we were going to hunt bears the next day.

It was just twelve o'clock when we knocked at Ebenezer's front door. Just at the moment when I should have been abstracting the fifteen hundred dollars from the box under the tree, according to the original proposition, Bill was counting out two hundred and fifty dollars into Dorset's hand.

When the kid found out we were going to leave him at home he started up a howl like a calliope and fastened himself as tight as a leech to Bill's leg. His father peeled him away gradually, like a porous plaster.

"How long can you hold him?" asks Bill.

"I'm not as strong as I used to be," says old Dorset, "but I think I can promise you ten minutes."

"Enough," says Bill. "In ten minutes I shall cross the Central, Southern, and Middle Western States, and be legging it trippingly for the Canadian border."

And, as dark as it was, and as fat as Bill was, and as good a runner as I am, he was a good mile and a half out of Summit before I could catch up with him.

JOHN SHELTON REED

Reed is an open Republican, but he is by no means included in this book for the sake of multiculturalism. I am myself what is known as a yellow-dog Democrat, but some—well, a few—of my favorite funny Southern writers are politically conservative, and Reed came by his Republicanism growing up in east Tennessee, a region which never identified itself with slavery, the Confederacy, or the Solid South. At any rate, Reed's reputation as a tough-mindedly witty defender and critical analyst of the South is well established. A professor of sociology and American studies at the

University of North Carolina, he writes columns for the monthly Chronicles: A
Magazine of American Culture, *which he has collected in* Whistling Dixie:
Dispatches from the South. *In one of those brief sprightly essays, "How to Get
Along in the South: A Guide for Yankees," he states "Reed's Rule for Successful
Adjustment to the South," which is "Don't think that you know what's going on."
"Never mind," Reed goes on, "that you think the Northern way is superior. Even if it
is—maybe especially if it is—we don't want to hear about it. Even the most
cosmopolitan Southerner is likely to bristle at that. Lewis Grizzard puts it eloquently:
'Delta is ready when you are.' "*

"Poetic Gems"   •

> Alas, for the South! Her books have grown fewer—
> She never was much given to literature.

Thus, South Carolina's J. Gordon Coogler—"the last bard of Dixie, at least in
the legitimate line," as H. L. Mencken put it in his scathing essay "Sahara of
the Bozart." Mencken's essay has by now introduced several generations of
readers to the Songbird of Dixie. No doubt many of those readers have
assumed that Mencken made him up, but he did not: the Bard of the Congaree
was all too real, the author of *Purely Original Verse* (1897), nearly all of it every
bit as lame as his immortal couplet on Southern belles lettres.

Coogler is a splendid example of what we might call a primitive poet, the
verbal equivalent of the folk artists whose paintings have lately come to command critical acclaim and inflated prices.

My region boasts many others. Heck, my state does. I place in evidence
Nematodes in My Garden of Verse, subtitled *A Little Book of Tar Heel Poems* and
edited by Richard Walser. Walser culled a number of these things from
turn-of-the-century North Carolina newspapers, which often printed their
readers' verse, dealing with presidential assassinations, train wrecks, the coming of spring, and other subjects of civic or personal interest. But the center-
piece of *Nematodes* is six poems from a little book called *Little Pansy* (1890), by
the Poetissima Laureatissima [*sic*] of Bladen County, North Carolina, Miss
Mattie J. Peterson, in whose masterwork "I Kissed Pa Twice After His
Death" are found the priceless lines:

> I saw him coming, stepping high,
> Which was of his walk the way.

Perfect.
I don't know why—or even whether—the South has produced more than

its share of primitive poets. (These days, of course, we have more than our share of the high-toned sort.) Even if we have a quantitative edge, of course, this folk-bardic tradition is not a Southern monopoly. In fact, the all-time record for sustained badness without surcease, year in and year out, a record unsurpassed and unsurpassable, must belong to a nineteenth-century Dundee weaver named William McGonagall. The inimitable McGonagall retired the cup.

A short summary of McGonagall's career may have some inspirational value for those not familiar with it. In 1877, by his own account, McGonagall was seized by a "strange kind of feeling [that] seemed to kindle up my entire frame, along with a strong desire to write poetry." He promptly penned a testimonial to a local clergyman, in verse that concluded:

> My blessing on his noble form,
> And on his lofty head,
> May all good angels guard him while living,
> And hereafter when he's dead.

The reverend gentleman responded tactfully that "Shakespeare never wrote anything like this," and it was onward and downward thereafter for McGonagall.

There was no stopping him. He didn't take hints. When he stepped up to recite his verse in pubs, people jeered him, threw peas at him, dumped flour on him. . . . His persistence amounted to a species of heroism, diminished only slightly by the fact that he seemed not to recognize ridicule and abuse for what it was. After the publication of his first book, *Poetic Gems,* for instance, some students wrote him a hoaxing letter from the "King of Burma" proclaiming him a "Knight of the Order of the White Elephant of Burma"; thereafter he signed himself, in perfect faith, "Sir William."

It is simply impossible to convey the effect produced by an entire book of McGonagall's verse. It is all dreadful. I swear to you that I have just now opened at random to this stanza, from a lengthy account of the Johnstown flood:

> The pillaging of the houses in Johnstown is fearful to describe,
>   By the Hungarians and ghouls, and woe betide
> Any person or party that interfered with them,
>   Because they were mad with drink, and yelling like tigers in a den.

There are pages and pages of this stuff.

It is estimated that a half-million copies of *Poetic Gems* have been sold since McGonagall's day—not, alas, to the profit of the author and his long-suffering wife and children. In 1965 the BBC held a competition to find a worthy successor to McGonagall, but the judges called it off. None of the entries, they said, was in the same league.

But of course none could have been. The BBC's contest was like asking people to do primitive paintings. People who paint the Apotheosis of Hank Williams do not think of their work as folk art. This kind of thing can't be done tongue-in-cheek. It must be turned out in dead earnest. (And by people who ought to know better: children can write like this, and sometimes do, but the effect isn't the same at all.)

So I proposed a different competition for the readers of my monthly letter in *Chronicles: A Magazine of American Culture.* I asked them to submit McGonagallisms from the work of poets who are or at one time were well-regarded. Even Homer nods, and isolated passages almost as bad as the ones I've quoted have been written by people who made better livings off their verse than poor Sir William ever did.

My candidate, to get things started, was from Whittier's eulogy for John Randolph of Roanoke:

> Too honest or too proud to feign
>   A love he never cherished,
> Beyond Virginia's border line
>   His patriotism perished.

(True, it scans, and the rhymes aren't bad. But you must admit that it has that Coogleresque quality, that Petersonian je ne sais quoi. William McGonagall would not have been ashamed of it.)

The contest elicited some truly dreadful entries, although none of them was awful in just the right bathetic way. The winner was this, from Byron's "Song to the Suliotes":

> Up to battle! Sons of Suli
> Up, and do your duty duly!
> There the wall—and there the Moat is:
> Bouwah! Bouwah! Suliotes,
> There is booty—there is Beauty,
> Up my boys and do your duty.

The Atlanta man who submitted that got to shake his booty; his prize was my copy of Whittier, which had cost me thirty-five cents some years back.

The runner-up was a Chicagoan, who submitted the entire text of Browning's "Why I Am a Liberal." (Look it up: it's every bit as sappy as it sounds.) A curious fact, for the record, is that this man was the only non-Southerner who entered the contest. Could he be the only non-Southerner who reads this sort of verse? In any case, he averred that Chicagoans do not have to yield to Southerners when it comes to *writing* it, and placed in evidence the work of Alderman John J. "Bathhouse John" Coughlin, author of "Ode to a Bath Tub," "Why Did They Build the Lovely Lake So Close to the Horrible Shore?," "They're Tearing Up Clark Street Again," "She Sleeps by the Side of the Drainage Canal," and many other works.

"Like Wallace Stevens," my correspondent wrote, "Bathhouse John had to devote most of his time to his career—in his case, political corruption—but surely his shade has earned the right to enjoy the company of Coogler and other immortals." Surely, indeed, as this sample of his verse attests:

To a Hod Carrier

'Tis not a ladder of fame he climbs
This rugged man of bricks and mortar;
The mason gets six for laying the bricks
While the hod carrier gets but two and a quarter.

Two other readers received, ah, Honorable Mention, although their entries didn't exactly meet the criteria. A Nashville lady sent a specimen of her own original verse (as well as several entries from her grandmother's 1860 edition of Longfellow which were, Lord knows, pretty bad). Did I say Coogleresque verse can't be written on purpose? This lady did it, thus:

In 1865 we tried to forget the Late Unpleasantness,
But the Reconstruction laws imposed were dirty as a pheasant nest.

Finally, among the many crimes for which anarchism must answer are some poems from *The Illustrious Life of William McKinley: Our Martyred President,* sent in by a reader in Savannah. The editor of this memorial volume observed that many of these samples from the spontaneous outpouring of folk verse evoked by McKinley's death express "the feeling that by too indulgent toleration of the infamous doctrines whose disciples slew the good President the nation has fallen into disgrace and incurred a stain upon its honor which must be effaced." Refreshing.

These verses had me wondering why John Kennedy's assassination produced no comparable effluence—until I suddenly realized that it had. Indeed, my state legislator at the time, the Honorable R. L. "Bobby" Peters of Kingsport, Tennessee, not only wrote something called "A Sunny Day in Dallas," but set it to music, and recorded it too. The tradition of McGonagall and Coogler (and, yes, of Coughlin) continues—where else but in country music?

J. GORDON COOGLER

"In Memorial"

(To a young lady who sought publicity by attempting to belittle in public print a poem by the author, entitled "Beautiful Snow"—She has never been heard from through the press since.)

> She died after the beautiful snow had melted,
> And was buried beneath the "slush";
> The last sad words she breathed upon earth
> Were these simple ones, "Oh, poet, do hush!"

HARRY CREWS

One of the best books by a living Southerner is also one of the most gothic, and furthermore it's nonfiction: A Childhood, Harry Crews's account of growing up poor in Bacon County, Georgia. He was playing pop-the-whip one day and "went flying into the steaming boiler of water beside a scalded, floating hog." When he was pulled out, all of his "cooked and glowing skin" came off, in sections: "I reached over and touched my right hand with my left, and the whole thing came off like a wet glove." And that was by no means untypical of his formative years. If I were you I would put this book down, as proud of it as I am so far, and go read that one. Then see if you think this opening chapter from Car, one of Crews's dozen or so fevered and sometimes hilarious novels, is anything you can call farfetched. "How much sense does it make for a 113-pound housewife to get into 4,000 pounds of machinery and drive 2 blocks for a 13-ounce loaf of bread?" Crews has noted. "That question and others like it made writing the book Car *inevitable."*

from *Car*

There was a taxi parked at the iron-grilled gate, closed and padlocked now. It was near enough dark that the taxi had its headlights on. A woman in a wide black hat and a black veil stood at the grilled gate with her hands on the bars. Mister sighed. God knows who she was. He was prepared to have anybody arrive at their gates. If it had been a woman come to take him away and butcher him and sell him as meat in the local supermarket, it would not have surprised him. But of course it was nothing so interesting and unusual as that, and he had known it wouldn't be.

"Where is Fred's car?" she asked through the gate.

Mister was close enough that he could see right through her veil even through the light was bad. He saw that her eyes were black and hollow and her nose was blunt and spoon-shaped. Without answering, he turned from her and looked back toward forty-three acres of wrecked cars, dark and jagged and indistinguishable one from the other now. He looked back at her. Why couldn't any of them see it was impossible?

"I don't know," said Mister.

She weaved gently on her black-shod, delicate feet. Then she turned loose the iron gate and opened a black purse, took out a piece of paper, and squinted at it in the bad light.

"Is this Auto-Town?" she asked.

"Yes," Mister said.

"Is this your place of business? Do you own it?" Her voice was light and, in its grief, lilting.

"My daddy owns it."

"His car was brought here," she said.

"Whose?"

"Fred's. My husband. The one he was . . . The one he had the accident in. They told me it was brought here. Please. If I could just see it? For a minute. Please help me."

"When was it brought here, lady?"

"Six days ago." Through the veil, he could see the little place between her eyes tighten. "In the afternoon."

"Make?"

"A Cadillac. A vinyl top. A paisley vinyl top."

"A new one?"

"This year's, yes, a new one."

It would have been that one naturally. Which other one could it have possibly been? And now it was a very solid suitcase, lumped in with two hundred and sixteen other suitcases on the dock waiting for the barge. Mister took a key ring out of his pocket. The ring was fastened to a leather strap attached to his belt. He unlocked the gate.

"This way, lady."

She looked at the taxi. "I'll be a little while. You can turn off your lights."

It was getting dark now, but she followed him all right, making only a little sound like rats scurrying over dried grain. Mister knew exactly where to take her. Less than fifty yards from Salvage House, laid out in one of the first rows, they came upon it, a foreshortened Cadillac car in perfect condition except that the front seat was filled with the engine and the windshield on the driver's side had a star-shaped shatter where, unmistakably, a head had stopped.

They stood in the darkness watching it. It was a sixty-nine and not a seventy, but Mister knew that even if the light had been good she probably would not have known. Women were emotional and full of gestures.

She walked closer to the Cadillac. She stopped by the back door. She looked at him. He knew exactly what to do. He took the handle of the door and pulled. The hinge was jammed. He pulled harder. It groaned and scraped, but it opened. She wedged into the back seat. He closed the door.

"I'll just sit here a while," she said.

"Right," he said. He left her there and went back to Salvage House and climbed the outside stairs to the second floor where he lived with his father, his sister Junell, and his twin brother Herman.

Herman was not there. But Mister had not expected him to be. The light was dim in the single vast room they used for kitchen, dining place, and living room. The wall was a solid bank of windows on the side next to the wrecked mountains and the river. His father, Easton Mack, whom everyone called Easy, stood at the windows looking down. Junell stood beside him. She was dressed in black motorcycle racing leathers. The long hair spilling down her back was red and burned like a light against the black jacket. Mister's father turned his head and glanced at him as he came through the door. His eyes were thin as knifeblades. Mister went over to where they were standing. They were looking down at the sixty-nine Cadillac where Fred's new widow sat. The three of them stood there a long time. The windows were open to the wind from the river. From this distance the wind was pleasantly warm and thick with an odor like ripe cheese.

A sound came to them from below. Metal on metal, a groaning. Easy Mack turned and walked quickly across the room and came back. He stared down into the gathering darkness where the sound had become more urgent, insistent. Fred's widow was trying to get out of what she thought was Fred's Cadillac.

"She won't be able to get out of there," Junell said.

"She'll get out," said Mister.

"Who died in it?" asked Easy.

"Husband," said Mister. "Name of Fred."

"Fred?" Easy said.

"Fred."

They could hear her voice now, faint, lilting, full of grief.

"Go down and get her out," said Easy Mack.

"She'll make it," Mister said.

"Go on down," Junell said. "Daddy caint stand it."

"I guess it's about time he stood *something,*" said Mister.

Easy Mack's knife-thin eyes touched Mister briefly about the face, but Easy said nothing. Mister was sorry for what he'd said. He knew that his father felt bad enough about what had happened without being made to feel worse. It had been Easy Mack who had finally made Mister's twin brother Herman give up his last venture, which had been called CAR DISPLAY: YOUR HISTORY ON PARADE. Fred's widow was sitting in part of the parade right now. And because Easy Mack hadn't been able to stand it, hadn't been able to stand the crowds, the arc lights at night, the laughter, the tears and angry accusations, his brother Herman was lost now for good.

The thing about Herman was that he couldn't take hold. He never had been able to. The others took hold and found their places, but not Herman. Junell drove Big Mama and ran Salvage House. Mister ran the disposal end of the business, operating the car-crusher, directing the hired man Paul on the crane, and overseeing the loading at the dock. Their father, who had founded Auto-Town, kept the books and tried to see into the future. But Herman was a dreamer. That was what his daddy, who loved him, said. But Herman's dreams never seemed to amount to much, or when they did amount to something, there was always somebody to stop him, somebody to say no.

Take CAR DISPLAY: YOUR HISTORY ON PARADE. They were turning money with both hands when their father said they had to stop.

"You got to stop," he said one morning. "I caint stand it anymore."

It had all started one day when a well-dressed man had come into Auto-Town and asked if they had a 1949 De Soto. Of course they had one. Could he see it? Mister and Herman took him back to look at it. The man climbed up the slope of wrecked cars to the place where the 1949 De Soto stuck out. Mister and Herman climbed up with him and sat on the crushed fender of a Plymouth, watching. The De Soto was in bad shape, not wrecked or mangled, but covered with a heavy skin of rust. The man looked in through the back window. He stared for a long time. When he finally straightened, he had tears in his eyes.

"I just lost my son in Vietnam," he said.

They got off the Plymouth fender. They didn't know what to say. Mister thought he might be crazy.

"In 1950, I had one of these," said the man, gently touching the rusty car. "A year old and ran like a dream. Had twenty-three coats of paint on her. Put them on myself. And every coat buffed—hand-buffed—before the next coat was put on." He looked at them, but not at them either, through them rather, on into something else. "You could comb your hair in the lid of the trunk." He looked toward the back seat again. His face was now away from them, his voice distant, muted. "And that's the only reason she ever married me. I've always known that. Right in the back seat of this *very* car on the first date. And she caught." He looked suddenly at Mister. "She caught. You believe that? She caught. You believe that?"

Mister didn't know what to say.

"The *first* time on the *first* date, she caught. Pregnant. And now the boy's dead." He looked back at the car. "Thanks. I wanted to see it again."

Walking back to Salvage House after the man was gone, Mister was about to cry. It was the saddest goddam thing he'd ever heard. But not Herman. That Herman was a dreamer.

"How many of the American people do you think fucked for their children in the back seat of a car?" asked Herman. "What percent?"

"Goddam, Herman," Mister said.

"I'd say ten percent," Herman said. Herman smiled at his brother. "Hell, the old man may have got *us* in a back seat."

That was his brother Herman, a dreamer of mad dreams. But Herman was never willing to let mad dreams remain just dreams. He insisted upon acting on them. And so when he thought about your history on parade, he mined the mountains for individual cars.

"Everything that's happened in this goddam country in the last fifty years," said Herman, "has happened in, on, around, with, or near a car." He smiled his dreamy smile. "And everybody wants to return to the scene of the crime."

And so he mined the mountains for cars, individual cars for each of the last fifty years, cleared off ten of his father's acres, and laid the cars in rows. From 1920 to 1970, the cars sat there rusted, broken, and mutilated with parts missing, but all still recognizable. And they *did* want to return to the scene of the crime. Thousands of people.

Herman put up a billboard: see the car it happened in—the event that changed your life. And they came: to relive the love affair, the accident, that first car, that last car, the time the tire went flat, the time he ran out of gas, the time he *said* he ran out of gas, the place where Junior was conceived ("You had your foot braced against the dash light and the other foot against the door handle, honey. Remember?").

But finally, his daddy couldn't stand it. Easy Mack was losing his balance over what was happening. A man stabbed his brother-in-law over the hood of a forty-seven Ford coupe. A woman lost her sanity when her husband opened the door of a forty Studebaker and said: "See!" So Easy Mack had told Herman that there was no alternative but to take the billboard down and close up the ten acres, close up YOUR HISTORY ON PARADE.

"But why?" his son had asked.

"There is no joy. No love," said Easy Mack.

Mister remembered it and was suddenly angry again. Insisting on love and joy had lost them Herman. Herman was gone, and they'd not get him back again. Whether he lived or died, he was gone.

There was an abrupt squeal of metal on metal, followed by the dry rush of feet over the glassy yard below.

"Thank God," said Easy Mack. "She got out."

"She's all right now," Junell said.

They heard the taxi fire up and roar away from the gate.

"Some people will do anything," said Easy Mack. "Come in here to set in a wrecked Cadillac. Goddam people are crazy. It's a puzzle to me."

Mister clenched his fists. "I wouldn't say a word if I was you," said Mister. "I just wouldn't say one word if I'd raised a son who was advertising in public that he was going to eat a car."

I will eat a car. I will eat a car from bumper to bumper, Herman was saying over the radio. On the television. In the Florida *Times-Union* newspaper.

Junell and the old man had jerked their heads to stare at Mister as though he had said some unimaginable obscenity. They had not spoken of it directly before this. They'd said things like, "Herman's a fool if he thinks he can do that." Or, "It's a unnatural thing and cannot be done." But they had avoided the actual words *eat a car.*

"You might as well say it, daddy," said Mister bitterly. "You might as well say it right out. You have raised a boy who is going to eat a car."

Soft and flat, as though it were some ritual thing memorized and only half understood, Easy Mack said: "I have raised a son who is going to eat a car."

LEE SMITH

Lee Smith as a teenager was Miss Grundy, Virginia. Since then we have become old friends—Lord knows she is fun to be around. Somewhere along the way I began to realize that her fiction had gone from poignant and amusing to really good. Now she is Ms. Contemporary Southern Novel, a model for any number of aspiring and newly established Southern women writers. Probably your best bet at getting a grip on her place in Southern humor would be to call her up and get her to tell you whatever happened to her this morning, which she may well largely make up. Don't actually do that, though, because she'd probably take the time to tell you, and her readership now is way too wide and expanding for her to have any business fooling with you. In her best writing the feeling takes you deeper than the comic elements swing you up (wait till you get to the last line—don't skip ahead—of her novel Fair and Tender Ladies*), but this short story from her 1981 collection* Cakewalk *is, though to be sure not merely, a stitch. She has taught at North Carolina State and Duke.*

"*Between the Lines*"

"Peace be with you from Mrs. Joline B. Newhouse" is how I sign my columns. Now I gave some thought to that. In the first place, I like a line that has a ring to it. In the second place, what I have always tried to do with my column is to uplift my readers if at all possible, which sometimes it is not. After careful thought, I threw out "Yours in Christ." I am a religious person and all my readers know it. If I put "Yours in Christ," it seems to me that they will think I am theirs because I am in Christ, or even that they and I are in Christ *together,* which is not always the case. I am in Christ but I know for a fact that a lot of them are not. There's no use acting like they are, but there's no use rubbing their faces in it, either. "Peace be with you," as I see it, is sufficiently religious without laying all the cards right out on the table in plain view. I like to keep an ace or two up my sleeve. I like to write between the lines.

This is what I call my column, in fact: "Between the Lines, by Mrs. Joline B. Newhouse." Nobody knows why. Many people have come right out and asked me, including my best friend, Sally Peck, and my husband, Glenn.

"Come on, now, Joline," they say. "What's this 'Between the Lines' all about? What's this 'Between the Lines' supposed to mean?" But I just smile a sweet mysterious smile and change the subject. I know what I know.

And my column means everything to folks around here. Salt Lick community is where we live, unincorporated. I guess there is not much that you would notice, passing through—the Post Office (real little), the American oil station, my husband Glenn's Cash 'N Carry Beverage Store. He sells more than beverages in there, though, believe me. He sells everything you can think of, from thermometers and rubbing alcohol to nails to frozen pizza. Anything else you want, you have to go out of the holler and get on the interstate and go to Greenville to get it. That's where my column appears, in the *Greenville Herald,* fortnightly. Now there's a word with a ring to it: fortnightly.

There are seventeen families here in Salt Lick—twenty, if you count those three down by the Five Mile Bridge. I put what they do in the paper. Anybody gets married, I write it. That goes for born, divorced, dies, celebrates a golden wedding anniversary, has a baby shower, visits relatives in Ohio, you name it. But these mere facts are not what's most important, to my mind.

I write, for instance: "Mrs. Alma Goodnight is enjoying a pleasant recuperation period in the lovely, modern Walker Mountain Community Hospital while she is sorely missed by her loved ones at home. Get well soon, Alma!" I do not write that Alma Goodnight is in the hospital because her husband hit her up the side with a rake and left a straight line of bloody little holes going from her waist to her armpit after she yelled at him, which Lord knows she did all the time, once too often. I don't write about how Eben Goodnight is all torn up now about what he did, missing work and worrying, or how Alma liked it so much in the hospital that nobody knows if they'll ever get her to go home or not. Because that is a *mystery,* and I am no detective by a long shot. I am what I am, I know what I know, and I know you've got to give folks something to hang on to, something to keep them going. That is what I have in mind when I say *uplift,* and that is what God had in mind when he gave us Jesus Christ.

My column would not be but a paragraph if the news was all I told. But it isn't. What I tell is what's important, like the bulbs coming up, the way the redbud comes out first on the hills in the spring and how pretty it looks, the way the cattails shoot up by the creek, how the mist winds down low on the ridge in the mornings, how my wash all hung out on the line of a Tuesday looks like a regular square dance with those pants legs just flapping and flapping in the wind! I tell how all the things you ever dreamed of, all changed and ghostly, will come crowding into your head on a winter night when you sit up late in front of your fire. I even made up these little characters to talk for me, Mr. and Mrs. Cardinal and Princess Pussycat, and often I have them voice my thoughts. Each week I give a little chapter in their lives. Or I might tell what was the message brought in church, or relate an inspirational word from a magazine, book, or TV. I look on the bright side of life.

I've had God's gift of writing from the time I was a child. That's what the B. stands for in Mrs. Joline B. Newhouse—Barker, my maiden name. My father was a patient strong God-fearing man despite his problems and it is in his honor that I maintain the B. There was a lot of us children around all the time—it was right up the road here where I grew up—and it would take me a day to tell you what all we got into! But after I learned how to write, that was that. My fingers just naturally curved to a pencil and I sat down to writing like a ball of fire. They skipped me up one, two grades in school. When I was not but eight, I wrote a poem named "God's Garden," which was published in the church bulletin of the little Methodist Church we went to them on Hunter's Ridge. Oh, Daddy was so proud! He gave me a quarter that Sunday, and then I turned around and gave it straight to God. Put it in the collection plate. Daddy almost cried he was so proud. I wrote another poem in school the next year, telling how life is like a maple tree, and it won a statewide prize.

That's me—I grew up smart as a whip, lively, and naturally good. Jesus came as easy as breathing did to me. Don't think I'm putting on airs, though: I'm not. I know what I know. I've done my share of sinning, too, of which more later.

Anyway, I was smart. It's no telling but what I might have gone on to school like my own children have and who knows what all else if Mama hadn't run off with a man. I don't remember Mama very well, to tell the truth. She was a weak woman, always laying in the bed having a headache. One day we all came home from school and she was gone, didn't even bother to make up the bed. Well, that was the end of Mama! None of us ever saw her again, but Daddy told us right before he died that one time he had gotten a postcard from her from Atlanta, Georgia, years and years after that. He showed it to us, all wrinkled and soft from him holding it.

Being the oldest, I took over and raised those little ones, three of them, and then I taught school and then I married Glenn and we had our own children, four of them, and I have raised them too and still have Marshall, of course, poor thing. He is the cross I have to bear and he'll be just like he is now for the rest of his natural life.

I was writing my column for the week of March 17, 1976, when the following events occurred. It was a real coincidence because I had just finished doing the cutest little story named "A Red-Letter Day for Mr. and Mrs. Cardinal" when the phone rang. It rings all the time, of course. Everybody around here knows my number by heart. It was Mrs. Irene Chalmers. She was all torn up. She said that Mr. Biggers was over at Greenville at the hospital very bad off this time, and that he was asking for me and would I please try to get over there today as the doctors were not giving him but a 20 percent chance to make it through the night. Mr. Biggers has always been a fan of mine, and he especially liked Mr. and Mrs. Cardinal. "Well!" I said. "Of course I will! I'll get Glenn on the phone right this minute. And you calm down, Mrs. Chalmers. You go fix yourself a Coke." Mrs. Chalmers said she would, and hung up. I knew what was bothering her, of course. It was that given the natural run of things, she would be the next to go. The next one to be over there dying. Without even putting down the receiver, I dialed the beverage store. Bert answered.

"Good morning," I said. I like to maintain a certain distance with the hired help although Glenn does not. He will talk to anybody, and any time you go in there, you can find half the old men in the county just sitting around that stove in the winter or outside on those wooden drink boxes in the summer, smoking and drinking drinks which I am sure they are getting free out of the cooler although Glenn swears it on the Bible they are not. Anyway, I said good morning.

"Can I speak to Glenn?" I said.

"Well now, Mrs. Newhouse," Bert said in his naturally insolent voice—he is just out of high school and too big for his britches—"he's not here right now. He had to go out for a while."

"Where did he go?" I asked.

"Well, I don't rightly know," Bert said. "He said he'd be back after lunch."

"Thank you very much, there will not be a message," I said sweetly, and hung up. I *knew* where Glenn was. Glenn was over on Caney Creek where his adopted half-sister Margie Kettles lived, having carnal knowledge of her in the trailer. They had been at it for thirty years and anybody would have thought they'd have worn it out by that time. Oh, I knew all about it.

The way it happened in the beginning was that Glenn's father had died of his lungs when Glenn was not but about ten years old, and his mother grieved so hard that she went off her head and began taking up with anybody who would go with her. One of the fellows she took up with was a foreign man out of a carnival, the James H. Drew Exposition, a man named Emilio something. He had this curly-headed dark-skinned little daughter. So Emilio stayed around longer than anybody would have expected, but finally it was clear to all that he never would find any work around here to suit him. The work around here is hard work, all of it, and they say he played a musical instrument. Anyway, in due course this Emilio just up and vanished, leaving that foreign child. Now that was Margie, of course, but her name wasn't Margie then. It was a long foreign name, which ended up as Margie, and that's how Margie ended up here, in these mountains, where she has been up to no good ever since. Glenn's mother did not last too long after Emilio left, and those children grew up wild. Most of them went to foster homes, and to this day Glenn does not know where two of his brothers are! The military was what finally saved Glenn. He stayed with the military for nine years, and when he came back to this area he found me over here teaching school and with something of a nest egg in hand, enabling him to start the beverage store. Glenn says he owes everything to me.

This is true. But I can tell you something else: Glenn is a good man, and he has been a good provider all these years. He has not ever spoken to me above a regular tone of voice nor raised his hand in anger. He has not been tight with the money. He used to hold the girls in his lap of an evening. Since I got him started, he has been a regular member of the church, and he has not fallen down on it yet. Glenn furthermore has that kind of disposition where he never knows a stranger. So I can count my blessings, too.

Of course I knew about Margie! Glenn's sister Lou-Ann told me about it before she died, that is how I found out about it originally. She thought I *should* know, she said. She said it went on for years and she just wanted me to know before she died. Well! I had had the first two girls by then, and I thought I was so happy. I took to my bed and just cried and cried. I cried for four days and then by gum I got up and started my column, and I have been writing on it ever since. So I was not unprepared when Margie showed up again some years after that, all gap-toothed and wild-looking, but then before you knew it she was gone, off again to Knoxville, then back working as a waitress at that truck stop at the county line, then off again, like that. She led an irregular life. And as for Glenn, I will have to hand it to him, he never darkened her door again until after the birth of Marshall.

Now let me add that I would not have gone on and had Marshall if it was left up to me. I would have practiced more birth control. Because I was old by that time, thirty-seven, and that was too old for more children I felt, even though I had started late of course. I had told Glenn many times, I said three normal girls is enough for anybody. But no, Glenn was like a lot of men, and I don't blame him for it—he just had to try one more time for a boy. So we went on with it, and I must say I had a feeling all along.

I was not a bit surprised at what we got, although after wrestling with it all for many hours in the dark night of the soul, as they say, I do not believe that Marshall is a judgment on me for my sin. I don't believe that. He is one of God's special children, is how I look at it. Of course he looks funny, but he has already lived ten years longer than they said he would. And has a job! He goes to Greenville every day on the Trailways bus, rain or shine, and cleans up the Plaza Mall. He gets to ride on the bus, and he gets to see people. Along about six o'clock he'll come back, walking up the holler and not looking to one side or the other, and then I give him his supper and then he'll watch something on TV like "The Brady Bunch" or "Family Affair," and then he'll go to bed. He would not hurt a flea. But oh, Glenn took it hard when Marshall came! I remember that night so well and the way he just turned his back on the doctor. This is what sent him back to Margie, I am convinced of it, what made him take up right where he had left off all those years before.

So since Glenn was up to his old tricks I called up Lavonne, my daughter, to see if she could take me to the hospital to see Mr. Biggers. Why yes she could, it turned out. As a matter of fact she was going to Greenville herself. As a matter of fact she had something she wanted to talk to me about anyway. Now Lavonne is our youngest girl and the only one that stayed around here. Lavonne is somewhat pop-eyed, and has a weak constitution. She is one of those people that never can make up their minds. That day on the phone, I heard a whine in her voice I didn't like the sound of. Something is up, I thought.

First I powdered my face, so I would be ready to go when Lavonne got there. Then I sat back down to write some more on my column, this paragraph I had been framing in my mind for weeks about how sweet potatoes are not what they used to be. They taste gritty and dry now, compared to how they were. I don't know the cause of it, whether it is man on the moon or pollution in the ecology or what, but it is true. They taste awful.

Then my door came bursting open in a way that Lavonne would never do it and I knew it was Sally Peck from next door. Sally is loud and excitable but she has a good heart. She would do anything for you. "Hold on to your hat, Joline!" she hollered. Sally is so loud because she's deaf. Sally was just huffing and puffing—she is a heavy woman—and she had rollers still up in her hair and her old housecoat on with the buttons off.

"Why, Sally!" I exclaimed. "You are all wrought up!"

Sally sat down in my rocker and spread out her legs and started fanning herself with my *Family Circle* magazine. "If you think I'm wrought up," she said finally, "it is nothing compared to what you are going to be. We have had us a suicide, right here in Salt Lick. Margie Kettles put her head inside her gas oven in the night."

"Margie?" I said. My heart was just pumping.

"Yes, and a little neighbor girl was the one who found her, they say. She went over to borrow some baking soda for her mama's biscuits at seven o'clock A.M." Sally looked real hard at me. "Now wasn't she related to you all?"

"Why," I said just as easily, "why yes, she was Glenn's adopted half-sister of course when they were nothing but a child. But we haven't had anything to do with her for years as you can well imagine."

"Well, they say Glenn is making the burial arrangements," Sally spoke up. She was getting her own back that day, I'll admit it. Usually I'm the one with all the news.

"I have to finish my column now and then Lavonne is taking me to Greenville to see old Mr. Biggers who is breathing his last,'' I said.

"Well," Sally said, hauling herself out of my chair, "I'll be going along then. I just didn't know if you knew it or not." Now Sally Peck is not a spiteful woman in all truth. I have known her since we were little girls sitting out in the yard looking at a magazine together. It is hard to imagine being as old as I am now, or knowing Sally Peck—who was Sally Bland then—so long.

Of course I couldn't get my mind back on sweet potatoes after she left. I just sat still and fiddled with the pigeonholes in my desk and the whole kitchen seemed like it was moving and rocking back and forth around me. Margie dead! Sooner or later I would have to write it up tastefully in my column. Well, I must say I had never thought of Margie dying. Before God, I never hoped for that in all my life. I didn't know what it would do to *me*, in fact, to me and Glenn and Marshall and the way we live because you know how the habits and the ways of people can build up over the years. It was too much for me to take in at one time. I couldn't see how anybody committing suicide could choose to stick their head in the oven anyway—you can imagine the position you would be found in.

Well, in came Lavonne at that point, sort of hanging back and stuttering like she always does, and that child of hers Bethy Rose hanging on to her skirt for dear life. I saw no reason at that time to tell Lavonne about the death of Margie Kettles. She would hear it sooner or later, anyway. Instead, I gave her some plant food that I had ordered two for the price of one from Montgomery Ward some days before.

"Are you all ready, Mama?" Lavonne asked in that quavery way she has, and I said indeed I was, as soon as I got my hat, which I did, and we went out and got in Lavonne's Buick Electra and set off on our trip. Bethy Rose sat in the back, coloring in her coloring book. She is a real good child. "How's Ron?" I said. Ron is Lavonne's husband, an electrician, as up and coming a boy as you would want to see. Glenn and I are as proud as punch of Ron, and actually I never have gotten over the shock of Lavonne marrying him in the first place. All through high school she never showed any signs of marrying anybody, and you could have knocked me over with a feather the day she told us she was secretly engaged. I'll tell you, our Lavonne was not the marrying sort! Or so I thought.

But that day in the car she told me, "Mama, I wanted to talk to you and tell you I am thinking of getting a d-i-v-o-r-c-e."

I shot a quick look into the back seat but Bethy Rose wasn't hearing a thing. She was coloring Wonder Woman in her book.

"Now, Lavonne," I said. "What in the world is it? Why, I'll bet you can work it out." Part of me was listening to Lavonne, as you can imagine, but part of me was still stuck in that oven with crazy Margie. I was not myself.

I told her that. "Lavonne," I said, "I am not myself today. But I'll tell you one thing. You give this some careful thought. You don't want to go off half-cocked. What is the problem, anyway?"

"It's a man where I work," Lavonne said. She works in the Welfare Department, part-time, typing. "He is just giving me a fit. I guess you can pray for me, Mama, because I don't know what I'll decide to do."

"Can we get an Icee?" asked Bethy Rose.

"Has anything happened between you?" I asked. You have to get all the facts.

"Why *no!*" Lavonne was shocked. "Why, I wouldn't do anything like that! Mama, for goodness' sakes! We just have coffee together so far."

That's Lavonne all over. She never has been very bright. "Honey," I said, "I would think twice before I threw up a perfectly good marriage and a new brick home for the sake of a cup of coffee. If you don't have enough to keep you busy, go take a course at the community college. Make yourself a new pantsuit. This is just a mood, believe me."

"Well," Lavonne said. Her voice was shaking and her eyes were swimming in tears that just stayed there and never rolled down her cheeks. "Well," she said again.

As for me, I was lost in thought. It was when I was a young married woman like Lavonne that I committed my own great sin. I had the girls, and things were fine with Glenn and all, and there was simply not any reason to ascribe to it. It was just something I did out of loving pure and simple, did because I wanted to do it. I knew and have always known the consequences, yet God is full of grace, I pray and believe, and his mercy is everlasting.

To make a long story short, we had a visiting evangelist from Louisville, Kentucky, for a two-week revival that year. John Marcel Wilkes. If I say it myself, John Marcel Wilkes was a real humdinger! He had the yellowest hair you ever saw, curly, and the finest singing voice available. Oh, he was something, and that very first night he brought two souls into Christ. The next day I went over to the church with a pan of brownies just to tell him how much I personally had received from his message. I thought, of course, that there would be other people around—the Reverend Mr. Clark, or the youth director, or somebody cleaning. But to my surprise that church was totally empty except for John Marcel Wilkes himself reading the Bible in the fellowship hall and making notes on a pad of paper. The sun came in a window on his head. It was early June, I remember, and I had on a blue dress with little white cap sleeves and open-toed sandals. John Marcel Wilkes looked up at me and his face gave off light like the sun.

"Why, Mrs. Newhouse," he said. "What an unexpected pleasure!" His voice echoed out in the empty fellowship hall. He had the most beautiful voice, too—strong and deep, like it had bells in it. Everything he said had a ring to it.

He stood up and came around the table to where I was. I put the brownies down on the table and stood there. We both just stood there, real close without touching each other, for the longest time, looking into each other's eyes. Then he took my hands and brought them up to his mouth and kissed them, which nobody ever did to me before or since, and then he kissed me on the mouth. I thought I would die. After some time of that, we went together out into the hot June day where the bees were all buzzing around the flowers there by the back gate and I couldn't think straight. "Come," said John Marcel Wilkes. We went out in the woods behind the church to the prettiest place, and when it was all over I could look up across his curly yellow head and over the trees and see the white church steeple stuck up against that blue, blue sky like it was pasted there. This was not all. Two more times we went out there during that revival. John Marcel Wilkes left after that and I have never heard a word of him since. I do not know where he is, or what has become of him in all these years. I do know that I never bake a pan of brownies, or hear the church bells ring, but what I think of him. So I have to pity Lavonne and her cup of coffee if you see what I mean, just like I have to spend the rest of my life to live my sinning down. But I'll tell you this: if I had it all to do over, I would do it all over again, and I would not trade it in for anything.

Lavonne drove off to look at fabric and get Bethy Rose an Icee, and I went in the hospital. I hate the way they smell. As soon as I entered Mr. Biggers' room, I could see he was breathing his last. He was so tiny in the bed you almost missed him, a poor little shriveled-up thing. His family sat all around.

"Aren't you sweet to come?" they said. "Looky here, honey, it's Mrs. Newhouse."

He didn't move a muscle, all hooked up to tubes. You could hear him breathing all over the room.

"It's Mrs. Newhouse," they said, louder. "Mrs. Newhouse is here. Last night he was asking for everybody," they said to me. "Now he won't open his eyes. You are real sweet to come," they said. "You certainly did brighten his days." Now I knew this was true because the family had remarked on it before.

"I'm so glad," I said. Then some more people came in the door and everybody was talking at once, and while they were doing that, I went over to the bed and got right up by his ear.

"Mr. Biggers!" I said. "Mr. Biggers, it's Joline Newhouse here."

He opened one little old bleary eye.

"Mr. Biggers!" I said right into his ear. "Mr. Biggers, you know those cardinals in my column? Mr. and Mrs. Cardinal? Well, I made them up! I made them up, Mr. Biggers. They never were real at all." Mr. Biggers closed his eye and a nurse came in and I stood up.

"Thank you so much for coming, Mrs. Newhouse," his daughter said.

"He is one fine old gentleman," I told them all, and then I left.

Outside in the hall, I had to lean against the tile wall for support while I waited for the elevator to come. Imagine, me saying such a thing to a dying man! I was not myself that day.

Lavonne took me to the big Kroger's in north Greenville and we did our shopping, and on the way back in the car she told me she had been giving everything a lot of thought and she guessed I was right after all.

"You're not going to tell anybody, are you?" she asked me anxiously, popping her eyes. "You're not going to tell Daddy, are you?" she said.

"Why, Lord, no honey!" I told her. "It's the farthest thing from my mind."

Sitting in the back seat among all the grocery bags, Bethy Rose sang a little song she had learned at school. "Make new friends but keep the old, some are silver but the other gold," she sang.

"I don't know what I was thinking of," Lavonne said.

Glenn was not home yet when I got there—making his arrangements, I supposed. I took off my hat, made myself a cup of Sanka, and sat down and finished off my column on a high inspirational note, saving Margie and Mr. Biggers for the next week. I cooked up some ham and red-eye gravy, which Glenn just loves, and then I made some biscuits. The time seemed to pass so slow. The phone rang two times while I was fixing supper, but I just let it go. I thought I had received enough news for *that* day. I still couldn't get over Margie putting her head in the oven, or what I had said to poor Mr. Biggers, which was not at all like me you can be sure. I buzzed around that kitchen doing first one thing, then another. I couldn't keep my mind on anything I did.

After a while Marshall came home and ate, and went in the front room to watch TV. He cannot keep it in his head that watching TV in the dark will ruin your eyes, so I always have to go in there and turn on a light for him. This night, though, I didn't. I just let him sit there in the recliner in the dark, watching his show, and in the pale blue light from that TV set he looked just like anybody else.

I put on a sweater and went out on the front porch and sat in the swing to watch for Glenn. It was nice weather for that time of year, still a little cold but you could smell spring in the air already and I knew it wouldn't be long before the redbud would come out again on the hills. Out in the dark where I couldn't see them, around the front steps, my crocuses were already up. After a while of sitting out there I began to take on a chill, due more to my age no doubt than the weather, but just then some lights came around the bend, two headlights, and I knew it was Glenn coming home.

Glenn parked the truck and came up the steps. He was dog-tired, I could see that. He came over to the swing and put his hand on my shoulder. A little wind came up, and by then it was so dark you could see lights on all the ridges where the people live. "Well, Joline," he said.

"Dinner is waiting on you," I said. "You go on in and wash up and I'll be there directly. I was getting worried about you," I said.

Glenn went on and I sat there swaying on the breeze for a minute before I went after him. Now where will it all end? I ask you. All this pain and loving, mystery and loss. And it just goes on and on, from Glenn's mother taking up with dark-skinned gypsies to my own daddy and his postcard to that silly Lavonne and her cup of coffee to Margie with her head in the oven, to John Marcel Wilkes and myself, God help me, and all of it so long ago out in those holy woods.

ROY BLOUNT, JR.

"*I Don't Eat Dirt Personally*"

When we read items in the *New York Times* about human behavior or the physical universe or so on, our reaction is, "Well, this is certainly On Solid Ground." Not long ago the *Times* revealed . . . that scientists had discovered . . . that people who were told not to think about a white bear had a lot more thoughts about a white bear than people who weren't told not to think about a white bear. I forget the exact figures. Any day I expect the *Times* to disclose research establishing that some very low percentage of people know you when you're down and out.

So when the *Times* runs something that reflects on me as a Southerner, I can't just dismiss it as off the wall. I have to explain it to the people I live among, which is to say Northerners. One morning I picked up the *Times* and saw my work cut out for me. Here was the headline: SOUTHERN PRACTICE OF EATING DIRT SHOWS SIGNS OF WANING.

"While it is not uncommon these days to find people here who eat dirt," the story said, many Southerners "are giving up dirt because of the social stigma attached to it."

Now, I would be willing to argue, in a quasi-agrarian way, that the giving up of dirt is part of the downside of modern life. The giving up of eating dirt, however, is a subject that I frankly kind of resent having to discuss. And not because it hits too close to home. The truth is, I never started eating dirt. The stigma attached to dirt-eating is one of a handful of stigmas that I have never even considered feeling. But try telling that to Northerners.

People who attend fashionable Northern soirées read the *New York Times*. The very night of the dirt-eating story, I was in someone's chic salon eating arugula. A woman with a crewcut heard my accent.

"What do you do?" she asked.

I said I was a writer.

"Ah, yes," she said. "Of course. Southerners are all natural storytellers. Sitting on the old screen porch, dog under the rocker, flies on the baby, everyone spitting and spinning yarns compounded of biblical cadences and allusions to animals named B'rer.

"One thing I never realized, though," she went on, "was that you eat dirt."

At that point there were two tacks I could take. One, what we might call the Jimmy Carter tack, I could tell the truth: "Well, I know there are some folks down South who like to chew on clay, but I never ate any myself and neither did any of my relatives or friends, and in point of fact I never even saw anybody eat dirt."

The response to that tack would have been a knowing look. "Here is a man who comes from people who eat dirt and he thinks he is better than they are." She would be thinking I couldn't handle stigma. Or that I was inauthentic. Southern *and* inauthentic: the worst of both worlds.

So I took what we might call the Billy Carter tack. "Hell, yes, we eat dirt," I said. "And if you never ate any blackened red dirt, you don't know what's good. I understand you people up here eat raw fish."

You know how sushi got started, don't you? Some Tokyo marketing people were sitting around thinking how they could create a whole new American market, and one of them said, "Restaurants."

And another one said, "Okay. What would these restaurants serve?"

"Oh, fish."

"What would be the most cost-effective way of cooking it?" asked another.

And the eyes of another one lit up, and he said, "You know what we could do . . . ?"

But of course sushi was dead now, I told this Northerner, and people were Cajuned out, and even New Zealand cuisine was about to go the way of Australian, and now this hot New Guinea place, Yam Yam, was so over-praised, I figured the time was ripe for investing in dirt restaurants.

None of the Northerners I used this tack on had realized that it was time to be Cajuned out, even. The best way to get a Northerner to believe something is to talk to him as if you assume that he knows it already and that most people don't. I raised $3,800 in one evening. I figured when these investors came to me wondering what had happened to their money, I could admit that dirt-dining wasn't quite happening yet after all—that when they had invested in it, it had been ahead of its time. Which would have consoled them more than you might think.

Then the *Times* came out with another headline: "QUIET CLAY REVEALED AS VIBRANT AND PRIMAL." According to some scientists, the first forms of life may have begun in clay. This was too close to what I learned as a boy back in Sunday school for comfort. And I didn't want to be explaining why Southerners eat life at its very source. But then I thought, what the heck. "Yep," I told Northerners at parties. "In fact, if there'd been a Southerner around at the time when the first forms of life were getting underway, he'd've been nipped in the mud." People who weren't put off by raw fish were certainly not dismayed to learn that dirt was, in a sense, their mother.

The *third* dirt-related *Times* headline was the one that made my position difficult. CLAY EATING PROVES WIDESPREAD BUT REASON IS UNCERTAIN, it said.

"Uh-oh," I thought, and I was right.

"The practice of eating dirt, usually fine clays, is so common in so many societies," the *Times* story began, "that it must be regarded as a normal human behavior rather than an oddity, according to scientists who are studying it."

Dirt-eating, the *Times* had now decided, was known by experts as geophagy, and was no more peculiarly Southern—or, for that matter, peculiar—than rabbits. "Historical records of earth-eating in Europe go back to 300 B.C., when Aristotle described it," said the newspaper of record.

And the Northerners wanted their money back. Some of them had reached the conclusion that there was no real prestige value in dirt. Others wanted to look into importing as-yet-underpriced French dirts. I told them I had plowed all their money into development.

What I had done was send the money to my Uncle Mullet, who did eat dirt. When I said I never had any relative who ate dirt, I wasn't counting my Uncle Mullet, who is not my blood uncle and I never felt responsible for him, because he did everything, up to and including worship through snakebite. He wasn't typical of anybody's family. He kept armadillos and lived with a woman named Valvoline. He always did just exactly what nobody wanted him to, and wouldn't even talk to anybody else in the family on the phone. Didn't have a phone. So no wonder I would feel free to say that I never had any relatives who ate dirt.

But Uncle Mullet did, and one afternoon he went over to his favorite clayhole to dig some up, and a man dressed all in freshly-ordered-looking L. L. Bean clothing came out from behind a tree to wave a POSTED sign at him.

"Stranger," the man said in a Northern accent, "you are eating my land."

"What do you mean, *'stranger'?*" my Uncle Mullet said. "I been coming here for generations."

The Northerner looked at him in a certain way.

"What do you mean, *'your land'?*" my Uncle Mullet said. "This spot has been free for folks to come to for clay ever since I don't know when."

The Northerner looked at him a certain way.

"And what do you mean, *'eating'?*" Uncle Mullet said. "I wouldn't . . ."

And that's what broke his spirit. After a lifetime of doing every awful thing he felt like, proudly, Uncle Mullet had denied to a Northerner that he did something that he had always done. Had denied it just because the Northerner had looked at him in a certain way enough times to make him feel looked at in a certain way.

And it disgusted Uncle Mullet to the point that he stopped trying to shift for himself, and everybody in the family had to start sending my Aunt Rayanne money to keep him up. (Valvoline dropped him.)

And of course the reason the man in the unbroken-in L. L. Bean outfit was protecting the old clayhole was that he had just bought all that area through there so he could get in on the ground floor of the chain of fine dirt restaurants that I had led him to believe, late one night in that chic salon, was about to happen.

We reap what we sow.

RANDALL JARRELL

Jarrell was born (1914) in Nashville, went to high school there (in between he was in California), and found his literary vocation there at Vanderbilt. His reputation rests on his poetry and his criticism, but he also wrote what is surely the only satirical novel to carry a blurb ("a delight of true understanding") from Wallace Stevens. Jarrell taught for many years at the University of North Carolina at Greensboro, but presumably Pictures from an Institution *was inspired by his year as a visiting professor at Sarah Lawrence. The novel's tony Eastern college, Benton, is out-toned—to a so-lo, as we used to say back home—by the skein of witty lines that constitutes the novel. But the character who comes off worst is the cold-eyed Southern novelist-in-residence Gertrude Johnson—her portrait is so coldly drawn that she might have written it herself. Jarrell died in 1965, struck by a car as he took a walk outside the hospital in Chapel Hill where he was trying to find some psychiatric peace.*

Gertrude

Dwight Robbins; President Robbins, that is; the President, that is—the President *interested* Gertrude. She realized, suddenly, that she was no longer between novels. She looked at the President as a weary, way-worn diamond-prospector looks at a vein of blue volcanic clay; she said to herself, rather coarsely—Gertrude was nothing if not coarse: "Why, girl, that Rift's *loaded.*" How can we expect novelists to be moral, when their trade forces them to treat every end they meet as no more than an imperfect means to a novel? The President was such invaluable material that Gertrude walked around and around him rubbing up and down against his legs, looking affectionately into the dish of nice fresh mackerel he wore instead of a face; and the dish looked back, uneasy, unsuspecting.

Mrs. Robbins, the Robbins' little boy Derek, the Robbins' two big Afghans: these and Benton—and Benton!—interested Gertrude too. Derek and the Afghans didn't really, except as properties: Gertrude thought children and dogs overrated, and used to say that you loved them so much only when you didn't love people as much as you should. *As much as you should* had a haunting overtone of *as much as I do*—an overtone, alas! too high for human ears. But bats heard it and knew, alone among living beings, that Gertrude loved.

.   .   .   .

Of any thousand pigs, or cats, or white rats, there are some who eat their litters and some, a good many more, who do not. Gertrude understood the first, the others she did not understand; she explained everything in terms of the first. They would all have behaved like the first except for—this, that, the other. She saw the worst: it was, indeed, her only principle of explanation. Consequently she seemed to most people a writer of extraordinary penetration—she appealed to the Original La Rochefoucauld in everybody. People looked up to her just as they look up to all those who know why everything is as it is: because of munitions makers, the Elders of Zion, agents of the Kremlin, Oedipus complexes, the class struggle, Adamic sin, *something;* these men can explain everything, and we cannot. People who were affectionate, cheerful, and brave—and human too, all too human—felt in their veins the piercing joy of Understanding, of pure disinterested insight, as they read Gertrude's demonstration that they did everything because of greed, lust, and middle-class hypocrisy. She told them that they were very bad and, because they were fairly stupid, they believed her.

It is partly our own fault—the fault of a great many of us, at least—that writers like Gertrude come into being and stay there: the baby does nothing but cry because, each time he cries, we go upstairs with a bottle, and bounce him on a tender knee. Gertrude was not, alas, a good woman; Gertrude had a style in which you couldn't tell the truth if you tried—and when, except when it was a shameful one, had Gertrude ever tried? But how many of her readers cared? Most of them went on admiring her in the tones of butchers from Gopher Prairie admiring the Murderer of Düsseldorf; they could not mention that style without using the vocabulary of a salesman of kitchen knives. If Gertrude had written another *Remembrance of Things Past,* they would only have murmured disappointedly that it wasn't the old Gertrude. They wanted her to tell them the worst about themselves, and after they had met her they whispered to one another the worst about *her.*

HUNTER S. THOMPSON

Thompson, a product of Louisville who has staunchly affirmed his Southernness, is clearly an heir of the old uproarious Southwestern humorists, but it's hard to find a bit of his crazed personal journalism that fits securely into a collection such as this. "The Kentucky Derby Is Decadent and Depraved" slashes vividly away at a Southern institution, but it's awfully long for our purposes and it doesn't make me laugh. His explanation of why Jimmy Carter's presidential candidacy caught his fancy includes some arresting passages:

> *I was still feeling weird around noon, when we started talking "seriously," and the tape of that first conversation is liberally sprinkled with my own twisted comments about "rotten fascist bastards" . . . and "these goddamn brainless fools who refuse to serve liquor in the Atlanta airport on Sunday."*
>
> *It was nothing more than my normal way of talking, and Carter was already familiar with it, but there are strange and awkward pauses here and there on the tape where I can almost hear Carter gritting his teeth and wondering whether to laugh or get angry at things I wasn't even conscious of saying at the time. . . . Most of the conversation is intensely rational, but every once in a while it slips over the line and all I can hear is the sound of my own voice yelling something like "Jesus Christ! What's that filthy smell?"*

But Thompson can be more, well, humorous than that. As I believe he shows in this encounter in New York with another Louisville native, Muhammad Ali.

Head to Head with the Champ

My way of joking is to tell the truth. That's the funniest
joke in the world.
                                              —Muhammad Ali

Indeed. . . . And that is also as fine a definition of "Gonzo Journalism" as
anything I've ever heard, for good or ill. But I was in no mood for joking when
my cab pulled up to the Plaza that night. I was half-drunk, fully cranked, and
pissed off at everything that moved. My only real plan was to get past this
ordeal that Conrad was supposedly organizing with Ali, then retire in shame to
my eighty-eight-dollar-a-night bed and deal with Conrad tomorrow.

But this world does not work on "real plans"—mine or anyone else's—so
I was not especially surprised when a total stranger wearing a *serious* black
overcoat laid a hand on my shoulder as I was having my bags carried into the
Plaza:

"Doctor Thompson?" he said.

"What?" I spun away and glared at him just long enough to know there was
no point in denying it. . . . He had the look of a rich undertaker who had once
been the Light-Heavyweight karate champion of the Italian Navy; a *very quiet*
presence that was far too heavy for a cop. . . . He was on *my* side.

And he seemed to understand my bad nervous condition; before I could ask
anything, he was already picking up my bags and saying—with a smile as
uncomfortable as my own: "We're going to the Park Lane; Mister Conrad is
waiting for you. . . ."

I shrugged and followed him outside to the long black limo that was parked
with the engine running so close to the front door of the Plaza that it was
almost up on the sidewalk . . . and about three minutes later I was face to face
with Hal Conrad in the lobby of the Park Lane Hotel, more baffled than ever
and not even allowed enough time to sign in and get my luggage up to the
room. . . .

"What took you so goddamn long?"

"I was masturbating in the limo," I said. "We took a spin out around
Sheepshead Bay and I—"

"Sober up!" he snapped. "Ali's been *waiting* for you since ten o'clock."

"Balls," I said, as the door opened and he aimed me down the hall. "I'm
tired of your bullshit, Harold—and where the hell is my luggage?"

"Fuck your luggage," he replied as we stopped in front of 904 and he
knocked, saying, "Open up, it's *me*."

The door swung open and there was Bundini, with a dilated grin on his face, reaching out to shake hands. "Welcome!" he said. "Come right in, Doc—make yourself at home."

I was still shaking hands with Bundini when I realized where I was—standing at the foot of a king-size bed where Muhammad Ali was laid back with the covers pulled up to his waist and his wife, Veronica, sitting next to him: they were both eyeing me with very different expressions than I'd seen on their faces in Chicago.

Muhammad leaned up to shake hands, grinning first at me and then at Conrad: "Is this *him?*" he asked. "You sure he's safe?"

Bundini and Conrad were laughing as I tried to hide my confusion at this sudden plunge into unreality by lighting two Dunhills at once, as I backed off and tried to get grounded . . . but my head was still whirling from this hurricane of changes and I heard myself saying, "What do you mean—*Is this him?* You bastard! I should have you *arrested* for what you did to me in Chicago!"

Ali fell back on the pillows and laughed. "I'm sorry, boss, but I just couldn't *recognize* you. I knew I was supposed to meet *somebody,* but—"

"Yeah!" I said. "That's what I was trying to *tell* you. What did you think I was *there* for—an autograph?"

Everybody in the room laughed this time, and I felt like I'd been shot out of a cannon and straight into somebody else's movie. I put my satchel down on the bureau across from the bed and reached in for a beer. . . . The pop-top came off with a hiss and a blast of brown foam that dripped on the rug as I tried to calm down.

"You *scared* me," Ali was saying. "You looked like some kind of a bum—or a hippie."

"What?" I almost shouted. " '*A bum? A hippie?*' " I lit another cigarette or maybe two, not realizing or even thinking about the gross transgressions I was committing by smoking *and* drinking in the presence of The Champ. (Conrad told me later that *nobody* smokes or drinks in the same room with Muhammad Ali—and Jesus Christ! Not—of all places—in the sacred privacy of *his own bedroom at midnight,* where I had no business being in the first place.) . . . But I was mercifully and obviously ignorant of what I was doing. Smoking and drinking and tossing off crude bursts of language are not *second* nature to me, but *first*—and my mood, at that point, was still so mean and jangled that it took me about ten minutes of foulmouthed raving before I began to get a grip on myself.

Everybody else in the room was obviously relaxed and getting a wonderful boot out of this bizarre spectacle—which was *me;* and when the adrenaline finally burned off I realized that I'd backed so far away from the bed and into the bureau that I was actually *sitting* on the goddamn thing, with my legs crossed in front of me like some kind of wild-eyed, dope-addled budda (Bhud-dah? Buddah? Budda? . . . Ah, fuck these wretched idols with unspellable names—let's use *Budda,* and to hell with Edwin Newman) . . . and suddenly I felt just fine.

And why not?

I was, after all, the undisputed heavyweight Gonzo champion of the world—and this giggling yoyo in the bed across the room from me was no longer the champion of *anything,* or at least nothing he could get a notary public to vouch for. . . . So I sat back on the bureau with my head against the mirror and I thought, "Well, shit—here I am, and it's definitely a weird place to be; but not *really,* and not half as weird as a lot of other places I've been. . . . Nice view, decent company, and no *real* worries at all in this tight group of friends who were obviously having a good time with each other as the conversation recovered from my flaky entrance and got back on the fast-break, bump-and-run track they were used to. . . .

Conrad was sitting on the floor with his back to the big window that looks out on the savage, snow-covered wasteland of Central Park—and one look at his face told me that he was *finished working* for the night; he had worked a major miracle, smuggling a hyena into the house of mirrors, and now he was content to sit back and see what happened. . . .

Conrad was as happy as a serious smoker without a serious smoke could have been right then. . . . And so was I, for that matter, despite the crossfire of abuse and bent humor that I found myself caught in, between Bundini and the bed.

Ali was doing most of the talking: his mind seemed to be sort of wandering around and every once in a while taking a quick bite out of anything that caught his interest, like a good-humored wolverine. . . . There was no talk about boxing, as I recall: we'd agreed to save that for the "formal interview" tomorrow morning, so this midnight gig was a bit like a warmup for what Conrad described as "the *serious* bullshit."

There was a lot of talk about "drunkards," the sacred nature of "unsweet-ened grapefruit" and the madness of handling money—a subject I told him I'd long since mastered: "How many acres do you own?" I kept asking him whenever he started getting too high on his own riffs. "Not as many as me," I assured him. "I'm richer than Midas, and nine times as shrewd—whole valleys and mountains of acres," I continued, keeping a very straight face: "Thousands of cattle, stallions, peacocks, wild boar, sloats. . . ." And then the final twist: "You and Frazier just never learned how to handle money—but for twenty percent of the nut I can make you almost as rich as I am."

I could see that he didn't believe me. Ali is a hard man to con—but when he got on the subject of his tragic loss of "all privacy," I figured it was time for the frill.

"You really want a cure for your privacy problem?" I asked him, ripping the top out of another Ballantine Ale.

He smiled wickedly. "Sure boss—what you got?"

I slid off the bureau and moved toward the door, "Hang on," I told him. "I'll be right back."

Conrad was suddenly alert. "Where the hell are you going?" he snapped.

"To my room," I said. "I have the ultimate cure for Muhammad's privacy problem."

"*What* room?" he asked. "You don't even know where it is, do you?"

More laughter.

"It's 1011," Conrad said, "right upstairs—but hurry back," he added. "And if you run into Pat, we never heard of you."

Pat Patterson, Ali's fearfully diligent bodyguard, was known to be prowling the halls and putting a swift arm on anything human or otherwise that might disturb Ali's sleep. The rematch with Spinks was already getting cranked up, and it was Patterson's job to make sure The Champ stayed deadly serious about his new training schedule.

"Don't worry," I said. "I just want to go up to the room and put on my pantyhose. I'll be a lot more comfortable."

The sound of raucous laughter followed me down the hall as I sprinted off toward the fire exit, knowing I would have to be fast or I'd never get back in that room—tonight *or* tomorrow.

But I knew what I wanted, and I knew where it was in my parachute bag: yes, a spectacularly hideous full-head, real-hair, seventy-five-dollar movie-style red devil mask—a thing so fiendishly *real* and ugly that I still wonder, in moments like these, what sort of twisted impulse caused me to even pack the goddamn thing, much less wear it through the halls of the Park Lane Hotel and back into Muhammad Ali's suite at this unholy hour of the night.

Three minutes later I was back at the door, with the mask zipped over my head and the neck-flap tucked into my shirt. I knocked twice, then leaped into the room when Bundini opened the door, screaming some brainless slogan like "DEATH TO THE WEIRD!"

For a second or two there was no sound at all in the room—then the whole place exploded in wild laughter as I pranced around, smoking and drinking through the molded rubber mouth and raving about whatever came into my head.

The moment I saw the expression on Muhammad's face, I knew my mask would never get back to Woody Creek. His eyes lit up like he'd just seen the one toy he'd wanted all his life, and he almost came out of the bed after me. . . .

"Okay," I said, lifting it off my head and tossing it across the room to the bed. "It's yours, my man—but let me warn you that not *everybody* thinks this thing is real funny."

("Especially *black* people," Conrad told me later. "Jesus," he said, "I just about flipped when you jumped into the room with that goddamn mask on your head. That *was* really pushing your luck.")

Ali put the mask on immediately and was just starting to enjoy himself in the mirror when . . . ye Gods, we all went stiff as the sound of harsh knocking came through the door, along with the voice of Pat Patterson. "Open up," he was shouting. "What the hell is going on in there?"

I rushed for the bathroom, but Bundini was two steps ahead of me. . . . Ali, still wearing the hideous mask, ducked under the covers and Conrad went to open the door.

It all happened so fast that we all simply *froze* in position as Patterson came in like Dick Butkus on a blood scent . . . and that was when Muhammad came out of the bed with a wild cry and a mushroom cloud of flying sheets, pointing one long brown arm and a finger like Satan's own cattle prod, straight into Pat Patterson's face.

And that, folks, was a moment that I'd just as soon not have to live through again. We were all lucky, I think, that Patterson didn't go for his gun and blow Muhammad away in that moment of madness before he recognized the body under the mask.

It was only a split second, but it could easily have been a hell of a lot longer for all of us if Ali hadn't dissolved in a fit of whooping laughter at the sight of Pat Patterson's face. . . . And although Pat recovered instantly, the smile he finally showed us was uncomfortably thin.

The problem, I think, was not so much the mask itself and the shock it had caused him but *why* The Champ was wearing the goddamn thing at all; where had it come from? And why? These were serious times, but a scene like this could have ominous implications for the future—particularly with Ali so pleased with his new toy that he kept it on his head for the next ten or fifteen minutes, staring around the room and saying with no hint of a smile in his voice that he would definitely wear it for his appearance on the Dick Cavett show the next day. "This is the new *me,*" he told us. "I'll wear it on TV tomorrow and tell Cavett that I promised Veronica that I won't take it off until I win my title back. I'm gonna wear this ugly thing everywhere I go—even when I get into the ring with Spinks next time." He laughed wildly and jabbed at himself in the mirror. "Yes indeed!" he chuckled. "They thought I was crazy *before,* but they ain't seen *nothin'* yet."

LARRY L. KING

The first blurb I ever gave was to Larry L. King for one of his collections of burly rollicking journalism. Actually I gave three of them: "He writes just like an angel would, if it came from west Texas and drank," "If this book had been a whorehouse, nobody could have shut it down," and "Ought to get the Nobel Prize, but they'll probably give it to some Mexican." I was surprised but proud to see that all three encomia made it onto the jacket. That was years ago, when I was still tickled to be asked for a blurb and before King got eminently solvent as the writer of the book of that highly successful musical—based on one of his magazine pieces—The Best Little Whorehouse in Texas. Since then he has settled down and written for the theater largely, and more power to him, but it sure was a treat back in the '70s to pick up the latest issue of Willie Morris's Harper's *and see that King had thrust himself heartily into the middle of some situation where he wasn't necessarily welcome but who was going to chase him away?*

Willie Didn't Want a Lot of Confusion Backstage

Though the concert lasted eighteen hours, I am critically disadvantaged in that I heard absolutely no music. This is partly because my day contained certain gaps and partly because The Press, and roughly 5,000 pretenders claiming to be The Press, were confined two or three fenced compounds away from the stage—and behind it—in what I came to think of as Andersonville Prison. Like its Civil War namesake, this new Andersonville exposed its residents to sunstroke, rain, dust, thirst, hunger, ticks, chiggers, and brutal keepers. But, then, I am getting ahead of my story. . . .

Willie and Dr. Jay D. Milner, his public relations genius, had provided The Press with individualized T-shirts bearing our powerful names and literary connections. These would permit us to roam at will, even breaking into song with Kris 'n' Rita or Willie himself if being onstage with them tempted our good judgments, and generally were advertised as guaranteeing everything but romance with the Pointer Sisters. "Willie don't want a lot of confusion backstage," Dr. Milner told The Press. "Accredited press people only will be admitted. You may visit with the stars at your leisure." *Rita! Hot damn! You in trouble, Kris!*

Dr. Milner depicted an oasis of trailer houses full of frigid air-conditioner breezes, warm-blooded hostesses, hot food, cold liquors, and maybe palm trees. When we ladies and gentlemen of The Press had gorged our souls on angel's music or celebrity contacts, we would be free to repair to this perfect oasis, where everything would be provided except house slippers; just don't forget to wear your Willie Nelson T-shirts. Ten minutes later Dr. Milner came back to say that, well, er, ah, our T-shirts might not mean all that much, since they'd apparently been copied and were going for $5 each all over Texas. Now we would have to make do with Press Passes; sorry about you having to stand in line to get 'em, but they'll do the job, yessir, don't you worry. My Press Pass was blue. Blue Press Passes were represented as passports to everything but heaven and Albania. These would eventually entitle the bearers, if otherwise qualified, to drive on public roads.

We inched toward Liberty Hill at speeds more indigenous to the tortoise than the hare. Signs only twelve miles from the concert site promised parking at $2; signs a mere two miles away proclaimed the same service for $8. People walked along burdened by beer coolers, tents, watermelons, crying kids, folding chairs, picnic hampers, and their hindsight judgments; walking cases of sunburn, drunkenness, and shell shock were noted. Cars overheated and were abandoned where they exploded; grim rustics, sure enough, guarded their private roads with barricades of pickup trucks, scowls, and shotguns. My car required less than three hours to conquer thirty miles, a statistic causing much envy. The last 100 yards included fording a swift stream. It would be the last water I would see until it rained on Andersonville Prison.

We swaggered to the special gate reserved for Lords of the Press, confident in our individualized T-shirts and flashing our blue Press Passes. These so impressed security guards that they turned their backs. We then had the good luck to be joined by Gino McCoslin, who proclaimed his importance as official promoter and vouched for us as his good friends of The Press. One of the security guards grinned, grabbed Gino's head, trapped it in a wire fence, and began to beat on it. Gino did not appear unduly surprised but reached into his belt and got us admitted at gunpoint. It didn't seem unusual at the time.

Turned out we'd broken into Andersonville Prison. It was heavily overpopulated. Security guards at gates leading to the next compound, nearer to the stage by 300 yards, had guns of their own and didn't seem to fear Gino's. Gino ran away and came back with a stamp machine, which he applied to our blue Press Passes, causing them to say PAYMENT APPROVED. He said this would permit us to go anyplace we wanted. He was full of shit.

But Shrake and I decided to break out of Andersonville; our escape gave us a view of a broiling mass then 70,000 strong. It was scary. Writhing human forms as far as the eye could see. Tents and banners and bonfires and scorched earth and burned asses. Garbage and litter. Fellini's version of hell. There were shanties reminiscent of Hoovervilles, where people hawked blue jeans, souvenir programs, and fireworks. People noting our official Willie Nelson T-shirts complained because beer wasn't available, their hair hurt, the temperature was 106 degrees Fahrenheit, and no big-name acts had appeared yet. Many appeared to be crazed, with or without artificial stimulants.

"They are going to rip our official T-shirts off and stuff 'em up our asses," Shrake whispered. We rapidly headed toward the relative safety of Andersonville Prison, smiling and waving like Nixon-Agnew going up to claim the nomination, making loud promises of all the shameful conditions we intended to improve. Now, however, Andersonville Prison was guarded by a 300-pound Samoan whose stick was big enough to please Teddy Roosevelt. He whopped my shoulders and neck with it awhile. Shrake squatted in the shade of the big fellow's considerable shadow, watching him work and frequently chuckling. I broke and ran.

We found a friendlier gate. It was in the charge of Paul English, a member of Willie's band who is also the boss's alter ego. English is a double for Satan, except for being too skinny: Willie has written such songs about him as "Devil in a Sleepin' Bag." Paul waved us in while accusing a security guard of pocketing gate proceeds. The fellow denied it. When a bystander shouted that the guard had, indeed, pocketed his $7.50, Paul English threw the guard to the ground and ripped out his pockets. What looked like $300 fell out. Paul kicked him in the jaw with a cowboy boot, prompting the guard to resign on the grounds of guilt by association. While Paul was recovering the money, several dozen music lovers decided to crash the gate. English produced a "bidness" of about .22 caliber, with a long barrel, and had the scientific satisfaction of seeing a moving mass immediately reverse its direction.

Ah, at last! The oasis of trailer houses Dr. Milner had reserved for The Press! They were stoutly locked from the inside and under siege from about 3,000 howling Andersonville inmates. By now we spat cotton and knew enough to whine and beg. A tall blond hostess named Cookie admitted us. Probably she only wanted to share her misery; somebody had forgotten to connect the air conditioning and to order food and drink. Cookie offered a choice of pretzels or salt tablets, though she couldn't provide water in either case. We gasped and made sweat and occasionally fainted. I do not recall any palm trees.

A friendly musician produced white powders from twin vials. One assumed them to be varied grains of cocaine. One should not have. One should have presumed them to be Methedrine and THC, or, more accurately, a bastard variety of the latter used to tranquilize hogs. One soon began to feel peculiar. One remembers trying to turn over somebody's camper, somehow shorting an electrical circuit in the process—sizzle! flash!—rooting in the dirt and oinking and being begged by friends to sit in the shade.

The Press was shrieking and whining to Gino McCoslin, of betrayals and brutality. Gino leaned against a tree he thought he was propping up, focused on Europe with a dazed smile, and said, "Wheah!" about every eight seconds. Had I been a narc, I'd have arrested him on the evidence of his eyes; they appeared to be made of red glazed tile.

Gino did his best to talk. We leaned in and cupped our ears as if taking a deathbed confession. Gino appeared to be talking in strange tongues. Shrake translated approximately as follows: "Fuck it, I paid the goddamn politicians twenty thousand dollars to ensure security, and all they done was provide a bunch of killer bikers ripping off gate receipts and stomping the customers. You spoiled and pampered Press shitasses might do well to avoid them mean bastards. Git away, I'm busy holding up this tree."

Somebody shouted, "Goddamn it, you promised commodious accommodations, and we're paying two dollars a warm can for bootleg beer." Gino mumbled that he'd take a six-pack hisself if somebody would fetch it.

There was elected a Committee of Unrest and Indignation. Its purpose was to locate Willie Nelson. Better it had gone looking for Judge Crater. Willie and the other big, bright stars had locked themselves in their private trailers and would not give out their addresses among the acres of cars, campers, and trucks. Somebody said he'd seen Willie come out and sniff what appeared to be baking soda but that he'd disappeared in a cow pony's lope when a giggling gang of groupies began ripping off his clothes. (Jerry Jeff would have stayed and fought, by God.) "Willie was grinning," the informant volunteered. Willie is always grinning. When you talk to him, he looks at you and grins and grins and nods and nods and appears to be the world's best listener, until you realize he is not listening at all.

We found Dr. Milner, wearing a false beard and pretending not to be himself. Unmasked, he cleverly touted us to his Press-trailer oasis, where—he proclaimed—refreshments had newly arrived. We broke in by main force amid much shouting and grappling. The lucky got one can of warm beer, two bell tomatoes, and leavings of potato chips. It was exactly 144 degrees in there. All the hostesses were crying and trying to garrote people with their WELCOME TO WILLIE's banners. No more than 150 people milled, cursed, and shoved in a space God had made for 20.

I spotted a tray of delicate steak sandwiches, dug in my heels, used my huge, swollen body as a shield, and wolfed them down quickly enough to qualify for the *Guinness Book of World Records*. A frail fellow in fruit boots began to beat my broad back with his tiny little fists and screamed, "You son of a

bitch, you just ate the Pointer Sisters' supper!'' I said there hadn't been
enough to sponsor a good burp, anyway, and why didn't he just send 'em
some watermelon? "Oh, you reprehensible racist *poot,*" he screeched. They
led him off burbling about steak sandwiches' being required in the Pointer
Sisters' contract.

We were herded back to the stifling open air of Andersonville Prison,
whereupon it began to rain like a tall cow pissing on a flat rock. The baked and
blistered thousands cheered. There was a sharp retort—unmistakably, gun-
fire—and the cheers increased. "My God," Shrake said, "somebody just got
shot, and people are celebrating it." Crouching in the rain and goofy with hog
chemicals, I fervently hoped it had been Willie Nelson and that he'd been
blown away as effectively as Ray Price's mean rooster. Unfortunately it had
only been Paul English firing into the tent roof above the stage to rid it of
dangerous water accumulations.

The Pointer Sisters' road manager appeared to announce that his charges
refused to go onstage. Wouldn't sing without their supper, huh? But it proved
not to be a food strike, merely a matter of pure terror. "Listen, you blame
'em? I mean, thousands of crazed honkies out there and them the only *blacks?*
And people shooting guns and shit!''

Scott Hale of the Willie Nelson group led the manager onstage to convince
him of security. "See how nice it is?" Scott beamed. "Everything's fine."

The manager said, "Yeah? Then how come your leg is on fire?"

Scott looked down to see that a bottle rocket had come out of the crowd
and lodged in his right boot, which was sending up enough smoke and flames
to lift off a moon shot. He immediately began to stomp and thresh across the
stage, making wild owl-hoot noises. Many cheered, thinking he was dancing a
spectacular cowboy polka.

The Pointer Sisters agreed to come out only if a flying wedge of 100
reasonably unzonked honkies would lead them onstage and off. The security
guard leading the flying wedge was so loaded on scotch and Quaaludes that he
fell backward at the top of the stage steps, causing a domino reaction. The
much-buffeted Pointer Sisters squealed and grabbed their wigs and probably
wished for Detroit City.

Along about midnight, sufficiently baked and wet and beaten, I decided I'd
had enough entertainment, even though I'd not heard any music, laid eyes on
Willie Nelson, or had a chance to strike on Rita Coolidge. It took only two
hours to bog through the sea of mud, past grungy bikers pissing in open fields
and assorted wounded groaning from the bushes in passion or despair, to find
that my rental car was missing. Just plain gone.

The fellow who gave me a lift toward civilization kindly consented to sell
the remains of his bottle of scotch for $27; by the time this good Samaritan

dropped me at my hotel it required two bellmen and a baggage cart to get me to my room.

Gino McCoslin later managed to make it sound as if the Willie Nelson concert had been an artistic triumph and a financial disaster.

How was that possible, with huge multitudes paying what theoretically had to approach a half million dollars?

Gino seemed to say that while maybe 100,000 people had heard the wonderful music, pitifully few had paid for the privilege. He spoke of gate crashers, counterfeit tickets; 8,000 or 12,000 or 17,000 tickets allegedly stolen; receipts pocketed by security men; record high expenses.

Tell me about the expenses, I said.

Gino mumbled huge sums rapidly, sticking to generalities and claiming he was not authorized to open the books for inspection.

How much had been spent on Press arrangements?

Gino said it was $15,000 or $25,000 or maybe $50,000; he remembered it had a five in it. I said if he spent over $2.98, other than for the goat fencing surrounding Andersonville Prison, then he'd been ripped off. Gino expressed absolute astonishment in saying mine was the first complaint he'd received. "Ol' Willie's generous," he said. "Willie spent so much money making sure his friends and fans would be comfortable he probably lost his ass." It was suggested that Gino might be rehearsing his speech to the IRS folks. "No shit, now," he said. "It'll take days to tote it up, but I'd bet my ass we didn't no more than break even."

I recalled Willie's comment after his second Independence Day picnic, where he also allegedly only broke even, when asked if he would hold another: "Hell, I guess so. I'd hate to throw four thousand thieves out of work."

Gino now was painting Willie Nelson as a good-hearted raggedy-ass, who might have to sell his horses or find his wife a part-time job, when two pistol-packing cowboys came in. They grunted under the burden of several sacks, which they dumped onto a table. One said, "This here's the forty thousand dollars from advance ticket sales in San Antonio." Gino had the grace to wince.

I wanted to see Willie, I said, to commiserate with him in his poverty and maybe to kick his ass for sponsoring such a confused show. "Willie?" Gino said, surprised. "Shit, man, *Willie* ain't here! Willie and his old lady went straight to the airport for two weeks in Hawaii."

Later, at my friend Dub's house, we drank beer and smoked with various youthfuls while listening to Willie Nelson sing to us of red-headed strangers wild in their sorrow, of how cold it is sleeping out on the ground, of life's rough and rocky traveling. People muttered, "Great, man," and, "Out-

tasight,'' and, ''Pick up on this 'un, baby,'' all around the worshipful circle.
I'd been a Willie Nelson fan for years, back when there had been so few of us
we took pride in being a cult; his mournful, melancholy music never had failed
to reach me. But now all I could think of was Willie picking up the telephone
in the Waikiki Hilton to call room service, he and God grinning together at the
irony of his poor-boy songs.

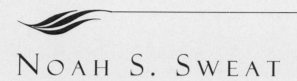

NOAH S. SWEAT

*Long after Prohibition staggered to defeat on the national level, a coalition of
bootleggers and Baptists kept liquor illegal in Mississippi. And yet it was not a wholly
abstinent state. Certainly it was not a state with a teetotaling legislature. So
candidates for public office had to approach the issue with some delicacy. When Noah
S. Sweat put himself forward in a bid to represent Alcorn County in 1948, he finessed
the question by composing a lasting model of the fence-straddling address. Evidently it
was a county with a sense of humor. He won, and went on to be a judge—whether
Solomonic or not, I don't know—in the 1970s.*

A Position on Whisky

My friends, I had not intended to discuss this controversial subject at this
particular time. However, I want you to know that I do not shun controversy.
On the contrary, I will take a stand on any issue at any time, regardless of how
fraught with controversy it might be. You have asked me how I feel about
whisky. All right, here is how I feel about whisky.

If when you say ''whisky'' you mean the devil's brew, the poison scourge,
the bloody monster that defiles innocence, dethrones reason, destroys the
home, creates misery and poverty, yea, literally takes the bread from the
mouths of little children; if you mean the evil drink that topples the Christian
man and woman from the pinnacle of righteous, gracious living into the
bottomless pit of degradation, and despair, and shame, and helplessness, and
hopelessness—then certainly I am against it.

But, if when you say ''whisky'' you mean the oil of conversation, the
philosophic wine, the ale that is consumed when good fellows get together,

that puts a song in their hearts and laughter on their lips, and the warm glow of contentment in their eyes; if you mean Christmas cheer; if you mean the stimulating drink that puts the spring into the old gentleman's step on a frosty, crispy morning; if you mean the drink that enables a man to magnify his joy, and his happiness, and to forget, if only for a little while, life's great tragedies, and heartaches, and sorrows; if you mean that drink the sale of which pours into our treasuries untold millions of dollars, which are used to provide tender care for our little crippled children, our blind, our deaf, our dumb, our pitiful aged and inform; to build highways and hospitals and schools—then certainly I am for it.

This is my stand. I will not retreat from it. I will not compromise.

Nunnally Johnson

Johnson was born in Columbus, Georgia, in 1897. "Where I come from," he once said hyperbolically, "the Tobacco Road people are the country club set." He went up to New York as a young man, worked for newspapers, hung out with James Thurber and Harold Ross, wrote short stories and humorous articles for The Smart Set *and* The Saturday Evening Post, *and then in the Depression went out to Hollywood, where he eventually made friends of everybody from Alec Guinness to Groucho Marx to Bogie and Bacall. He wrote fifty screenplays, including adaptations of* The Grapes of Wrath *and* Tobacco Road *(director John Ford, he complained, "turned the crackers into Irishmen") and* The Three Faces of Eve, *which he also directed. He found rapport with Joanne Woodward as a fellow cracker and approved of Faulkner's screenwriting ethic: "Bill came out to Hollywood like a plumber with all his tools, did the very best job he could, got his pay from the man, and went back to Oxford, Mississippi." Johnson didn't go back to Columbus, but the humor in his letters to various friends, collected in 1981, hearkens amiably back to his origins. He died in 1976.*

Letters from Hollywood

To Pete Martin

April 19, 1949

. . . I remembered a nice sample of [Gary] Cooper's rather nice dry humor that might interest you.

When we were making *Along Came Jones* on location, there was a quickie outfit working in the neighborhood. One day the star of this outfit, a western hero named Wild Bill Elliott, rode over to pay his respects to us. Like all quickie western heroes, Elliott was a brilliant spectacle. He rode a magnificent horse, his saddle and bridle were one hundred percent silver, and he himself was decked out in a $150 Stetson, a fine tailor-made western hero suit with white piping around the pockets and shoulders and his initials on his chest. He was really a sight to behold. Cooper was wearing a worn cowhand's outfit and was really a dilapidated looking fellow as he talked to Elliott and inspected his paraphernalia. Presently Elliott galloped off handsomely and Cooper came back to me and stood with his eyes on the ground for a moment. Then he said sadly, "They give him *two* guns."

To Thornton Delehanty

January 26, 1954

. . . You may want to hear what happened to my friend Zsa Zsa the other evening. Christmas Eve, in fact. George Sanders, who tells the story, said that his lawyers and Zsa Zsa's had come to a property settlement agreeable to both parties until it came to the point of Zsa Zsa's signing the paper. Then she refused and began to ask for more and more and more. This irked George. But he figured it wouldn't be difficult to get something on her.

So on Christmas Eve, that holy day, he prepared to raid her home to catch [Porfirio] Rubirosa in the hay with her. He planned to lean a ladder against a second-floor balcony and enter her bedroom through the French doors there, but he couldn't remember whether the doors opened in or out, so, being a careful fellow, he sent a gift over to Zsa Zsa that afternoon by his butler, who was also instructed to nip upstairs and get information on the door situation. They opened out.

Around two-thirty that night, while every son-of-a-bitch and his brother in town was singing "Silent Night," George got in a car with four Sam Spades and set out for the house in Bel-Air. His operatives were such horrible looking fellows that he thought it best to take along something in the shape of a gift for Mrs. Sanders by way of alibi if the Bel-Air cops stopped him. So he wrapped up a brick in some holly paper. They found Rubirosa's car parked outside and the Sam Spades all went through a "Dragnet" routine of jotting numbers and photographing fingerprints and then George and his friends sneaked around the house and set up the ladder.

The rules, it seems, call for the husband to enter first. Otherwise, charges of breaking and entering can be lodged against outsiders. The ladder turned out to be a little shaky and George got quite nervous. As he explained, "I felt it would be most embarrassing if I fell and broke my leg and Rubirosa had to take me to the hospital." But he made it to the balcony all right and found the windows open. Zsa Zsa likes fresh air. So he dashed in bravely and found himself in a scramble with a Venetian blind. Through them he saw two naked forms break the record for the dash to the bathroom, where the light was on. As soon as he could untangle himself from the blinds, George rallied at the head of his operatives and all made a dash for the privileged sanctuary. Rubi and Zsa Zsa had slammed the door shut but in their excitement they forgot that it could also be locked. The door opened inward and it then became a head-on push between George and Rubi, Rubi trying to hold the door shut, George trying to bull it open. Now according to George, he was hitting low, just like Knute Rockne always said, and with a powerful lunge he managed to get the door open about a foot, which to his astonishment brought him face to face with Rubirosa's organ, whereupon, in a moment of whimsy, he shook it heartily and called Merry Christmas to them both. This mortified Rubirosa. It was then that Zsa Zsa called out, "Now, George, really! Please be seated and I'll be out in just a moment." She emerged in a diaphanous negligee, leaving the shy Mr. Rubirosa skulking in the can.

George says her conduct then was above and beyond reproach. In the most elegant fashion, like a veritable Clare Luce, she greeted her husband and his four thugs and invited them to sit down and talk it over. While the thugs stared, George mentioned the lateness of the hour and that he felt that they should be pushing on. But when they started to exit by way of the balcony and the ladder, Zsa Zsa was shocked that they should believe she would not show them to the front door as she would any guest in her home. So she led them downstairs and was reminded on the way of the Christmas tree. "You haven't seen it, George! You must! It's perfectly beautiful!" So she led them all into the living room and they all admired it. "Did you get your gift?" she asked. George said he hadn't, but the evening could be taken as an entirely adequate gift so far as he was concerned. "Never mind, it'll be there bright and early in the morning," she assured him. Then she opened the front door for them, shook hands all around, and they all exchanged God bless you's.

To Gene Fowler

March 17, 1955

. . . Alva Johnston told me once that while there had been hundreds of fights in Bleeck's, no human standing directly in front of a gladiator had ever been harmed; the dead and dying had always been felled by elbows. There was a time, during Prohibition, when Bleeck's was incorporated as a club, the Artists and Writers Club. Only one member was ever posted throughout this period, Mrs. Dick Maney [wife of the theatrical press agent], who, according to Alva, was barred for biting other members. I don't know the lady but she must have been what they call quite a character. Stanley told me he went into the backroom one night on the way to the can and found her methodically piling all the furniture up in the middle of the floor. When he came out of the can she had crumpled up a newspaper and lighted it with the apparent purpose of burning down the whole building. When Stanley stomped out the fire, she looked at him in some disgust and said, "Well, you would seem to have very little to do." . . .

To Robert Goldstein

October 22, 1957

Did you want to know about Tallulah Bankhead? I sat at a dinner table with her the other night. She's really a caution. Inflamed with wine, she was attacking Josh Logan, far down the table, for being solvent, which seemed to be an unpardonable crime to her. You never heard such screams and yells and walloping around, while poor Josh, to whom the charges never became quite clear, tried to crawl up the wall behind him. Mrs. Jennifer Selznick, our hostess, kept signalling frantically to me to talk, talk, talk! Anything to create a diversion. But as all men know, and most women, there is a limit to my courage, and Tallulah is well out in front of this limit. I had just as soon walk in front of a Sherman tank. Later, in case you haven't already turned the page, she called across the dance floor to Cecil Beaton, "Don't try to show off in front of me, Mr. Beaton! Don't forget that it was I who taught you how to make up your eyes!" That's the way to make a party go!

Beaton told Dorris (assuming you are still with us) that he sat between Hedda and Tallulah at a dinner a few nights before. He said Hedda recounted her first view of Tallulah, a vivid drama in which Hedda claimed to have been in the audience the night that Tallulah made her debut in London. "The curtain rose on the most beautiful girl in the world: you, Tallulah!" To which

Tallulah replied with a short ugly word, described Hedda as a Republican bitch, and declared that the occasion was of such social elegance that Hedda would not have been allowed in the same neighborhood, much less the theatre. Hedda retorted in kind, and since her voice isn't many decibels below Tallulah's, poor Beaton must have been threatened with concussion. The shouting got more and more acrimonious, and when finally Tallulah offered to bet a thousand dollars that Hedda was not present on that occasion, Hedda made the very good point that Tallulah didn't have a thousand dollars, whereupon Tallulah looked around the room and replied, "No, but I will make a thousand dollars before I leave this house tonight." . . .

And now in conclusion, all I care to say about this winsome Alabama belle is that I'll bet there are no black children who would like to go to school with her. . . .

To Groucho Marx

December 17, 1962

. . . John [Steinbeck] was on his way back from getting the Nobel Prize in Stockholm. He says he holds one record anyway, he's the only American male winner to be both sober and perpendicular when he accepted the prize. He said Red Lewis was in such a state [in 1930] that he forgot the acceptance speech he'd worked so hard on and ad libbed an entirely different one. The committee [in 1949], after observing Faulkner at work on the local booze for a couple of days, resorted to deception to assure his being sober. They shook him into listening and then told him that he was due on the platform that afternoon. But Faulkner, whom they don't call the Old Fox for nothing (in fact, they don't call him the Old Fox), just smiled. Even while the Swede double-domes were explaining to him that it was Thursday, the Big Day, Bill could hear the churchbells ringing; it was Sunday, not Thursday, and either he had three more days of wassail or he had skipped the whole affair on the previous Thursday. In either case, all was well and he ordered up schnapps for all. John said the Swedes had great admiration for Faulkner, the way he was propped up and spoke slowly but indistinctly. . . .

EUDORA WELTY

Eudora Welty, a Jackson, Mississippian, born in 1909, is the foremost living Southern writer and sometimes one of the funniest. You can scarcely find an anthology of humor, Southern writing, or the short story that doesn't include her "Why I Live at the P.O." "Petrified Man" is almost as much of a standard, so I thought the author might appreciate it if I picked something else; but then I read it again, and decided that whether she is tired of seeing it reprinted or not, Miss Welty wouldn't be able to pry it away from me with a crowbar. But I have also picked the more darkly comic "Keela, the Outcast Indian Maiden," which at least Keela her/himself gets a laugh out of. Once I called Miss Welty on the phone and she said, "I appreciated your refrence in Gentleman's Quotully." Never one to pass up a magazine assignment purely on the grounds that its concept is profoundly tacky on its face, I had agreed to write for GQ on the topic "What Makes a Woman Sexy." One of my criteria was a woman's ability to recognize a certain number of names from a list of my favorite cultural figures, one of whom was Keela. Knowing that Miss Welty might be reading any given old thing I am peddling to magazines has made me feel somehow sexier myself. Later I visited her at home. She said she had just had to turn away a woman who appeared on her doorstep to declare that her life story would be the ideal Welty subject. Though I have no doubt she was quite politely rebuffed, the woman left saying, "Girl, you don't know what you're missing." On the contrary, I believe that if there is a heaven, the Almighty will receive Miss Welty by saying, "Girl, you didn't miss a trick."

"Petrified Man"

"Reach in my purse and git me a cigarette without no powder in it if you kin, Mrs Fletcher, honey," said Leota to her ten o'clock shampoo-and-set customer. "I don't like no perfumed cigarettes."

Mrs Fletcher gladly reached over to the lavender shelf under the lavender-framed mirror, shook a hair net loose from the clasp of the patent-leather bag, and slapped her hand down quickly on a powder puff which burst out when the purse was opened.

"Why, look at the peanuts, Leota!" said Mrs Fletcher in her marveling voice.

"Honey, them goobers has been in my purse a week if they's been in it a day. Mrs Pike bought them peanuts."

"Who's Mrs Pike?" asked Mrs Fletcher, settling back. Hidden in this den of curling fluid and henna packs, separated by a lavender swing door from the other customers, who were being gratified in other booths, she could give her curiosity its freedom. She looked expectantly at the black part in Leota's yellow curls as she bent to light the cigarette.

"Mrs Pike is this lady from New Orleans," said Leota, puffing, and pressing into Mrs Fletcher's scalp with strong red-nailed fingers. "A friend, not a customer. You see, like maybe I told you last time, me and Fred and Sal and Joe all had us a fuss, so Sal and Joe up and moved out, so we didn't do a thing but rent out their room. So we rented it to Mrs Pike. And Mr Pike." She flicked an ash into the basket of dirty towels. "Mrs Pike is a very decided blonde. *She* bought me the peanuts."

"She must be cute," said Mrs Fletcher.

"Honey, 'cute' ain't the word for what she is. I'm tellin' you, Mrs Pike is attractive. She has her a good time. She's got a sharp eye out, Mrs Pike has."

She dashed the comb through the air, and paused dramatically as a cloud of Mrs Fletcher's hennaed hair floated out of the lavender teeth like a small storm cloud.

"Hair fallin'."

"Aw, Leota."

"Uh-huh, commencin' to fall out," said Leota, combing again, and letting fall another cloud.

"Is it any dandruff in it?" Mrs Fletcher was frowning, her hair-line eyebrows diving down toward her nose, and her wrinkled, beady-lashed eyelids batting with concentration.

"Nope." She combed again. "Just fallin' out."

"Bet it was that last perm'nent you gave me that did it," Mrs Fletcher said cruelly. "Remember you cooked me fourteen minutes."

"You had fourteen minutes comin' to you," said Leota with finality.

"Bound to be somethin'," persisted Mrs Fletcher. "Dandruff, dandruff. I couldn't of caught a thing like that from Mr Fletcher, could I?"

"Well," Leota answered at last, "you know what I heard in here yestiddy, one of Thelma's ladies was settin' over yonder in Thelma's booth gittin' a machineless, and I don't mean to insist or insinuate or anything, Mrs Fletcher, but Thelma's lady just happ'med to throw out—I forgotten what she was talkin' about at the time—that you was p-r-e-g., and lots of times that'll make your hair do awful funny, fall out and God knows what all. It just ain't our fault, is the way I look at it."

There was a pause. The women stared at each other in the mirror.

"Who was it?" demanded Mrs Fletcher.

"Honey, I really couldn't say," said Leota. "Not that you look it."

"Where's Thelma? I'll get it out of her," said Mrs Fletcher.

"Now, honey, I wouldn't go and git mad over a little thing like that," Leota said, combing hastily, as though to hold Mrs Fletcher down by the hair. "I'm sure it was somebody didn't mean no harm in the world. How far gone are you?"

"Just wait," said Mrs Fletcher, and shrieked for Thelma, who came in and took a drag from Leota's cigarette.

"Thelma, honey, throw your mind back to yestiddy if you kin," said Leota, drenching Mrs Fletcher's hair with a thick fluid and catching the overflow in a cold wet towel at her neck.

"Well, I got my lady half wound for a spiral," said Thelma doubtfully.

"This won't take but a minute," said Leota. "Who is it you got in there, old Horse Face? Just cast your mind back and try to remember who your lady was yestiddy who happ'm to mention that my customer was pregnant, that's all. She's dead to know."

Thelma drooped her blood-red lips and looked over Mrs Fletcher's head into the mirror. "Why, honey, I ain't got the faintest," she breathed. "I really don't recollect the faintest. But I'm sure she meant no harm. I declare, I forgot my hair finally got combed and thought it was a stranger behind me."

"Was it that Mrs Hutchinson?" Mrs Fletcher was tensely polite.

"Mrs Hutchinson? Oh, Mrs Hutchinson." Thelma batted her eyes. "Naw, precious, she come on Thursday and didn't ev'm mention your name. I doubt if she ev'm knows you're on the way."

"Thelma!" cried Leota staunchly.

"All I know is, whoever it is 'll be sorry some day. Why, I just barely knew it myself!" cried Mrs Fletcher. "Just let her wait!"

"Why? What 're you gonna do to her?"

It was a child's voice, and the women looked down. A little boy was making tents with aluminum wave pinchers on the floor under the sink.

"Billy Boy, hon, mustn't bother nice ladies," Leota smiled. She slapped him brightly and behind her back waved Thelma out of the booth. "Ain't Billy Boy a sight? Only three years old and already just nuts about the beauty-parlor business."

"I never saw him here before," said Mrs Fletcher, still unmollified.

"He ain't been here before, that's how come," said Leota. "He belongs to Mrs Pike. She got her a job but it was Fay's Millinery. He oughtn't to try on those ladies' hats, they come down over his eyes like I don't know what. They just git to look ridiculous, that's what, an' of course he's gonna put 'em on:

hats. They tole Mrs Pike they didn't appreciate him hangin' around there. Here, he couldn't hurt a thing.''

"Well! I don't like children that much,'' said Mrs Fletcher.

"Well!'' said Leota moodily.

"Well! I'm almost tempted not to have this one,'' said Mrs Fletcher. "That Mrs Hutchinson! Just looks straight through you when she sees you on the street and then spits at you behind your back.''

"Mr Fletcher would beat you on the head if you didn't have it now,'' said Leota reasonably. "After going this far.''

Mrs Fletcher sat up straight. "Mr Fletcher can't do a thing with me.''

"He can't!'' Leota winked at herself in the mirror.

"No siree, he can't. If he so much as raises his voice against me, he knows good and well I'll have one of my sick headaches, and then I'm just not fit to live with. And if I really look that pregnant already—''

"Well, now, honey, I just want you to know—I habm't told any of my ladies and I ain't goin' to tell 'em—even that you're losin' your hair. You just get you one of those Stork-a-Lure dresses and stop worryin'. What people don't know don't hurt nobody, as Mrs Pike says.''

"Did you tell Mrs Pike?'' asked Mrs Fletcher sulkily.

"Well, Mrs Fletcher, look, you ain't ever goin' to lay eyes on Mrs Pike or her lay eyes on you, so what diffunce does it make in the long run?''

"I knew it!'' Mrs Fletcher deliberately nodded her head so as to destroy a ringlet Leota was working on behind her ear. "Mrs Pike!''

Leota sighed. "I reckon I might as well tell you. It wasn't any more Thelma's lady tole me you was pregnant than a bat.''

"Not Mrs Hutchinson?''

"Naw, Lord! It was Mrs Pike.''

"Mrs Pike!'' Mrs Fletcher could only sputter and let curling fluid roll into her ear. "How could Mrs Pike possibly know I was pregnant or otherwise, when she doesn't even know me? The nerve of some people!''

"Well, here's how it was. Remember Sunday?''

"Yes,'' said Mrs Fletcher.

"Sunday, Mrs Pike an' me was all by ourself. Mr Pike and Fred had gone over to Eagle Lake, sayin' they was goin' to catch 'em some fish, but they didn't, a course. So we was settin' in Mrs Pike's car, is a 1939 Dodge———''

"1939, eh,'' said Mrs Fletcher.

"———An' we was gettin' us a Jax beer apiece—that's the beer that Mrs Pike says is made right in N.O., so she won't drink no other kind. So I seen you drive up to the drugstore an' run in for just a secont, leavin' I reckon Mr Fletcher in the car, an' come runnin' out with looked like a perscription. So I says to Mrs Pike, just to be makin' talk, 'Right yonder's Mrs Fletcher, and I reckon that's Mr Fletcher—she's one of my regular customers,' I says.''

"I had on a figured print," said Mrs Fletcher tentatively.

"You sure did," agreed Leota. "So Mrs Pike, she give you a good look—she's very observant, a good judge of character, cute as a minute, you know—and she says, 'I bet you another Jax that lady's three months on the way.' ''

"What gall!" said Mrs Fletcher. "Mrs Pike!"

"Mrs Pike ain't goin' to bite you," said Leota. "Mrs Pike is a lovely girl, you'd be crazy about her, Mrs Fletcher. But she can't sit still a minute. We went to the travelin' freak show yestiddy after work. I got through early—nine o'clock. In the vacant store next door? What, you ain't been?"

"No, I despise freaks," declared Mrs Fletcher.

"Aw. Well, honey, talkin' about bein' pregnant an' all, you ought to see those twins in a bottle, you really owe it to yourself."

"What twins?" asked Mrs Fletcher out of the side of her mouth.

"Well, honey, they got these two twins in a bottle, see? Born joined plumb together—dead a course." Leota dropped her voice into a soft lyrical hum. "They was about this long—pardon—must of been full time, all right, wouldn't you say?—an' they had these two heads an' two faces an' four arms an' four legs, all kind of joined *here*. See, this face looked this-a-way, and the other face looked that-a-way, over their shoulder, see. Kinda pathetic."

"Glah!" said Mrs Fletcher disapprovingly.

"Well, ugly? Honey, I mean to tell you—their parents was first cousins and all like that. Billy Boy, git me a fresh towel from off Teeny's stack—this 'n's wringin' wet—an' quit ticklin' my ankles with that curler. I declare! He don't miss nothin'."

"Me and Mr Fletcher aren't one speck of kin, or he could never of had me," said Mrs Fletcher placidly.

"Of course not!" protested Leota. "Neither is me an' Fred, not that we know of. Well, honey, what Mrs Pike liked was the pygmies. They've got these pygmies down there, too, an' Mrs Pike was just wild about 'em. You know, the tee-niniest men in the universe? Well, honey, they can just rest back on their little bohunkus an' roll around an' you can't hardly tell if they're sittin' or standin'. That'll give you some idea. They're about forty-two years old. Just suppose it was your husband!"

"Well, Mr Fletcher is five foot nine and one half," said Mrs Fletcher quickly.

"Fred's five foot ten," said Leota, "but I tell him he's still a shrimp, account of I'm so tall." She made a deep wave over Mrs Fletcher's other temple with the comb. "Well, these pygmies are a kind of a dark brown, Mrs Fletcher. Not bad lookin' for what they are, you know."

"I wouldn't care for them," said Mrs Fletcher. "What does that Mrs Pike see in them?"

"Aw, I don't know," said Leota. "She's just cute, that's all. But they got this man, this petrified man, that ever'thing ever since he was nine years old, when it goes through his digestion, see, somehow Mrs Pike says it goes to his joints and has been turning to stone."

"How awful!" said Mrs Fletcher.

"He's forty-two too. That looks like a bad age."

"Who said so, that Mrs Pike? I bet she's forty-two," said Mrs Fletcher.

"Naw," said Leota, "Mrs Pike's thirty-three, born in January, an Aquarian. He could move his head—like this. A course his head and mind ain't a joint, so to speak, and I guess his stomach ain't, either—not yet anyways. But see—his food, he eats it, and it goes down, see, and then he digests it"— Leota rose on her toes for an instant—"and it goes out to his joints and before you can say 'Jack Robinson,' it's stone—pure stone. He's turning to stone. How'd you like to be married to a guy like that? All he can do, he can move his head just a quarter of an inch. A course he *looks* just *terrible*."

"I should think he would," said Mrs Fletcher frostily. "Mr Fletcher takes bending exercises every night of the world. I make him."

"All Fred does is lay around the house like a rug. I wouldn't be surprised if he woke up some day and couldn't move. The petrified man just sat there moving his quarter of an inch though," said Leota reminiscently.

"Did Mrs Pike like the petrified man?" asked Mrs Fletcher.

"Not as much as she did the others," said Leota deprecatingly. "And then she likes a man to be a good dresser, and all that."

"Is Mr Pike a good dresser?" asked Mrs Fletcher skeptically.

"Oh, well, yeah," said Leota, "but he's twelve-fourteen years older 'n her. She ast Lady Evangeline about him."

"Who's Lady Evangeline?" asked Mrs Fletcher.

"Well, it's this mind reader they got in the freak show," said Leota. "Was real good. Lady Evangeline is her name, and if I had another dollar I wouldn't do a thing but have my other palm read. She had what Mrs Pike said was the 'sixth mind' but she had the worst manicure I ever saw on a living person."

"What did she tell Mrs Pike?" asked Mrs Fletcher.

"She told her Mr Pike was as true to her as he could be and besides, would come into some money."

"Humph!" said Mrs Fletcher. "What does he do?"

"I can't tell," said Leota, "because he don't work. Lady Evangeline didn't tell me near enough about my nature or anything. And I would like to go back and find out some more about this boy. Used to go with this boy got married to this girl. Oh, shoot, that was about three and a half years ago, when you was still goin' to the Robert E. Lee Beauty Shop in Jackson. He married her for her money. Another fortune teller tole me that at the time. So I'm not in love with him any more, anyway, besides being married to Fred, but Mrs Pike thought, just for the hell of it, see, to ask Lady Evangeline was he happy.''

''Does Mrs Pike know everything about you already?'' asked Mrs Fletcher unbelievingly. ''Mercy!''

''Oh yeah, I tole her ever'thing about ever'thing, from now on back to I don't know when—to when I first started goin' out,'' said Leota. ''So I ast Lady Evangeline for one of my questions, was he happily married, and she says, just like she was glad I ask her, 'Honey,' she says, 'naw, he idn't. You write down this day, March 8, 1941,' she says, 'and mock it down: three years from today him and her won't be occupyin' the same bed.' There it is, up on the wall with them other dates—see, Mrs Fletcher? And she says, 'Child, you ought to be glad you didn't git him, because he's so mercenary.' So I'm glad I married Fred. He sure ain't mercenary, money don't mean a thing to him. But I sure would like to go back and have my other palm read.''

''Did Mrs Pike believe in what the fortune teller said?'' asked Mrs Fletcher in a superior tone of voice.

''Lord, yes, she's from New Orleans. Ever'body in New Orleans believes ever'thing spooky. One of 'em in New Orleans before it was raided says to Mrs Pike one summer she was goin' to go from state to state and meet some gray-headed men, and, sure enough, she says she went on a beautician convention up to Chicago. . . .''

''Oh!'' said Mrs Fletcher. ''Oh, is Mrs Pike a beautician too?''

''Sure she is,'' protested Leota. ''She's a beautician. I'm goin' to git her in here if I can. Before she married. But it don't leave you. She says sure enough, there was three men who was a very large part of making her trip what it was, and they all three had gray in their hair and they went in six states. Got Christmas cards from 'em. Billy Boy, go see if Thelma's got any dry cotton. Look how Mrs Fletcher's a-drippin'.''

''Where did Mrs Pike meet Mr Pike?'' asked Mrs Fletcher primly.

''On another train,'' said Leota.

''I met Mr Fletcher, or rather he met me, in a rental library,'' said Mrs Fletcher with dignity, as she watched the net come down over her head.

''Honey, me an' Fred, we met in a rumble seat eight months ago and we was practically on what you might call the way to the altar inside of a half an hour,'' said Leota in a guttural voice, and bit a bobby pin open. ''Course it don't last. Mrs Pike says nothin' like that ever lasts.''

''Mr Fletcher and myself are as much in love as the day we married,'' said Mrs Fletcher belligerently as Leota stuffed cotton into her ears.

''Mrs Pike says it don't last,'' repeated Leota in a louder voice. ''Now go git under the dryer. You can turn yourself on, can't you? I'll be back to comb you out. Durin' lunch I promised to give Mrs Pike a facial. You know—free. Her bein' in the business, so to speak.''

"I bet she needs one," said Mrs Fletcher, letting the swing door fly back against Leota. "Oh, pardon me."

A week later, on time for her appointment, Mrs Fletcher sank heavily into Leota's chair after first removing a drugstore rental book, called *Life Is Like That,* from the seat. She stared in a discouraged way into the mirror.

"You can tell it when I'm sitting down, all right," she said.

Leota seemed preoccupied and stood shaking out a lavender cloth. She began to pin it around Mrs Fletcher's neck in silence.

"I said you sure can tell it when I'm sitting straight on and coming at you this way," Mrs Fletcher said.

"Why, honey, naw you can't," said Leota gloomily. "Why, I'd never know. If somebody was to come up to me on the street and say, 'Mrs Fletcher is pregnant!' I'd say, 'Heck, she don't look it to me.' "

"If a certain party hadn't found it out and spread it around, it wouldn't be too late even now," said Mrs Fletcher frostily, but Leota was almost choking her with the cloth, pinning it so tight, and she couldn't speak clearly. She paddled her hands in the air until Leota wearily loosened her.

"Listen, honey, you're just a virgin compared to Mrs Montjoy," Leota was going on, still absent-minded. She bent Mrs Fletcher back in the chair and, sighing, tossed liquid from a teacup onto her head and dug both hands into her scalp. "You know Mrs Montjoy—her husband's that premature-gray-headed fella?"

"She's in the Trojan Garden Club, is all I know," said Mrs Fletcher.

"Well, honey," said Leota, but in a weary voice, "she come in here not the week before and not the day before she had her baby—she come in here the very selfsame day, I mean to tell you. Child, we was all plumb scared to death. There she was! Come for her shampoo an' set. Why, Mrs Fletcher, in a hour an' twenty minutes she was layin' up there in the Babtist Hospital with a seb'm-pound son. It was that close a shave. I declare, if I hadn't been so tired I would of drank up a bottle of gin that night."

"What gall," said Mrs Fletcher. "I never knew her at all well."

"See, her husband was waitin' outside in the car, and her bags was all packed an' in the back seat, an' she was all ready, 'cept she wanted her shampoo an' set. An' havin' one pain right after another. Her husband kep' comin' in here, scared-like, but couldn't do nothin' with her a course. She yelled bloody murder, too, but she always yelled her head off when I give her a perm'nent."

"She must of been crazy," said Mrs Fletcher. "How did she look?"

"Shoot!" said Leota.

"Well, I can guess," said Mrs Fletcher. "Awful."

"Just wanted to look pretty while she was havin' her baby, is all," said Leota airily. "Course, we was glad to give the lady what she was after—that's our motto—but I bet an hour later she wasn't payin' no mind to them little end curls. I bet she wasn't thinkin' about she ought to have on a net. It wouldn't of done her no good if she had."

"No, I don't suppose it would," said Mrs Fletcher.

"Yeah man! She was a-yellin'. Just like when I give her her perm'nent."

"Her husband ought to could make her behave. Don't it seem that way to you?" asked Mrs Fletcher. "He ought to put his foot down."

"Ha," said Leota. "A lot he could do. Maybe some women is soft."

"Oh, you mistake me, I don't mean for her to get soft—far from it! Women have to stand up for themselves, or there's just no telling. But now you take me—I ask Mr Fletcher's advice now and then, and he appreciates it, especially on something important, like is it time for a permanent—not that I've told him about the baby. He says, 'Why dear, go ahead!' Just ask their *advice.*"

"Huh! If I ever ast Fred's advice we'd be floatin' down the Yazoo River on a houseboat or somethin' by this time," said Leota. "I'm sick of Fred. I tole him to go over to Vicksburg."

"Is he going?" demanded Mrs Fletcher.

"Sure. See, the fortune teller—I went back and had my other palm read, since we've got to rent the room agin—said my lover was goin' to work in Vicksburg, so I don't know who she could mean, unless she meant Fred. And Fred ain't workin' here—that much is so."

"Is he going to work in Vicksburg?" asked Mrs Fletcher. "And———"

"Sure, Lady Evangeline said so. Said the future is going to be brighter than the present. He don't want to go, but I ain't gonna put up with nothin' like that. Lays around the house an' bulls—did bull—with that good-for-nothin' Mr Pike. He says if he goes who'll cook, but I says I never get to eat anyway—not meals. Billy Boy, take Mrs Grover that *Screen Secrets* and leg it."

Mrs Fletcher heard stamping feet go out the door.

"Is that that Mrs Pike's little boy here again?" she asked, sitting up gingerly.

"Yeah, that's still him." Leota stuck out her tongue.

Mrs Fletcher could hardly believe her eyes. "Well! How's Mrs Pike, your attractive new friend with the sharp eyes who spreads it around town that perfect strangers are pregnant?" she asked in a sweetened tone.

"Oh, Mizziz Pike." Leota combed Mrs Fletcher's hair with heavy strokes.

"You act like you're tired," said Mrs Fletcher.

"Tired? Feel like it's four o'clock in the afternoon already," said Leota. "I ain't told you the awful luck we had, me and Fred? It's the worst thing you ever heard of. Maybe *you* think Mrs Pike's got sharp eyes. Shoot, there's a limit! Well, you know, we rented out our room to this Mr and Mrs Pike from New Orleans when Sal an' Joe Fentress got mad at us 'cause they drank up some home-brew we had in the closet—Sal an' Joe did. So, a week ago Sat'day Mr and Mrs Pike moved in. Well, I kinda fixed up the room, you know—put a sofa pillow on the couch and picked some ragged robbins and put in a vase, but they never did say they appreciated it. Anyway, then I put some old magazines on the table.''

"I think that was lovely," said Mrs Fletcher.

"Wait. So, come night 'fore last, Fred and this Mr Pike, who Fred just took up with, was back from they said they was fishin', bein' as neither one of 'em has got a job to his name, and we was all settin' around in their room. So Mrs Pike was settin' there, readin' a old *Startling G-Man Tales* that was mine, mind you, I'd bought it myself, and all of a sudden she jumps!—into the air—you'd 'a' thought she'd set on a spider—an' says, 'Canfield'—ain't that silly, that's Mr Pike—'Canfield, my God A'mighty,' she says, 'honey,' she says, 'we're rich, and you won't have to work.' Not that he turned one hand anyway. Well, me and Fred rushes over to her, and Mr Pike, too, and there she sets, pointin' her finger at a photo in my copy of *Startling G-Man*. 'See that man?' yells Mrs Pike. 'Remember him, Canfield?' 'Never forget a face,' says Mr Pike. 'It's Mr Petrie, that we stayed with him in the apartment next to ours in Toulouse Street in N.O. for six weeks. Mr Petrie.' 'Well,' says Mrs Pike, like she can't hold out one secont longer, 'Mr Petrie is wanted for five hundred dollars cash, for rapin' four women in California, and I know where he is.' ''

"Mercy!" said Mrs Fletcher. "Where was he?"

At some time Leota had washed her hair and now she yanked her up by the back locks and sat her up.

"Know where he was?"

"I certainly don't," Mrs Fletcher said. Her scalp hurt all over.

Leota flung a towel around the top of her customer's head. "Nowhere else but in that freak show! I saw him just as plain as Mrs Pike. *He* was the petrified man!"

"Who would ever have thought that!" cried Mrs Fletcher sympathetically.

"So Mr Pike says, 'Well whatta you know about that,' an' he looks real hard at the photo and whistles. And she starts dancin' and singin' about their good luck. She meant our bad luck! I made a point of tellin' that fortune teller the next time I saw her. I said, 'Listen, that magazine was layin' around the house for a month, and there was five hundred dollars in it for somebody. An' there was the freak show runnin' night an' day, not two steps away from my own beauty parlor, with Mr Petrie just settin' there waitin'. An' it had to be Mr and Mrs Pike, almost perfect strangers.' ''

"What gall," said Mrs Fletcher. She was only sitting there, wrapped in a turban, but she did not mind.

"Fortune tellers don't care. And Mrs Pike, she goes around actin' like she thinks she was Mrs God," said Leota. "So they're goin' to leave tomorrow, Mr and Mrs Pike. And in the meantime I got to keep that mean, bad little ole kid here, gettin' under my feet ever' minute of the day an' talkin' back too."

"Have they gotten the five hundred dollars' reward already?" asked Mrs Fletcher.

"Well," said Leota, "at first Mr Pike didn't want to do anything about it. Can you feature that? Said he kinda liked that ole bird and said he was real nice to 'em, lent 'em money or somethin'. But Mrs Pike simply tole him he could just go to hell, and I can see her point. She says, 'You ain't worked a lick in six months, and here I make five hunderd dollars in two seconts, and what thanks do I get for it? You go to hell, Canfield,' she says. So," Leota went on in a despondent voice, "they called up the cops and they caught the ole bird, all right, right there in the freak show where I saw him with my own eyes, thinkin' he was petrified. He's the one. Did it under his real name—Mr Petrie. Four women in California, all in the month of August. So Mrs Pike gits five hunderd dollars. And my magazine, and right next door to my beauty parlor. I cried all night, but Fred said it wasn't a bit of use and to go to sleep, because the whole thing was just a sort of coincidence—you know: can't do nothin' about it. He says it put him clean out of the notion of goin' to Vicksburg for a few days till we rent out the room agin—no tellin' who we'll git this time."

"But can you imagine anybody knowing this old man, that's raped four women?" persisted Mrs Fletcher, and she shuddered audibly. "Did Mrs Pike *speak* to him when she met him in the freak show?"

Leota had begun to comb Mrs Fletcher's hair. "I says to her, I says, 'I didn't notice you fallin' on his neck when he was the petrified man—don't tell me you didn't recognize your fine friend?' And she says, 'I didn't recognize him with that white powder all over his face. He just looked familiar,' Mrs Pike says, 'and lots of people look familiar.' But she says that ole petrified man did put her in mind of somebody. She wondered who it was! Kep' her awake, which man she'd ever knew it reminded her of. So when she seen the photo, it all come to her. Like a flash. Mr Petrie. The way he'd turn his head and look at her when she took him in his breakfast."

"Took him in his breakfast!" shrieked Mrs Fletcher. "Listen—don't tell me. I'd 'a' felt something."

"Four women. I guess those women didn't have the faintest notion at the time they'd be worth a hunderd an' twenty-five bucks apiece someday to Mrs Pike. We ast her how old the fella was then, an' she says he musta had one foot in the grave, at least. Can you beat it?"

"Not really petrified at all, of course," said Mrs Fletcher meditatively. She drew herself up. "I'd 'a' felt something," she said proudly.

"Shoot! I did feel somethin'," said Leota. "I tole Fred when I got home I felt so funny. I said, 'Fred, that ole petrified man sure did leave me with a funny feelin'.' He says, 'Funny-haha or funny-peculiar?' and I says, 'Funny-peculiar.' " She pointed her comb into the air emphatically.

"I'll bet you did," said Mrs Fletcher.

They both heard a crackling noise.

Leota screamed, "Billy Boy! What you doin' in my purse?"

"Aw, I'm just eatin' these old stale peanuts up," said Billy Boy.

"You come here to me!" screamed Leota, recklessly flinging down the comb, which scattered a whole ash tray full of bobby pins and knocked down a row of Coca-Cola bottles. "This is the last straw!"

"I caught him! I caught him!" giggled Mrs Fletcher. "I'll hold him on my lap. You bad, bad boy, you! I guess I better learn how to spank little old bad boys," she said.

Leota's eleven o'clock customer pushed open the swing door upon Leota paddling him heartily with the brush, while he gave angry but belittling screams which penetrated beyond the booth and filled the whole curious beauty parlor. From everywhere ladies began to gather round to watch the paddling. Billy Boy kicked both Leota and Mrs Fletcher as hard as he could, Mrs Fletcher with her new fixed smile.

"There, my little man!" gasped Leota. "You won't be able to set down for a week if I knew what I was doin'."

Billy Boy stomped through the group of wild-haired ladies and went out the door, but flung back the words, "If you're so smart, why ain't you rich?"

"Keela, the Outcast Indian Maiden"

One morning in summertime, when all his sons and daughters were off picking plums and Little Lee Roy was all alone, sitting on the porch and only listening to the screech owls away down in the woods, he had a surprise.

First he heard white men talking. He heard two white men coming up the path from the highway. Little Lee Roy ducked his head and held his breath; then he patted all around back of him for his crutches. The chickens all came out from under the house and waited attentively on the steps.

The men came closer. It was the young man who was doing all of the talking. But when they got through the fence, Max, the older man, interrupted him. He tapped him on the arm and pointed his thumb toward Little Lee Roy.

He said, "Bud? Yonder he is."

But the younger man kept straight on talking, in an explanatory voice.

"Bud?" said Max again. "Look, Bud, yonder's the only little clubfooted nigger man was ever around Cane Springs. Is he the party?"

They came nearer and nearer to Little Lee Roy and then stopped and stood there in the middle of the yard. But the young man was so excited he did not seem to realize that they had arrived anywhere. He was only about twenty years old, very sunburned. He talked constantly, making only one gesture— raising his hand stiffly and then moving it a little to one side.

"They dressed it in a red dress, and it ate chickens alive," he said. "I sold tickets and I thought it was worth a dime, honest. They gimme a piece of paper with the thing wrote off I had to say. That was easy. 'Keela, the Outcast Indian Maiden!' I call it out through a pasteboard megaphone. Then ever' time it was fixin' to eat a live chicken, I blowed the sireen out front."

"Just tell me, Bud," said Max, resting back on the heels of his perforated tan-and-white sport shoes. "Is this nigger the one? Is that him sittin' there?"

Little Lee Roy sat huddled and blinking, a smile on his face. . . . But the young man did not look his way.

"Just took the job that time. I didn't mean to—I mean, I meant to go to Port Arthur because my brother was on a boat," he said. "My name is Steve, mister. But I worked with this show selling tickets for three months, and I never would of knowed it was like that if it hadn't been for that man." He arrested his gesture.

"Yeah, what man?" said Max in a hopeless voice.

Little Lee Roy was looking from one white man to the other, excited almost beyond respectful silence. He trembled all over, and a look of amazement and sudden life came into his eyes.

"Two years ago," Steve was saying impatiently. "And we was travelin' through Texas in those ole trucks.—See, the reason nobody ever come clost to it before was they give it a iron bar this long. And tole it if anybody come near, to shake the bar good at 'em, like this. But it couldn't say nothin'. Turned out they'd tole it it couldn't say nothin' to anybody ever, so it just kind of mumbled and growled, like a animal."

"Hee! hee!" This from Little Lee Roy, softly.

"Tell me again," said Max, and just from his look you could tell that everybody knew old Max. "Somehow I can't get it straight in my mind. Is this the boy? Is this little nigger boy the same as this Keela, the Outcast Indian Maiden?"

Up on the porch, above them, Little Lee Roy gave Max a glance full of hilarity, and then bent the other way to catch Steve's next words.

"Why, if anybody was to even come near it or even bresh their shoulder against the rope it'd growl and take on and shake its iron rod. When it would eat the live chickens it'd growl somethin' awful—you ought to heard it."

"Hee! hee!" It was a soft, almost incredulous laugh that began to escape from Little Lee Roy's tight lips, a little mew of delight.

"They'd throw it this chicken, and it would reach out an' grab it. Would sort of rub over the chicken's neck with its thumb an' press on it good, an' then it would bite its head off."

"O.K.," said Max.

"It skint back the feathers and stuff from the neck and sucked the blood. But ever'body said it was still alive." Steve drew closer to Max and fastened his light-colored, troubled eyes on his face.

"O.K."

"Then it would pull the feathers out easy and neat-like, awful fast, an' growl the whole time, kind of moan, an' then it would commence to eat all the white meat. I'd go in an' look at it. I reckon I seen it a thousand times."

"That was you, boy?" Max demanded of Little Lee Roy unexpectedly.

But Little Lee Roy could only say, "Hee! hee!" The little man at the head of the steps where the chickens sat, one on each step, and the two men facing each other below made a pyramid.

Steve stuck his hand out for silence. "They said—I mean, I said it, out front through the megaphone, I said it myself, that it wouldn't eat nothin' but only live meat. It was supposed to be an Indian woman, see, in this red dress an' stockin's. It didn't have on no shoes, so when it drug its foot ever'body could see. . . . When it come to the chicken's heart, it would eat that too, real fast, and the heart would still be jumpin'."

"Wait a second, Bud," said Max briefly, "Say, boy, is this white man here crazy?"

Little Lee Roy burst into hysterical, deprecatory giggles. He said, "Naw suh, don't think so." He tried to catch Steve's eye, seeking appreciation, crying, "Naw suh, don't think he crazy, mista."

Steve gripped Max's arm. "Wait! Wait!" he cried anxiously. "You ain't listenin'. I want to tell you about it. You didn't catch my name—Steve. You never did hear about that little nigger—all that happened to him? Lived in Cane Springs, Miss'ippi?"

"Bud," said Max, disengaging himself, "I don't hear anything. I got a juke box, see, so I don't have to listen."

"Look—I was really the one," said Steve more patiently, but nervously, as if he had been slowly breaking bad news. He walked up and down the bare-swept ground in front of Little Lee Roy's porch, along the row of princess feathers and snow-on-the-mountain. Little Lee Roy's turning head followed him. "I was the one—that's what I'm tellin' you."

"Suppose I was to listen to what every dope comes in Max's Place got to say, *I'd* be nuts," said Max.

"It's all me, see," said Steve. "I know that. I was the one was the cause for it goin' on an' on an' not bein' found out—such an awful thing. It was me, what I said out front through the megaphone.''

He stopped still and stared at Max in despair.

''Look,'' said Max. He sat on the steps, and the chickens hopped off. ''I know I ain't nobody but Max. I got Max's Place. I only run a place, understand, fifty yards down the highway. Liquor buried twenty feet from the premises, and no trouble yet. I ain't ever been up here before. I don't claim to been anywhere. People come to my place. Now. You're the hitchhiker. You're tellin' me, see. You claim a lot of information. If I don't get it I don't get it and I ain't complainin' about it, see. But I think you're nuts, and did from the first. I only come up here with you because I figured you's crazy.''

''Maybe you don't believe I remember every word of it even now,'' Steve was saying gently. ''I think about it at night—that an' drums on the midway. You ever hear drums on the midway?'' He paused and stared politely at Max and Little Lee Roy.

''Yeh,'' said Max.

''Don't it make you feel sad. I remember how the drums was goin' and I was yellin', 'Ladies and gents! Do not try to touch Keela, the Outcast Indian Maiden—she will only beat your brains out with her iron rod, and eat them alive!' '' Steve waved his arm gently in the air, and Little Lee Roy drew back and squealed. '' 'Do not go near her, ladies and gents! I'm warnin' you!' So nobody ever did. Nobody ever come near her. Until that man.''

''Sure,'' said Max. ''That fella.'' He shut his eyes.

''Afterwards when he come up so bold, I remembered seein' him walk up an' buy the ticket an' go in the tent. I'll never forget that man as long as I live. To me he's a sort of—well—''

''Hero,'' said Max.

''I wish I could remember what he looked like. Seem like he was a tallish man with a sort of white face. Seem like he had bad teeth, but I may be wrong. I remember he frowned a lot. Kept frownin'. Whenever he'd buy a ticket, why, he'd frown.''

''Ever seen him since?'' asked Max cautiously, still with his eyes closed. ''Ever hunt him up?''

''No, never did,'' said Steve. Then he went on. ''He'd frown an' buy a ticket ever' day we was in these two little smelly towns in Texas, sometimes three-four times a day, whether it was fixin' to eat a chicken or not.''

''O.K., so he gets in the tent,'' said Max.

''Well, what the man finally done was, he walked right up to the little stand where it was tied up and laid his hand out open on the planks in the platform. He just laid his hand out open there and said, 'Come here,' real low and quick, that-a-way.''

Steve laid his open hand on Little Lee Roy's porch and held it there, frowning in concentration.

"I get it," said Max. "He'd caught on it was a fake."

Steve straightened up. "So ever'body yelled to git away, git away," he continued, his voice rising, "because it was growlin' an' carryin' on an' shakin' its iron bar like they tole it. When I heard all that commotion—boy! I was scared."

"You didn't know it was a fake."

Steve was silent for a moment, and Little Lee Roy held his breath, for fear everything was all over.

"Look," said Steve finally, his voice trembling. "I guess I was supposed to feel bad like this, and you wasn't. I wasn't supposed to ship out on that boat from Port Arthur and all like that. This other had to happen to me—not you all. Feelin' responsible. You'll be O.K., mister, but I won't. I feel awful about it. That poor little old thing."

"Look, you got him right here," said Max quickly. "See him? Use your eyes. He's O.K., ain't he? Looks O.K. to me. It's just you. You're nuts, is all."

"You know—when that man laid out his open hand on the boards, why, it just let go the iron bar," continued Steve, "let it fall down like that—bang—and act like it didn't know what to do. Then it drug itself over to where the fella was standin' an' leaned down an' grabbed holt onto that white man's hand as tight as it could an' cried like a baby. It didn't want to hit him!"

"Hee! hee! hee!"

"No sir, it didn't want to hit him. You know what it wanted?"

Max shook his head.

"It wanted him to help it. So the man said, 'Do you wanna get out of this place, whoever you are?' An' it never answered—none of us knowed it could talk—but it just wouldn't let that man's hand a-loose. It hung on, cryin' like a baby. So the man says, 'Well, wait here till I come back.' "

"Uh-huh?" said Max.

"Went off an' come back with the sheriff. Took us all to jail. But just the man owned the show and his son got took to the pen. They said I could go free. I kep' tellin' 'em I didn't know it wouldn't hit me with the iron bar an' kep' tellin' 'em I didn't know it could tell what you was sayin' to it."

"Yeh, guess you told 'em," said Max.

"By that time I felt bad. Been feelin' bad ever since. Can't hold on to a job or stay in one place for nothin' in the world. They made it stay in jail to see if it could talk or not, and the first night it wouldn't say nothin'. Some time it cried. And they undressed it an' found out it wasn't no outcast Indian woman a-tall. It was a little clubfooted nigger man."

"Hee! hee!"

"You mean it was this boy here—yeh. It was him."

"Washed its face, and it was paint all over it made it look red. It all come off. And it could talk—as good as me or you. But they'd tole it not to, so it never did. They'd tole it if anybody was to come near it they was comin' to git it—and for it to hit 'em quick with that iron bar an' growl. So nobody ever come near it—until that man. I was yellin' outside, tellin' 'em to keep away, keep away. You could see where they'd whup it. They had to whup it some to make it eat all the chickens. It was awful dirty. They let it go back home free, to where they got it in the first place. They made them pay its ticket from Little Oil, Texas, to Cane Springs, Miss'ippi."

"You got a good memory," said Max.

"The way it *started* was," said Steve, in a wondering voice, "the show was just travelin' along in ole trucks through the country, and just seen this little deformed nigger man, sittin' on a fence, and just took it. It couldn't help it."

Little Lee Roy tossed his head back in a frenzy of amusement.

"I found it all out later. I was up on the Ferris wheel with one of the boys—got to talkin' up yonder in the peace an' quiet—an' said they just kind of happened up on it. Like a cyclone happens: it wasn't nothin' it could do. It was just took up." Steve suddenly paled through his sunburn. "An' they found out that back in Miss'ippi it had it a little bitty pair of crutches an' could just go runnin' on 'em!"

"And there they are," said Max.

Little Lee Roy held up a crutch and turned it about, and then snatched it back like a monkey.

"But if it hadn't been for that man, I wouldn't of knowed it till yet. If it wasn't for him bein' so bold. If he hadn't knowed what he was doin'."

"You remember that man this fella's talkin' about, boy?" asked Max, eying Little Lee Roy.

Little Lee Roy, in reluctance and shyness, shook his head gently.

"Naw suh, I can't say as I remembas that ve'y man, suh," he said softly, looking down where just then a sparrow alighted on his child's shoe. He added happily, as if on inspiration, "Now I remembas *this* man."

Steve did not look up, but when Max shook with silent laughter, alarm seemed to seize him like a spasm in his side. He walked painfully over and stood in the shade for a few minutes, leaning his head on a sycamore tree.

"Seemed like that man just studied it out an' knowed it was somethin' wrong," he said presently, his voice coming more remotely than ever. "But I didn't know. I can't look at nothin' an' be sure what it is. Then afterwards I know. Then I see how it was."

"Yeh, but you're nuts," said Max affably.

"You wouldn't of knowed it either!" cried Steve in sudden boyish, defensive anger. Then he came out from under the tree and stood again almost pleadingly in the sun, facing Max where he was sitting below Little Lee Roy on the steps. "You'd of let it go on an' on when they made it do those things—just like I did."

"Bet I could tell a man from a woman and an Indian from a nigger though," said Max.

Steve scuffed the dust into little puffs with his worn shoe. The chickens scattered, alarmed at last.

Little Lee Roy looked from one man to the other radiantly, his hands pressed over his grinning gums.

Then Steve sighed, and as if he did not know what else he could do, he reached out and without any warning hit Max in the jaw with his fist. Max fell off the steps.

Little Lee Roy suddenly sat as still and dark as a statue, looking on.

"Say! Say!" cried Steve. He pulled shyly at Max where he lay on the ground, with his lips pursed up like a whistler, and then stepped back. He looked horrified. "How you feel?"

"Lousy," said Max thoughtfully. "Let me alone." He raised up on one elbow and lay there looking all around, at the cabin, at Little Lee Roy sitting cross-legged on the porch, and at Steve with his hand out. Finally he got up.

"I can't figure out how I could of ever knocked down an athaletic guy like you. I had to do it," said Steve. "But I guess you don't understand. I had to hit you. First you didn't believe me, and then it didn't bother you."

"That's all O.K., only hush," said Max, and added, "Some dope is always giving me the low-down on something, but this is the first time one of 'em ever got away with a thing like this. I got to watch out."

"I hope it don't stay black long," said Steve.

"I got to be going," said Max. But he waited. "What you want to transact with Keela? You come a long way to see him." He stared at Steve with his eyes wide open now, and interested.

"Well, I was goin' to give him some money or somethin', I guess, if I ever found him, only now I ain't got any," said Steve defiantly.

"O.K.," said Max. "Here's some change for you, boy. Just take it. Go on back in the house. Go on."

Little Lee Roy took the money speechlessly, and then fell upon his yellow crutches and hopped with miraculous rapidity away through the door. Max stared after him for a moment.

"As for you"—he brushed himself off, turned to Steve and then said, "When did you eat last?"

"Well, I'll tell you," said Steve.

"Not here," said Max. "I didn't go to ask you a question. Just follow me. We serve eats at Max's Place, and I want to play the juke box. You eat, and I'll listen to the juke box."

"Well . . ." said Steve. "But when it cools off I got to catch a ride some place."

"Today while all you all was gone, and not a soul in de house," said Little Lee Roy at the supper table that night, "two white mens come heah to de house. Wouldn't come in. But talks to me about de ole times when I use to be wid de circus—"

"Hush up, Pappy," said the children.

ALICE WALKER

Walker was born in 1944 in Eatonton, Georgia. (Also the home of Joel Chandler Harris.) Her novels have established her as an important American writer, but she won my heart some years ago when she collected the money to erect a headstone for Zora Neale Hurston, still a neglected figure at that time. Walker also edited a Hurston reader. The following drolly counter-cooptational fable inspired by Elvis and Big Mama Thornton appears in Walker's second collection of short stories, You Can't Keep a Good Woman Down. *When Elvis died, Big Mama was asked what she thought about the fact that her original version of "You Ain't Nothing but a Hound Dog" earned her a hundred dollars whereas Elvis's cover of it earned him millions. She said, "I'm still here to spend my hundred dollars."*

"Nineteen Fifty-five"

1955

The car is a brandnew red Thunderbird convertible, and it's passed the house more than once. It slows down real slow now, and stops at the curb. An older gentleman dressed like a Baptist deacon gets out on the side near the house, and a young fellow who looks about sixteen gets out on the driver's side. They are white, and I wonder what in the world they doing in this neighborhood.

Well, I say to J. T., put your shirt on, anyway, and let me clean these glasses offa the table.

We had been watching the ballgame on TV. I wasn't actually watching, I was sort of daydreaming, with my foots up in J. T.'s lap.

I seen 'em coming on up the walk, brisk, like they coming to sell something, and then they rung the bell, and J. T. declined to put on a shirt but instead disappeared into the bedroom where the other television is. I turned down the one in the living room; I figured I'd be rid of these two double quick and J. T. could come back out again.

Are you Gracie Mae Still? asked the old guy, when I opened the door and put my hand on the lock inside the screen.

And I don't need to buy a thing, said I.

What makes you think we're sellin'? he asks, in that hearty Southern way that makes my eyeballs ache.

Well, one way or another and they're inside the house and the first thing the young fellow does is raise the TV a couple of decibels. He's about five feet nine, sort of womanish looking, with real dark white skin and a red pouting mouth. His hair is black and curly and he looks like a Loosianna creole.

About one of your songs, says the deacon. He is maybe sixty, with white hair and beard, white silk shirt, black linen suit, black tie and black shoes. His cold gray eyes look like they're sweating.

One of my songs?

Traynor here just *loves* your songs. Don't you, Traynor? He nudges Traynor with his elbow. Traynor blinks, says something I can't catch in a pitch I don't register.

The boy learned to sing and dance livin' round you people out in the country. Practically cut his teeth on you.

Traynor looks up at me and bites his thumbnail.

I laugh.

Well, one way or another they leave with my agreement that they can record one of my songs. The deacon writes me a check for five hundred dollars, the boy grunts his awareness of the transaction, and I am laughing all over myself by the time I rejoin J. T.

Just as I am snuggling down beside him though I hear the front door bell going off again.

Forgit his hat? asks J. T.

I hope not, I say.

The deacon stands there leaning on the door frame and once again I'm thinking of those sweaty-looking eyeballs of his. I wonder if sweat makes your eyeballs pink because his are sure pink. Pink and gray and it strikes me that nobody I'd care to know is behind them.

I forgot one little thing, he says pleasantly. I forgot to tell you Traynor and I would like to buy up all of those records you made of the song. I tell you we sure do love it.

Well, love it or not, I'm not so stupid as to let them do that without making 'em pay. So I says, Well, that's gonna cost you. Because, really, that song never did sell all that good, so I was glad they was going to buy it up. But on the other hand, them two listening to my song by themselves, and nobody else getting to hear me sing it, give me a pause.

Well, one way or another the deacon showed me where I would come out ahead on any deal he had proposed so far. Didn't I give you five hundred dollars? he asked. What white man—and don't even need to mention colored—would give you more? We buy up all your records of that particular song: first, you git royalties. Let me ask you, how much you sell that song for in the first place? Fifty dollars? A hundred, I say. And no royalties from it yet, right? Right. Well, when we buy up all of them records you gonna git royalties. And that's gonna make all them race record shops sit up and take notice of Gracie Mae Still. And they gonna push all them other records of yourn they got. And you no doubt will become one of the big name colored recording artists. And then we can offer you another five hundred dollars for letting us do all this for you. And by God you'll be sittin' pretty! You can go out and buy you the kind of outfit a star should have. Plenty sequins and yards of red satin.

I had done unlocked the screen when I saw I could get some more money out of him. Now I held it wide open while he squeezed through the opening between me and the door. He whipped out another piece of paper and I signed it.

He sort of trotted out to the car and slid in beside Traynor, whose head was back against the seat. They swung around in a u-turn in front of the house and then they was gone.

J. T. was putting his shirt on when I got back to the bedroom. Yankees beat the Orioles 10–6, he said. I believe I'll drive out to Paschal's pond and go fishing. Wanta go?

While I was putting on my pants J. T. was holding the two checks.

I'm real proud of a woman that can make cash money without leavin' home, he said. And I said Umph. Because we met on the road with me singing in first one little low-life jook after another, making ten dollars a night for myself if I was lucky, and sometimes bringin' home nothing but my life. And J. T. just loved them times. The way I was fast and flashy and always on the go from one town to another. He loved the way my singin' made the dirt farmers cry like babies and the womens shout Honey, hush! But that's mens. They loves any style to which you can get 'em accustomed.

1 9 5 6

My little grandbaby called me one night on the phone: Little Mama, Little
Mama, there's a white man on the television singing one of your songs! Turn
on channel 5.

Lord, if it wasn't Traynor. Still looking half asleep from the neck up, but
kind of awake in a nasty way from the waist down. He wasn't doing too bad
with my song either, but it wasn't just the song the people in the audience was
screeching and screaming over, it was that nasty little jerk he was doing from
the waist down.

Well, Lord have mercy, I said, listening to him. If I'da closed my eyes, it
could have been me. He had followed every turning of my voice, side streets,
avenues, red lights, train crossings and all. It give me a chill.

Everywhere I went I heard Traynor singing my song, and all the little white
girls just eating it up. I never had so many ponytails switched across my line of
vision in my life. They was so *proud*. He was a *genius*.

Well, all that year I was trying to lose weight anyway and that and high
blood pressure and sugar kept me pretty well occupied. Traynor had made a
smash from a song of mine, I still had seven hundred dollars of the original one
thousand dollars in the bank, and I felt if I could just bring my weight down,
life would be sweet.

1 9 5 7

I lost ten pounds in 1956. That's what I give myself for Christmas. And J. T.
and me and the children and their friends and grandkids of all description had
just finished dinner—over which I had put on nine and a half of my lost
ten—when who should appear at the front door but Traynor. Little Mama,
Little Mama! It's that white man who sings ——— ——— ———. The
children didn't call it my song anymore. Nobody did. It was funny how that
happened. Traynor and the deacon had bought up all my records, true, but on
his record he had put "written by Gracie Mae Still." But that was just another
name on the label, like "produced by Apex Records."

On the TV he was inclined to dress like the deacon told him. But now he
looked presentable.

Merry Christmas, said he.

And same to you, Son.

I don't know why I called him Son. Well, one way or another they're all
our sons. The only requirement is that they be younger than us. But then
again, Traynor seemed to be aging by the minute.

You looks tired, I said. Come on in and have a glass of Christmas cheer.

J. T. ain't never in his life been able to act decent to a white man he wasn't working for, but he poured Traynor a glass of bourbon and water, then he took all the children and grandkids and friends and whatnot out to the den. After while I heard Traynor's voice singing the song, coming from the stereo console. It was just the kind of Christmas present my kids would consider cute.

I looked at Traynor, complicit. But he looked like it was the last thing in the world he wanted to hear. His head was pitched forward over his lap, his hands holding his glass and his elbows on his knees.

I done sung that song seem like a million times this year, he said. I sung it on the Grand Ole Opry, I sung it on the Ed Sullivan show. I sung it on Mike Douglas, I sung it at the Cotton Bowl, the Orange Bowl. I sung it at Festivals. I sung it at Fairs. I sung it overseas in Rome, Italy, and once in a submarine *underseas.* I've sung it and sung it, and I'm making forty thousand dollars a day offa it, and you know what, I don't have the faintest notion what that song means.

Whatchumean, what do it mean? It mean what it says. All I could think was: These suckers is making forty thousand a *day* offa my song and now they gonna come back and try to swindle me out of the original thousand.

It's just a song, I said. Cagey. When you fool around with a lot of no count mens you sing a bunch of 'em. I shrugged.

Oh, he said. Well. He started brightening up. I just come by to tell you I think you are a great singer.

He didn't blush, saying that. Just said it straight out.

And I brought you a little Christmas present too. Now you take this little box and you hold it until I drive off. Then you take it outside under that first streetlight back up the street always in front of that green house. Then you open the box and see . . . Well, just *see.*

What had come over this boy, I wondered, holding the box. I looked out the window in time to see another white man come up and get in the car with him and then two more cars full of white mens start out behind him. They was all in long black cars that looked like a funeral procession.

Little Mama, Little Mama, what it is? One of my grandkids come running up and started pulling at the box. It was wrapped in gay Christmas paper—the thick, rich kind that it's hard to picture folks making just to throw away.

J. T. and the rest of the crowd followed me out the house, up the street to the streetlight and in front of the green house. Nothing was there but somebody's gold-grilled white Cadillac. Brandnew and most distracting. We got to looking at it so till I almost forgot the little box in my hand. While the others were busy making 'miration I carefully took off the paper and ribbon and folded them up and put them in my pants pocket. What should I see but a pair of genuine solid gold caddy keys.

Dangling the keys in front of everybody's nose, I unlocked the caddy, motioned for J.T. to git in on the other side, and us didn't come back home for two days.

1 9 6 0

Well, the boy was sure nuff famous by now. He was still a mite shy of twenty but already they was calling him the Emperor of Rock and Roll.

Then what should happen but the draft.

Well, says J. T. There goes all this Emperor of Rock and Roll business.

But even in the army the womens was on him like white on rice. We watched it on the News.

> Dear Gracie Mae [*he wrote from Germany*],
>
> How you? Fine I hope as this leaves me doing real well. Before I come in the army I was gaining a lot of weight and gitting jittery from making all them dumb movies. But now I exercise and eat right and get plenty of rest. I'm more awake than I been in ten years.
>
> I wonder if you are writing any more songs?
>
> Sincerely,
> Traynor

I wrote him back:

> Dear Son,
>
> We is all fine in the Lord's good grace and hope this finds you the same. J. T. and me be out all times of the day and night in that car you give me—which you know you didn't have to do. Oh, and I do appreciate the mink and the new self-cleaning oven. But if you send anymore stuff to eat from Germany I'm going to have to open up a store in the neighborhood just to get rid of it. Really, we have more than enough of everything. The Lord is good to us and we don't know Want.
>
> Glad to here you is well and gitting your right rest. There ain't nothing like exercising to help that along. J. T. and me work some part of every day that we don't go fishing in the garden.
>
> Well, so long Soldier.
>
> Sincerely,
> Gracie Mae

He wrote:

Dear Gracie Mae,

I hope you and J. T. like that automatic power tiller I had one of the stores back home send you. I went through a mountain of catalogs looking for it—I wanted something that even a woman could use.

I've been thinking about writing some songs of my own but every time I finish one it don't seem to be about nothing I've actually lived myself. My agent keeps sending me other people's songs but they just sound mooney. I can hardly git through 'em without gagging.

Everybody still loves that song of yours. They ask me all the time what do I think it means, really. I mean, they want to know just what *I* want to know. Where out of your life did it come from?

SINCERELY,
TRAYNOR

1 9 6 8

I didn't see the boy for seven years. No. Eight. Because just about everybody was dead when I saw him again. Malcolm X, King, the president and his brother, and even J. T. J. T. died of a head cold. It just settled in his head like a block of ice, he said, and nothing we did moved it until one day he just leaned out the bed and died.

His good friend Horace helped me put him away, and then about a year later Horace and me started going together. We was sitting out on the front porch swing one summer night, dusk-dark, and I saw this great procession of lights winding to a stop.

Holy Toledo! said Horace. (He's got a real sexy voice like Ray Charles.) Look *at* it. He meant the long line of flashy cars and the white men in white summer suits jumping out on the drivers' sides and standing at attention. With wings they could pass for angels, with hoods they could be the Klan.

Traynor comes waddling up the walk.

And suddenly I know what it is he could pass for. An Arab like the ones you see in storybooks. Plump and soft and with never a care about weight. Because with so much money, who cares? Traynor is almost dressed like someone from a storybook too. He has on, I swear, about ten necklaces. Two sets of bracelets on his arms, at least one ring on every finger, and some kind of shining buckles on his shoes, so that when he walks you get quite a few twinkling lights.

Gracie Mae, he says, coming up to give me a hug. J. T.

I explain that J. T. passed. That this is Horace.

Horace, he says, puzzled but polite, sort of rocking back on his heels, Horace.

That's it for Horace. He goes in the house and don't come back.

Looks like you and me is gained a few, I say.

He laughs. The first time I ever heard him laugh. It don't sound much like a laugh and I can't swear that it's better than no laugh a'tall.

He's gitting fat for sure, but he's still slim compared to me. I'll never see three hundred pounds again and I've just about said (excuse me) fuck it. I got to thinking about it one day an' I thought: aside from the fact that they say it's unhealthy, my fat ain't never been no trouble. Mens always have loved me. My kids ain't never complained. Plus they's fat. And fat like I is I looks distinguished. You see me coming and know somebody's *there*.

Gracie Mae, he says, I've come with a personal invitation to you to my house tomorrow for dinner. He laughed. What did it sound like? I couldn't place it. See them men out there? he asked me. I'm sick and tired of eating with them. They don't never have nothing to talk about. That's why I eat so much. But if you come to dinner tomorrow we can talk about the old days. You can tell me about that farm I bought you.

I sold it, I said.

You did?

Yeah, I said, I did. Just cause I said I liked to exercise by working in a garden didn't mean I wanted five hundred acres! Anyhow, I'm a city girl now. Raised in the country it's true. Dirt poor—the whole bit—but that's all behind me now.

Oh well, he said, I didn't mean to offend you.

We sat a few minutes listening to the crickets.

Then he said: You wrote that song while you was still on the farm, didn't you, or was it right after you left?

You had somebody spying on me? I asked.

You and Bessie Smith got into a fight over it once, he said.

You *is* been spying on me!

But I don't know what the fight was about, he said. Just like I don't know what happened to your second husband. Your first one died in the Texas electric chair. Did you know that? Your third one beat you up, stole your touring costumes and your car and retired with a chorine to Tuskegee. He laughed. He's still there.

I had been mad, but suddenly I calmed down. Traynor was talking very dreamily. It was dark but seems like I could tell his eyes weren't right. It was like some*thing* was sitting there talking to me but not necessarily with a person behind it.

You gave up on marrying and seem happier for it. He laughed again. I married but it never went like it was supposed to. I never could squeeze any of my own life either into it or out of it. It was like singing somebody else's record. I copied the way it was sposed to be *exactly* but I never had a clue what marriage meant.

I bought her a diamond ring big as your fist. I bought her clothes. I built her a mansion. But right away she didn't want the boys to stay there. Said they smoked up the bottom floor. Hell, there were *five* floors.

No need to grieve, I said. No need to. Plenty more where she came from.

He perked up. That's part of what that song means, ain't it? No need to grieve. Whatever it is, there's plenty more down the line.

I never really believed that way back when I wrote that song, I said. It was all bluffing then. The trick is to live long enough to put your young bluffs to use. Now if I was to sing that song today I'd tear it up. 'Cause I done lived long enough to know it's *true.* Them words could hold me up.

I ain't lived that long, he said.

Look like you on your way, I said. I don't know why, but the boy seemed to need some encouraging. And I don't know, seem like one way or another you talk to rich white folks and you end up reassuring *them.* But what the hell, by now I feel something for the boy. I wouldn't be in his bed all alone in the middle of the night for nothing. Couldn't be nothing worse than being famous the world over for something you don't even understand. That's what I tried to tell Bessie. She wanted that same song. Overheard me practicing it one day, said, with her hands on her hips: Gracie Mae, I'ma sing your song tonight. I *likes* it.

Your lips be too swole to sing, I said. She was mean and she was strong, but I trounced her.

Ain't you famous enough with your own stuff? I said. Leave mine alone. Later on, she thanked me. By then she was Miss Bessie Smith to the World, and I was still Miss Gracie Mae Nobody from Notasulga.

The next day all these limousines arrived to pick me up. Five cars and twelve bodyguards. Horace picked that morning to start painting the kitchen.

Don't paint the kitchen, fool, I said. The only reason that dumb boy of ours is going to show me his mansion is because he intends to present us with a new house.

What you gonna do with it? he asked me, standing there in his shirtsleeves stirring the paint.

Sell it. Give it to the children. Live in it on weekends. It don't matter what I do. He sure don't care.

Horace just stood there shaking his head. Mama you sure looks *good,* he says. Wake me up when you git back.

Fool, I say, and pat my wig in front of the mirror.

The boy's house is something else. First you come to this mountain, and then you commence to drive and drive up this road that's lined with magnolias. Do magnolias grow on mountains? I was wondering. And you come to lakes and you come to ponds and you come to deer and you come up on some sheep. And I figure these two is sposed to represent England and Wales. Or something out of Europe. And you just keep on coming to stuff. And it's all pretty. Only the man driving my car don't look at nothing but the road. Fool. And then *finally,* after all this time, you begin to go up the driveway. And there's more magnolias—only they're not in such good shape. It's sort of cool up this high and I don't think they're gonna make it. And then I see this building that looks like if it had a name it would be The Tara Hotel. Columns and steps and outdoor chandeliers and rocking chairs. Rocking chairs? Well, and there's the boy on the steps dressed in a dark green satin jacket like you see folks wearing on TV late at night, and he looks sort of like a fat dracula with all that house rising behind him, and standing beside him there's this little white vision of loveliness that he introduces as his wife.

He's nervous when he introduces us and he says to her: This is Gracie Mae Still, I want you to know me. I mean . . . and she gives him a look that would fry meat.

Won't you come in, Gracie Mae, she says, and that's the last I see of her.

He fishes around for something to say or do and decides to escort me to the kitchen. We go through the entry and the parlor and the breakfast room and the dining room and the servants' passage and finally get there. The first thing I notice is that, altogether, there are five stoves. He looks about to introduce me to one.

Wait a minute, I say. Kitchens don't do nothing for me. Let's go sit on the front porch.

Well, we hike back and we sit in the rocking chairs rocking until dinner.

Gracie Mae, he says down the table, taking a piece of fried chicken from the woman standing over him, I got a little surprise for you.

It's a house, ain't it? I ask, spearing a chitlin.

You're getting *spoiled,* he says. And the way he says *spoiled* sounds funny. He slurs it. It sounds like his tongue is too thick for his mouth. Just that quick he's finished the chicken and is now eating chitlins *and* a pork chop. *Me* spoiled, I'm thinking.

I already got a house. Horace is right this minute painting the kitchen. I bought that house. My kids feel comfortable in that house.

But this one I bought you is just like mine. Only a little smaller.

I still don't need no house. And anyway who would clean it?

He looks surprised.

Really, I think, some peoples advance *so* slowly.

I hadn't thought of that. But what the hell, I'll get you somebody to live in.

I don't want other folks living 'round me. Makes me nervous.

You *don't?* It *do?*

What I want to wake up and see folks I don't even know for?

He just sits there downtable staring at me. Some of that feeling is in the song, ain't it? Not the words, the *feeling*. What I want to wake up and see folks I don't even know for? But I see twenty folks a day I don't even know, including my wife.

This food wouldn't be bad to wake up to though, I said. The boy had found the genius of corn bread.

He looked at me real hard. He laughed. Short. They want what you got but they don't want you. They want what I got only it ain't mine. That's what makes 'em so hungry for me when I sing. They getting the flavor of something but they ain't getting the thing itself. They like a pack of hound dogs trying to gobble up a scent.

You talking 'bout your fans?

Right. Right. He says.

Don't worry 'bout your fans, I say. They don't know their asses from a hole in the ground. I doubt there's a honest one in the bunch.

That's the point. Dammit, that's the point! He hits the table with his fist. It's so solid it don't even quiver. You need a honest audience! You can't have folks that's just gonna lie right back to you.

Yeah, I say, it was small compared to yours, but I had one. It would have been worth my life to try to sing 'em somebody else's stuff that I didn't know nothing about.

He must have pressed a buzzer under the table. One of his flunkies zombies up.

Git Johnny Carson, he says.

On the phone? asks the zombie.

On the phone, says Traynor, what you think I mean, git him offa the front porch? Move your ass.

So two weeks later we's on the Johnny Carson show.

Traynor is all corseted down nice and looks a little bit fat but mostly good. And all the women that grew up on him and my song squeal and squeal. Traynor says: The lady who wrote my first hit record is here with us tonight, and she's agreed to sing it for all of us, just like she sung it forty-five years ago. Ladies and Gentlemen, the great Gracie Mae Still!

Well, I had tried to lose a couple of pounds my own self, but failing that I had me a very big dress made. So I sort of rolls over next to Traynor, who is dwarfted by me, so that when he puts his arm around the back of me to try to hug me it looks funny to the audience and they laugh.

I can see this pisses him off. But I smile out there at 'em. Imagine squealing for twenty years and not knowing why you're squealing? No more sense of endings and beginnings than hogs.

It don't matter, Son, I say. Don't fret none over me.

I commence to sing. And I sound —— wonderful. Being able to sing good ain't all about having a good singing voice a'tall. A good singing voice helps. But when you come up in the Hard Shell Baptist church like I did you understand early that the fellow that sings is the singer. Them that waits for programs and arrangements and letters from home is just good voices occupying body space.

So there I am singing my own song, my own way. And I give it all I got and enjoy every minute of it. When I finish Traynor is standing up clapping and clapping and beaming at first me and then the audience like I'm his mama for true. The audience claps politely for about two seconds.

Traynor looks disgusted.

He comes over and tries to hug me again. The audience laughs.

Johnny Carson looks at us like we both weird.

Traynor is mad as hell. He's supposed to sing something called a love ballad. But instead he takes the mike, turns to me and says: Now see if my imitation still holds up. He goes into the same song, *our* song, I think, looking out at his flaky audience. And he sings it just the way he always did. My voice, my tone, my inflection, everything. But he forgets a couple of lines. Even before he's finished the matronly squeals begin.

He sits down next to me looking whipped.

It don't matter, Son, I say, patting his hand. You don't even know those people. Try to make the people you know happy.

Is that in the song? he asks.

Maybe. I say.

1 9 7 7

For a few years I hear from him, then nothing. But trying to lose weight takes all the attention I got to spare. I finally faced up to the fact that my fat is the hurt I don't admit, not even to myself, and that I been trying to bury it from the day I was born. But also when you git real old, to tell the truth, it ain't as pleasant. It gits lumpy and slack. Yuck. So one day I said to Horace, I'ma git this shit offa me.

And he fell in with the program like he always try to do and Lord such a procession of salads and cottage cheese and fruit juice!

One night I dreamed Traynor had split up with his fifteenth wife. He said: *You meet 'em for no reason. You date 'em for no reason. You marry 'em for no reason. I do it all but I swear it's just like somebody else doing it. I feel like I can't remember Life.*

The boy's in trouble, I said to Horace.

You've always said that, he said.

I have?

Yeah. You always said he looked asleep. You can't sleep through life if you wants to live it.

You not such a fool after all, I said, pushing myself up with my cane and hobbling over to where he was. Let me sit down on your lap, I said, while this salad I ate takes effect.

In the morning we heard Traynor was dead. Some said fat, some said heart, some said alcohol, some said drugs. One of the children called from Detroit. Them dumb fans of his is on a crying rampage, she said. You just ought to turn on the t.v.

But I didn't want to see 'em. They was crying and crying and didn't even know what they was crying for. One day this is going to be a pitiful country, I thought.

DONALD BARTHELME

I grant you that the surrealistic, parodistic, bankshot-behind-the-back New Yorker *stories and novels of Donald Barthelme do not constitute the first body of work that comes to mind when you think of Southern humor. But surely one reason he was so slick was that he hailed from Houston. And way back down behind his poker-face obliquity, Barthelme had—as I think you can divine from this story about a Mississippian getting over—a lot of good old down-to-earth, wanting-to-grin heart. He just had a funny way of showing it, that's all. I know I felt a pang in 1989 when he died, back in Houston, at the age of fifty-eight.*

"The King of Jazz"

Well I'm the king of jazz now, thought Hokie Mokie to himself as he oiled the slide on his trombone. Hasn't been a 'bone man been king of jazz for many years. But now that Spicy MacLammermoor, the old king, is dead, I guess I'm it. Maybe I better play a few notes out of this window here, to reassure myself.

"Wow!" said somebody standing on the sidewalk. "Did you hear that?"

"I did," said his companion.

"Can you distinguish our great homemade American jazz performers, each from the other?"

"Used to could."

"Then who was that playing?"

"Sounds like Hokie Mokie to me. Those few but perfectly selected notes have the real epiphanic glow."

"The what?"

"The real epiphanic glow, such as is obtained only by artists of the caliber of Hokie Mokie, who's from Pass Christian, Mississippi. He's the king of jazz, now that Spicy MacLammermoor is gone."

Hokie Mokie put his trombone in its trombone case and went to a gig. At the gig everyone fell back before him, bowing.

"Hi Bucky! Hi Zoot! Hi Freddie! Hi Thad! Hi Roy! Hi Dexter! Hi Jo! Hi Willie! Hi Greens!"

"What we gonna play, Hokie? You the king of jazz now, you gotta decide."

"How 'bout 'Smoke'?"

"Wow!" everybody said. "Did you hear that? Hokie Mokie can just knock a fella out, just the way he pronounces a word. What a intonation on that boy! God Almighty!"

"I don't want to play 'Smoke,' " somebody said.

"Would you repeat that, stranger?"

"I don't want to play 'Smoke.' 'Smoke' is dull. I don't like the changes. I refuse to play 'Smoke.' "

"He refuses to play 'Smoke.' But Hokie Mokie is the king of jazz and he says 'Smoke'!"

"Man, you from outa town or something? What do you mean you refuse to play 'Smoke'? How'd you get on this gig anyhow? Who hired you?"

"I am Hideo Yamaguchi, from Tokyo, Japan."

"Oh, you're one of those Japanese cats, eh?"

"Yes I'm the top trombone man in all of Japan."

"Well you're welcome here until we hear you play. Tell me, is the Tennessee Tea Room still the top jazz place in Tokyo?"

"No, the top jazz place in Tokyo is the Square Box now."

"That's nice. O.K., now we gonna play 'Smoke' just like Hokie said. You ready, Hokie? O.K., give you four for nothin'. One! Two! Three! Four!"

The two men who had been standing under Hokie's window had followed him to the club. Now they said:

"Good God!"

"Yes, that's Hokie's famous 'English sunrise' way of playing. Playing with lots of rays coming out of it, some red rays, some blue rays, some green rays, some green stemming from a violet center, some olive stemming from a tan center—''

''That young Japanese fellow is pretty good, too.''

''Yes, he is pretty good. And he holds his horn in a peculiar way. That's frequently the mark of a superior player.''

''Bent over like that with his head between his knees—good God, he's sensational!''

He's sensational, Hokie thought. Maybe I ought to kill him.

But at that moment somebody came in the door pushing in front of him a four-and-one-half-octave marimba. Yes, it was Fat Man Jones, and he began to play even before he was fully in the door.

''What're we playing?''

'' 'Billie's Bounce.' ''

''That's what I thought it was. What're we in?''

''F.''

''That's what I thought we were in. Didn't you use to play with Maynard?''

''Yeah I was on that band for a while until I was in the hospital.''

''What for?''

''I was tired.''

''What can we add to Hokie's fantastic playing?''

''How 'bout some rain or stars?''

''Maybe that's presumptuous.''

''Ask him if he'd mind.''

''You ask him. I'm scared. You don't fool around with the king of jazz. That young Japanese guy's pretty good, too.''

''He's sensational.''

''You think he's playing in Japanese?''

''Well I don't think it's English.''

This trombone's been makin' my neck green for thirty-five years, Hokie thought. How come I got to stand up to yet another challenge, this late in life?

''Well, Hideo—''

''Yes, Mr. Mokie?''

''You did well on both 'Smoke' and 'Billie's Bounce.' You're just about as good as me, I regret to say. In fact, I've decided you're *better* than me. It's a hideous thing to contemplate, but there it is. I have only been king of jazz for twenty-four hours, but the unforgiving logic of this art demands we bow to Truth, when we hear it.''

''Maybe you're mistaken.''

''No, I got ears. I'm not mistaken. Hideo Yamaguchi is the new king of jazz.

''You want to be king emeritus?''

"No, I'm just going to fold up my horn and steal away. This gig is yours, Hideo. You can pick the next tune."

"How 'bout 'Cream'?"

"O.K., you heard what Hideo said, it's 'Cream.' You ready, Hideo?"

"Hokie, you don't have to leave. You can play too. Just move a little over to the side there—"

"Thank you, Hideo, that's very gracious of you. I guess I will play a little, since I'm still here. Sotto voce, of course."

"Hideo is wonderful on 'Cream'!"

"Yes, I imagine it's his best tune."

"What's that sound coming in from the side there?"

"Which side?"

"The left."

"You mean that sound that sounds like the cutting edge of life? That sounds like polar bears crossing Arctic ice pans? That sounds like a heard of musk ox in full flight? That sounds like male walruses diving to the bottom of the sea? That sounds like fumaroles smoking on the slopes of Mt. Katmai? That sounds like the wild turkey walking through the deep, soft forest? That sounds like beavers chewing trees in an Appalachian marsh. That sounds like an oyster fungus growing on an aspen trunk? That sounds like a mule deer wandering a montane of the Sierra Nevada? That sounds like prairie dogs kissing? That sounds like witchgrass tumbling or a river meandering? That sounds like manatees munching seaweed at Cape Sable? That sounds like coatimundis moving in packs across the face of Arkansas? That sounds like—"

"Good God, it's Hokie! Even with a cup mute on, he's blowing Hideo right off the stand!"

"Hideo's playing on his knees now! Good God, he's reaching into his belt for a large steel sword—Stop him!"

"Wow! That was the most exciting 'Cream' ever played. Is Hideo all right?"

"Yes, somebody is getting him a glass of water."

"You're my man, Hokie. That was the dadblangedest thing I ever saw!"

"You're the king of jazz once again!"

"Hokie Mokie is the most happening thing there is!"

"Yes, Mr. Hokie sir, I have to admit, you blew me right off the stand. I see I have many years of work and study before me still."

"That's O.K., son. Don't think a thing about it. It happens to the best of us. Or it almost happens to the best of us. Now I want everybody to have a good time because we're gonna play 'Flats.' 'Flats' is next."

"With your permission, sir, I will return to my hotel and pack. I am most grateful for everything I have learned here."

"That's O.K., Hideo. Have a nice day. He-he. Now, 'Flats.' "

NICK TOSCHES

Tosches has written a compelling biography of Dean Martin (believe it or not) and a number of articles about country music and other strange heartland institutions for leading magazines. He is also the author of a full-length biography of Jerry Lee Lewis, Hellfire, *but the glimpse of the Killer that stays with me is this one from Tosches' 1978 book* Country: The Biggest Music in America, *which gets into several aspects of country-and-western more pungent than apple pie.*

A Jerry Lee Session

Patsy Lynn Kochin, esteemed deposed president of the Jerry Lee Lewis Fan Club, told in her *Newsletter* of a night she spent with Jerry Lee in a Boston Ramada Inn. It is one of my favorite passages.

"Jerry would play the piano with one hand and sing while he found what he was looking for in the Bible using the other hand. He then read Acts Ch. 2. . . . Jerry also spoke on the last days which he says we are living in—the end almost here. . . . Then he told us why the South lost the war. . . . Jerry then explained the difference in a 99 year sentence and a 100 year sentence. . . ."

The truth is that Jerry Lee has always known the end is almost here, must be almost here, and that the almost-here end is the heart of it all; without it, there is no rock-and-roll, no jukebox epiphany, just pale, soft people looking from the window.

Writers have not had much success interviewing Jerry Lee. One night in Brooklyn in 1973, an editor of *Country Music* asked Jerry Lee a question. The interviewee responded by leaping across the table, breaking off the butt of his pint-bottle of Heaven Hill, and sticking the interviewer in the neck with it.

Armed, I attended a Jerry Lee Lewis recording session in Memphis. Pappy Lewis was there. On his way to the studio, Pappy had been chased down the highway by the Memphis police as he rushed along in Jerry Lee's white, custom-built Lincoln (1-FZ541) at a speed of 110 miles per hour. Pappy's reaction to his situation was ingenious. He increased his speed until he put enough distance between himself and the police so that he was invisible to them. Then he skidded the car to the side of the road, jumped in the back seat, and waited. The police arrived in a moment. "Glad you showed up, boys," Pappy said. "That crazy man drivin' this car was like to get us killed. When he saw your light flashin', he stopped the car and ran off into them trees there." The cops stared dully at the vacant driver's seat. "My son's Jerry Lee Lewis. He's makin' a record on Popular Avenue, and I gotta be there. This is his car. I'm in no condition to drive myself. How's about one you boys takin' me? Jerry be purty mad I don't git his car back to him." He was driven to the studio.

Earlier in the day, at Jerry Lee's office, the scene was something like this: Jerry was on the telephone, shouting. "He's gonna sue *me?* You tell that sonofabitch husband of yours that if he tries to sue me I'm gonna come over there and give him the biggest ass-whuppin' he ever got in his life." There were perhaps 12 other people in the room. Everyone was drunk, and a few were falling asleep as Jerry shouted into the phone. It was ten o'clock in the morning. For some reason, Jerry Lee was drinking bourbon and orange juice, a combination the color of wan excrement. "He's on a health kick," somebody suggested. Pappy Lewis decided to try some orange juice in his bourbon, so he asked someone to give him the Tropicana container from Jerry's desk. Jerry Lee banged the hand with the receiver as it was about to touch the orange juice. From the wielded receiver, a woman's voice was faint and shrill: "What the fuck was that?" Jerry was indignant. "What the hell you doin' my orange juice?" A voice attached to the hand, a drunken voice, answered, "It's for your father." Jerry Lee returned the receiver to his ear. "Shoot. Tell him to go buy his own fuckin' orange juice. You still there, darlin'?"

At the recording session was a one-armed man named Paul. He introduced himself. "Mr. Lewis, you probably don't remember me—"

"Right," Jerry said. . . .

Pappy Lewis seemed to be speaking in Hittite. Only Jerry could comprehend him, or perhaps he was merely faking. "You know you ain't supposed to drink." Pappy responded in Hittite and spilled an eight-ounce Dixie cup of whiskey into his lap, a deed he loudly regretted, in Hittite. With Pappy was the son of his girlfriend. The future son-in-law was about 30, drunk but not in the Hittite fashion. It surfaced that Pappy could not remember his fiancée's name, but he was sure the fiancée was mad with him. "Get a dime; call your mama," he said, in English, or something like it.

An obviously psychopathic youth with eyes the size of gull eggs ran about telling anyone he could catch, "I'm a writer for *TV Guide.* I write about country artisez. Did you ever hear of the Grateful Dead? They played at my wedding. My wife's a model. She poses for artisez. She poses naked: tits, hiney, everything. She makes more money than you and me both.'' . . .

A woman with bleached hair was referred to by all as ''the curse of the family,'' a distinction of awesome implication.

A man dressed in black and carrying a bottle of Peter Pan Port introduced himself to the curse of the family. ''Don't get fresh,'' she said, frequently. He was the drummer with Bobby and the Spotlites, the house band at Hernando's Hideaway. There was a pack of cigarettes sticking from each of his pockets. Every pack was open, and he smoked from them variously. Memphis session organist James Brown was in the studio. The drummer from Hernando's Hideaway saw him and screamed, ''Oh, my God, don't tell me Jerry Lee's got spooks in his band!'' The curse of the family applied lipstick.

Judd fell asleep on the floor. Jerry Lee gently kicked him awake and said, ''Take out your teeth and I'll marry ya.'' Judd returned to sleep.

Through all this, Huey Meaux was trying to produce a record. Carl Perkins was in the studio, playing guitar in several cuts. Every few minutes a large, barefoot, suet-thighed lady turned to Huey Meaux and yelled, ''Make Carl Perkins play the 'Blue Suede Shoes'! Please!'' Carl, a reformed alky, seemed ill at ease.

Billy Lee Riley, the man who cut ''Flying Saucers Rock 'n' Roll'' for Sun in 1957, materialized, looking like 5,000 concentrated volts. He spread his hands before him as if holding a birthday cake. ''Man, I got me a pill this big, and when I take a bite the damn thing grows right back.'' Then he smiled, baring a large space between his teeth, and departed quickly.

It was the only recording session I ever saw that was fun.

RICHARD PENNIMAN
AND BUMPS BLACKWELL

Good golly, Miss Molly, what do you want me to tell you about Macon, Georgia, native Little Richard that you don't already know? I think I talked to him on the phone once nearly thirty years ago when I was working the police beat for the Atlanta Journal. *He had reported the theft from his Atlanta hotel room of a paper bag containing several thousand dollars. I called the hotel, was connected to his room, and I say I think I talked to him because it sounded like him but I was shyer back then and somehow it seemed overfamiliar to say ''Little Richard?'' and lame to say ''Mr.*

Penniman?" So it may have been his valet or somebody. Anyway, I got the details. Here are the details of the recording of "Tutti Frutti," and some prefatory information, as related by the man himself and by Robert "Bumps" Blackwell, the conservatory-educated black musician who produced that session, in Charles White's eyebrow-raising biography The Life and Times of Little Richard.

Womp Bomp a-Loo Momp

LITTLE RICHARD

My mother had all these kids, and I was the only one born deformed. My right leg is shorter than the left. I didn't realize that my leg was small. I never knew about it. Yet looking back, I can see why my mother and them was always so careful about me . . . cos they knew something I didn't. My mother used to let me get away with so much. I lived through a lot, and a lot of it was the way I walked. The kids didn't realize I was crippled. They thought I was trying to twist and walk feminine. But I had to take short steps cos I had a little leg. I used to walk with odd strides, like long-short, long-short. The kids would call me faggot, sissy, freak, punk. They called me everything.

One time my brother Peyton said to me, "Oh, Richard, where'd you get this body? Boy, you got a curious body," and I said to Mother, "Why is it that one of my legs is shorter than the other?" She answered, "Shut up, boy. You go and get the dishes washed and don't worry about it." But I *wanted* to hear someone talk about it. I wanted some explanation. I had this great big head and little body, and I had one big eye and one little eye.

But God gave me a strong mind, and a strong will. I've always had a fierce determination to excel. If we were cleaning the yard I would try to make my part better. It was like I had to, cos I was in competition with my brothers, and they were all good-looking.

I was the one at home that everybody thought was a nut. I would do some *silly* things. Like when Mother was cooking and I would slip a piece of chicken in my pants pocket and burn my thigh. Or, she'd send me out to do the washing, and I'd just throw the clothes in the water and wring them out. I had everybody dirty for a week! Momma didn't trust my washing *or* my cooking. She'd say, "Bro (all my family called me that. They didn't say Brother, they'd say Bro), you're a nasty cook."

I used to give people rocks and things as presents, but I once did something worse than that. I had a bowel movement in a box, in a shoebox or something like that, and I packed it up like a present and gave it to an old lady next to Mathis Groceries, on Monroe Street, in Pleasant Hill. I went to her on her birthday and I said, "Miz Ola, how you bin?" And she said, "Oh, Richard, I feel so fine. Richard, you're such a nice child.'' I said, ''Miz Ola, I've just come to wish you a happy birthday, and I've brought you a present. Look.'' She said, ''Ohhh, thank you so much.'' So she took this big old shoebox with the stuff in it. I went off and waited around the corner of the house to listen for her reactions. I was hoping that she would open it while the other ladies were there, and she did. She wanted to show them what I had brought her. She said, ''Let us see what Richard has brought for me.'' Then I just heard somebody say, ''Aaaaaaa, aaaaaaahhh—I'm gonna kill him. I'll kill him!'' She was crippled, but she leaped off that porch and she was walking without her stick! I laughed like a cuckoo! God bless Miz Ola, she's dead now.

Me and my cousin, Bertha May, we used to run together. We were a little team. A little evil, devilish team. I used to call her Boodlum. She had a big old black scar on her face, cos she had fallen and cut her face. And the old people back then, they didn't take her to the doctor. They just took some soot out of the stove and packed it on her face and it got well. It turned black though. That's what they used to do in those days. Well, me and Boodlum were going past Mathis Groceries and there was this big padlock hanging open on the door. I said, ''Well, we might just as well lock him up in there,'' so we locked him up in his own store.

One day we went up the hill, and we saw my daddy's car parked, the old Model T Ford, and we said, ''Well, we might as well push it on down the hill.'' So we pushed it, and we jumped in and were going to drive it, but it was going so fast that we had to jump out and just let it roll down the hill. . . .

I was crazy, you know. Crazy. I don't know why I did all these awful things. Momma used to complain to the ladies who came round to the house, ''I don't know why he does such evil dirty things like that. It must be the Devil.'' One lady put the bad-mouth on me—like putting on a curse—that I would die at twenty-one. I always thought that I would never live past twenty-one because she had told me I would die. I always believed that, but it just made me wilder.

I was glad to go to school though. It meant a lot to me. I had so many friends at school. Didn't trust none of 'em, though. All the kids would call me Big Head. The boys would want to fight me because I didn't like to be with them. I wanted to play with the girls. See, I *felt* like a girl. I used to play house with my cousins and I'd say, ''I'm the momma,'' and they'd say, ''Hey, Richard, you was the momma yesterday.'' But I wanted to be the momma, you know? So the boys wouldn't play with me cos I'd been saying stuff like that.

I had always loved Mother more than Daddy. I think it was because my mother was so close to me. I just wanted to be like her. I loved her so much. I idolized her. Every movement. I used to just love it when she put powder on her face. I used to watch her, and later I'd sneak up into her bedroom and just sit there, putting rosewater and stuff on myself. I'd imitate the things she said and the way she said them. She'd say, "Ooh, it's *so* hot." Then I would go outside and sit with my friends and say, "Ooh, it's *so* hot." I would practice it. I just felt that I wanted to be a girl more than a boy. . . .

I went through a lot when I was a boy. They called me sissy, punk, freak, and faggot. If I ever went out to friends' houses on my own, the guys would try to catch me, about eight or twenty of them together. They would run me. I never knew I could run so fast, but I was *scared*. They would jump on me, you know, cos they didn't like my *action*.

BUMPS BLACKWELL

When I got to New Orleans, Cosimo Matassa, the studio owner, called and said, "Hey, man, this boy's down here waiting for you." When I walked in, there's this cat in this loud shirt, with hair waved up six inches above his head. He was talking wild, thinking up stuff just to be different, you know? I could tell he was a megapersonality. So we got to the studio, on Rampart and Dumaine. . . .

Well, the first session was to run six hours, and we planned to cut eight sides. Richard ran through the songs on his audition tape. "He's My Star" was very disappointing. I did not even record it. But "Wonderin' " we got in two takes. Then we got "I'm Just a Lonely Guy," which was written by a local girl called Dorothy La Bostrie who was always pestering me to record her stuff. Then "The Most I Can Offer," and then "Baby." So far so good. But it wasn't really what I was looking for. I had heard that Richard's stage act was really wild, but in the studio that day he was very inhibited. Possibly his ego was pushing him to show his spiritual feeling or something, but it certainly wasn't coming together like I had expected and hoped.

The problem was that what he looked like, and what he sounded like didn't come together. If you look like Tarzan and sound like Mickey Mouse it just doesn't work out. So I'm thinking, Oh, Jesus . . . You know what it's like when you don't know what to do? It's "Let's take a break. Let's go to lunch." I had to think. I didn't know what to do. I couldn't go back to Rupe with the material I had because there was nothing there that I could put out. Nothing that I could ask anyone to put a promotion on. Nothing to merchandise. And I was paying out serious money.

So here we go over to the Dew Drop Inn, and, of course, Richard's like any other ham. We walk into the place and, you know, the girls are there and the boys are there and he's got an audience. There's a piano, and that's his crutch. He's on stage reckoning to show Lee Allen his piano style. So WOW! He gets to going. He hits that piano, didididididididididi . . . and starts to sing "Awop-bop-a-Loo-Mop a-good Goddam—Tutti Frutti, good booty . . ." I said,

"Wow! That's what I want from you, Richard. That's a hit!" I knew that the lyrics were too lewd and suggestive to record. It would never have got played on the air. So I got hold of Dorothy La Bostrie, who had come over to see how the recording of her song was going. I brought her to the Dew Drop.

Dorothy was a little colored girl so thin she looked like six o'clock. She just had to close one eye and she looked like a needle. Dorothy had songs stacked this high and was always asking me to record them. She'd been singing these songs to me, but the trouble was they all sounded like Dinah Washington's "Blowtop Blues." They were all composed to the same melody. But looking through her words, I could see that she was a prolific writer. She just didn't understand melody. So I said to her, "Look. You come and write some lyrics to this, cos I can't use the lyrics Richard's got." He had some terrible words in there. Well, Richard was embarrassed to sing the song and she was not certain that she wanted to hear it. Time was running out, and I *knew* it could be a hit. I talked, using every argument I could think of. I asked him if he had a grudge against making money. I told her that she was over twenty-one, had a houseful of kids and no husband and needed the money. And finally, I convinced them. Richard turned to face the wall and sang the song two or three times and Dorothy listened.

Break time was over, and we went back to the studio to finish the session, leaving Dorothy to write the words. I think the first thing we did was "Directly from My Heart to You." Now that, and "I'm Just a Lonely Guy," could have made it. Those two I could have gotten by with—just by the skin of my teeth. Fifteen minutes before the session was to end, the chick comes in and puts these little trite lyrics in front of me. I put them in front of Richard. Richard says he ain't got no voice left. I said, "Richard, you've *got* to sing it."

There had been no chance to write an arrangement, so I had to take the chance on Richard playing the piano himself. That wild piano was essential to the success of the song. It was impossible for the other piano players to learn it in the short time we had. I put a microphone between Richard and the piano and another inside the piano, and we started to record. It took three takes, and in fifteen minutes we had it. "Tutti Frutti."

TUTTI FRUTTI
(Penniman/La Bostrie/Lubin)

First Specialty Record

Womp-Bomp-a-Loo-Momp Alop-Bomp-Bomp

Tutti Frutti, Aw-Rootie (5 times)
Awop-Bop-a-Loo-Mop Alop-Bomp-Bomp

I Got A Girl, Named Sue
She Knows Just What To Do
I Got A Girl, Named Sue
She Knows Just What To Do
She Rock To The East, She Rock To The West
But She's The Girl That I Love Best

Tutti Frutti, Aw-Rootie (5 times)
Awop-Bop-a-Loo-Mop Alop-Bam-Boom

I've Got A Gal, Named Daisy
She Almost Drives Me Crazy
I've Got A Gal, Named Daisy
She Almost Drives Me Crazy
She Knows How To Love Me, Yes Indeed
Boy You Don't Know What She's Doin' To Me

Tutti Frutti, Aw-Rootie (5 times)
Awop-Bop-a-Loo-Mop Alop-Bam-Boom

TOM WOLFE

Except notably in his profile of stock-car legend Junior Johnson, which is available in The Norton Book of Sports, *Virginian Tom Wolfe has seldom cast his satirical eye on Southern matters. But if he doesn't mind following Little Richard, I thought I might favor you with this bit of high psychedelic nonsense from Wolfe's estimable book about the travels of Ken Kesey and his Merry Pranksters,* The Electric Kool-Aid Acid Test.

Alabama Dimensions

On into the flatlands of Mississippi and Alabama, Biloxi, Mobile, U.S. Route 90, the flatlands and the fields and the heat doesn't let up ever. They are heading for Florida. Sandy hasn't slept in days:::::how many:::::like total insomnia and everything is *bending* in curvy curdling lines. Sun and flatlands.

So damned hot—and everything is getting torn into opposites. The dead-still heat-stroked summertime deep Southland—and Sandy's heart racing at a constant tachycardia and his brain racing and reeling out and so essential to . . . *keep moving, Cassady!* . . . but there are two Cassadys. One minute Cassady looks 58 and crazy—*speed!*—and the next, 28 and peaceful—*acid*—and Sandy can tell the peaceful Cassady in an instant, because his nose becomes . . . long and smooth and almost patrician, whereas the wild Cassady looks beat-up. And Kesey—*always Kesey!* Sandy looks . . . and Kesey is old and haggard and his face is lopsided . . . and then Sandy looks and Kesey is young, serene, and his face is lineless, and round and smooth as a baby's as he sits for hours on end reading comic books, absorbed in the plunging purple Steve Ditko shadows of Dr. Strange attired in capes and chiaroscuro, saying: "How could they have known that this gem was merely a device to bridge DIMENSIONS! It was a means to enter the dread PURPLE DIMENSION—from our own world!" Sandy may wander . . . off the bus, but it remains all Kesey. Dr. Strange! Always seeing two Keseys. Kesey the Prankster and Kesey the organizer. Going through the steams of southern Alabama in late June and Kesey rises up from out of the comic books and becomes Captain Flag. He puts on a pink kilt, like a miniskirt, and pink socks and patent-leather shoes and pink sunglasses and wraps an American flag around his head like a big turban and holds it in place with an arrow through the back of it and gets up on top of the bus roaring through Alabama and starts playing the flute at people passing by. The Alabamans drawn into the PINK DIMENSION do a double-freak take for sure and it is *Too Much!* as George Walker always says, too mullyfogging much. They pull into a gas station in Mobile and half the Pranksters jump out of the bus, blazing red and white stripes and throwing red rubber balls around in a crazed way like a manic ballet of slick Servicenter flutter decoration while the guy fills up the tank, and he looks from them to Captain Flag to the bus itself, and after he collects for the gas he looks through the window at Cassady in the driver's seat and shakes his head and says:

"No wonder you're so nigger-heavy in California."

FORNIA - FORNIA - FORNIA - FORNIA - FORNIA - FORNIA - FORNIA - FORNIA as it picked up inside the bus in variable lag, and that breaks everybody up.

BLIND BLAKE

The man known as Blind Blake may have been born in Jacksonville, Florida, in the early 1890s and may have died somewhere in Florida in 1933. He was also known as Blind Arthur, Georgeous Weed, Billy James, and Blind George Martin, but his real name was probably Arthur Phelps. He hoboed extensively and sang and played guitar on many streets and at many fish fries. His other compositions include "Chump Man Blues," "Come on Boys Let's Do That Messin' Around," "Goodby Mama Moan," "Hard Pushing Papa," "Police Dog Blues," "Rope Stretching Blues," "Search Warrant Blues," "Skeedle Loo Doo Blues," and "That Will Never Happen No More." This arrangement of Blake's lines on the page is from Eric Sackheim's admirable 1969 compilation of blues lyrics, The Blues Line.

"Diddie Wa Diddie"

There's a great big mystery
And it surely is worrying me
        This diddie wa diddie
        This diddie wa diddie
        I wish somebody would tell me what diddie wa diddie means

The little girl about four feet four:
"Come on papa and give me some more
        Of your diddie wa diddie
        Your diddie wa diddie"
        I wish somebody would tell me what diddie wa diddie means

I went out and walked around
Somebody yelled, said: "Look who's in town—
        Mister diddie wa diddie
        Mister diddie wa diddie
        I wish somebody would tell me what diddie wa diddie means

Went to church, put my hand on the seat
Lady sat on it, said: "Daddy you sure is sweet,
      Mister diddie wa diddie
      Mister diddie wa diddie"
   I wish somebody would tell me what diddie wa diddie means

I said: "Sister I'll soon be gone
Just gimme that thing you setting on
      My diddie wa diddie
      My diddie wa diddie"
   I wish somebody would tell me what diddie wa diddie means

Then I got put out of church
'Cause I talk about diddie wa diddie too much
      Mister diddie wa diddie
      Mister diddie wa diddie
   I wish somebody would tell me what diddie wa diddie means

SECTION FOUR

BLACK AND WHITE, AND OTHER POLITICAL STRIPES

Sir, I understand that you have called me a "bob-tail" politician. I wish to know if it be true; and if true, your meaning.

—William B. Giles
(Governor of Virginia, 1827–30)

Sir, I do not recollect having called you a bob-tail politician at any time, but think it probable I have. Not recollecting the time or occasion, I can't say what I did mean, but if you will tell me what you think I meant, I will say whether you are correct or not. Very respectfully,

—Patrick Henry

JULIAN BOND

Atlanta native Bond is a writer, professor, former Georgia legislator, and one of the founders of the Student Nonviolent Coordinating Committee, the avant-garde of the civil rights movement. On display in the Civil Rights Museum in Memphis is a sportive memo written by Bond in those scary halcyon days entitled "HOW TO BE SNCCY," a guide for new members of the organization, which says in part, "There are several auxiliary habits that one should pick up. One is dancing—extremely hard for some—and another is hand-clapping. A note to the wise: when in a mass meeting, watch some Negro staff member and try to make your hands come together at the same time his do. UNDER NO CIRCUMSTANCES SHOULD YOU WATCH JAMES FORMAN OR JULIAN BOND!" The following verse appeared in Langston Hughes's 1966 anthology The Book of Negro Humor.

"Look at That Gal . . ."

Look at that gal
Shake that thing.
We cannot all be
Martin Luther King.

ISHMAEL REED

Novelist, poet, editor, controversialist Reed has long lived in the Bay Area, but he is originally a Chattanoogan. This is an excerpt from his satirical novel Flight to Canada, *which remythifies the War Between the States.*

Bookie Odds Favored the Union

The Master's study. Arthur Swille has just completed the push-ups he does after his morning nourishment, two gallons of slave mothers' milk. Uncle Robin, his slave, is standing against the wall, arms folded. He is required to dress up as a Moorish slave to satisfy one of Swille's cravings.

"Robin?"

"Yessir, Massa Swille."

"What are the people down in the quarters saying about those kinks who took off with themselves?"

"Don't get down to the slave village much any more, Massa Swille. After you and Cato the Graffado put out directions that none was to tarry there, I tain't. We were gettin all of our information from Stray Leechfield, the runner, but now that he's . . . well, after he . . ."

"Yes, you don't have to say it, Robin. He's gone. Stray Leechfield, 40s and [voice drops] Quickskill. They contracted *Drapetomania,* as that distinguished scientist Dr. Samuel Cartwright described in that book you read to me . . ."

"*Dysaethesia Aethipica,* Mr. Swille?"

"Exactly, Robin, that disease causing Negroes to run away. Of course, I'm not a sentimentalist. I won't sleep until they've returned. I mean, I'm the last man to go against science, and if a slave is sick, then he must be rejuvenated— but I just can't permit anyone to run over me like that. The other slaves will get ideas. So, even though they're sick—they must be returned."

"But suppose they paid you off. Would you try to recover even then?"

"Look, Robin, if they'd came to me and if they'd asked to buy themselves, perhaps we could have arranged terms. But they didn't; they furtively pilfered themselves. Absconded. They have committed a crime, and no amount of money they send me will rectify the matter. I'd buy all the niggers in the South before I'd accept a single dime for or from them . . . Quickskill, I'll never be able to figure out. Why, he ate in the house and was my trusted bookkeeper. I allowed him to turn the piano pages when we had performers in the parlor, even let him wear a white wig—and he'd give all of this up. Well," he said, pounding on the top of his desk, "they won't get away with it. One thing my father told me: never yield a piece of property. Not to a man, not to the State. Before he died, that's what he told me and my brothers."

Dressed in his robes, Swille reaches out his hand, which embraces a wine-glass. Uncle Robin walks over to the spirits cabinet, returns and pours him a gobletful, goes back to his place. Uncle Robin knows his place—his place in the shadows.

"Robin, what have you heard about this place up North, I think they call it Canada?" Swille says, eying Robin slyly.

"Canada. I do admit I have heard about the place from time to time, Mr. Swille, but I loves it here so much that . . . that I would never think of leaving here. These rolling hills. Mammy singing spirituals in the morning before them good old biscuits. Watching 'Sleepy Time Down South' on the Late Show. That's my idea of Canada. Most assuredly, Mr. Swille, this my Canada. You'd better believe it."

"Uncle Robin, I'm glad to hear you say that. Why, I don't know what I'd do without you. I can always count on you not to reveal our little secret. Traveling around the South for me, carrying messages down to the house slaves, polishing my boots and drawing my bath water. All of these luxuries. Robin, you make a man feel like . . . well, like a God."

"Thank you, Massa Swille. I return the compliment. It's such a honor to serve such a mellifluous, stunning and elegant man as yourself, Massa Swille; indeed an honor. Why . . . why, you could be President if you wanted to."

"I toyed with the idea, Robin. But my brothers made me think of the Family. It would be a disgrace to the Swilles if I ever stooped so low as to offer myself to this nation. I'm afraid, Robin, that that office is fit only for rapscal-lions, mobocrats, buckrahs, coonskinners and second-story men. Before Grand-dad died, they elected that Irishman Andrew Jackson, a cut-up and a barroom brawler, to office—why, I remained in exile during his entire term. Refused even to speak the language, spoke French for those years. It was only after Dad died that I returned to manage this land."

"You're a very busy man, Mr. Swille. The presidency would only be a waste of time for you."

There's a knock on the door. Mammy Barracuda enters. "Arthur," then, noticing Uncle Robin, "Oh, I mean Massa Swille."

"Yes, Barracuda?"

Barracuda has a silk scarf tied about her head. A black velvet dress. She wears a diamond crucifix on her bosom. It's so heavy she walks with a stoop. Once she went into the fields and the sun reflected on her cross so, two slaves were blinded.

"It's your wife, Ms. Swille, sir. She say she tired of being a second-class citizen and she say she don't want to feed herself no mo. She say it's anti-suffragette. She say she shouldn't have to exert herself to feed herself and she say she wont to be fed extravenous, I mean, fed intravenous, somethin. Grumph. When she do get out of bed, we have to rock her in the rocking chair. We have to wash her feet and then empty her spoils. The room ain't been aired out in months. She say she boycott somethin. Humph!"

"If it isn't one thing, it's another. You mean she won't eat at all?"

"She told me to mail this letter. I thought I'd show it to you. See what you thought about it before I mailed it."

"Very thoughtful of you, Barracuda."

He takes the letter, opens it.

"What you lookin at?"

"I was just admiring your new apron, Mammy Barracuda, that's all," Uncle Robin says.

"Better be. Humph. Grumph."

"Destroy this letter, Barracuda. A one-year subscription to that *National Era* which carried the work by that fanatical Beecher woman."

"I will burn it first chance I get, Massa Swille. What about him?"

"I trust Robin second only to you, Barracuda. Lying curled up fetuslike in your lap is worth a hundred shrinks on Park Avenue."

"Humph. Whew. Wheeew," utters Barracuda, of whom it once was rumored "she stared a man to death," as she goes out.

"Wonderful old soul, Mammy Barracuda."

"You can second that twice for me, Massa Swille."

"What's that, Robin?"

"That part about her being a wonderful old soul. You can second that twice for me."

There's a knock at the door. It's Moe, the white house slave—Mingy Moe, as the mammies in the kitchen call him. He looks like an albino: tiny pink pupils, white Afro.

"Sorry to disturb you, Master Swille, but Abe Lincoln, the President of the so-called Union, is outside in the parlor waiting to see you. He's fiddling around and telling corny jokes, shucking the shud and husking the hud. I told him that you were scheduled to helicopter up to Richmond to shake your butt at the Magnolia Baths tonight, but he persists. Says, 'The very survival of the Union is at stake.' "

"Hand me my jacket, Uncle Robin," Swille says as he stands in the middle of the room.

"Which one do you wont, suh—the one with the spangly fritters formal one or the silvery-squilly festooned street jacket?"

"Give me the spangly one." Turning to Moe, Swille says, "Now, Moe, you tell this Lincoln gentleman that he won't be able to stay long. Before I fly up to Richmond, I have to check on my investments all over the world."

"Yessir, Mr. Swille."

Momentarily, Lincoln, Gary Cooper-awkward, fidgeting with his stovepipe hat, humble-looking, imperfect—a wart here and there—craw and skuttlecoat, shawl, enters the room. "Mr. Swille, it's a pleasure," he says, extending his hand to Swille, who sits behind a desk rumored to have been owned by Napoleon III. "I'm a small-time lawyer and now I find myself in the room of the mighty, why—"

"Cut the yokel-dokel, Lincoln, I don't have all day. What's on your mind?" Swille rejects Lincoln's hand, at which Lincoln stares, hurt.

"Yokel-dokel? Why, I don't get you, Mr. Swille."

"Oh, you know—log-cabin origin. That's old and played out. Why don't you get some new speech writers? Anyway, you're the last man I expected to see down here. Aren't you supposed to be involved in some kind of war? Virginia's off limits to your side, isn't it? Aren't you frightened, man?"

"No, Mr. Swille. We're not frightened because we have a true cause. We have a great, a noble cause. Truth is on our side, marching to the clarion call. We are in the cause of the people. It is a people's cause. This is a great, noble and people period in the history of our great Republic. We call our war the Civil War, but some of the fellows think we ought to call it the War Between the States. You own fifty million dollars' worth of art, Mr. Swille. What do you think we ought to call it?"

"I don't feel like naming it, Lanky—and cut the poppy-cock."

"Lincoln, sir."

"Oh yes, Lincoln. Well, look, Lincoln, I don't want that war to come up here because, to tell you the truth, I'm not the least bit interested in that war. I hate contemporary politics and probably will always be a Tory. Bring back King George. Why would a multinational like myself become involved in these queer crises? Why, just last week I took a trip abroad and was appallingly and disturbingly upset and monumentally offended by the way the Emperor of France was scoffing at this . . . this nation, as you call it. They were snickering about your general unkempt, hirsute and bungling appearance—bumping into things and carrying on. And your speeches. What kind of gibberish are they? Where were you educated, in the rutabaga patch? Why don't you put a little pizazz in your act, Lanky? Like Davis . . . Now that Davis is as nit as a spit with his satin-embroidered dressing case, his gold tweezers and Rogers & Sons strap. He's just bananas about Wagner and can converse in German, French and even that bloody Mexican patois. Kindly toward the 'weak' races, as he referred to them in that superb speech he made before the Senate criticizing Secretary of State Seward and other celebrities for financing that, that . . . maniac, John Brown. And when he brought in that savage, Black Hawk, on the steamboat *Winnebago,* he treated the primitive overlord with the respect due an ethnic celebrity. You can imagine the Americans taunting this heathen all decked out in white deerskins. Davis' slaves are the only ones I know of who take mineral baths, and when hooped skirts became popular he gave some to the slave women, and when this made it awkward for them to move through the rows of cotton, he widened the rows.''

"That's quite impressive, Mr. Swille. I have a worthy adversary.''

. . . .

Lincoln salutes the Confederate soldiers Lee has sent up to escort him and his party back to *The River Queen.* He climbs into the carriage and sits next to an aide.

"Did you sell him some bonds?'' the aide asks.

"Yeah,'' Lincoln says, leaning back in his carriage, removing his stovepipe hat and boots; he takes off his white gloves last.

"Gilded Age ding-dong if there ever was. Hands like a woman's. I feel like a minstrel . . .''

"But you did sell him some bonds?''

"Yes. First I gave him the yokel-dokel—he saw through that. And then he went on about my lack of culture and poked fun at my clothes. Talked about my shiny suitcoat and pants. Then he said some nasty things about Mary. Well, I know that she's . . . she's odd. Well, you know, I couldn't stand there and listen to that, so I blew my top.''

"And he still gave you the gold?''

"Yeah. You know, if we lost this war we wouldn't be able to repay Swille. We're sticking our necks out, but with the cost of things these days, we have to turn to him.''

"Look, sir.''

On the side of the road some of the colored contraband were appearing. They started waving their handkerchiefs at the President. The President waved back. One man ran up to the carriage; Lincoln stuck his hand out to shake the slave's hand, but instead of shaking the President's hand the man began kissing it until he dropped back behind the carriage. He stood in the road waving.

"They love you, sir.''

"Curious tribe. There's something, something very human about them, something innocent and . . . Yet I keep having the suspicion that they have another mind. A mind kept hidden from us. They had this old mammy up there. She began singing and dancing me around. The first time in these years I took my mind off the war. I felt like crawling into her lap and going to sleep. Just sucking my thumb and rolling my hair up into pickaninny knots. I never even gave spooks much thought, but now that they've become a subplot in this war, I can't get these shines off my mind. My dreams . . . She must do Swille a lot of good." . . .

Lincoln rested his head against the window and looked out into the Virginia night, the blackest night in the South. There was an old folk art cemetery with leaning tombstones behind an ornate black wrought-iron fence. A woman in white floated across the cemetery. A wolf howled. Bats flew into the dark red sun.

"Aide, did you see that?"

"I can't see anything for the fog, sir. But I think I did hear some screaming. As soon as we entered Virginia we heard the screaming. First a little screaming and then a whole lot. As soon as the sun goes up out here you hear the screaming until the moon goes down, I hear tell, Mr. Lincoln."

"Like hell."

"What's that, Mr. President?"

"The screaming, it reminds you of hell. This man Swille was talking about whips and said something about people being humiliated. Is that some kind of code?"

"Grant said it was decadent down here, Mr. Lincoln. Said it was ignoble. Others call it 'immoral.' William Wells Brown, the brown writer, called it that."

"Grant said ignoble?" Lincoln laughs. "Swille offered me a barony. What's that all about?"

"I heard talk, Mr. President. The proceedings from the Montgomery Convention where the slaveholders met to map the Confederacy have never been released, but there are rumors that somebody offered Napoleon III the Confederate Crown, and he said he'd think about it. It was in *The New York Times,* August—"

"The Crown!"

"But Nappy Three said that slavery was an anachronism."

"Hey!" Lincoln said, snapping his fingers. "I got it! Of course."

"What's that, Mr. President?"

"Look, it's common sense. Why, I'll be a jitterbug in a hogcreek. Aide, when we return to Washington, I want you to return Swille's gold. We don't need it."

"But, Mr. President, we just risked our lives coming through Confederate lines to get the gold. Now you don't want it? I don't understand."

"We change the issues, don't you see? Instead of making this some kind of oratorical minuet about States' Rights versus the Union, what we do is make it so that you can't be for the South without being for slavery! I want you to get that portrait painter feller Denis Carter to come into the office, where he'll show me signing the . . . the Emancipation Proclamation. That's it. The Emancipation Proclamation. Call in the press. Get the Capitol calligrapher who's good at letterin to come in and draw this Proclamation. Phone the networks. We'll put an end to this Fairy Kingdom nonsense. Guenevere, Lancelot, Arthur and the whole dang-blasted genteel crew.''

"A brilliant idea, Mr. President. A brilliant idea.'' . . .

"Did you send Major Corbett away?''

"We put Major Corbett on active duty, Mr. President.''

"Good. Invite Mrs. Corbett to review the troops with me and General Hooker tomorrow. Tell her afterwards we'll take tea. Give my boots a little lick of grease and go to the drugstore and get me some of that Golden Fluid hair slick.''

"But what will I do about Mrs. Lincoln, Mr. President? The press will be there. Suppose they take a picture?''

"Oh, tell Mother . . . tell her that I was detained. I don't know which one's going to be the death of me, Mother or the niggers.''

"How much gold did Mr. Swille give you, Mr. President?''

Lincoln counts. "He was supposed to give me five, but I only count four.''

"What could have happened, sir? The nigger?''

"I doubt it. Poor submissive creature. You should have seen him shuffle about the place. Yessirring and nosirring. Maybe he didn't intend to give me but four. I'm tired. Can't you make this thing go faster?''

"Yessir,'' the aide says. "Right away, sir.''

He leans out of the window and instructs the coachman to go faster. Lincoln opens his purse and examines the five-dollar Confederate bill. Bookie odds favored the Union, but you could never tell when you might need carfare.

WILLIAM ALEXANDER PERCY

William Alexander Percy, who was born in 1885 in Greenville, Mississippi, and died there in 1942, led an extraordinarily vigorous life. Son of a plantation-owning U.S.

Senator, he took a law degree at Harvard, was decorated by King Albert of Belgium for his relief work in that country in 1916, won a Croix de Guerre with gold star for his service as a U.S. infantry officer in France, fought alongside his father to keep the Ku Klux Klan from controlling Greenville, succeeded his father as manager of the 3,343-acre plantation and its six hundred workers, wrote volumes of poetry, traveled around the world, lived for a time on the beach in Bora Bora, and adopted and reared (though he was a lifelong bachelor) three orphaned second cousins, including Walker Percy, who loved him dearly. In the course of my researches for this book I came to a disturbing realization: I found William Alexander's writing—at least in his memoir, Lanterns on the Levee—more of a pleasure to read than Walker's.

This was disturbing because Walker Percy is very important to most of my Southern writer friends. Whereas William Alexander Percy is a bit of an embarrassment, today, to Southern culture. Perhaps my preference was a humor anthologist's bias: I had expected to include Walker Percy's essay on whiskey in this book, until I reread it and realized that fine as it is, only a few lines of it are funny. And although people recommended several passages from his novels, none of these ever struck me as standing alone humorously.

On the other hand, when people would rather hesitantly recall something from Lanterns ("Probably seems dated now, but my parents used to cite it a lot when I was a kid, and it sure was funny then"), I would check it out and it would be funny, still. For instance, there was the time young W.A.P. went to dine at a Harvard professor's house and accidentally, in flipping open his folded napkin, sent a "small brown roll shaped like a torpedo" flying across the room to clang up against a parakeet cage, causing the birds to "burst into a paean of dismay or applause," and yet no person at the table let out a peep; Percy appreciated this Northern politeness, but would have preferred what he imagined happening at a polite Southern table: all the other diners would have thrown their rolls at the birdcage, or at least would have laughed and cheered.

The problem with enjoying the elder Percy's sense of humor now is that William Alexander—although far more progressive in his thinking and his actions, for his time, than Walker for his—was prone to paternalistic race-relations statements that make the contemporary Southern reader's heart sink.

Which makes him all the more interesting as a figure in Southern humor. He was a brave man. He made an enemy of the local sheriff by suing him, successfully, for abusing one of the Percy plantation workers in jail. The reason this Percy could be so unabashedly, feelingly condescending is that he was also a bit of a baby. A rich kid all his life, he is put out that people whose parents or grandparents were slaves don't act more like people whose parents or grandparents owned them. However, Percy was an honest enough humorist and Negrophile to hand himself down to posterity not only as a natural aristocrat but also as black people saw him: an easy if irritable touch and a natural fool. When—as in the following excerpts from Lanterns—the rolls start rattling not only the perceivedly mutual Southern or human birdcage but also the

author's particular one, you can feel the white man's burden taking comic wing,
uncertainly, in company with the weary load of black experience.

Relating to Skillet and Fode

Any little boy who was not raised with little Negro children might just as well
not have been raised at all. My first boon-companion was Skillet, the small
dark son of Mère's cook. . . . As a conversationalist he outdistanced any white
child in inventiveness, absurdity, and geniality. In Mère's back yard we would
sit in a row-boat, a relic of the last overflow, and for hours ply imaginary oars
toward an imaginary land that we described and embellished as we approached. These voyages afforded endless opportunity for discussions. One in
particular drifts back to me across long years. It was one of those still, hot days
when earth things lie tranced at the bottom of a deep sea of summer sun. We
were resting on our oars at the moment. Far, far up buzzards circled dreamily,
their black wings motionless, tilting, banking, coasting in wide arcs, somnam-
bulistic symbols of the drowse and delight of deep summer. Watching them,
Skillet observed in a singsong: "If they was to ever light, the world would
burn up." As the birds seemed fixed at their vast altitude, this was a safe
prophecy. But I was skeptical, as could have been expected of any horrid little
white realist. Skillet, though, was so eloquent in citing reasons and authorities
that my disbelief weakened and by degrees I was convinced, for the old
excellent reason that I wanted to be. As we watched, the buzzards, careening
and narrowing their circles, began to descend. It was exciting to see them
drop lower and lower and to think what might happen. At last we could
discern their horrible necks and heads. Skillet rose in a kind of ecstasy, thrust-
ing out his arms, flexing his knees, and chanting: "Don't let 'em light, God,
don't let 'em light." The flames of a consuming world were practically around
us. Only the fire music as it came to Mime about the time Siegfried rushed in
with the bear could have expressed our abject and delicious terror. They were
hovering over our own back yard and, last touch of horror, there lay one of
Mère's chickens dead—indeed, more than dead—their target, stark and un-
tidy on the crust of the earth so unconcerned and so doomed. One of the
ghastly creatures suddenly rocked, flapped its wings, and settled down awkwardly on the fence between us and the Fergusons'. "Look, I told you so, the
world didn't burn up," I almost sobbed, torn between relief and disappointment. "He lit on a fence. He ain't never teched the ground," whispered
Skillet. The buzzard gave an ungainly bound and landed on the too, too solid
earth. "Look," I wailed. "He lit on a chip," Skillet observed affably. I was
outraged.

.   .   .   .

In the South every white man worth calling white or a man is owned by some Negro, whom he thinks he owns, his weakness and solace and incubus. Ford is mine. There is no excuse for talking about him except that I like to. He started off as my caddy, young, stocky, strong, with a surly expression, and a smile like the best brand of sunshine. For no good reason he rose to be my chauffeur; then houseboy; then general factotum; and now, without any contractual relation whatever, my retainer, which means to say I am retained for life by him against all disasters, great or small, for which he pays by being Ford. It was not because of breaking up the first automobile, coming from a dance drunk, or because of breaking up the second automobile, coming from a dance drunk, that our contractual relation was annulled, but for a subtler infamy. I was in the shower, not a position of dignity at best, and Ford strolled in, leaned against the door of the bathroom, in the relaxed pose of the Marble Faun, and observed dreamily: "You ain't nothing but a little old fat man."

A bit of soap was in my eye and under the circumstances it was no use attempting to be haughty anyway, so I only blurted: "You damn fool."

Ford beamed: "Jest look at your stummick."

When one had fancied the slenderness of one's youth had been fairly well retained! Well, taking advantage of the next dereliction and one occurred every week, we parted; that is to say, I told Ford I was spoiling him and it would be far better for him to battle for himself in this hostile world, and Ford agreed, but asked what he was going to do "seeing as how nobody could find a job nohow." As neither of us could think of the answer, I sent him off to a mechanics' school in Chicago. He returned with a diploma and a thrilling tale of how nearly he had been married against his vehement protest to a young lady for reasons insufficient surely in any enlightened community with an appreciation of romance. With Ford's return the demand for mechanics fell to zero—he always had an uncanny effect on the labor market—so he took to house-painting. His first week he fell off the roof of the tallest barn in the county and instead of breaking his neck, as Giorgione or Raphael would have done, he broke only his ankle and had to be supplied with crutches, medical care, and a living for six weeks. It was then that I left for Samoa. . . .

That I have any dignity and self-respect is not because of but in spite of Ford. We were returning from a directors' meeting in a neighboring town and he was deeply overcast. At last he became communicative:

"Mr. Oscar Johnston's boy says Mr. Oscar won't ride in no car more'n six months old and he sho ain't goin' to ride in nothin' lessen a Packard."

I received this calmly, it was only one more intimation that my Ford was older than need be and congenitally unworthy. Ford continued:

"He says Mr. Oscar says you ain't got near as much sense as your pa." I agreed, heartily. "He says you ain't never goin' to make no money." I agreed, less heartily. "En if you don't be keerful you goin' to lose your plantation." I agreed silently, but I was nettled, and observed:

"And you sat there like a bump on a log, saying nothing, while I was being run down?"

"Well, I told him you had traveled a lot, a lot more'n Mr. Oscar; you done gone near 'bout everywhere, en he kinder giggled and says: 'Yes, they tells me he's been to Africa,' en I says: 'He is,' en he says: 'You know why he went to Africa?' en I says: ' 'Cause he wanted to go there,' en he says: 'That's what he tells you, but he went to Africa to 'range to have the niggers sent back into slavery.' "

I exploded: "And you were idiot enough to believe that?"

"I'se heard it lots of times," Ford observed mildly, "but it didn't make no difference to me, you been good to me en I didn't care."

Having fancied I had spent a good portion of my life defending and attempting to help the Negro, this information stunned me and, as Ford prophesied, it hurt. But hiding my wounded vanity as usual in anger, I turned on Ford with:

"You never in your life heard any Negro except that fool boy of Oscar Johnston's say I was trying to put the Negroes back in slavery."

"Lot of 'em," reiterated Ford.

"I don't believe you," I said. "You can't name a single one."

We finished the drive in silence; spiritually we were not en rapport.

The next morning when Ford woke me he was wreathed in smiles, suspiciously pleased with himself. He waited until one eye was open and then announced triumphantly:

"Louisa!" (pronounced with a long *i*).

"What about Louisa?" I queried sleepily.

"She says you'se goin' to send the niggers back into slavery!"

Louisa was our cook, the mainstay and intimate of the household for fifteen years.

"God damn!" I exploded, and Ford fairly tripped out, charmed with himself.

.   .   .   .

My bitter tutelage didn't conclude here. In late autumn we drove to the plantation on settlement day. Cotton had been picked and ginned, what cash had been earned from the crop was to be distributed. The managers and bookkeeper had been hard at work preparing a statement of each tenant's account for the whole year. As the tenant's name was called he entered the office and was paid off. The Negroes filled the store and overflowed onto the porch, milling and confabulating. As we drove up, one of them asked: "Whose car is dat?" Another answered: "Dat's *us* car." I thought it curious they didn't recognize my car, but dismissed the suspicion and dwelt on the thought of how sweet it was to have the relation between landlord and tenant so close and affectionate that to them my car was their car. Warm inside I passed through the crowd, glowing and bowing, the lord of the manor among his faithful retainers. My mission concluded, I returned to the car, still glowing. As we drove off I said:

"Did you hear what that man said?"

Ford assented, but grumpily.

"It was funny," I continued.

"Funnier than you think," observed Ford sardonically.

I didn't understand and said so.

Ford elucidated: "He meant that's the car *you* has bought with *us* money. They all knew what he meant, but you didn't and they knew you didn't. They wuz laughing to theyselves."

. . . .

Although nothing further was said and Ford asked no questions, he understood my depression and felt the duty on him to cheer me up. He drove to my favorite spot on the levee and parked where I could watch across the width of waters a great sunset crumbling over Arkansas. As I sat moody and worried, Ford, for the first and only time in his life, began to tell me Negro stories. . . .

"There wuz a cullud man en he died en went to hevven en the Lawd gevvum all wings, en he flew en he flew" (here Ford hunched his shoulders and gave a superb imitation of a buzzard's flight). "After he flew round there fur 'bout a week he looked down en saw a reel *good*-lookin' lady, a-settin' on a cloud. She wuz *reel* good-lookin'. En he dun the loop-the-loop.

"The Lawd cum en sez: 'Don't you know how to act? There ain't nuthin' but nice people here, en you beehavin' like that. Git out.' But he told the Lawd he jest didn't know en he wuzzent never gonner do nuthin' like that no mo', en please let him stay. So the Lawd got kinder pacified en let him stay. En he flew en he flew. En after he had been flying round fur 'bout a week, he ups en sees that same good-lookin' lady a-settin' on a cloud en he jest couldn't hep it—he dun the loop-the-loop.

"So the Lawd stepped up en he sez: 'You jest don't know how to act, you ain't fitten fur to be with decent folks, you'se a scanlus misbeehavor. Git out.' En he got.

"He felt mighty bad en hung round the gate three or four days tryin' to ease up on St. Peter, but St. Peter 'lowed there wuzn't no way, he jest couldn't let him in en the onliest way he might git in wuz to have a *conference* with the Lawd. Then the man asked if he couldn't 'range fur a conference en they had a

lot of back-and-forth. En finally St. Peter eased him in fur a conference.''
(Ford loved that word, it made him giggle.) ''But the Lawd wuz mad, He wuz
mad sho-nuff, he wuz hoppin' mad en told him flatfooted to git out en stay
out. Then the cullud man sez:

'' 'Well, jest remember this, Lawd: while I wuz up here in yo' place I wuz
the flyin'est fool you had.' '' . . .

The second story is just as inconsequential:

''A fellow cum to a cullud man en promised him a whole wagen-load of
watermelons if he would go en set by hisself in a hanted house all night long.
Well, the man he liked watermelons en he promised, though he sho didn't like
no hanted house, en he sho didn't wanter see no hants. He went in en drug up
a cheer en set down en nuthin' happened. After so long a time, in walked a
black cat en set down in front of him en jest looked at him. He warn't so
skeered because it warn't much more'n a kitten, en they both uvvem jest set
there en looked at each uther. Then ernurther cat cum in, a big black 'un, en
he set by the little 'un en they jest set there lookin' at him, en ain't sed
nothin'. Then ernurther one cum en he wuz big as a dawg en all three uvvem
jest set there en looked at him en sed nuthin'. Ernurther one cum, still bigger,
en ernurther, en ernurther, en the last one wuz big as a hoss. They all jest set
there in a row en sed nuthin' en looked at him. That cullud man he wuz plum
skeered en he had ter say sumpin so he 'lowed all nice en p'lite:

'' 'Whut us gwiner do?'

''En the big 'un sed: 'Us ain't gwiner do nuthin', till Martin comes.'

''The cullud man says reel nice en p'lite: 'Jest tell Martin I couldn't wait,'
en he busted out the winder en tore down the big road fast as he could en
faster, en he ain't never taken no more interest in watermelons since.'' . . .

And now the last:

''A cullud man cum to the white folks' house in the country en sed to the
man:

'' 'Boss, I'se hongry; gimme sumpin t'eat.'

''The man sed: 'All right, go round to the back do' en tell the cook to feed
you.'

''The cullud man sed: 'Boss, I'se neer 'bout starved, I ain't et fur a whole
week.'

''The man sed: 'All right, all right, go round to the kitchen.'

''The cullud man sed: 'Boss, if you gimme sumpin t'eat I'll split up all that
stove wood you got in yo' back yard.'

''The man sed: 'All right, all right, go en git that grub like I tole yer.'

''So he went. After 'bout three hours the man went to his back yard en saw
the cullud man, who wuz jest settin'. So he sed:

" 'Has you et?'

"En he sed: 'Yassir.'

"En he sed: 'Has you chopped up that wood-pile?'

"En he sed: 'Boss man, if you jest let me res' round till dinner time, after dinner I'll go en chop out that patch of cotton fur you.'

"So the man sed: 'All right, but don't you fool me no more.'

"After the cullud man had et him a big dinner he started out to the cotton patch en he met him a cooter [a mud-turtle] en the cooter sed to him:

" 'Nigger, you talks too much.'

"The nigger goes tearin' back to the big house en when he gits there the man cums out en sez:

" 'Nigger, has you chopped out that cotton?'

"En the nigger sez:

" 'Lawd, boss, I wuz on my way, fo' God I wuz, en I met a cooter en he started talkin' to me en I lit out from there en here I is.'

"The boss man was plenty riled and he sez:

" 'Nigger, take me to that cooter en if he don't start talkin', I'se goin' to cut your throat frum year to year."

"So they bof uvvem started fur the cotton patch en there in the middle of the big road set that cooter. En he never opened his mouth, he ain't sed nuthin'. So the man hopped on the nigger en whupped him sumpin' scand'lous en left fur the big house mighty sore at niggers en cooters. Well, the cullud man wuz neer 'bout through breshing hisself off en jest fo' moseying on off when the cooter poked his head out en looks at him en sez:

" 'Nigger, I tole you you talks too much.' "

STERLING A. BROWN

Brown was born in Washington, D.C., in 1901. His father, born a slave in Tennessee, had gone on to become a professor of religion at Howard University; Brown himself was a Phi Beta Kappa at Williams, took a Harvard master's degree, and became a legendary professor of English at several colleges including Fisk, Atlanta University, Vassar, and Howard. He was a pioneering folklorist, poetry scholar, and anthologist of black writing. He was also a first-rate poet. Brown's coolness, his wit, his unidealistic common touch, and his deft low-key use of dialect may have denied him that broad audience which looks to black poetry for the fire next time, but no one is

*less accommodating to prejudice than he, and the economical resonance of his verse is
like that of the blues. He can, I would venture to say, make an appreciative white or
black or Northern or Southern reader wince profoundly, but he can also—often
simultaneously—be heartily funny. He died in 1989.*

"Slim in Atlanta"

>   Down in Atlanta,
>   De whitefolks got laws
>   For to keep all de niggers
>   From laughin' outdoors.
>
>   Hope to Gawd I may die
>   If I ain't speakin' truth
>   Make de niggers do deir laughin
>   In a telefoam booth.
>
>   Slim Greer hit de town
>   An' de rebs got him told,—
>   "Dontcha laugh on de street,
>   If you want to die old."
>
>   Den dey showed him de booth,
>   An' a hundred shines
>   In front of it, waitin'
>   In double lines.
>
>   Slim thought his sides
>   Would bust in two,
>   Yelled, "Lookout, everybody,
>   I'm coming through!"
>
>   Pulled de other man out,
>   An' bust in de box,
>   An' laughed four hours
>   By de Georgia clocks.
>
>   Den he peeked through de door,
>   An' what did he see?
>   *Three* hundred niggers there
>   In misery.—

Some holdin' deir sides,
    Some holdin' deir jaws,
To keep from breakin'
    De Georgia laws.

An' Slim gave a holler,
    An' started again;
An' from three hundred throats
    Come a moan of pain.

An' everytime Slim
    Saw what was outside,
Got to whoopin' again
    Till he nearly died.

An' while de poor critters
    Was waitin' deir chance,
Slim laughed till dey sent
    Fo' de ambulance.

De state paid de railroad
    To take him away;
Den, things was as usural
    In Atlanta, Gee A.

"Slim Hears 'The Call'"

I

Down at the barbershop
    Slim had the floor,
"Ain't never been so
    Far down before.

"So ragged, I make a jaybird
    About to moult,
Look like he got on gloves
    An' a overcoat.

"Got to walk backwards
    All de time

Jes' a-puttin' on front
Wid a bare behime.

"Been down to skin and bones
Gittin' down to de gristle,
So de call sounds louder
Dan a factory whistle.

"Big holes is the onlies'
Things in my pocket,
So bein' a bishop
Is next on de docket.

"Lawd, lawd, yas Lawd,
I hears de call,
An' I'll answer, good Lawd,
Don't fret none atall.

"I heard it once
An' I hears it again
Broadcast from the station
W-I-N!

"Gonna be me a bishop
That ain't no lie,
Get my cake down here,
An' my pie in the sky.

II

"Saw a buddy th' other day,
Used to know him well
Best coon-can player
This side of hell.

"Had a voice as deep
As a bellerin' bull,
Called hogs in a way
Jes' beautiful.

"Ran across him down
In Caroline

Folks interduced him
    As a 'great divine.'

      "Had on a jimswinger
        Hangin' low,
      An' a collar put on
        Hindparts befo'.

"At first I jes' couldn't
    Fix his face,
Then I remembered him dealin'
    In Shorty Joe's place.

      " 'You got de advantage
        Of me, I fear—'
      Then all of a sudden
        'My dear—Brother Greer!'

"He let out a roar
    An' grabbed my hand:
'Welcome, thou Pilgrim
    To our Pleasant Land!'

      "Took me to a house
        Like de State Capitol:
      'Jes' a shanty, not fit
        Fo' you, at all

" 'Brother Greer, but if
    You'll stay wid me
I'll try to make it up
    In hosspitality.'

      "Called in his wife
        As purty as sin,
      An' his secketary, twict
        As purty again.

"When dey went out, he winked
    An' said—'Well, Slim?'
An' he looked at me,
    An' I looked at him.

III

"Little fatter an' greasier
Than when we had been
Side pardners together
In de ways of sin.

"Ran a great big school,
Was de president,
'Brother Greer, jus' see
What de Lawd hath sent!'

"An' he de kind of guy
Was sich a fool
Dey had to burn down de shack
To get him out of school.

"When de other pupils
Was doin' history
He was spellin' cat
With a double p.

"Couldn't do no problems,
But was pretty good
At beatin' out erasers
An' bringin' in wood.

"But he knew what side de bread
You put de butter on,
An' he could figger all right
For number one.

"So here he was de head man
Of de whole heap—
Wid dis solemn charge dat
He had to keep:

"A passel of Niggers
From near an' far
Bringin' in de sacred bucks
Regular.

"Stayed wid him a while,
　Watched him do his stuff,
Wid a pint of good sense,
　An' a bushel of bluff.

　　"Begged fo' his dyin' school
　　　At de conference
　　Took up nine thousand dollars
　　　An' eighty cents.

"An' I swear, as sure
　As my name's Slim Greer,
He repohted to de school
　Sixteen dollars clear.

　　" 'Expenses pretty high,'
　　　He said with a frown.
　　An' de conference held
　　　In de very next town!

"Ordered the convention
　To Los Angeles,
'Ain't no members out there,'
　Said his enemies.

　　" 'Dat's jes' de reason
　　　Why we gotta go,
　　Gotta missionize de heathen
　　　On de Western Sho'.

　" 'Furrin parts is callin','
　　De Bishop says,
'Besides, I got a cravin'
　　Fo' oranges.'

　　　"Filled a Pullman wid de delegates
　　　　He liked de best,
　　　An' took a private plane
　　　　Fo' de Golden West.

"Las' words he said
　As he rose in de air:

'Do lak me; take you' troubles
    To de Lord in prayer.

    " 'Brother Greer, do that,
        An' you will see,
    De Lawd'll be wid you,
        Like he's been wid me.'

IV

"I remembers his words
    Now de North Wind blows
Like de Memphis special
    Through my holy clothes.

    "Now dat thinkin' of ham an' eggs
        Makes me sick
    Got me a longin'
        Fo' de bishopric.

"I kin be a good bishop,
    I got de looks,
An' I ain't spoiled myself
    By readin' books.

    "Don't know so much
        'Bout de Holy Ghost,
    But I likes de long green
        Better'n most.

"I kin talk out dis worl'
    As you folks all know,
An' I'm good wid de women,
    Dey'll tell you so . . .

V

    "An' I says to all de Bishops,
        What is hearin' my song—
    Ef de cap fits you, brother,
        Put it on."

"*Sporting Beasley*"

Good glory, give a look at Sporting Beasley
Strutting, oh my Lord.

    Tophat cocked one side his bulldog head,
    Striped four-in-hand, and in his buttonhole
    A red carnation; Prince Albert coat
    Form-fitting, corset like; vest snugly filled,
    Gray morning trousers, spotless and full-flowing,
    White spats and a cane.

Step it, Mr. Beasley, oh step it till the sun goes down.

    Forget the snippy clerks you wait upon,
    Tread clouds of glory above the heads of pointing children,
    Oh, Mr. Peacock, before the drab barnfowl of the world.

    Forget the laughter when at the concert
    You paced down the aisle, your majesty,
    Down to Row A, where you pulled out your opera glasses.

    Majesty. . . .

    It's your turn now, Sporting Beasley,
    Step it off.

    The world is a ragbag; the world
    Is full of heathens who haven't seen the light;
    Do it, Mr. Missionary.

Great glory, give a look.

    Oh Jesus, when this brother's bill falls due,
    When he steps off the chariot
    And flicks the dust from his patent leathers with his silk handkerchief,
    When he stands in front of the jasper gates, patting his tie,

    And then paces in
    Cane and knees working like well-oiled slow-timed pistons;

Lord help us, give a *look* at him.

Don't make him dress up in no night gown, Lord.
Don't put no fuss and feathers on his shoulders, Lord.

Let him know it's heaven.

Let him keep his hat, his vest, his elkstooth, and everything.

Let him have his spats and cane
Let him have his spats and cane.

HARRY GOLDEN

Golden is not much read anymore, but his book Only in America *was an enormous best-seller in the '50s. Back before the civil rights movement he edited and also wrote a monthly newspaper,* The Carolina Israelite, *which drolly advanced a number of commonsense liberal notions without getting firebombed. John Egerton has reminded me that Golden once reported seeing three thermometers in an emergency room in the South—one marked "white," one "colored," and one "rectal." Golden said that "is what I call gradual integration."*

"The Vertical Negro Plan"

One of the factors involved in our tremendous industrial growth and economic prosperity is the fact that the South, voluntarily, has all but eliminated VERTICAL SEGREGATION. The tremendous buying power of the twelve million Negroes in the South has been based wholly on the absence of racial segregation. The white and Negro stand at the same grocery and supermarket counters; deposit money at the same bank teller's window; pay phone and light bills to the same clerk; walk through the same dime and department stores, and stand at the same drugstore counters.

It is only when the Negro "sets" that the fur begins to fly.

Now, since we are not even thinking about restoring VERTICAL SEGREGA-TION, I think my plan would not only comply with the Supreme Court decisions, but would maintain "sitting-down" segregation. Now here is the GOLDEN VERTICAL NEGRO PLAN. Instead of all those complicated proposals, all the next session needs to do is pass one small amendment which would provide *only* desks in all the public schools of our state—*no seats.*

The desks should be those standing-up jobs, like the old-fashioned book-keeping desk. Since no one in the South pays the slightest attention to a VERTICAL NEGRO, this will completely solve our problem. And it is not such a terrible inconvenience for young people to stand up during their classroom studies. In fact, this may be a blessing in disguise. They are not learning to read sitting down, anyway; maybe standing up will help. This will save more millions of dollars in the cost of our remedial English course when the kids enter college. In whatever direction you look, with the GOLDEN VERTICAL NEGRO PLAN you save millions of dollars, to say nothing of eliminating forever any danger to our public education system upon which rests the destiny, hopes, and happiness of this society.

My WHITE BABY PLAN offers another possible solution to the segregation problem—this time in a field other than education.

Here is an actual case history of the "White Baby Plan to End Racial Segregation":

Some months ago there was a revival of the Laurence Olivier movie, *Hamlet,* and several Negro schoolteachers were eager to see it. One Saturday afternoon they asked some white friends to lend them two of their little children, a three-year-old girl and a six-year-old boy, and, holding these white children by the hands, they obtained tickets from the movie-house cashier without a moment's hesitation. They were in like Flynn.

This would also solve the baby-sitting problem for thousands and thousands of white working mothers. There can be a mutual exchange of references, then the people can sort of pool their children at a central point in each neighborhood, and every time a Negro wants to go to the movies all she need do is pick up a white child—and go.

Eventually the Negro community can set up a factory and manufacture white babies made of plastic, and when they want to go to the opera or to a concert, all they need do is carry that plastic doll in their arms. The dolls, of course, should all have blond curls and blue eyes, which would go even further; it would give the Negro woman and her husband priority over the whites for the very best seats in the house.

While I still have faith in the WHITE BABY PLAN, my final proposal may prove to be the most practical of all.

Only after a successful test was I ready to announce formally the GOLDEN "OUT-OF-ORDER" PLAN.

I tried my plan in a city of North Carolina, where the Negroes represent 39 per cent of the population.

I prevailed upon the manager of a department store to shut the water off in his "white" water fountain and put up a sign, "Out-of-Order." For the first day or two the whites were hesitant, but little by little they began to drink out of the water fountain belonging to the "coloreds"—and by the end of the third week everybody was drinking the "segregated" water; with not a single solitary complaint to date.

I believe the test is of such sociological significance that the Governor should appoint a special committee of two members of the House and two Senators to investigate the GOLDEN "OUT-OF-ORDER" PLAN. We kept daily reports on the use of the unsegregated water fountain which should be of great value to this committee. This may be the answer to the necessary uplifting of the white morale. It is possible that the whites may accept desegregation if they are assured that the facilities are still "separate," albeit "Out-of-Order."

As I see it now, the key to my Plan is to keep the "Out-of-Order" sign up for at least two years. We must do this thing gradually.

MARSHALL FRADY

Besides his big books about George Wallace, Billy Graham, and what we call in the South the Holy Land, Marshall Frady of North Carolina has written scores of articles, many of them rhetorically venturous in a highly Southern way, for publications ranging from Life *to the* New York Review of Books. Southerners, *his collection of many of these pieces, includes a long straight-faced consideration of a man without whom no book of Southern comedy would be complete. When old Lester was governor of Georgia, I reviled him regularly in the* Atlanta Journal, *and Lord knows many of his pronouncements were objectively hateful as well as foolish, but he was antiestablishment, he seemed once in power to have a pretty good heart (he appointed more blacks to office than any Georgia governor had before), and in retrospect there is something touching about his ingenuousness. "They call me a clown," he told an enthusiastic audience while running unsuccessfully for reelection, "but what is wrong with being a clown once in awhile? Clowns are happy, humorous and witty; and I don't know any in prison." His politics were pretty much the same as Ronald*

Reagan's only less broadly palatable because more genuinely of the folk. This part of Frady's piece traces the Maddox ascendancy.

The Rise of Lester Maddox

In retrospect, the Sixties now seem a decade in the life of this country which passed like a malarial dream, in which the unthinkable became the commonplace, the surreal the familiar. It may seem, then, a reckless proposition, but there was perhaps no more astral occurrence during those bewitched ten years than the ascension of Lester Garfield Maddox—erstwhile fried-chicken peddler and pick-handle Dixie patriot—to the governorship of Georgia. The nation's only notice of him up till to then had been a single brief glimpse, in the summer of 1964, of a flushed, bespectacled figure with an onion-bulb head lunging gawkily about the parking lot of his Atlanta restaurant, a small black pistol clenched at his waist, shrilly shooing back into their car three black students who had presented themselves as customers. The next time everybody saw him, about two and a half years later, he was being inaugurated governor of the state.

There had been several affrays at his restaurant, beginning almost immediately after the 1964 civil-rights bill was signed—Lester on one occasion yelping at two black students seeking entrance, "You no-good dirty devils! You dirty Communists!" On another occasion, Lester merely stood in the doorway with a finger thoughtfully rummaging in one nostril as he watched, on a streetcorner twenty yards away, another small delegation of young blacks being persuaded by a gaggle of whites that a notable case of indigestion could ensue from eating his fried chicken; among the crowd surrounding the three youths—filling-station attendants, Georgia Tech students in tattered sweatshirts and bermudas, businessmen in shirt-sleeves and loosened ties licking ice-cream cones—were Lester's two stout sisters, one of whom demanded of the youths, "Have you boys been born into God's family? Have you been regenerated?" The rest of the crowd was less theological: "C'mon down to Mississippi, niggers! Six feet under, that's all!"

But that afternoon produced one of Lester's more memorable moments. He and his faithful were expecting a climactic confrontation, and Lester stalked up and down the street in front of his restaurant in the warm August sundown, trailed in his every move by a cheering multitude of some five hundred people. They soon created a colossal, horn-blaring traffic jam. When police began diverting cars down side streets at each end of the block, Lester suddenly became convinced it was all a conspiratorial maneuver to flush customers away from his restaurant, and he charged from one corner to the other to protest, the crowd happily tumbling after him. He tried to shove one patrolman out of the street, and then, to the admonitions of a police captain, squalled, "Shut your big mouth!" with the captain answering gently, "Now, Mr. Maddox . . ." But he was a man now mightily besieged, lost in a great, giddy, reckless transport of outrage. He finally screeched his glassy new black Pontiac out of his parking lot and swiftly barricaded one street through which police had been redirecting traffic, locking the car, pocketing the keys, and, with horns now wailing fearfully behind him, marched back down to his place at the bottom of the hill to deploy the rest of his family's fleet of cars to blockade the other side streets.

It was a countermaneuver that was triumphant for another hour or two. Once he hopped on a small bicycle and pedaled up to one corner to check on the situation there, then flagged a passing bus which police had let through and rode back to the other corner, standing tall and imperious right behind the windshield with his arms rigidly spread before him, holding onto the railing, his pose whimsically suggestive of Lord Nelson on the bridge of his warship as it heaved toward Cape Trafalgar. The police at last called wreckers to haul away his cars, and when the first arrived the crowd converged to block it, with Lester himself swinging up on the heavy dangling coupler and clinging there grimly. Finally the driver, caught up in the occasion's spirit of merry uproar, climbed up on the top of his cab and sat there, plump, legs folded under him Buddha-fashion, chugging on his cigar and waving as the throng applauded him.

As it turned out, no Negroes materialized, but that really didn't matter anymore. Walking back to his restaurant, his shirt limp and gray with sweat and the back of his coat smudged with rust and dirt from the coupler, Lester somehow brought to mind the mayor of some small provincial French town who had suddenly taken it on himself to flamboyantly, if futilely, defy in the town square the forces of Paris' federal officialdom. He strode right down the center of the street, his head cocked high, his face flushed and his balding head shining with sweat, his long legs resolutely scissoring and his arms swinging, as the crowd cheered him from the sidewalks, "Attaway, Lester! Oh, man— whatta man!" Reaching his restaurant again, Lester was met by his wife, and he hugged her, shouting, "Don't worry, hon," as the crowd pressed around them, still whooping in the soft summer dusk—"Don't get knocked down, sugar," he advised her. He paused to pose with her under his flickering neon restaurant sign for photographers, and then on an impulse hugged her to him again and gave her a great smack on her cheek. And his eyes suddenly twinkled with tears.

.   .   .   .

When he arose on winter mornings as a small boy, before he could eat breakfast, on a cold stomach he had to start a fire in the kitchen, get eggs from the henhouse, heat water, and take his bath in a tin tub. His father was a laborer at the Atlantic Steel Company, and Lester grew up, with three brothers and three sisters, in the same drab smoky neighborhood where one day he was to build his famous restaurant. But then he was just a boy riding his bicycle—the weightless, effortless glide, the exquisite flickering of light through the spokes—on his daily newspaper route, sometimes hovering at the back of a Coca-Cola truck to snitch a bottle, then veering away, madly pedaling off into the calm flare of a Georgia afternoon.

"I tried to play ball," he once recollected, "but the other boys used to make fun of me, you know, 'cause of my being nearsighted. They used to call me 'Cocky' 'cause of my eyes." He sold newspapers for a while on downtown streetcorners, three cents a copy, but "I never could get me a good spot. Somebody else would always take the good spots." Later he worked at a jeweler's supply house, then as an apprentice dental technician, a soda jerk, a bicycle delivery boy—coasting disembodied, the silent wheels strumming the long afternoon light. His career as a restaurateur had its beginnings in a drink stand in an old pigeon coop, which he stocked with a case of Coca-Cola, a case of NuGrape, mint candy, and bread. His love was then borne to him there on a bicycle, eating an Eskimo Pie. She rode past his drink stand several times, and finally he asked her if he could borrow her bike—he fell off. A few years later they were married.

He was nineteen then, and working, as his father had, at Atlantic Steel—a clanging, fierce, cheerless place, with stark heaps of scrap metal rusting in weeds beneath a murderous sun. He earned ten dollars a week. "Men were afraid to get a drink of water, to go to the bathroom, for fear of losing their jobs," he would later remember.

During World War II, he worked in a plant near Atlanta that produced fleets of B-29 bombers, among them, he later reported, the one that dropped the first atomic bomb. He also gave chicken farming a fling for a while. "I had several thousand broilers once. But I lost every one of 'em. They got involved in this cannibalism, you know." On the whole, it was an accurate assessment, as Lester himself later reflected in one speech, that "if anyone ever had a perfect background for failure, I did."

But then he opened his restaurant on an off-street downtown—a fried-chicken emporium he dubbed the Pickrick ("You PICK them out, we'll RICK them up!")—and began, for the first time in his life, to prosper modestly. All the while, he continued his zest for riding bicycles. Shortly before that pandemonious confrontation with the Atlanta police in front of the Pickrick, he won a neighborhood bicycle race, pumping furiously and ecstatically, quickly gathering the wind and leaving all the others, a middle-aged man in his shirtsleeves skimming off into the blue summer twilight. . . .

Nevertheless, after the melees at his restaurant following the passage of the public-accommodations law, Lester elected to shut his restaurant rather than serve Negroes. Over the succeeding months, something seemed to fade within him. His voice became not exactly quieter but tinier, his smiles somewhat pale and fleeting. One summer afternoon in 1964, not long after closing down the Pickrick, he showed a visitor around his rambling home of brick and glass, which was situated among the lilting lawns and shaded quiet of Atlanta's expensive northwest section. A sign at the doorway warned, "Beware of Dog" (it turned out to be a collie with a peculiarly hoarse and unconvincing bark that ended in a squeak), and another sign over the carport curtly advised, "Stay in Car and Blow Horn." But inside, among the deep mist-green carpets and the cold glow of indirect lighting, Lester shuffled about somewhat droopily. "I really love this place," he said at one point, "but I'm probably going to lose it all too." He stepped out once on his wide back porch where, in a corner, a myna bird was flicking from perch to perch in a small cage, and as Lester went by, the bird croaked, "Hello, you rascal!" Lester paused, grinned fondly, and replied, "Yeah, you ole rascal," but with an odd unaccustomed dullness in his voice.

He eventually reopened his place downtown, but this time the mild dining music was replaced by doughty fifes and drums flurrying through "Yankee Doodle Dandy," and he was peddling crates of ax handles instead of plates of drumsticks, his stock including a complete family backlash kit of "mama-sized drumsticks and junior-sized drumsticks—those clubs, you know, that railway switchmen used to carry." He now considered going into the patriotism business full-time. "I think I'll probably turn the Pickrick into a national shrine," he speculated, a glimmer of excitement setting his damp eyes to blinking behind his glasses. "We'll take people through on tours, and I'll have an eternal light burning inside. . . ." Instead, he had to sell the place after a short, indifferent spell of business. He opened a furniture store which he also called the Pickrick, advertising, "You will want Pickrick furniture, because our furniture is for families who live better."

But he was becoming restless again. Whenever the legislature was in session, he could be found in the capitol's corridors almost every morning—a solitary, forlorn, but deathlessly eager figure, handing out patriotism tracts with the indefatigable vigor of a streetcorner evangelist, totally impervious to the snickers and impatient condescensions of the legislators. The doorkeeper to the house was notified he would be fired for only two reasons: "Laying down on your job, or if you ever let Lester Maddox get past you and loose in this chamber." Nevertheless, Lester possessed that peculiar redoubtability, a ferocious fidelity to purpose, that is one of the askance fortitudes of absolute hopelessness. There was, in truth, a kind of valiantness about him; he was like a cracker Don Quixote. And in 1965, he decided he would run for governor.

"I didn't see any way in the world I was gonna lose," he declared later. "I kept telling the politicians, 'I'm gonna beat every one of you. You either gonna come in now or come in later.' " Believing the secret of genius to be directness, he commenced by drawing up a platform and printing fifty thousand copies, which he mailed to people over the state. Then he got into his dusty white Pontiac station wagon and, with a four-foot ladder tied to the top, disappeared into the backlands beyond Atlanta. It wasn't long before one began to notice along thin country highways a spattering of small cardboard signs tacked up high on telephone poles and pine trees, announcing in simple black print, "THIS IS MADDOX COUNTRY." "I used the ladder," Lester related afterward, "to climb up on and fasten the signs way up there so people couldn't come along and tear 'em off. I'd go down the highway and see all these big two-thousand-dollar billboards put up by my opponents, and I'd just pull off the road and get my ladder and hammer up ten little signs of my own and ruin 'em all—and it wouldn't cost me but a quarter."

His campaign staff at this point consisted, in its entirety, of himself, his wife, his daughter, and a sister. In his odyssey around the state, he stopped for occasional speaking engagements, and slept—raggedly, in two-hour snatches—in a succession of bleary little motels, frequently lunging from his bed in the middle of the night, fumbling on his glasses, and scribbling out a suddenly inspired phrase of fulmination in the small harsh glare of a metal desk lamp. The following day, he would stop at telephone booths along the road and call in publicity releases to the AP and UPI—insistent, unreal, dimly crackling little notifications out of the obscure interior of Georgia ("Oh, hell, it's Lester on the phone again") that were largely ignored.

Astoundingly, he bobbed up as one of the run-off contenders in the Democratic primary. With that, he drove across Atlanta to the oak-bowered knoll where the new governor's mansion was under construction. He got out and chatted convivially with the workmen, shortly inquiring as to about when they figured they'd be finished with it. They told him, and he got back in his station wagon and drove away. A certain change now seemed to settle over him. "You used to see Lester running around with his eyes wide open with outrage, kind of hysterical all the time, you know," said one veteran reporter. "But then there was a picture of him the morning after he had gotten into the run-off. His eyelids had dropped a full inch, he had this hazy little beatific smile on his face, his lips just parted a little bit—he had the drowsy, peaceful look of a lizard that has just swallowed a blue-bottle fly."

Immediately after winning the run-off, he made another trip out to the mansion site to check on the progress. Satisfied, he now struck off after Callaway. By this point he had a lot more company, and other folks' cars, and other folks' planes. He carried with him everywhere a basket of apples, and as his party approached a town, he would toot happily, "Buster, give me an apple from back there!"

. He was hardly dispirited by the fact that, in the general election, he actually trailed Callaway by some 3,100 votes. Showing up for that Jaycee banquet in a downtown Atlanta hotel the night before the legislature was to name him governor of Georgia, Lester—although this was not precisely a gathering of his sort of people—was hugely expansive, slapping backs and shouting, "How are you, boy, you doin' all right?" Then he discovered that he was seated right across the table from the Callaways, at point-blank conversational range. But he was in an invincibly amiable mood. Presently, sitting with an almost military erectness, both forearms lying perfectly straight and parallel on the table, one hand holding a cookie and the other hand wrapped around a glass of milk, he addressed himself to the Callaways: "Bo, yawl ski, don't you?"

This sally met with icy politeness from the Callaways—Mrs. Callaway, in fact, simply didn't speak. Undaunted, Lester continued nibbling on his cookie, beaming and nodding at others up and down the table. But once, for a long moment, as Callaway was whispering to his wife, Lester stared silently at the two of them, a light little quizzical smile on his face, as if he were puzzled by their remoteness, by the fact they would not heartily include him in their conversation. Mrs. Callaway, a handsome, tanned, tawny woman wearing a royal-blue sheath dress, turned to a reporter behind her and breathed, "I don't know whether it's the heat or the food or the situation, but it's stifling in here." She managed to maintain a semblance of a smile, though, her jaw set. For a while, Lester and the Callaways studiously avoided each other's eyes. Lester now was spooning down his food with a kind of absent half-mindful haste, not quite getting his mouthfuls of coffee swallowed as he turned to greet well-wishers leaning over him, his chin discreetly dribbling. Then, for another long moment, he gazed at the Callaways again, bemused, and abruptly said, "Well, did yawl have a nice Christmas?" Callaway murmured something, and Lester listened with a very grave and attentive expression on his face. Holding his coffee cup poised midway to his mouth, he then turned to Callaway's wife and inquired, "How about you, Mrs. Callaway?" She gave him a small, sweet smile. "No, we didn't," she snapped, "thanks to you." He stared at her a second longer, blinked twice, and finally raised his cup up to his lips, took a long sip, and set it down, glancing up at the ceiling was an expression of airy, angelic innocence.

There had been a moment back during his campaign: late one dull gray autumn afternoon after a rally in a small north-Georgia village, Lester had instructed his driver to stop the car, and got out and engaged in a brief, low conversation with a small boy who had a bicycle. Lester then shakily mounted the undersized bike and, as his aides sat patiently in the car, he went wobbling down the sidewalk to the corner, then back, his expression absolutely serene and composed, almost blissful, his knees pumping high as a light snow began to fall like a noiseless benediction everywhere around him in the dim, hushed afternoon. . . .

The following Saturday evening, Lester set out to make his first official appearance as governor at a national Jaycee banquet on Jekyll Island—a moss-drifted resort along Georgia's southern coastline. Strapped in his seat in a state plane, looking a bit uncomfortably pent in a tuxedo and black tie, with his pink face gleaming and his spectacles polished and his thin faint hair combed back behind his balding dome, he could have been George F. Babbitt setting forth for a Zenith dinner party. Immediately after takeoff, a state trooper brought him a Coke, and he cradled it in his lap with both hands as he continued a discursive, running review of his fortunes.

". . . Yessir. Then when it looked like I was gonna win after all, some of these politicians and so forth starting coming out for me—after 'long soul-searching,' they said." There came a scampish twinkle in his eye, and he briefly scratched his ear. "You know how they search their souls, don't you?" Holding his Coke in one hand, he raised up slightly from his seat and word-lessly, with the barest hint of a smile, his eyebrows arching prankishly, reached his other hand around to grab his hip pocket. Then he settled back in the seat and took a quick pull at his Coke, watching the other passengers chuckle around him. "Gonna have to sell my house, though," Lester abruptly an-nounced. "Just can't keep up the payments. I was out there to the new mansion the other day, and the workmen told me they ought to be finished around March. Probably be longer, though. I'll probably have to make two more house payments." He mused a moment. "We aren't gonna be serving any liquor there, you know. I have seen liquor destroy a lot of good people. I've experienced some of it in my own family. . . ."

He looked out of his window for a while. Then he turned back to the passengers in the cabin and, his face touched with a certain grave wonder, launched into a peculiar recital of various manglings and accidents he had witnessed, narrating them in the most elaborate, reverent detail. "I've seen several people killed before. One dropped right in front of me once when I was working at the steel mill, fella was electrocuted. My brother, he was burned horribly, and he's suffered ever since. One hundred and ten opera-tions. Then, my son, when he was just a little thing, I threw him once right through the front windshield of my car when I had to stop real quick. When I went to pick him up, the whole side of his face here"—Lester carefully traced a diagram on his own cheek with his forefinger—"hung down. I carried him to the hospital like that, holding the meat on with my hand. Then, 'nother time"—he took a swallow of his Coke—"he was out playing in the yard and caught on fire somehow. When the maid looked out the window, he was just standing there with his hands up in the air like this"—he threw both arms up as high as he could in his tuxedo—''burning all over. Then, 'nother time, he was playing up in some rafters on the back porch and fell, and caught his chin on a nail up there. It went all the way through here''—Lester lifted his chin and pointed—''and came out''—he bared his lower gum and pointed—''right here. He was just hanging there in the air on that nail through his chin. You look at him now, the next time you see him, you can see the scar there.''

Despite this odd little Grand Guignol recountal, Lester was in an irrepressibly buoyant humor. ''I guess in the Thirties was when I got interested in government, attending neighborhood political rallies—I wasn't but about eighteen, nineteen at the time. But my first real intense desire was in 1957, when a friend of mine was running for mayor and wasn't making the race I thought he should—he wouldn't work. So I decided I'd get into it. I read one of those ads about Dale Carnegie, and I went over there to check it out. I got halfway through that class, and I announced I was gonna run for mayor of Atlanta.'' There was an instant of silence as the plane lurched, bumped. Lester quickly glanced around and lifted his eyebrows alertly. Then the plane smoothed back out, and Lester went on, ''When I got in that first mayor's campaign, they thought I was funny. Yessir. But the people didn't think so. Nosir. Everybody thought I was funny but the people.'' He meditated for a moment. '' 'Course, it's been hard for my wife to get used to, my running all over the state. But I told her once, 'Honey, every man should accomplish more than his daddy did. If I was just somebody who wanted to work at a job like everybody else, wanted to just run a private business like everybody else, come home every night and eat supper and go to bed like everybody else, then I'm gonna *be* like everybody else.' Yessir, taking that Dale Carnegie course . . .''

He blinked. The plane was bumping again, and again his eyes widened slightly in suspense. He waited for it to steady. ''. . . uh, taking that Dale Carnegie course, that was the greatest thing I ever did. My daddy told me one time, said, 'You better be careful, you gonna bite off more than you can chew one of these days.' I told him, 'Dad, there's not a job in this state I can't handle.' I still think I can do any job in this state, right this minute—'cept maybe doctor. That's something different, you know, being a doctor. But anything else, I can sho do. You can go to the top in anything.'' He turned to the state trooper who was sitting on the arm of the seat behind him, tilted forward and listening intently. ''You remember that, young man. You just set your mind to it, you can do *anything.*'' The trooper nodded vigorously. ''I'm listening, governor, I'm listening.''

The plane was riding level and resistless now, and there was a sensation in the cabin of motionless suspension—like the sensation, almost, of floating along on a bicycle. Lester presently reported, ''You know, though, I told President Johnson at least forty times that the trouble going on in the country today was gonna happen. After the civil-rights bill was signed, I sent him must've been forty letters and telegrams. One of 'em I sent cost me *thirty* dollars. But you know what? He never answered a single one of my letters or telegrams. Nosir!'' He leaned forward then, his elbows on his knees, and inquired in a low, earnest voice, ''Johnson and all these others—I wonder sometimes. Do you reckon they thought I was a nut?''

ALICE CHILDRESS

Childress, born in South Carolina in 1920, is best known as the author of the novel A Hero Ain't Nothing but a Sandwich, *which was made into a movie. The following selections are from her 1956 book* Like One of the Family: Conversations from a Domestic's Life.

''Mrs. James''

Well, Marge, you haven't heard anything! You should hear the woman I work for . . . she's really something. Calls herself ''Mrs. James!'' All the time she says ''Mrs. James.''

The first day I was there she come into the kitchen and says, ''Mildred, Mrs. James would like you to clean the pantry.'' Well, I looked 'round to see if she meant her mother-in-law or somebody, and then she adds, ''If anyone calls, Mrs. James is out shopping,'' and with that she sashays out the door.

Now she keeps on talking that way all the time, the whole time I'm there. That woman wouldn't say ''I'' or ''me'' for nothing in the world. The way I look at it . . . I guess she thought it would be too personal.

Now, Marge, you know I don't work Saturdays for nobody! Well, sir! Last Friday she breezed in the kitchen and fussed around a little . . . movin' first the salt and then the pepper. I could feel something brewin' in the air. Next thing you know she speaks up. ''Mildred,'' she says, ''Mrs. James will need you this Saturday.'' I was polishin' silver at the time, but I turned around and looked her dead in the eye and said, ''Mildred does not work on Saturdays.''

Well, for the rest of the day things went along kind of quiet—like but just before time for me to go home she drifted by the linen closet to check the ruffle on a guest towel and threw in her two cents more. "Mildred," she says, "a depression might do this country some good, then some people might work eight days a week and be glad for the chance to do it."

I didn't bat an eyelash, but about fifteen minutes later, when I was headin' for home, I stopped off at the living room and called to her, "That's very true, but on the other hand some folks might be doin' their own housework . . . don'tcha know." With that and a cool "good night" I gently went out the front door. . . .

Oh, but we get along fine now. Just fine!

"The Pocketbook Game"

Marge . . . day's work is an education! Well, I mean workin' in different homes you learn much more than if you was steady in one place . . . I tell you, it really keeps your mind sharp tryin' to watch for what folks will put over on you.

What? . . . No, Marge, I do not want to help shell no beans, but I'd be more than glad to stay and have supper with you, and I'll wash the dishes after. Is that all right?

Who put anything over on who? . . . Oh, yes! It's like this . . . I been working for Mrs. E. one day a week for several months and I notice that she has some peculiar ways. Well, there was only one thing that really bothered me and that was her pocketbook habit . . . No, not those little novels . . . I mean her purse—her handbag.

Marge, she's got a big old pocketbook with two long straps on it, and whenever I'd go there, she'd be propped up in a chair with her handbag double wrapped tight around her wrist, and from room to room she'd roam with that purse hugged to her bosom. . . . Yes, girl! This happens every time! No, there's *nobody* there but me and her. . . . Marge, I couldn't say nothin' to her! It's her purse, ain't it? She can hold onto it if she wants to!

I held my peace for months, tryin' to figure out how I'd make my point: . . . Well, bless Bess! *Today was the day!* . . . Please, Marge, keep shellin' the beans so we can eat! I know you're listenin', but you listen with your ears, not your hands. . . . Well, anyway, I was almost ready to go home when she steps in the room hangin' onto her bag as usual and says, "Mildred will you ask the super to come up and fix the kitchen faucet?" "Yes, Mrs. E.," I says, "as soon as I leave." "Oh, no," she says, "he may be gone by then. Please go now." "All right," I says, and out the door I went, still wearin' my Hoover apron.

I just went down the hall and stood there a few minutes . . . and then I rushed back to the door and knocked on it as hard and frantic as I could. She flung open the door, sayin', "What's the matter? Did you see the super?" "No," I says, gaspin' hard for breath, "I was almost downstairs when I remembered . . . *I left my pocketbook!*"

With that I dashed in, grabbed my purse, and then went down to get the super! Later, when I was leavin', she says real timid-like, "Mildred, I hope that you don't think I distrust you because . . ." I cut her off real quick. "That's all right, Mrs. E., I understand. 'Cause if I paid anybody as little as you pay me, I'd hold my pocketbook, too!"

Marge, you fool, lookout! You gonna drop the beans on the floor!

MARILYN NELSON WANIEK

"Tuskegee Airfield"

For the Tuskegee Airmen

These men,
these proud black men:
our first to touch
their fingers to the sky.

The Germans learned to call them
Die Schwarzen Vogelmenschen.
They called themselves
The Spookwaffe.

Laughing.
And marching to class under officers
whose thin-lipped ambition
was to *wash the niggers out.*

Sitting at attention
for lectures about ailerons, airspeed, altimeters

from boring lieutenants who believed
you monkeys ain't meant to fly.

Oh, there were parties,
cadet-dances, guest appearances
by the Count
and the lovely Lena.

There was the embarrassing
adulation of Negro civilians.
A woman approached my father in a bar
where he was drinking with his buddies.
Hello, Airman. She held out her palm.
Will you tell me my future?

There was that,
like a breath of pure oxygen.
But first
they had to earn wings.

There was this one instructor
who was pretty nice.
I mean, we just sat around
and *talked* when a flight had gone well.

But he was from Minnesota,
and he made us sing
the Minnesota Fight Song
before we took off.

If you didn't sing it,
your days were numbered.
"Minnesota, hats off to thee . . ."
That bastard!

One time I had a check-flight
with an instructor from Louisiana.
As we were about to head for base,
he chopped the power.

Force-landing, nigger.
There were trees everywhere I looked.

Except on that little island . . .
I began my approach.

The instructor said, *Pull Up.*
That was an excellent approach.
Real surprised.
But where would you have taken off, wise guy?

I said, *Sir,*
I was ordered
to land the plane.
Not take off.

The instructor grinned.
Boy, if your ass
is as hard as your head,
you'll go far in this world.

"Women's Locker Room"

The splat of bare feet on wet tile
breaks the incredible luck
of my being alone in here.
I snatch a stingy towel
and sidle into the shower. I'm already soaped
by the time a white hand turns the neighboring knob.
I recognize the arm as one that flashed
for many rapid laps while I dogpaddled at the shallow end.
I dart an appraising glance: She arches down
to wash her lifted heel, and is beautiful.
As she straightens, I look into her eyes.

For an instant I remember human sacrifice:
The female explorer led skyward,
her blond tresses loose on her neck;
the drums of our pulses grew louder;
I raised the obsidian knife.
Violets bloomed in the clefts of the stairs.

I could freeze her name in an ice cube,
bottle the dirt from her footsteps

with potent graveyard dust.
I could gather the combings from her hairbrush
to burn with her fingernail clippings,
I could feed her Iago powder.
Childhood taunts, branded ears,
a thousand insults swirl through my memory
like headlines in a city vacant lot.

I jump, grimace, divide like an amoeba
into twin rages that stomp around
with their lips stuck out,
then come suddenly face to face.
They see each other and know that they
are mean mamas.
Then I bust out laughing
and let the woman live.

CHARLES W. CHESNUTT

Around the time Mark Twain was born, a prosperous white Fayetteville, North Carolina, tobacco merchant named Cade was siring and supporting but not acknowledging five children by a free woman of color named Ann Chesnutt. By virtue of their light skin these children enjoyed certain economic advantages in the slave South, but Charles Chesnutt's father did not enjoy them enough to keep him from moving to Cleveland, where Charles was born in 1858. In 1866, however, the family returned to Fayetteville, where Charles lived until he was twenty-five. He could have passed for white but didn't, so got little education. But he taught himself shorthand, moved to Cleveland, worked as a court reporter, studied the law, and became an attorney. He also wrote comic sketches for magazines and newspapers. These evolved into more ambitious stories told in dialect by an ex-slave raconteur, Uncle Julius, which were published by The Atlantic Monthly *and collected along with others of Chesnutt's dialect tales in a book,* The Conjure Woman. *Uncle Julius, who always has something up his sleeve as he spins folk reminiscences for a Northern couple who have bought a Carolina plantation, is an African-American's version of Uncle Remus, and the difference is instructive. "Dave's Neckliss," the best of these tales, is, in fact, in Uncle Julius's particulars, tragic. I include it here as a triumph of comic wiliness* against a heritage of agony: Julius's use of this over-the-top horror story (how strictly true, how cannily conjured?) to get over on his boggled white listeners is the more deeply delicious for the undismissable shock of the material. I say "delicious"; every time I take a bite of ham now, I taste this story. Chesnutt has taken a convention from which white writers derived quaintness and made it reek of slavery—that twist, I submit, is darkly delightful. Moving on from dialect tales to racial-issue novels, Chesnutt became a literary figure of some prominence and a member of Booker T. Washington's Committee of Twelve, but eventually he returned to court reporting to make a living. He died, having been honored by a medal from the NAACP, in 1932.

"Dave's Neckliss"

"Have some dinner, Uncle Julius?" said my wife.

It was a Sunday afternoon in early autumn. Our two women-servants had gone to a camp-meeting some miles away, and would not return until evening. My wife had served the dinner, and we were just rising from the table when Julius came up the lane, and, taking off his hat, seated himself on the piazza.

The old man glanced through the open door at the dinner-table, and his eyes rested lovingly upon a large sugar-cured ham, from which several slices had been cut, exposing a rich pink expanse that would have appealed strongly to the appetite of any hungry Christian.

"Thanky, Miss Annie," he said, after a momentary hesitation. "I dunno ez I keers ef I does tas'e a piece er dat ham, ef yer 'll cut me off a slice un it."

"No," said Annie, "I won't. Just sit down to the table and help yourself; eat all you want, and don't be bashful."

Julius drew a chair up to the table, while my wife and I went out on the piazza. Julius was in my employment; he took his meals with his own family, but when he happened to be about our house at mealtimes, my wife never let him go away hungry.

I threw myself into a hammock, from which I could see Julius through an open window. He ate with evident relish, devoting his attention chiefly to the ham, slice after slice of which disappeared in the spacious cavity of his mouth. At first the old man ate rapidly, but after the edge of his appetite had been taken off he proceeded in a more leisurely manner. When he had cut the sixth slice of ham (I kept count of them from a lazy curiosity to see how much he *could* eat) I saw him lay it on his plate; as he adjusted the knife and fork to cut it into smaller pieces, he paused, as if struck by a sudden thought, and a tear rolled down his rugged cheek and fell upon the slice of ham before him. But the emotion, whatever the thought that caused it, was transitory, and in a moment he continued his dinner. When he was through eating, he came out

on the porch, and resumed his seat with the satisfied expression of countenance that usually follows a good dinner.

"Julius," I said, "you seemed to be affected by something a moment ago.
Was the mustard so strong that it moved you to tears?"

"No, suh, it wa'n't de mustard; I wuz studyin' 'bout Dave."

"Who was Dave, and what about him?" I asked.

The conditions were all favorable to storytelling. There was an autumnal
languor in the air, and a dreamy haze softened the dark green of the distant
pines and the deep blue of the Southern sky. The generous meal he had made
had put the old man in a very good humor. He was not always so, for his
curiously undeveloped nature was subject to moods which were almost childish in their variableness. It was only now and then that we were able to study,
through the medium of his recollection, the simple but intensely human inner
life of slavery. His way of looking at the past seemed very strange to us; his
view of certain sides of life was essentially different from ours. He never
indulged in any regrets for the Arcadian joyousness and irresponsibility which
was a somewhat popular conception of slavery; his had not been the lot of the
petted houseservant, but that of the toiling fieldhand. While he mentioned
with a warm appreciation the acts of kindness which those in authority had
shown to him and his people, he would speak of a cruel deed, not with the
indignation of one accustomed to quick feeling and spontaneous expression,
but with a furtive disapproval which suggested to us a doubt in his own mind as
to whether he had a right to think or to feel, and presented to us the curious
psychological spectacle of a mind enslaved long after the shackles had been
struck off from the limbs of its possessor. Whether the sacred name of liberty
ever set his soul aglow with a generous fire; whether he had more than the
most elementary ideas of love, friendship, patriotism, religion—things which
are half, and the better half, of life to us; whether he even realized, except in a
vague, uncertain way, his own degradation, I do not know. I fear not; and if
not, then centuries of repression had borne their legitimate fruit. But in the
simple human feeling, and still more in the undertone of sadness which per-
vaded his stories, I thought I could see a spark which, fanned by favoring
breezes and fed by the memories of the past, might become in his children's
children a glowing flame of sensibility, alive to every thrill of human happiness
or human woe.

"Dave use' ter b'long ter my old marster," said Julius; "he wuz raise' on
dis yer plantation, en I kin 'member all erbout 'im, fer I wuz old 'nuff ter chop
cotton w'en it all happen'. Dave wuz a tall man, en monst'us strong: he could
do mo' wuk in a day dan any yuther two niggers on de plantation. He wuz one
er dese yer solemn kine er men, en nebber run on wid much foolishness, like
de yuther darkies. He use' ter go out in de woods en pray; en w'en he hear de
han's on de plantation cussin' en gwine on wid dere dancin' en foolishness, he

use' ter tell 'em 'bout religion en jedgmen'-day, w'en dey would haf ter gin account fer eve'y idle word en all dey yuther sinful kyarin's-on.

"Dave had l'arn' how ter read de Bible. Dey wuz a free nigger boy in de settlement w'at wuz monst'us smart, en could write en cipher, en wuz alluz readin' books er papers. En Dave had hi'ed dis free boy fer ter l'arn 'im how ter read. Hit wuz 'g'in' de law, but co'se none er de niggers did n' say nuffin ter de w'ite folks 'bout it. Howsomedever, one day Mars Walker—he wuz de overseah—foun' out Dave could read. Mars Walker wa'n't nuffin but a po' bockrah, en folks said he could n' read ner write hisse'f, en co'se he did n' lack ter see a nigger w'at knowed mo' d'n he did; so he went en tole Mars Dugal'. Mars Dugal' sont fer Dave, en ax' 'im 'bout it.

"Dave did n't hardly knowed w'at ter do; but he could n' tell no lie, so he 'fessed he could read de Bible a little by spellin' out de words. Mars Dugal' look' mighty solemn.

" 'Dis yer is a se'ious matter,' sezee; 'it 's 'g'in' de law ter l'arn niggers how ter read, er 'low 'em ter hab books. But w'at yer l'arn out'n dat Bible, Dave?'

"Dave wa'n't no fool, ef he wuz a nigger, en sezee:

" 'Marster, I l'arns dat it 's a sin fer ter steal, er ter lie, er fer ter want w'at doan b'long ter yer; en I l'arns fer ter love de Lawd en ter 'bey my marster.'

"Mars Dugal' sorter smile' en laf' ter hisse'f, like he 'uz might'ly tickle' 'bout sump'n, en sezee:

" 'Doan 'pear ter me lack readin' de Bible done yer much harm, Dave. Dat's w'at I wants all my niggers fer ter know. Yer keep right on readin', en tell de yuther han's w'at yer be'n tellin' me. How would yer lack fer ter preach ter de niggers on Sunday?'

"Dave say he'd be glad fer ter do w'at he could. So Mars Dugal' tole de overseah fer ter let Dave preach ter de niggers, en tell 'em w'at wuz in de Bible, en it would he'p ter keep 'em fum stealin' er runnin' erway.

"So Dave 'mence' ter preach, en done de han's on de plantation a heap er good, en most un 'em lef' off dey wicked ways, en 'mence' ter love ter hear 'bout God, en religion, en de Bible; en dey done dey wuk better, en did n' gib de overseah but mighty little trouble fer ter manage 'em.

"Dave wuz one er dese yer men w'at did n' keer much fer de gals— leastways he did n' 'tel Dilsey come ter de plantation. Dilsey wuz a monst'us peart, good-lookin', gingybread-colored gal—one er dese yer high-steppin' gals w'at hol's dey heads up, en won' stan' no foolishness fum no man. She had b'long' ter a gemman over on Rockfish, w'at died, en whose 'state ha' ter be sol' fer ter pay his debts. En Mars Dugal' had be'n ter de oction, en w'en he seed dis gal a-cryin' en gwine on 'bout bein' sol' erway fum her ole mammy, Aun' Mahaly, Mars Dugal' bid 'em bofe in, en fotch 'em ober ter our plantation.

"De young nigger men on de plantation wuz des wil' atter Dilsey, but it did n' do no good, en none un 'em could n' git Dilsey fer dey junesey,* 'tel Dave 'mence' fer ter go roun' Aun' Mahaly's cabin. Dey wuz a fine-lookin' couple, Dave en Dilsey wuz, bofe tall, en well-shape', en soopl'. En dey sot a heap by one ernudder. Mars Dugal' seed 'em tergedder one Sunday, en de nex' time he seed Dave atter dat, sezee:

" 'Dave, w'en yer en Dilsey gits ready fer ter git married, I ain' got no rejections. Dey 's a poun' er so er chawin' terbacker up at de house, en I reckon yo' mist'iss kin fine a frock en a ribbin er two fer Dilsey. Youer bofe good niggers, en yer neenter be feared er bein' sol' 'way fum one ernudder long ez I owns dis plantation; en I 'spec's ter own it fer a long time yit.'

"But dere wuz one man on de plantation w'at did n' lack ter see Dave en Dilsey tergedder ez much ez ole marster did. W'en Mars Dugal' went ter de sale whar he got Dilsey en Mahaly, he bought ernudder han', by de name er Wiley. Wiley wuz one er dese yer shiny-eyed, double-headed little niggers, sha'p ez a steel trap, en sly ez de fox w'at keep out'n it. Dis yer Wiley had be'n pesterin' Dilsey 'fo' she come ter our plantation, en had nigh 'bout worried de life out'n her. She did n' keer nuffin fer 'im, but he pestered her so she ha' ter th'eaten ter tell her marster fer ter make Wiley let her 'lone. W'en he come ober to our place it wuz des ez bad, 'tel bimeby Wiley seed dat Dilsey had got ter thinkin' a heap 'bout Dave, en den he sorter hilt off aw'ile, en purten' lack he gin Dilsey up. But he wuz one er dese yer 'ceitful niggers, en w'ile he wuz laffin' en jokin' wid de yuther han's 'bout Dave en Dilsey, he wuz settin' a trap fer ter ketch Dave en git Dilsey back fer hisse'f.

"Dave en Dilsey made up dere min's fer ter git married long 'bout Christmas time, w'en dey 'd hab mo' time fer a weddin'. But 'long 'bout two weeks befo' dat time ole mars 'mence' ter lose a heap er bacon. Eve'y night er so somebody 'ud steal a side er bacon, er a ham, er a shoulder, er sump'n, fum one er de smoke'ouses. De smoke'ouses wuz lock', but somebody had a key, en manage' ter git in some way er 'nudder. Dey 's mo' ways 'n one ter skin a cat, en dey 's mo' d'n one way ter git in a smoke'ouse—leastways dat 's w'at I hearn say. Folks w'at had bacon fer ter sell did n' hab no trouble 'bout gittin' rid un it. Hit wuz 'g'in de law fer ter buy things fum slabes; but Lawd! dat law did n' 'mount ter a hill er peas. Eve'y week er so one er dese yer big covered waggins would come 'long de road, peddlin' terbacker en w'iskey. Dey wuz a sight er room in one er dem big waggins, en it wuz monst'us easy fer ter swop off bacon fer sump'n ter chaw er ter wa'm yer up in de wintertime. I s'pose de peddlers did n' knowed dey wuz breakin' de law, caze de niggers alluz went at night, en stayed on de dark side er de waggin; en it wuz mighty hard fer ter tell *w'at* kine er folks dey wuz.

*Sweetheart.

"Atter two er th'ee hund'ed er meat had be'n stole', Mars Walker call all de niggers up one ebenin', en tol' 'em dat de fus' nigger he cot stealin' bacon on dat plantation would git sump'n fer ter 'member it by long ez he lib'. En he say he'd gin fi' dollars ter de nigger w'at 'skiver' de rogue. Mars Walker say he s'picion' one er two er de niggers, but he could n' tell fer sho, en co'se dey all 'nied it w'en he 'cuse em un it.

"Dey wa'n't no bacon stole' fer a week er so, 'tel one dark night w'en somebody tuk a ham fum one er de smoke'ouses. Mars Walker des cusst awful w'en he foun' out de ham wuz gone, en say he gwine ter sarch all de niggers' cabins; w'en dis yer Wiley I wuz tellin' yer 'bout up'n say he s'picion' who tuk de ham, fer he seed Dave comin' 'cross de plantation fum to'ds de smoke'ouse de night befo'. W'en Mars Walker hearn dis fum Wiley, he went en sarch' Dave's cabin, en foun' de ham hid under de flo'.

"Eve'ybody wuz 'stonish'; but dere wuz de ham. Co'se Dave 'nied it ter de las', but dere wuz de ham. Mars Walker say it wuz des ez he 'spected: he did n' b'lieve in dese yer readin' en prayin' niggers; it wuz all 'pocrisy, en sarve' Mars Dugal' right fer 'lowin' Dave ter be readin' books w'en it wuz 'g'in' de law.

"W'en Mars Dugal' hearn 'bout de ham, he say he wuz might'ly 'ceived en dissapp'inted in Dave. He say he would n' nebber hab no mo' conference in no nigger, en Mars Walker could do des ez he wuz a mineter wid Dave er any er de res' er de niggers. So Mars Walker tuk'n tied Dave up en gin 'im forty; en den he got some er dis yer wire clof w'at dey uses fer ter make sifters out'n, en tuk'n wrap' it roun' de ham en fasten it tergedder at de little een'. Den he tuk Dave down ter de blacksmif shop, en had Unker Silas, de plantation blacksmif, fasten a chain ter de ham, en den fasten de yuther een' er de chain roun' Dave's neck. En den he says ter Dave, sezee:

" 'Now, suh, yer 'll wear dat neckliss fer de nex' six mont's; en I 'spec's yer ner none er de yuther niggers on dis plantation won' steal no mo' bacon dyoin' er dat time.'

"Well, it des 'peared ez if fum dat time Dave did n' hab nuffin but trouble. De niggers all turnt ag'in' 'im, caze he be'n de 'casion er Mars Dugal' turnin' 'em all ober ter Mars Walker. Mars Dugal' wa'n't a bad marster hisse'f, but Mars Walker wuz hard ez a rock. Dave kep' on sayin' he did n' take de ham, but none un 'em did n' b'lieve 'im.

"Dilsey wa'n't on de plantation w'en Dave wuz 'cused er stealin' de bacon. Ole mist'iss had sont her ter town fer a week er so fer ter wait on one er her darters w'at had a young baby, en she did n' fine out nuffin 'bout Dave's trouble 'tel she got back ter de plantation. Dave had patien'ly endyoed de finger er scawn, en all de hard words w'at de niggers pile' on 'im, caze he wuz sho' Dilsey would stan' by 'im, en would n' b'lieve he wuz a rogue, ner none er de yuther tales de darkies wuz tellin' 'bout 'im.

"W'en Dilsey come back fum town, en got down fum behine de buggy whar she b'en ridin' wid ole mars, de fus' nigger 'ooman she met says ter her—

" 'Is yer seed Dave, Dilsey?'

" 'No, I ain' seed Dave,' says Dilsey.

" 'Yer des oughter look at dat nigger; reckon yer would n' want 'im fer yo' junesey no mo'. Mars Walker cotch 'im stealin' bacon, en gone en fasten' a ham roun' his neck, so he can't git it off'n hisse'f. He sut'nly do look quare.' En den de 'ooman bus' out laffin' fit ter kill herse'f. W'en she got thoo laffin' she up'n tole Dilsey all 'bout de ham, en all de yuther lies w'at de niggers be'n tellin' on Dave.

"W'en Dilsey started down ter de quarters, who should she meet but Dave, comin' in fum de cotton-fiel'. She turnt her head ter one side, en purten' lack she did n' seed Dave.

" 'Dilsey!' sezee.

"Dilsey walk' right on, en did n' notice 'im.

" '*Oh,* Dilsey!'

"Dilsey did n' paid no 'tention ter 'im, en den Dave knowed some er de niggers be'n tellin' her 'bout de ham. He felt monst'us bad, but he 'lowed ef he could des git Dilsey fer ter listen ter 'im for a minute er so, he could make her b'lieve he did n' stole de bacon. It wuz a week er two befo' he could git a chance ter speak ter her ag'in; but fine'ly he cotch her down by de spring one day, en sezee:

" 'Dilsey, w'at fer yer won' speak ter me, en purten' lack yer doan see me? Dilsey, yer knows me too well fer ter b'lieve I'd steal, er do dis yuther wick'ness de niggers is all layin' ter me—yer *knows* I would n' do dat, Dilsey. Yer ain' gwine back on yo' Dave, is yer?'

"But w'at Dave say did n' hab no 'fec' on Dilsey. Dem lies folks b'en tellin' her had p'isen' her min' 'g'in' Dave.

" 'I doan wanter talk ter no nigger,' says she, 'w'at be'n whip' fer stealin', en w'at gwine roun' wid sich a lookin' thing ez dat hung roun' his neck. I's a 'spectable gal, *I* is. W'at yer call dat, Dave? Is dat a cha'm fer to keep off witches, er is it a noo kine er neckliss yer got?'

"Po' Dave did n' knowed w'at ter do. De las' one he had 'pended on fer ter stan' by 'im had gone back on 'im, en dey did n' 'pear ter be nuffin mo' wuf libbin' fer. He could n' hol' no mo' pra'r-meetin's, fer Mars Walker would n' 'low 'im ter preach, en de darkies would n' 'a' listen' ter 'im ef he had preach.' He did n' eben hab his Bible fer ter comfort hisse'f wid, fer Mars Walker had tuk it erway fum 'im en burnt it up, en say ef he ketch any mo' niggers wid Bibles on de plantation he 'd do 'em wuss'n he done Dave.

"En ter make it still harder fer Dave, Dilsey tuk up wid Wiley. Dave could see him gwine up ter Aun' Mahaly's cabin, en settin' out on de bench in de

moonlight wid Dilsey, en singin' sinful songs en playin' de banjer. Dave use'
ter scrouch down behine de bushes, en wonder w'at de Lawd sen' 'im all dem
tribberlations fer.

"But all er Dave's yuther troubles wa'n't nuffin side er dat ham. He had
wrap' de chain roun' wid a rag, so it did n' hurt his neck; but w'eneber he
went ter wuk, dat ham would be in his way; he had ter do his task, howsomedever, des de sam ez ef he did n' hab de ham. W'eneber he went ter lay
down, dat ham would be in de way. Ef he turn ober in his sleep, dat ham
would be tuggin' at his neck. It wuz de las' thing he seed at night, en de fus'
thing he seed in de mawnin'. W'eneber he met a stranger, de ham would be
de fus' thing de stranger would see. Most un 'em would 'mence' ter laf, en
whareber Dave went he could see folks p'intin' at him, en year 'em sayin':

" 'W'at kine er collar dat nigger got roun' his neck?' er, ef dey knowed
'im, 'Is yer stole any mo' hams lately?' er 'W'at yer take fer yo' neckliss,
Dave?' er some joke er 'nuther 'bout dat ham.

"Fus' Dave did n' mine it so much, caze he knowed he had n' done nuffin.
But bimeby he got so he could n' stan' it no longer, en he'd hide hisse'f in de
bushes w'eneber he seed anybody comin', en alluz kep' hisse'f shet up in his
cabin atter he come in fum wuk.

"It wuz monst'us hard on Dave, en bimeby, w'at wid dat ham eberlastin'
en etarnally draggin' roun' his neck, he 'mence' fer ter do en say quare things,
en make de niggers wonder ef he wa'n't gittin' out'n his mine. He got ter
gwine roun' talkin' ter hisse'f, en singin' cornshuckin' songs, en laffin' fit ter
kill 'bout nuffin. En one day he tole one er de niggers he had 'skivered a noo
way fer ter raise hams—gwine ter pick 'em off'n trees, en save de expense er
smoke'ouses by kyoin' 'em in de sun. En one day he up'n tole Mars Walker he
got sump'n pertickler fer ter say ter 'im; en he tuk Mars Walker off ter one
side, en tole 'im he wuz gwine ter show 'im a place in de swamp whar dey wuz
a whole trac' er lan' covered wid ham trees.

"W'en Mars Walker hearn Dave talkin' dis kine er fool-talk, en w'en he
seed how Dave wuz 'mencin' ter git behine in his wuk, en w'en he ax' de
niggers en dey tole 'im how Dave be'n gwine on, he 'lowed he reckon' he 'd
punish' Dave ernuff, en it mou't do mo' harm dan good fer ter keep de ham on
his neck any longer. So he sont Dave down ter de blacksmif shop en had de
ham tuk off. Dey wa'n't much er de ham lef' by dat time, fer de sun had melt
all de fat, en de lean had all swivel' up, so dey wa'n't but th'ee er fo' poun's
lef'.

"W'en de ham had be'n tuk off'n Dave, folks kinder stopped talkin' 'bout
'im so much. But de ham had be'n on his neck so long dat Dave had sorter got
use' ter it. He look des lack he'd los' sump'n fer a day er so atter de ham wuz
tuk off, en did n' 'pear ter know w'at ter do wid hisse'f; en fine'ly he up'n
tuk'n tied a lighterd-knot ter a string, en hid it under de flo' er his cabin, en

w'en nobody wuz n' lookin' he'd take it out en hang it roun' his neck, en go off in de woods en holler en sing; en he allus tied it roun' his neck w'en he went ter sleep. Fac', it 'peared lack Dave done gone clean out'n his mine. En atter a w'ile he got one er de quarest notions you eber hearn tell un. It wuz 'bout dat time dat I come back ter de plantation fer ter wuk—I had be'n out ter Mars Dugal's yuther place on Beaver Crick for a mont' er so. I had hearn 'bout Dave en de bacon, en 'bout w'at wuz gwine on on de plantation; but I did n' b'lieve w'at dey all say 'bout Dave, fer I knowed Dave w'n't dat kine er man. One day atter I come back, me'n Dave wuz choppin' cotton tergedder, w'en Dave lean' on his hoe, en motion' fer me ter come ober close ter 'im; en den he retch ober en w'ispered ter me.

" 'Julius,' sezee, 'did yer knowed yer wuz wukkin' long yer wid a ham?'

"I could n' 'magine w'at he meant. 'G'way fum yer, Dave,' says I. 'Yer ain' wearin' no ham no mo'; try en fergit 'bout dat; 't ain' gwine ter do yer no good fer ter 'member it.'

" 'Look a-yer, Julius,' sezee, 'kin yer keep a secret?'

" 'Co'se I kin, Dave,' says I. 'I doan go roun' tellin' people w'at yuther folks says ter me.'

" 'Kin I trus' yer, Julius? Will yer cross yo' heart?'

"I cross' my heart. 'Wush I may die ef I tells a soul,' says I.

"Dave look' at me des lack he wuz lookin' thoo me en 'way on de yuther side er me, en sezee:

" 'Did yer knowed I wuz turnin' ter a ham, Julius?'

"I tried ter 'suade Dave dat dat wuz all foolishness, en dat he ought n't ter be talkin' dat-a-way—hit wa'n't right. En I tole 'im ef he'd des be patien', de time would sho'ly come w'en eve'ything would be straighten' out, en folks would fine out who de rale rogue wuz w'at stole de bacon. Dave 'peared ter listen ter w'at I say, en promise' ter do better, en stop gwine on dat-a-way; en it seem lack he pick' up a bit w'en he seed dey wuz one pusson did n' b'lieve dem tales 'bout 'im.

"Hit wa'n't long atter dat befo' Mars Archie McIntyre, ober on de Wimbleton road, 'mence' ter complain 'bout somebody stealin' chickens fum his hen'ouse. De chickens kep' on gwine, en at las' Mars Archie tole de han's on his plantation dat he gwine ter shoot de fus' man he ketch in his hen'ouse. In less'n a week atter he gin dis warnin', he cotch a nigger in de hen'ouse, en fill' 'im full er squir'l-shot. W'en he got a light, he 'skivered it wuz a strange nigger; en w'en he call' one er his own sarven's, de nigger tole 'im it wuz our Wiley. W'en Mars Archie foun' dat out, he sont ober ter our plantation fer ter tell Mars Dugal' he had shot one er his niggers, en dat he could sen' ober dere en git w'at wuz lef' un 'im.

"Mars Dugal' wuz mad at fus'; but w'en he got ober dere en hearn how it all happen', he did n' hab much ter say. Wiley wuz shot so bad he wuz sho' he wuz gwine ter die, so he up'n says ter ole marster:

" 'Mars Dugal,' sezee, 'I knows I's be'n a monst'us bad nigger, but befo' I go I wanter git sump'n off'n my mine. Dave did n' steal dat bacon w'at wuz tuk out'n de smoke'ouse. *I* stole it all, en I hid de ham under Dave's cabin fer ter th'ow de blame on him—en may de good Lawd fergib me fer it.'

"Mars Dugal' had Wiley tuk back ter de plantation, en sont fer a doctor fer ter pick de shot out'n 'im. En de ve'y next' mawnin' Mars Dugal' sont fer Dave ter come up ter de big house; he felt kinder sorry fer de way Dave had be'n treated. Co'se it wa'n't no fault er Mars Dugal's, but he wuz gwine ter do w'at he could fer ter make up fer it. So he sont word down ter de quarters fer Dave en all de yuther han's ter 'semble up in de yard befo' de big house at sunup nex' mawnin'.

"Yearly in de mawnin' de niggers all swarm' up in de yard. Mars Dugal' wuz feelin' so kine dat he had brung up a bairl er cider, en tole de niggers all fer ter he'p deyselves.

"All de han's on de plantation come but Dave; en bimeby, w'en it seem lack he wa'n't comin', Mars Dugal' sont a nigger down ter de quarters ter look fer 'im. De sun wuz gittin' up, en dey wuz a heap er wuk ter be done, en Mars Dugal' sorter got ti'ed waitin'; so he up'n says:

" 'Well, boys en gals, I sont fer yer all up yer fer ter tell yer dat all dat 'bout Dave's stealin' er de bacon wuz a mistake, ez I s'pose yer all done hearn befo' now, en I's mighty sorry it happen'. I wants ter treat all my niggers right, en I wants yer all ter know dat I sets a heap by all er my han's w'at is hones' en smart. En I want yer all ter treat Dave des lack yer did befo' dis thing happen', en mine w'at he preach ter yer; fer Dave is a good nigger, en has had a hard row ter hoe. En de fus' one I ketch sayin' anythin' 'g'in' Dave, I'll tell Mister Walker ter gin 'im forty. Now take ernudder drink er cider all roun', en den git at dat cotton, fer I wanter git dat Persimmon Hill trac' all pick' ober terday.'

"W'en de niggers wuz gwine 'way, Mars Dugal' tole me fer ter go en hunt up Dave, en bring 'im up ter de house. I went down ter Dave's cabin, but could n' fine 'im dere. Den I look' roun' de plantation, en in de aidge er de woods, en 'long de road; but I could n' fine no sign er Dave. I wuz 'bout ter gin up de sarch, w'en I happen' fer ter run 'cross a foot-track w'at look' lack Dave's. I had wukked 'long wid Dave so much dat I knowed his tracks: he had a monst'us long foot, wid a holler instep, w'ich wuz sump'n skase 'mongs' black folks. So I follered dat track 'cross de fiel' fum de quarters 'tel I get ter de smoke'ouse. De fus' thing I notice' wuz smoke comin' out'n de cracks: it wuz cu'ous, caze dey had n' be'n no hogs kill' on de plantation fer six mont' er so, en all de bacon in de smoke'ouse wuz done kyoed. I could n' 'magine fer ter sabe my life w'at Dave wuz doin' in dat smoke'ouse. I went up ter de do' en hollered:

"'Dave!'

"Dey did n' nobody answer. I did n' wanter open de do', fer w'ite folks is monst'us pertickler 'bout dey smoke'ouses; en ef de oberseah had a-come up en cotch me in dere, he mou't not wanter b'lieve I wuz des lookin' fer Dave. So I sorter knock at de do' en call' out ag'in:

"'O Dave, hit's me—Julius! Doan be skeered. Mars Dugal' wants yer ter come up ter de big house—he done 'skivered who stole de ham.'

"But Dave did n' answer. En w'en I look' roun' ag'in en did n' seed none er his tracks gwine way fum de smoke'ouse, I knowed he wuz in dere yit, en I wuz 'termine' fer ter fetch 'im out; so I push de do' open en look in.

"Dey wuz a pile er bark burnin' in de middle er de flo', en right ober de fier, hangin' fum one er de rafters, wuz Dave; dey wuz a rope roun' his neck, en I did n' haf ter look at his face mo' d'n once fer ter see he wuz dead.

"Den I knowed how it all happen'. Dave had kep' on gittin' wusser en wusser in his mine, 'tel he des got ter b'lievin' he wuz all done turnt ter a ham; en den he had gone en built a fier, en tied a rope roun' his neck, des lack de hams wuz tied, en had hung hisse'f up in de smoke'ouse fer ter kyo.

"Dave wuz buried down by the swamp, in de plantation buryin' groun'. Wiley did n' died fum de woun' he got in Mars McIntyre's hen'ouse; he got well atter a w'ile, but Dilsey would n' hab nuffin mo' ter do wid 'im, en 't wa'n't long 'fo' Mars Dugal' sol' 'im ter a spekilater on his way souf—he say he did n' want no sich a nigger on de plantation, ner in de county, ef he could he'p it. En w'en de een' er de year come, Mars Dugal' turnt Mars Walker off, en run de plantation hisse'f atter dat.

"Eber sence den," said Julius in conclusion, "w'eneber I eats ham, it min's me er Dave. I lacks ham, but I nebber kin eat mo' d'n two er th'ee poun's befo' I gits ter studyin' 'bout Dave, en den I has ter stop en leab de res' fer ernudder time."

There was a short silence after the old man had finished his story, and then my wife began to talk to him about the weather, on which subject he was an authority. I went into the house. When I came out, half an hour later, I saw Julius disappearing down the lane, with a basket on his arm.

At breakfast, next morning, it occurred to me that I should like a slice of ham. I said as much to my wife.

"Oh, no, John," she responded, "you shouldn't eat anything so heavy for breakfast."

I insisted.

"The fact is," she said, pensively, "I couldn't have eaten any more of that ham, so I gave it to Julius."

CHARLES HENRY SMITH

Born in 1826 in Lawrenceville, Georgia, Smith became a lawyer and the mayor of Rome, Georgia, before the War. From 1861 till his death in 1903 he wrote letters from his creation, Bill Arp, that were published in various Southern newspapers and reprinted around the country. During the War, Smith tried traitors and served as an officer in the Army of Northern Virginia. This letter, written five months after Appomattox from a defeated humorist to a Northern one, his friend, is kind of sweet. Unbowed, Smith pursued law, politics, and business until he was able as of 1877 just to farm and live off Arp.

"Bill Arp Addresses Artemus Ward"

Rome, Ga., September 1, 1865

Mr. Artemus Ward, *Showman*—

SIR: The reason I write to you in perticler, is because you are about the only man I know in all "God's country," *so-called.* For some several weeks I have been wantin' to say sumthin'. For some several years we rebs, *so-called,* but now late of said country deceased, have been tryin' mighty hard to do somethin'. We didn't quite do it, and now it's very painful, I assure you, to dry up all of a sudden, and make out like we wasn't there.

My friend, I want to say somethin'. I suppose there is no law agin' thinkin', but thinkin' don't help me. It don't let down my thermomyter. I must explode myself generally so as to feel better. You see I'm tryin' to harmonize. I'm tryin' to soften down my feelin's. I'm endeavoring to subjugate myself to the level of surroundin' circumstances, *so-called.* But I can't do it until I am allowed to say somethin'. I want to quarrel with somebody and then make friends. I ain't no giant-killer. I ain't no Norwegian bar. I ain't no boa-constrickter, but I'll be hornswaggled if the talkin' and writin' and slanderin' has got to be all done on one side any longer. Sum of your folks have got to dry up or turn our folks loose. It's a blamed outrage, *so-called.* Ain't you editors got nothin' else to do but peek at us, and squib at us, and crow over us? Is every man what can write a paragraph to consider us bars in a cage, and be always a-jobbin' at us to hear us growl? Now, you see, my friend, that's what's disharmonious, and do you jest tell 'em, one and all, e pluribus unum, so-called, that if they don't stop it at once or turn us loose to say what we please, why, we rebs, so-called, have unanimously and jointly and severally resolved to—to—to—think very hard of it—if not harder.

That's the way to talk it. I ain't agoin' to commit myself. I know when to put on the brakes. I ain't goin' to say all I think. Nary time. No, sir. But I'll jest tell you, Artemus, and you may tell it to your show. If we ain't allowed to express our sentiments, we can take it out in hatin'; and hatin' runs heavy in my family, sure. I hated a man once so bad that all the hair cum off my head, and the man drowned himself in a hog-waller that night. I could do it agin, but you see I'm tryin' to harmonize, to acquiess, to becum calm and sereen.

Now, I suppose that, poetically speakin',

> In Dixie's fall,
> We sinned all.

But talkin' the way I see it, a big feller and a little feller, so-called, got into a fite, and they fout and fout a long time, and everybody all 'round kept hollerin', "hands off," but helpin' the big feller, until finally the little feller caved in and hollered enuf. He made a bully fite, I tell you. Well, what did the big feller do? Take him by the hand and help him up, and brush the dirt off his clothes? Nary time! No, sur! But he kicked him arter he was down, and throwed mud on him, and drugged him about and rubbed sand in his eyes, and now he's gwine about huntin' up his poor little property. Wants to confiscate it, so-called. Blame my jacket if it ain't enuf to make your head swim.

But I'm a good Union man, so-called. I ain't agwine to fight no more. I shan't vote for the next war. I ain't no gurrilla. I've done tuk the oath, and I'm gwine to keep it, but as for my bein' subjugated, and humilayted, and amalgamated, and enervated, as Mr. Chase says, it ain't so—nary time. I ain't ashamed of nuthin' neither—ain't repentin'—ain't axin' for no one-horse, short-winded pardon. Nobody needn's be playin' priest around me. I ain't got no twenty thousand dollars. Wish I had; I'd give it to these poor widders and orfins. I'd fatten my own numerous and interestin' offspring in about two minutes and a half. They shouldn't eat roots and drink branch-water no longer. Poor unfortunate things! to cum into this subloonary world at such a time. There's four or five of them that never saw a sirkis or piece of chees, nor a reesin. There's Bull Run Arp, and Harper's Ferry Arp, and Chicahominy Arp, that never saw the pikters in a spellin' book. I tell you, my friends, we are the poorest people on the face of the earth—but we are poor and proud. We made a bully fite, and the whole American nation ought to feel proud of it. It shows what

Americans can do when they think they are imposed upon. Didn't our four fathers fight, bleed and die about a little tax on tea, when not one in a thousand drunk it? Bekaus they succeeded, wasn't it glory? But if they hadn't, I suppose it would have been treason, and they would have been bowin' and scrapin' round King George for pardon. So it goes, Artemus, and to my mind, if the whole thing was stewed down it would make about half a pint of humbug. We had good men, great men, Christian men, who thought we was right, and many of them have gone to the undiscovered country, and have got a pardon as is a pardon. When I die I am mighty willing to risk myself under the shadow of their wings, whether the climate be hot or cold. So mote it be.

Well, maybe I've said enough. But I don't feel easy yet. I'm a good Union man, certain and sure. I've had my breeches died *blue,* and I've bot a *blue* bucket, and I very often feel *blue,* and about twice in a while I go to the doggery and git *blue,* and then I look up at the *blue* cerulean heavens and sing the melancholy chorus of the *Blue*-tailed Fly. I'm doin' my durndest to harmonize, and think I could succeed if it wasn't for sum things.

I don't want much. I ain't ambitious, as I used to was. You all have got your shows and monkeys and sircusses and brass bands and organs, and can play on the patrolyum and the harp of a thousand strings, and so on, but I've only got one favor to ax you. I want enough powder to kill a big yaller stump-tail dog that prowls around my premises at night. Pon my honor, I won't shoot at anything blue or black or mulatter. Will you send it? Are you and your folks so skeered of me and my folks that you won't let us have any ammunition? Are the squirrels and crows and black racoons to eat up our little corn-patches? Are the wild turkeys to gobble all around with impunity? If a mad dog takes the hiderphoby, is the whole community to run itself to death to get out of the way? I golly! it looks like your people had all took the rebelfoby for good, and was never gwine to get over it. See here, my friend, you must send me a litle powder and a ticket to your show, and me and you will harmonize sertin.

With these few remarks I think I feel better, and I hope I han't made nobody fitin' mad, for I'm not on that line at this time.

I am truly your friend, all present or accounted for.

A. J. LIEBLING

Liebling, who wrote rousingly of food, war, boxing, politics, and the press for The New Yorker *from the 1930s until he died in 1964, was no Southerner, but like H. L. Mencken, only far more sympathetically, he relished at least one aspect of Southern color. Liebling came to Louisiana in 1959 to scoff at Earl Long, but stayed to appreciate. This is an excerpt from the resultant classic of impressionistic political reporting,* The Earl of Louisiana.

''Earl Long's Finest Moment''

Since the Governor was not available in the flesh, my friends took me after dinner to see and hear him on film. In the projection room of television station WDSU, which is off a handsome Creole courtyard in the French Quarter, they had arranged for a showing of a documentary composed of various television-newsreel shots, and from this encounter I date my acquaintance with Uncle Earl. The cameramen had covered all the great moments of that fulminating May session of the legislature, which began with the Governor riding high and ended, for him, when he was led from the floor, tired and incoherent, by Margaret Dixon, the managing editor of the Baton Rouge *Advocate*.

A day later he was under heavy sedation and on his way to Texas, where he arrived, he subsequently said, with ''not enough clothes on me to cover a red bug, and a week later I was enjoying the same wardrobe.'' But within a fortnight he had talked a Texas judge into letting him return to Louisiana on his promise to matriculate at a private hospital in New Orleans. After signing himself in and out of the New Orleans hospital, the Governor had started for Baton Rouge to assume power, only to be stopped by sheriff's deputies at the behest of his wife, Miz Blanche, who had then committed him to the State Hospital at Mandeville. Thence he had been rescued by a faithful retainer, the lawyer Joe Arthur Sims, who sought a writ of habeas corpus. Once the Governor had regained temporary liberty, he completed the job by firing the director of the Department of Hospitals and the superintendent of the hospital, who, in the normal course of events, might have appeared against him to contend that he was insane.

In the opening newsreel shots Long appeared a full-faced, portly, peppery, white-haired man, as full of *hubris* as a dog of ticks in spring, sallying out on the floor of the Legislature to wrest the microphone from the hands of opposition speakers. "Let him talk, Governor, let him talk," a man in the foreground of the picture—perhaps the Speaker—kept saying during these episodes, but the Governor never would. He would shake his finger in his subjects' faces, or grab the lectern with both hands and wag his bottom from side to side. He interrupted one astonished fellow to ask, "What's your name?"

"John Waggoner, from Plain Dealing." (This is the name of a town.)

"Well, well, you look like a fine man. Don't let nothing run over you."

Some of the newsreel clips were of the Governor's press conferences, and in one, when a reporter asked him whether he thought he could manage his legislators, he said, "You know, the Bible says that before the end of time billy goats, tigers, rabbits and house cats are all going to sleep together. My gang looks like the Biblical proposition is here." This was the first good sample of his prose I had had a chance to evaluate, and I immediately put him on a level with my idol Colonel John R. Stingo, the Honest Rainmaker, who, at the age of eighty-five, is selling lots at Massena, New York, a community he predicts will be the Pittsburgh of the future.

In another remark to a reporter I thought I detected a clue to what was to set him off. The Governor said he had reduced 29 pounds, from 203 to 174, in a few months at his doctor's behest. To do this he must have been hopped up with thyroid and Dexedrine, and his already notorious temper, continually sharpened by ungratified appetite, had snapped like a rubber band pulled too hard.

Khrushchev, too, looks like the kind of man his physicians must continually try to diet, and historians will some day correlate these sporadic deprivations, to which he submits "for his own good," with his public tantrums. If there is to be a world cataclysm, it will probably be set off by skim milk, Melba toast, and mineral oil on the salad.

The newsreel also included a sequence in which the Governor sounded off on Mayor deLesseps S. Morrison of New Orleans, who for years had been his rival in Democratic primaries. "I hate to say this—I hate to boost old Dellasoups—but he'll be second again." (Long beat Morrison badly in the 1956 race for Governor. He always referred to him as "Dellasoups" and represented him as a city slicker.) "I'd rather beat Morrison than eat any blackberry, huckleberry pie my mama ever made. Oh, how I'm praying for that stump-wormer to get in there. I want him to roll up them cuffs, and get out that little old tuppy, and pull down them shades, and make himself up. He's the easiest man to make a nut out of I've ever seen in my life." The "tuppy," for "toupee," was a slur on Morrison's hair, which is thinning, though only Long has ever accused him of wearing a wig. As for the make-up, Morrison occasionally used it for television. Earl's Morrison bit was a standard feature of his repertoire, and I could see from the mobile old face how he enjoyed it. Morrison took the "dude" attacks so to heart that in his last campaign he performed dressed like Marlon Brando in deshabille.

And, as if to illustrate the old Long vote-getting method, which had worked in Louisiana ever since Huey took the stump in 1924, the newsreel anthologist had included part of a speech of the Governor's, evidently favoring a higher license fee for heavy (rich men's) vehicles. "Don't you think the people that use the roads ought to pay for building them? Take a man out in the country, on an old-age pension. He don't own an automobile, can't even drive one— do you think he should pay for highways for overloaded trucks that tear up the highways faster than you can build them? We got a coffee-ground formation in south Louisiana—it cost three times more to build a road in south Louisiana than it does in west Texas—but still the *Picayune* says they don't know, they can't understand. Well, there's a hell of a lot that they don't understand—that they *do* understand but they don't want *you* to understand. And you can say this, as long as I've got the breath and the life and the health, I've got the fortitude and the backbone to tell 'em, and dammit they know I'll tell 'em, and that's why they're against me. You can only judge the future by the past."

Almost all the elements of the Long appeal are there, starting with the pensions, which Huey conceived and sponsored, and on which a high propor-tion of the elderly people in Louisiana live—seventy-two dollars a month now, a fine sum in a low-income state. "But still the *Picayune* says they don't know, they can't understand" refers to the good roads whose high price the *Times-Picayune* constantly carps at, because, the Longs always imply, the *Pica-yune,* organ of the czarists, secretly wants *bad* roads. "They know I'll tell them, and that's why they're against me" means that the press—a monopoly press in New Orleans now—has always been against the Longs, the champions of the poor; when all the press consistently opposes one skillful man, he can turn its opposition into a backhanded testimony to his unique virtue.

"You can only judge the future by the past" is a reminder that the past in Louisiana, before Huey, was painful for the small farmers in the northern hills and along the southern bayous. It is not hard to select such an all-inclusive passage from a Long speech; they recur constantly, the mixture as before.

Then followed clips showing the crucial scrimmages on the floor of the Legislature. In the beginning, I could see, the Governor was as confident as Oedipus Tyrannus before he got the bad news. He felt a giant among pygmies, a pike among crappies, as he stood there among the legislators, most of whom owed him for favors—special bills passed for their law clients, state jobs for constituents, "contributions" for their personal campaign funds, and so on. But that day the Governor was rushing in where the dinner-party liberals who represent one or two Southern states in Washington have steadily refused to tread. Old Earl was out to liberalize the registration law, passed in Reconstruction times, that gives parish (i.e., county) registrars the power to disqualify voters arbitrarily on "educational" grounds. Except in a few rural parishes, the effect of this law has been on the decline for decades, but now a white-supremacy group in the legislature had moved for its strict enforcement—against colored voters, of course. It took me a minute or two to realize that the old "demagogue" was actually making a civil-rights speech.

"Now, this registration you're talking about," he said. "That was put through in carpetbag days, when colored people and scalawags were running rampant in our country. You got to interpret the Constitution. There ain't ten people looking at me, including myself, who, if properly approached or attacked, could properly qualify to vote. They say this a nigger bill—ain't no such." (The old law, if enforced impartially, would also have disqualified a number—large but hard to estimate—of older white men and women who had been on the rolls since they were twenty-one but were not Ph.Ds. Needless to say, the bill's proponents did not expect enforcement to be impartial.)

At this point, the camera focused on a young man with slick black hair and a long upper lip who was wearing a broad necktie emblazoned with a Confederate flag and who addressed a microphone with gestures appropriate to mass meetings. "It's Willie Rainach, the Citizens' Council boy," one of my mentors told me. Rainach, who is a state senator from Summerfield, in Claiborne Parish, pleaded with his colleagues not to let Long "sell Louisiana down the river." (I felt another concept crumbling; I had always thought it was Negroes who got sold down rivers.)

Long, grabbing for a microphone—probably he had no legal right to be in the argument at all—remonstrated, "I think there's such a thing as being overeducated. Scientists tell me there's enough wrinkles up there—" tapping his head—"to take care of all kinds of stuff. Maybe I'm getting old—I'm losing some of mine. I hope that don't happen to Rainach. After all this over, he'll probably go up there to Summerfield, get up on his front porch, take off his shoes, wash his feet, look at the moon and get close to God." This was gross comedy, a piece of miming that recalled Jimmy Savo impersonating the Mississippi River. Then the old man, changing pace, shouted in Rainach's direction, "And when you *do,* you got to *recognize* that *niggers* is human beings!"

It was at this point that the legislators must have decided he'd gone off his crumpet. Old Earl, a Southern politician, was taking the Fourteenth Amendment's position that "No State shall make or enforce any law which shall abridge the privileges or immunities of citizens of the United States . . . nor

deny to any person within its jurisdiction the equal protection of the laws.''
. . . So sporadic was my interest in Southern matters then that I did not know
the Federal Department of Justice had already taken action against Washington
Parish, over near the Mississippi line, because the exponents of the law that
Earl didn't like had scratched the names of 1,377 Negro voters, out of a total
of 1,510, from the rolls. (When, in January 1960, six months later, United
States District Judge J. Skelly Wright, a Louisianian, ordered the Negroes'
names put back on the rolls, no dispatch clapped old Earl on the back for
having championed them. Nor, in February, when Louisiana appealed Judge
Wright's decision and the Supreme Court sustained it, did anybody give the
old battler credit for having battled. The main feature of the civil-rights bill
passed by Congress was, in fact, an affirmation of the Earl Long argument that
led to his sojourn in Texas, but nobody recalled the trouble that his fight for
civil rights had cost him.)

''There's no longer *slavery!*'' Long shouted at Rainach. ''There wasn't but
two people in Winn Parish that was able to own slaves—one was my grandpa,
the other was my uncle—and when they were freed, they stayed on'' (here his
voice went tenor and sentimental, then dropped again) ''and two of those fine
old colored women more or less died in my Christian mother's arms—Black
Alice and Aunt Rose.'' He sounded like a blend of David Warfield and Morton
Downey. ''To keep fine, honorable grayheaded men and women off the registration rolls, some of whom have been voting as much as sixty or sixty-five
years—I plead with you in all candor. I'm a candidate for Governor. If it hurts
me, it will just have to hurt.''

He didn't believe it would hurt, but it did. In any case, he was taking a
chance, which put him in a class by himself among Southern public men.

This was the high point of the Governor's performance, an Elizabethan
juxtaposition of comedy and pathos; weeks after witnessing it, I could still
visualize Senator Rainach up on his porch in Summerfield, looking at the
moon, foot in hand, and feeling integrated with his Creator. As the session
continued, the old man, blundering into opposition he hadn't expected, became bitter and hardly coherent.

The theme of one long passage was that many legislators had Negro or at
least part-Negro relatives in the bar sinister category, to whom they now
wanted to deny the vote. He told a story about his own uncle who, climbing
into bed with a Negro woman, had given umbrage to her husband, then
present.

Here the Governor's voice was sad, like the voice of a man recounting the
death of Agamemnon: ''He shot my poor uncle—'' a one-beat pause—''and
he died.'' If white men had let Negro women alone, he said, there wouldn't
be any trouble.

The squabble continued, Uncle Earl growing progressively less effective, but with flashes of humor: of some fellow on his own side, he said once, "Why does the *Picayune* hate him—is why I like him. When he makes the *Picayune* scratch and wiggle, he is putting anointed oil on my head."

The others snarled him down, and Mrs. Dixon led him from the floor.

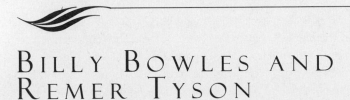

BILLY BOWLES AND REMER TYSON

Bowles and Tyson, both with deep backgrounds in Southern newspapering, went around in 1989 gathering yarns about Southern politicians of the old, pre-TV, unblow-dried school. Another veteran newspaperman, Virginian Johnny Popham, summed up the ethic of a reporter who could get the good stuff of this tradition: "Always distinguish between the rogue and the criminal and love and enjoy the rogue. . . . The rogue's the guy who gets the information for you. He's got a foot in the other camp, he's playing a little bit, he's loose, he isn't quite bad. And your rule with him is, Joe, I love you, I'm with you all the way. I'll take you right down until they close the gates at Sing Sing. When they do, you and I are through, goddammit, it's all over then." Rogues abound in Bowles and Tyson's They Love a Man in the Country: Saints and Sinners in the South.

Rogue Truth

His voice preceded his presence. Jim Cummings was talking on the telephone in the next room, but we could hear him as we conversed with his secretary, Linda Brown, in the waiting room of his law office on the square in Woodbury.

"He'll just talk, talk, talk, and he won't let you talk back to him," she told us.

We had driven 600 miles to see this little pot-bellied man who tormented city bosses and Tennessee governors for more years than any other man in history. He started his political career as a Cannon County Circuit Court clerk in 1914, campaigning for the office on horseback, and he rose no higher than a state legislator from rural Tennessee. But he and his wily confederates took on the city slickers from Nashville and Memphis and Knoxville and picked them clean, until the Supreme Court changed the rules of the game.

When we visited them on a warm April day in 1977, Linda Brown was secretary, caretaker and companion to the eighty-seven-year-old country lawyer. She was a friendly, outgoing woman, married to the local postmaster for thirty-two years. She acted as judge and jury for Cummings when he tried out his arguments before taking them to court. If he failed to convince her of his client's innocence, he plea bargained. She also helped him keep track of his whiskey.

"Mister Jim takes a nip every once in a while," she told us as we waited for him to get off the phone. "Not very often. But when he takes a nip it lasts for about two or three days. He comes in and says, 'Well, Miss Linda, let's you and me take a little ride. Hell, I got to go home.' I know right then we're heading for the beer place." The beer place, we would learn in due time, was where you bought bootleg whiskey.

Linda said that if she located a bottle for Mister Jim at the office, he would say, "Nooooo, I don't have to go home."

Mister Jim talked on the phone like he talked in his parlor, at the top of his lungs. George Barker, a reporter for the Nashville *Tennessean,* said that Cummings "speaks as if against the wind." His voice, high-pitched and piping, demanded you pay attention to it.

Linda said Mister Jim was talking on a wall phone installed next to his desk because he was always losing the desk phone under the debris.

"When I started working here we had a home telephone system," Linda informed us. "You just cranked the phone and told the operator you wanted to talk to George Brown. But a few years back we got a modern dialing system. Well, Mister Jim refuses to let me dial for him. And he constantly gets the wrong number, but he finds out who it is and has a long conversation."

Linda first came to Cummings' office to operate an insurance business, then an income-tax business, with Cummings' late wife, Hesta. Years later, when Hesta Cummings got sick and quit coming to the law office, Linda quit a $600-a-month job to work for Mister Jim full time.

She said that when she offered to join him, "He said, 'That will suit me 200 percent. Now I may not be able to pay you *hardly* as much, but I'll pay you every penny I can.' So I said, 'Okay,' and I resigned the job and came to work. Well, about a month later, I said, 'Mr. Jim, it's time for me to get paid. How much are you going to pay me?' He said, 'Well, I figured about $60 a week.' I said, 'Hell, I'm not going to work for that.' Well, I finally got him up to $75. Six days a week."

We were in luck with Miss Linda. She had none of the protective veneer of the big city secretary. Not only was she an accommodating Southern woman, she also took pride in this old man and saw nothing to be ashamed of.

She told us of a busy week in the office doing income tax returns.

"He stayed in my office might near all day long," she said, "and to every one of my income tax people he'd say, 'Honey, let me hold your hand while she does your income tax.' And he would hold her hand. One girl said, 'You know, this is the first time Mister Jim has ever paid any attention to me.' I said, 'He's drunk.' "

Judges asked Linda to accompany Mister Jim to the courtroom because he was always handing them the wrong papers. One day when he went to court alone to testify in a land case, she got worried about him because he was gone so long.

"Directly I went over there," she said, "and the judge was standing out in the hall taking a break. I said, 'Judge, what on earth is going on?' He said, 'Mister Jim has not hushed all day. His attorney got up and said, "State your—" and he didn't even get "name" out before Mister Jim started. Mister Jim said, "My name is Jim Cummings." His lawyer has never said another word.' "

Linda said her husband, George Brown, had just retired as postmaster, and she confided: "Course, I don't need to be working here, but I can't leave Mister Jim. He's lost without me. When I'm on vacation, they say he won't even come to the office."

We heard the phone being slammed into the wall receiver, and moments later James Harvey Cummings walked into the waiting room hitching up his britches under his belly.

"I been talking to a damn recording," he announced.

Jim Cummings came out of his office just like Linda said he would, like a hurricane. It was hard to get in a word. The voice we had been hearing belonged to a small man wearing a bow tie, slender except for a bulge in his middle that made it difficult for him to keep his pants up. He exuded mirth and high spirits and a devilish nature. He had the kind of voice that would make a dog howl.

"Come in here, let me talk to you," he said, loud and shrill, ordering us into his law office. "Come in here! Come right in, and we'll get ahold of this and see what I can do to be helpful to you. I'm cooperative, I'll say that. I'll try to help you if I can."

As we walked into his small, cluttered law office, Linda seized the opportunity to break in: "I've been entertaining these people," she said. "I told them a story or two about your telephoning and your lawsuit. I'm going to 'fess up about that."

"About *what,* honey?"

She repeated her confession but left out the incriminating parts.

"Oh, that recording," Mister Jim said. "This pretty, sweet voice said—and I'm not hearing good, maybe—that I'd gotten the wrong number and to hang up. I said, 'Thank you.' To a damn recording."

"And I told them about Sam frequenting the house of ill repute," Linda said.

Cummings explained that Sam was a client arrested in a whorehouse raid. While cross-examining Sam, the prosecutor had asked, "On this night, were you frequenting this house?"

"No, sir," Sam replied. " 'I was not frequenting. All I was doing was sitting down there strumming my guitar."

Miss Linda was enjoying herself. She was invaluable to us as prompter, reminding the eighty-seven year old raconteur of stories she had heard him tell for years. Even when she suggested them, she reacted to the stories as if she were hearing them for the first time.

"Who were the two guys who woke up in the penitentiary?" she prompted.

Mister Jim straightened up in his chair as if startled, his eyebrows rose and his face lit up.

"Oh, that was my *BROTHER!*" he roared. "And Barton Dement. Look over there: that picture."

He pointed to a wall filled with pictures:

"Barton Dement's over there, he and Governor Clement, right at the far end, RIGHT AT THE FAR END! Do you see a picture right at the bottom, in this corner. RIGHT THERE! THAT FELLA!"

Clarence Cummings and Barton Dement were well-known lawyers from Murfreesboro who served in the Tennessee Legislature.

"They went to Nashville," Mister Jim recalled with glee, "and in the course of their day's work, they got to drinking, fooling around, overindulged. And they had some friend who was a guard out at the penitentiary."

As the night went on, Mister Jim said, "the guard realized that he needed to do something for my brother and Barton Dement. They were overloaded. So he took them out there and bedded them down in his quarters at the state prison. They fell into a deep sleep, of course. And the next morning they woke up and looked out the window and hell! Damn! They looked and saw they were inside the walls. Convicts were walking around."

It was as if Mister Jim were looking through a crosshatch of bars out across the exercise yard to the high walls.

"One of them said to the other, 'Whur in the hell *are* we? WE'RE IN THE PENIT—THAT'S the penitentiary. We're in the *penitentiary.*' Barton says, 'Clarence'—that's my brother's name—'Do you remember being put in here?' And Clarence said, 'Hell, I don't even remember having a trial.' "

As he told us these stories, Cummings chain smoked filter tip cigarettes, puffing on them till the butts were so short he had to slide them to the side of his mouth to keep from scorching his nose. Yet he had fretted that his late wife was wrecking her health with cigarettes in her later years.

"One day I said, 'Miss Hesta, you know what I believe? I do a little drinking and smoking, and I believe that smoking hurts me worse than drinking.' She smoked but didn't drink. She told me, 'Well, I don't doubt it, but I'll remind you of one thing, smoking don't make you act quite as big a fool.' That wound up my lecture to her about smoking."

.   .   .   .

In Texas, the Harris County district attorney in Houston once rivaled the governor in power and influence. Texans still talk about a D.A.'s race just after World War I between Tom Branch and Tom Clark.

Branch was a country lawyer and legal scholar. He wore celluloid collars and galluses. Clark was a political hanger-on. They clashed in debate on a hot Saturday afternoon in Baytown, Texas.

Farmers cooled themselves with funeral home fans and the barbecue simmered off to the side as the candidates mounted a specially built platform.

Branch spoke first, then Clark, who saved a sucker punch for the end:

"I had promised myself I'd never mention this," Clark said, "but this job is so important I have to. I fought for my country in the war. But let me tell you what Tom Branch did. When the Army was fixing to get him, Tom Branch went out behind the barn and he took the axe and he cut off his trigger finger."

Turning to face his opponent, Clark thrust his own trigger finger into the air and cried out: "Show 'em your trigger finger, Tom Branch, show 'em your trigger finger!"

Everyone in the crowd knew that Branch had lost his index finger in a childhood accident. But he made a mistake. Instinctively, he clapped his hand over the stub, and the crowd saw him.

Rising for his rebuttal, Branch mopped away the sweat on his face and began slowly:

"Yes, it's true. When the Army came to get me I went out behind the barn, and like Tom Clark says, I took the axe and I cut off my trigger finger."

The crowd stirred.

"But let me tell you why I did it. You all knew my daddy. You know he fought in the War Between the States. You remember when he died. On his death bed he turned to me, his oldest boy, and he made me promise I would never leave my mama and my sisters and my brothers. So when the war came, I had a choice. I could go and fight for my country, or I could break the promise I made to my daddy on his death bed. I decided I had to keep my word. So I went out behind the barn and I took the axe and, like Tom Clark says, I cut off my trigger finger."

It was so quiet you could hear the barbecue sizzling.

"But let me tell you how Tom Clark got in the Army. When the Army came for him, they didn't find Tom Clark. His mother was so ashamed she told them where Tom Clark was hiding in the brush. They had to go out and get him. They took him by the collar and they drug him through the brambles. The marks of those brambles are still there."

Wheeling to face his opponent, Branch pointed the stub of his trigger finger and bellowed: "Show 'em your ass, Tom Clark, show 'em your ass!"

.   .   .   .

Marvin Griffin, who commanded fierce loyalty himself when he was governor, told us about another strong supporter of old Gene [Eugene Talmadge, governor of Georgia] in Berrien County, deep in south Georgia.

"Gene came down there in 1940 when he was running for governor, in Nashville, on a Saturday afternoon, to make a speech," Griffin told us. "One of the first ones that came up to him at the Confederate monument there on the square was George Rowan. Gene said, 'George, how you been getting along? George, I want you to help me beat this crowd. I don't just mean in Berrien County. George, ain't you got a pickup truck?' George said, 'Yeah.' Gene says, 'I want you to get in that pickup truck and cover all the counties that adjoin Berrien. And George, you look a little seedy. You got a job?' George said, 'No.' "

In 1940, the Depression still had a grip on south Georgia, Griffin said.

"Nobody had a job much," Griffin said, "except what you could scratch out of the ground. Gene said, 'George, when I get elected and get back in the governor's office in January, you come up there and I'll give you a job. You look like you need one.'

"Of course, George got out there and about wore out the rest of that pickup truck, tacking up signs and handing out handbills when Gene was going to speak in that section. Gene was elected. The day he was to take office, George was one of the ones who would get to the cafe at about five o'clock in the morning to drink coffee. A fellow said, 'George, you going to Atlanta today?' He said, 'No, Gene's got plenty to do today. He's going to be inaugurated today. He ain't got no time to mess with me about no job. I'm going to give him time to get his feet on the ground, and then I'm going up there to see him.' The fellow said, 'We heard him promise you the job. We heard him. If I were you, I'd go up there and get me a good job.'

"He waited about a week or ten days, and he come up there about five o'clock all dressed up and said, 'I'm going to Atlanta today to see Gene.' The truck broke down about Barnesville, but he got it fixed with some baling wire and stuff and made it in to the Capitol. There was a thousand folks milling around in there, wanting to see Gene about a job. George waited about half the day, and finally he got in.

"George said, 'Well, governor, I reckon you know what I came up here to see you about. You promised me a job if I helped you and you got elected, and

I damn sure holp you.' Gene said, 'I know you did, George, I know you did. But I ain't got no job. I just, dammit, told you a lie. I ain't got a job. I just lied to you. That's all.' Gene had run out of patience by that time. George said, 'All right.'

"So he got in his truck and he come on home. The next morning, he was up there drinking coffee with the fellows. One of them said, 'You go to Atlanta yesterday, George?' George said, 'Yep.' Said, 'You see Gene?' George said, 'Yeah, saw him.' The fellow said, 'You get the job?' George said, 'No, didn't get the job, but I'll tell you one damn thing. Gene Talmadge will damn sure tell you the truth.' "

. . . .

In 1975, when George Corley Wallace, Jr., was governor of Alabama, the state's general fund was about out of money, but the separate education fund was bulging with a $150 million surplus. Wallace wanted to divert $48 million for highways and mental hospitals.

"Of course, the educators were bad against it," political consultant Tom Cork told us. "They raised hell. They lobbied. They got the Alabama Education Association to come up to the Capitol. They had every teacher in the state, you know, to call their representatives and the press. All these educators were talking about was, 'The poor little school children are going to suffer.' The little school children this. The little school children that. 'They're not going to have any milk if Governor Wallace has his way. Not going to have any books.'

"So the bill got hung up in the Legislature, and Wallace called about seven of the legislators into his office. He started off very calmly, 'Now, gentlemen, I think I have offered here what is a good sound program to help us out of this emergency, and it will not hurt education in the long run. I just want to hear your views on it. I think what I proposed is good. If you will examine it very carefully, I think you will agree with me. I don't know why you oppose me so. I want to hear every one of your views on it.'

"And every one of them just sounded like a parrot. They said the same thing. They said, 'Oh, governor, these teachers have been calling us about the little school children. We just can't go against the little school children.'

"The governor said, 'Yes, I understand that.' He asked the next legislator, and he said the same thing: 'Oh, I'm telling you, they brought a whole bunch of little school children to see me, you know, and they said all these little school children are going to suffer if you do this, and we're going to beat you the next time you run.'

"The governor says, 'I understand.' He goes on to the next one. He listens to them all. All of them were alike."

Cork interrupted the story to tell us: "I need to give you this little tip note of information. About a month before this issue had come up, they had a local referendum in Montgomery about raising taxes for the schools. They wanted to put a half mill on, something like that. They had a local vote on it, raising taxes for the same purpose, little school children, see. It was beat about ten to one. Just beat the hell out of it.''

He went on with his story:

''The governor very calmly listened to all the legislators he had called into his office. When they got through, he said, 'I'm going to tell you something. Y'all keep talking about the little school children, how they're going to suffer, how the people are going to get mad at us. I want to tell you a little story. Right here in Montgomery, about a month ago, they had a vote on this issue over raising taxes for schools. All these educators went on TV, and they told everybody, 'If you don't vote for this tax increase, the schools are going to shut down, and the little school children will suffer. They ain't going to get no education. You'd better vote for this tax increase or these little school children are going to suffer.'

''That amendment was beat ten to one, and I'll tell you why. It was because the average Alabamian has spent eight hours working out in the hot sun, comes in at five o'clock in the afternoon, he sits down in front of the TV set, mad as hell, all hot and sweaty, and he's got a beer in one hand and a baloney sandwich in the other. And he turns on the TV, and some educator in some three-piece suit comes on the air and says, *If you don't vote this tax increase, the little school children are going to suffer.*

''Now I'm going to tell you what that fellow watching that TV thinks. He says, *Fuck the little school children.*''

.   .   .   .

During the Central High crisis in Little Rock in 1957, out-of-state newsmen flooded into the city to cover the story.

''They came in here for weeks and weeks,'' said [Harry Ashmore, editor of the *Arkansas Gazette*]. ''I'd go over to the Little Rock Club for lunch, and I'd wind up with eight or ten of them, drinking with both hands, eating lunch. It was genuinely a club, and they couldn't pay for anything. I had to sign the checks, which the paper was paying for.

''Hell, this had been going on for a month or two months, and I suddenly realized when the bill came in from the club it wasn't any higher than it usually was.

''All the attendants at the Little Rock Club were black, including Herbert Douglas, who was the chief bartender. I went over to see Herbert and said, 'I just noticed this bill from the club isn't running any higher than it usually does. I think I know what's happening. I've been bringing all these goddamned newspapermen over here, and you've been writing it off. Y'all can't do that.'

"He said, 'Nah, it ain't hurting the club any. The club is collecting.' I said, 'What do you mean, the club is collecting?' He said, 'We just lay it off on the segs.'

"They had all these goddamn drinks I was signing for, and they had all these drunken segs around. The attendants would add some on this one's bill and some on that one's."

RUSSELL BAKER

People associate Russell Baker, who has been writing the "Observer" column for the New York Times for over thirty years, with Baltimore, to which city his mother moved him, via New Jersey, when he was eleven. But he was born in the village of Morrisonville, Virginia, in 1925, his people were from there, his parents are buried there, and he lives in that state now. Baker has won a Pulitzer Prize for his column and another one for his first memoir, Growing Up. *In that book's sequel,* The Good Times, *Baker favored us with what is anything but a snooty Northern-media recollection of another small-town boy, God's and Texas's gift to the Oval Office, Lyndon Baines Johnson.*

"Johnson"

On a spring morning in 1958, Mimi answered the phone and said it was Senator Johnson's office asking for me. It was Saturday. We were eating a late breakfast, and Senator Johnson didn't know me from Herb, Uncle Gene, or the Jolly Green Giant.

. . . .

A woman with a lovely, soft southern accent said good morning, Mr. Baker, Senator Johnson wants to speak to you, please, and gave way to a big male voice that said, "Russ, this is Lyndon Johnson."

It was, indeed. Lyndon Johnson, the genuine article, Democratic leader of the Senate, nobody could doubt that. He had one of the most distinctive voices in town.

"Russ, I hear you're going to be working up here on the Hill, covering the Senate . . ."

I was saying something, but didn't know what. By now I had covered a lot of famous people and was used to talking easily with them, but this strange Saturday-morning call from Lyndon Johnson had me too flustered to keep command of the conversation.

Maybe it was the unabashed heartiness with which Johnson kept calling me "Russ," as though we had been pals ever since boyhood down on the "Purd'-nallis" River, and never mind that he wouldn't recognize me if I tapped him on the shoulder at this very moment.

He said they'd been telling him I was taking over Bill White's job covering the Senate for the *Times.* Bill White was a wonderful man as well as a wonderful reporter and he'd done a wonderful job for the *Times,* and he'd been able to do it so well because he understood the Senate, knew how it worked . . .

.   .   .   .

So the politics of this Saturday-morning call was amply clear. I'd been around Washington long enough now to understand that politics was fundamental to the human condition everywhere, only more so in Washington.

Johnson was saying, Russ, the two of us are going to get along just fine.

I sure hope so, Senator, I was saying, while thinking this man is really a piece of work. Just last night I hear I'm going to be the new Bill White, he probably knows it before I get to bed, probably has to be restrained from telephoning me in the middle of the night to say, "Russ, we're going to get along just fine, you and me . . ."

It was no secret around town that Lyndon Johnson wanted to be president. Big-time television was still in the wings waiting for the 1960s, so it was no secret among men who wanted to be president that being written about with awe and wonder in *The New York Times* was one of the most wonderful things that could happen to you.

"When there's something in the Senate you want to know about, I want you to feel you can come ask me, and I'll be glad . . ."

This kind of talk made me edgy. You didn't have to be terribly Washington-wise to know that Lyndon Johnson, if not actually offering a deal, was probing to find out if I was willing to trade favors. He was saying he could make me look good at the *Times.* He didn't have to tell me what my end of the deal would be: to make Lyndon Johnson look good in the *Times.*

.   .   .   .

During this eerie Saturday morning phone conversation, I didn't think things out so carefully as I now suggest, but I was instinctively trying to keep distance between us. This was never an easy thing to do with Lyndon Johnson, even on the telephone. One of his favorite postures for conversation was leaning down over you and pressing his nose down toward yours until your spine was bent so far back that you couldn't think of anything but your aching vertebrae.

So while he went on calling me "Russ," I kept saying "Senator," determined not to get palsy by saying "Lyndon." Toward the end, I suddenly became aware that this was not a phone conversation. It was a broadcast.

The phone company sold a device that sat on your desk and worked as both mouthpiece and earpiece. You could lean back and talk from a distance and still be clearly heard, and the reply from the person you were talking to came through it so loud and clear it was heard all over the room. The defect was that it sometimes transmitted an echo. Johnson, who loved all gadgets, had one, of course, but I didn't suspect it until I heard my own voice echoing in my earpiece a millisecond after I'd spoken.

This prompted me to listen more closely, and—what do you know!—I could hear the shuffling of bodies moving around in chairs, and even a faint laugh from somebody not Lyndon Johnson. Johnson's phone call was a performance being given for an audience. I was not having a phone conversation; I was playing to a crowd.

This left me feeling clammy. That faint laugh had been especially unnerving. Was Johnson making a fool of me to amuse his audience? Who was in that audience? Any reporters who covered the Senate for other papers?

Johnson returned to his major theme: his eagerness to do me immense kindnesses, to dole out the most secret information. All I had to do was come to him, tell him what I needed, it would be mine for the asking, that was how kindly disposed he felt toward me. Then he concluded with a line I hear clearly in my head to this day because it made me laugh so many times in the years that followed:

"For you, Russ, I'd leak like a sieve."

In my four years covering the Senate, he never "leaked" me a single piece of information that had the slightest news value.

Maybe he wrote me off as useless after that first phone talk. More likely, I suspect, he never "leaked" anything to any journalist unless it was something self-serving. The most useful information for a Senate reporter in those years was what Lyndon Johnson was up to, and I soon learned that Johnson was the last person to ask.

.   .   .   .

A year before I took up the Senate beat, Bill White wrote a long portrait of him for the *Times Sunday Magazine*. To call it flattering would have been understatement. Bill believed Johnson could be one of the nation's great presidents, though at that time, the mid-1950s, there seemed little chance that an oil Texan with a southern accent could ever get to the White House. Bill's

Magazine piece emphasized Johnson's statesmanlike qualities so fully that it never got around to suggesting Johnson might have a defect or two of the most trivial sort.

Normally Bill talked to Johnson at least once a day, but for three days after publication of the famously flattering *Magazine* piece, Johnson refused to see him. On the fourth day, Johnson relented, Bill went to his office, they discussed business, and, since Johnson obviously didn't intend to raise the subject, Bill asked if he had seen the *Times* magazine article.

Yes, Johnson had seen it. He spoke now in his tragic voice, a tone he often fell into when reflecting on the persecutions to which he was subjected. He had seen the piece, all right. To his sorrow, he had seen the piece.

Was something wrong with it?

Johnson's reply was so outrageous that Bill, one of Johnson's oldest friends, couldn't resist telling us about it back in the office. Johnson said:

"If I thought I was the kind of man you wrote about in that piece, I wouldn't like myself very much."

Old friendship got Bill off easy compared to the punishment visited on Sam Shaffer, who did the reporting on an unabashedly flattering *Newsweek* cover story on Johnson. Johnson did not leave Sam dangling, but called him into his office the day the magazine appeared, abused him extensively, and declared, "Anybody who'd write something like that about me would rape my wife."

Sam sat in Coventry for three weeks before Johnson would speak to him again. Then they resumed relations as though nothing had happened.

.   .   .   .

He had a gift for finessing the awkward question with a comic vulgarity.

"Don't you think the Senate ought to be discussing this situation in Laos?" I asked him one day when that mysterious little Southeast Asian country was in the news.

This was in the 1950s when most senators, including Lyndon Johnson, I suspect, couldn't have found Laos on a map. Instead of admitting he didn't have a single idea about Laos in his head, Johnson went on the attack, came out of his chair, leaned into my face, and whacking his hands on his buttocks in rhythm with his words, shouted:

"Low Ass! Low Ass! Low Ass! All the things I've got on my mind and you come in here wanting to talk about Low Ass!"

.   .   .   .

[One] day in 1962 I spent nearly an hour alone with him in his Capitol office listening to one of his marathon monologues. I had known him seven years by then. He had become vice-president, knew he was the butt of cruel humor among many of President Kennedy's people, and was trying to pretend it wasn't so, that he still counted as he had counted back in the Fifties when he was Johnson the Genius Who Ran the Senate.

He spotted me outside the Senate this day, clapped my back, mauled my hand, massaged my ribs, just as he'd always done in the glory days of old, all the time hailing me as though I were a long lost friend and simultaneously hauling me into a big office he kept across the corridor from the Senate chamber. He sat me down and launched his monologue. The part he obviously wanted me to note, in case I published some of this in the *Times,* dealt with a private dinner for three at the White House at which he had supped alone with the president and Mrs. Kennedy.

He had been profoundly moved when Mrs. Kennedy had reached across the table, touched his hand, and said, "We need you, Lyndon."

I strongly suspected this story was about eighty percent fiction, but his eyes glittered so happily that he seemed to have persuaded himself every word was God's truth, and I wasn't disposed to ask skeptical questions. For one thing, he'd told me I couldn't quote him directly on anything he said, and I had no intention of reporting this touching story of Jackie Kennedy's dinner-table endorsement on my own say-so.

For another thing, I felt sorry for him. If you had once been the great Lyndon Johnson, master of the Senate, it was hard being the nonentity called vice-president, it was painful to be laughed at and called "Cornpone" by people you thought of as arrogant, smart-ass Ivy League pipsqueaks.

Looking for something that could be printed, I shifted ground slightly toward the famous frustrations other powerful men had experienced in the vice-presidency. His fellow Texan, "Cactus Jack" Garner, Franklin Roosevelt's vice-president, had said, "The vice-presidency isn't worth a jar of warm piss." It was the only memorable line Garner had ever uttered.

No such thing, said Johnson. John Garner had never said any such thing. He had known John Garner very well, had often talked to the old gentleman back in the early New Deal days. Garner had always known the job was vitally important. Nothing as silly as that statement about a jar of warm piss could ever have been spoken by John Garner.

And so it went, on and on. During our chat Johnson scrawled a few words on a piece of memo paper and sent it to his outer office. A few minutes later his secretary brought him back a message on a small piece of paper. Johnson looked at it, crumpled it, and threw it in a wastebasket. A reporter who knew me happened to be idling in Johnson's outer office during this exchange of messages, so knew what it was about and told me as we walked away from the office together.

"Do you know what was in that message Johnson sent out while you were in there?"

"No. What did it say?"

"It said, 'Who is this I'm talking to?' "

.   .   .   .

I first met Johnson in 1955. It was at a dinner party in the garden at Bill White's house on one of those early-summer Washington nights still soft enough to dine out of doors. I had been with the *Times* only a few months, and Bill had taken an interest in me. This was flattering because he was one of the bright stars of American journalism.

.   .   .   .

Arriving at his place for dinner that night, Mimi and I were dismayed to find we were the only people there that nobody had ever heard of. We knew it was going to be a heavy evening when we stepped through the gate and saw Dean Acheson, former secretary of state and architect of the Western world's cold-war policy. It was that kind of crowd: famous congressmen, a famous judge, a famous newspaperwoman. Except for Mimi and me, the least famous guests were a couple of lawyers named Abe Fortas and Edward Bennett Williams, and I knew they were big-time, too, because I'd seen their names in newspaper stories about big-timers.

Lyndon Johnson was only moderately famous. He must have felt almost as out of place as I did. Why else could he be chain-smoking one cigarette on top of another and pouring down Scotch whisky like a man who had a date with a firing squad? During the drinking hour before dinner, I watched him taking in rivers of smoke and whisky and waving his hands and weaving his long, skinny torso this way and that, all the while talking nonstop to a group of four or five who seemed enthralled by the performance. It was just Lyndon Johnson being himself, of course. He always operated like a runaway motor, but I didn't know that at the time.

There were four or five tables for dinner, and when we finally sat down to eat I discovered Bill White had done me another favor by seating me next to Johnson. Bill's wife, June, introduced us and told him I'd been working in London. As food arrived, he stubbed out a cigarette, lit another, finished his Scotch, called for another, and asked how the House of Commons compared with what little I had seen of the Senate.

I'd been surprised at the lack of debate in the Senate, and said so. In the House of Commons, debate seemed to be far more important than in the Senate, where, I said, most talk seemed commonplace, inaudible, and inconsequential, as though it didn't really matter.

Johnson had taken only two or three mouthfuls of food, and now he shoved his plate aside, stubbed out his cigarette in the food, lit another smoke, drained his whisky, and called for another.

Speechmaking didn't count for anything when it came to passing bills, he said. What mattered was who had the votes.

He was being the forthright schoolteacher, trying to instruct an innocent pupil about life's realities.

But what about the history books with their stories of the great debaters? What about Webster and Clay? What about . . . ?

Johnson had a child on his hands.

"You want to hear a speech? I can get somebody to make any kind of speech you want to hear. What kind of speech do you want?"

Another cigarette was being stubbed out in the food, another cigarette was being lit, the Scotch was getting low in his glass again.

"You want to hear a great speech about suffering humanity? I've got Hubert Humphrey back in the cloakroom. I've got Herbert Lehman. I've got Paul Douglas . . ."

This man obviously absolutely hated oratory. As he talked on, another butt fizzled out in the green beans, another match flared, the empty glass was replaced with a filled glass. . . .

"You want to hear about government waste? I can give you Harry Byrd, States' rights? I've got Jim Eastland, I've got Olin Johnston, I've got . . ."

Another cigarette was squashed, another lit.

.   .   .   .

He did for an instant know me by name one afternoon several years later. It was during the 1964 presidential campaign. He knew he was going to win big, big, big, and he was euphoric about it. One of the few things troubling him was a scandal involving Bobby Baker, a young man, said some, whom he had once loved like a son. Bobby was now out of his life, except as a political embarrassment, and Johnson was enjoying probably the supreme moment of his life. He was running for president, and everybody, absolutely everybody, was going to vote for him.

Flying across the country on Air Force One, he often sat up far into the night drinking Scotch and savoring the miracle of it all. You didn't sleep through a time of glory and happiness as wonderful as this. You stayed up, enjoying it, talking about it. He talked about it one night with the handful of pool reporters assigned to his plane, telling them that all the great leaders of the world were dead now, replaced by minor figures. He, Lyndon Johnson, was the last of the big men left on the international scene. One reporter said what about President de Gaulle of France, who had just completed an unexciting visit to several South American capitals.

"Aren't you forgetting General de Gaulle?" he asked Johnson.

Johnson snorted in contempt.

"De Gaulle! He's just an old man who went to South America and fell on his ass."

Flying the country in this extraordinary state of elation, he landed at Los Angeles a few minutes behind the chartered jetliner the rest of the press was flying. As Air Force One rolled to a stop, I stood back from the photographers to get a long view of the scene and saw him come down the ramp laughing and talking and waving for the cameras.

As his feet touched the tarmac, he glanced into the distance and saw my face. Some extraordinary chemistry, produced no doubt by the joy of the season, helped him match my name to my face at that instant. Waving happily at me, he shouted, "Baker for president! Baker for president!"

Then, an instant of dreadful recognition! This film, shown on television, could be a disaster. Everybody would think he was shouting about the scandalous Bobby Baker. So he waved again, and again shouted, in an even louder voice:

"RUSSELL Baker for president! RUSSELL Baker for president!"

A year and a half later, mired fatally in Vietnam, his presidency was already headed for ruin, though he didn't know it. Except for that brief campaign moment, I hadn't covered him as president. I had been writing a newspaper column, which was often critical of his Vietnam policy. On a May day, eleven years after I had first met him, he recognized my name on a list of guests invited to a large, not very special White House reception.

The document is in his presidential library in Austin. It is a memorandum from the office of Eric Goldman, who was Johnson's house intellectual:

"Jim Jones phoned to say that the President has okayed everyone on the guest list for the Presidential Scholars ceremony except in category 17, newspapermen.

"On that list the President wants removed the following:

"Russell Baker, Art Buchwald, Robert Donovan, Walter Lippman, Peter Lisagor, James Reston."

It was a pretty distinguished company to find myself in. The chief qualification for membership, I suspected, was having got under Johnson's skin by criticizing his Vietnam policy. I didn't learn about it, however, until some fifteen years later when a friend doing research in the Johnson library found it in the files.

Funny thing, though: I remembered going to that reception. It was the only time I'd gone to the White House socially since Eisenhower had left. Somebody had slipped up, and I had got an invitation in spite of Johnson's veto. It must often be like that, even after you are president.

Unaware that we were supposed to be scratched, Mimi and I went. I followed Mimi through the reception line, coming up toward Mrs. Johnson and Lyndon in the Blue Room, wondering if, when my name was announced, he might stop me for a word of reminiscence about the old days.

He didn't. He just looked at me with his official, brief reception-line expression as we shook hands. It was the look you get from people who look you right in the eye and haven't the faintest idea who you are. After all those years, he still didn't know me from Herb, Uncle Gene, or the Jolly Green Giant.

MOLLY IVINS

I first began noticing things by Molly Ivins in the Texas Observer *in the early '70s. In one column, headed "Stomp Out Whackers," she told of a Texas gubernatorial candidate named Robert Looney, whose call for strong regulation of utilities was couched in these terms: "The fact that the light companies always have a monopoly and the water companies always have a monopoly and send out what a lot of people call the whackers and without any notice whatsoever the whackers come and whack the lights and whack the gas and whack whatever else. The whackers, they whack it off and they bar no defense whatsoever and there is no process of law involved and the citizens of this state should have the right to have due process of law and that the whackers don't come and whack their lights, whack their gas, whack their telephone and that the utilities companies are invincible and giants that they are." Looney, Ivins reported, was also a poet; for example:*

> Hip, hip, hooray!
> Hip, hip, hooray!
> For the attorney general of the U.S.A.,
> The Honorable big John (Martha's husband) Mitchell
> Hip, hip hooray
> And twitchell, twitchell.

Molly, who is one of the best people in America to drink beer with, is also the only contributor to Ms. *and* The Progressive *and* Mother Jones *who would quote an old Texas Ranger as saying, "The three most overrated things in the world are young pussy, Mack trucks and the FBI." Her column in the* Fort Worth Star-Telegram *is syndicated, and her collections,* Molly Ivins Can't Say That, Can She? *and* Nothin' but Good Times Ahead, *have been best-sellers.*

"Tough as Bob War and Other Stuff"

We've just survived another political season largely unscathed. I voted for Bobby Locke for governor: he's the one who challenged Col. Muammar el-Qaddafi to hand-to-hand combat. In the Gulf of Sidra. On the Line of Death. At high noon. Next Fourth of July. "Only one of us will come out of the water alive," said Locke. Locke thinks the trouble with America is that we've lost respect for our leaders and this would be a good way to restore same. Me too. Besides, you should have seen the other guys.

The Republicans had a congressman running who thinks you get AIDS through your feet. That's Representative Tom Loeffler of Hunt, who is smarter than a box of rocks. His television advertisements proudly claimed, "He's tough as bob war" (bob war is what you make fences with), and also that in his youth Loeffler played football with two broken wrists. This caused uncharitable persons to question the man's good sense, so he explained he didn't know his wrists were broken at the time. Loeffler went to San Francisco during the campaign to make a speech. While there, he wore shower caps on his feet while showering lest he get AIDS from the tile in the tub. He later denied that he had spent the entire trip in his hotel room. He said: "I did walk around the hotel. I did see people who do have abnormal tendencies. I'd just as soon not be associated with abnormal people." If that's true, what was he doing running for governor of Texas?

Perhaps Loeffler's most enduring contribution to Texas political lore was a thought that seemed to him so profound he took to repeating it at every campaign stop and during televised debates as well: "As I have traveled around this state, many people have said to me, 'Texas will never be Texas again.' But I say they are wrong. I say Texas will *always* be Texas." Hard to add anything to that.

On the Democratic side, the nerd issue was dominant. The ugly specter of nerditude was raised by A. Don Crowder, a candidate from Dallas. Crowder's platform consisted of vowing to repeal the no-pass, no-play rule on account of it has seriously damaged high school football and is un-American, un-Texan, and probably communist inspired. No pass, no play was part of the education reform package enacted last year by Governor Mark White and the State Legislature. If you don't pass all your school subjects, you can't participate in any extracurricular activities—including football. Quite naturally, this has caused considerable resentment and could cost White the governorship. So A. Don Crowder holds this press conference in which he says the reason Mark White favors no pass, no play is because White was "one of the first nerds in Texas." As evidence, Crowder produces White's high school annual, and there it was: the guy was zip in extracurricular activities in his school days. We're talking not even Booster Club. Not Glee Club or Stage Crew. Not even the Prom Poster Committee. According to Crowder, this explains "the psychological reasoning behind White's dislike of football."

There were headlines all over the state: "Gov. White Called 'Nerd' By Yearbook Wielding Foe." "Nerd Charge Merits Scrutiny." Meanwhile, we tracked down Donnie Crowder's high school annual and guess what? He was captain of the football team. Played baseball. Ran track. And was in the French Club. French Club! Need I say more? *Quel fromage.*

White's initial response to this slanderous aspersion was to whine about how tacky it was for Crowder to be so ugly right after the explosion of the *Challenger* shuttle. Nerd City. Then his campaign manager tries to pull it out by saying, So the guy was not real active in high school—but he was superinvolved in after-school activities at the Baptist Church. Nerd! Nerd! Finally White gets his act together, comes out, and says, "Look, I grew up poor. My daddy had an accident when I was just a sophomore and he couldn't work after that, so I spent my high school years working summers and after school." While A. Don Crowder was in French Club, doubtlessly conjugating highly irregular verbs with busty cheerleaders over the pâté and vin rouge, our governor was out mowing lawns, frying burgers, and pumping gas to help his dear old silver-haired mother. Great stuff. Besides, Bubba never joined no French Club.

Marko Blanco, as we call him in South Texas, will meet former Governor Bill Clements for a rematch in November. Clements was defeated by White four years ago on account of he's an awful grouch. Grumpy versus the Nerd— what a match-up.

Also contributing to the political festivities of late is that peerless, fearless commie-hater Charlie Wilson of Lufkin. It's possible to get used to Charlie. He has a certain charm. When I called him to verify some of the more bloodthirsty quotations attributed to him in the *Houston Post*'s account of his latest trip to the Afghanistan border, the first thing he said was, "The only thing those cocksuckers understand is hot lead and cold steel." I was especially pleased that he took his lady friend, Annelise Ilschenko, a former Miss World U.S.A., along on the Afghan jaunt. According to the *Houston Post,* she is a "dark-haired and sloe-eyed beauty," and you hardly ever find a good case of sloe-eyed beauty in the newspapers anymore. The *Post* said, "[She] went everywhere with Wilson, not even flinching as she sank her high-heeled white leather boots into the thick brown ooze of Darra's main street." No sacrifice is too great when you're fighting for freedom.

Charlie told the *Post* reporter he went over there hoping to "kill Russians, as painfully as possible." Myself, I think it had more to do with an observation he made after he got back: "Hell, they're still lining up to see *Rambo* in

Lufkin.'' Patriotism is always in good smell in East Texas. The night El Presidente started bombing Libya, the deejay at Benny B's, a honky-tonk in Lufkin, made all the patrons stand on their chairs and sing ''The Star-Spangled Banner.'' He said if anybody refused to do it, ''We'll know you're a commie faggot.'' Of course, they do the same thing at Benny B's for David Allan Coe's song ''You Never Even Called Me By My Name.'' Living in East Texas can be a real challenge.

Living anywhere in Texas is getting to be a challenge as the price of oil slides gracefully toward single digits. Texas-bashing seems to be a popular new national pastime. ''Let 'Em Rot in the Sun,'' said a cordial headline in the *New Republic*. Some Northern papers ran stories on our oil woes with heads the likes of ''Sorry About That, J.R.'' I don't see that we've got any cause to whine about this vein of snottiness: some of the Bubbas did put bumper stickers on their pickups a few years back that said, ''Let the Yankee Bastards Freeze in the Dark.'' Somehow I forebode that Yankees going and doing likewise is not going to teach Bubba any manners. The rest of us down here been having poor luck at it for a long time.

I would point out, though, that Texas is not a rich state, never has been. Never even made it up to the national average in per capita income until the tail end of the oil boom, and then we slid right down again. Poverty level here is always among the nation's highest and, according to a recent study by a team from Harvard University, Texas has more counties beset by hunger and mal-nutrition than any other state. Our second-biggest industry after oil is agricul-ture, and you've maybe read something about how it's going for farmers these days. Citrus crop in the Rio Grande Valley was wiped out by a freeze three years ago. Now they got drought and 40 percent unemployment, and the peso is still going down. Our banks had their money in oil, agriculture, and Mex-ico. We're losing a lot of banks.

There is no social support system for the poor in Texas. Adults get nothing; children get $57.50 a month. Bubba's got a beer-gut he can let shrink some and not be hurting, but almost half the children in this state are black or brown and they have no cushion. If Eddie Chiles goes broke, it's Don't Cry for Me Texarkana; John Connally and Ben Barnes on hard times, search me for sympathy; and I could give a shit about J.R. But that's not who's hurting.

Good thing we've still got politics in Texas—finest form of free entertain-ment ever invented.

"*Hair Dupe*"

I don't know about y'all, but what I hate most about moving is finding a new hair colorist. Last time I moved was from Dallas, where I had spent three years in the hands of a hair-coloring artiste. The man had made me a redhead, a condition to which I had never aspired and for which I have no natural talent, but you cannot argue with an artiste. You also have to pay artistes a lot. "It's the way I *see* you," he explained.

I moved to South Austin, home of the Bubbas and the Bubbettes, where our municipal motto is "South Austin, Texas, a Great Place to Buy Auto Parts." Figured I'd find some nice lady in a beauty parlor and I could tell her what color I thought my hair should be. Off I went to Groner Pitts's sister's La Delle's Beauty Shoppe, spelled with two P's and an E, on south First Street, and a hair colorist named Esther Ann. Me and Esther Ann are settin' there lookin' at my roots in the mirror. I say, "Esther Ann, I want to dye my hair natural. Let's color the whole thing silver-gray and then I can let it grow out and I won't have to worry about it anymore."

Esther Ann said, "Honey, I cain't."

I said, "Esther Ann, how come?"

She said, "Dear, you're sprang."

I said, "Do what?"

She said, "You're sprang. You can't have a winter color like silver next to your face, it won't go." Esther Ann is into color charts based on the seasons, just like the makeup ladies at Bergdorf Goodman in New York City. Creeping chic has come to South Austin.

Next Esther Ann and I had to decide what color blonde I was going to be. The range of choices is staggering. How do women make up their minds about all these colors, I asked Esther Ann. She informs me that some women get their hair dyed to match their dogs. If you had an Irish setter or a golden retriever, or even an apricot poodle, that might be okay, but my dog is black with a white spot on her chest. Might be sharp if I ran with a punk set. Wonder what it would look like if someone matched her bluetick hound?

Since blonde is also a popular color for cabinets, you could conceivably dye your hair to match your cupboards and truly blend into the woodwork.

I have a friend who recently stopped dyeing her hair just to find out what color it is. It had been thirty years since she'd seen its natural shade and she was curious. Turned out to be a nice browny-blonde and she likes it so well she kept it. It looks real natural too.

Some shades you never see anymore: a good bleached blonde is hard to find nowadays. Marilyn Monroe, Jean Harlow—where are those blondes of yesteryear? You have to find a five-and-dime in a small town, the kind where the waitresses still sport colored handkerchiefs folded like flowers on their chests, to find that shade of blonde. I like the punk mockery of letting the dark roots show, like Madonna. But Esther Ann informs me sternly that Madonna looks tacky. I'm living in the middle of the White Trash Hall of Fame, but I'm not allowed to look like Madonna. The fashion magazines often ask, "What does your 'look' say about you?" Madonna's says: "Slut!," which is a clear fashion statement, just what the magazines advise.

I'm now a strawberry blonde because Esther Ann didn't want me to make too dramatic a departure from my former condition of redheadedness. I used to cry and wish I were dead for several weeks when somebody changed my hair color. But we live in an era when California bodybuilders dye their hair two-tone, like old convertibles: dark on the sides and blonde on the top. It's hard to look strange anymore.

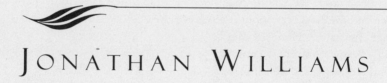

JONATHAN WILLIAMS

Williams, born in Asheville, North Carolina, in 1929, runs from the Great Smokies his Jargon Press, which has published such poets as Robert Creeley and Denise Levertov and such other contributions to the culture as the late Ernie Mickler's classic, The White Trash Cookbook. *He is a student of painting, particularly Southern folk art, and the writer of poems which sometimes consist of artfully arranged quotes from highway signs, burger-palace menus, small-town phonebooks, and the talk of mountain folk.*

"*Cracker-Barrel Reveries on the Tune 'Pax Americana'*"

"Us common people run this country!"
—George Wallace

feller over in
franklin
says hes got thishere book

says that fbi feller hoover
says that nigger preacher kings
nothin
but a tarnation communist

and i reckon you boys
heared on the tv this
walter jenkins hes
some kind of unnatchrul sex prevert why
you know them seven chillun
must be lightbulbs
you just know it

just like you know ol castro
and them jew boys in new york
got us into veetnam

some things be's plain obvious

why the barber feller was sayin
just yesterday
he said put the bombs to em boys drop em
all over them russkis and
the dadblame chinamens too and
might as well drop em on ol dee gawl
too hes got the big mouth dont he

i mean put it to em all
i mean buddy we could stop all this foolishness up north

why some things be's plain obvious

people get
what they want

"Uncle Iv Surveys His Domain from His Rocker of a Sunday Afternoon as Aunt Dory Starts to Chop the Kindling"

Mister Williams
lets youn me move
tother side the house

the woman
choppin woods
mite nigh the awkerdist thing
I seen

DAVE GARDNER

If this were a book about Southern humor, I would want to include in it Larry L. King's terrific article, published in Harper's *in 1970 (and reprinted in King's 1974 collection* The Old Man and Lesser Mortals*), entitled "Whatever Happened to Brother Dave?" Gardner was an obscure strip-joint comedian in 1957 when, at the age of thirty-one, he appeared on the Jack Paar talk show for the first time and became a national sensation. King's description of Gardner: "Andy Griffith running downhill with the brakes off, slightly zonked, and maybe plotting a practical joke to severely embarrass nice old Aunt Bea—or maybe more than embarrass her: his routines had a way of stressing humor in death. There was about him some combination of fun and menace, one sensed, slices of the high school dropout who perhaps had read Shakespeare on his own but who still might efficiently (and not always fairly) clean your pockets at the pool hall, or deliberately direct Yankee tourists to the wrongest possible road should they be foolish enough to inquire the most direct road to Birmingham." TV appearances, college-campus gigs, and albums with titles like* Rejoice, Dear Hearts *and* Kick Thine Own Self *set Gardner up with a yacht, several Cadillacs, and luxury homes in Hollywood and Biloxi. But as the civil rights movement, and Brother Dave's drug use, gained momentum, his comedy became more* and more reactionarily political and he lost his mainstream audience. In the past he had defused objections to his adept imitation of black voices by asserting that he believed "in one race—the human race," but by the time King caught his near-fugitive act in a Charlotte club, Brother Dave had gone way unbrotherly. He denounced "old liberal commie long-haired traitor hippies" and avowed, "I'd join the Klan, only I ain't got enough morals" as respectable locals demanded their money back and veritable Kluxers cheered him on. If I were to quote the most egregiously distasteful punch lines cited by King (who established a certain joint-sharing rapport with Brother Dave himself, but had reason to fear some of his supporters mortally), you might quite apolitically throw this book down in disgust. If there could be such a thing as a redneck Lennie Bruce, however, Gardner was it. Jimmy Buffett doing Lord Buckley's "God's Own Drunk" monologue is perhaps the closest anyone has come to Gardner's far-out/ol' boy fusion. Brother Dave was surely the wiggiest racist in Southern cultural history (one of his albums was called Reality: What a Concept), he never descended to gentility, and even at his right-wing nuttiest the range of his affinities blithely defied categorization. I thought it might be nice, for this book, to transcribe some quite characteristic bits of his, whose leanings might be labeled "politically correct," disapprovingly, by conservatives today. He died in 1983.

"The Spoon Story"

I think everything that we can think of ought to be legal, see, and let ever'body have the choice of going to hell the only way they wanted to, if they want to; if there's any place like that; I don't know. There was this one cat that went.

And he went down there you know and he studied it, see, and he loved to eat, I mean he was hung up on eatin' food, he loved good food; and he looked all around and he sees all these folks sitting at this great big table with these long spoons on their hands—just, oh, they was about, oh, well, about fourteen, fifteen, oh, 'bout twenty-five . . . oh about thirty-six inches long, them spoons was. I mean that's a pretty long spoon; and they was tied onto their hand, and the other hand was tied behind 'em don'tcha know.

And this was like Hades, see, they was reaching for that food but they couldn't make it to their mouth, you know; so—and then he said, "Wait a minute," said, "I don't like this kick, I wanta go see what it is in heaven, it's gotta be better." So he goes to heaven, man, it's just a step over,

bap.

And he gets over there, you know, and there's a great big table and all the folks sitting around with the big long spoons the same way, onliest difference is they're feeding one another.

"*Chicken Every Sunday*"

Now rocks are interesting to me. I love rocks because mineral, you know, is considered dense. Mineral, you know, mineral, and vegetable, and you know animal, see, and uh, yeah, and uh, us is supposed to be animals, but we're more than animals—because we're that vain. See, that's another tromp at ignernce. . . . I tell ya I got myself a handful of it the other day. I did that, I went out there and I just found all the ignernce in the whole world and I got it right in my hand and I squeezed it and I hung on to it, and I said, "I gotcha. Gotcha trapped." Went out and buried it—now don't nobody start poking round and digging it up, man. We ain't going to see nothing but intelligent things around us. Everybody's intelligent—dogs, cats, chickens, woodchucks, hogs, mules, chickens.

Chickens?

Well certainly, chickens is bright. Imagine old Grandmama, 'member how she used to say, "Now you chillun love one another, and go on off to Sunday school and church. And I'll have you somethin' other to eat when you get home.

"*Come 'ere, chicken!*"

"*BLAWWWWK!*"

I've seen 'em take that biddy's head and put their foot on their legs and pull briskly—*zip*.

I don't bleeve we have to devour the flesh of animals in order to sustain a happy, swinging frame.

And some folks are talking about, "Well my goodness," says, "Texas is cow country, you mean to tell me that we ain't supposed to whup them bovines in the head and eat their carcass no more? . . ."

[Voice from the audience: "Take care."]

That's all right, you never be careful. You see if you be careful you might break it.

[Same voice: "What?"]

Anything. Don't make no difference. Don't make no difference.

"*The Rolls-Royce Story*"

Money is power, but wisdom surpasses it. Goes higher. 'Cause the wise cat can always free-load off the rich cat.

Did you notice the millionaires today . . . ?

Going around saying, "Well, damn, I want a Rolls-Royce."

A woman says, "You don't want one of them old tacky *English* cars, do you? Well they're old-looking. Got that old square hood on 'em."

"But honey they *run* good. I mean they run *good*—when you set down in one of them Rolls-Royces and drop it down there in whatever gear you can find on it, and you just ride along . . . you can't hear anything but the tickin' of the clock."

She says, "But time *bugs* me."

"Observations on American Indians"

There's lots of folks that's hung up on that intellectual kick, you know, 'cause they don't know that the intellect is only a tool of the ego. And we're supposed to suppress that. Lest we become vain. And ignernt. And arrogant. Can you imagine the vanity and the ignernce of the white man to think that the Indians had a great white father?

Sure he was an Indian. Settin' down there beatin' on his drum, *k'toong toong toong toong.*

They're the only true Americans. The Indians. Bless their hearts, hallelujah. American Indians. Wh'shew, hehh hehh: Oh don't it give you strength to know what Sittin' Bull did to Custer? He was a smart aleck. Man, Sittin' Bull said, "Get 'im Junior and Willie," *whap,* man, that was all. Send his saddle home. Well, they gave him a haircut.

Friends, the Indian still can't vote; they ain't got no candidate running.

SECTION FIVE

HOME ON THE ROAD

Got on de train didn't have no fare
But I rode some
Yes I rode some
Got on de train didn't have no fare
Conductor ast me what I'm doing there
But I rode some.
Yes I rode some.

Well, he grabbed me by de collar and he led me to de door
But I rode some
Yes I rode some.
Well, he grabbed me by de collar and he led me to de door
He rapped me over de head with a forty-four
But I rode some
Yes I rode some.

—ANONYMOUS

BILLY JOE SHAVER

When Billy Joe Shaver was eleven, he caught two of his fingers in some mill machinery and had to rip them off to keep from losing his arm. They might have been reattachable, but before he got to the hospital a person he knew only as "a Negro woman" asked if she could have them and he said he guessed so, and he never saw her or them again. "It's not important," he told me in Nashville once. "The kids like it." Then he held the stubs up to his nostrils so that it looked like the fingers were way up his nose. But he can play guitar well enough to accompany himself on his songs, which have some of the most memorable lyrics—gracefully metrical lines turned out of plain country vernacular—ever recorded by Willie Nelson or Waylon Jennings or Shaver himself. "The devil made me do it the first time, | The second time I done it on my own" (from "Black Rose") stands out, and so does this bit of autobiography.

"Georgia on a Fast Train"

On a rainy Wednesday mornin',
That's the day that I was born in
That old sharecropper's one-room country shack.
They say my mammy left me
The day before she had me,
Said she hit the road and never once looked back.

Well I just thought I'd mention
My grandma's old-age pension
Is the reason why I'm standing here today.
I got all my country learnin'
Milkin' and a-churnin',
Pickin' cotton, raisin' hell and balin' hay.

I been to Georgia on a fast train honey,
I wuddn't born no yesterday.

I got a good Christian raisin'
And a 8th-grade education,
Ain't no need in y'all treatin' me this way.

Now sweet Carolina,
I don't guess I'll ever find a—
Nother woman put together like you are.
I love your wiggle in your walkin'
And your big city talkin'
And your brand new shiny Plymouth ragtop car.

LOUIS ARMSTRONG

On an Empty Stomach

It was a useful experience for me to work on the boat with all those big-shots in music. From some of them I learned valuable methods of playing, from others I learned to guard against acquiring certain nasty traits. I was interested in their way of handling money. David Jones, for instance, starved himself the whole summer we worked on the *Saint Paul*. He saved every nickel and sent all his money to a farm down South where employees and relatives were raising cotton for him and getting away with as much of his money as they could, since he was not there to look after his own interests. Every day he would eat an apple instead of a good hot meal. What was the result? The boll weevils ate all of his cotton before the season was over. He did not even have a chance to go down and look his farm over before a telegram came saying everything had been shot to hell. After that David Jones used to stand at the boat rail during every intermission looking down at the water and thinking about all the jack he had lost.

I often said to Fate Marable:

"Fate, keep an eye on David Jones. He's liable to jump in the water most any minute."

This incident taught me never to deprive my stomach. As a kid I had never believed in "cutting off my nose to spite my face," which is a true expression if there ever was one. I'll probably never be rich, but I will be a fat man.

CHARLES PORTIS

I hate it when people ask me what my favorite book is (there are so many books: War
and Peace, The Joy of Cooking, Ecclesiastes . . .*), but the truth of the matter
is, it's* Norwood. *In fact, once when somebody in an audience asked me which writer
I would like to be if I weren't myself, I responded that even if I were myself, it would
be Charles Portis. Since then we have gotten to be friends. He served as a Marine in
the Korean War, graduated from the University of Arkansas, worked as a reporter for
the* Arkansas Gazette *and the* New York Herald Tribune, *resigned his post as the*
Trib's *London bureau chief in 1966 to become a free-lance writer, resides now in
Little Rock, has never married, frequently drives down to Mexico, and once interviewed
Elvis (who was worried about his mother's condition: "She's yaller as a lemon," Elvis
said). Portis is the author of five novels:* True Grit *(which was a big best-seller and
was fairly faithfully adapted into the movie that won John Wayne his Oscar),*
Masters of Atlantis, The Dog of the South, Gringos, *and* Norwood, *which is
the text reread most often by Portis devotees, who say things like "The way I decided
to marry my wife, I gave her* Norwood *and waited. And then I heard her laughing
upstairs." Norwood Pratt is an old boy who gets out of the Marines and returns to his
hometown of Ralph, Texas (actually not "right in Ralph but just the other side of
Ralph"), to look after his sister Vernell. Then Vernell marries and brings into their
home an opinionated Michigan man named Bill Bird who "left hairs stuck around in
the soap—short, gray, unmistakable Bill Bird hairs." What with one thing and
another, Norwood takes off for New York City to collect a seventy-dollar debt from an
old Army buddy. Along the way he meets a lot of interesting people, including the
world's smallest perfect fat man and Joann the Wonder Hen, who is not strictly a
person but has a lot of personality for a hen that is not in the best of health. Norwood
rescues her from a cage where she is compelled to answer questions by pulling on a
lanyard with her beak when you deposit a nickel. The following excerpt is from before
he gets that far north, though.*

from *Norwood*

The sun was coming up before he got a ride. It was a bread truck. The driver
was a round sloping man who was wearing an official bread hat with a sunburst
medallion and a T-shirt that was so thin hairs were breaking through it. A
bulldozer watch fob lay on his lap. Norwood thought at first he had rubber
bands around his wrists. They were fat and dimpled like baby wrists.

"This is against the rules," said the bread man, "but I just can't pass a man
up. My wife says I'm too kind for my own good."

"Well, I sure appreciate it," said Norwood. "I was getting pretty tired."

The truck was a delivery model with no passenger seat and Norwood had to
sit on a wooden bread box. He laid the guitar across his knees. There was a bad
shimmy in the front wheels and this made the guitar bounce and hum.

"I'll have to make a few stops, but a man begging a ride ought to be glad to
get whatever he can."

"This is fine. I appreciate it too."

"Have you got a dollar to help on the gas?"

Norwood gave him a dollar. "Do you have to pay for your own gas?"

The man looked straight ahead. "Sometimes I do."

"How much does a job like this pay?" said Norwood. "A bread job?"

"Well, it don't pay as much as heavy construction work but you don't have
to work as hard neither. I used to drive a D-8 cat till I hurt my back. Didn't do
anything while I was on workmen's compensation. Just went to the show all
the time. I like *The Road Runner*."

"Yeah, I do too."

"I could watch that scutter for an hour."

"I believe I could too."

The bread man began to rumble with quiet laughter. "That coyote or
whatever he is, a wolf or something, every time he gets up on a clift or
somewhere with a new plan, why the Road Runner comes along on some
skates or has him some new invention like a rocket or a big wrecker's ball and
just busts that coyote a good one." He laughed some more, then fell into
repose. In a minute or two his face clouded with a darker memory. "Novel-
toons are not any good at all," he said. "It's usually a shoemaker and a bunch
of damn mice singing. When one of them comes on I get up and go get me a
sack of corn or something."

They shimmied on down the road. At the first stop, a roadside grocery
store, Norwood got a quart of milk and had the grocer make him a couple of
baloney and cheese sandwiches with mayonnaise. He leaned on the meat box

and ate and watched the bread man do his stuff. The bread man carried old bread out and brought new bread in. He squatted down and arranged it on the rack. Norwood noticed that he was poking finger holes in the competitors' loaves. Their eyes met, just for a second, and the bread man looked away. He tried to recover by doing peculiar things with his hands, as though he had a funny way of arranging bread. Norwood was not deceived. The bread man had no gift for pantomime and he did not seem to consider that from a range of eight or nine feet it is easy enough to tell whether someone is or is not punching holes in bread.

He said nothing about it and neither did Norwood. But back on the road the guilty knowledge hung heavy over the conversation. The bread man tried to get something going again. He asked Norwood if that was a Gibson guitar, but before Norwood could answer the man said, "My whole family is musical. Some families are like that. My sister used to play trombone solos in church. Daddy played the accordion and we would all sing. He could really play that thing. And didn't know note one."

"They're hard to beat," said Norwood, agreeably. "I like to hear a good accordion."

"Daddy passed on two days after Labor Day of 1951," said the bread man, forestalling any suggestion that they go hear the old gentleman play.

They picked up another hitchhiker. This one was carrying a sack of garden tomatoes. Norwood made room for him on the box. The man was grateful and deeply apologetic and he insisted on shaking their hands. Norwood had never seen a man so happy to get a ride. "This sure is nice of you," he kept saying.

"I'm not supposed to do it," said the bread man. "I just don't like to pass anybody up. Might need a ride myself sometime. How far are you going?"

"I'm going on in to Indianapolis. My wife is in the hospital there. She doesn't have any sweat glands."

"I never had a cold in my life," said the bread man.

"It was sure nice of you to stop like that. A lot of people are scared of hitchhikers. I guess you can't blame 'em."

"Have you got a dollar to help on the gas?"

The man looked frightened. "No sir, I sure don't. All I got is sixty cents and I was going to get my wife some ice cream with that. That's why I'm thumbing. I'm supposed to get a little check Friday."

The bread man stopped the truck and nodded at Norwood. "Well, it wouldn't be fair to him if I let you ride. He paid his dollar."

"I don't care," said Norwood. "It's all right with me."

But the bread man made no move to get the truck going again. He looked impassively into the distance.

"I tell you what, if you'll let me ride I'll try to do something nice for somebody else on down the road. I'll return the favor that way. I'll do somebody else a good deed and tell them to pass it on. . . . Maybe it'll go all the way around the world. . . ."

It was no use. The man got out with his sack of tomatoes after riding fifty yards. "Well . . . thank you anyway. . . . I'm sorry . . . if it was Friday I would have the money." He was pained at having caused trouble. Everybody was right but him.

The bread man drove away and glanced at Norwood to see how he was taking it. "He wasn't going to do anything for anybody down the road. That was a load of crap."

"I think he would have," said Norwood. "You ought to let him ride."

"You think so, huh? Why didn't you pay his dollar?"

"I didn't think about that. I guess I could have. . . . Let's go back and get him."

"I'm not running a bus service. Anyway, I didn't like his personality."

"You should of let him ride."

"Maybe *you* don't like *my* personality."

"I don't know you very well."

"Maybe you think I have personality trouble."

"I just don't know you."

"That's not any kind of answer. Why don't you say what you think? You think I don't know that some people don't like me because of my personality? I know that. My wife wants me to take a course. They're giving one at the hotel next week that's supposed to help you in sales work. It makes people like you."

"Why don't you take it?"

"What do you know about it? You're just a hitchhiker begging rides."

"Well . . ."

"You saw me back there roughing up that bread, didn't you?"

"Yeah, I did."

"I got nothing to hide. *They* started it. What do you want me to do?"

"It's none of my business."

"You mighty right it's not. The Vita-White guys *step* on my bread. Mash it all in with their feet. No telling what kind of germs is on their shoes. They don't care. A little child's death don't mean anything to them."

"I believe I'll get out along here, just anywhere."

"I'm going on in to town."

"I believe I'll get out anyway."

"That's fine with me. I'll be glad to get rid of you. You're not friendly."

He pulled over on the shoulder and stopped short. Norwood said, "much oblige," and got out.

"You need to do something about your personality, hitchhiker. That's what you need."

"What *you* need is about forty dollars worth of front end work on this truck," said Norwood. "Some new kingpins."

"I hope don't nobody pick you up."

"No use in you hoping that. Somebody will."

At a pool hall in Indianapolis a rack boy with a Junior Tracy haircut and a good opinion of himself told Norwood that if he was going to New York he wouldn't bother with hitchhiking, he would go out to the Pennsylvania yards and catch him a freight train. Norwood shot snooker with him most of the afternoon and lost $2.75, then downed two chili dogs and went out to the rail yards and wandered around in the dark.

He had never done this before. There were tracks and more tracks and empty flatcars and switch engines banging around and trains coming in and trains going out. The thing was to ask somebody. He walked over to the station and talked to a Negro man in coveralls who was pushing a mail buggy. The man pointed out a freight train that was being made up for Philadelphia and said be careful. Norwood circled all the way around to the end of the train—instead of just crawling over a coupling—and came back up the other side where it was darker. He walked along like an inspector giving all the boxcar hatches a shake, and finally found one he liked. It was a faded blue L & N car with a banged-up door that wouldn't close all the way. No one could lock that door on him. He slid it back and struck a match and looked in. Big sacks of flour, hundred-pounders, were stacked high at each end of the car, almost to the roof. There was an open space in the middle of the car. He pushed his bag and guitar in and climbed in after them.

It was pitch-dark inside and hot, close, airless. Well, he would be riding at night. It would be cooler when they started moving. The floor was nothing but splinters. He wished he had a flashlight. It was probably dangerous striking matches with all that flour. He pulled some of the sacks down and fashioned himself a place to sleep. It looked like a nest for some bird that never lived on this earth. He slipped his boots off and settled back into it and tipped his hat over his eyes range style. No. Better be ready for a fast move. Better put the boots back on. Like getting caught by the gooks in one of those sleeping bags that zipped only halfway down. A suicide bag. He ate a dime Payday and then peeled an orange and ate it and lay there quiet and watchful in that ghostly Pillsbury darkness until the train moved.

It started with a clanging jerk. Norwood was half asleep. He turned on his side and adjusted his hat. Drops of sweat ran across his back and tickled. He was sweating like a hog. Did hogs sweat? No. That's why they like mudholes. Mules did, and horses. Out in the sun they had shiny wet skins. He tried to remember what a hog's skin looked like out in the sun. He couldn't remember seeing a hog in the sun. For any length of time. Hogs didn't have to work. Had anybody ever tried to *make* one work? Maybe they tried it a long time ago in history, and just gave up. And told their sons not to bother with it any more. Better not leave the guitar out loose like that. All kinds of folks riding trains. He looped the shoulder cord around his wrist a couple of times. The bag was under his head, safe. Everything was secured. The head is secured. Some boot standing there at the door with a swab at port arms trying to keep you out. Even when it was secured for regimental inspection they had to keep one bowl and one urinal open. Everybody knew that. Why did they keep on trying to pull that swab on you? Norwood dozed and woke and blew flour out of his nose and slept and groaned and dreamed crazy dreams about Miss Phillips. The train stopped and started all night long. It seemed to last about three days.

The train was slowing for the block in Philadelphia when Norwood suddenly awoke. He was asleep one second and wide awake the next. A thin wall of sunlight was coming through the doorway crack, with a lot of stuff dancing around in it. Something was wrong. It was his feet. He felt air on his feet. He sat up and there wasn't anything on them except a pair of J. C. Penney Argyles. Somebody had taken his thirty-eight-dollar stovepipe boots right off his feet. *"Son of a bitch!"* He got up and climbed over the floor and pulled sacks this way and that way but there was no one to be found, and no boots.

Soon it was so thick with flour dust in the car that he had to slam one of the doors back and stick his head out for air. The trouble was, two of the sacks had broken. After he caught his breath he dragged them over and pushed them out. The second one snagged on the bad door and hung there for a moment blowing flour up in his face. Then he began *flinging* sacks out, good ones, till he got a cramp in his neck.

The train entered the yard with long blats from the diesel horn and as it lurched in for a stop Norwood grabbed up his gear and bailed out in his sock feet. It stung. He squatted there and looked long and hard up and down the train, through the wheels, to see if anybody else was jumping off. Nobody. He dusted himself off, whacking his trousers with his hat, and decided to do some backtracking along the roadbed.

He couldn't walk far. The rocks and clinkers hurt his feet and he sat down on a stack of crossties to put on another layer of socks. While he was sitting there smoking a cigarette he saw two men in the distance coming up the tracks. One of them was wearing a luminous orange jacket. It was blinding. He might have had some job that required him to be easily spotted by aircraft. Norwood waited.

The one with the jacket was a tall whiskery man. He was also wearing a St. Louis Cardinal's baseball cap. By his side, stepping smartly along with a knotty walking stick, was a short angry little man with a knapsack on his back. He was covered from head to toe with flour, except right around his eyes and mouth.

"What happened to you, neighbor?" said Norwood.

"You should of seen it," said the man with the Cardinal cap. "Some thug was throwing flour out of a boxcar and Eugene here was walking along not thinking about anything when one of 'em hit him. One of them sacks."

"Was he hurt?"

"Well, it didn't hurt him, but it didn't help him none either."

He wanted to stop and talk about it some more, the sexagenarian Cardinal, but his short chum kept moving. He didn't even glance at Norwood. He looked like a man who was going somewhere to report something. Norwood had to run around in front of him to stop him. "Hey wait a minute. I better have a look in that pack. Somebody got my boots last night." The flour man looked up and fixed Norwood with two evil red eyes, but said nothing. The Cardinal did not like the turn things had taken. Maybe he could explain it again.

"We don't know anything about any boots. Eugene got hit with some flour, that's all. Some thug was throwing it off the train. I got hit with a mail pouch myself once but it wasn't anything like this. This was like a flour bomb went off."

Norwood moved around behind the flour man and reached up to undo the straps on the knapsack. With that, the flour man went into action. He was like lightning. He was a tiger. He spun around and hit Norwood on the arms three or four times with his stick and when it broke he popped Norwood in the mouth with a straight left and then he jumped up on his back and stuck there like a small white bear. The knapsack on *his* back was like a yet smaller bear.

"Look out! Look out!" the Cardinal was saying. He had jumped back well clear of the action. "Turn him loose, Eugene! He's another Hitler!"

Norwood was dancing around jabbing at the man with his elbows trying to shake him off. He backed him up and bumped him against the crossties. The man's ankles were locked together in front and Norwood broke them loose but the man had a hold on his neck that wouldn't quit. "You better get him off before I bust his head open," said Norwood, stopping to rest a minute. He was breathing hard. His upper lip was bloody.

The Cardinal moved in a little closer. Maybe something could be worked out now. "Eugene don't weigh very much, does he?" he said.

"I still don't want him on my back."

"He's light enough to be a jockey. Of course he's way too old."

"How long does he generally hang on?"

"I don't know. I never seen him do that before. . . . They say a snapping turtle won't let go till it thunders. That's what I've heard. I never was bit by a turtle. My oldest sister was bit by a mad fox. They didn't have any screens on their house and it come in a window one night and nipped her on the leg like a little dog will do. They carried that fox's head on in to Birmingham in some ice and said it was mad and she had to take all them shots. She said she hoped she never did get bit by nair another one.''

Norwood kicked his feet forward and fell backward on the flour man and they hit the deck in a puff of white. The flour man was squeezed between Norwood and the pack and it knocked the wind out of him. He made a lung noise like *gunh!* He turned loose and sat up and brushed himself off a little, still defiant but not fighting any more. Norwood opened the knapsack and poked around in it. There were rolled-up clothes and a cast-iron skillet and pie pans and a can of Granger and cotton blankets and copies of *True Police Cases* and a mashed store cake and crackers and cans of chili and lima beans and an insulated plastic cup and a bottle of 666 Tonic and a clock and an old five-shot top-breaking .32 revolver with a heavy fluted barrel and taped-on grips. No boots. But in one of the side pouches he did find some shoes.

They were old-timers' high tops with elastic strips on the sides. Norwood tried them on and walked around flexing them and looking at them in profile. They were plenty loose. Eugene didn't have feet, he had flippers. Norwood said, ''I'll give you two dollars for these dudes.''

''Those are my house shoes,'' said Eugene, speaking for the first time and the last.

''A man comes along and needs some shoes, you ought to want to help him. You already got some good shoes on.''

''Eugene doesn't want to sell his house shoes,'' said the Cardinal.

''You stay out of this,'' said Norwood.

''You international thug. You're just like Hitler and Tojo wrapped up into one.''

Norwood tried Eugene once more. ''Look, you can get another pair of these dudes easy for six bits at the Goodwill Store. I'm offering you two dollars. What about me? I don't have any shoes. I lost some thirty-eight-dollar boots last night. They took 'em right off my feet. They didn't give *me* anything.''

''You better give Tojo what he wants, Eugene. He'll terrorize you if you don't. That's the way he does business.''

''Don't call me Tojo any more.''

''This is a free country, *thug.* You can call people anything you want to. Can't you, Eugene?''

Norwood rolled the two dollar bills into a cylinder and pushed it into Eugene's shirt pocket. ''I ought not to give you anything. Jumping up on people's backs. They'll put you in a home somewhere if you don't watch out.''

WILLIAM FAULKNER

How often do we think about the fact that Faulkner's middle name was Cuthbert?
Well, never mind that. He was a fine comic writer when he took a mind to be. I don't
know of any parody of Faulkner that is much good; Faulkner over the top is too far
out there to be sent up, and Faulkner on his game is hard to touch. Faulkner wrote a
parody of himself, in fact, under the name Ernest V. Trueblood (" 'Are you hurt, Mr.
Faulkner?' I cried. I shall not attempt to reproduce Mr. Faulkner's reply, other than to
indicate that it was couched in that pure ancient classic Saxon which the best of our
literature sanctions and authorizes and which, due to the exigencies of Mr. Faulkner's
style and subject matter, I often employ but which I myself never use although Mr.
Faulkner even in his private life is quite addicted to it and which . . ."), which is not
much good either. The title of that piece is "Afternoon of a Cow." According to
Dwight Macdonald, who reprinted it in his anthology Parodies, *it was first*
published, around 1947, in an Algerian magazine called Fontaine. *Macdonald was*
unable to say what caused Faulkner to appear in such a venue. Trueblood is presented
as the person who writes all of Faulkner's fiction. In the movie Barton Fink, *it may*
be noted, a Faulkner-like character, well played by John Mahoney, is portrayed as
letting his secretary, well played by Judy Davis, do all his writing. That is the only
part of Barton Fink, *I might mention, that I liked. I wonder whether it would be*
amusing if I tried to rewrite this whole note in a Faulknerian style. Nah.

"Uncle Willy"

I know what they said. They said I didn't run away from home but that I was
tolled away by a crazy man who, if I hadn't killed him first, would have killed
me inside another week. But if they had said that the women, the good women
in Jefferson had driven Uncle Willy out of town and I followed him and did
what I did because I knew that Uncle Willy was on his last go-round and this
time when they got him again it would be for good and forever, they would
have been right. Because I wasn't tolled away and Uncle Willy wasn't crazy,
not even after all they had done to him. I didn't have to go; I didn't have to go
any more than Uncle Willy had to invite me instead of just taking it for granted

that I wanted to come. I went because Uncle Willy was the finest man I ever knew, because even women couldn't beat him, because in spite of them he wound up his life getting fun out of being alive and he died doing the thing that was the most fun of all because I was there to help him. And that's something that most men and even most women too don't get to do, not even the women that call meddling with other folks' lives fun.

He wasn't anybody's uncle, but all of us, and grown people too, called him (or thought of him) as Uncle Willy. He didn't have any kin at all except a sister in Texas married to an oil millionaire. He lived by himself in a little old neat white house where he had been born on the edge of town, he and an old nigger named Job Wylie that was older than he was even, that cooked and kept the house and was the porter at the drugstore which Uncle Willy's father had established and which Uncle Willy ran without any other help than old Job; and during the twelve or fourteen years (the life of us as children and then boys), while he just used dope, we saw a lot of him. We liked to go to his store because it was always cool and dim and quiet inside because he never washed the windows; he said the reason was that he never had to bother to dress them because nobody could see in anyway, and so the heat couldn't get in either. And he never had any customers except country people buying patent medicines that were already in bottles, and niggers buying cards and dice, because nobody had let him fill a prescription in forty years I reckon, and he never had any soda fountain trade because it was old Job who washed the glasses and mixed the syrups and made the ice cream ever since Uncle Willy's father started the business in eighteen-fifty-something and so old Job couldn't see very well now, though papa said he didn't think that old Job took dope too, it was from breathing day and night the air which Uncle Willy had just exhaled.

But the ice cream tasted all right to us, especially when we came in hot from the ball games. We had a league of three teams in town and Uncle Willy would give the prize, a ball or a bat or a mask, for each game though he would never come to see us play, so after the game both teams and maybe all three would go to the store to watch the winner get the prize. And we would eat the ice cream and then we would all go behind the prescription case and watch Uncle Willy light the little alcohol stove and fill the needle and roll his sleeve up over the little blue myriad punctures starting at his elbow and going right on up into his shirt. And the next day would be Sunday and we would wait in our yards and fall in with him as he passed from house to house and go on to Sunday school, Uncle Willy with us, in the same class with us, sitting there while we recited. Mr. Barbour from the Sunday school never called on him. Then we would finish the lesson and we would talk about baseball until the bell rang and Uncle Willy still not saying anything, just sitting there all neat and clean, with his clean collar and no tie and weighing about a hundred and ten pounds and his eyes behind his glasses kind of all run together like broken eggs. Then we would all go to the store and eat the ice cream that was left over from Saturday and then go behind the prescription case and watch him again: the little stove and his Sunday shirt rolled up and the needle going slow into his blue arm and somebody would say, "Don't it hurt?" and he would say, "No. I like it."

II

Then they made him quit dope. He had been using it for forty years, he told us once, and now he was sixty and he had about ten years more at the outside, only he didn't tell us that because he didn't need to tell even fourteen-year-old boys that. But they made him quit. It didn't take them long. It began one Sunday morning and it was finished by the next Friday; we had just sat down in our class and Mr. Barbour had just begun, when all of a sudden Reverend Schultz, the minister, was there, leaning over Uncle Willy and already hauling him out of his seat when we looked around, hauling him up and saying in that tone in which preachers speak to fourteen-year-old boys that I don't believe even pansy boys like: "Now, Brother Christian, I know you will hate to leave Brother Barbour's class, but let's you and I go in and join Brother Miller and the men and hear what he can tell us on this beautiful and heartwarming text," and Uncle Willy still trying to hold back and looking around at us with his run-together eyes blinking and saying plainer than if he had spoke it: "What's this? What's this, fellows? What are they fixing to do to me?"

We didn't know any more than he did. We just finished the lesson; we didn't talk any baseball that day; and we passed the alcove where Mr. Miller's men's Bible class met, with Reverend Schultz sitting in the middle of them like he did every Sunday, like he was just a plain man like the rest of them yet kind of bulging out from among the others like he didn't have to move or speak to keep them reminded that he wasn't a plain man; and I would always think about April Fool's one year when Miss Callaghan called the roll and then stepped down from her desk and said, "Now I'm going to be a pupil today," and took a vacant seat and called out a name and made them go to her desk and hold the lesson and it would have been fun if you could have just quit remembering that tomorrow wouldn't be April Fool's and the day after that wouldn't be either. And Uncle Willy was sitting by Reverend Schultz looking littler than ever, and I thought about one day last summer when they took a country man named Bundren to the asylum at Jackson but he wasn't too crazy not to know where he was going, sitting there in the coach window handcuffed to a fat deputy sheriff that was smoking a cigar.

Then Sunday school was over and we went out to wait for him, to go to the store and eat the ice cream. And he didn't come out. He didn't come out until church was over too, the first time that he had ever stayed for church that any of us knew of—that anybody knew of, papa told me later—coming out with Mrs. Merridew on one side of him and Reverend Schultz on the other still holding him by the arm and he looking around at us again with his eyes saying again only desperate now: "Fellows, what's this? What's this, fellows?" and Reverend Schultz shoving him into Mrs. Merridew's car and Mrs. Merridew saying, loud, like she was in the pulpit: "Now, Mr. Christian, I'm going to take you right out to my house and I'm going to fix you a nice glass of cool lemonade and then we will have a nice chicken dinner and then you are going to take a nice nap in my hammock and then Brother and Sister Schultz are coming out and we will have some nice ice cream," and Uncle Willy saying, "No. Wait, ma'am, wait! Wait! I got to go to the store and fill a prescription I promised this morning—"

So they shoved him into the car and him looking back at us where we stood there; he went out of sight like that, sitting beside Mrs. Merridew in the car like Darl Bundren and the deputy on the train, and I reckon she was holding his wrist and I reckon she never needed any handcuffs and Uncle Willy giving us that single look of amazed and desperate despair.

Because now he was already an hour past the time for his needle and that afternoon when he finally slipped away from Mrs. Merridew he was five hours past it and so he couldn't even get the key into the lock, and so Mrs. Merridew and Reverend Schultz caught him and this time he wasn't talking or looking either: he was trying to get away like a half-wild cat tries to get away. They took him to his home and Mrs. Merridew telegraphed his sister in Texas and Uncle Willy didn't come to town for three days because Mrs. Merridew and Mrs. Hovis took turn about staying in the house with him day and night until his sister could get there. That was vacation then and we played the game on Monday and that afternoon the store was still locked and Tuesday it was still locked, and so it was not until Wednesday afternoon and Uncle Willy was running fast.

He didn't have any shirt on and he hadn't shaved and he could not get the key into the lock at all, panting and whimpering and saying, "She went to sleep at last; she went to sleep at last," until one of us took the key and unlocked the door. We had to light the little stove too and fill the needle and this time it didn't go into his arm slow, it looked like he was trying to jab it clean through the bone. He didn't go back home. He said he wouldn't need anything to sleep on and he gave us the money and let us out the back door and we bought the sandwiches and the bottle of coffee from the café and we left him there.

Then the next day, it was Mrs. Merridew and Reverend Schultz and three more ladies; they had the marshal break in the door and Mrs. Merridew holding Uncle Willy by the back of the neck and shaking him and kind of whispering, "You little wretch! You little wretch! Slip off from *me*, will you?"

and Reverend Schultz saying, "Now, Sister; now, Sister; control yourself," and the other ladies hollering Mr. Christian and Uncle Willy and Willy, according to how old they were or how long they had lived in Jefferson. It didn't take them long.

The sister got there from Texas that night and we would walk past the house and see the ladies on the front porch or going in and out, and now and then Reverend Schultz kind of bulging out from among them like he would out of Mr. Miller's Bible class, and we could crawl up behind the hedge and hear them through the window, hear Uncle Willy crying and cussing and fighting to get out of the bed and the ladies saying, "Now, Mr. Christian; now, Uncle Willy," and "Now, Bubber," too, since his sister was there; and Uncle Willy crying and praying and cussing. And then it was Friday, and he gave up. We could hear them holding him in the bed; I reckon this was his last go-round, because none of them had time to talk now; and then we heard him, his voice weak but clear and his breath going in and out.

"Wait," he said. "Wait! I will ask it one more time. Won't you please quit? Won't you please go away? Won't you please go to hell and just let me come on at my own gait?"

"No, Mr. Christian," Mrs. Merridew said. "We are doing this to save you."

For a minute we didn't hear anything. Then we heard Uncle Willy lay back in the bed, kind of flop back.

"All right," he said. "All right."

It was like one of those sheep they would sacrifice back in the Bible. It was like it had climbed up onto the altar itself and flopped onto its back with its throat held up and said: "All right. Come on and get it over with. Cut my damn throat and go away and let me lay quiet in the fire."

III

He was sick for a long time. They took him to Memphis and they said that he was going to die. The store stayed locked all the time now, and after a few weeks we didn't even keep up the league. It wasn't just the balls and the bats. It wasn't that. We would pass the store and look at the big old lock on it and at the windows you couldn't even see through, couldn't even see inside where we used to eat the ice cream and tell him who beat and who made the good plays and him sitting there on his stool with the little stove burning and the dope boiling and bubbling and the needle waiting in his hand, looking at us with his eyes blinking and all run together behind his glasses so you couldn't even tell where the pupil was like you can in most eyes. And the niggers and the country folks that used to trade with him coming up and looking at the lock too, and asking us how he was and when he would come home and open up again. Because even after the store opened again, they would not trade with the clerk that Mrs. Merridew and Reverend Schultz put in the store. Uncle Willy's sister said not to bother about the store, to let it stay shut because she would take care of Uncle Willy if he got well. But Mrs. Merridew said no, she not only aimed to cure Uncle Willy, she was going to give him a complete rebirth, not only into real Christianity but into the practical world too, with a place in it waiting for him so he could hold up his head not only with honor but pride too among his fellow men; she said that at first her only hope had been to fix it so he would not have to face his Maker slave body and soul to morphine, but now since his constitution was stronger than anybody could have believed, she was going to see that he assumed that position in the world which his family's name entitled him to before he degraded it.

She and Reverend Schultz found the clerk. He had been in Jefferson about six months. He had letters to the church, but nobody except Reverend Schultz and Mrs. Merridew knew anything about him. That is, they made him the clerk in Uncle Willy's store; nobody else knew anything about him at all. But Uncle Willy's old customers wouldn't trade with him. And we didn't either. Not that we had much trade to give him and we certainly didn't expect him to give us any ice cream and I don't reckon we would have taken it if he had offered it to us. Because it was not Uncle Willy, and pretty soon it wasn't even the same ice cream because the first thing the clerk did after he washed the windows was to fire old Job, only old Job refused to quit. He stayed around the store anyhow, mumbling to himself and the clerk would run him out the front door and old Job would go around to the back and come in and the clerk would find him again and cuss him, whispering, cussing old Job good even if he did have letters to the church; he went and swore out a warrant and the marshal told old Job he would have to stay out of the store. Then old Job moved across the street. He would sit on the curb all day where he could watch the door and every time the clerk came in sight old Job would holler, "I ghy tell um! I ghy do hit!" So we even quit passing the store. We would cut across the corner not to pass it, with the windows clean now and the new town trade the clerk had built up—he had a lot of trade now—going in and out, just stopping long enough to ask old Job about Uncle Willy, even though we had already got what news came from Memphis about him every day and we knew that old Job would not know, would not be able to get it straight even if someone told him, since he never did believe that Uncle Willy was sick, he just believed that Mrs. Merridew had taken him away somewhere by main force and was holding him in another bed somewhere so he couldn't get up and come back home; and old Job sitting on the curb and blinking up at us with his little watery red eyes like Uncle Willy would and saying, "I ghy tell um! Holting him up dar whilst whipper-snappin' trash makin' free wid Marse Hoke Christian's sto. I ghy tell um!"

IV

Uncle Willy didn't die. One day he came home with his skin the color of tallow and weighing about ninety pounds now and with his eyes like broken eggs still but dead eggs, eggs that had been broken so long now that they didn't even smell dead any more—until you looked at them and saw that they were anything in the world except dead. That was after he got to know us again. I don't mean that he had forgotten about us exactly. It was like he still liked us as boys, only he had never seen us before and so he would have to learn our names and which faces the names belonged to. His sister had gone back to Texas now, because Mrs. Merridew was going to look after him until he was completely recovered, completely cured. Yes. Cured.

I remember that first afternoon when he came to town and we walked into the store and Uncle Willy looked at the clean windows that you could see through now and at the town customers that never had traded with him, and at the clerk and said, "You're my clerk, hey?" and the clerk begun to talk about Mrs. Merridew and Reverend Schultz and Uncle Willy said, "All right, all right," and now he ate some ice cream too, standing at the counter with us like he was a customer too and still looking around the store while he ate the ice cream, with those eyes that were not dead at all and he said, "Looks like you been getting more work out of my damned old nigger than I could," and the clerk began to say something else about Mrs. Merridew and Uncle Willy said, "All right, all right. Just get a holt of Job right away and tell him I am going to expect him to be here every day and that I want him to keep this store looking like this from now on." Then we went on behind the prescription case, with Uncle Willy looking around here too, at how the clerk had it neated up, with a big new lock on the cabinet where the drugs and such were kept, with those eyes that wouldn't anybody call dead, I don't care who he was, and said, "Step up there and tell that fellow I want my keys." But it wasn't the stove and the needle. Mrs. Merridew had busted both of them that day. But it wasn't that anyway, because the clerk came back and begun to talk about Mrs. Merridew and Reverend Schultz, and Uncle Willy listening and saying, "All right, all right," and we never had seen him laugh before and his face didn't change now but we knew that he was laughing behind it. Then we went out. He turned sharp off the square, down Nigger Row to Sonny Barger's store and I took the money and bought the Jamaica ginger from Sonny and caught up with them and we went home with Uncle Willy and we sat in the pasture while he drank the Jamaica ginger and practiced our names some more.

And that night we met him where he said. He had the wheelbarrow and the crowbar and we broke open the back door and then the cabinet with the new lock on it and got the can of alcohol and carried it to Uncle Willy's and buried it in the barn. It had almost three gallons in it and he didn't come to town at all for four weeks and he was sick again, and Mrs. Merridew storming into the house, jerking out drawers and flinging things out of closets and Uncle Willy lying in the bed and watching her with those eyes that were a long way from being dead. But she couldn't find anything because it was all gone now, and besides she didn't know what it was she was looking for because she was looking for a needle. And the night Uncle Willy was up again we took the crowbar and went back to the store and when we went to the cabinet we found that it was already open and Uncle Willy's stool sitting in the door and a quart bottle of alcohol on the stool in plain sight, and that was all. And then I knew that the clerk knew who got the alcohol before but I didn't know why he hadn't told Mrs. Merridew until two years later.

I didn't know that for two years, and Uncle Willy a year now going to Memphis every Saturday in the car his sister had given him. I wrote the letter with Uncle Willy looking over my shoulder and dictating, about how his health was improving but not as fast as the doctor seemed to want and that the doctor said he ought not to walk back and forth to the store and so a car, not an expensive car, just a small car that he could drive himself or maybe find a negro boy to drive for him if his sister thought he ought not to: and she sent the money and he got a burr-headed nigger boy about my size named Secretary to drive it for him. That is, Secretary said he could drive a car; certainly he and Uncle Willy both learned on the night trips they would make back into the hill country to buy corn whisky and Secretary learned to drive in Memphis pretty quick, too, because they went every Saturday, returning Monday morning with Uncle Willy insensible on the back seat, with his clothes smelling of that smell whose source I was not to discover at first hand for some years yet, and two or three half-empty bottles and a little notebook full of telephone numbers and names like Lorine and Billie and Jack. I didn't know it for two years, not until that Monday morning when the sheriff came and padlocked and sealed what was left of Uncle Willy's stock and when they tried to find the clerk they couldn't even find out what train he had left town on; a hot morning in July and Uncle Willy sprawled out on the back seat, and on the front seat with Secretary a woman twice as big as Uncle Willy, in a red hat and a pink dress and a dirty white fur coat over the back of the seat and two straw suitcases on the fenders, with hair the color of a brand new brass hydrant bib and her cheeks streaked with mascara and caked powder where she had sweated.

It was worse than if he had started dope again. You would have thought he had brought smallpox to town. I remember how when Mrs. Merridew telephoned Mamma that afternoon you could hear her from away out at her house, over the wire, clean out to the back door and the kitchen: "Married! *Married!* Whore! Whore! *Whore!*" like the clerk used to cuss old Job, and so maybe the church can go just so far and maybe the folks that are in it are the ones that know the best or are entitled to say when to disconnect religion for a minute or two. And Papa was cussing too, not cussing anybody; I knew he was not cussing Uncle Willy or even Uncle Willy's new wife, just like I knew that I wished Mrs. Merridew could have been there to hear him. Only I reckon if she had been there she couldn't have heard anything because they said she still had on a house dress when she went and snatched Reverend Schultz into her car and went out to Uncle Willy's, where he was still in bed like always on Monday and Tuesday, and his new wife run Mrs. Merridew and Reverend Schultz out of the house with the wedding license like it was a gun or a knife. And I remember how all that afternoon—Uncle Willy lived on a little quiet side street where the other houses were all little new ones that country people who had moved to town within the last fifteen years, like mail carriers and little storekeepers, lived—how all that afternoon mad-looking ladies with sun-bonnets on crooked came busting out of that little quiet street dragging the little children and the grown girls with them, heading for the mayor's office and Reverend Schultz's house, and how the young men and the boys that didn't work and some of the men that did would drive back and forth past Uncle Willy's house to look at her sitting on the porch smoking cigarettes and drinking something out of a glass; and how she came down town the next day to shop, in a black hat now and a red-and-white striped dress so that she looked like a great big stick of candy and three times as big as Uncle Willy now, walking along the street with men popping out of the stores when she passed like she was stepping on a line of spring triggers and both sides of her behind kind of pumping up and down inside the dress until somebody hollered, threw back his head and squalled: "YIPPEEE!" like that and she kind of twitched her behind without even stopping and then they hollered sure enough.

And the next day the wire came from his sister, and Papa for the lawyer and Mrs. Merridew for the witness went out there and Uncle Willy's wife showed them the license and told them to laugh that off, that Manuel Street or not she was married as good and tight as any high-nosed bitch in Jefferson or anywhere else and Papa saying, "Now, Mrs. Merridew; now, Mrs. Christian," and he told Uncle Willy's wife how Uncle Willy was bankrupt now and might even lose the house too, and his wife said how about that sister in Texas, was Papa going to tell her that the oil business was bankrupt too and not to make her laugh. So they telegraphed the sister again and the thousand dollars came and they had to give Uncle Willy's wife the car too. She went back to Memphis that same afternoon, driving across the square with the straw suitcases, in a black lace dress now and already beginning to sweat again under her new makeup because it was still hot, and stopping where the men were waiting at the post office for the afternoon mail and she said, "Come on up to Manuel Street and see me sometime and I will show you hicks what you and this town can do to yourselves and one another."

And that afternoon Mrs. Merridew moved back into Uncle Willy's house and Papa said the letter she wrote Uncle Willy's sister had eleven pages to it because Papa said she would never forgive Uncle Willy for getting bankrupted. We could hear her from behind the hedge: "You're crazy, Mr. Christian; crazy. I have tried to save you and make something out of you besides a beast but now my patience is exhausted. I am going to give you one more chance. I am going to take you to Keeley and if that fails, I am going to take you myself to your sister and force her to commit you to an asylum." And the sister sent papers from Texas declaring that Uncle Willy was incompetent and making Mrs. Merridew his guardian and trustee, and Mrs. Merridew took him to the Keeley in Memphis. And that was all.

V

That is, I reckon they thought that that was all, that this time Uncle Willy would surely die. Because even Papa thought that he was crazy now because even Papa said that if it hadn't been for Uncle Willy I would not have run away, and therefore I didn't run away, I was tolled away by a lunatic; it wasn't Papa, it was Uncle Robert that said that he wasn't crazy because any man who could sell Jefferson real estate for cash while shut up in a Keeley institute wasn't crazy or even drunk. Because they didn't even know that he was out of Keeley, even Mrs. Merridew didn't know it until he was gone two days and they couldn't find him. They never did find him or find out how he got out and I didn't either until I got the letter from him to take the Memphis bus on a certain day and he would meet me at a stop on the edge of Memphis. I didn't even realize that I had not seen Secretary or old Job either in two weeks. But he didn't toll me away. I went because I wanted to, because he was the finest man I ever knew, because he had had fun all his life in spite of what they had tried to do to him or with him, and I hoped that maybe if I could stay with him a while I could learn how to, so I could still have fun too when I had to get old. Or maybe I knew more than that, without knowing it, like I knew that I would do anything he asked me to do, no matter what it was, just like I helped him break into the store for the alcohol when he took it for granted that I would without asking me to at all and then helped him hide it from Mrs. Merridew. Maybe I even knew what old Job was going to do. Not what he did do, but that he would do it if the occasion arose, and that this would have to be Uncle Willy's last go-round and if I wasn't there it would be just him against all the old terrified and timid clinging to dull and rule-ridden breathing which Jefferson was to him and which, even though he had escaped Jefferson, old Job still represented.

So I cut some grass that week and I had almost two dollars. I took the bus on the day he said and he was waiting for me at the edge of town, in a Ford now without any top on it and you could still read the chalk letters, $85 *cash* on the windshield, and a brand new tent folded up in the back of it and Uncle Willy and old Job in the front seat, and Uncle Willy looked fine with a checked cap new except for a big oil stain, with the bill turned round behind and a pair of goggles cocked up on the front of it and his celluloid collar freshly washed and no tie in it and his nose peeling with sunburn and his eyes bright behind his glasses. I would have gone with him anywhere; I would do it over again right now, knowing what was going to happen. He would not have to ask me now any more than he did then. So I got on top of the tent and we didn't go toward town, we went the other way. I asked where we were going but he just said wait, rushing the little car along like he couldn't get there quick enough himself, and I could tell from his voice that this was fine, this was the best yet, better than anybody else could have thought about doing, and old Job hunched down in the front seat, holding on with both hands and yelling at Uncle Willy about going so fast. Yes. Maybe I knew from old Job even then that Uncle Willy may have escaped Jefferson but he had just dodged it; he hadn't gotten away.

Then we came to the sign, the arrow that said Airport, and we turned and I said: "What? What is it?" but Uncle Willy just said: "Wait; just wait," like he couldn't hardly wait himself, hunched over the wheel with his white hair blowing under his cap and his collar riding up behind so you could see his neck between the collar and the shirt; and old Job saying (Oh yes, I could tell even then): "He got hit, all right. He done done hit. But I done tole him. Nemmine. I done warned him." Then we came to the airport and Uncle Willy stopped quick and pointed up without even getting out and said, "Look."

It was an airplane flying around and Uncle Willy running up and down the edge of the field waving his handkerchief until it saw him and came down and landed and rolled up to us, a little airplane with a two-cylinder engine. It was Secretary, in another new checked cap and goggles like Uncle Willy's and they told me how Uncle Willy had bought one for old Job too but old Job wouldn't wear it. And that night—we stayed in a little tourist camp about two miles away and he had a cap and goggles all ready for me too; and then I knew why they hadn't been able to find him—Uncle Willy told me how he had bought the airplane with some of the money he had sold his house for after his sister saved it because she had been born in it too, but that Captain Bean at the airport wouldn't teach him to run it himself because he would need a permit from a doctor ("By God," Uncle Willy said, "damn if these Republicans and

Democrats and XYZ's ain't going to have it soon where a man can't even flush the toilet in his own bathroom.'') and he couldn't go to the doctor because the doctor might want to send him back to the Keeley or tell Mrs. Merridew where he was. So he just let Secretary learn to run it first and now Secretary had been running it for two weeks, which was almost fourteen days longer than he had practiced on the car before they started out with it. So Uncle Willy bought the car and tent and camping outfit yesterday and tomorrow we were going to start. We would go first to a place named Renfro where nobody knew us and where there was a big pasture that Uncle Willy had found out about and we would stay there a week while Secretary taught Uncle Willy to run the airplane. Then we would head west. When we ran out of the house money we would stop at a town and take up passengers and make enough to buy gasoline and food to get to the next town, Uncle Willy and Secretary in the airplane and me and old Job in the car; and old Job sitting in a chair against the wall, blinking at Uncle Willy with his little weak red sullen eyes, and Uncle Willy reared up on the cot with his cap and goggles still on and his collar without any tie (it wasn't fastened to his shirt at all: just buttoned around his neck) sometimes sideways and sometimes even backward like an Episcopal minister's, and his eyes bright behind his glasses and his voice bright and fine. "And by Christmas we will be in California!" he said. "Think of that. California!"

VI

So how could they say that I had to be tolled away? How could they? I suppose I knew then that it wouldn't work, couldn't work, that it was too fine to be true. I reckon I even knew how it was going to end just from the glum way Secretary acted whenever Uncle Willy talked about learning to run the airplane himself, just as I knew from the way old Job looked at Uncle Willy, not what he did of course, but what he would do if the occasion arose. Because I was the other white one. I was white, even if old Job and Secretary were both older than me, so it would be all right; I could do it all right. It was like I knew even then that, no matter what might happen to him, he wouldn't ever die and I thought that if I could just learn to live like he lived, no matter what might happen to me I wouldn't ever die either.

So we left the next morning, just after daylight because there was another fool rule that Secretary would have to stay in sight of the field until they gave him a license to go away. We filled the airplane with gas and Secretary went up in it just like he was going up to practice. Then Uncle Willy got us into the car quick because he said the airplane could make sixty miles an hour and so Secretary would be at Renfro a long while before we got there. But when we got to Renfro Secretary wasn't there and we put the tent up and ate dinner and he still didn't come and Uncle Willy beginning to cuss and we ate supper and dark came but Secretary didn't and Uncle Willy was cussing good now. He didn't come until the next day. We heard him and ran out and watched him fly right over us, coming from the opposite direction of Memphis, going fast and us all hollering and waving. But he went on, with Uncle Willy jumping up and down and cussing, and we were loading the tent into the car to try to catch him when he came back. We didn't hear him at all now and we could see the propeller because it wasn't running and it looked like Secretary wasn't even going to light in the pasture but he was going to light in some trees on the edge of it. But he skinned by them and kind of bumped down and we ran up and found him still sitting in the airplane with his eyes closed and his face the color of wood ashes and he said, "Captain, will you please tell me where to find Ren——" before he even opened his eyes to see who we were. He said he had landed seven times yesterday and it wouldn't be Renfro and they would tell him how to get to Renfro and he would go there and that wouldn't be Renfro either and he had slept in the airplane last night and he hadn't eaten since we left Memphis because he had spent the three dollars Uncle Willy gave him for gasoline and if he hadn't run out of gas when he did he wouldn't never have found us.

Uncle Willy wanted me to go to town and get some more gas so he could start learning to run it right away but Secretary wouldn't. He just refused. He said the airplane belonged to Uncle Willy and he reckoned he belonged to Uncle Willy too, leastways until he got back home, but that he had flown all he could stand for a while. So Uncle Willy started the next morning.

I thought for a while that I would have to throw old Job down and hold him and him hollering, "Don't you git in dat thing!" and still hollering, "I ghy tell um! I ghy tell um!" while we watched the airplane with Secretary and Uncle Willy in it kind of jump into the air and then duck down like Uncle Willy was trying to take the short cut to China and then duck up again and get to going pretty straight at last and fly around the pasture and then turn down to land, and every day old Job hollering at Uncle Willy and field hands coming up out of the fields and folks in wagons and walking stopping in the road to watch them and the airplane coming down, passing us with Uncle Willy and Secretary side by side and looking exactly alike, I don't mean in the face but exactly alike like two tines of a garden fork look exactly like just before they chop into the ground; we could see Secretary's eyes and his mouth run out so you could almost hear him saying, "Hooooooooo!" and Uncle Willy's glasses shining and his hair blowing from under his cap and his celluloid collar that he washed every night before he went to bed and no tie in it and they would go by, fast, and old Job hollering, "You git outer dar! You git outer dat thing!" and we could hear Secretary too: "Turn hit loose, Unker Willy! Turn hit *loose!*" and the airplane would go on, ducking up one second and down the next and with one wing higher than the other one second and lower the next and then it would be traveling sideways and maybe it would hit the ground sideways the first time, with a kind of crashing sound and the dust spurting up and then bounce off again and Secretary hollering, "Unker Willy! *Turn loose!*" and at night in the tent Uncle Willy's eyes would still be shining and he would be too excited to stop talking and go to sleep and I don't believe he even remembered that he had not taken a drink since he first thought about buying the airplane.

Oh yes, I know what they said about me after it was all over, what Papa said when he and Mrs. Merridew got there that morning, about me being the white one, almost a man, and Secretary and old Job just irresponsible niggers, yet it was old Job and Secretary who tried to prevent him. Because that was it; that was what they couldn't understand.

I remember the last night and Secretary and old Job both working on him, when old Job finally made Secretary tell Uncle Willy that he would never learn to fly, and Uncle Willy stopped talking and stood up and looked at Secretary. "Didn't you learn to run it in two weeks?" he said. Secretary said yes. "You, a damn, trifling, worthless, ignorant, burr-headed nigger?" and Secretary said yes. "And me that graduated from a university and ran a fifteen-thousand-dollar business for forty years, yet you tell me I can't learn to run a damn little fifteen-hundred-dollar airplane?" Then he looked at me. "Don't you believe I can run it?" he said. And I looked at him and I said, "Yes. I believe you can do anything."

VII

And now I can't tell them. I can't say it. Papa told me once that somebody said that if you know it you can say it. Or maybe the man that said that didn't count fourteen-year-old boys. Because I must have known it was going to happen. And Uncle Willy must have known it too, known that the moment would come. It was like we both had known it and we didn't even have to compare notes, tell one another that we did: he not needing to say that day in Memphis, "Come with me so you will be there when I will need you," and me not needing to say, "Let me come so I can be there when you will."

Because old Job telephoned Mrs. Merridew. He waited until we were asleep and slipped out and walked all the way to town and telephoned her; he didn't have any money and he probably never telephoned in his life before, yet he telephoned her and the next morning he came up running in the dew (the town, the telephone, was five miles away) just as Secretary was getting the engine started and I knew what he had done even before he got close enough to holler, running and stumbling along slow across the pasture, hollering, "Holt um! Holt um! Dey'll be here any minute! Jest holt um ten minutes en dey'll be here," and I knew and I ran and met him and now I did hold him and him fighting and hitting at me and still hollering at Uncle Willy in the airplane. "You telephoned?" I said. "Her? *Her?* Told her where he is?"

"Yes," Uncle Job hollered. "En she say she gonter git yo pappy and start right away and be here by six o'clock," and me holding him; he felt like a handful of scrawny dried sticks and I could hear his lungs wheezing and I could feel his heart, and Secretary came up running too and old Job begun to holler at Secretary, "Git him outer dar! Dey comin! Dey be here any minute if you can jest holt um!" and Secretary saying, "Which? Which?" and old Job hollered at him to run and hold the airplane and Secretary turned and I tried to grab his leg but I couldn't and I could see Uncle Willy looking toward us and Secretary running toward the airplane and I got onto my knees and waved and I was hollering too. I don't reckon Uncle Willy could hear me for the engine. But I tell you he didn't need to, because we knew, we both knew; and so I knelt there and held old Job on the ground and we saw the airplane start, with Secretary still running after it, and jump into the air and duck down and then jump up again and then it looked like it had stopped high in the air above the trees where we thought Secretary was fixing to land that first day before it ducked down beyond them and went out of sight and Secretary was already running and so it was only me and Uncle Job that had to get up and start.

Oh, yes, I know what they said about me; I knew it all that afternoon while we were going home with the hearse in front and Secretary and old Job in the Ford next and Papa and me in our car coming last and Jefferson getting nearer and nearer; and then all of a sudden I began to cry. Because the dying wasn't anything, it just touched the outside of you that you wore around with you for comfort and convenience like you do your clothes: it was because the old garments, the clothes that were not worth anything had betrayed one of the two of us and the one betrayed was me, and Papa with his other arm around my shoulders now, saying, "Now, now; I didn't mean that. You didn't do it. Nobody blames you."

You see? That was it. I did help Uncle Willy. He knows I did. He knows he couldn't have done it without me. He knows I did; we didn't even have to look at one another when he went. That's it.

And now they will never understand, not even Papa, and there is only me to try to tell them and how can I ever tell them, and make them understand? How can I?

"A Guest's Impression of New England"

It is not the country which impressed this one. It is the people—the men and women themselves so individual, who hold individual integration and privacy as high and dear as they do liberty and freedom; holding these so high that they take it for granted that all other men and women are individuals, too, and treat them as such, doing this simply by letting them alone with absolute and complete dignity and courtesy.

Like this. One afternoon (it was October, the matchless Indian summer of New England) Malcolm Cowley and I were driving through back roads in western Connecticut and Massachusetts. We got lost. We were in what a Mississippian would call mountains but which New Englanders call hills; the road was not getting worse yet: just hillier and lonelier and apparently going nowhere save upward, toward a range of hills. At last, just as we were about to turn back, we found a house, a mailbox, two men, farmers or in the costume of farmers—sheep-lined coats and caps with earflaps tied over the crown—standing beside the mailbox, and watching us quietly and with perfect courtesy as we drove up and stopped.

'Good afternoon,' Cowley said.

'Good afternoon,' one of the men said.

'Does this road cross the mountain?' Cowley said.

'Yes,' the man said, still with that perfect courtesy.

'Thank you,' Cowley said and drove on, the two men still watching us quietly—for perhaps fifty yards, when Cowley braked suddenly and said, 'Wait,' and backed the car down to the mailbox again where the two men still watched us. 'Can I get over it in this car?' Cowley said.

'No,' the same man said. 'I dont think you can.' So we turned around and went back the way we came.

That's what I mean. In the West, the Californian would have been a farmer only by hobby, his true dedication and calling being that of a car trader, who would assure us that our car could not possibly make the crossing but that he had not only a car that could make it, but the only car west of the Rocky Mountains that could do it; in the Central States and the East we would have been given directions to circumvent the mountain, based on obscure third-count road forks and distant houses with lightning rods on the northeast chimney and creek crossings where if you looked carefully you could discern the remains of bridges vanished these forty years ago, which Gabriel himself could not have followed; in my own South the two Mississippians would have adopted us before Cowley could have closed his mouth and put the car in motion again, saying (one of them; the other would already be getting into the car): 'Why sure, it wont be no trouble at all; Jim here will go with you and I'll telephone across the mountain for my nephew to meet you with his truck where you are stuck; it'll pull you right on through and he'll even have a mechanic waiting with a new crankcase.'

But not the New Englander, who respects your right to privacy and free will by telling, giving you only and exactly what you asked for, and no more. If you want to try to take your car over that road, that's your business and not his to ask you why. If you want to wreck it and spend the night on foot to the nearest lighted window or disturbed watchdog, that's your business, too, since it's your car and your legs, and if you had wanted to know if *the car* could cross the mountain, you would have asked that. Because he is free, private, not made so by the stern and rockbound land—the poor thin soil and the hard long winters—on which his lot was cast, but on the contrary: having elected deliberately of his own volition that stern land and weather because he knew he was tough enough to cope with them; having been bred by the long tradition which sent him from old worn-out Europe so he could be free; taught him to believe that there is no valid reason why life should be soft and docile and amenable, that to be individual and private is the thing and that the man who cannot cope with any environment anywhere had better not clutter the earth to begin with.

To stand out against that environment which has done its worst to him, and failed, leaving him not only superior to it but its master, too. He quits it occasionally of course, but he takes it with him, too. You will find him in the Middle West, you will find him in Burbank and Glendale and Santa Monica in sunglasses and straw sandals and his shirt-tail outside his pants. But open the aloha bed-jacket and scratch him a little and you will find the thin soil and the rocks and the long snow and the man who had not at all been driven from his birthplace because it had beaten him at last, but who had left it because he himself was the victor and the spirit was gone with his cooling and slowing blood, and now is simply using that never-never land of mystics and astrologers and fire-worshippers and raw-carrot fiends as a hobby for his declining years.

WILLIAM TAPPAN THOMPSON

Thompson (1812–82) worked for A. B. Longstreet on the States' Rights Sentinel *in Augusta, Georgia, founded the* Augusta Mirror, *fought the Seminoles, turned the* Mirror *into the* Family Companion and Ladies' Mirror, *edited the* Southern Miscellany *in Madison, Georgia, and founded the* Savannah Morning News. *He also created the dialect character Major Joseph Jones, whom I will spare you. I like this story, though.*

"The Hoosier and the Salt Pile"

It is very refreshin in these days of progress, after rattlin over the country for days and nights, at the rate of twenty miles a ower in a railroad car—with your mouth full of dust and smoke, and with sich a everlastin clatter in your ears that you can't hear yourself think—to git into a good, old-fashioned stage-coach. Ther's something sociable and cosey in stage-coach travelin, so different from the bustle and confusion of a railroad, whar people are whirled along "slam bang to eternal smash," like they wer so many bales and boxes of dry-goods and groceries, without so much as a chance of seein whar they're gwine, or of takin any interest in the feller sufferers. I love to hear the pop of the whip and the interestin conversation between the driver and his horses; and I like the constant variation in the motion of the stage, the rattle of the wheels over the stones, the stillness of the drag through the heavy sand, the lunging and pitching into the ruts and gullies, the slow pull up the steep hills, the rush down agin, and the splashin of the horses' feet and the wheels in the water and mud. And then one has time to see the country he's passin through, to count the rails in the panels of the fences, and the wimen and children in the doors of the houses, to notice the appearance of the craps and the condition of the stock on the farms, and now and then to say a word to the people on the roadside. All these things is pleasant, after a long voyage on the railroad. But what's still more agreeable about stage-coach travelin, is that we have a oppertunity of makin the acquaintance of our feller passengers, of conversin with 'em and studdyin ther traits of character, which from the strikin contrast they often present, never fail to amuse if they don't interest our mind.

Some years ago I had a tolerably fair specimen of a stage-coach ride from Warrenton to Milledgeville. The road wasn't the best in the world, and didn't run through the most interestin part of Georgia, but we had a good team, a good stage, and a first-rate driver, what could sing like a camp-meetin and whistle like a locomotive, and the company was jest about as good a one as could be jumped up for sich a occasion. Ther was nine of us besides the driver, and I don't believe ther ever was a crowd of the same number that presented a greater variety of characters. Ther was a old gentleman in black, with big round spectacles, and a gold headed cane; a dandy gambler, with a big diamond breast-pin and more gold chains hangin round him than would hang him; a old hardshell preacher, as they call 'em in Georgia, with the biggest mouth and the ugliest teeth I ever seed; a circus clown, whose breath smelled strong enough of whiskey to upset the stage; a cross old maid, as ugly as a tar-bucket; a butiful young school-gall, with rosy cheeks and mischievous bright eyes; a cattle-drover from Indiany, who was gwine to New Orleans to git a army contract for beef, and myself.

For a while after we started from Warrenton nobody didn't have much to say. The young lady put her green vail over her face and leaned her head back in the corner; the old maid, after a row with the driver about her band-boxes, sot up straight in her seat and looked as sharp as a steel-trap; the old gentleman with the spectacles drummed his fingers on his cane and looked out of the coach-winder; the circus-man tried to look interestin; the gambler went to sleep; the preacher looked solemn; and the hoosier stuck his head out of the winder on his side to look at the cattle what we passed every now and then.

"This aint no great stock country," ses he to the old gentleman with the specs.

"No, sir," ses the old gentleman. "There's very little grazing here. The range in these parts is pretty much worn out."

Then ther was nothing said for some time. Bimeby the hoosier opened again.

"It's the d———st place for 'simmon-trees and turkey-buzzards I ever did see."

The old gentleman didn't say nothin, and the preacher fetched a long groan. The young lady smiled through her vail, and the old maid snapped her eyes and looked sideways at the speaker.

"Don't make much beef down here, I reckon," ses the hoosier.

"No," ses the old gentleman.

"Well, I don't see how in the h———l they manage to live in a country whar ther aint no ranges, and they don't make no beef. A man aint considered worth a cuss in Indiany what hasn't got his brand on a hundred head or so of cattle.''

"Your's is a great beef country, I believe," ses the old gentleman.

"Well, sir, it aint nothing else. A man that's got sense enough to foller his own cow-bell, with us, aint no danger of starvin. I'm gwine down to Orleans to see if I can't git a contract out of Uncle Sam, to feed the boys what's been lickin them infernal Mexicans so bad. I spose you've seed them cussed lies what's been in the newspapers about the Indiany boys at Bona Vista?''

"I've read some accounts of the battle," ses the old gentleman, "that didn't give a very flattering account of the conduct of some of our troops.''

With that, the Indiany man went into a full explanation of the affair, and gittin warmed up as he went along, begun to cuss and swear like he'd been through a dozen campaigns himself.

The old preacher listened to him with evident signs of displeasure, twistin and groanin every time he uttered a big oath, until he couldn't stand it no longer.

"My friend," ses he, "you must excuse me, but your conversation would be a great deal more interestin to me, and I'm sure it would please the company much better, if you wouldn't swear so terribly. It's very wicked to swear so, and I hope you'll have respect for our religious feelins, if you hain't got no respect for your Maker.''

If the hoosier had been struck with a clap of thunder and lightning he couldn't been more completely tuck aback. He shut his mouth right in the middle of what he was sayin, and looked at the preacher, while his face got as red as fire.

"Swearin," continued the old hardshell, "is a terrible bad practise, and ther aint no use in it no how. The Bible says 'swear not at all,' and I spose you know the commandments about taking the Lord's name in vain.''

The hoosier didn't open his mouth.

"I know," ses the old preacher, "a great many people swear without thinkin, and that some people don't believe in the Bible.''

And then he went on to preach a regular sermon agin, and to quote the Scripture like he knowed the whole Bible by heart. In the course of his argyments he undertook to prove the Scriptures to be true, and told us all about the miracles and prophecies and their fulfillment. The old gentleman with the cane tuck a part in the conversation, and the hoosier listened without ever once openin his head.

"I've jest heard of a gentleman," sed the preacher, "what has been to the Holy Land, and went all over the Bible country. It's astonishin what wonderful things he seed thar. He was at Soddom and Gomorrow, and seed the place whar Lot's wife fell!''

"Ah?" ses the old gentleman with the specs.

"Yes," ses the preacher. "He went to the very spot, and what's the most remarkablest thing of all, he seed the pillar of salt what she was turned into."

"Is it possible?" ses the old gentleman.

The hoosier's countenance all at once brightened up, and he opened his mouth wide.

"Yes, sir; he seed the salt standin thar to this day."

The hoosier's curiosity was raised to a pint beyond endurance.

"What!" ses he, "real genewine good salt?"

"Yes, sir, a pillar of salt jest as it was when that wicked woman was punished for her disobedience."

All but the gambler, who was snoozin in the corner of the coach, looked at the preacher—the hoosier with an expression of countenance that plainly told that his mind was powerfully convicted of a important fact.

"Standin right out in the open air?" he axed.

"Yes, sir,—right out in the open field where she fell."

"Well," ses the hoosier, "all I've got to say is, *if she'd drap'd in Indiany, the cattle would lick'd her up long ago!*"

VERTAMAE
SMART-GROSVENOR

In the autobiographical note in the Ballantine edition of Vibration Cooking, or the Travel Notes of a Geechee Girl, *it says that Vertamae Smart-Grosvenor was "a space goddess with Sun Ra and his Intergalactic Solar Myth Science Orkestra." I might mention that Sun Ra was from Mississippi and his Christian name was Herbert "Sonny" Blount. Smart-Grosvenor has also written articles for the* New York Times, Essence, Redbook, *and* Ebony *and done commentary on National Public Radio's* All Things Considered. *As to what she and her life are like, she can tell you that a lot better than I can.*

from *Vibration Cooking*

I'm from the village of Fairfax, Allendale County, South Carolina, so is Jasper Johns. Don't know how many people in the town. I do know I'm kin to most of them. The Ritters and the Myerses and the Smarts are from Luray and Estill. I was born across the branch from where Uncle Bubba lives now. . . .

I was so weak they put me in a shoe box and put the box on the wood-stove oven door. That was a kind of incubator. My mother says it was a case of touch and go for a while, cause she got the childbirth fever. She said, "I'm sorry child you'll have to fend for yourself" and started to throw me in the fireplace but all praises due to the gods Aunt Rose caught me. When I go down south now they treat me so good, cause they know that I wasn't but three pounds when I was born. Everyone always says, "Well do Jesus. To think that you wasn't no bigger than a minute when you was born and now you six feet tall and strong and healthy and got two fine children of your own."

.   .   .   .

When we go south by train, I always get excited around Denmark cause after Denmark is Ulmers and after Ulmers is Sycamore and after Sycamore is Fairfax. From Sycamore I can see Uncle Bill's house and between Sycamore and Fairfax I pass the house I was born in. It's falling apart but in my mind's eye I can see it as it used to be. Right near to it is where my mother and father got married. The house burned down but the trees are still there. Uncle Bubba always tells of how pretty Mama looked standing under that tree in her white dress. After Uncle Bubba meets us in Fairfax we pass the same road by car and I always lean out and yell and act crazy. On the same road we pass Uncle Costen's house and I always yell out to Serge and Miss Belle. They always wave back and shake their heads and say, "That fool doll is home again."

After we pass there I get quiet cause it is a swamp and there are big tall Spanish moss trees and I'm scared of the way they look. Also Modestine and Bozie and Sister and Juanita left me in that swamp once. I never got over that. They left me cause they said I was acting too citified. I was complaining about how far we had to walk to get from Miss Nuit's house to Uncle Bubba's. I said in Philadelphia we got trolley cars. So they ran ahead and left me in the swamp. When I came out I was mad and didn't talk to them for two days. I played by myself.

Modestine and Bozie are my mother's sister Luella's children. John and Jerry, Betty and Helen and Juanita and Brenda are Uncle Bubba's children. Glen and Debbie, Barb and Brother are Uncle Bill's children. Sinah and Sister are Uncle Simmie's. Fester is Aunt Rose's son. They are my first cousins on the Ritter side. We grew up together and have had some wonderful times. I just never forgave them for leaving me in that swamp.

.   .   .   .

Once Daddy had an accident on his motorcycle and broke his collarbone and his right arm and his left leg. When he left the hospital with his casts he decided that since he would be laid up for a while he should spend the time in a place with good vibrations. So he got on his motorcycle and went to Fairfax. Years later we drove south for a visit and as we were getting gas in a filling station in one of those real cracker towns I began to feel nervous—the man was looking at my father very strangely and I was worried. *The Smarts are famous for their long legs and short tempers.* My father noticed the strange vibrations the man was throwing out at him and said, "Wonder if that bukra is ready to come up missing cause that's what's going to happen if he don't stop looking at me." Finally the man walked up to my father and said, "Are you the nigger who pass through here in '47 with his right arm in a cast and his left leg in a cast and his neck in a brace?" My father said, "Yeah, I'm the nigger and Frank Smart's my name." The man said, "I thought it was you. I ain't never forgot your face. Mr. Smart, let me shake your hand cause you a bad nigger."

.   .   .   .

I love fish. You know the expression, "The blacker the berry, the sweeter the juice." Well the fishier the fish, the better I like it. Straight up fishy. There was a fish store on Ridge Avenue in Philadelphia called Porgy and Bass. . . .

FISH HEAD STEW

Is delicious. My mother used to get the heads from the fish market on Ridge Avenue for five cents a pound. She would stew them down with onions and bell pepper. Served over grits, head stew is an epicurean delight. I had other fish stews and my mother's head stew is the best.

.   .   .   .

A lot of new foods were brought to this country via the slave trade like watermelons. They were cultivated thousands of years ago in the Nile Valley. When David Livingston got to Central Africa he found watermelons growing wild and sweet. Egyptians make salted roasted watermelon seed. The Russians make a beer.

Some other things brought via the slave trade were sesame seeds (sometimes called benne seeds), yams, cow peas (black-eyed peas), peanuts and

So-Called Okra

Boil your meat and then add washed and carefully trimmed so-called okra. Do not cut the tip. Cook for 20 minutes.

If you are wondering how come I say so-called okra it is because the African name of okra is gombo. Just like so-called Negroes. We are Africans. Negroes only started when they got here. I am a black woman. I am tired of people calling me out of my name. Okra must be sick of that mess too. So from now on call it like it is.

.   .   .   .

Wilson Pickett found him a love and I found me a way . . . to get a taxi—I use Black Flag roach spray. My heart has been hurt by taxi drivers. . . .

One time I almost got killed cause I rode on the door from Houston to Second Street. The driver told my grandmother that he didn't have to take people like her. We had just had a wonderful engagement party for her and she was leaving to go back home. People think taxis just don't want to go to Harlem but that driver didn't want to take my grandmother to Penn Station. Well, when he said that, I saw red. I thought of all the years my grandmother personally had put up with the whims of white folks and told the driver that this night he would go to Penn Station or I would go to my grave. He went. I grabbed the door handle and he pulled off and I pulled my legs up and I held on. People were screaming and I held on. I thought of Sam and Dave, just keep holding on. And I did. He stopped at Second Street and my grandmother got in. He said, "Who do you people think you are?" and I said, "We are."

I think my next book will be the notes of a black woman trying to hail a taxi. Any taxi story you got I can top. This spring I just got fed up. People talking about colored people are late, half the time the reason is that they can't get a taxi.

Anyhow what happened was that I was on my way to AB's house, it was Thanksgiving and we was having a big dinner. Everybody brought a dish. I brought

Feijoada

1 pound black beans (wash and soak overnight). Next day put the beans and 1 pound Spanish sausages, ½ pound salt pork, 1 smoked tongue (cut in cubes) and 1 pound stew beef in a pot and bring to a boil. After it boils, cover and simmer for 2 hours or until the beans are tender. In a skillet, add ¼ cup palm oil (or use

peanut oil) and sauté onions and garlic and about 2 cups beans mashed up and then put all back in the pot and cook for ½ hour more. Some people then take the meat out of the pot and put it on a separate platter, but I leave it all together and serve with rice, collard greens and

THIRD WORLD ONIONS

Take

    1 small Bermuda onion
    1 large red onion and
    1 large yellow onion and slice thin.

Cover with boiling water, then drain, then add salt, Louisiana Hot Sauce, vinegar and palm or peanut oil and marinate for 1 hour.

Back to the taxi. I stood for forty-five minutes and all the taxis were "off duty." The children were so happy. They love parties and they were excited. One taxi pulled right up to us and said he was going to lunch. I said that I only wanted to go across Houston (from Avenue C about six blocks to Elizabeth Street). He said, "Too bad. Take the bus." Now, everybody knows that the phantom bus runs on Houston Street and it takes forever to come.

So I reached my hand in the open window and he started to roll up the window on my arm and called me a nigger bitch and pulled away. In the meantime, Chandra thought that we could get in and she was leaning on the back door so that when he pulled away she fell. My hands were full of food and it was a mess. She was hurt, not physically but inside. She said, "We only want to go to the party, why doesn't that taxi want to take us?" That did it. I made a vow it would be the last time I couldn't get some satisfaction!!!

Now I carry rocks in my purse for the drivers who have closed windows and when I approach a driver with an open window who says he is going to lunch, I take him right out with my poor man's mace.

Once in New York as Dorothy and I were walking in the Port Authority terminal a woman came running up to me and started preaching and shouting and just acting like a nut. She was yelling, "Who do you think you are? What do you people want? Are you trying to make me a victim of the people in Harlem? Why do you have on those clothes? You are an American. You aren't African. Join the Pepsi generation."

The other time somebody went crazy was at the Sorbonne when I was helping Julia sell the *pouvoir noir* material in the stall in the courtyard. It was during the occupation in '68. The whole courtyard was bustling. Everybody was selling everything. The Marxists were selling their stuff. The Jeune Nation was selling their propaganda. People were making speeches on the loud speaker. They even had some Africans selling Billy Graham Bibles. Lena Horne was singing "Now" on record, coming out of another loud-speaker. One guy was walking around with a sword tied on his hip and a baseball bat in one hand and a transistor radio in the other with a loaf of bread under his arm. I had on all my do and was feeling very good because I had been speaking only French all day and was able to talk to a lot of the brothers and sisters of the Third World who didn't speak English.

I was sitting there minding my own business when I hear this cracker voice say, "Do you speak English?" and I said, "I sho do honey." "Well, why are you wearing those African clothes, you are a Negro." I said, "I am who I think I am. I am free and free to define myself." "No you are not. You are a Negro. You are of American descent. I'm from Georgia and have spent all my life with Negroes and had a black mammy when I was a child." So I got mad and said, "So did I."

Now I have done a lot of research on food and found out that Long Island ducks are not from Long Island at all. They are the descendants of ducks imported from Peking around 1870. Georgia peaches are descendants of peaches brought from China. Potatoes are native to South America and were taken to Europe by the Spanish explorers when they "discovered" South America. They discovered "Indians and potatoes and squash and peppers and turkeys and tomatoes and corn and chocolate." They took everything back to Europe except the Indians. The settlers who later came from Europe brought the descendants of these vegetables to North America. Now, if a squash and a potato and a duck and a pepper can grow and look like their ancestors, I know damn well that I can walk around dressed like mine.

.   .   .   .

I love bon voyage parties. One year I had one planned on the *Leonardo da Vinci.* I was going to have this big "bon voyage," invite all my friends and when they cried and said how sorry they were that I was leaving, I'd leave, too. Truth being that I wasn't planning to really leave since I didn't have a ticket anyhow. I just wanted to have a different kind of party—but I told so many people of my plot that nobody came. . . .

But we did have a bon voyage party that March day we left the country "for good!!" That was some party. Seventy-five adults, forty-five children. We had the whole lounge. I thought that I would be out of the country for good so I invited EVERYBODY! Black folks, white folks, the man from the candy store on Third Street, militants, Uncle Toms, racists, Black Nationalists, Yorubas, hustlers, gamblers, actors, writers, husbands, wives, ex-husbands, ex-wives, mistresses and ex-mistresses and so on. I figured since I was leaving that they would have it. Well, the party was a smash!! They all showed up and some brought their friends. Everybody brought something. White brought three bottles of Half and Half. Bob Stocking brought a bottle of gin and his camera but he forgot his film.

Vinnie brought oatmeal cookies.

Vinie's Oatmeal Cookies

Cream 1 cup butter and 1 cup sugar. Add 2 beaten eggs and 2 cups flour, 2 cups oatmeal, 1 teaspoon baking powder, pinch of salt and some cinnamon, raisins and some chopped nuts. Mix together and add enough milk to make a stiff dough. Then drop on a buttered cooky sheet 1 inch apart.

Bake in hot oven for 8 to 10 minutes.

And Bernard Boston brought Gypsy Rose.
André brought champagne.
C♯ and China brought some sweet wine.
Gregory brought Coke and ginger ale (for the children).
David brought a bottle of Jack Daniel's.
Oscar brought a gallon of Gallo. . . .
Mrs. Jackson was going to bring some sweet potato pies but Johnnie Mae thought that would be too colored. As a matter of fact Mrs. Jackson was going to give us a couple of shoe-box lunches but Johnnie Mae said that would definitely be too too colored. Mrs. Jackson can cook chocolate cake—Lord she can cook chocolate cake. . . . She also used to make wine.

.   .   .   .

Mrs. Jackson's Wine

Gather your berries where you can and fill a large stone jar with the ripe berries. Cover with water and tie a cloth over the jar and let stand for 4 days to ferment. Then mash and press berries through a cloth. To every gallon of berry juice add 2 pounds sugar—1 brown and 1 white.

Put the mixture back in stone jar. Cover and close.
    For 9 days skim each morning.

Skim each morning for the next 9 days or until it clears.
When clear, carefully pour into another vessel.
Cork tightly and put in a cool place for 3 months.

We had flowers and candies and fruits. Barbara Carter arrived just as they were ready to sail but they waited for her to come aboard. She gave us a jar of hair grease. Sulphur 8, a hard thing to find in Europe, a drawing from Vigo. The whistle sounded, Chandra and Kali started to cry and I was wailing, and we were all hugging and kissing and falling out. We set sail and waved good-by to fun city.

Everyone on the pier was waving and crying and yelling and throwing kisses and then all of a sudden they started disappearing one at a time. Bob Stocking was acting weird. He was gesturing with his fist all clenched and jumping up and down. I didn't know what the hell was going on and it was a few years before the black power fist was popular. So I keep on waving and throwing up my fist too. The mystery was solved the very next morning. I called Johnnie Mae from the ship to see if I had left a missing bag in her car, since she and Fred had driven us to the pier.

Johnnie Mae started screaming. "Child, you should have been on the pier yesterday after you left. Lord, it was a straight-up race riot." She said that Dean was standing on a car bumper trying to see over Fred's back and a white man wearing a black suit, a rifle tie pin in his red tie and an American flag in his lapel said, "Get off that car." Dean said, "Is it your car?" "No, but I know you people—you have no respect for other people's property and you smell bad and you don't want to go to the war in Vietnam either." Well, child, that was it! Dean said, "Here, Vinie, take Sojourner [then a four-month-old baby]." Vinie said, "No, dear, no." Dean said, "Woman, I said take the girl, I got to fight." She did. While this was happening, Oscar spit on the flag in his lapel. Then the man walked away to get some of his friends. Oscar and Dean and Johnnie Mae organized. That's the reason I saw them leaving one at a time. Anyhow, the man and his troops lined up and came back to fight. Oscar and Dean took the offensive and before you could say "John Birch," the manure hit the fan and Johnnie Mae says all she remembers when she was holding the man down on the ground is that she thought Oscar had put out one of his eyes. But Dean says that was the friend of the guy in the black suit that she was holding and that it wasn't Oscar it was Sol who was punching him. Johnnie Mae says it's all blurred cause they all looked alike. Anyhow, they made a hasty retreat and Johnnie Mae says she heard his wife say, "George, I told you not to discuss politics up here."

JILL CONNER BROWNE

Back in the late '80s and early '90s a Jackson, Mississippi, music promoter and blues club operator named Malcolm White put out a lively alternative monthly called Diddy Wah Diddy. *My favorite writer in it was a columnist identified as Betty Fulton. This was a nom de plume for Browne, who got the name from a high school annual put out by Don Novello, which was pretty much like any traditional yearbook except that all the pictures were of sheep. Betty Fulton was by far the most popular ewe. "She of course was just everything," says Browne, who now writes a column under her own name for* The Jackson Clarion-Ledger *and another one as Betty for* The Mississippi Business Journal.

The Neshoba County Fair

I suppose I could tell you about the Neshoba County Fair which was pretty entertaining. And I wasn't even there when Dowdy shot himself in the foot. Me and Pie and Peep went up Friday night, followed by the diminutive Brenda Avery and JoJo the Wonderboy. It was their First Fair. They did good. They brought lawn chairs and coffee for Lallah. This was our first car trip with BoPeep in which she was old enough to ask every 5 seconds, "When're we gonna GET THERE??!!" So that was fun. Then the diminutive B.A., who usually drives like a bat, was like creeping along behind us—possibly suffering from some pretty heavy distraction by the charms of JoJo the WB—I don't know but we kept almost losing them. Then they had to stop to go to the bathroom in Carthage. It took about 4 hours to get to Philadelphia. But get there we did. We were staying one night at Lallah Perry's cabin in Happy Hollow. We had 4 bags of clothes, lawn chairs, a tub of lasagna, a gallon of homemade lemonade, 4,000 homemade blueberry muffins, Crawfish Monica for hundreds, two caramel cakes, assorted juices and coffees and a 5-pound pan of Chocolate Stuff. This is commonly known as "Protecting Supply." We felt pretty safe.

Me and Allen waited til everybody else went to bed and then we got out the Chocolate Stuff and two spoons. Actually, we carry our spoons with us at all times, just in case something tasty presents itself. We betook ourselves to the back porch swing. JoJo the WB ventured out but declined our somewhat weak offer to share the Chocolate Stuff. We heaved a mighty sigh of relief when he said, he actually said, "Oh no, I'm so full. I couldn't eat another bite of anything." HA! Like that has anything to do with it! But, as I said, it was his First Fair. He just didn't know any better. Yet Allen and I were getting pretty wired on the Chocolate and it didn't take long to run JoJo off to bed. We were plotting money-making schemes. We came up with what we thought at the time, were some pretty good ones. FRIED CHICKEN SKIN. Am I right, or what? I mean get honest. It's the best part. All this broiled skinless crap. Blech. But you eat it because it's "healthy" and Lord knows, we all want to do the "healthy" thing, don't we? Hell no, we don't want to. We get bullied into it or shamed into it, or scared into it—but we don't WANT to do it. Denial is our favorite pastime, right? But if you could go to a drive-in (read: anonymous) window and order up a bucket of nothing but fried chicken skin—tell me you wouldn't be wearing out the pavement. We figure we can get it dirt cheap since every place else is now supposedly discarding it and cooking "healthy"—read: rubbery, bland but oh, so good for you. Like hell they're discarding it. Somebody somewhere I guarantee you has already thought of this and is HOARDING chicken skin by the ton against the day that we all come to our senses—taste being the first one. Either that or Colonel Sanders is somewhere—probably with Elvis—having a veritable feast—finally having all the fried chicken skin he can eat. Sounds like heaven to me.

.   .   .   .

. . . Well, about the time we were really rolling on this theory, JoJo the WB surfaced. . . . JoJo allowed as how he ALMOST got a tattoo when he got out of boot camp at Parris Island. He and a bunch of his buddies got liquored up (naturally) and went in search of a tattoo parlor and of course, found one. JoJo was last in line and by the time they got to him, he was so drunk he was crying and the guy refused to do him. He said he'd tattooed Marines who were drunk, passed out, even DEAD but be damned if he'd tattoo one that was CRYING!

.   .   .   .

Me and BoPeep brought (wheeled) MoonPie home late Saturday night. He wins Most Improved Player but he is still not quite up to our Marathon Standards of Eating. After 24 hours, he's got to have a nap. Peep and I blared it back up there Monday. Monday night is pageant night. Miss Neshoba County Fair. Likely I would miss that! HA! I made 5 (five) batches of Chocolate Stuff. Had to leave one for Pie, he was greatly displeased at having slept through the other. We ate one on my arrival. Allen took the largest one up and secreted it in his suitcase—just to be on the safe side.

. . . .

. . . Anyway, the pageant exceeded my wildest dreams. They don't have a talent competition, which is just TOO BAD but they do tell all the contestants' FAVORITE COLOR AND THEIR FAVORITE FOOD!!! So it went something like, "Betty is the daughter of Martha-Fred and Earl "HoeHandle" Fulton. She has (big tits) BROWN HAIR AND BROWN EYES. Her favorite color is PURPLE and her favorite food is CHEEZY PERTATERS. Her hobbies are WALKING AND BEING WITH FRIENDS." Allen and I thought we had for sure picked the winner—there was only one with tits—imagine our surprise when she didn't even place. Everybody was surprised. Go figger. Allen had wisely brought along a pan of chocolate stuff for us to nibble on. . . .

The next day, after a leisurely breakfast at Lallah's, we returned to Alice's—shortly before lunch-time. Of course, we always think it is lunchtime before Alice does. She requires only gentle nudging however to get things rolling. So we retrieved the cleverly concealed pan of The Stuff and provided Alice with a spoon, ours already being well in hand. It was just the appetizer she'd been looking for. She was buzzing around that kitchen and in no time at all, had a blackberry cobbler coming out of the oven. That sight sent Allen flying down the hill (rolling) to fetch the ice cream we'd foolishly left at Lallah's. So we polished off ¾ of the cobbler and ice cream. Alice and Billy W. were ready to really get to cooking—Howard and Luran were coming for lunch—so we thought it best that we leave for a little bit. So we went back to Lallah's and had a little left-over Monica and a few chicken wings, a little crabmeat stuff and oh, just a nibble of this and that—it was really too hot to eat, you know. Someone drifted past our line of vision and said that Luran and Howard had, in fact, arrived so we beat feet back up the hill. Howard's been a little poley lately and had kinda mealy-mouthed around about not making the the Fair this year so Alice, sly fox, lured him up there with a Promise we knew he'd never be able to resist. Food. She vowed to have all his Fair Favorites if he could just get it up to appear. Alice swore she wasn't gonna put it on the table til he got there so we were panicking for him to COME ON! We had (besides our little Chocolate/Blackberry/Ice Cream appetizers)—Alice's Lasagna (didja get any onya, onya, onya?), boiled shrimp, field peas, lima beans, fried corn, Billy W.'s Famous Ho-Made Biscuits, some kind of fancy pasta stuff, the remains of the Blackberry Cobbler and a Cherry Dump Cake. Mercifully, someone brought some more ice cream. Pete came in and said, "Alice, I forgot to tell you—Betty brought you something last night. I think it's put up somewhere . . ." Alice looked him right in the eye and without flinching said,

"It's already been served." Allen, Alice and I are getting married. It will be a triple spoon ceremony. We asked Alice what we would have had to eat if Howard and Luran hadn't shown—"pimento cheese." We thought we were glad to see Howard BEFORE!

IRVIN S. COBB

Native of Paducah, Kentucky, son of a Civil War vet, Cobb (1876–1944) wrote a column called "Sour Mash" for the Louisville Evening Post, *became a topnotch New York newspaperman and highly popular humorist in the 1920s, then moved to Hollywood, where he wrote screenplays and acted in movies. He costarred with his friend Will Rogers in John Ford's 1935* Steamboat Round the Bend. *Rogers portrayed a country judge character created by Cobb in* Judge Priest, *which Ford called his favorite of all his own movies. Cobb's books, many of them deriving from Kentucky recollections, had titles like* Snake Doctor and Other Stories, Red Likker, *and* Exit Laughing, *his 1941 autobiography.*

from *Eating in Two or Three Languages*

On my way home from overseas I spent many happy hours mapping out a campaign. To myself I said: The day I land is going to be a great day for some of the waiters and a hard day on some of the cooks. Persons who happen to be near by when I am wrestling with my first ear of green corn will think I am playing on a mouth organ. My behaviour in regard to hothouse asparagus will be reminiscent of the best work of the late Bosco. In the matter of cantaloupes I rather fancy I shall consume the first two on the half shell, or *au naturel,* as we veteran correspondents say; but the third one will contain about as much vanilla ice cream as you could put in a derby hat.

And when, as I am turning over my second piece of fried chicken, with Virginia ham, if H. Hoover should crawl out from under it, and, shaking the gravy out of his eyes, should lift a warning hand, I shall say to him: "Herb," I shall say, "Herb, stand back! Stand well back to avoid being splashed, Herb.

Please desist and do not bother me now, for I am busy." Kindly remember that I am but just returned from over there and that for months and months past, as I went to and fro across the face of the next hemisphere that you'll run into on the left of you if you go just outside of Sandy Hook and take the first turn to the right, I have been storing up a great, unsatisfied longing for the special dishes of my own, my native land. Don't try, I pray you, to tell me a patriot can't do his bit and eat it too, for I know better.

"Shortly I may be in a fitter frame of mind to listen to your admonitions touching on rationing schemes; but not to-day, and possibly not to-morrow either, Herb. At this moment I consider food regulations as having been made for slaves and perhaps for the run of other people; but not for me. As a matter of fact, what you may have observed up until now has merely been my preliminary attack—what you might call open warfare, with scouting operations. But when they bring on the transverse section of watermelon I shall take these two trenching tools which I now hold in my hands, and just naturally start digging in. I trust you may be hanging round then; you'll certainly overhear something.

"Kindly pass the ice water. That's it. Thank you. Join me, won't you, in a brimming beaker? It may interest you to know that I am now on my second carafe of this wholesome, delicious and satisfying beverage. Where I have lately been, in certain parts of the adjacent continent, there isn't any ice, and nobody by any chance ever drinks water. Nobody bathes in it either, so far as I have been able to note. You'll doubtless be interested in hearing what they do do with it over on that side. It took me months to find out.

"Then finally, one night in a remote interior village, I went to an entertainment in a Y. M. C. A. hut. A local magician came out on the platform; and after he had done some tricks with cards and handkerchiefs which were so old that they were new all over again, he reached up under the tails of his dress coat and hauled out a big glass globe that was slopping full of its crystal-pure fluid contents, with a family of goldfish swimming round and round in it, as happy as you please.

"So then, all in a flash, the answer came and I knew the secret of what the provincials in that section of Europe do with water. They loan it to magicians to keep goldfish in. But I prefer to drink a little of it while I am eating and to eat a good deal while I am drinking it; both of which, I may state, I am now doing to the best of my ability, and without let or hindrance, Herb."

MARK TWAIN

The first Twain selection here—originally written for Huckleberry Finn *but published in* Life on the Mississippi *because that book came together first—is the finest rendering of what might be called Early Buckra Dozens, and the third is as funny an essay as Twain ever wrote and yet is seldom anthologized. But the second selection, "The Private History of a Campaign That Failed," is the one that gives us most to think about: we wonder what American culture would be like today if Sam Clemens hadn't had the prudence to desert the Confederate Army after a couple of weeks—or if he'd been caught and hauled as a traitor before a military court like the one Charles Henry "Bill Arp" Smith was running in Georgia, and shot. Even assuming he would have survived the War—which seems unlikely in view of his military aptitude as portrayed in "The Private History"—he would surely have been left with a less ebullient opportunism than that which bore him away from the War, to California and later to New England and literary greatness. All of modern American literature, said Ernest Hemingway, flows from the fusion of backwoods vernacular and formal English in* Huckleberry Finn, *which ends with Huck planning to light out for the territory as Sam lit out for something that he could stand better than the War Between the States. I want to make it clear that I am glad Sam Clemens cut and run. One of the best things you can say about the South is that its greatest writer (Clemens was conceived in Tennessee by Southern parents and reared in slave-holding Missouri) is also its funniest. You could say the same thing about America.*

Raftmen's Passage

But you know a young person can't wait very well when he is impatient to find a thing out. We talked it over, and by and by Jim said it was such a black night, now, that it wouldn't be no risk to swim down to the big raft and crawl aboard and listen—they would talk about Cairo, because they would be calculating to go ashore there for a spree, maybe, or anyway they would send boats ashore to buy whiskey or fresh meat or something. Jim had a wonderful level head, for a nigger: he could most always start a good plan when you wanted one.

I stood up and shook my rags off and jumped into the river, and struck out

for the raft's light. By and by, when I got down nearly to her, I eased up and
went slow and cautious. But everything was all right—nobody at the sweeps.
So I swum down along the raft till I was most abreast the camp fire in the
middle, then I crawled aboard and inched along and got in amongst some
bundles of shingles on the weather side of the fire. There was thirteen men
there—they was the watch on deck of course. And a mighty rough-looking
lot, too. They had a jug, and tin cups, and they kept the jug moving. One man
was singing—roaring, you may say; and it wasn't a nice song—for a parlor
anyway. He roared through his nose, and strung out the last word of every line
very long. When he was done they all fetched a kind of Injun war-whoop, and
then another was sung. It begun:

> 'There was a woman in our towdn,
>   In our towdn did dwed'l (dwell,)
> She loved her husband dear-i-lee,
>   But another man twyste as wed'l.

> Singing too, riloo, riloo, riloo,
>   Ri-too, riloo, rilay---e,
> She loved her husband dear-i-lee,
>   But another man twyste as wed'l.'

And so on—fourteen verses. It was kind of poor, and when he was going to
start on the next verse one of them said it was the tune the old cow died on;
and another one said, 'Oh, give us a rest.' And another one told him to take a
walk. They made fun of him till he got mad and jumped up and begun to cuss
the crowd, and said he could lame any thief in the lot.

They was all about to make a break for him, but the biggest man there
jumped up and says—

'Set whar you are, gentlemen. Leave him to me; he's my meat.'

Then he jumped up in the air three times and cracked his heels together
every time. He flung off a buckskin coat that was all hung with fringes, and
says, 'You lay thar tell the chawin-up's done;' and flung his hat down, which
was all over ribbons, and says, 'You lay thar tell his sufferins is over.'

Then he jumped up in the air and cracked his heels together again and
shouted out—

'Whoo-oop! I'm the old original iron-jawed, brass-mounted, copper-bel-
lied corpse-maker from the wilds of Arkansaw!—Look at me! I'm the man
they call Sudden Death and General Desolation! Sired by a hurricane; dam'd
by an earthquake, half-brother to the cholera; nearly related to the small-pox
on the mother's side! Look at me! I take nineteen alligators and a bar'l of
whiskey for breakfast when I'm in robust health, and a bushel of rattlesnakes

and a dead body when I'm ailing! I split the everlasting rocks with my glance, and I squench the thunder when I speak! Whoo-oop! Stand back and give me room according to my strength! Blood's my natural drink, and the wails of the dying is music to my ear! Cast your eye on me, gentlemen!—and lay low and hold your breath, for I'm bout to turn myself loose!'

All the time he was getting this off, he was shaking his head and looking fierce, and kind of swelling around in a little circle, tucking up his wrist-bands, and now and then straightening up and beating his breast with his fist, saying, 'Look at me, gentlemen!' When he got through, he jumped up and cracked his heels together three times, and let off a roaring 'whoo-oop! I'm the bloodiest son of a wildcat that lives!'

Then the man that had started the row tilted his old slouch hat down over his right eye; then he bent stooping forward, with his back sagged and his south end sticking out far, and his fists a-shoving out and drawing in in front of him, and so went around in a little circle about three times, swelling himself up and breathing hard. Then he straightened, and jumped up and cracked his heels together three times, before he lit again (that made them cheer), and he begun to shout like this—

'Whoo-oop! bow your neck and spread, for the kingdom of sorrow's a-coming! Hold me down to the earth, for I feel my powers a-working! whoo-oop! I'm a child of sin, *don't* let me get a start! Smoked glass, here, for all! Don't attempt to look at me with the naked eye, gentlemen! When I'm playful I use the meridians of longitude and parallels of latitude for a seine, and drag the Atlantic Ocean for whales! I scratch my head with the lightning, and purr myself to sleep with the thunder! When I'm cold, I bile the Gulf of Mexico and bathe in it; when I'm hot I fan myself with an equinoctial storm; when I'm thirsty I reach up and suck a cloud dry like a sponge; when I range the earth hungry, famine follows in my tracks! Whoo-oop! Bow your neck and spread! I put my hand on the sun's face and make it night in the earth; I bite a piece out of the moon and hurry the seasons; I shake myself and crumble the mountains! Contemplate me through leather—*don't* use the naked eye! I'm the man with a petrified heart and biler-iron bowels! The massacre of isolated communities is the pastime of my idle moments; the destruction of nationalities the serious business of my life! The boundless vastness of the great American desert is my enclosed property, and I bury my dead on my own premises!' He jumped up and cracked his heels together three times before he lit (they cheered him again), and as he come down he shouted out: 'Whoo-oop! bow your neck and spread, for the pet child of calamity's a-coming!'

Then the other one went to swelling around and blowing again—the first one—the one they called Bob; next, the Child of Calamity chipped in again, bigger than ever; then they both got at it at the same time, swelling round and round each other and punching their fists most into each other's faces, and whooping and jawing like Injuns; then Bob called the Child names, and the Child called him names back again: next, Bob called him a heap rougher names and the Child come back at him with the very worst kind of language; next, Bob knocked the Child's hat off, and the Child picked it up and kicked Bob's ribbony hat about six foot; Bob went and got it and said never mind, this warn't going to be the last of this thing, because he was a man that never forgot and never forgive, and so the Child better look out, for there was a time a-coming, just as sure as he was a living man, that he would have to answer to him with the best blood in his body. The Child said no man was willinger than he was for that time to come, and he would give Bob fair warning, *now,* never to cross his path again, for he could never rest till he had waded in his blood, for such was his nature, though he was sparing him now on account of his family, if he had one.

Both of them was edging away in different directions, growling and shaking their heads and going on about what they was going to do; but a little black-whiskered chap skipped up and says—

'Come back here, you couple of chicken-livered cowards, and I'll thrash the two of ye!'

And he done it, too. He snatched them, he jerked them this way and that, he booted them around, he knocked them sprawling, faster than they could get up. Why, it warn't two minutes till they begged like dogs—and how the other lot did yell and laugh and clap their hands all the way through, and shout 'Sail in, Corpse-Maker!' 'Hi! at him again, Child of Calamity!' 'Bully for you, little Davy!' Well, it was a perfect pow-wow for a while. Bob and the Child had red noses and black eyes when they got through. Little Davy made them own up that they were sneaks and cowards and not fit to eat with a dog or drink with a nigger; then Bob and the Child shook hands with each other, very solemn, and said they had always respected each other and was willing to let bygones be bygones. So then they washed their faces in the river; and just then there was a loud order to stand by for a crossing, and some of them went forward to man the sweeps there, and the rest went aft to handle the after-sweeps.

I laid still and waited for fifteen minutes, and had a smoke out of a pipe that one of them left in reach; then the crossing was finished, and they stumped back and had a drink around and went to talking and singing again. Next they got out an old fiddle, and one played and another patted juba, and the rest turned themselves loose on a regular old-fashioned keel-boat breakdown. They couldn't keep that up very long without getting winded, so by and by they settled around the jug again.

They sung 'jolly, jolly raftman's the life for me,' with a rousing chorus, and then they got to talking about differences betwixt hogs, and their different kinds of habits; and next about women and their different ways: and next about the best ways to put out houses that was afire; and next about what ought to be done with the Injuns; and next about what a king had to do, and how much he got; and next about how to make cats fight; and next about what to do when a man has fits; and next about differences betwixt clear-water rivers and muddy-water ones. The man they called Ed said the muddy Mississippi water was wholesomer to drink than the clear water of the Ohio; he said if you let a pint of this yaller Mississippi water settle, you would have about a half to three quarters of an inch of mud in the bottom, according to the stage of the river, and then it warn't no better than Ohio water—what you wanted to do was to keep it stirred up—and when the river was low, keep mud on hand to put in and thicken the water up the way it ought to be.

The Child of Calamity said that was so; he said there was nutritiousness in the mud, and a man that drunk Mississippi water could grow corn in his stomach if he wanted to. He says—

'You look at the graveyards; that tells the tale. Trees won't grow worth shucks in a Cincinnati graveyard, but in a Sent Louis graveyard they grow upwards of eight hundred foot high. It's all on account of the water the people drunk before they laid up. A Cincinnati corpse don't richen a soil any.'

And they talked about how Ohio water didn't like to mix with Mississippi water. Ed said if you take the Mississippi on a rise when the Ohio is low, you'll find a wide band of clear water all the way down the east side of the Mississippi for a hundred mile or more, and the minute you get out a quarter of a mile from shore and pass the line, it is all thick and yaller the rest of the way across. Then they talked about how to keep tobacco from getting moldy, and from that they went into ghosts, and told about a lot that other folks had seen; but Ed says—

'Why don't you tell something that you've seen yourselves? Now let me have a say. Five years ago I was on a raft as big as this, and right along here it was a bright moonshiny night, and I was on watch and boss of the stabboard oar forrard, and one of my pards was a man named Dick Allbright, and he come along to where I was sitting, forrard—gaping and stretching, he was—and stooped down on the edge of the raft and washed his face in the river, and come and set down by me and got out his pipe, and had just got it filled, when he looks up and says—

' "Why looky-here," he says, "ain't that Buck Miller's place, over yander in the bend?"

' "Yes," says I, "it is—why?" He laid his pipe down and leant his head on his hand, and says—

' "I thought we'd be furder down." I says—

' "I thought it too, when I went off watch"—we was standing six hours on and six off—"but the boys told me," I says, "that the raft didn't seem to hardly move, for the last hour," says I, "though she's a slipping along all right, now," says I. He give a kind of a groan, and says—

' "I've seed a raft act so before, along here," he says, " 'pears to me the current has most quit above the head of this bend durin' the last two years," he says.

'Well, he raised up two or three times, and looked away off and around on the water. That started me at it, too. A body is always doing what he sees somebody else doing, though there mayn't be no sense in it. Pretty soon I see a black something floating on the water away off to stabboard and quartering behind us. I see he was looking at it, too. I says—

' "What's that?" He says, sort of pettish,—

' "Tain't nothing but an old empty bar'l."

' "An empty bar'l!" says I, "why," says I, "a spy-glass is a fool to *your* eyes. How can you tell it's an empty bar'l?" He says—

' "I don't know; I reckon it ain't a bar'l, but I thought it might be," says he.

' "Yes," I says, "so it might be, and it might be anything else, too; a body can't tell nothing about it, such a distance as that," I says.

'We hadn't nothing else to do, so we kept on watching it. By and by I says—

' "Why looky-here, Dick Allbright, that thing's a-gaining on us, I believe."

'He never said nothing. The thing gained and gained, and I judged it must be a dog that was about tired out. Well, we swung down into the crossing, and the thing floated across the bright streak of the moonshine, and, by George, it *was* a bar'l. Says I—

' "Dick Allbright, what made you think that thing was a bar'l, when it was a half a mile off," says I. Says he—

' "I don't know." Says I—

' "You tell me, Dick Allbright." He says—

' "Well, I knowed it was a bar'l; I've seen it before; lots has seen it; they says it's a haunted bar'l."

'I called the rest of the watch, and they come and stood there, and I told them what Dick said. It floated right along abreast, now, and didn't gain any more. It was about twenty foot off. Some was for having it aboard, but the rest didn't want to. Dick Allbright said rafts that had fooled with it had got bad luck by it. The captain of the watch said he didn't believe in it. He said he reckoned the bar'l gained on us because it was in a little better current than what we was. He said it would leave by and by.

'So then we went to talking about other things, and we had a song, and then a breakdown; and after that the captain of the watch called for another song; but it was clouding up, now, and the bar'l stuck right thar in the same place, and the song didn't seem to have much warm-up to it, somehow, and so they didn't finish it, and there warn't any cheers, but it sort of dropped flat, and nobody said anything for a minute. Then everybody tried to talk at once, and one chap got off a joke, but it warn't no use, they didn't laugh, and even the chap that made the joke didn't laugh at it, which ain't usual. We all just settled down glum, and watched the bar'l, and was oneasy and oncomfortable. Well, sir, it shut down black and still, and then the wind begin to moan around, and next the lightning begin to play and the thunder to grumble. And pretty soon there was a regular storm, and in the middle of it a man that was running aft stumbled and fell and sprained his ankle so that he had to lay up. This made the boys shake their heads. And every time the lightning come, there was that bar'l with the blue lights winking around it. We was always on the look-out for it. But by and by, towards dawn, she was gone. When the day come we couldn't see her anywhere, and we warn't sorry, neither.

'But next night about half-past nine, when there was songs and high jinks going on, here she comes again, and took her old roost on the stabboard side. There warn't no more high jinks. Everybody got solemn; nobody talked; you couldn't get anybody to do anything but set around moody and look at the bar'l. It begun to cloud up again. When the watch changed, the off watch stayed up, 'stead of turning in. The storm ripped and roared around all night, and in the middle of it another man tripped and sprained his ankle, and had to knock off. The bar'l left towards day, and nobody see it go.

'Everybody was sober and down in the mouth all day. I don't mean the kind of sober that comes of leaving liquor alone—not that. They was quiet, but they all drunk more than usual—not together—but each man sidled off and took it private, by himself.

'After dark the off watch didn't turn in; nobody sung, nobody talked; the boys didn't scatter around, neither; they sort of huddled together, forrard; and for two hours they set there, perfectly still, looking steady in the one direction, and heaving a sigh once in a while. And then, here comes the bar'l again. She took up her old place. She staid there all night; nobody turned in. The storm come on again, after midnight. It got awful dark; the rain poured down, hail, too; the thunder boomed and roared and bellowed; the wind blowed a hurricane; and the lightning spread over everything in big sheets of glare, and showed the whole raft as plain as day; and the river lashed up white as milk as far as you could see for miles, and there was that bar'l jiggering along, same as ever. The captain ordered the watch to man the after sweeps for a crossing, and nobody would go—no more sprained ankles for them, they said. They wouldn't even *walk* aft. Well then, just then the sky split wide open, with a crash, and the lightning killed two men of the after watch, and crippled two more. Crippled them how, says you? Why, *sprained their ankles!*

'The bar'l left in the dark betwixt lightnings, towards dawn. Well, not a body eat a bite at breakfast that morning. After that the men loafed around, in twos and threes, and talked low together. But none of them herded with Dick Allbright. They all give him the cold shake. If he come around where any of the men was, they split up and sidled away. They wouldn't man the sweeps with him. The captain had all the skiffs hauled up on the raft, alongside of his wigwam, and wouldn't let the dead men be took ashore to be planted; he didn't believe a man that got ashore would come back; and he was right.

'After night come, you could see pretty plain that there was going to be trouble if that bar'l come again; there was such a muttering going on. A good many wanted to kill Dick Allbright, because he'd seen the bar'l on other trips, and that had an ugly look. Some wanted to put him ashore. Some said, let's all go ashore in a pile, if the bar'l comes again.

'This kind of whispers was still going on, the men being bunched together forrard watching for the bar'l, when, lo and behold you, here she comes again. Down she comes, slow and steady, and settles into her old tracks. You could a heard a pin drop. Then up comes the captain, and says:—

' "Boys, don't be a pack of children and fools; I don't want this bar'l to be dogging us all the way to Orleans, and *you* don't; well, then, how's the best way to stop it? Burn it up,—that's the way. I'm going to fetch it aboard,'' he says. And before anybody could say a word, in he went.

'He swum to it, and as he come pushing it to the raft, the men spread to one side. But the old man got it aboard and busted in the head, and there was a baby in it! Yes, sir, a stark naked baby. It was Dick Allbright's baby; he owned up and said so.

' "Yes,'' he says, a-leaning over it, "yes, it is my own lamented darling, my poor lost Charles William Allbright deceased,'' says he,—for he could curl his tongue around the bulliest words in the language when he was a mind to, and lay them before you without a jint started, anywheres. Yes, he said he used to live up at the head of this bend, and one night he choked his child, which was crying, not intending to kill it,—which was prob'ly a lie,—and then he was scared, and buried it in a bar'l, before his wife got home, and off he went, and struck the northern trail and went to rafting; and this was the third year that the bar'l had chased him. He said the bad luck always begun light, and lasted till four men was killed, and then the bar'l didn't come come any more after that. He said if the men would stand it one more night,—and was a-going on like that,—but the men had got enough. They started to get out a boat to take him ashore and lynch him, but he grabbed the little child all of a sudden and jumped overboard with it hugged up to his breast and shedding tears, and we never see him again in this life, poor old suffering soul, nor Charles William neither.'

'*Who* was shedding tears?' says Bob; 'was it Allbright or the baby?'

'Why, Allbright, of course; didn't I tell you the baby was dead? Been dead three years—how could it cry?'

'Well, never mind how it could cry—how could it *keep* all that time?' says Davy. 'You answer me that.'

'I don't know how it done it,' says Ed. 'It done it though—that's all I know about it.'

'Say—what did they do with the bar'l?' says the Child of Calamity.

'Why, they hove it overboard, and it sunk like a chunk of lead.'

'Edward, did the child look like it was choked?' says one.

'Did it have its hair parted?' says another.

'What was the brand on that bar'l, Eddy?' says a fellow they called Bill.

'Have you got the papers for them statistics, Edmund?' says Jimmy.

'Say, Edwin, was you one of the men that was killed by the lightning?' says Davy.

'Him? O, no, he was both of 'em,' says Bob. Then they all haw-hawed.

'Say, Edward, don't you reckon you'd better take a pill? You look bad—don't you feel pale?' says the Child of Calamity.

'O, come, now, Eddy,' says Jimmy, 'show up; you must a kept part of that bar'l to prove the thing by. Show us the bunghole—*do*—and we'll all believe you.'

'Say, boys,' says Bill, 'less divide it up. Thar's thirteen of us. I can swaller a thirteenth of the yarn, if you can worry down the rest.'

Ed got up mad and said they could all go to some place which he ripped out pretty savage, and then walked off aft cussing to himself, and they yelling and jeering at him, and roaring and laughing so you could hear them a mile.

'Boys, we'll split a watermelon on that,' says the Child of Calamity; and he come rummaging around in the dark amongst the shingle bundles where I was, and put his hand on me. I was warm and soft and naked; so he says 'Ouch!' and jumped back.

'Fetch a lantern or a chunk of fire here, boys—there's a snake here as big as a cow!'

So they run there with a lantern and crowded up and looked in on me.

'Come out of that, you beggar!' says one.

'Who are you?' says another.

'What are you after here? Speak up prompt, or overboard you go.'

'Snake him out, boys. Snatch him out by the heels.'

I began to beg, and crept out amongst them trembling. They looked me over, wondering, and the Child of Calamity says—

'A cussed thief! Lend a hand and less heave him overboard!'

'No,' says Big Bob, 'less get out the paint-pot and paint him a sky blue all over from head to heel, and *then* heave him over!'

'Good! that's it. Go for the paint, Jimmy.'

When the paint come, and Bob took the brush and was just going to begin, the others laughing and rubbing their hands, I begun to cry, and that sort of worked on Davy, and he says—

' 'Vast there! He's nothing but a cub. I'll paint the man that fetches him!'

So I looked around on them, and some of them grumbled and growled, and Bob put down the paint, and the others didn't take it up.

'Come here to the fire, and less see what you're up to here,' says Davy. 'Now set down there and give an account of yourself. How long have you been aboard here?'

'Not over a quarter of a minute, sir,' says I.

'How did you get dry so quick?'

'I don't know, sir. I'm always that way, mostly.'

'Oh, you are, are you? What's your name?'

I warn't going to tell my name. I didn't know what to say, so I just says—

'Charles William Allbright, sir.'

Then they roared—the whole crowd; and I was mighty glad I said that, because maybe laughing would get them in a better humor.

When they got done laughing, Davy says—

'It won't hardly do, Charles William. You couldn't have growed this much in five year, and you was a baby when you come out of the bar'l, you know, and dead at that. Come, now, tell a straight story, and nobody'll hurt you, if you ain't up to anything wrong. What *is* your name?'

'Aleck Hopkins, sir. Aleck James Hopkins.'

'Well, Aleck, where did you come from, here?'

'From a trading scow. She lays up the bend yonder. I was born on her. Pap has traded up and down here all his life; and he told me to swim off here, because when you went by he said he would like to get some of you to speak to a Mr. Jonas Turner, in Cairo, and tell him—'

'Oh, come!'

'Yes, sir, it's as true as the world; Pap he says—'

'Oh, your grandmother!'

They all laughed, and I tried again to talk, but they broke in on me and stopped me.

'Now, looky-here,' says Davy; 'you're scared, and so you talk wild. Honest, now, do you live in a scow, or is it a lie?'

'Yes, sir, in a trading scow. She lays up at the head of the bend. But I warn't born in her. It's our first trip.'

'Now you're talking! What did you come aboard here, for? To steal?'

'No, sir, I didn't.—It was only to get a ride on the raft. All boys does that.'

'Well, I know that. But what did you hide for?'

'Sometimes they drive the boys off.'

'So they do. They might steal. Looky-here; if we let you off this time, will you keep out of these kind of scrapes hereafter?'

' 'Deed I will, boss. You try me.'

'All right, then. You ain't but little ways from shore. Overboard with you, and don't you make a fool of yourself another time this way.—Blast it, boy, some raftsmen would rawhide you till you were black and blue!'

I didn't wait to kiss good-bye, but went overboard and broke for shore. When Jim come along by and by, the big raft was away out of sight around the point. I swum out and got aboard, and was mighty glad to see home again.

"The Private History of a Campaign That Failed"

You have heard from a great many people who did something in the war; is it not fair and right that you listen a little moment to one who started out to do something in it, but didn't? Thousands entered the war, got just a taste of it, and then stepped out again permanently. These, by their very numbers, are respectable, and are therefore entitled to a sort of voice—not a loud one, but a modest one; not a boastful one, but an apologetic one. They ought not to be allowed much space among better people—people who did something. I grant that; but they ought at least to be allowed to state why they didn't do anything, and also to explain the process by which they didn't do anything. Surely this kind of light must have a sort of value.

Out West there was a good deal of confusion in men's minds during the first months of the great trouble—a good deal of unsettledness, of leaning first this way, then that, then the other way. It was hard for us to get our bearings. I call to mind an instance of this. I was piloting on the Mississippi when the news came that South Carolina had gone out of the Union on the 20th of December, 1860. My pilot mate was a New Yorker. He was strong for the Union; so was I. But he would not listen to me with any patience; my loyalty was smirched, to his eye, because my father had owned slaves. I said, in palliation of this dark fact, that I had heard my father say, some years before he died, that slavery was a great wrong, and that he would free the solitary negro he then owned if he could think it right to give away the property of the family when he was so straitened in means. My mate retorted that a mere impulse was nothing—anybody could pretend to a good impulse; and went on decrying my Unionism and libeling my ancestry. A month later the secession atmosphere had considerably thickened on the Lower Mississippi, and I became a rebel; so did he. We were together in New Orleans the 26th of January, when Louisiana went out of the Union. He did his full share of the rebel shouting, but was bitterly opposed to letting me do mine. He said that I came of bad stock—of a father who had been willing to set slaves free. In the following summer he was piloting a Federal gunboat and shouting for the Union again, and I was in the Confederate army. I held his note for some borrowed money. He was one of the most upright men I ever knew, but he repudiated that note without hesitation because I was a rebel and the son of a man who owned slaves.

In that summer—of 1861—the first wash of the wave of war broke upon the shores of Missouri. Our State was invaded by the Union forces. They took possession of St. Louis, Jefferson Barracks, and some other points. The Governor, Claib Jackson, issued his proclamation calling out fifty thousand militia to repel the invader.

I was visiting in the small town where my boyhood had been spent—Hannibal, Marion County. Several of us got together in a secret place by night and formed ourselves into a military company. One Tom Lyman, a young fellow of a good deal of spirit but of no military experience, was made captain; I was made second lieutenant. We had no first lieutenant; I do not know why; it was long ago. There were fifteen of us. By the advice of an innocent connected with the organization we called ourselves the Marion Rangers. I do not remember that any one found fault with the name. I did not; I thought it sounded quite well. The young fellow who proposed this title was perhaps a fair sample of the kind of stuff we were made of. He was young, ignorant, good-natured, well-meaning, trivial, full of romance, and given to reading chivalric novels and singing forlorn love-ditties. He had some pathetic little nickel-plated aristocratic instincts, and detested his name, which was Dunlap; detested it, partly because it was nearly as common in that region as Smith, but mainly because it had a plebeian sound to his ear. So he tried to ennoble it by writing it in this way: *d'Unlap.* That contented his eye, but left his ear unsatisfied, for people gave the new name the same old pronunciation—emphasis on the front end of it. He then did the bravest thing that can be imagined—a thing to make one shiver when one remembers how the world is given·to resenting shams and affectations; he began to write his name so: *d'Un Lap.* And he waited patiently through the long storm of mud that was flung at this work of art, and he had his reward at last; for he lived to see that name accepted, and the emphasis put where he wanted it by people who had known him all his life, and to whom the tribe of Dunlaps had been as familiar as the rain and the sunshine for forty years. So sure of victory at last is the courage that can wait. He said he had found, by consulting some ancient French chronicles, that the name was rightly and originally written d'Un Lap; and said that if it were translated into English it would mean Peterson: *Lap,* Latin or Greek, he said, for stone or rock, same as the French *pierre,* that is to say, Peter; *d',* of or from; *un,* a or one; hence, d'Un Lap, of or from a stone or a Peter; that is to say, one who is the son of a stone, the son of a Peter—Peterson. Our militia company were not learned, and the explanation confused them; so they called him Peterson Dunlap. He proved useful to us in his way; he named our camps for us, and he generally struck a name that was "no slouch," as the boys said.

That is one sample of us. Another was Ed Stevens, son of the town jeweler—trim-built, handsome, graceful, neat as a cat; bright, educated, but given over entirely to fun. There was nothing serious in life to him. As far as he was concerned, this military expedition of ours was simply a holiday. I should say that about half of us looked upon it in the same way; not consciously perhaps, but unconsciously. We did not think; we were not capable of it. As for myself, I was full of unreasoning joy to be done with turning out of bed at midnight and four in the morning for a while; grateful to have a change, new scenes, new occupations, a new interest. In my thoughts that was as far as I went; I did not go into the details; as a rule, one doesn't at twenty-four.

Another sample was Smith, the blacksmith's apprentice. This vast donkey had some pluck, of a slow and sluggish nature, but a soft heart; at one time he would knock a horse down for some impropriety, and at another he would get homesick and cry. However, he had one ultimate credit to his account which some of us hadn't: he stuck to the war, and was killed in battle at last.

Jo Bowers, another sample, was a huge, good-natured, flax-headed lubber; lazy, sentimental, full of harmless brag, a grumbler by nature; an experienced, industrious, ambitious, and often quite picturesque liar, and yet not a successful one, for he had had no intelligent training, but was allowed to come up just any way. This life was serious enough to him, and seldom satisfactory. But he was a good fellow anyway, and the boys all liked him. He was made orderly sergeant; Stevens was made corporal.

These samples will answer—and they are quite fair ones. Well, this herd of cattle started for the war. What could you expect of them? They did as well as they knew how; but really what was justly to be expected of them? Nothing, I should say. That is what they did.

We waited for a dark night, for caution and secrecy were necessary; then, towards midnight, we stole in couples and from various directions to the Griffith place, beyond the town; from that point we set out together on foot. Hannibal lies at the extreme southeastern corner of Marion County, on the Mississippi River; our objective point was the hamlet of New London, ten miles away, in Ralls County.

The first hour was all fun, all idle nonsense and laughter. But that could not be kept up. The steady trudging came to be like work; the play had somehow oozed out of it; the stillness of the woods and the somberness of the night began to throw a depressing influence over the spirits of the boys, and presently the talking died out and each person shut himself up in his own thoughts. During the last half of the second hour nobody said a word.

Now we approached a log farmhouse where, according to report, there was a guard of five Union soldiers. Lyman called a halt; and there, in the deep gloom of the overhanging branches, he began to whisper a plan of assault upon that house, which made the gloom more depressing than it was before. It was a crucial moment; we realized, with a cold suddenness, that here was no jest—we were standing face to face with actual war. We were equal to the occasion. In our response there was no hesitation, no indecision: we said that if Lyman wanted to meddle with those soldiers, he could go ahead and do it; but if he waited for us to follow him, he would wait a long time.

Lyman urged, pleaded, tried to shame us, but it had no effect. Our course was plain, our minds were made up: we would flank the farmhouse—go out around. And that was what we did.

We struck into the woods and entered upon a rough time, stumbling over roots, getting tangled in vines, and torn by briers. At last we reached an open place in a safe region, and sat down, blown and hot, to cool off and nurse our scratches and bruises. Lyman was annoyed, but the rest of us were cheerful; we had flanked the farmhouse, we had made our first military movement, and it was a success; we had nothing to fret about, were feeling just the other way. Horse-play and laughing began again; the expedition was become a holiday frolic once more.

Then we had two more hours of dull trudging and ultimate silence and depression; then, about dawn, we straggled into New London, soiled, heel-blistered, fagged with our little march, and all of us except Stevens in a sour and raspy humor and privately down on the war. We stacked our shabby old shotguns in Colonel Ralls's barn, and then went in a body and breakfasted with that veteran of the Mexican War. Afterwards he took us to a distant meadow, and there in the shade of a tree we listened to an old-fashioned speech from him, full of gunpowder and glory, full of that adjective-piling, mixed metaphor, and windy declamation which were regarded as eloquence in that ancient time and that remote region; and then he swore us on the Bible to be faithful to the State of Missouri and drive all invaders from her soil, no matter whence they might come or under what flag they might march. This mixed us considerably, and we could not make out just what service we were embarked in; but Colonel Ralls, the practiced politician and phrase-juggler, was not similarly in doubt; he knew quite clearly that he had invested us in the cause of the Southern Confederacy. He closed the solemnities by belting around me the sword which his neighbor, Colonel Brown, had worn at Buena Vista and Molino del Rey; and he accompanied this act with another impressive blast.

Then we formed in line of battle and marched four miles to a shady and pleasant piece of woods on the border of the far-reaching expanses of a flowery prairie. It was an enchanting region for war—our kind of war.

We pierced the forest about half a mile, and took up a strong position, with some low, rocky, and wooded hills behind us, and a purling, limpid creek in front. Straightway half the command were in swimming and the other half fishing. The ass with the French name gave this position a romantic title, but it was too long, so the boys shortened and simplified it to Camp Ralls.

We occupied an old maple sugar camp, whose half-rotted troughs were still propped against the trees. A long corn-crib served for sleeping quarters for the battalion. On our left, half a mile away, were Mason's farm and house; and he was a friend to the cause. Shortly after noon the farmers began to arrive from several directions, with mules and horses for our use, and these they lent us for as long as the war might last, which they judged would be about three months. The animals were of all sizes, all colors, and all breeds. They were mainly young and frisky, and nobody in the command could stay on them long at a time; for we were town boys, and ignorant of horsemanship. The creature that fell to my share was a very small mule, and yet so quick and active that it could throw me without difficulty; and it did this whenever I got on it. Then it would bray—stretching its neck out, laying its ears back, and spreading its jaws till you could see down to its works. It was a disagreeable animal in every way. If I took it by the bridle and tried to lead it off the grounds, it would sit down and brace back, and no one could budge it. However, I was not entirely destitute of military resources, and I did presently manage to spoil this game; for I had seen many a steamboat aground in my time, and knew a trick or two which even a grounded mule would be obliged to respect. There was a well by the corn-crib; so I substituted thirty fathom of rope for the bridle, and fetched him home with the windlass.

I will anticipate here sufficiently to say that we did learn to ride, after some days' practice, but never well. We could not learn to like our animals; they were not choice ones, and most of them had annoying peculiarities of one kind or another. Stevens's horse would carry him, when he was not noticing, under the huge excreseences which form on the trunks of oak trees, and wipe him out of the saddle; in this way Stevens got several bad hurts. Sergeant Bowers's horse was very large and tall, with slim, long legs, and looked like a railroad bridge. His size enabled him to reach all about, and as far as he wanted to, with his head; so he was always biting Bowers's legs. On the march, in the sun, Bowers slept a good deal; and as soon as the horse recognized that he was asleep he would reach around and bite him on the leg. His legs were black and blue with bites. This was the only thing that could ever make him swear, but this always did; whenever his horse bit him he always swore, and of course Stevens, who laughed at everything, laughed at this, and would even get into such convulsions over it as to lose his balance and fall off his horse; and then Bowers, already irritated by the pain of the horse-bite, would resent the laughter with hard language, and there would be a quarrel; so that horse made no end of trouble and bad blood in the command.

However I will get back to where I was—our first afternoon in the sugar-camp. The sugar-troughs came very handy as horse-troughs, and we had plenty of corn to fill them with. I ordered Sergeant Bowers to feed my mule; but he said that if I reckoned he went to war to be a dry-nurse to a mule, it wouldn't take me very long to find out my mistake. I believed that this was insubordination, but I was full of uncertainties about everything military, and so I let the thing pass, and went and ordered Smith, the blacksmith's apprentice, to feed the mule; but he merely gave me a large, cold, sarcastic grin, such as an ostensibly seven-year-old horse gives you when you lift his lip and find he is fourteen, and turned his back on me. I then went to the captain, and asked if it was not right and proper and military for me to have an orderly. He said it was, but as there was only one orderly in the corps, it was but right that he himself should have Bowers on his staff. Bowers said he wouldn't serve on anybody's staff; and if anybody thought he could make him, let him try it. So, of course, the thing had to be dropped; there was no other way.

Next, nobody would cook; it was considered a degradation; so we had no dinner. We lazied the rest of the pleasant afternoon away, some dozing under the trees, some smoking cob-pipes and talking sweethearts and war, some playing games. By late supper-time all hands were famished; and to meet the difficulty all hands turned to, on an equal footing, and gathered wood, built fires, and cooked the meal. Afterwards everything was smooth for a while; then trouble broke out between the corporal and the sergeant, each claiming to rank the other. Nobody knew which was the higher office; so Lyman had to settle the matter by making the rank of both officers equal. The commander of an ignorant crew like that has many troubles and vexations which probably do not occur in the regular army at all. However, with the song-singing and yarn-spinning around the camp-fire, everything presently became serene again; and by and by we raked the corn down level in one end of the crib, and all went to bed on it, tying a horse to the door, so that he would neigh if any one tried to get in.

We had some horsemanship drill every forenoon; then, afternoons, we rode off here and there in squads a few miles, and visited the farmers' girls, and had a youthful good time, and got an honest good dinner or supper, and then home again to camp, happy and content.

For a time life was idly delicious, it was perfect; there was nothing to mar it. Then came some farmers with an alarm one day. They said it was rumored that the enemy were advancing in our direction from over Hyde's prairie. The result was a sharp stir among us, and general consternation. It was a rude awakening from our pleasant trance. The rumor was but a rumor—nothing definite about it; so, in the confusion, we did not know which way to retreat. Lyman was for not retreating at all in these uncertain circumstances; but he found that if he tried to maintain that attitude he would fare badly, for the command were in no humor to put up with insubordination. So he yielded the point and called a council of war—to consist of himself and the three other officers; but the privates made such a fuss about being left out that we had to allow them to remain, for they were already present, and doing the most of the talking too. The question was, which way to retreat; but all were so flurried that nobody seemed to have even a guess to offer. Except Lyman. He explained in a few calm words that, inasmuch as the enemy were approaching from over Hyde's prairie, our course was simple: all we had to do was not to retreat *towards* him; any other direction would answer our needs perfectly. Everybody saw in a moment how true this was, and how wise; so Lyman got a great many compliments. It was now decided that we should fall back on Mason's farm.

It was after dark by this time, and as we could not know how soon the enemy might arrive, it did not seem best to try to take the horses and things with us; so we only took the guns and ammunition, and started at once. The route was very rough and hilly and rocky, and presently the night grew very black and rain began to fall; so we had a troublesome time of it, struggling and stumbling along in the dark; and soon some person slipped and fell, and then the next person behind stumbled over him and fell, and so did the rest, one after the other; and then Bowers came with the keg of powder in his arms, while the command were all mixed together, arms and legs, on the muddy slope; and so he fell, of course, with the keg, and this started the whole detachment down the hill in a body, and they landed in the brook at the bottom in a pile, and each that was undermost pulling the hair and scratching and biting those that were on top of him; and those that were being scratched and bitten scratching and biting the rest in their turn, and all saying they would die before they would ever go to war again if they ever got out of this brook this time, and the invader might rot for all they cared, and the country along with him—and all such talk as that, which was dismal to hear and take part in, in such smothered, low voices, and such a grisly dark place and so wet, and the enemy, maybe, coming any moment.

The keg of powder was lost, and the guns, too; so the growling and complaining continued straight along while the brigade pawed around the pasty hillside and slopped around in the brook hunting for these things; consequently we lost considerable time at this; and then we heard a sound, and held our breath and listened, and it seemed to be the enemy coming, though it could have been a cow, for it had a cough like a cow; but we did not wait, but left a couple of guns behind and struck out for Mason's again as briskly as we could scramble along in the dark. But we got lost presently among the rugged little ravines, and wasted a deal of time finding the way again, so it was after nine when we reached Mason's stile at last; and then before we could open our mouths to give the countersign several dogs came bounding over the fence, with great riot and noise, and each of them took a soldier by the slack of his trousers and began to back away with him. We could not shoot the dogs without endangering the persons they were attached to; so we had to look on helpless, at what was perhaps the most mortifying spectacle of the Civil War. There was light enough, and to spare, for the Masons had now run out on the porch with candles in their hands. The old man and his son came and undid the dogs without difficulty, all but Bowers's; but they couldn't undo his dog, they didn't know his combination; he was of the bull kind, and seemed to be set with a Yale time-lock; but they got him loose at last with some scalding water, of which Bowers got his share and returned thanks. Peterson Dunlap afterwards made up a fine name for this engagement, and also for the night march which preceeded it, but both have long ago faded out of my memory.

We now went into the house, and they began to ask us a world of questions, whereby it presently came out that we did not know anything concerning who or what we were running from, so the old gentleman made himself very frank, and said we were a curious breed of soldiers, and guessed we could be depended on to end up the war in time, because no government could stand the expense of the shoe-leather we should cost it trying to follow us around. "Marion *Rangers!* good name, b'gosh!" said he. And wanted to know why he hadn't had a picket-guard at the place where the road entered the prairie, and why we hadn't sent out a scouting party to spy out the enemy and bring us an account of his strength, and so on, before jumping up and stampeding out of a strong position upon a mere rumor—and so on, and so forth, till he made us all feel shabbier than the dogs had done, not half so enthusiastically welcome. So we went to bed shamed and low-spirited; except Stevens. Soon Stevens began to devise a garment for Bowers which could be made to automatically display his battle-scars to the grateful, or conceal them from the envious, according to his occasions; but Bowers was in no humor for this, so there was a fight, and when it was over Stevens had some battle-scars of his own to think about.

Then we got a little sleep. But after all we had gone through, our activities were not over for the night; for about two o'clock in the morning we heard a shout of warning from down the lane, accompanied by a chorus from all the dogs, and in a moment everybody was up and flying around to find out what the alarm was about. The alarmist was a horseman who gave notice that a detachment of Union soldiers was on its way from Hannibal with orders to capture and hang any bands like ours which it could find, and said we had no time to lose. Farmer Mason was in a flurry this time himself. He hurried us out of the house with all haste, and sent one of his negroes with us to show us where to hide ourselves and our telltale guns among the ravines half a mile away. It was raining heavily.

We struck down the lane, then across some rocky pasture-land which offered good advantages for stumbling; consequently we were down in the mud most of the time, and every time a man went down he black-guarded the war, and the people that started it, and everybody connected with it, and gave himself the master dose of all for being so foolish as to go into it. At last we reached the wooded mouth of a ravine, and there we huddled ourselves under the streaming trees, and sent the negro back home. It was a dismal and heart-breaking time. We were like to be drowned with the rain, deafened with the howling wind and the booming thunder, and blinded by the lightning. It was, indeed, a wild night. The drenching we were getting was misery enough, but a deeper misery still was the reflection that the halter might end us before we were a day older. A death of this shameful sort had not occurred to us as being among the possibilities of war. It took the romance all out of the campaign, and turned our dreams of glory into a repulsive nightmare. As for doubting that so barbarous an order had been given, not one of us did that.

The long night wore itself out at last, and then the negro came to us with the news that the alarm had manifestly been a false one, and that breakfast would soon be ready. Straightway we were lighthearted again, and the world was bright, and life as full of hope and promise as ever—for we were young then. How long ago that was! Twenty-four years.

The mongrel child of philology named the night's refuge Camp Devastation, and no soul objected. The Masons gave us a Missouri country breakfast, in Missourian abundance, and we needed it: hot biscuits; hot "wheat bread," prettily criss-crossed in a lattice pattern on top; hot corn pone; fried chicken; bacon, coffee, eggs, milk, buttermilk, etc.; and the world may be confidently challenged to furnish the equal of such a breakfast, as it is cooked in the South.

We stayed several days at Mason's; and after all these years the memory of the dullness, and stillness, and lifelessness of that slumberous farmhouse still oppresses my spirit as with a sense of the presence of death and mourning. There was nothing to do, nothing to think about; there was no interest in life. The male part of the household were away in the fields all day, the women were busy and out of our sight; there was no sound but the plaintive wailing of a spinning-wheel, forever moaning out from some distant room—the most lonesome sound in nature, a sound steeped and sodden with homesickness and the emptiness of life. The family went to bed about dark every night, and as we were not invited to intrude any new customs we naturally followed theirs. Those nights were a hundred years long to youths accustomed to being up till twelve. We lay awake and miserable till that hour every time, and grew old and decrepit waiting through the still eternities for the clock-strikes. This was no place for town boys. So at last it was with something very like joy that we received news that the enemy were on our track again. With a new birth of the old warrior spirit we sprang to our places in line of battle and fell back on Camp Ralls.

Captain Lyman had take a hint from Mason's talk, and he now gave orders that our camp should be guarded against surprise by the posting of pickets. I was ordered to place a picket at the forks of the road in Hyde's prairie. Night shut down black and threatening. I told Sergeant Bowers to go out to that place and stay till midnight; and, just as I was expecting, he said he wouldn't do it. I tried to get others to go, but all refused. Some excused themselves on account of the weather; but the rest were frank enough to say they wouldn't go in any kind of weather. This kind of thing sounds odd now, and impossible, but there was no surprise in it at the time. On the contrary, it seemed a perfectly natural thing to do. There were scores of little camps scattered over Missouri where the same thing was happening. These camps were composed of young men who had been born and reared to a sturdy independence, and who did not know what it meant to be ordered around by Tom, Dick, and Harry, whom they had known familiarly all their lives, in the village or on the farm. It is quite within the probabilities that this same thing was happening all over the South. James Redpath recognized the justice of this assumption, and furnished the following instance in support of it. During a short stay in East Tennessee he was in a citizen colonel's tent one day talking, when a big private appeared at the door, and, without salute or other circumlocution, said to the colonel:

"Say, Jim, I'm a-goin' home for a few days."

"What for?"

"Well, I hain't b'en there for a right smart while, and I'd like to see how things is comin' on."

"How long are you going to be gone?"

" 'Bout two weeks."

"Well, don't be gone longer than that; and get back sooner if you can."

That was all, and the citizen officer resumed his conversation where the private had broken it off. This was in the first months of the war, of course. The camps in our part of Missouri were under Brigadier-General Thomas H. Harris. He was a townsman of ours, a first-rate fellow, and well liked; but we had all familiarly known him as the sole and modest-salaried operator in our telegraph office, where he had to send about one dispatch a week in ordinary times, and two when there was a rush of business; consequently, when he appeared in our midst one day, on the wing, and delivered a military command of some sort, in a large military fashion, nobody was surprised at the response which he got from the assembled soldiery:

"Oh, now, what'll you take to *don't*, Tom Harris?"

It was quite the natural thing. One might justly imagine that we were hopeless material for war. And so we seemed, in our ignorant state; but there were those among us who afterwards learned the grim trade; learned to obey like machines; became valuable soldiers; fought all through the war, and came out at the end with excellent records. One of the very boys who refused to go out on picket duty that night, and called me an ass for thinking he would expose himself to danger in such a foolhardy way, had become distinguished for intrepidity before he was a year older.

I did secure my picket that night—not by authority, but by diplomacy. I got Bowers to go by agreeing to exchange ranks with him for the time being, and go along and stand the watch with him as his subordinate. We stayed out there a couple of dreary hours in the pitchy darkness and the rain, with nothing to modify the dreariness but Bowers's monotonous growlings at the war and the weather; then we began to nod, and presently found it next to impossible to stay in the saddle; so we gave up the tedious job, and went back to the camp without waiting for the relief guard. We rode into camp without interruption or objection from anybody, and the enemy could have done the same, for there were no sentries. Everybody was asleep; at midnight there was nobody to send out another picket, so none was sent. We never tried to establish a watch at night again, as far as I remember, but we generally kept a picket out in the daytime.

In that camp the whole command slept on the corn in the big corn-crib; and there was usually a general row before morning, for the place was full of rats, and they would scramble over the boys' bodies and faces, annoying and irritating everybody; and now and then they would bite some one's toe, and the person who owned the toe would start up and magnify his English and begin to throw corn in the dark. The ears were half as heavy as bricks, and when they struck they hurt. The persons struck would respond, and inside of five minutes every man would be locked in a death-grip with his neighbor. There was a grievous deal of blood shed in the corn-crib, but this was all that was spilt while I was in the war. No, that is not quite true. But for one circumstance it would have been all. I will come to that now.

Our scares were frequent. Every few days rumors would come that the enemy were approaching. In these cases we always fell back on some other camp of ours; we never stayed where we were. But the rumors always turned out to be false; so at last even we began to grow indifferent to them. One night a negro was sent to our corn-crib with the same old warning: the enemy was hovering in our neighborhood. We all said let him hover. We resolved to stay still and be comfortable. It was a fine warlike resolution, and no doubt we all felt the stir of it in our veins—for a moment. We had been having a very jolly time, that was full of horse-play and school-boy hilarity; but that cooled down now, and presently the fast-waning fire of forced jokes and forced laughs died out altogether, and the company became silent. Silent and nervous. And soon uneasy—worried—apprehensive. We had said we would stay, and we were committed. We could have been persuaded to go, but there was nobody brave enough to suggest it. An almost noiseless movement presently began in the dark by a general but unvoiced impulse. When the movement was completed each man knew that he was not the only person who had crept to the front wall and had his eye at a crack between the logs. No, we were all there; all there with our hearts in our throats, and staring out towards the sugar-troughs where the forest footpath came through. It was late, and there was a deep woodsy stillness everywhere. There was a veiled moonlight, which was only just strong enough to enable us to mark the general shape of objects. Presently a muffled sound caught our ears, and we recognized it as the hoof-beats of a horse or horses. And right away a figure appeared in the forest path; it could have been made of smoke, its mass had so little sharpness of outline. It was a man on horseback, and it seemed to me that there were others behind him. I got hold of a gun in the dark, and pushed it through a crack between the logs, hardly knowing what I was doing, I was so dazed with fright. Somebody said "Fire!" I pulled the trigger. I seemed to see a hundred flashes and hear a hundred reports; then I saw the man fall down out of the saddle. My first feeling was of surprised gratification; my first impulse was an apprentice-sportsman's impulse to run and pick up his game. Somebody said, hardly audibly, "Good—we've got him!—wait for the rest." But the rest did not come. We waited—listened—still no more came. There was not a sound, not the whisper of a leaf; just perfect stillness; an uncanny kind of stillness, which was all the more uncanny on account of the damp, earthy, late-night smells now rising and pervading it. Then, wondering, we crept stealthily out, and approached the man. When we got to him the moon revealed him distinctly. He was lying on his back, with his arms abroad; his mouth was open and his chest heaving with long gasps, and his white shirt-front was all splashed with blood. The thought shot through me that I was a murderer; that I had killed a man—a man who had never done me any harm. That was the coldest sensation that ever went through my marrow. I was down by him in a moment, helplessly stroking his forehead; and I would have given anything then—my own life freely—to make him again what he had been five minutes before. And all the boys seemed to be feeling in the same way; they hung over him, full of pitying interest, and tried all they could to help him, and said all sorts of regretful things. They had forgotten all about the enemy; they thought only of this one forlorn unit of the foe. Once my imagination persuaded me that the dying man gave me a reproachful look out of his shadowy eyes, and it seemed to me that I could rather he had stabbed me than done that. He muttered and mumbled like a dreamer in his sleep about his wife and his child; and I thought with a new despair, "This thing that I have done does not end with him; it falls upon *them* too, and they never did me any harm, any more than he."

In a little while the man was dead. He was killed in war; killed in fair and legitimate war; killed in battle, as you may say; and yet he was as sincerely mourned by the opposing force as if he had been their brother. The boys stood there a half-hour sorrowing over him, and recalling the details of the tragedy, and wondering who he might be, and if he were a spy, and saying that if it were to do over again they would not hurt him unless he attacked them first. It soon came out that mine was not the only shot fired; there were five others—a division of the guilt which was a great relief to me, since it in some degree lightened and diminished the burden I was carrying. There were six shots fired at once; but I was not in my right mind at the time, and my heated imagination had magnified my one shot into a volley.

The man was not in uniform, and was not armed. He was a stranger in the country; that was all we ever found out about him. The thought of him got to preying upon me every night; I could not get rid of it. I could not drive it away, the taking of that unoffending life seemed such a wanton thing. And it seemed an epitome of war; that all war must be just that—the killing of strangers against whom you feel no personal animosity; strangers whom, in other circumstances, you would help if you found them in trouble, and who would help you if you needed it. My campaign was spoiled. It seemed to me that I was not rightly equipped for this awful business; that war was intended for men, and I for a child's nurse. I resolved to retire from this avocation of sham soldiership while I could save some remnant of my self-respect. These morbid thoughts clung to me against reason; for at bottom I did not believe I had touched that man. The law of probabilities decreed me guiltless of his blood; for in all my small experience with guns I had never hit anything I had tried to hit, and I knew I had done my best to hit him. Yet there was no solace in the thought. Against a diseased imagination demonstration goes for nothing.

The rest of my war experience was of a piece with what I have already told of it. We kept monotonously falling back upon one camp or another, and eating up the country. I marvel now at the patience of the farmers and their families. They ought to have shot us; on the contrary, they were as hospitably kind and courteous to us as if we had deserved it. In one of these camps we found Ab Grimes, an Upper Mississippi pilot, who afterwards became famous as a dare-devil rebel spy, whose career bristled with desperate adventures. The look and style of his comrades suggested that they had not come into the war to play, and their deeds made good the conjecture later. They were fine horsemen and good revolver shots; but their favorite arm was the lasso. Each had one at his pommel, and could snatch a man out of the saddle with it every time, on a full gallop, at any reasonable distance.

In another camp the chief was a fierce and profane old blacksmith of sixty, and he had furnished his twenty recruits with gigantic home-made bowie-knives, to be swung with two hands, like the *machetes* of the Isthmus. It was a grisly spectacle to see that earnest band practicing their murderous cuts and slashes under the eye of that remorseless old fanatic.

The last camp which we fell back upon was in a hollow near the village of

Florida, where I was born—in Monroe County. Here we were warned one day that a Union colonel was sweeping down on us with a whole regiment at his heel. This looked decidedly serious. Our boys went apart and consulted; then we went back and told the other companies present that the war was a disappointment to us, and we were going to disband. They were getting ready themselves to fall back on some place or other, and were only waiting for General Tom Harris, who was expected to arrive at any moment; so they tried to persuade us to wait a little while, but the majority of us said no, we were accustomed to falling back, and didn't need any of Tom Harris's help; we could get along perfectly well without him—and save time, too. So about half of our fifteen, including myself, mounted and left on the instant; the others yielded to persuasion and stayed—stayed through the war.

An hour later we met General Harris on the road, with two or three people in his company—his staff, probably, but we could not tell; none of them were in uniform; uniforms had not come into vogue among us yet. Harris ordered us back; but we told him there was a Union colonel coming with a whole regiment in his wake, and it looked as if there was going to be a disturbance; so we had concluded to go home. He raged a little, but it was of no use; our minds were made up. We had done our share; had killed one man, exterminated one army, such as it was; let him go and kill the rest, and that would end the war. I did not see that brisk young general again until last year; then he was wearing white hair and whiskers.

In time I came to know that Union colonel whose coming frightened me out of the war and crippled the Southern cause to that extent—General Grant. I came within a few hours of seeing him when he was as unknown as I was myself; at a time when anybody could have said, "Grant?—Ulysses S. Grant? I do not remember hearing the name before." It seems difficult to realize that there was once a time when such a remark could be rationally made; but there *was,* and I was within a few miles of the place and the occasion, too, though proceeding in the other direction.

The thoughtful will not throw this war paper of mine lightly aside as being valueless. It has this value: it is a not unfair picture of what went on in many and many a militia camp in the first months of the rebellion, when the green recruits were without discipline, without the steadying and heartening influence of trained leaders; when all their circumstances were new and strange, and charged with exaggerated terrors, and before the invaluable experience of actual collision in the field had turned them from rabbits into soldiers. If this side of the picture of that early day has not before been put into history, then history has been to that degree incomplete, for it had and has its rightful place there. There was more Bull Run material scattered through the early camps of this country than exhibited itself at Bull Run. And yet it learned its trade presently, and helped to fight the great battles later. I could have become a soldier myself if I had waited. I had got part of it learned; I knew more about retreating than the man that invented retreating.

"Taming the Bicycle"

I

I thought the matter over, and concluded I could do it. So I went down and bought a barrel of Pond's Extract and a bicycle. The Expert came home with me to instruct me. We chose the back yard, for the sake of privacy, and went to work.

Mine was not a full-grown bicycle, but only a colt—a fifty-inch, with the pedals shortened up to forty-eight—and skittish, like any other colt. The Expert explained the thing's points briefly, then he got on its back and rode around a little, to show me how easy it was to do. He said that the dismounting was perhaps the hardest thing to learn, and so we would leave that to the last. But he was in error there. He found, to his surprise and joy, that all that he needed to do was to get me on to the machine and stand out of the way; I could get off, myself. Although I was wholly inexperienced, I dismounted in the best time on record. He was on that side, shoving up the machine; we all came down with a crash, he at the bottom, I next, and the machine on top.

We examined the machine, but it was not in the least injured. This was hardly believable. Yet the Expert assured me that it was true; in fact, the examination proved it. I was partly to realize, then, how admirably these things are constructed. We applied some Pond's Extract, and resumed. The Expert got on the *other* side to shove up this time, but I dismounted on that side; so the result was as before.

The machine was not hurt. We oiled ourselves up again, and resumed. This time the Expert took up a sheltered position behind, but somehow or other we landed on him again.

He was full of surprised admiration; said it was abnormal. She was all right, not a scratch on her, not a timber started anywhere. I said it was wonderful, while we were greasing up, but he said that when I came to know these steel spider-webs I would realize that nothing but dynamite could cripple them. Then he limped out to position, and we resumed once more. This time the Expert took up the position of short-stop, and got a man to shove up behind. We got up a handsome speed, and presently traversed a brick, and I went out over the top of the tiller and landed, head down, on the instructor's back, and saw the machine fluttering in the air between me and the sun. It was well it came down on us, for that broke the fall, and it was not injured.

Five days later I got out and was carried down to the hospital, and found the

Expert doing pretty fairly. In a few more days I was quite sound. I attribute this to my prudence in always dismounting on something soft. Some recommend a feather bed, but I think an Expert is better.

The Expert got out at last, brought four assistants with him. It was a good idea. These four held the graceful cobweb upright while I climbed into the saddle; then they formed in column and marched on either side of me while the Expert pushed behind; all hands assisted at the dismount.

The bicycle had what is called the "wabbles," and had them very badly. In order to keep my position, a good many things were required of me, and in every instance the thing required was against nature. Against nature, but not against the *laws* of nature. That is to say, that whatever the needed thing might be, my nature, habit, and breeding moved me to attempt it in one way, while some immutable and unsuspected law of physics required that it be done in just the other way. I perceived by this how radically and grotesquely wrong had been the lifelong education of my body and members. They were steeped in ignorance; they knew nothing—nothing which it could profit them to know. For instance, if I found myself falling to the right, I put the tiller hard down the other way, by a quite natural impulse, and so violated a law, and kept on going down. The law required the opposite thing—the big wheel must be turned in the direction in which you are falling. It is hard to believe this, when you are told it. And not merely hard to believe it, but impossible; it is opposed to all your notions. And it is just as hard to do it, after you do come to believe it. Believing it, and knowing by the most convincing proof that it is true, does not help it: you can't any more *do* it than you could before; you can neither force nor persuade yourself to do it at first. The intellect has to come to the front, now. It has to teach the limbs to discard their old education and adopt the new.

The steps of one's progress are distinctly marked. At the end of each lesson he knows he has acquired something, and he also knows what that something is, and likewise that it will stay with him. It is not like studying German, where you mull along, in a groping, uncertain way, for thirty years; and at last, just as you think you've got it, they spring the subjunctive on you, and there you are. No—and I see now, plainly enough, that the great pity about the German language is, that you can't fall off it and hurt yourself. There is nothing like that feature to make you attend strictly to business. But I also see, by what I have learned of bicycling, that the right and only sure way to learn German is by the bicycling method. That is to say, take a grip on one villainy of it at a time, and learn it—not ease up and shirk to the next, leaving that one half learned.

When you have reached the point in bicycling where you can balance the machine tolerably fairly and propel it and steer it, then comes your next task—how to mount it. You do it in this way: you hop along behind it on your right foot, resting the other on the mounting-peg, and grasping the tiller with your hands. At the word, you rise on the peg, stiffen your left leg, hang your other one around in the air in a general and indefinite way, lean your stomach against the rear of the saddle, and then fall off, maybe on one side, maybe on the other; but you fall off. You get up and do it again; and once more; and then several times.

By this time you have learned to keep your balance; and also to steer without wrenching the tiller out by the roots (I say tiller because it *is* a tiller; "handle-bar" is a lamely descriptive phrase). So you steer along, straight ahead, a little while, then you rise forward, with a steady strain, bringing your right leg, and then your body, into the saddle, catch your breath, fetch a violent hitch this way and then that, and down you go again.

But you have ceased to mind the going down by this time; you are getting to light on one foot or the other with considerable certainty. Six more attempts and six more falls make you perfect. You land in the saddle comfortably, next time, and stay there—that is, if you can be content to let your legs dangle, and leave the pedals alone a while; but if you grab at once for the pedals, you are gone again. You soon learn to wait a little and perfect your balance before reaching for the pedals; then the mounting-art is acquired, is complete, and a little practice will make it simple and easy to you, though spectators ought to keep off a rod or two to one side, along at first, if you have nothing against them.

And now you come to the voluntary dismount; you learned the other kind first of all. It is quite easy to tell one how to do the voluntary dismount; the words are few, the requirement simple, and apparently undifficult; let your left pedal go down till your left leg is nearly straight, turn your wheel to the left, and get off as you would from a horse. It certainly does sound exceedingly easy; but it isn't. I don't know why it isn't, but it isn't. Try as you may, you don't get down as you would from a horse, you get down as you would from a house afire. You make a spectacle of yourself every time.

II

During eight days I took a daily lesson of an hour and a half. At the end of this twelve working-hours' apprenticeship I was graduated—in the rough. I was pronounced competent to paddle my own bicycle without outside help. It seems incredible, this celerity of acquirement. It takes considerably longer than that to learn horseback-riding in the rough.

Now it is true that I could have learned without a teacher, but it would have been risky for me, because of my natural clumsiness. The self-taught man seldom knows anything accurately, and he does not know a tenth as much as he could have known if he had worked under teachers; and, besides, he brags, and is the means of fooling other thoughtless people into going and doing as he himself has done. There are those who imagine that the unlucky accidents of life—life's "experiences"—are in some way useful to us. I wish I could find out how. I never knew one of them to happen twice. They always change off and swamp around and catch you on your inexperienced side. If personal experience can be worth anything as an education, it wouldn't seem likely that you could trip Methuselah; and yet if that old person could come back here it is more than likely that one of the first things he would do would be to take hold of one of these electric wires and tie himself all up in a knot. Now the surer thing and the wiser thing would be for him to ask somebody whether it was a good thing to take hold of. But that would not suit him; he would be one of the self-taught kind that go by experience; he would want to examine for himself. And he would find, for his instruction, that the coiled patriarch shuns the electric wire; and it would be useful to him, too, and would leave his education in quite a complete and rounded-out condition, till he should come again, some day, and go to bouncing a dynamite-can around to find out what was in it.

But we wander from the point. However, get a teacher; it saves much time and Pond's Extract.

Before taking final leave of me, my instructor inquired concerning my physical strength, and I was able to inform him that I hadn't any. He said that that was a defect which would make up-hill wheeling pretty difficult for me at first; but he also said the bicycle would soon remove it. The contrast between his muscles and mine was quite marked. He wanted to test mine, so I offered my biceps—which was my best. It almost made him smile. He said, "It is pulpy, and soft, and yielding, and rounded; it evades pressure, and glides from under the fingers; in the dark a body might think it was an oyster in a rag." Perhaps this made me look grieved, for he added, briskly: "Oh, that's all right; you needn't worry about that; in a little while you can't tell it from a petrified kidney. Just go right along with your practice; you're all right."

Then he left me, and I started out alone to seek adventures. You don't really have to seek them—that is nothing but a phrase—they come to you.

I chose a reposeful Sabbath-day sort of a back street which was about thirty yards wide between the curbstones. I knew it was not wide enough; still, I thought that by keeping strict watch and wasting no space unnecessarily I could crowd through.

Of course I had trouble mounting the machine, entirely on my own responsibility, with no encouraging moral support from the outside, no sympathetic instructor to say, "Good! now you're doing well—good again—don't hurry—there, now, you're all right—brace up, go ahead." In place of this I had some other support. This was a boy, who was perched on a gate-post munching a hunk of maple sugar.

He was full of interest and comment. The first time I failed and went down he said that if he was me he would dress up in pillows, that's what he would do. The next time I went down he advised me to go and learn to ride a tricycle first. The third time I collapsed he said he didn't believe I could stay on a horse-car. But next time I succeeded, and got clumsily under way in a weaving, tottering, uncertain fashion, and occupying pretty much all of the street. My slow and lumbering gait filled the boy to the chin with scorn, and he sung out, "My, but don't he rip along!" Then he got down from his post and loafed along the sidewalk, still observing and occasionally commenting. Presently he dropped into my wake and followed along behind. A little girl passed by, balancing a wash-board on her head, and giggled, and seemed about to make a remark, but the boy said, rebukingly, "Let him alone, he's going to a funeral."

I had been familiar with that street for years, and had always supposed it was a dead level; but it was not, as the bicycle now informed me, to my surprise. The bicycle, in the hands of a novice, is as alert and acute as a spirit-level in the detecting of delicate and vanishing shades of difference in these matters. It notices a rise where your untrained eye would not observe that one existed; it notices any decline which water will run down. I was toiling up a slight rise, but was not aware of it. It made me tug and pant and perspire; and still, labor as I might, the machine came almost to a standstill every little while. At such times the boy would say: "That's it! take a rest—there ain't no hurry. They can't hold the funeral without *you*."

Stones were a bother to me. Even the smallest ones gave me a panic when I went over them. I could hit any kind of a stone, no matter how small, if I tried to miss it; and of course at first I couldn't help trying to do that. It is but natural. It is part of the ass that is put in us all, for some inscrutable reason.

I was at the end of my course, at last, and it was necessary for me to round to. This is not a pleasant thing, when you undertake it for the first time on your own responsibility, and neither is it likely to succeed. Your confidence oozes away, you fill steadily up with nameless apprehensions, every fiber of you is tense with a watchful strain, you start a cautious and gradual curve, but your squirmy nerves are all full of electric anxieties, so the curve is quickly demoralized into a jerky and perilous zigzag; then suddenly the nickel-clad horse takes the bit in its mouth and goes slanting for the curbstone, defying all prayers and all your powers to change its mind—your heart stands still, your breath hangs fire, your legs forget to work, straight on you go, and there are but a couple of feet between you and the curb now. And now is the desperate moment, the last chance to save yourself; of course all your instructions fly out of your head, and you whirl your wheel *away* from the curb instead of *toward* it, and so you go sprawling on that granite-bound inhospitable shore. That was my luck; that was my experience. I dragged myself out from under the indestructible bicycle and sat down on the curb to examine.

I started on the return trip. It was now that I saw a farmer's wagon poking along down toward me, loaded with cabbages. If I needed anything to perfect the precariousness of my steering, it was just that. The farmer was occupying the middle of the road with his wagon, leaving barely fourteen or fifteen yards of space on either side. I couldn't shout at him—a beginner can't shout; if he opens his mouth he is gone; he must keep all his attention on his business. But in this grisly emergency, the boy came to the rescue, and for once I had to be grateful to him. He kept a sharp lookout on the swiftly varying impulses and inspirations of my bicycle, and shouted to the man accordingly:

"To the left. Turn to the left, or this jackass'll run over you!" The man started to do it. "No, to the right, to the right! Hold on! *that* won't do!—to the left!—to the right!—to the *left!*—right! left—ri— Stay where you *are,* or you're a goner!"

And just then I caught the off horse in the starboard and went down in a pile. I said, "Hang it! Couldn't you *see* I was coming?"

"Yes, I see you was coming, but I couldn't tell which *way* you was coming. Nobody could—now, *could* they? You couldn't yourself—now, *could* you? So what could *I* do?"

There was something in that, and so I had the magnanimity to say so. I said I was no doubt as much to blame as he was.

Within the next five days I achieved so much progress that the boy couldn't keep up with me. He had to go back to his gate-post, and content himself with watching me fall at long range.

There was a row of low stepping-stones across one end of the street, a measured yard apart. Even after I got so I could steer pretty fairly I was so afraid of those stones that I always hit them. They gave me the worst falls I ever got in that street, except those which I got from dogs. I have seen it stated that no expert is quick enough to run over a dog; that a dog is always able to skip out of his way. I think that that may be true: but I think that the reason he couldn't run over the dog was because he was trying to. I did not try to run over any dog. But I ran over every dog that came along. I think it makes a great deal of difference. If you try to run over the dog he knows how to calculate, but if you are trying to miss him he does not know how to calculate, and is liable to jump the wrong way every time. It was always so in my experience. Even when I could not hit a wagon I could hit a dog that came to see me practise. They all liked to see me practise, and they all came, for there was very little going on in our neighborhood to entertain a dog. It took time to learn to miss a dog, but I achieved even that.

I can steer as well as I want to, now, and I will catch that boy out one of these days and run over *him* if he doesn't reform.

Get a bicycle. You will not regret it, if you live.

LYLE LOVETT

"I work in traditional forms of music," says Lovett. "I love blues, and I love the straightforwardness of the country lyric. And you can be sneaky with both, which I enjoy." He is from old east Texas stock on both sides of his family, was born outside Houston, grew up on the family farm, and attended Texas A&M. He calls his daddy Daddy. At least as recently as 1992 he was telling an interviewer that, to his regret, he still couldn't dance. And yet in 1993 he surprised the world by marrying Julia Roberts, who is a lot prettier Georgian than you would expect an Aggie to win. You wouldn't call Lovett a country singer today, because his songs are as shifty and sly and peculiar—and, yet, direct—as country music used to be.

"If I Had a Boat"

And if I had a boat
I'd go out on the ocean,
And if I had a pony
I'd ride him on my boat.
And we would all together
Go out on the ocean,
Sit me up on my pony
On my boat.

And if I were Roy Rogers
I'd sho' enough be single—
I couldn't bring myself
To marryin' no Dale.
It'd just be me and Trigger,
Go a-ridin' through the movies,
And we'd buy a boat and on the sea we'd sail.

Now myst'ry masked man was smarter,
He got himself a Tonto,

Cause Tonto did the dirty work for free.
Tonto he was smarter,
One day said: "Kemosabe,
Kiss my ass I bought a boat I'm going out to sea."

And if I were like lightnin'
I wouldn't need no sneakers,
I'd come and go whenever I would please.
And I'd scare 'em by the shade tree
And scare 'em by the light pole,
But would not scare my pony
On my boat out on the sea.

And if I had a boat
I'd go out on the ocean,
And if I had a pony
I'd ride him on my boat.
And we could all together
Go out on the ocean,
Sit me up on my pony
On my boat.

JUSTIN WILSON

When it comes to Cajun humor, Justin Wilson of Amite, Louisiana, is the man, I ga-ron-tee. The following tales were got down on paper by Howard Jacobs, veteran columnist of the New Orleans Times-Picayune. *In his introduction to* Justin Wilson's Cajun Humor, *Jacobs says, "I once remarked to one of his innumerable 'frien's' that Wilson was unquestionably one of the greatest embellishers I had ever met. 'You don't mean to tole me,' exclaimed the frien'. 'An' I never t'ought he aver stole a nickel in his life.'"*

"*Confused Motorist*"

We got a town down in Sout' Lewisana how—you—call Loff-i-yette. De engineer w'at laid Loff-i-yette out was dronk eight week befo' he drew de firs' line. Iss de only town in de U.S. an' A. where you can get los' in one block.

I never will forgot, de firs' time I brought ma'se'f to Loff-i-yette I was so los' I didn't know where I was los' from, an' dass bad, you year? Soon I come to a crossin' road I later foun' out was name Four Corner. I cas' an eye on a li'l boy stoodin' dair an' I brought my car to a dead still.

Den I say, "Son, brought you'se'f here, I wanna ax you somet'ing."

He say, "W'at dat is?"

"You can tole me where dis road on de r'at han' will took me if I got on dat, hanh?"

"Mister, I hate to tole you, but me, I don't know."

"How 'bout dis road on de lef', hanh? Can you tole me where dat road will took me if I got on dat?"

"Ag'in I hate to tole you, but me, I don't know dat too, no."

"How 'bout dat road straight ahead like I'm look? Can you tole me where dis road will took me if I stayed jus' like dat, hanh?"

"It broke ma' heart to tole you dis, but me, I don' know dat too, no."

"Son, I ain't gonna did it, but s'pose I turn ma'se'f aroun' an' go jus' like I come from. Can you tole me where dat road would took me if I dues dat, hanh?"

"On de groun' my heart is in a milyun li'l bitty pieces, iss broke so bad. But me, I don't know dat also too besides."

"Son, you don't know a damn t'ing."

"Dass r'at, but I ain't los', no!"

"*Sizing Him Up*"

I got a frien' w'at brought hisse'f to Church Point, an' he cass an eye on a man stoodin' by de corner and he ax him like dis, "Ma' frien', you can tole me where François Prudhomme live, hanh?"

He say, "François Prudhomme? Lessee. Yeah. You go fo' 'bout a mile dair an' you gonna see a oak tree, an' on de lef' is dat li'l yallow house where he live."

Ma' frien' say, "T'ank you vary much," an' de man say, "Wait. François Prudhomme, you say?"

Ma' frien' say, "Dass r'at."

An' de man say, "Dat instruc' I give you don't right. François live on de islan' part, him. You got to brought you'se'f aroun' de behin' side an' you goin' see a li'l yellow house wit' a chinaball tree. Dass where he live."

Ma' frien' say, "T'ank you so much."

"Wait a minute," de fallow say, "you specify François Prudhomme?"

"Dass r'at."

"Well," de man say, "dass me. Whut you want?"

JOHN OLIVER KILLENS

John Oliver Killens was born in Macon in 1916 and grew up in the South. His early novels, including Youngblood *(1954), from which this selection is taken, dealt with Southern injustice, but he has been associated with Brown, Columbia, and NYU, he founded the Harlem Writers Guild, and his 1971 novel* The Cotillion *dealt with hypocrisy within Northern black society. He is also the author of a book of essays,* The Black Man's Burden.

"Georgia Dust"

"Where you headed for, Young Blood?"

"Going to New York."

Skinny looked hard at the boy and laughed softly. "I don't blame you, Young Blood. I'm gonna shake this Georgia dust off my heels, too, and I ain't gon want to see any part of the South no more, not even in a picture show."

Another man laughed. "Skinny, you sure is hard on the South, I swear 'fore God."

Skinny didn't laugh. "I ain't hard on no South. She hard on me. Last southern town I spent any time in was in Mississippi. We called it Laughing, Mississippi. Man, I'm telling you. If a colored man walking up the main street he had to walk in the gutter when a white man pass. They got a big old garbage can in the middle of each block. If a colored man see anything funny and he wanna laugh he have to run to that can and stick his head in it."

Some of the men laughed. "Man, you ought to stop that stuff."

"I ain't lying," Skinny insisted. "They got a great big sign in one uppidy section of town, it says—White Trash Read and Walk Fast—Niggers Read and Haul Ass."

The men laughed and Robby laughed, too, but Skinny didn't laugh, and Robby looked into Skinny's fat face and tried to figure out if the man was serious.

Scotty was smiling but his eyes weren't smiling. "Remind me the time I was passing through Tipkin, Georgia, about a hundred miles down the road from here. I went into one of them little stores on the outskirts of town and asked the man for a can of Prince Albert tobacco. He say, 'What you say, boy?' 'I say I want a can of Prince Albert.' He say, 'Nigger, you better say Mister Prince Albert.' "

.   .   .   .

The buzzing noise of the clippers almost put him to sleep. He watched a good-looking baby-faced country boy get down from the chair next to him dressed to kill from head to foot in brand-new overalls. The young fellow paid the barber and he looked in the mirror long and hard, and he threw up his arms and stretched his slim body. "Whoo-weee," he shouted softly. "I would holler but the town too small." He looked around him and walked out of the shop. The man who got into the chair behind him shook his head and looked at the back of the boy. "Ain't that a damn shame. You can get the feller out the country but you can't get the country out the feller. He comes from so fur in the sticks he ain't never heard a train whistle. He on his way down to the railroad tracks right now to see the trains come in. Crackers catch him down there and run him loose."

RICHARD CHASE

I thought I would find more folk tales that fit into this book, but—well, I wish I could have gotten more of them from folk themselves. Some folklore scholars seem to pride themselves on being terrible storytellers; maybe they don't think it's authentic to be spinners as well as gatherers. Richard Chase, on the other hand, was not only good at searching out folk tales in the North Carolina, Virginia, and Kentucky mountains, he was good at retelling them in a book. He heard versions of this one from three different Wise County Kentuckians, and then for his 1948 collection Grandfather Tales, *he made a piece of writing, the way somebody might make a piece of furniture* out of various authentic pieces of wood. Damned if I see what's inauthentic about that, if you have any aptitude for it. And if you don't have any aptitude for telling folktales, you ought to publish books of something else. What's inauthentic is setting down various oral renditions of stories and saying, "There, there's the evidence, I didn't touch it." That ain't no way to preserve stories.

"Old Dry Frye"

One time there was an old man named Dry Frye. He was a preacher but all he preached for was revival collections and all the fried chicken he could eat. And one time he stayed for supper and he was eatin' fried chicken so fast he got a chicken bone stuck in his throat. Choked him to death. Well, the man of the house he was scared. "Law me!" he says, "they'll find old Dry Frye here and they'll hang me for murder sure!" So he took old Dry Frye to a house down the road a piece and propped him up against the door. Somebody went to go out the door directly old Dry Frye fell in the house. "Law me!" says the man of the house. "Hit's old Dry Frye!" (Everybody knew old Dry Frye.) "We got to get shet of him quick or we're liable to be hung for murder!"

So he took old Dry Frye and propped him up in the bresh 'side the road. And way up in the night some men come along, thought it was a highway robber layin' for 'em. So they chunked rocks at him, knocked him down, and when they seen who it was (everybody knew old Dry Frye) they thought they'd killed him, and they got scared they'd be hung for murder 'cause they'd passed several people on the road who'd 'a knowed who was along there that night.

Well, they took old Dry Frye and propped him up against a man's corn-house. And that man he went out early the next mornin'; and he'd been missin' corn—so when he seen there was somebody over there at his corn-house he ran and got his gun. Slipped around, hollered, "Get away from there or I'll shoot!"

And when old Dry Frye never moved he shot and Dry Frye tumbled over and hit the ground.

"Law me!" says the man. "I believe that was old Dry Frye." (Everybody knew old Dry Frye.) "Now I've done killed him and I'll sure get hung for murder."

So he went and saw it *was* him and seen how dead he was, and went to studyin' up some way to get shet of him. Well, he throwed him in the cornhouse to hide him, and that night he took old Dry Frye down to a baptizin' place 'side a bend in the river where they were fixin' to have a big baptizin' the next day, propped him up on a stump on the riverbank—over a right deep place where the bank was pretty high—propped his elbows on his knees and his chin in his hands. Made him look awful natural. Left him there, went on home and slept sound.

So early the next mornin', 'fore anybody else, a little old feisty boy came down there foolin' around the baptizin' place. Saw old Dry Frye, hollered, "Howdy, Mr. Frye."

Went over closer.

"Howdy, Mr. Dry Frye."

Old Dry Frye sat right on.

"I said Howdy, Dry Frye."

Old Dry Frye kept on sittin'. That boy, now he was just as feisty as he could be. He didn't care how he spoke to nobody.

"Look-a-here, Old Dry Frye, if you don't answer me Howdy I'm goin' to knock your elbows out from under you.—Howdy, Mr. Frye!"

So that feisty boy he reached over and swiped old Dry Frye a lick and over in the river the old man went, right down the bank into that deep water, sunk clean out of sight. Then that boy thought sure he'd drownded Dry Frye. He got scared about bein' hung for murder but he couldn't do nothin' about it right then 'cause he'd seen folks comin' down the road for the baptizin'. So he hung around and directly everybody gathered for the baptizin', and they waited and waited for old Dry Frye to come and preach, but he didn't come and didn't come and when they got to askin' who'd seen old Dry Frye, one man said he'd left his place right after supper, and another man said why, no, he'd not seen old Dry Frye since last meetin'. And that feisty boy he 'uld let out a giggle where he was sittin' on one of the benches in the back, and the other boys 'uld ask him what he was laughin' at but he'd just get tickled again and not tell 'em nothin'. So fin'lly the folks sung a few hymns and took up a collection. So meetin' broke and everybody went on home, and that boy he went on home, too.

Then 'way along late that night he went down and hooked old Dry Frye out of the river and put him in a sack. Got his shoulder under it and started down the road to hide him somewhere. Well, there were a couple of rogues comin' along that same night, had stole a couple of hogs and had 'em sacked up carryin' 'em on their shoulders. Them rogues came over a little rise in the road, saw that boy and they got scared, dropped their sacks and run back lickety-split and hid in the bresh. The boy he never saw the two rogues so he came on, saw them two sacks and set old Dry Frye down to see what was in the other sacks. Then he left old Dry Frye layin' there, picked up one of the hogs and went on back home.

So the two rogues they slipped out directly and when they saw the two sacks still layin' there, they picked 'em up and kept on goin'. Got in home and hung the sacks up in the meathouse. Then the next mornin' the old woman got up to cook breakfast, went out to the smokehouse to cut some meat. Ripped open one of them sacks and there hung old Dry Frye. Well, she hollered and dropped her butcher knife and she got away from there in such a hurry she tore down one side of the smokehouse, broke out two posts on the back porch, and knocked the kitchen door clean off the hinges. She was sorta scared. She hollered and squalled and the men come runnin' in their shirt-tails and fin'lly looked out in the smokehouse, saw old Dry Frye hangin' up there in the place of a hog.

"Law me!" says one of 'em. "Hit's old Dry Frye!" (Everybody knew old Dry Frye.) "We'll sure be hung for murder if we don't get shet of him some way or other."

Well, they had some wild horses in a wilderness out on the mountain. So they rounded up one of 'em, got him in the barn. Then, they put an old no-'count saddle on him and an old piece of bridle, and put old Dry Frye on. Stropped his legs to the bellyband, tied his hands to the saddlehorn and pulled the reins through, stuck his old hat on his head; and then they slipped out and opened all the gates. Opened the barn door and let the horse go. He shot out of there and down the road he went with that old preacher-man a-bouncin' first one side and then the other. And them rogues run out and went to shootin' and hollerin', "He's stole our horse! Stop him! Somebody stop him yonder! Horse thief! Horse thief!"

Everybody down the road come runnin' out their houses a-shoutin' and hollerin' and a-shootin' around, but that horse had done jumped the fence and took out up the mountain and it looked like he was headed for Kentucky.

And as far as I know old Dry Frye is over there yet a-tearin' around through the wilderness on that wild horse.

GREGORY JAYNES

"Lamar Fountain Is Free"

I see by the news that Lamar Fountain, my fellow shut-in, has been paroled. High time! Mr. Fountain was imprisoned, unjustly, I hasten to say, many years ago. He himself made matters worse—aggravated his situation as a boy does a scabby knee—by refusing to serve out his sentence. Time and time again, Mr.

Fountain ran lickety-split from our state's penal institutions. I have maintained close monitor on his struggle.

Believe it was a year ago this month when I read an account of Mr. Fountain's seventh, make that eighth, escape, and found myself in the following week driving through his county on my way elsewhere. The word was he had never been caught. The law said his pattern was to stay gone about six weeks, drink bottle upon bottle of whisky, then come dragging himself back to jail, frazzle worn as a bent-dicked dog. I am a sucker for this manner of behavior; it interests me far more than, say, Sunday football on television.

The egg-shaped man at the general store in the town Mr. Fountain calls home told me the sheriff's name was Gaskins, Walter Gaskins, and that he could be found down to the courthouse most anytime, day or night. So I went down to the courthouse in the daylight and a deputy let me in the door and showed me into Sheriff Gaskins' office. Sheriff Gaskins was on the telephone. He made a wipe sweep of his hand and motioned me to sit on a green Naugahyde couch. I noticed the sheriff had a yellow nose, the only man I've ever seen who had such. This is what the sheriff was saying on the telephone:

"Did he do anything other'n pinch you on the titty? Uh-hmmm. I see. Put your hand on his private. I see. Well, hmmmm, uh, how did his private feel to you? No, ma'am. I don't mean good or bad . . ." Directly, the sheriff polished off the delicate complaint. "Well," he said to the caller, "come on down and we'll take out a warrant on the bastard."

In response to his first question, I told the sheriff no, I did not have a complaint. I asked him to tell me about Lamar Fountain. The sheriff is a brusque man. Here is what he said:

"I'm going down there tonight in my old '52 Chevrolet and I'm not gonna take a gun and I'm not gonna take a deputy and I'm gonna come back with Lamar or I ain't. Anybody don't like what I'm doing, they can kiss my ass." Given the alternative, I assured the sheriff of my firm, unshakable support.

Sheriff Gaskins rose, came round front of his desk, leaned back on it, looked at me sternly and told me the only reason Lamar was out of jail again was to spend his inheritance. A tractor turned over on his daddy and killed him, and Lamar stood to get eight hundred dollars and a nice piece of land, so the sheriff said. The sheriff said Lamar's relatives had already fronted him to the eight hundred and that the escapee had been flashing money all over town. "Leland Kent will tell you," the sheriff said. He gave me directions to Leland Kent's grocery store.

"He come in here the other day," Mr. Kent said of Mr. Fountain. "He got some beanie weenies, Vienna sausage, pork 'n' beans, light bread, sardines, some of them little ol' oatmeal cookies, and a quart of buttermilk. He got some Clorox, too. Said he wanted it for his athlete's foot, but I knowed different. I knowed what he wanted it for. Tell me if you put that Clorox on your shoes it'll keep the dogs off your trail.

"So he gets ten, twelve dollars' worth and he laid a hundred-dollar bill on the counter. I said, 'Lamar, I don't believe I can change that.' He said, 'Just jot it down. I'll be back tomorrow.' And he did, too. Musta been fifty officers and two, three high sheriffs around here lookin' for him, and Lamar walked right on into my store and bought some more beanie weenies and such. Course, I been knowin' him ever since he was little bitty . . ."

I asked Mr. Kent where a thirsty man might find a beer, here in swamp country, and, on his recommendation, I drove to the Silver Dollar Restaurant, a roadside establishment that does not sell food. The Silver Dollar sits on sand beneath tall slash pines that look sick. Mr. Fountain may find beauty in it, but I could not. Where the land isn't thick with gallberry bushes and huckleberry bushes and palmettos, it is planted in tobacco, corn and peanuts. There isn't a hill within one hundred miles of that county. Everyone inside the concrete block Silver Dollar was talking about Lamar Fountain.

Jimmy the bartender, a man with no neck to speak of, was saying, "Ol' Lamar is kinda like that, what's that fellow in the movie? Cool Hand Luke. Yeah, that's Ol' Lamar for you," when I pulled a stool up to the black-padded bar. There was red shag carpeting on the wall behind the bar and spaced three feet apart along the carpeting were diamond-shaped mirrors.

"I growed up with Lamar," said Earl, a customer who sat to my left, sucking on a Miller's. "Course he's older'n me. Guess Lamar's about forty-eight now. I bet he's prob'ly up in New York City right this minute havin' himself a drink at some bar."

"And he'll prob'ly come back here," said Jimmy the bartender, "in an Eldorado Cadillac and take the sheriff out to lunch."

"Naw," said Ernest, the janitor, who is six feet nine or better. No egg, Ernest. "Lamar hauled ass. He won't be back."

"Now that's where you're wrong," said a man with red hair and a nail body with tight, knotty muscles all over it. A backhoe driver for the county, I learned later. "This is home to Lamar."

"Tell me," Jimmy the bartender said, wiping clean the counter, and then he dropped the sentence and looked at me. "Beg pardon," he said. "Didn't notice you come in. Somethin' for you?"

"Draft."

"You got it," Jimmy said, drawing one. "Tell me Lamar's been usin' tar cups. Them cups of turpentine they get off the pine trees. Say he heats it up, puts it on the soles of his shoes, lets it cool and then he walks pretty as you please anyplace he wants to in them swamps. No scent."

"Pepper, too," Earl said. "Black pepper'll flat THOW a dog off a track."

"They run him with the dogs four days straight," Jimmy said. "Next day,

Lamar showed up out back of his sister's place, washin' the sweat out of his clothes. Tol' the boys down at the store the dogs come within ten foot of him, and he was settin' on a log, eatin' oatmeal cookies and drinkin' buttermilk. Went right by him. Another beer, Earl?"

I had business in a neighboring state, and thus could spend no more than an afternoon in that county far to the south of us. At the Silver Dollar, the talk turned to mules right after Jimmy said, "Sheriff Gaskins took Lamar to prison one day and Lamar come on back home that night." There was time left to visit Sheriff Gaskins one short while more.

> Lamar Fountain was not a bad man;
> He went to prison in this great land.
> Whisky and women were the cause of it all;
> That's been many a man's downfall.
> Poor Lamar Fountain!

The sheriff was singing, accompanying himself on guitar, chording it with one finger. It was his own composition, "The Ballad of Lamar Fountain."

> Many days and nights have come and gone
> Since Lamar left his loved ones at home
> He suffered many days and nights away,
> Thinking of his parents who were old and gray.
> Poor Lamar Fountain.

The sheriff stood the guitar in a corner and explained that back in 1968 Lamar got drunk with another fellow. The other fellow gave Lamar a twenty-dollar bill and told him to fetch more whisky. "Lamar didn't come back in the proper time," he said. The drinking partner got a warrant, charging Lamar with robbery. He was advised—ill advised, it is thought—to plead guilty and accept a suspended sentence. He did so, and got euchred, sentenced to go to jail. No one said anything about a suspended sentence. "Ever' time he escapes," the sheriff said, "they give him one to five years more. Here lately, I think they've been givin' him five years ever' time."

At the time I was there, Lamar Fountain, six foot three, 180 pounds and a "pretty boy to look at," had been loose over a month. The Law was embarrassed, even though Sheriff Gaskins was more than sympathetic. "Lamar ain't no damned escape artist," the sheriff said. "It's negligence on somebody's part, I can tell you that. You just peck on concrete long enough and you peck a hole in it. You take out the block and you get away. That's all Lamar done. We'll get him."

Night after night, the posse had formed outside Leland Kent's Grocery, where the sign on the door said, "If You Owe Me Please Pay Me As I Need It." Time after time, members of the posse bought soft drinks and cigars and Goody's Headache Powders and prepared for work. Sheriff Gaskins got astride his horse, his Doberman pinscher at his side. A great howling began and the bloodhounds were loosed. There was a mad dash across the two-lane blacktop and the manhunt was in the swamp.

By midnight, two nights before I was there, the dogs had turned up one old swamp rabbit. Wet, tuckered men were heaving for breath. They had followed paths so thickly overgrown, according to the sheriff's account, that they had to travel them on hands and knees. They had found three camps Lamar had used. They gave up for the evening.

Next day, Sheriff Gaskins was out on his horse when he found Lamar Fountain's current hiding place. There was a bed of hay, with a tin roof supported by six pine saplings. Beanie weenie and Vienna sausage cans were piled all around, filled with cigarette butts.

"I heard him hit the woods," the sheriff said. "My dog hadn't run but one man, and I didn't trust him. So I called back for the bloodhounds." All the dogs and the sweating men plunged in after Lamar, who was leading by less than five minutes. They ran him all afternoon. They did not catch him.

Now it has been a year, and Lamar has been caught and freed, legally. They had found him peacefully fishing for bream and crappie in a pond not far from his sister's house. According to the newspapers, he threw up his hands and said he was tired.

A great Free Lamar Fountain wave struck the south of the state. Petitions were signed and delivered. Attorneys went to work in his behalf without pay. And today, success. Lamar is quoted as saying, "I am tickled to death." He said he has stopped drinking, and that he intends to farm and live a quiet, respectable life. I am told that Sheriff Gaskins, and all who know Lamar Fountain, believe he will live a free man the rest of his days.

JAMES SEAY

My friend Seay, head of the creative writing program at the University of North Carolina, has been honored for his poetry by the American Academy and Institute of

Arts and Letters. One night after I wrote him of my desire to have his poem about the fate of Punk Kincaid in this book, I came home to this message on my answering machine:

"Hey Roy, this is Jim on Saturday night. I was actually going to call you earlier and tell you that we had been swimming in the Atlantic Ocean, and then, five minutes later, well, ten minutes later, we were grilling steaks and looking at the Atlantic Ocean from our deck, on the coast in our house on Emerald Isle. And we want you to come and do the same thing with us.

"I want to thank you for including me in your book. Though I feel like a failure, a total failure, because I never meant Punk to be in any way comic. I had in mind you know just anybody in the world going to a ballgame after reading my poem and breaking down and crying in the bleachers, like a, like a broken coach, from the thought of Punk Kincaid down there; but, if you think that's comic, I guess that's the comic vision, the comic sensibility.

"But, I had hoped to write you something that was, you know, like sitting on the porch.

"Well, the thing about that—you know you always hear this stuff about growing up sitting on the porch at night in the South, and hearing people telling stories. Well I know I sat on the porch a lot at night when I was a kid, especially at my grandparents' at Senatobia, Mississippi, up in Tate County, Mississippi, and I'm sure there was storytelling going on, but I don't remember a story in the world. I just remember the sounds and the trees and the night air and the summer and the wind in the cedars and the pines. I know there were stories going on, but I think that's a lot of bullshit, people talking about remembering stories from on the porch when they were kids; and I spoke to that in something I wrote once; but I was thinking about elaborating on that. . . .

"In fact I'm sure the story was told many times when I was a kid, sitting on the porch, at night, in the summer, but it was not until recently, I guess about two years ago, that my mother told me that my granddaddy, her father, my maternal grandfather, Dock Joe Page, was in fact sitting out on the porch in Como, Mississippi, home of Stark Young, *So Red the Rose*, and also of the linguist (or medievalist?) Kemp Malone—at any rate, also, more importantly, the home of my mother.

"Anyway Dock Joe was sitting out on the porch after he had come in from work and was trying to relax and had his feet up on the porch railing, and he was hit by a bullet. I think I've told you about this. And what it was, one of his best friends—who was the sheriff, who lived next door—had gone out and shot at a mad dog, a mad dog that had been reported coming along the railroad track—the railroad was nearby—and the bullet had ricocheted and hit my granddaddy Dock Joe in the ankle.

"And my grandmother, Cora Mattie, she came out there and said, 'Doc Joe, you're bleeding from the ankle,' and he sure was, and they set up a holler, and the sheriff was nearby who had shot at the mad dog, like Atticus Finch in To Kill a

Mockingbird, *and the ricochet off the railroad track had hit Dock Joe in the ankle—he came over. Understand that this was a* small-town *Southern sheriff, the prototype of manliness and all—Southern manliness—"*

At that point, my answering machine tape ran out.

I called Jim to say that my machine had cut off the end of his story. He said he realized that. I asked him to tell me the rest. He said:

"Well, the sheriff, who had shot at the mad dog, and was one of my granddaddy's best friends—and this was a small-town *sheriff, Southern sheriff—he came over there to the porch and saw my granddaddy's ankle bleeding, where the ricochet had hit him.*

"And he started crying. *He'd shot one of his best friends in the ankle. My grandparents ended up having to comfort* him.*"*

"One Last Cheer for Punk Kincaid"

We never believed that any judge's word
Could send Punk Kincaid to Parchman Farm,
But when Punk broke and wept
On the last night of his trial a year ago
We knew that he was guilty as accused
And never again would we run interference
As he brought back a down-field punt
Or took a hand-off on a sweeper play
And moved on out into an open field.
Today we are watching Negro trusties
Drag a lake near Parchman Farm
For his body.
Word had come that Punk went down
To help recover a drowned man;
We drove all morning into the Delta
Thinking he might rise grinning
Near the sidelines
And josh about this trick
He had pulled
Or simply say the names of towns
He cruised the rustled cattle through—
Anguilla, Rolling Fork, Redwood, on to Natchez—
And with the Negroes from the boat
Gathered with us in a circle

We would help him mile by mile
Through the outlaw past.
They drag the lake with net and hook
But it will not give him up—
Below their boat
The drowned are running interference
For Punk Kincaid
As he returns a punt
From deep inside his own territory.

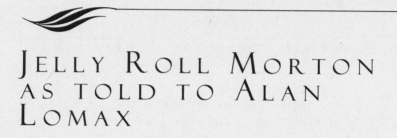

Jelly Roll Morton as told to Alan Lomax

Ferdinand Joseph La Menthe Morton was born a Creole of Color on the Gulf Coast near New Orleans in 1885. By the age of fifteen he was one of the best ragtime-blues pianists in the whorehouses of New Orleans, which is of course to say one of the best ragtime-blues pianists. He composed some sublime music, most notably "The Pearls," and his claim that he invented jazz probably carries more weight than any other single person's claim to have invented jazz. In 1938 he sat down with the folklorist Alan Lomax to record the story of his life for the Library of Congress. "It took me four years of rewriting to render his prose on the page so that at times you can almost hear him talking," wrote Lomax in his introduction to the book he fashioned out of those tapes, Mister Jelly Roll.

Hustling Here and There

You see, there wasn't no certain neighborhood for nobody to live in in New Orleans, only for the St. Charles Avenue millionaires' district, and that's why anybody could go any place they wanted to. So in those days in honkey-tonks the St. Charles millionaires would bump up against the fellows that was on the levee, some of whom didn't bathe more than once in six months and, I'll go so far as to say, were even lousy. They would reach up in their collars, when they saw anyone that was dressed up, get one of these educated louses and throw it on that person when his back was turned. Then maybe a St. Charles Avenue millionaire would be in the same situation they were—lousy—and didn't know how they got to be that way. It was a funny situation. And away in the dark there would always be an old broke-down piano and somebody playing the blues and singing something like this . . .

I'm a levee man,
I'm a levee man,
I'm a levee man,
I'm a levee man.

Captain, captain,
Let me make this trip,
I need some money
To fill my grip.
Yes I need the money

And I need it bad,
Wants a lot of things
That I never had.

. . . .

If they didn't clean [a] sucker by legitimate cheating, one of the tough guys would take his money anyhow—men like Chicken Dick, who had shoulders and arms on him much more stronger-looking than Joe Louis—and Toodlum and Toodoo Parker, guys you couldn't afford to bother with—and Sheep Eye (I was raised with him), he was real loud-mouthed and, if he could bluff you, he might murder you. Sheep Eye was a raider around these little Cotch games and when he would walk in, everybody would quit—

"Cash in my checks here, I've got to go."

And Sheep Eye would holler, "You gonna play! Sheep Eye's here and I'm the baddest sonofabitch that ever moved. Set down there and play. If you don't, I'm taking this pot."

Of course, it made no difference whether Sheep Eye won or lost. He'd take all the money anyway. Curse you, kick you, and slap you cross the head with a pistol. He was the toughest guy in the world until Aaron Harris showed up, but, when Aaron entered, Sheep Eye would become the nicest little boy anywhere—just lovely.

Aaron was the toughest of them all—a known and dangerous killer that had very little to say. The policemen wanted Aaron, but they couldn't afford to say much to him unless they intended to kill him. They were afraid to try that, because it seemed he never missed any time he got ready to kill anyone. Man or woman, it made no difference to Aaron. He had eleven killings to his credit, including his sister and his brother-in-law. I believe Aaron Harris was, no doubt, the most heartless man I've ever heard of or ever seen. . . .

It was known that Madame Papaloos always backed him when he got in trouble—not with funds or anything like that—money wasn't really in it. Madame Papaloos was a hoodoo woman. She was supposed, from certain evidences, to tumble up Aaron's house to discourage the judge from prosecuting—take all the sheets off the bed, turn the mattresses over, hang sheets in front of the mirrors, turn the chairs over, which was said and known to confuse the judge. Then she would get lamb and beef and veal tongues from the markets and stick pins and needles all through them in order to tie the tongues of the prosecuting attorney and the witnesses and the juries so they couldn't talk against whoever the victim's supposed to be—not the victim, but the one that's arrested. That way, Aaron Harris, the ready killer, was always successful in getting out of his troubles . . .

> Aaron Harris was a bad, bad man,
> Baddest man ever was in this land.
>
> Killed his sweet little sister and his brother-in-law,
> About a cup of coffee, he killed his sister and his brother-in-law.

Now listen to the story of the man who was maybe even more dangerous than Aaron. This was a seemingly harmless little fellow, but he tore up the entire city of New Orleans for a week.

Robert Charles sold newspapers on the corner of Dryad and Melpomene, back there around 1900. He never made any noise bigger than "Get your *Picayune,* Get your paypire!" until the day he had an argument with his wife and she called the police. According to authentic information that I gathered, Robert Charles was arrested and the policeman wouldn't let him go back after his hat. He was a very orderly seeming guy, but this arose him to fury. He broke away, taken a Winchester rifle, killed the policeman and from that the riot started, in which all sorts of innocent people were killed.

Seemingly Robert Charles must have been a marksman. It was later learned that he had a couple of barrels of bullets in his house that he had made himself. Well, if you shoot one officer like Robert Charles had, it's no more than right that another one should take his place, but the way that newsboy was killing them off it looked like the department might run out of officers. . . .

The first day after the killing, which I believe was on a Sunday, the newspapers were full of it. Then the riot broke out. Men were beat up on streetcars—both white and colored. Any place a white man seen a colored man or a colored man seen a white man there was a fight. The streetcars had to stop.

Transportation absolutely quit. Finally, B. A. Baldwin, considered one of the biggest ammunition dealers in the world, issued a statement that if they didn't quit killing the colored people, he would arm them all to fight back for their own rights. Through this there came a halt to the Robert Charles Riot.

After the riot, nobody knows for sure what became of Robert Charles. . . . Anyhow, like many other bad men, he had a song originated on him. This song was squashed very easily by the department, and not only by the department but by anyone else who heard it, due to the fact that it was a trouble breeder. So that song never did get very far. I once knew the Robert Charles song, but I found out it was best for me to forget it and that I did in order to go along with the world on the peaceful side.

. . . .

There was a man standing at the bar, a little bit of a short fellow. Seemingly he was sick with rheumatism. A great big husky guy steps on this little guy's foot (I was just in between them) and they got into an argument and the little guy didn't want to stand for it and pulled out a great big gun, almost as long as he was old, and shot, and if I hadn't pulled my stomach back, I wouldn't be here to tell you the history of jazz.

. . . .

Oftentimes the girls would ask me to perform my *Animule Dance*. I wrote this in 1906 and ten thousand has claimed it; it's never been published and it never will be, because nobody can do it but myself . . .

> *Ladies and gentlemen, we are now in the jungles.*
> *Everyone of you are animules.*
> *You should be walking on four legs,*
> *But you're now walking on two.*
> *You know you come directly from the animule famulee.*
>
> *Yes, we're right here in the animule field.*
> *And I want to tell you people with clothes on*
> *You have tails just the same.*
> *But you wear clothes and you can't see them . . .*
> *   Way down in jungle town,*
> *   For miles around . . .*
> *They used to give a ball every night at the animule hall.*
> *The band began to play, they began to shout.*
> *You'd laugh—Haw-haw-haw—, Lord, till your sides*
> *   would crack.*
> *How they'd call them doggone figures out!*
> *   The monkey hollered, "Run, I say!"*

The wildcat did the bambochay;
The tiger did the mooch;
The elephant did the hooch-ama-cooch;
The pan'ter did the eagle rock and began to prance,
    Down in the jungle,
    At that animule dance.

Well, the lion came through the door,
Ugh, you could tell that lion was posilutely sore.
"Let me in the hall." "What you gwine do?"
"I'm gonna break up this doggone animule ball.
    Yes, don't you think I want to dawnce?
    Give me one more chawnce . . ."
    The lion give a roar,
    Broke down the door,
    Broke up the animule ball. . . .

Then I'd carry on some of my scat . . .

Bee-la-bah-bee-bab-a-lee-ba.

People believe Louis Armstrong originated scat. I must take that credit away from him, because I know better. Tony Jackson and myself were using scat for novelty back in 1906 and 1907 when Louis Armstrong was still in the orphan's home.

Those days I hung out at Eloise Blackenstein and Louise Aberdeen's place—the rendezvous of all the big sports like Pensacola Kid, who later came to be the champion pool player of the world. Bob Rowe, the man who didn't know how many suits he had, and his wife, Ready Money, were regulars, also the Suicide Queen, who used to take poison all the time. Tony Jackson also hung out there and was the cause of me not playing much piano. When Tony came in, the guys would tell me, "Get off that piano stool. You're hurting the piano's feelings."

.   .   .   .

. . . I dropped down to Houston, Texas, to see whether they had anybody could shoot a game of pool. I did a good bit of winning and then I started shooting left-handed so I could get more bets. They slipped a shark by the name of Joe Williams in on me, but right at the end of the game I switched over to my right hand and ran the game out. His backer, who had lost heavily, said I was robbing him (which was true), pulled out a pistol and started shooting. Somehow I got under the pool table, but that cured me of playing pool in Houston.

.   .   .   .

. . . I left New Orleans with a guy from Jackson, Mississippi, who had named himself Jack the Bear. I found out later he should have called himself Jack the Lamb. He was a little bit of a guy and it seems like he must have stolen his name from some other big guy. Very often the boys, to be recognized as somebody, would use alias names like that.

Anyhow Jack the Bear proposed that we hobo.

I said, "No, I can't hobo. I tried that once. When I got off the train I thought it was slowing down and I fell headforemost and tore the knees out of the trousers of my sixty-dollar, brand-new suit. So I don't have to do that no more."

.   .   .   .

Going up on the train, Jack the Bear had some kind of a fake pin in the lapel of his coat, and everytime he would get to one of those real simple colored people who had on any kind of a pin, he would walk up to him and cover the pin with his hands and say, "I got you covered now. If you can't tell me the secret oath of the fiftieth degree of this order, I will have to remove your pin. You are really violating the lodge rules, and I will have to have some money not to condemn you. . . ."

From time to time Jack would pick up a couple of dollars doing that kind of thing.

.   .   .   .

We got into Memphis, all right, which Jack was supposed to know all about. He was going to take me around and introduce me to the different personnels of Memphis. But the big, lying dog—I found out he hadn't ever been to Memphis before. So, anyhow, after I was in Memphis, safe and sound, on the shores of Memphis, Tennessee, I decided to go to this Beale Street I had heard a lot of talk about. I first inquired was there any piano players in the city and they told me that absolutely the best in the whole state of Tennessee was there. I asked them had they heard about Tony Jackson, Alfred Carroll, Albert Wilson, or Winding Boy, and they said they had never heard of them guys. "Them guys wouldn't be able to play with this fellow, Benny Frenchy, the best in the whole state." Well, that kind of frightened me and I wouldn't even try to touch a piano until I could hear Benny Frenchy.

This guy, Benny Frenchy, was playing in a place on Beale Street, near Fourth. Nothing went into that place but pimps, robbers, gamblers, and whores—(it's really a shame to think of some of those environments I drifted into)—which it was run by a white fellow who was the tough guy of Memphis, Tennessee.

It seems like Benny Frenchy had certain days he came to the place and he was a natural drawing-card. The bunch would come up from the honkeytonks, with tough killers hanging around and prizefighters of a low caliber that would probably kill you for an argument. When Benny would show up, there would be a type of those lowclass women and some that was a little better class. They would have a special way of dancing when he played and I never seen that dance before or since. They would run right directly up to the wall and with a kind of little bitty shuffle and clap their hands together and kick back their right leg. And they'd say, "O play it, Benny, play it."

Well, there was this piano right in the Monarch. Benny Frenchy was playing it. All those lowclass whores were doing that dance. I was talking to the fellow who was running the dice game on the daytime watch. I didn't even know who I was talking to, only that he was the gentleman that ran the games. I said to him—it was Bad Sam, only I didn't know who it was—I said,

"Who is this fellow?"

He said, "This is Benny Frenchy."

I said, "I never heard of him."

"Where in hell you been, never heard of Benny Frenchy?"

I said, "What is he? Supposed to be good?"

He said, "He is the best in the whole State of Tennessee."

I said, "Why, that damn fool can't hit a piano with a brick."

So he said to me, he says, "Can you play?"

I said, "Well, I'm not supposed to be good, but if that is playing I can beat all them kind of suckers."

He hollered to Benny, "Wait a minute, Benny. There's one of them little upstarts around here, thinks he can play. Would you mind lettin him get down there to show what he can do?"

And he says to me, "Will you play?"

I said, "Sure, there is no worry about playing with a palooka like that. Why, certainly."

Bad Sam said, "Okay, Benny, here is a little bum thinks he can play piano. Let him try his hand. See what he can do, because, if he can't play, I'll kick him in the ass."

There was a kind of chill came over me when he said that. Bad Sam was a very tough man, but I didn't know it at the time. I found out later he was really the toughest Negro in Memphis, no doubt the toughest man in the whole section, black or white. . . . But courage came to me because I knew that no matter how I played I could beat Benny Frenchy because he couldn't play at all. I got up a lot of courage and I said, "You won't kick me in the ass, because I can beat this palooka."

And Bad Sam said, "He's a game kid, all right, so let him go down."

Well, I sat down and began to play the New Orleans *Naked Dance*. All the girls begin to do high kicks and they told me, "O play it, mister, play it. Play that thing, boy." Of course I never was a great singer, but I could do better than now. I told 'em I certainly would and then sung something like this:

> *All that I ask is love,*
> *All that I want is you,*
> *And I swear by all the stars*
> *I'll be forever true. . . .*

I swung out on that number in my style and, when I looked around, Benny Frenchy was standing all by himself looking like he wanted to put a knife in me; Bad Sam was sort of smiling in his deal and all them little whores was running directly up to the wall and kicking back in that funny little Memphis dance. Man, I brought the house down with that thing. Don't you believe me? Think I'm kidding? I brought it *down,* man. After that Beale Street belonged to me.

KATHERINE ANNE PORTER

Katherine Anne Porter's Indian Creek, Texas, parents named her Callie Russell Porter. She was born in 1890 and married a railway clerk at sixteen. Eight years later she went alone to Chicago to be a movie actress. She lived in Denver, Mexico, Bermuda, Madrid, Paris, Berlin, New Orleans, New York, Hollywood—she had an interesting life, and she was a distinguished Southern writer. What is she doing in a book of Southern humor, though? Well, her acceptance speech to the American Academy of Arts and Letters on receiving the Gold Medal for Fiction began, "I was told to write a speech and I did, but I'm not sure I'm going to read it. Oh, I'll start," and ended, "One of my favorite characters in literature is the Wife of Bath . . . : 'It tickleth me about my heart's root, That I have seen the world as in my time.' " And she wrote for The Ladies Home Journal *a recollection of Hemingway (from which the following is excerpted) that I count as Texas lady putting Illinois guy (both of them in Paris) drolly in his place.*

Meeting Hemingway

Sylvia [Beach] loved her hundreds of friends, and they all loved her—many of whom loved almost no one else except perhaps himself—apparently without jealousy, each one sure of his special cell in the vast honeycomb of her heart; sure of his welcome in her shop with its exhilarating air of something pretty wonderful going on at top speed. Her genius was for friendship; her besetting virtue, generosity, an all-covering charity in its true sense; and courage that reassured even Hemingway, the distrustful, the wary, the unloving, who sized people up on sight, who couldn't be easy until he had somehow got the upper hand. Half an hour after he was first in her shop, Hemingway was sitting there with a sock and shoe laid aside, showing Sylvia the still-painful scars of his war wounds got in Italy.

.   .   .   .

As I say, Sylvia's friends did not always love each other even for her sake, nor could anyone but Sylvia expect them to, yet it is plain that she did. At parties especially, or in her shop, she had a way, figuratively, of taking two of her friends, strangers to each other, by the napes of their necks and cracking their heads together, saying in effect always, and at times in so many words, "My dears, you *must* love one another," and she could cite the best of reasons for this hope. . . .

.   .   .   .

I had dropped into Sylvia's shop looking for something to read, just at early dark on a cold, rainy winter evening, maybe in 1934, I am not sure. We were standing under the light at the big round table piled up with books, talking; and I was just saying good-bye when the door burst open, and Hemingway unmistakably Ernest stood before us, looking just like the snapshots of him then being everywhere published—tall, bulky, broadfaced (his season of boy-ish slenderness was short), cropped black moustache, watchful eyes, all reas-suringly there.

He wore a streaming old raincoat and a drenched floppy rain hat pulled over his eyebrows. Sylvia ran to him calling like a bird, both arms out; they embraced in a manly sort of way (quite a feat, sizes and sexes considered), then Sylvia turned to me with that ominous apostolic sweetness in her eyes.

Still holding one of Hemingway's hands, she reached at arm's length for mine. "Katherine Anne Porter," she said, pronouncing the names in full, "this is Ernest Hemingway . . . Ernest, this is Katherine Anne, and I want the two best modern American writers to know each other!"

Our hands were not joined.

"Modern" was a talismanic word then, but this time the magic failed. At that instant the telephone rang in the back room, Sylvia flew to answer, calling back to us merrily, merrily, "Now you two just get acquainted, and I'll be right back." Hemingway and I stood and gazed unwinkingly at each other with poker faces for all of ten seconds, in silence. Hemingway then turned in one wide swing and hurled himself into the rainy darkness as he had hurled himself out of it, and that was all. I am sorry if you are disappointed. All personal lack of sympathy and attraction aside, and they were real in us both, it must have been galling to this most famous young man to have his name pronounced in the same breath as writer with someone he had never heard of, and a woman at that. I nearly felt sorry for him.

A. R. AMMONS

Ammons was born in 1926 in Columbus County, North Carolina, graduated from Wake Forest in 1949, was a Hatteras, North Carolina, elementary school principal, worked for a company that manufactured biological glassware, got a teaching job at Cornell, became a distinguished professor, and finally in the 1970s became recognized as an important poet. Who hadn't lost his sense of humor.

"First Carolina Said-Song"
(as told me by an aunt)

In them days
    they won't hardly no way to know if
     somebody way off
    died
      till they'd be
      dead and buried

     and Uncle Jim

hitched up a team of mules to the wagon
and he cracked the whip over them

and run them their dead-level best
the whole thirty miles to your great grandma's funeral
                down there in
                Green Sea County

                and there come up this
awfulest rainstorm
                you ever saw in your whole life
                and your grandpa
                was setting
                in a goat-skin bottomed chair

and them mules a-running
and him sloshing round in that chairful of water

                till he got scalded
                he said

                and ev-
ery
anch of skin come off his behind:

we got there just in time to see her buried
                in an oak grove up
                back of the field:

it's growed over with soapbushes and huckleberries now.

"Second Carolina Said-Song"
(as told me by a patient, Ward 3-B,
Veterans Hospital, Fayetteville, August
1962)

                I was walking down by the old
Santee
                River
                one evening, foredark
                fishing I reckon,

           when I come on this
swarm of
bees
        lit in the fork of a beech limb
           and they werz

           jest a swarming:

        it was too late to go home
           and too far
and brang a bee-gum

           so I waited around
             till the sun went
down,
most dark,

        and cut me off a pinebough,
           dipped it in the river
              and sprankled water

on 'em: settled 'em right down,
        good and solid,
about
           a bushel of
           them:

           when it got dark I first cut off
the fork branches and
then cut about four foot back toward
              the trunk

and I
        throwed the limb over my shoulder and
           carried 'em home.

SECTION SIX

MIND AND HEART AND SOUL

A young pastor took a rural church. Being recently out of the seminary with its heady theological discussions, he set up a series of lectures to deliver to his flock on Thursday evenings. His first topic was "Immaculate Conception," and he gave what he imagined to be an inspired and thorough lecture on the subject. When he had finished, he asked if there were questions, not really expecting any. A little old lady in the back raised her hand and inquired timidly, "Uh, what are its advantages?"

—LOYAL JONES

There was a rumor about a tumor
Nestled at the base of his brain.
He was settin' up there with his .36 Magnum,
Laughing wildly as he bagged 'em.
Who are we to say the boy's insane?

Now Charley was awful disappointed,
Else he thought he was anointed
To do a deed so lowdown and so mean.
The students looked up from their classes,
Had to stop and rub their glasses.
Who'd believe he'd once been . . . a Marine?

.   .   .   .

Some were dyin', some were weepin',
Some were studyin', some were sleepin',
Some were shoutin' "Texas number one!"
Some were runnin', some were fallin',
Some were screamin', some were bawlin',
Some thought the Revolution had begun.

The doctors tore his poor brain down,
But not a snitch of illness could be found.
Most folks couldn't figger just a-why he did it,
And them that could would not admit it.
There's still a lot of Eagle Scouts around.

There was a rumor about a tumor
Nestled at the base of his brain.
He was settin' up there with his .36 Magnum,
Laughin' wildly as he bagged 'em.
Who are we to say the boy's in-
Who are we to say the boy's in-
Who are we to say the boy's insane?

JOHN SHELTON REED

"Precious Memories"

George Garrett, in a splendidly cranky and very wise essay, observes that a nearly universal characteristic of Southern writers is their sense of loss, of "the dimming of many bright things and the falling away of familiar certainties." He notes that this is one of Southerners' most attractive traits, but that "it is mildly strange that what the very youngest generation of Southern writers laments and regrets the passing of has to be, in fact, among the crowd of new things whose arrival and presence on the scene was roundly deplored by the previous generation."

I know what he means. Older readers may not believe me, but I swear it's possible to be nostalgic about white bread and lunch meat sandwiches. For me, a Dolly Madison cupcake can set off a Proustian reverie of driving through a steamy Southern night, with WLAC blasting Hank Ballard songs. One can actually believe, deep down, that the decline of Western civilization dates from the death of Buddy Holly. I know. I do.

At the same time, I can be scornful about those younger folks who feel the same way about Simon and Garfunkel. And I am absolutely distraught when I think about what my own children may remember fondly. Izod shirts? Disco? The new Episcopal prayer book? (Actually, I may have inoculated my kids. "What's in life jackets, Daddy?" my daughter asked one day. "It used to be something called kapok," I told her. "I don't know what they use now." "But it's not as good, is it?" she said.)

Of course, Garrett's point is that we need to remember that our own parents looked on Buddy Holly much as the Romans must have regarded Alaric. Indeed, that was part of Buddy's appeal. Our folks, in their turn, were given to lamenting that nothing had been the same since the War—meaning World War II, by which time the Golden Age was long past, according to *their* parents. This elegiac stance was certainly evident in the aftermath of Appomattox. Oscar Wilde, during his American tour, remarked that you couldn't admire the moon in Georgia without being told how much better it looked before the War. I gather, though, that antebellum Southerners harked back to Ole Virginny, of the seventeenth and eighteenth centuries, if not to Merrie Englande.

Maybe Garrett is right when he traces this trope to the Anglo-Saxon ballad. Lord knows it's alive and well in the latter-day Anglo-Saxon ballads of country music, where vanished scenes of our childhood and home make up much of the subject matter. Coupled with that pervasive nostalgia is a celebration of continuity, sometimes disconcerting, as when Hank Williams, Jr., rejoices that Florida girls still don't wear underwear, folks still get drunk at football games, his woman "still looks good in her T-shirt, standin' in the Georgia rain"—and "the New South, thank God, is still the same." It may be significant that one of the few songs even somewhat skeptical about the singer's own rose-colored memories is sung by one of the very few black country-music singers around. In "I Wonder Could I Live There Any More," Charlie Pride doesn't deny the feeling, but he does recognize that actuality was grimmer than he realized at the time.

There are really two sides to Garrett's anthropological observation: on the one hand, Southerners' regret at the passing of familiar things; on the other, our readiness to adopt new things, to naturalize them and turn them into familiar things—Southern things—whose passing we shall regret. It's startling to consider how many of what seem bedrock Southern institutions are actually recent innovations. In *The Strange Career of Jim Crow*, C. Vann Woodward even argued that that was so for racial segregation. Maybe he exaggerated, for rhetorical effect, but there are other examples. For instance, I dare say few of us now could imagine the South without stock-car racing, although we know, deep down, that it didn't exist before stock cars did. A happy historical amnesia can help this tendency along. I don't doubt that there are younger Southerners who think the Atlanta Braves were founded about the same time as the Ku Klux Klan.

Joe Gray Taylor has some nice examples in his informal history of Southern foodways, *Eating, Drinking, and Visiting in the South.* Heavily sweetened iced tea, for instance, the staple potation of the Southern summer, wasn't widely consumed until there were reliable supplies of ice in the Southern countryside. And however great Grandma's biscuits were, you can bet her grandmother didn't bake many of them: she didn't have the wheat flour and baking powder to do it with. . . .

A fragment of speech I recently overheard in a local grocery store seems somehow to the point. One of the checkers, responding to an inquiry from a high-toned lady customer, turned toward the manager's booth and hollered: "Hey Bobby—where's the couscous at?"

KINKY FRIEDMAN

I guess I should try to find out what Kinky Friedman's real first name is. But hey, the important things are that Kinky's father was a University of Texas professor, Kinky himself was a Peace Corps volunteer who claims to have introduced the Frisbee to Borneo, and Kinky used to be an outlaw country singer in Austin—Kinky Friedman and the Texas Jewboys was the name of his act. His memorable songs include "Sold American," "High on Jesus," "Get Your Biscuits in the Oven and Your Buns in the Bed," and the following kinky historical ballad. Now he lives in New York and writes mystery novels.

"The Ballad of Charles Whitman"

He was sittin' up there for more than an hour,
Way up there on the Texas Tower,
Shootin' from the 27th floor.
He didn't choke or slash or slit them,
Not our Charles Joseph Whitman.
He won't be an architect no more.

Got up that mornin', calm and cool,
He picked up his guns and walked to school.
All the while he smiled so sweetly
That it blew their minds completely—
They never seen an Eagle Scout so cruel.

Think of the shame and degradation
For the school's administration,
Who put on such a bold and brassy show.
The chancellor cried, "It's adolescent,
And of course it's most unpleasant,
But I gotta admit, it's a lovely way to go."

BARRY HANNAH

When Airships, Barry Hannah's book of short stories, came out in 1978, I thought, "Whoa! I ought to be doing something like this." Philip Roth's blurb said, "These stories are wonderful in the ways Mark Twain, Faulkner, and Flannery O'Connor are wonderful when they are working the great vein of fierce and pitiless Southern comedy." This is one of those stories. Hannah is from Mississippi, and teaches at Ole Miss.

"Knowing He Was Not My Kind yet I Followed"

It makes me sick when we kill them or ride horses over them. My gun is blazing just like the rest of them, but I hate it.

One day I rode up on a fellow in blue and we were both out of ammunition. He was trying to draw his saber and I was so outraged I slapped him right off his horse. The horseman behind me cheered. He said I'd broken the man's neck. I was horrified. Oh, life, life—you kill what you love. I have seen such handsome faces with their mouths open, their necks open to the Pennsylvania sun. I love stealing for forage and food, but I hate this murdering business that goes along with it.

Some nights I amble in near the fire to take a cup with the boys, but they chase me away. I don't scold, but in my mind there are the words: All right, have your way in this twinkling mortal world.

Our Jeb Stuart is never tired. You could wake him with a message any time of night and he's awake on the instant. He's such a bull. They called him "Beauty" at West Point. We're fighting and killing all his old classmates and even his father-in-law, General Philip St. George Cooke. Jeb wrote about this man once when he failed to join the Confederacy: "He will regret it but once, and that will be continuously."

Gee, he can use the word, Jeb can. I was with him through the ostrich feathers in his hat and the early harassments, when we had nothing but shot-guns and pretty horses. He was always a fool at running around his enemy. I was with him when we rode down a lane around a confused Yank picket, risking the Miniés. But he's a good family man too, they say.

I was with him when he first went around McClellan and scouted Porter's wing. That's when I fell in love with burning and looting. We threw ourselves on railroad cars and wagons, we collected carbines, uniforms and cow steaks that we roasted on sticks over the embers of the rails. Jeb passed right by when I was chewing my beef and dipping water out of the great tank. He had his banjo man and his dancing nigger with him. Jeb has terrific body odor along with his mud-spattered boots, but it rather draws than repels, like the musk of a woman.

When we were celebrating in Richmond, even I was escorted by a woman out into the shadows and this is why I say this. She surrendered to me, her hoop skirt was around her eyebrows, her white nakedness lying under me if I wanted it, and I suppose I did, because I went laboring at her, head full of smoke and unreason. I left her with her dress over her face like a tent and have no clear notion of what her face was like, though my acquaintance Ruppert Longstreet told me in daylight she was a troll.

That was when young Pelham set fire to the Yank boat in the James with his one Napoleon cannon. We whipped a warship from the shore. Pelham was a genius about artillery. I loved that too.

It's killing close up that bothers me. Once a blue-suited man on the ground was holding his hands out after his horse fell over. This was at Manassas. He seemed to be unclear about whether this was an actual event; he seemed to be asking for directions back to his place in a stunned friendly way. My horse, Pardon Me, was rearing way high and I couldn't put the muzzle of my shotgun at him. Then Jeb rode in, plumes shivering. He slashed the man deep in the shoulder with his saber. The man knelt down, closing his eyes as if to pray. Jeb rode next to me. What a body odor he had. On his horse, he said:

"Finish that poor Christian off, soldier."

My horse settled down and I blew the man over. Pardon Me reared at the shot and tore away in his own race down a vacant meadow—fortunate for me, since I never had to look at the carnage but only thought of holding on.

After McClellan placed himself back on the York, we slipped through Mary-land and here we are in Pennsylvania. We go spying and cavorting and looting. I'm wearing out. Pardon Me, I think, feels the lunacy even in this smooth countryside. We're too far from home. We are not defending our beloved Dixie anymore. We're just bandits and maniacal. The gleam in the men's eyes tells this. Everyone is getting crazier on the craziness of being simply too far from home for decent return. It is like Ruth in the alien corn, or a troop of men given wings over the terrain they cherished and taken by the wind to trees they do not know.

Jeb leads us. Some days he has the sneer of Satan himself.

Nothing but bad news comes up from home, when it comes.

Lee is valiant but always too few.

All the great bullies I used to see out front are dead or wounded past use.

The truth is, not a one of us except Jeb Stuart believes in anything any longer. The man himself the exception. There is nobody who does not believe in Jeb Stuart. Oh, the zany purposeful eyes, the haggard gleam, the feet of his lean horse high in the air, his rotting flannel shirt under the old soiled grays, and his heroic body odor! He makes one want to be a Christian. I wish I could be one. I'm afraid the only things I count on are chance and safety.

The other night I got my nerve up and asked for him in his tent. When I went in, he had his head on the field desk, dead asleep. The quill was still in his hand. I took up the letter. It was to his wife, Flora. A daguerreotype of her lay next to the paper. It was still wet from Jeb's tears. At the beginning of the letter there was small talk about finding her the black silk she'd always wanted near Gettysburg. Then it continued: "After the shameful defeat at Gettysburg," etc.

I was shocked. I always thought we won at Gettysburg. All the fellows I knew thought we had won. Further, he said:

"The only thing that keeps me going on my mission is the sacred inalienable right of the Confederacy to be the Confederacy, Christ Our Lord, and the memory of your hot hairy jumping nexus when I return."

I placed the letter back on the table. This motion woke him.

I was incredulous that he knew my first name. He looked as if he had not slept a second.

The stories were true.

"Corporal Deed Ainsworth," he said.

"Sorry to wake you, General."

"Your grievance?" he said.

"No one is my friend," I mumbled.

"Because the Creator made you strange, my man. I never met a chap more loyal in the saddle than you. God made us different and we should love His differences as well as His likenesses."

"I'd like to kiss you, General," I said.

"Oh, no. He made me abhor that. Take to your good sleep, my man. We surprise the railroad tomorrow."

"Our raids still entertain you?" I asked.

"Not so much. But I believe our course has been written. We'll kill ten and lose two. Our old Bobbie Lee will smile when we send the nigger back to him with the message. I'll do hell for Lee's smile.''

The nigger came in the tent about then. He was highfalutin, never hardly glanced at me. They had a magnificent bay waiting for the letters. Two soldiers came in and took an armload of missives from General Stuart's trunk, pressing them into the saddlebags. The nigger, in civilian clothes, finally looked at me.

''Who dis?'' he said.

''Corporal Deed Ainsworth; shake hands,'' said General Stuart.

I have a glass shop in Biloxi. I never shook hands with any nigger. Yet the moment constrained me to. He was Jeb's best minstrel. He played the guitar better than anything one might want to hear, and the banjo. His voice singing ''All Hail the Power'' was the only feeling I ever had to fall on my knees and pray. But now he was going back down South as a rider with the messages.

''Ain't shaking hands with no nancy,'' said the nigger. ''They say he lay down with a Choctaw chief in Mississip, say he lick a heathen all over his feathers.''

''You're getting opinions for a nigger, George,'' said Jeb, standing. ''I don't believe Our Lord has room for another nigger's thoughts. You are tiring God when you use your mouth, George.''

''Yessuh,'' said George.

''Do you want to apologize to Corporal Ainsworth?''

''I real sorry. I don't know what I say,'' the nigger said to me. ''General Jeb taught me how to talk and sometimes I justs go on talking to try it out.''

''Ah, my brother George,'' Jeb suddenly erupted.

He rushed to the nigger and threw his arms around him. His eyes were full of tears. He embraced the black man in the manner of my dreams of how he might embrace me.

''My chap, my chum. Don't get yourself killed,'' said Jeb to George. ''Try to look ignorant when you get near the road pickets, same as when I found you and saved you from drink.''

''I loves you too, General Jeb. I ain't touched nothing since you saved me. Promise. I gon look ignorant like you say, tills I get to Richmond. Then I might have me a beer.''

''Even Christ wouldn't deny you that. Ah, my George, there's a heaven where we'll all prosper together. Even this sissy, Corporal Ainsworth.''

They both looked at me benevolently. I felt below the nigger.

George got on the horse and took off South.

At five the next morning we came out of a stand of birches and all of us flew high over the railroad, shooting down the men. I had two stolen repeaters on my hip in the middle of the rout and let myself off Pardon Me. A poor torn Yank, driven out of the attack, with no arm but a kitchen fork, straggled up to me. We'd burned and killed almost everything else.

Stuart rode by me screaming in his rich bass to mount. The blue cavalry was coming across the fire toward us. The wounded man was stabbing me in the chest with his fork. Jeb took his saber out in the old grand style to cleave the man from me. I drew the pistol on my right hip and put it almost against Jeb's nose when he leaned to me.

"You kill him, I kill you, General," I said.

There was no time for a puzzled look, but he boomed out: "Are you happy, Corporal Ainsworth? Are you satisfied, my good man Deed?"

I nodded.

"Go with your nature and remember our Savior!" he shouted, last in the retreat.

I have seen it many times, but there is no glory like Jeb Stuart putting spurs in his sorrel and escaping the Minié balls.

They captured me and sent me to Albany prison, where I write this.

I am well fed and wretched.

A gleeful little floorwipe came in the other day to say they'd killed Jeb in Virginia. I don't think there's much reservoir of self left to me now.

This earth will never see his kind again.

JIMMIE RODGERS

Jimmie Rodgers (1897–1933) of near Meridian, Mississippi, was called not only the Singing Brakeman but also the Father of Country Music. I would no more want to argue with the latter than with the former. America's Blue Yodeler (another thing he was called) pulled commercial hillbilly and black country blues together back in the 1920s, and yet it wasn't until 1964 that a civil rights act passed. One of his songs was called "Whipping That Old TB," but that's what he died of. "His last recording session is one of the most heart-rending episodes in show-business history," writes Bill Malone in Country Music, U.S.A. *"He had become so weak that the Victor company provided him a special cot in a room near the studio. At the conclusion of each recorded take, he lay down until he regained adequate strength for another performance. He recorded almost to the very end; his last session was on May 24, two days before he succumbed in the Taft Hotel. On the day of his death he went to Coney Island on a sight-seeing tour with his private nurse, Cora Bedell, and while there suffered an attack of spasms." Earlier he had performed in blackface with a medicine show, toured in vaudeville, shared a tent-theater bill with a fan dancer, and been named an honorary Texas Ranger. The Taft Hotel no longer exists, but I used to work around the corner from it; on the thirty-seventh anniversary of the Blue Yodeler's death I went up to the desk clerk, identified myself as a writer, and said, "Do you know which room Jimmie Rodgers died in?" The desk clerk said, "You're the second one today. There was some yelling up there, but nobody died."*

"T for Texas (Blue Yodel No. 1)"

T for Texas, T for Tennessee
T for Texas, T for Tennessee
T for Thelma, that gal that made a wreck out of me.

If you don't want me, Mama, you sure don't have to stall
If you don't want me, Mama, you sure don't have to stall
'Cause I can get more women than a passenger train can haul.

I'm gonna buy me a pistol just as long as I'm tall
I'm gonna buy me a pistol just as long as I'm tall
I'm gonna shoot poor Thelma just to see her jump and fall.

I'm going where the water drinks like cherry wine
I'm going where the water drinks like cherry wine
'Cause the Georgia water tastes like turpentine.

I'm gonna buy me a shotgun with a great long shiny barrel
I'm gonna buy me a shotgun with a great long shiny barrel
I'm gonna shoot that rounder that stole away my gal.

Rather drink muddy water and sleep in a hollow log
Rather drink muddy water and sleep in a hollow log
Than to be in Atlanta, treated like a dirty dog.

BILLY EDD WHEELER AND JERRY LIEBER

A product of West Virginia, Wheeler was struggling to make a living writing songs in New York when he saw Who's Afraid of Virginia Woolf?, *which starts off bang-bang-bang right away. This contradicted what he had learned at Yale Drama School: that a play should start slow and build to a climax. But it got him to thinking about how a couple will "go at each other." Which got him started writing "Jackson." He tried out his lengthy first version on Jerry Lieber, of the great Lieber and Stroller songwriting team. Lieber didn't perk up until the last verse, the pepper-sprout one. "Start with that!" cried Lieber. So Billy Edd went back, commenced with the climax, and worked up most of what became a classic lyric best rendered by Johnny Cash and June Carter. The song's co-writer has heretofore been identified as Gaby Rogers, but that was a pseudonym for Lieber, whose added touches included the Japan fan. Nancy Sinatra sang it as "Japan flan," but never mind that.*

"Jackson"

> *Him and Her:*
> We got married in a fever,
> Hotter than a pepper sprout.
> We've been talkin' 'bout Jackson
> Ever since the fire went out.
>
> *Him:*
> I'm goin' to Jackson,
> I'm gonna mess around,
> Yeah, I'm goin' to Jackson,
> Look out, Jackson town.
>
> *Her:*
> Well, go on down to Jackson,

Go ahead and wreck your health.
Go play your hand, ya big-talkin' man,
Make a big fool of yourself.

Yeah, yeah, go to Jackson,
But go comb your hair.
Go and snowball Jackson,
Go ahead and see if I care.

Him:

When I go into that city,
People gonna stoop and bow.
All them women gonna beg me
Teach 'em what they don't know how—

I'm goin' to Jackson,
You turn aloose my coat.
'Cause I'm goin' to Jackson,
"Good bye," that's all she wrote.

Her:

They'll laugh at you in Jackson,
And I'll be dancin' on a pony keg.
They'll lead you 'round town like a scalded hound
With your tail a-tucked between your legs,

Yeah, yeah, go to Jackson,
You big talkin' man.
I'll be waitin' in Jackson
Behind my Japan fan.

BESSIE SMITH

One of the great figures in American music was born in Chattanooga in 1894 and died in Clarksdale, Mississippi, in 1937. Both of her parents died before she was eight. She was billed as the Empress of the Blues. You can go to the Riverside Hotel in

Clarksdale, a Mecca/boardinghouse, and spend the night in the room where Bessie died, because back then it was what passed for a black hospital. She was taken there—not because a white hospital turned her away, as legend would have it, but because nobody even considered taking her to a white hospital—after the car wreck in which she suffered the injuries she died of. I spent the night there myself a couple of years ago, or else I wouldn't pretend to be qualified to edit this anthology. The problem with trying to represent Bessie Smith's humor on the page is the problem with trying to represent the humor of the blues in general on the page: the words are grim or graphic, the humor is in the way they were sung. But the notion of capturing screwing in figures of speech is in itself pretty droll, and these are some authoritative figures.

"Empty Bed Blues"

Bought me a coffee grinder,
The best one I could find.
Bought me a coffee grinder,
The best one I could find.
Oh, he could grind my coffee,
'Cause he had a brand-new grind.

He's deep, deep diver,
With a stroke that can't go wrong.
He's deep, deep diver,
With a stroke that can't go wrong.
Oh, he can touch the bottom,
And his wind holds out so long.

.   .   .   .

He gave me a lesson
That I never had before.
He gave me a lesson
That I never had before.
When he got through teachin',
From my elbows down was sore.

He boiled first my cabbage,
And he made it awful hot.

He boiled first my cabbage,
And he made it awful hot.
When he put in the bacon,
It overflowed the pot.

ERSKINE CALDWELL

Okay, now, Erskine Caldwell. (Born in Newnan, Georgia, 1902.) Generally in Southern humor I go for the salty over the sweet, but when I read Tobacco Road *and* God's Little Acre *I think, "These people put the T in Trashy." Caldwell's minister father and teacher mother were quality folks, intellectually serious and socially conscious, and I can't help feeling that a morbid downlooking fascination on their son's part helped to put that T in there.* Georgia Boy *(1944), in which this story appeared, has more fellow-feeling.*

"My Old Man and the Grass Widow"

When my old man got up earlier than usual and left the house, he did not say where he was going, and Ma was so busy getting ready to do the washing she did not think to ask him.

Usually when he went off like that, and Ma asked him where he was going, he would say he had to see somebody about something on the other side of town, or that he had a little job to attend to not far off. I don't know what he would have said that morning if Ma hadn't been too busy to ask him.

Anyway, he had got up before anybody else and went straight to the kitchen and cooked his own breakfast. By the time I was up and dressed, he had finished hitching Ida to the cart. He climbed up on the seat and started driving out into the street.

"Can't I go, Pa?" I asked him. I ran down the street beside the cart, holding on to the sideboard and begging to go along. "Please let me go, Pa!" I said.

"Not now, son," he said, slapping Ida with the reins and whipping her into a trot. "If I need you later, I'll send for you."

They clattered down the street and turned the corner out of sight.

When I got back to the house, Ma was in the kitchen working over the cook-stove. I sat down and waited for something to eat, but I did not say anything about Pa. It made me feel sad to be left behind like that when Pa and Ida were going some place, and I didn't feel like talking, even to Ma. I just sat at the table by the stove and waited.

Ma ate in a hurry and went out into the yard to kindle the fire underneath the washpot.

Early that afternoon one of the neighbors, Mrs. Singer, who lived on the corner below us, came walking into our backyard. I saw her before Ma did, because I had been sitting on the porch steps almost all day waiting for Pa to come back.

Mrs. Singer went over to the bench where Ma was washing. She stood and didn't say anything for a while. Then all at once she leaned over the tub and asked Ma if she knew where Pa was.

"Most likely sleeping in the shade somewhere," Ma said, not even straightening up from the scrub board. "Unless he's too lazy to move out of the sun."

"I'm in dead earnest, Martha," Mrs. Singer said, coming closer to Ma. "I really am."

Ma turned around and looked at me on the porch.

"Run along into the house, William," she said crossly.

I went up on the porch as far as the kitchen door. I could hear there just as good.

"Now, Martha," Mrs. Singer said, leaning over and putting her hands on the edge of the tub. "I'm not a gossip, and I don't want you to think I'm anything like one. But I thought you would want to hear the truth."

"What is it?" Ma asked.

"Mr. Stroup is out at that Mrs. Weatherbee's this very minute," she said quickly. "And that's not all, either. He's been out there at her house all day long, too. Just him and her!"

"How do you know?" Ma asked, straightening up.

"I passed there and saw him with my own eyes, Martha," Mrs. Singer said. "I decided right then and there that it was my duty to tell you."

Mrs. Weatherbee was a young grass widow who lived all alone just outside of town. She had been married for only two months when her husband left her one morning and never came back.

"What is Morris Stroup doing out there at that place?" Ma said, raising her voice just as if she were blaming everything on Mrs. Singer.

"That's not for me to say, Martha," she said, backing away from Ma. "But I considered it my Christian duty to warn you."

She left the yard and hurried out of sight around the corner of the house. Ma leaned over and sloshed the water in the tub until a lot of it splashed out. After a minute or two she turned around and started across the yard, drying her hands on her apron as she went.

"William," she said, calling me, "you go inside the house and stay there until I come back. I want to think you are obeying me, William. Do you hear me, William?"

"I hear you, Ma," I said, backing toward the door.

She walked out of the yard in a hurry and went up the street. That was the direction to take to get to Mrs. Weatherbee's house. She lived about three-fourths of a mile from where we did.

I stood on the back porch out of sight until Ma crossed the street at the next corner, and then I ran around the house and cut across Mr. Joe Hammond's vacant lot toward the creek. I knew a short cut to Mrs. Weatherbee's house, because I had passed by it a lot of times going rabbit hunting with Handsome Brown. Handsome had always said it was a good idea to know short cuts to every place, because there was no telling when one would come in handy just when it was needed the most. I was glad I knew a short cut to Mrs. Weatherbee's, because Ma would have seen me if I had gone behind her.

I ran all the way out there, keeping close to the willows along the creek just like Handsome and I had done every time we went out there looking for rabbits. Just before I got to Mrs. Weatherbee's house I stopped and looked around for Pa. I couldn't see him anywhere about Mrs. Weatherbee's house. I couldn't even see her.

Then I crossed the creek and ran up the lane toward the house, keeping close to the fence that was covered over with honeysuckle vines.

It didn't take long to get as far as the garden, and as soon as I looked around the corner post I saw Ida standing at the garden gate. All she was doing was standing there switching flies with her tail. I think she must have recognized me right away, because she pricked up both ears and held them straight up in the air while she watched me.

I had started crawling around the garden fence when I looked across Mrs. Weatherbee's backyard and saw Ma coming jumping. She was leaping over the cotton rows, headed straight for the backyard.

Just then I heard Mrs. Weatherbee giggle. I looked toward the house, and I didn't even have to get up off my knees to see her and my old man. Mrs. Weatherbee kept it up, giggling as if she were out of her head, just exactly like the girls at school did when they knew a secret about something. At first all I could see was Mrs. Weatherbee's bare legs and feet dangling over the side of the porch. Then I saw my old man standing on the ground tickling her with a chicken feather. Mrs. Weatherbee was lying on her back on the porch, and he was standing there tickling her bare toes for all he was worth. Every once in a while he would sort of leap off the ground when she giggled the loudest. She had taken off her shoes and stockings, because I could see them in a heap on the porch.

Mrs. Weatherbee was not old like the other married women, because she had been going to high school in town when she got married that spring, and she had been a grass widow for only three or four months. She lay there on the porch squirming on her back, kicking her feet over the edge, and screaming and giggling like she was going to die if my old man didn't stop tickling her with the chicken feather. Every once in a while she would laugh as loud as she could, and that made everything funnier than ever, because when she did that my old man would leap up into the air like a kangaroo.

I had forgotten all about Ma, because I was so busy listening to Mrs. Weatherbee and watching my old man, but just then I looked across the yard and saw Ma coming. She made straight for the porch where they were.

Everything happened so fast from then on that it was hard to follow what was taking place. The first thing I knew after that was when Ma grabbed my old man by the hair on his head and slung him backward, clear off his feet. Then she grabbed one of Mrs. Weatherbee's bare feet and bit it as hard as she could. Mrs. Weatherbee let out a scream that must have been heard all the way to Sycamore.

Mrs. Weatherbee sat up then, and Ma grabbed at her, getting a good grip on the neck of her calico dress. It ripped away from her just like a piece of loose wallpaper. Mrs. Weatherbee screamed again when she saw her dress go.

By that time Ma had turned on my old man. He was sitting on the ground, too scared to move an inch.

"What do you mean by this, Morris Stroup!" she yelled at him.

"Why, Martha, I only just come out here to do a good deed for a poor widow woman," he said, looking up at Ma the way he does when he's scared. "Her garden sass needed cultivating, and so I just hitched up Ida and came out here to plow it a little for her."

Ma whirled around and grabbed at Mrs. Weatherbee again. This time the only way she could get a grip on Mrs. Weatherbee was to clutch her by the hair.

"I reckon, Morris Stroup," Ma said, turning her head and looking down at my old man, "that tickling a grass widow's toes with a chicken feather makes the garden sass grow better!"

"Now, Martha," he said, sliding backward on the ground away from her, "I didn't think of it that way at all. I just wanted to do the widow woman a kindly deed when I saw her sass growing weedy."

"Shut up, Morris Stroup!" Ma said. "The next thing you'll be doing will be putting the blame on Ida."

"Now, Martha," my old man said, sliding away some more on the seat of his pants, "that ain't no way to look at things. She's a poor widow woman."

"I'll look at it the way I please," Ma said, stamping her foot. "I have to go out and strip the leaves off milk weeds for enough food to keep body and soul together while you go around the country with a mule and plow cultivating grass widows' gardens. Not to mention tickling their bare toes with chicken feathers, besides. That's a pretty howdy-do!''

My old man opened his mouth as though he wanted to say something, but Ma turned Mrs. Weatherbee loose and grabbed him by his overall straps before he could speak a single word. Then she led him at a fast pace to the garden post where Ida was tied up. She took Ida by the bridle with one hand, still pulling my old man with the other, and started across the cotton field toward home. Ida knew something was wrong, because she trotted to keep up with Ma without being told to.

I raced down the lane to the creek, and hurried home by the short cut. I got there only a minute ahead of them.

When Ma came into our backyard leading Ida and my old man, I couldn't keep from snickering a little at the way both of them looked. Ida looked every bit as sheepish as my old man.

Ma glanced up at me standing on the porch.

"Stop that going-on, William," she said crossly. "Sometimes I think you're just as bad as your Pa."

My old man cut his eyes around and looked up at me. He winked with his right eye and went across the yard to Ida's stall, following Ma as meek as a pup. Just before they went into the shed, my old man stooped down and picked up a chicken feather that one of the hens had shed. While Ma was leading Ida inside, he stuffed the feather into his pocket out of sight.

ROGER MILLER

I just love Roger Miller, who wrote wonderful lyrics and said things like "If your toes and fingers fail you, Baby, you can always count on me" and "How can a chicken eat all the time and never get fat in the face?" In 1992, the year before he died, I had the pleasure of appearing with him on Garrison Keillor's radio show. Miller was amiable, sober, every now and then saying something like "I'm looking for my second wind. I broke the first one." Back in the 1960s when he was writing and recording songs like "King of the Road," "Engine, Engine, Number Nine," "My Uncle Used to Love Me but She Died," and "I've Been a Long Time Leaving but I'll Be a Long Time Gone," somebody asked a member of his band, "How long has Roger been up?" and the bandmember's answer was "Well, I've only been with him for three years. I don't know how long he'd been up, up to then." He was one of the original Nashville roarers. After he settled down, he wrote the score for Big River, *a musical based on* Huckleberry Finn. *He was born in Fort Worth in 1936. Charles Portis wanted him to play Norwood in the movie of* Norwood, *but of course Hollywood had to have Glen Campbell.*

"Dang Me"

Well here I sit high, gettin' ideas,
Ain't nothin' but a fool would live like this.
Out all night and runnin' wild
Woman sittin' home with a month-old child.

Dang me, dang me,
They oughta take a rope and hang me
High from the highest tree—
Woman would you weep for me.

Just sittin' 'round drinkin' with the rest of the guys,
Six rounds bought and I bought five.
Spent the groceries and half the rent,
Lack fourteen dollars havin' twenty-seven cents.

Dang me, dang me,
They oughta take a rope and hang me,
High from the highest tree—
Woman would you weep for me.

They say roses are red and violets are purple,
Sugar is sweet and so's maple syrple,
And I'm the seventh out of seven sons.
My Pappy was a pistol, I'm a son of a gun.

Dang me, dang me,
They oughta take a rope and hang me,
High from the highest tree—
Woman would you weep for me.

FERROL SAMS

There's a story by Dr. Sams—a practicing physician in Fayetteville, Georgia—called "The Widow's Mite" that I recommend to you, but I'm going to tell you something now, and you don't have to agree with me, but hear me out: Southern humor is just about a long-winded something or other, isn't it? Reading it, over the course of a lifetime, is one thing, if you have the time for it, but collecting it into one package that a body could lift—I tell you, there are times when I believe to my soul I wish I'd been given Noah's charge to keep instead. That aforesaid widow's blessed contribution to our region's store of merriment is over twice as long as anything else in this book but the Faulkner story and it's half again as long as that. So I'm representing Dr. Sams with two little snippets from his collection of reminiscences The Passing, *which aren't longer than anything except this note here, which I guess is saying something at that.*

"Saint Roxie"

All farm families have their memories of the washplace, of Monday morning, but I think my wife's grandmother was the most likely candidate for sainthood in that department. It may take another hundred years or so for the remembrances of her to be smoothed and softened enough, but she deserves it; she could quite capably fill the role.

I never saw her. She lived and died three hundred miles and ten years from my awareness, but I know her. So vivid is her memory among her descendants, so real her legend in her native community, that I have the same reverence, respect, affection and fear that she engendered in all of them. Her genes swim in my wife and my children and are awesome when they surface. It will wear a man out just to behold them.

Her name was Roxie. She was born into the farming culture of northwest Florida after The War, but wasted little time either pondering the privilege of gentle birth or bemoaning the loss of previous opulence. Roxie was a pioneer woman but did not have to leave home to be one. She would have been a pioneer no matter where she was. She took fate by the scruff of the neck, shook it into a shape that suited her, and went vigorously about her business, her family in her train. Reconstruction may have been overwhelming the South, but it was of peripheral concern to her. Reconstruction to Roxie was an active pursuit of her own, an opportunity to change people and events that fell short of her expectations.

She snatched up the threads of Southern sun, long-leaf pines, sandy fields, cypress-stained creeks, Federal oppression, Baptist morality, hard labor; laid them all into the loom of family pride with inflexible opinion; and wove a tapestry that will endure for ages. She asked no mercy; she made her way.

Roxie married a man as well connected as she. He was named Badger, a pleasant man, friendly, tolerant and easygoing. They sent all their sons to college and graduate school from a farm in Gadsden County, Florida, before shade tobacco made the area prosperous. If they felt this a boastful accomplishment, they never let on; they just kept working and going to church. Roxie's supervising eye never flickered.

One Monday in her youth, she was at the washplace. The recurring trips to the washpot, the pounding block, the scrub board and the rinsing tub were rhythmically under way. She had broken a sweat and was competently disposing of Monday. Over the fence in the adjacent sandy field, Badger was steadily plowing corn. The lark was on the wing, and all was right with Roxie's world. In unexpected reversal, the snail became impaled on the thorn.

Badger had a visitor. A neighbor from a distant farm came by in his wagon and hailed him. While Roxie worked, Badger whoa-ed his mule and propped on the handle of his plowstock, feet crossed in a fresh-turned furrow as he ignored the unplowed corn and visited with his friend. Courtesy was a cardinal virtue to Badger.

Roxie's step became faster; she beat the work pants more vigorously; she scrubbed in a frenzy with elbows high. The visit continued. Roxie poked her boiling clothes so hard that water spilled over and hissed in the hot ashes. Still Badger played the role of the gracious host in the cornfield, neighborly and cordial.

Roxie endured it as long as she could. She flung a stickload of clothes from the pot into the scrubbing tub and stepped with purpose to the fence. She cupped her hands around her mouth, never acknowledging the neighbor's presence.

"Badger!" she bellowed. "You, Badger! You keep that mule a-turning!"

"A Little Full"

Before I was born we had saloons in Georgia. My granddaddy told me. After I was born we had Prohibition. My daddy told me. Each of them was an expert, and they knew what they were talking about.

My granddaddy said that every little settlement of any note used to have a wooden building where a man could buy a drink of red liquor and visit with neighbors over the course of a rainy afternoon that precluded farming. Sometimes it was a long rainy spell, and sometimes a man got carried away in conviviality, and sometimes a man just plain had a hankering for it. Not infrequently a citizen would get a dram or two too many, a condition my granddaddy referred to as being "a little full."

He loved to tell about the night his nephew came home when he was more than a little full. He never referred to that nephew by just his first name, but always as "Will Sams." Will Sams had married a Hodnett, a fact that gave a man forever a certain stature and luster of respectability in our community that could be diminished but never erased by misdeeds on his part. The Hodnett girls were ladies, they had been raised right, they were the supreme example of "Blood will tell," and blood was what counted in Fayette County because the environment was the same for everyone and didn't amount to much.

"Will Sams came home well after dark one night; his wife and children were already in bed. Mamie (she was a Hodnett) heard him bumping up the steps and falling against the doorjamb and got up to let him in.

"Will Sams evidently had got hold of some bad liquor that evening, and more than likely had more than a bait of it, for he was pretty full. Will Sams was bad to drink every now and then. He just fell in the door that night and grabbed his wife.

" 'Mamie, I'm sick.'

"Mamie (she was a saint as well as a Hodnett) said, 'Yes, darling, I know you're sick.' And Will Sams begged, 'Help me, Mamie.'

"Mamie was leading him to the bed fast as she could, with him as limber-legged as he was, and she said. 'Yes, darling, I'm helping you.' She got him to the bed and laid out on it, and Will Sams said, 'Mamie, I tell you I'm sick. I mean, I'm sick enough to die. Mamie, I want you to pray for me.'

"And Mamie was pulling off his shoes and socks and she said, 'Of course, darling, I'll pray for you.'

"And Will Sams hollered, 'Mamie, I mean it when I say I want you to pray for me. I really think I'm dying. I want you to pray for me now. Quit messing around with them shoes and socks, and pray for me right now, this very minute. Before it's too late.'

"And that sweet, patient Mamie did as she was told. She knelt down by the side of the bed, folded her hands, bowed her head and said, 'Dear Lord, look down in thy infinite love and mercy and take pity on my poor drunken husband.'

"And Will Sams raised his head up off of the pillow and hollered, 'Hell, Mamie! Don't tell Him I'm drunk!' "

MARILYN NELSON WANIEK

"Grass Turned Out Green"

On the morning of the seventh day
God didn't plan to rest.
God was disgusted.
God looked around
and God said,
What's going on?
Things I'd planned to fly
walk, things I'd planned to swim
crawl around in the grass.
Grass turned out green,
water wet, everything's
all mixed up.

And God sat down
on a big rock
to think about
the long task of correction.
Then God saw
a shimmer on the water,

sky curdling into clouds
and all the innocent ugliness
of the world.
And God said,
Maybe that's good enough.
I'll let it be.
And God lay down and rested.
This was the seventh day.

This is our seventh year together.
Our plans are mouse tracks in a field of snow.
Shadows circle like owls around us and the fox is near.
We lie in the grass,
embrace each other's weakness,
have one thing God forgot:
someone to rest with
and to blame.

ZORA NEALE HURSTON

"Love"

So much for what I know about the major courses in love. However, there are some minor courses which I have not grasped so well, and would be thankful for some coaching and advice.

First is the number of men who pant in my ear on short acquaintance, "You passionate thing! I can see you are just *burning* up! Most men would be disappointing to you. It takes a man like me for you. Ahhh! I know that you will just wreck me! Your eyes and your lips tell me a lot. You are a walking furnace!" This amazes me sometimes. Often when this is whispered gustily into my ear, I am feeling no more amorous than a charter member of the Union League Club. I may be thinking of turnip greens with dumplings, or more royalty checks, and here is a man who visualizes me on a divan sending the world up in smoke. It has happened so often that I have come to expect it. There must be something about me that looks sort of couchy. Maybe it is a birthmark. My mother could have been frightened by a bed. There is nothing to be done about it, I suppose. But, I must say about these mirages that seem to rise around me, that the timing is way off on occasion.

Number two is, a man may lose interest in me and go where his fancy leads him, and we can still meet as friends. But if I get tired and let on about it, he is certain to become an enemy of mine. That forces me to lie like the cross-ties from New York to Key West. I have learned to frame it so that I can claim to be deserted and devastated by him. Then he goes off with a sort of twilight tenderness for me, wondering what it is that he's got that brings so many women down! I do not even have to show real tears. All I need to do is show my stricken face and dash away from him to hide my supposed heartbreak and renunciation. He understands that I am fleeing before his allure so that I can be firm in my resolution to save the pieces. He knew all along that he was a hard man to resist, so he visualized my dampened pillow. It is a good thing that some of them have sent roses as a poultice and stayed away. Otherwise, they might have found the poor, heartbroken wreck of a thing all dressed to kill and gone out for a high-heel time with the new interest, who has the new interesting things to say and do. Now, how to break off without acting deceitful and still keep a friend?

Number three is kin to Number two, in a way. Under the spell of moonlight, music, flowers, or the cut and smell of good tweeds, I sometimes feel the divine urge for an hour, a day or maybe a week. Then it is gone and my interest returns to corn pone and mustard greens, or rubbing a paragraph with a soft cloth. Then my ex-sharer of a mood calls up in a fevered voice and reminds me of every silly thing I said, and eggs me on to say them all over again. It is the third presentation of turkey hash after Christmas. It is asking me to be a seven-sided liar. Accuses me of being faithless and inconsistent if I don't. There is no inconsistency there. I was sincere for the moment in which I said the things. It is strictly a matter of time. It was true for the moment, but the next day or the next week, is not that moment. . . .

I have a strong suspicion, but I can't be sure, that much that passes for constant love is a golded-up moment walking in its sleep. Some people know that it is the walk of the dead, but in desperation and desolation, they have staked everything on life after death and the resurrection, so they haunt the graveyard. . . .

But pay no attention to what I say about love, for as I said before, it may not mean a thing. It is my own bathtub singing. Just because my mouth opens up like a prayer book, it does not just have to flap like a Bible. And then again, anybody whose mouth is cut cross-ways is given to lying, unconsciously as well as knowingly. So pay my few scattering remarks no mind as to love in general. I know only my part.

Anyway, it seems to be the unknown country from which no traveler ever returns. What seems to be a returning pilgrim is another person born in the strange country with the same-looking ears and hands. He is a stranger to the person who fared forth, and a stranger to family and old friends. He is clothed in mystery henceforth and forever. So, perhaps nobody knows, or can tell, any more than I. Maybe the old Negro folk rhyme tells all there is to know:

> Love is a funny thing; Love is a blossom;
> If you want your finger bit, poke it at a possum.

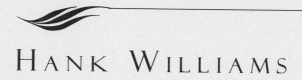

HANK WILLIAMS

Old Hank. Born near Georgiana, Alabama, in 1923, died on New Year's Day, 1953, somewhere between Montgomery, Alabama, and Oak Hill, West Virginia, in the backseat of his Cadillac. Which was being driven by a man named Charles Carr—how'd you like for it to have been you? "Hank? I'm stopping for gas, you want me to get you a Coke? Hank?" Did you ever hear a robin weep. . . . Aw, man.

"Jambalaya (on the Bayou)"

> Good-bye Joe, me gotta go,
> Me oh my oh,
> Me gotta go pole the pirogue
> Down the bayou.
>
> My Yvonne, the sweetest one,
> Me oh my oh,
> Son of a gun, we'll have big fun
> On the bayou.
>
> Jambalaya, crawfish pie,
> Filet gumbo,

'Cause tonight I'm gonna see
Ma cher ami-o.

Pick guitar, fill fruit jar
And be gay-o.
Son of a gun, we'll have big fun
On the bayou.

Thibodaux, Fontaineaux,
The place is buzzin'.
Kinfolk come to see Yvonne
By the dozen.

Dress in style, go hog wild,
Me oh my oh,
Son of a gun, we'll have big fun
On the bayou.

WILLIE NELSON

Well it's three in the morning and I'm getting to where I can almost see the end of all the notes for this book, and I just put an old Willie album on. The night life ain't no good life, but . . . Willie was born in Fort Worth in 1933, grew up in Abbott, Texas, and moved in 1972 from Nashville to Austin, where he established what they called outlaw country music and where he continues to out-outlaw everybody else without really pushing it. A close friend of his told me once, "You can't predict him. Well, sometimes you can."

"Sister's Comin' Home/Down at the Corner Beer Joint"

Sister's comin' home
Mama's gon' let her sleep the whole day long

The whole day long
Sister's comin' home
Mama's gon' let her sleep the whole day long

Sister's comin' home
Mama don't like the man who done her wrong
    Who done her wrong
Sister's comin' home
Mama don't like the man who done her wrong

Sister's comin' home
Mama's gon' let her sleep the whole day long
The mirror's gonna tell her just how long she's been gone

Down at the corner beer joint
Dancin' to the rock and roll
Sister likes to do it Lord, Sister likes to move her soul

Down at the corner beer joint
Dancin' on the hardwood floor
Her jeans fit a little bit tighter than they did before
    Than they did before
    Than they did before
Her jeans fit a little bit tighter than they did before

Down at the corner beer joint
Dancin' to the rock and roll
Sister likes to do it Lord, Sister likes to move her soul
    Likes to move her soul
    Likes to move her soul
Sister likes to do it Lord, Sister likes to move her soul

SARAH GILBERT

One of my favorite lines by Sarah Gilbert is when the eponymous narrator of Dixie
Riggs—*after telling about a boyfriend who doesn't sound like he was half worth her*

while—observes to the reader: "You wouldn't have liked him. Still, I did." This selection is from Gilbert's first novel, which inspired Vanity Fair *to call her "the funniest woman writer from the South since Flannery O'Connor." Unless Bailey White and Willie Nelson, or somebody (I just pick those names out of the air), have run off together without my knowing about it, Gilbert and her fellow South Carolinian William Price Fox are the only two people in this anthology, here, who are married to each other.*

from *Hairdo*

"Why, I'll be," said Ronder, handing Thurston the tray of cold cuts and wiping her hands in the air. "There's old Louise Stokes. I've been trying to get in touch with that old fool for days." She walked away, just like that, infuriating Miss Ruby, happy to get away from her and on to Louise.

Louise was just as happy to see Ronder. "Ronder!" she squealed. She pulled her into the bathroom, along with a woman named Millie Loudermilk. Ronder had never met her, but like a true beautician, the first thing she noticed was her hair. It looked horrible. It looked like she had slept in pink dimestore sponge rollers and then not bothered to brush out the roller marks.

"Honey!" Louise squealed again, slamming the door and clutching Ronder's hands. "Did somebody tell me right? Are you really going back to work?"

"That's what you heard all right," said Ronder, proudly.

"Well let me ask you this," Louise said, lowering her voice, "you and Buck aren't having any marital troubles now, are you?" Her gold rings glinted as she squeezed Ronder's hands even tighter.

"Buck and me?" laughed Ronder. "Absolutely not! Where'd you ever get an idea like that?"

"Well," said Louise, dropping her hands and pulling a tube of lipstick out of her purse. She began circling her lips with it. "That's not what Earline said. She said you were practically divorced." She pulled the lipstick away from her mouth and focused in hard on Ronder as she said the word "divorced."

"Ha! Buck and me, divorced?" Ronder laughed a small, hollow laugh. "You have got to be kidding. She said that?"

Louise's head bounced up and down, eager for the news, her eyes sparkling like her rings.

"Hon," said Ronder, flipping her hand at Louise, "put your mind to rest. We're doing just fine. As a matter of fact, Buck's taking me to Myrtle Beach the next free minute he's got."

"Well, from what Earline tells me," said Louise, pressing her newly painted lips together, "I understand he's got all the free time in the world right now." She popped her lips right in front of Ronder's face. "Hand me that Kleenex Millie, hon, would you?" asked Louise, pushing her purse at Millie to hold. "According to Earline," she said, "he fell off a ladder and hasn't painted since."

Louise took the Kleenex from Millie without even looking at her, pushing her away from the mirror so she could blot her lips.

"Oh, Louise," said Ronder, "it was just a tiny accident. He'll be back to work this week."

Someone knocked on the bathroom door and Louise shouted, "SOMEone is IN here! Millie, hon, reach in my pocketbook and hand me my powder, will you?" She began powdering the back of her neck and said, "Is that so? That isn't what I heard."

"Rest assured, Louise, we're doing just fine." Suddenly Ronder couldn't breathe. She had to get out of the bathroom. She opened the door to leave, but Louise snapped her compact shut, grabbed her purse and darted out ahead of her all in the same motion, past a line of women all waiting to use the bathroom.

With Louise, it was Louise first, always.

"Well, well," said Earline, who had been standing in line but was now descending on Ronder like a bad nightmare, her feathers rustling as she patted Ronder on the back, "some little angel told me that Buck didn't come home the other night."

"Some little angel told you wrong," Ronder said, walking away. She couldn't take one more bad news Buck line.

"Let's not talk about Buck," said Louise, picking up on this, motioning for Earline to follow, leaving Millie behind. "Let him drag his own name through the mud. What I want to know about is this Gladys Bessinger thing. Some story, isn't it?"

They went over to the food and began filling their paper plates with green bean casserole, three bean salad, cole slaw, honey baked ham, and other entrées and side dishes. Ronder listened to Louise go on and on about Gladys while she watched Earline eat a little of her cole slaw and then a little of her ham and then just enough of her mashed potatoes until they were leveled and in even proportion to everything else. Then she watched her go around her plate one more time with the same precision, careful to keep her feathers out of her food.

Louise, on the other hand, was eating all of one thing before she started in on another.

"But the real Gladys story," said Louise, finishing her green beans, "is that she closed down her shop because she was on drugs."

"Louise, that can't be true," said Ronder. "Gladys? I just couldn't believe that."

"Well believe it," said Earline, coming in with her two cents worth, taking another bite of ham. "I know for a fact that she went to the doctor's and he gave her some pills to help her lose weight. She just started taking them all the time."

"That's right," said Louise, dabbing at the corner of her lips with the corner of her napkin. "She got to the point where she was always talking, talking, talking, so fast you could barely understand her. You couldn't get a word in edgewise."

Earline had one eye on her mashed potatoes and one eye on Millie, sitting across the room with Riley. "Just look at her, would you," she said, interrupting, "she's got him pulling out his swords now."

"He must be in heaven," said Louise.

A woman they didn't know walked up to the table and everyone quit talking. The woman, who had come up for a whole plate of food, felt so uncomfortable by their silence that she just picked up a small brownie and left.

Earline eyed the woman's hips as she left and said, not particularly whispering, "Honey, you'd have done better with some of that cole slaw."

Ronder, who had just taken a sip of her Coke, almost choked. "You are so funny, Earline," she said, wiping her mouth.

"She is though, isn't she?" said Louise, not laughing.

Ronder looked over at Millie, who seemed to be making great progress with Riley. He had her on the couch now and they were looking at a big coffee table book together.

"Isn't that something," said Earline, still trying to make Ronder laugh. "I've seen that book three times now and all it is is a bunch of black and white pictures of a bunch of soldiers standing around."

Ronder pointed her plastic fork over at Millie. "Well, if you ask me, she sure looks like she's enjoying it."

"She's like a little dog," said Earline. "She follows anyone around who pays her the slightest bit of attention. Which reminds me," she said, putting down her plate and digging in her pocketbook and pulling out an 8½ by 11 pink flyer with hand drawn flowers bordering the edges. "How about this?" She held it up for everybody to read:

CELEBRITY STYLING
presents . . .
Madame Ronder!
She does makeovers, manicures,
pedicures and yes even

bikini waxings!
Now is the season to tell your husband,
"YES, I go to Mademoiselle Ronder and
am a new woman from head to toe!"
Grand Opening of CHEZ Ronder Room!

Ronder took a deep breath and grabbed the announcement. "Umm, can I have this?" She didn't even wait for a reply.

She found Miss Ruby in front of the Blueberry Bundt Cake that Millie Loudermilk had brought, examining the piece she had just sliced.

"Miss Ruby," she said, furious. She was waving the flyer at her. "Miss Ruby, I didn't tell you I was coming back yet. How could you? How could you, Miss Ruby? I am so embarrassed!"

"I don't know who made this cake but it isn't even near ready. Would you take a look at this," said Miss Ruby, pointing to the gray pastey looking dough in the middle of the cake. Then she looked up at Ronder and saw the tears. "Oh don't go getting all sensitive about it dear. Just think of the money you're going to be making. And did I tell you?" Miss Ruby put her arm around Ronder and they walked together. "We are going to be expanding, and not only that, we're going to Atlanta to that famous Hair Show. I'm paying everybody's way and we're going to have a real good time. Here here, don't cry now."

She gave Ronder a handkerchief that had the silhouette of her updo monogrammed on it. "Wipe your eyes now." They stopped walking and she pulled Ronder's head onto her massive chest. "I'll tell you what. We'll get us a penthouse suite and live it up just the way we used to. Would you like that?"

Miss Ruby had always been very generous with her girls. Every Christmas she gave them elaborate gifts. Lockets with diamonds, gold chains with lockets, rings with opals and pearls, and these were just the stocking stuffers. The big present came when Miss Ruby rented out the fanciest suite there was at the downtown Thunderbird Motor Inn and pretended that she and her girls were far away at some exotic place. Once she'd even decorated a suite to look like a Las Vegas Casino and brought in a roulette wheel and Ruby and her girls gambled all night long.

Ronder missed those times more than anything, and before she knew it, Buck was fuzzing out of her head, being replaced with the good old Miss Ruby days, and she was nodding her head and drying her eyes.

That's when all the commotion began.

Someone yelled, "It's Gladys! It's got to be Gladys!"

Then someone else said, "That wasn't Gladys. It just looked like Gladys."

"Come on," said Thurston, "who else do you know that drives a little red Corvette?"

On hearing this, Miss Ruby flounced to the front door and saw the tail end of what she was sure was Gladys' tiny sports car drive by.

"That was Gladys, all right," said Ronder, who was looking over her shoulder. "That was her plain as day."

"All she had to do was talk to me and tell me what was going on. I would've gladly helped her," said Louise.

Earline took Ruby's arm. "Miss Ruby, I bought her the cutest little birthday present, I swear I did. Just a darling little scarf, but you know what I'm going to do? I'm going to give it to you instead. I'll bring it my next appointment."

Miss Ruby pushed at her hair and picked at her stomach and, in her best celebrity posture, she began walking around Riley's house comforting all of Bebe Pointer's friends. Not so much comforting them about Bebe, though, as about Gladys, who had, they all felt, abandoned them. And as she did so, Miss Ruby went off into a daydream. She knew that right now, right this very minute, the contractors were in her shop working away like busy little ants. She had this perfect image of what her place was going to look like when Tuesday rolled around. Never again would these women ever have to worry about going some other place to have their hair done. From now on, the world of hair was going to belong to Ruby McSwain, and only to Ruby McSwain.

A small woman in a forest green pant suit tapped Miss Ruby right out of her dream, saying, "If I didn't know any better, Miss Ruby, I'd think somebody ordered this weather for the funeral. The rain has just ruined my hair!"

"I guarantee it," said an even smaller woman dressed in a seersucker suit. "You know, I remember a time when I was on a business trip and my boss and I were coming in out of the rain, on our way to a very important dinner meeting, I must add. And when we got in the elevator, his eyes got real big and he said, 'What happened to you?!' He was horrified. You should have seen his face. So I got to the ladies room as fast as I could, and the first thing I saw was my Red Flame temporary rinse running all down my neck, soaking into my collar and my shirt, straight through. Imagine how embarrassing that was." She nodded knowing everyone else knew exactly what she was talking about. "Since then," she continued, "I've gotten a little grayer and switched to White Minx, but I swear, if my girl puts too much on, even that will rub off on my pillowcases at night."

"Ain't it the truth!" joined in another woman. "And another thing about these rinses. They may make us look good, but have you ever noticed how when you go to the beach, that salt water makes that rinse get all sticky?"

"No, hon, that's the hairspray," said Thurston, walking up to them, trying to drum up some business. "Hairspray always does that. Now mousse, mousse is where it's at."

The woman who had told the business trip story started laughing and said,

"Now isn't this just something? Wouldn't Bebe just love to know that we were all sitting around in her living room talking about hair? It would be just like her, wouldn't it, to want to talk about her hair at her own funeral?"

H. L. MENCKEN

Well now of course old evil Teutonic Baltimorean Mencken vilified the South, but he vilified it with a feeling. And some people want to give him some credit for stimulating the Southern Literary Renaissance, which followed fairly hard upon his 1917 essay "The Sahara of the Bozart," which argued zestfully that there wasn't anything in the South that any person of taste could get enthusiastic about. Reading Mencken made Richard Wright decide he wanted to be a writer—his first step was to read every book mentioned in Mencken's book Prejudices. *You might call Mencken expansively narrow-minded, or you might say he painted the narrow-mindedness of others with a mighty broad brush. Whatever you call him, you can't tell me he wasn't funny. He wrote the following closely observed diatribe in July 1925, "on a roaring hot Sunday afternoon in a Chattanooga hotel room," according to him, "naked above the waist and with only a pair of BVDs below."*

"The Hills of Zion"

It was hot weather when they tried the infidel Scopes at Dayton, Tenn., but I went down there very willingly, for I was eager to see something of evangelical Christianity as a going concern. In the big cities of the Republic, despite the endless efforts of consecrated men, it is laid up with a wasting disease. The very Sunday-school superintendents, taking jazz from the stealthy radio, shake their fire-proof legs; their pupils, moving into adolescence, no longer respond to the proliferating hormones by enlisting for missionary service in Africa, but resort to necking instead. Even in Dayton, I found, though the job was up to do execution upon Scopes, there was a strong smell of antinomianism. The nine churches of the village were all half empty on Sunday, and weeds choked their yards. Only two or three of the resident pastors managed to sustain themselves by their ghostly science; the rest had to take orders for mail-order pantaloons or work in the adjacent strawberry fields; one, I heard, was a barber. On the courthouse green a score of sweating theologians debated the darker passages of Holy Writ day and night, but I soon found that they were all volunteers, and that the local faithful, while interested in their exegesis as an intellectual exercise, did not permit it to impede the indigenous debaucheries. Exactly twelve minutes after I reached the village I was taken in tow by a Christian man and introduced to the favorite tipple of the Cumberland Range: half corn liquor and half Coca-Cola. It seemed a dreadful dose to me, but I found that the Dayton illuminati got it down with gusto, rubbing their tummies and rolling their eyes. I include among them the chief local proponents of the Mosaic cosmogony. They were all hot for Genesis, but their faces were far too florid to belong to teetotalers, and when a pretty girl came tripping down the main street, which was very often, they reached for the places where their neckties should have been with all the amorous enterprise of movie actors. It seemed somehow strange.

An amiable newspaper woman of Chattanooga, familiar with those uplands, presently enlightened me. Dayton, she explained, was simply a great capital like any other. That is to say, it was to Rhea county what Atlanta was to Georgia or Paris to France. That is to say, it was predominantly epicurean and sinful. A country girl from some remote valley of the county, coming into town for her semi-annual bottle of Lydia Pinkham's Vegetable Compound, shivered on approaching Robinson's drug-store quite as a country girl from up-state New York might shiver on approaching the Metropolitan Opera House. In every village lout she saw a potential white-slaver. The hard sidewalks hurt her feet. Temptations of the flesh bristled to all sides of her, luring her to Hell. This newspaper woman told me of a session with just such a visitor, holden a few days before. The latter waited outside one of the town hot-dog and Coca-Cola shops while her husband negotiated with a hardware merchant across the street. The newspaper woman, idling along and observing that the stranger was badly used by the heat, invited her to step into the shop for a glass of Coca-Cola. The invitation brought forth only a gurgle of terror. Coca-Cola, it quickly appeared, was prohibited by the country lady's pastor, as a levantine and Hell-sent narcotic. He also prohibited coffee and tea—and pies! He had his doubts about white bread and boughten meat. The newspaper woman, interested, inquired about ice-cream. It was, she found, not specifically prohibited, but going into a Coca-Cola shop to get it would be clearly sinful. So she offered to get a saucer of it, and bring it out to the sidewalk. The visitor vacillated—and came near being lost. But God saved her in the nick of time. When the newspaper woman emerged from the place she was in full flight up the street. Later on her husband, mounted on a mule, overtook her four miles out the mountain pike.

This newspaper woman, whose kindness covered city infidels as well as Alpine Christians, offered to take me back in the hills to a place where the old-time religion was genuinely on tap. The Scopes jury, she explained, was composed mainly of its customers, with a few Dayton sophisticates added to leaven the mass. It would thus be instructive to climb the heights and observe the former at their ceremonies. The trip, fortunately, might be made by automobile. There was a road running out of Dayton to Morgantown, in the mountains to the westward, and thence beyond. But foreigners, it appeared, would have to approach the sacred grove cautiously, for the upland worshipers were very shy, and at the first sight of a strange face they would adjourn their orgy and slink into the forest. They were not to be feared, for God had long since forbidden them to practise assassination, or even assault, but if they were alarmed a rough trip would go for naught. So, after dreadful bumpings up a long and narrow road, we parked our car in a little woodpath a mile or two beyond the tiny village of Morgantown, and made the rest of the approach on foot, deployed like skirmishers. Far off in a dark, romantic glade a flickering light was visible, and out of the silence came the rumble of exhortation. We could distinguish the figure of the preacher only as a moving mote in the light: it was like looking down the tube of a dark-field microscope. Slowly and cautiously we crossed what seemed to be a pasture, and then we stealthily edged further and further. The light now grew larger and we could begin to make out what was going on. We went ahead on all fours, like snakes in the grass.

From the great limb of a mighty oak hung a couple of crude torches of the sort that car inspectors thrust under Pullman cars when a train pulls in at night. In the guttering glare was the preacher, and for a while we could see no one else. He was an immensely tall and thin mountaineer in blue jeans, his collarless shirt open at the neck and his hair a tousled mop. As he preached he paced up and down under the smoking flambeaux, and at each turn he thrust his arms into the air and yelled "Glory to God!" We crept nearer in the shadow of the cornfield, and began to hear more of his discourse. He was preaching on the Day of Judgment. The high kings of the earth, he roared, would all fall down and die; only the sanctified would stand up to receive the Lord God of Hosts. One of these kings he mentioned by name, the king of what he called Greec-y. The king of Greece-y, he said, was doomed to Hell. We crawled forward a few more yards and began to see the audience. It was seated on benches ranged round the preacher in a circle. Behind him sat a row of elders, men and women. In front were the younger folk. We crept on cautiously, and individuals rose out of the ghostly gloom. A young mother sat suckling her baby, rocking as the preacher paced up and down. Two scared little girls hugged each other, their pigtails down their backs. An immensely huge mountain woman, in a gingham dress, cut in one piece, rolled on her heels at every "Glory to God!" To one side, and but half visible, was what appeared to be a bed. We found afterward that half a dozen babies were asleep upon it.

The preacher stopped at last, and there arose out of the darkness a woman with her hair pulled back into a little tight knot. She began so quietly that we couldn't hear what she said, but soon her voice rose resonantly and we could follow her. She was denouncing the reading of books. Some wandering book agent, it appeared, had come to her cabin and tried to sell her a specimen of his wares. She refused to touch it. Why, indeed, read a book? If what was in it was true, then everything in it was already in the Bible. If it was false, then reading it would imperil the soul. This syllogism from the Caliph Omar complete, she sat down. There followed a hymn, led by a somewhat fat brother wearing silver-rimmed country spectacles. It droned on for half a dozen stanzas, and then the first speaker resumed the floor. He argued that the gift of tongues was real and that education was a snare. Once his children could read the Bible, he said, they had enough. Beyond lay only infidelity and damnation. Sin stalked the cities. Dayton itself was a Sodom. Even Morgantown had begun to forget God. He sat down, and a female aurochs in gingham got up. She began quietly, but was soon leaping and roaring, and it was hard to follow her. Under cover of the turmoil we sneaked a bit closer.

A couple of other discourses followed, and there were two or three hymns. Suddenly a change of mood began to make itself felt. The last hymn ran longer than the others, and dropped gradually into a monotonous, unintelligible chant. The leader beat time with his book. The faithful broke out with exultations. When the singing ended there was a brief palaver that we could not hear, and two of the men moved a bench into the circle of light directly under the flambeaux. Then a half-grown girl emerged from the darkness and threw herself upon it. We noticed with astonishment that she had bobbed hair. "This sister," said the leader, "has asked for prayers." We moved a bit closer. We could now see faces plainly, and hear every word. At a signal all the faithful crowded up to the bench and began to pray—not in unison, but each for himself. At another they all fell on their knees, their arms over the penitent. The leader kneeled facing us, his head alternately thrown back dramatically or buried in his hands. Words spouted from his lips like bullets from a machine-gun—appeals to God to pull the penitent back out of Hell, defiances of the demons of the air, a vast impassioned jargon of apocalyptic texts. Suddenly he rose to his feet, threw back his head and began to speak in the tongues—blub-blub-blub, gurgle-gurgle-gurgle. His voice rose to a higher register. The climax was a shrill, inarticulate squawk, like that of a man throttled. He fell headlong across the pyramid of supplicants.

From the squirming and jabbering mass a young woman gradually detached herself—a woman not uncomely, with a pathetic homemade cap on her head.

Her head jerked back, the veins of her neck swelled, and her fists went to her throat as if she were fighting for breath. She bent backward until she was like half a hoop. Then she suddenly snapped forward. We caught a flash of the whites of her eyes. Presently her whole body began to be convulsed—great throes that began at the shoulders and ended at the hips. She would leap to her feet, thrust her arms in the air, and then hurl herself upon the heap. Her praying flattened out into a mere delirious caterwauling. I describe the thing discreetly, and as a strict behaviorist. The lady's subjective sensations I leave to infidel pathologists, privy to the works of Ellis, Freud and Moll. Whatever they were, they were obviously not painful, for they were accompanied by vast heavings and gurglings of a joyful and even ecstatic nature. And they seemed to be contagious, too, for soon a second penitent, also female, joined the first, and then came a third, and a fourth, and a fifth. The last one had an extraordinary violent attack. She began with mild enough jerks of the head, but in a moment she was bounding all over the place, like a chicken with its head cut off. Every time her head came up a stream of hosannas would issue out of it. Once she collided with a dark, undersized brother, hitherto silent and stolid. Contact with her set him off as if he had been kicked by a mule. He leaped into the air, threw back his head, and began to gargle as if with a mouthful of BB shot. Then he loosed one tremendous, stentorian sentence in the tongues, and collapsed.

By this time the performers were quite oblivious to the profane universe and so it was safe to go still closer. We left our hiding and came up to the little circle of light. We slipped into the vacant seats on one of the rickety benches. The heap of mourners was directly before us. They bounced into us as they cavorted. The smell that they radiated, sweating there in that obscene heap, half suffocated us. Not all of them, of course, did the thing in the grand manner. Some merely moaned and rolled their eyes. The female ox in gingham flung her great bulk on the ground and jabbered an unintelligible prayer. One of the men, in the intervals between fits, put on his spectacles and read his Bible. Beside me on the bench sat the young mother and her baby. She suckled it through the whole orgy, obviously fascinated by what was going on, but never venturing to take any hand in it. On the bed just outside the light the half a dozen other babies slept peacefully. In the shadows, suddenly appearing and as suddenly going away, were vague figures, whether of believers or of scoffers I do not know. They seemed to come and go in couples. Now and then a couple at the ringside would step out and vanish into the black night. After a while some came back, the males looking somewhat sheepish. There was whispering outside the circle of vision. A couple of Model T Fords lurched up the road, cutting holes in the darkness with their lights. Once someone out of sight loosed a bray of laughter.

All this went on for an hour or so. The original penitent, by this time, was buried three deep beneath the heap. One caught a glimpse, now and then, of her yellow bobbed hair, but then she would vanish again. How she breathed down there I don't know; it was hard enough six feet away, with a strong five-cent cigar to help. When the praying brothers would rise up for a bout with the tongues their faces were streaming with perspiration. The fat harridan in gingham sweated like a longshoreman. Her hair got loose and fell down over her face. She fanned herself with her skirt. A powerful old gal she was, plainly equal in her day to a bout with obstetrics and a week's washing on the same morning, but this was worse than a week's washing. Finally, she fell into a heap, breathing in great, convulsive gasps.

Finally, we got tired of the show and returned to Dayton. It was nearly eleven o'clock—an immensely late hour for those latitudes—but the whole town was still gathered in the courthouse yard, listening to the disputes of theologians. The Scopes trial had brought them in from all directions. There was a friar wearing a sandwich sign announcing that he was the Bible champion of the world. There was a Seventh Day Adventist arguing that Clarence Darrow was the beast with seven heads and ten horns described in Revelation XIII, and that the end of the world was at hand. There was an evangelist made up like Andy Gump, with the news that atheists in Cincinnati were preparing to descend upon Dayton, hang the eminent Judge Raulston, and burn the town. There was an ancient who maintained that no Catholic could be a Christian. There was the eloquent Dr. T. T. Martin, of Blue Mountain, Miss., come to town with a truck-load of torches and hymn-books to put Darwin in his place. There was a singing brother bellowing apocalyptic hymns. There was William Jennings Bryan, followed everywhere by a gaping crowd. Dayton was having a roaring time. It was better than the circus. But the note of devotion was simply not there; the Daytonians, after listening a while, would slip away to Robinson's drug-store to regale themselves with Coca-Cola, or to the lobby of the Aqua Hotel, where the learned Raulston sat in state, judicially picking his teeth. The real religion was not present. It began at the bridge over the town creek, where the road makes off for the hills.

ROBERT PENN WARREN

As far as I know, Warren never wrote anything funny, although some of his poems' titles—for instance, "Little Black Heart of the Telephone"—lead me to believe that he could have. Lord knows this poem isn't the least bit funny, but I thought as we're coming down here toward the end, it might do us good to take on some sobering perspective. Just so we don't forget how narrow the ledge is between profound humor and the pit. Warren (1905–1989) came out of Guthrie, Kentucky, and Clarksville, Tennessee. In 1985 he was named America's first Poet Laureate. He is the only person ever to win a Pulitzer Prize in both fiction (All the King's Men) and poetry (Promises). Just read this, if you will, and then we'll let some other folks lift our souls back up.

"Last Laugh"

The little Sam Clemens, one night back in Hannibal,
Peeped through the dining-room keyhole, to see, outspread
And naked, the father split open, lights, liver, and all
Spilling out from that sack of mysterious pain, and the head

Sawed through, where his Word, like God's, held its deepest den,
And candlelight glimmered on blood-slick, post-mortem steel,
And the two dead fish-eyes stared steadily ceilingward—well, then,
If you yourself were, say, twelve, just how would you feel?

Oh, not that you'd loved him—that ramrod son of Virginia,
Though born for success, failing westward bitterly on.
"Armed truce"—that was all, years later, you could find to say in you.
But still, when a father's dead, an umbrella's gone

From between the son and the direful elements.
No, Sam couldn't turn from the keyhole. It's not every night
You can see God butchered in such learned dismemberments,
And when the chance comes you should make the most of the sight.

Though making the most, Sam couldn't make terms with the fact
Of the strangely prismatic glitter that grew in his eye,
Or climbing the stairs, why his will felt detached from the act,
Or why stripping for bed, he stared so nakedly

At the pore little body and thought of the slick things therein.
Then he wept on the pillow, surprised at what he thought grief,
Then fixed eyes at darkness while, slow, on his face grew a grin,
Till suddenly something inside him burst with relief,

Like a hog-bladder blown up to bust when the hog-killing frost
Makes the brats' holiday. So took then to laughing and could not
Stop, and so laughed himself crying to sleep. At last,
Far off in Nevada, by campfire or sluice or gulch-hut,

Or in roaring S.F., in an acre of mirror and gilt,
Where the boys with the dust bellied-up, he'd find words come,
His own face stiff as a shingle, and him little-built.
Then whammo!—the back-slapping riot. He'd stand, looking dumb.

God was dead, for a fact. He knew, in short, the best joke.
He had learned its thousand forms, and since the dark stair-hall
Had learned what was worth more than bullion or gold-dust-plump poke.
And married rich, too, with an extra spin to the ball;

For Livy loved God, and he'd show her the joke, how they lied.
Quite a tussle it was, but hot deck or cold, he was sly
And won every hand but the last. Then at her bedside
He watched dying eyes stare up at a comfortless sky,

And was left alone with his joke, God dead, till he died.

MELISSA FAY GREENE

*In the 1970s Greene was helping folks to organize for their rights in McIntosh
County, Georgia, which a state law enforcement officer called "the most different place
I've ever been to in my life." In 1991 her account of those days in that place,*
Praying for Sheetrock, *was published and deservingly praised. If you haven't read
it, I hope this excerpt will move you to.*

from *Praying for Sheetrock*

The black community of McIntosh was so isolated that, like a few others on
America's southern coast, its language was distinctive and was called Gullah, a

unique blend of eighteenth-century English, Scottish, and African tongues with modern Black English. The old people in particular spoke this rich brogue. Because the people lived far from any city, and because the old people and the middle-aged people had grown up without television and had as their chief form of entertainment the bombastic and vividly euphemistic preachings of the local home-schooled ministers, their speech was full of original and biblical-sounding constructions.

A Georgia peach, a real Georgia peach, a backyard great-grandmother's-orchard peach, is as thickly furred as a sweater, and so fluent and sweet that once you bite through the flannel, it brings tears to your eyes. The voices of the coastal people were like half-wild and lovely local peaches, compared to the bald, dry, homogeneous peaches displayed at a slant in the national chain supermarkets.

"Come in! Come in! Let's have some gossip and slander!" cried an old man living near the sea, whenever a passerby roamed within sight of his porch. "I believe these young ladies of today might clothe themselves more modestly," he said. "Of course, I am getting on and it has been many years since I was conversant with the wherewithal and nomenclature of the female."

.   .   .   .

There is a moment in Autumn when the leaves still curling on the trees and the leaves which have fallen are in equilibrium: dry gold pools spreading under gold-crested oaks. Then the yards and the forest floor seem to mirror the treetops, as if all the trunks rose out of ankle-deep water on which a palette of red-gold leaves reflected. Then the old women in the county bang down their windows and bend to twist the keys of their space heaters; the tall wood rooms fill with the woolly heat; and the old women get back in bed, groaning. The old men draw on long-sleeve flannel shirts, one on top of another, and let their whiskers coarsen. They eat nearly-burnt toast over a paper towel on the kitchen table, and drink a glass of tap water. The wives, after a time, get up, knot their robes, and shuffle into the kitchen, smelling of Mentholatum.

"You eat?"

"Yep."

"Well lemme cook." The old wives swing iron skillets up onto the gas burners, and bacon hisses in the heat.

The flawless autumn sky is lit from below by the fiery treetops. The trees could be snapping candle flames, the ground a bright tablecloth, and the sky a blue porcelain platter. If the Messiah were to arrive today, this cloudless, radiant county would be magnificent enough to receive Him. It is quiet. From the pine woods comes the high, continuous growl of a buzz saw, and on the dirt roads crows pace and argue. If the Messiah did arrive today, the old black people of McIntosh would be the *least* astonished group in America. They might send a young person to go look, and those with telephones might call their daughters, but the rest would remain in their upholstered rockers near their space heaters with their quilts across their laps, finish their coffee and their Bible chapters, and wait to be called upon Personally.

Then there would be ancient cookies in dusty tins extracted from high closet shelves, and teacups trembling on a proffered tray, and lamps carried up front from the bedrooms and plugged in, and a dozen more amenities until the Guest has had a moment to look around and have a sip of tea. Then there would come the complaints: "Did y'all have to cause my Raymond to lose that job back in '81? You know he was fixing to change his habits, and he never did make good after that"—the big women aproned, standing, hands on hips; the men shushing them, embarrassed, but swinging around to hear the reply nonetheless. "Excuse me, Lord, but my old Buick only had eighty thousand miles on it. You couldn't have given me another year out of it?"

The old people of McIntosh County have lived on close, practical, and well-understood terms with God all their lives, a matter of some seventy, eighty, or ninety years. If a messenger of God were to appear on their porch one morning, there'd be no awkwardness of address, no groping for greetings of sufficient splendor, no fumbling for religious rituals last exercised in child-hood, and no exaggerated prostration either: "Gertie?! Angel of the Lord's here!"

JOHN PRINE

John Prine was born, in 1946, in Maywood, Illinois, but his family and musical roots are in Kentucky coal country.

> *And daddy won't you take me back to Muhlenberg County*
> *Down by the Green River where Paradise lay*
> *Well I'm sorry my son, but you're too late in asking*
> *Mr. Peabody's coal train has hauled it away.*

That's from "Paradise." The following is from a song of his that's a sight more cheerful.

"Spanish Pipedream"

She was a levelheaded dancer
On the road to alcohol
And I was just a soldier
On my way to Montreal
Well, she pressed her chest against me
About the time the jukebox broke
Yeah, she gave me a peck
On the back of my neck
And these are the words she spoke

Blow up your T.V.
Throw away your paper
Go to the country
Build you a home
Plant a little garden
Eat a lot of peaches
Try and find Jesus
On your own

Well, I sat there at the table
And I acted real naive
For I knew that topless lady
Had something up her sleeve
Well she danced around the barroom
And she did the hootchy coo
Yeah, she sang her song
All night long
Telling me what to do

Blow up your T.V. . . . .

JERRY CLOWER

"Judgment in the Sky"

Down at East Fork Community of Amite County, Mississippi, I had the privilege of growing up with a gentleman by the name of Kirk Garner. Kirk Garner was a very religious fellow. He was in church every time them church doors opened.

One day he walked out on his front porch and an airplane had just finished doing some skywriting. Kirk didn't know that no airplane could do that. The airplane was gone, and the words what that plane wrote was kinda fading out. Kirk stood on the front porch and looked at it, then broke and run back in the house and told his wife, "Cally, it's Judgment. God done wrote it in the sky."

Cally said, "I don't hear no horns blowing and no bells ringing. I don't believe it's Judgment."

It aggravated Kirk to the extent he broke and run, jumped off the front porch, tripped and fell over a faucet he had drove into the ground to make folks think he had running water. (Actually, Kirk toted water a mile and a half from a branch back behind his house. He had a great big antenna stretched across the roof of his house, and Kirk didn't even know what a radio was.) He hit that road and he started running toward my daddy's house, and he was kicking up dust, brother. He was scared to death that Judgment was there.

Mr. Halley, a man down the road, saw him coming and knew something was bad wrong with Kirk running that fast, kicking up that much dust. He got out in the middle of the road and bear-hugged him when he come by. "Slow down, Kirk. What in the world is happening?"

He said, "Mr. Halley, it's Judgment."

"Why would you say that, Kirk?"

"I saw it wrote in the sky. God's done wrote it up there."

Mr. Halley said, "Kirk, that's Pepsi Cola."

"Sir?"

"That's Pepsi Cola, Kirk. An airplane wrote that up there. The airplane's been gone for several minutes, and you just saw that writing."

"Oh, Mr. Halley, you know that ain't no Pepsi Cola."

"Yes, it is. That plane wrote it and has done gone. You just calm down, it ain't Judgment."

The next morning Kirk came down to my daddy's house, and they were standing out in the back yard and Kirk was telling my daddy this story. Daddy asked him, "Kirk, what would you have done had it been Judgment?"

He said, "I was just gonna keep running till Judgment overtook me."

Benediction

Dear God:
We ain't what we ought to be.
We ain't what we gonna be.

We ain't what we wanta be.
But, thank God,
We ain't what we was.

—Anonymous

INDEX

Selection titles appearing in quotation marks are the original titles; those without quotation marks have been devised by the editor for this volume.

According to Bubba, 72
Alabama Dimensions, 405
"Alligators," 190
Alther, Lisa, 101
Ammons, A. R., 599
Animal Deals, 204
Armstrong, Louis, 50, 504
"Aunt Tempy's Story," 213

Baby Doll, from, 134
Baker, Russell, 479
"Ballad of Charles Whitman, The," 609
Barry, Dave, 200
Barthelme, Donald, 394
"Beard, The," 147
"Between the Lines," 331
"Bill Arp Addresses Artemus Ward," 463
Biloxi Indian, A (as told to James Owen Dorsey), 217
Blackwell, Bumps, 400
Blind Blake, 407
Blount, Roy, Jr., 172, 232, 341
Bond, Julian, 413
Bookie Odds Favored the Union, 414
Bowles, Billy, 471
"Brother Rabbit Conquers Brother Lion," 208

Brown, Sterling A., 427
Browne, Jill Conner, 541

Caldwell, Erskine, 620
Car, from, 326
Chappell, Fred, 147
Chase, Richard, 580
Chesnutt, Charles W., 452
"Chicken Every Sunday," 496
"Chicken Story, A," 197
Childress, Alice, 447
Clower, Jerry, 183, 651
Cobb, Irvin S., 544
"Coley Moke," 270
Confederacy of Dunces, A, from, 126
Confessions of a Failed Southern Lady, from, 105
"Confused Motorist," 578
Coogler, J. Gordon, 325
"Coon Huntin' Story, A," 184
"Country Golf," 258
"Cracker-Barrel Reveries on the Tune 'Pax Americana'," 492
Crews, Harry, 325
Crockett, Davy, 245

"Dang Me," 625
"Dave's Neckliss," 453
"Day with the Vet, A," 241
Dead Solid Perfect, from, 253
"Dickey Story, A," 264
"Diddie Wa Diddie," 407
Dozens, 292
Dying Properly, 101

Earl Long's Finest Moment, 466
Eating in Two or Three Languages, from, 544
Edgerton, Clyde, 59
"Empty Bed Blues," 619

"False Alarm," 201
Faulkner, William, 513
Fernandez, Roberto G., 304
Fighting for Folks, 116
"First Carolina Said-Song," 599
"Fish and the Edsel, The," 186
"Fortunate Spill, The," 114
Fort Worth Golf, 253
Fox, William Price, 266
Frady, Marshall, 438
Friedman, Kinky, 609

Gannon, Frank, 242
Gardner, Dave, 494
Garrett, George, 264
"Georgia Dust," 579
"Georgia on a Fast Train," 503
"Georgia Theatrics," 251
Gertrude, 345
Gilbert, Sarah, 634
Giovanni, Nikki, 116
Golden, Harry, 436
"Grass Turned Out Green," 629
Greene, Melissa Fay, 647
"Guest's Impression of New England, A," 528

Hairdo, from, 635
"Hair Dupe," 491
Hannah, Barry, 611
Harris, George Washington, 235
Harris, Joel Chandler, 208
Head to Head with the Champ, 347
"He Is My Horse," 200
Henry, O., 311

" 'Heyo, House!'," 211
"Hills of Zion, The," 640
Hooper, Johnson J., 295
"Hoosier and the Salt Pile, The," 530
Hurston, Zora Neale, 55, 277, 630
Hustling Here and There, 590
Hyman, Mac, 66

"I Blame It All on Mamma," 44
"I Don't Eat Dirt Personally," 341
"If I Had a Boat," 576
"I Get Born," 56
"In Memorial," 325
Ivins, Molly, 487

"Jackson," 617
"Jambalaya (on the Bayou)," 632
Jarrell, Randall, 344
Jaynes, Gregory, 241, 583
Jenkins, Dan, 72, 253
Jerry Lee Session, A, 398
"Johnson," 479
Johnson, Nunnally, 359
"Judgment in the Sky," 651

"Keela, the Outcast Indian Maiden," 375
Keeper of the Moon, from, 233
Keillor, Garrison, 257
Killens, John Oliver, 579
King, B. B., 41
King, Florence, 104
King, Larry L., 352
"King of Jazz, The," 394
"King of the Birds, The," 224
"Knowing He Was Not My Kind Yet I
    Followed," 611
"Kudzu East and West and South," 242

"Lamar Fountain Is Free," 583
"Last Laugh," 646
"Late Encounter with the Enemy, A," 84
Lemann, Nancy, 139
Letters from Hollywood, 360
"Levitation with Baby," 115
Lieber, Jerry, 617
Liebling, A. J., 466
"Little Full, A," 628
Longstreet, A. B., 251
"Look at That Gal . . .," 413

"Love," 630
Lovett, Lyle, 576
Lum, Ray (as told to William Ferris), 203

Making the Honky-tonks with Mama, 50
"Mama's Memoirs," 42
Mary Grace's Reception, 139
McLaurin, Tim, 233
Meeting Hemingway, 598
Memphis Minnie, 294
Mencken, H. L., 640
Miller, Roger, 624
Mitchell, Joseph, 43
Modern Baptist Bible Study, 157
"More Carters," 173
Morton, Jelly Roll (as told to Alan Lomax), 590
"Mrs. James," 447
Mules and Men, from, 277
"My Old Man and the Grass Widow," 620

Nelson, Willie, 633
Neshoba County Fair, The, 541
"New Dirty Dozen," 295
"Newgene and the Lion," 187
"Night at the Ugly Man's, A," 296
"Nineteen Fifty-five," 382
"Nobody Loves Me but My Mother," 41
Norwood, from, 506
No Time for Sergeants, from, 66

"Observations on American Indians," 497
O'Connor, Flannery, 84, 224
"Old Dry Frye," 581
On an Empty Stomach, 504
"One Last Cheer for Punk Kincaid," 589
"Ordeal of Lonnie Register, The," 266

"Papa Was a Democrat," 77
"Parson John Bullen's Lizards," 235
Penniman, Richard, 400
Percy, William Alexander, 420
"Petrified Man," 364
"Pocketbook Game, The," 448
Poe, Edgar Allan, 305
"Poetic Gems," 321
Porter, Katherine Anne, 597
Portis, Charles, 505
Position on Whisky, A, 358

Poston, Ted, 77
Powell, Padgett, 164
Praying for Sheetrock, from, 647
"Precious Memories," 607
Prine, John, 649
"Private History of a Campaign That Failed, The," 556

Raftmen's Passage, 546
Raney, from, 59
"Ransom of Red Chief, The," 312
"Rat Killin'," 188
"Rats in the Corn Crib," 189
Rawlings, Marjorie Kinnan, 190
Redneck Bride, The, from, 92
Reed, Ishmael, 414
Reed, John Shelton, 320, 607
Relating to Skillet and Fode, 422
Rise of Lester Maddox, The, 439
Rodgers, Jimmie, 615
Rogue Truth, 471
"Rolls-Royce Story, The," 496
Ryan, John Fergus, 92

"Saint Roxie," 626
Sams, Ferrol, 626
Seay, James, 587
"Second Carolina Said-Song," 600
"Sensible Varmint, A," 245
Shaver, Billy Joe, 503
Shuckin' and Jivin', from, 287
"Simon Slick's Mule," 207
"Sister's Comin' Home/Down at the Corner Beer Joint," 633
"Sizing Him Up," 578
"Slim Hears 'The Call'," 429
"Slim in Atlanta," 428
Smart-Grosvenor, Vertamae, 533
Smith, Bessie, 618
Smith, Charles Henry, 463
Smith, Lee, 331
"Song to Oysters," 232
"Spanish Pipedream," 650
"Spoon Story, The," 495
"Sporting Beasley," 435
Sweat, Noah S., 358

"Taming the Bicycle," 570
"T for Texas (Blue Yodel)," 616

Thompson, Hunter S., 346
Thompson, William Tappan, 530
Toole, John Kennedy, 126
"Toot and Teat," 220
Tosches, Nick, 398
"Tough as Bob War and Other Stuff," 488
"Turkeys," 222
"Tuskegee Airfield," 449
Twain, Mark, 546
"Typical," 164
Tyson, Remer, 471

"Uncle Iv Surveys His Domain from His Rocker of a Sunday Afternoon as Aunt Dory Starts to Chop the Kindling," 494
"Uncle Willy," 513

"Vertical Negro Plan, The," 436
Vibration Cooking, from, 534
Virginians, Various Black (as told to Daryl Cumber Dance), 286

Walker, Alice, 382
Waniek, Marilyn Nelson, 113, 449, 629

Warren, Robert Penn, 645
Washington, Ray, 197
Welty, Eudora, 364
Wheeler, Billy Edd, 617
White, Bailey, 41, 220
"Why the 'Possum's Tail Is Bony," 218
Wilcox, James, 157
Wilder, Roy, Jr., 299
Williams, Hank, 632
Williams, Jonathan, 492
Williams, Tennessee, 133
Willie Didn't Want a Lot of Confusion Backstage, 352
Wilson, Justin, 577
Wolfe, Tom, 405
"Women's Locker Room," 451
Womp Bomp a-Loo Momp, 401
Wright, Richard, 292
"Wrong Number," 304

"X-ing a Paragrab," 306

You All Spoken Here, from, 300